RESTRUCTURING EURO

Restructuring Europe

Centre formation, system building and political structuring between the nation-state and the European Union

STEFANO BARTOLINI

OXFORD

UNIVERSITY PRESS

OXFORD
UNIVERSITY PRESS

Great Clarendon Street, Oxford OX2 6DP

Oxford University Press is a department of the University of Oxford.
It furthers the University's objective of excellence in research, scholarship,
and education by publishing worldwide in

Oxford New York

Auckland Cape Town Dar es Salaam Hong Kong Karachi
Kuala Lumpur Madrid Melbourne Mexico City Nairobi
New Delhi Shanghai Taipei Toronto

With offices in

Argentina Austria Brazil Chile Czech Republic France Greece
Guatemala Hungary Italy Japan Poland Portugal Singapore
South Korea Switzerland Thailand Turkey Ukraine Vietnam

Oxford is a registered trade mark of Oxford University Press
in the UK and in certain other countries

Published in the United States
by Oxford University Press Inc., New York

British Library Cataloguing in Publication Data
Data available

Library of Congress Cataloging in Publication Data
Data available

Typeset by SPI Publisher Services, Pondicherry, India.
Printed in Great Britain
on acid-free paper by Biddles Ltd., King's Lynn, Norfolk.

ISBN 978-0-19-928643-0 (Hbk.)
978-0-19-923187-4 (Pbk.)

A Sandro e Martine, Sara e Alessandro

Am Ende hängen wir doch ab
Von Kreaturen, die wir machten
Goethe, *Faust*

ACKNOWLEDGEMENTS

The preparation of this book has been greatly helped by the financial support offered by the Research Council of the European University Institute in Florence during 2000–4, and it has profited from the research assistance of Guido Legnante and Goran von Sidow. The book could not have appeared without the careful English language editing by Nicola Owtram, and without the continuous help offered by Elisabeth Webb. The anonymous reviewers of the manuscript presented me with an extensive set of corrections of factual mistakes and with lots of suggestions for improving the presentation of the argument, and for this also I am grateful.

I have presented preliminary versions and parts of the content of this work in many conferences, papers and seminars—so many that I now can hardly remember all those to whom I am indebted. I want to thank Adrienne Héritier, Hanspeter Kriesi, Maurizio Ferrera, Philippe Schmitter, Thomas Risse, Peter Flora, Vivien Schmidt, Peter Mair, Colin Crouch, and Fritz Sharpf, to whom I have so often listened, and with whom I have so often exchanged views about the EU. Although I have learned much from all of these various colleagues, there are nevertheless two in particular who deserve a special word of gratitude: Adrienne Héritier, who has helped me intensely during the preparation of this work and who has worked harder on the draft manuscript than could have been expected of any colleague—in fact, only real friends can offer this sort of help to you; and Maurizio Ferrera, with whom I had numerous intellectual exchanges about Rokkan's and Hirschman's work while we were both drafting manuscripts on the EU, and who has proved a constant source of inspiration and reflection.

This book would not exist without the 'people' of the European University Institute in Florence—all of them, the students and the administrative staff, the colleagues and the many visitors. Without this unique environment, my interest for the EU would not have emerged, and my scepticism about its development would not be forced to confront the rigours of academic work.

PREFACE

Given the difficulty of defining the EU as a political formation, and given the virtually unanimous opinion that the EU is not a 'state', the literature tends to use a variety of different terms. Some see the EU as a classic 'confederation', while some feel the need to specify this further by adding the label of 'consociationalism'. Other scholars define the EU as a 'political system', while yet others prefer to classify it as a 'regime'. There are scholars who prefer to stress the opposition between 'government' and 'governance', while among those who do use the term 'state', various caveats are added to suggest that it is a special type of state—a 'policymaking state' or a 'regulatory state'. Finally, there are those who resort to the term 'system', speaking of 'a system of multilevel governance' or of 'a system of liberal intergovernmentalism'. One particular scholar who coins neologisms with great creativity defines it as 'post-sovereign, polycentric, incongruent and neo-medieval'.[1] Yet, despite its variety, this list is clearly incomplete, and leaves aside the most daring of these conceptual combinations.

As well as the multiplicity of definitions, there is also a multiplicity of approaches. If we focus on the institutions of the EU, European integration can be seen as involving the growth of the competences and powers of a new layer of government whose directives and regulations may replace, change,

---

[1] Respectively by Warleigh, W., 'Better the Evil You Know? Synthetic and Confederal Understandings of European Unification', *West European Politics*, 21 (1994), 1–18; Chryssochoou, D. N., 'Democracy and Symbiosis in the European Union: Towards a Confederal Consociation?', *West European Politics*, 17 (1994), 1–14; Bogaards, M., 'Consociational Interpretations of the EU: A Critical Appraisal', *European Union Politics*, 3 (2002), 357–81; Hix, S., *The Political System of the European Union* (Basingstoke: Macmillan, 1999); Breckenridge, R. E., 'Reassessing Regimes: The International Regime Aspects of the European Union', *Journal of Common Market Studies*, 35 (1997), 173–87; Eising, R. and Kohler-Koch, B., 'Introduction: Network Governance in the European Union'; and Kohler-Koch, B., 'The Evolution and Transformation of European Governance', in B. Kohler-Koch and Eising, R. (eds.), *The Transformation of Governance in the European Union* (London: Routledge, 1999), 3–13 and 14–35; Richardson, J., 'Policymaking in the EU: Interests, Ideas and Garbage Cans of Primeval Soup', in J. Richardson (ed.), *European Union: Power and Policy-making* (London: Routledge, 1996), 3–23; Majone, G., 'The Rise of the Regulatory State in Europe', *West European Politics*, 17 (1994), 77–101; Marks, G., Hooghe, L. and Blank, K. 'European Integration from the 1980s: State Centric v. Multi-level Governance', *Journal of Common Market Studies*, 34 (1996), 341–78; Moravcsik, A., *The Choice for Europe: Social Purpose and State Power from Messina to Maastricht* (London: UCL Press, 1998); Schmitter, P., 'Imagining the Future of the Euro-Polity with the Help of New Concepts', in G. Marks et al., *Governance in the European Union* (London: Sage, 1996), 121–50.

or complement national laws; or as the emergence of a set of political institutions that formalize and routinize interactions among actors; or as the growth of policy networks specializing in the creation of authoritative European rules; or as a gigantic coordination game among different kinds of actors to regulate the negative externalities of an enlarged area of free trade and market interactions. If we focus on the constitutive components of the Union—the nation-states—then integration can be conceptualized as a process of internalization of new and previously environmental inputs; as the adaptation of national institutions and regimes, and of national routine patterns of conflict resolution, competition and mediation to EU-level changes and to a new environment. If we focus instead on the actors, European integration can be seen as a major change in their institutional opportunity structure; as a growing horizontal interaction between cross-border firms, citizens, networks of experts and lobbyists, and the like; or as a convergence process through which formal and informal behaviour and values are becoming increasingly similar to one another.

This is obviously a rich and complex set of definitions and perspectives, and one which will be filled out even further with this particular book. In this study, I focus on the historical configuration of territorial borders and functional boundaries of the European nation-state, and I present integration as a process of territorial and functional boundary transcendence, redefinition, shift, and change that fundamentally alters the nature of the European states. Broadening the perspective even further, I see integration as a new historical phase in the development of Europe, characterized by a powerful trend towards legal, economic, and cultural territorial de-differentiation that follows after a five-century long process of differentiation that led to the territorial structuring of the European system of nation-states. The core concern of this study is the relationship between the specific institutional design of the new Brussels centre of territorial integration (as it stands roughly at the time of the Nice Treaty),[2] the boundary redefinitions that result from the political production of this new centre, and, finally, the consequences of both of these processes on the already established national and the newly developing European political structures. Although my interest in European

---

[2] The 'Treaty establishing a Constitution for Europe' (TCE) was elaborated by the European Convention (18 July 2003), approved by the European Council (17–18 June 2004) and signed by the Head of States (29 October 2004) while this book was drafted. It is now in the ratification process by all member states following their national prescribed procedures. The final approval is uncertain. There are many institutional innovations in the TCE, but most of them do not significantly alter the key features of the EU, particularly when these are seen in a rather long term developmental perspective as it is done in this work. Reference to the TCE will therefore be limited to the most relevant prospects of change (such as, for instance, the Chart of Fundamental Rights included in Part II of the Treaty).

integration is of relatively recent origin, it is nevertheless closely connected with my previous work, which was mainly devoted to the historical configuration of national cleavages as specific political structures articulating voice within the closed territorial entities of the European nation-states. If the EU can be seen as a process of boundary redefinition, is it almost inevitable that we ask about the implications for the historical forms of articulation of national voice.

Taking the EU as a case of the formation of an enlarged territorial system, this work recovers some of the central and classic issues of political modernization theory. Three questions in particular lie at the core of this work.[3] First, is the EU an attempt at state formation? The EU is often depicted as a novelty that departs so radically from previous forms of political organization that very little—if anything at all—can be learned from previous historical models of large-scale territorial enlargement/integration and retrenchment/differentiation. In sharp contrast with this view, I argue that a great deal can be learned about the EU and its future development, about its mode of structuring and about the kind of problematic pressures it is subject to, by looking at past experiences of large-scale territorial formations. The EU has not developed through war or through the acquisition of territory, but to the extent that supranational powers have accumulated and functional transfers can already be seen, it can be defined as a state-formation attempt that is characterized to date by limited administrative capabilities, by strong regulatory powers in selected fields, by very weak fiscal capabilities, and by strong juridical capabilities that have grown from the early spheres of competences.

From the historical point of view, there is nothing exceptional or new in this configuration of subsystemic differentiation. Even if the configuration is not structurally stable and the final outcomes are as yet far from clear, past experiences may help to conceptualize the problems arising from it. It is claimed here, on the one hand, that interesting insights can be gained by locating EU integration within the broader scheme of European development that has lasted from the collapse of the Roman Empire to the formation of modern states; and, on the other, that this new expansion in the range and scope of cross-territorial communication can only properly be understood against the background of the territorial, cultural, economic, and administrative differentiation brought about by the emergence of a system of states. *centre* Throughout this book I use the concept of *centre formation* as a more general *formation.* category than *state formation* (or state building). The formation of states was the formation of a particular type of centre, but there have been and there might still be different types of 'centres'. In short, the question is not whether

---

[3] See Flora, P., 'The National Welfare State and European Integration', in L. Moreno (ed.), *Social Exchange and Welfare Development* (Madrid: CSIC, 1993), 18.

the EU is a 'state', but rather whether its development can be fruitfully interpreted with the analytical categories of the 'centre formation' process, once those categories are adapted and separated from the historical experience of the 'state formation'.

Second, is the EU an attempt at centre formation without nation building? The concept of 'state' is often equated with that of 'nation-state', and the connotation characterizing the term 'nation' is often added implicitly to that of the state. It is difficult to dispute that the EU is not a nation-state. However, this does not rule out the investigation of the kind of relationships that can exist between a non-nation-state and its constitutive nations, in that states have existed which were not nation-states. Reminding ourselves of how European cultural boundaries came to be defined in relation to military, politico-administrative, and economic boundaries may help to clear up some of the questions surrounding the historical sequence and relationship between *demos*, *telos*, and *kratos*. Once again, the original question needs to be reformulated. The issue is not whether integration rests on, builds, or even requires a 'nation', but rather the more general question as to whether the EU is developing those features that force its components to stay within it beyond the 'contractual' agreements based on mere instrumental calculations, and, of course, without resorting to force. In other words, the issue is whether the EU is producing 'loyalty', which I interpret to be those structures and processes of system maintenance represented by cultural integration, social sharing institutions, and participation rights. This aspect is identified in this work with the concept of *system building*, as opposed to 'centre formation'. In this respect, the core argument of the book is that for any new centre a balance must exist between its system building capacity and the scope and reach of its political production, and that the ambitious political production of the EU centre is clearly out of balance with its weak system building capacity.

Third, is the EU a process of centre formation without democratization? Conflicts, opposition formation and institutional democratization have taken place within territorially consolidated states and have rested on a sense of cultural 'nationalization'. Closer consideration of past 'democratization processes' may help to clarify our ideas about the requirements, limits and possibilities of the internal democratization on the EU. However, before dealing with questions of institutional democratization, we need to conceptualize the forms of interest differentiation, the corresponding conflict lines, and the resulting political oppositions and alliances among individuals, collectivities, membership organizations, territories, corporate groups, and bureaucracies that are stimulated by the integration process itself. This means concentrating on the more deeply rooted process of institutionalization of conflict lines within the newly devised boundaries and borders of the

EU, so as to understand how they relate to national conflict lines, and which political structures can be created at the new level. I use the general concept of *political structuring* to identify this process, which is analytically distinct from both centre formation and system building processes. My argument through the book is that institutional democratization without political structuring may turn into façade electioneering, at best, or dangerous experiments, at worst.

Centre formation, system building, and *political structuring* are the three key conceptual tools that I use to interpret the EU. To apply them fruitfully requires, however, a considerable reworking of each. This book, in fact, is not based on original empirical research and relies on secondary literature; it also focuses more on general trends than on systematic cross-country variations. But it also has the theoretical ambition to sharpen the conceptual tools that are currently available to deal with processes of territorial enlargement and unification. The integration literature has produced many studies focusing on the explanation of specific sectoral outcomes. These sectoral theories are then generally evaluated with reference to the theories of supranationalism/neofunctionalism, on the one hand, and realism/intergovernmentalism, on the other. It is likely that not enough attention has been given to macro-level theorizing regarding the systemic significance of these subsystem developments, and the general constellation in which they take on their meaning and show their potential implications for the broader problems of social and systemic integration.

We lack a general theoretical framework for political structuring beyond the nation-state which is capable of linking the various aspects of EU integration—the persistent intergovernmentalism, the unbalanced definition of rights, the odd 'constitutionalization' of its treaties, the tensions between the need for legitimacy of the new territorial hierarchy and the nation-states, and so on. To use a term that is now largely discredited, we need a 'holistic' approach to integration in the form of a theory that gives us an idea of the whole model, and from which hypotheses can be generated, even if it is not possible to test all of its components. This theoretical framework needs (*a*) to overcome the rigid distinction between domestic politics and international relations; (*b*) to link actors' orientations, interests and motivations with macro outcomes; and (*c*) to relate structural profiles with dynamic processes of change.

The interpretation of the integration process needs to combine domestic relations *within* countries with international relations *among* countries. Before the formation of the European system of states, the neat distinction between domestic politics and international relations did not exist; indeed, the distinction came about as a result of this process. That is to say, a clear-cut separation between the 'external relations' of a territorial unit and its internal role differentiation and political dynamics is the contingent historical result of a specific configuration of the unit's boundaries. It comes into being when an internal hierarchical order manages to control the external territorial and functional boundaries so closely that it insulates domestic structuring processes from external influences. In this case, the internal hierarchy presents itself as the single organizing principle of the internal domestic structuring and, at the same time, as the single autonomous centre for external relations. Any deviation from this pure type makes the distinction between 'international' and 'domestic' politics of limited use, and sometimes renders it misleading. The deviation is obvious and macroscopic for advanced regional integration projects like the EU, in which boundaries between the internal developments and external relations of the states no longer exist in certain areas, or have become very loose in others, or are still closed and monitored in yet others. To the extent that both international relations and comparative politics theories rest on the 'reification' of the single political unit—either as a unified set of external preferences and interactions, or as an independent set of internal structures and developments—they are both challenged by issues of territorial and functional boundary redefinition.

The theory we need for the study of territorial system retrenchment and enlargement should also provide a micro and macro framework, linking the individual actor's options and choices to aggregate outcomes, as well as a structure and dynamics framework, linking structural profiles and dynamic processes. These links should be capable of generating hypotheses and scenarios about the variations in territorial groups and membership group responses to the integration process. At any given time, key individual and collective actors' preferences/values/interests can be identified and the set of institutions or rules constraining their options can be studied. Each choice decision, or each single outcome may, therefore, be rationalized in terms of a game equilibrium or of a specific structural profile. Over time, dynamic processes are characterized by the emergence of new actors who have not participated in the earlier 'games', by changes in actors' preferences, or by new institutional arrangements which all produce unintended and unexpected consequences. These consequences then continuously modify the relevant actors, their preferences, and their institutional constraints. In the long run, then, it is hard to explain a dynamic process of development by a consecutive set of structural profiles and individual choices, even if at each moment they result in new structural profiles.

In order to sketch the components of a theory with these requirements I build on the work of Stein Rokkan and Albert Hirschman, with both being approached in the light of Weber's insights into the relationship between the external consolidation and internal role differentiation of every 'political formation'. Neither Hirschman nor Rokkan has dealt with European integration. Rokkan does not mention it in his work, which focuses on the cosmos of nation-states in Europe, including the historically failed as well as the successful examples. Hirschman does not extend his exit-voice-loyalty framework outside or beyond the capsule of the nation-state. The work of both these authors therefore needs to 'travel to Brussels'—or at least be transported there. I maintain that this is a profitable exercise. Rokkan's theory provides a macro interpretation of the formation of modern states and nations in Europe since the sixteenth century, while Hirschman's 'exit-voice' paradigm provides a micro theory of individual actor's choices under different conditions of confinement. That is, Hirschman's exploration of exit and voice represents a micro-level theory of individual actors choices in relation to the quality of output in bounded territories, while Rokkan's enquiry constitutes a macro-level historical developmental theory of actors/ resources reactions to territorial confinement. In the work of both these two scholars there is a consistent set of key concepts and concerns, as well as an implicit theoretical framework that can be exploited to move beyond the crisis of the nation-state.

To argue that the theoretical framework developed in this book meets these demanding requirements would be immodest. Instead, it is hoped that this is a work that moves in this direction, and that represents a push for European studies to become more rooted in general theories of politics and to acquire a more developmental perspective.

Chapter 1 of this book is largely analytical and sketches the elements of a theory of voice structuring under different conditions of the territorial confinement of actors and resources. It formulates theoretical propositions about how processes of internal conflict generation and opposition development ('political structuring') relate to the processes of boundary demarcation in a large-scale territorial polity, and how the two relate to the internal institutional hierarchy of the same territory.

In Chapter 2 this analytical framework is used to review the history of state formation in Europe from the sixteenth to the twentieth century. The purpose is to interpret the specific historical configuration of the boundaries of the European nation-state and then to explain variations in the forms of centre–periphery structuring, interest intermediation structuring, and cleavage structuring.

From Chapter 3 onwards the book investigates the extent to which the analytical framework and the historical reconstruction of the nation-state experience can be fruitfully extended to the interpretation of the fifty-year-long development of the integration process. Chapter 3 interprets the EU as the formation of a new centre and focuses on the peculiarities of its institutional design.

Chapter 4 analyses how the political production of this new centre impacts on the traditional configuration of boundaries of the nation-states. The activities and the political production of the EU are also interpreted in their capacity of system building.

Chapters 5 and 6 then move on to analyse the implications of the process of boundary redrawing for the different types of actors and resources active in the territorial, corporate and political-electoral channels of representation. These chapters discuss both the consequences for established national political structures and the prospects of the development of new, European-wide political structures.

Finally, Chapter 7 recalls the trajectory of the analytical model and of the historical interpretation, discussing the implications of the peculiar model of centre formation, system building, and political structuring prevalent at the EU level to date.

In studying European integration, we retrace the ruins of previous attempts to integrate this part of the world. The half-a-century-long process of new large-scale territorial integration is characterized by the progressive lowering of internal boundaries and the slow rise of new external boundaries. The process liberates conflicting and contradictory energies and requests for exit and, at the same time, new demands for closure. Which specific systemic boundaries are lowered internally and which are raised externally is, and will be, of paramount importance for the internal forms of voice structuring and institutional differentiation. As usual, the specificity of the process that is unfolding before our eyes seems so complex and momentous as to defeat any comparison with previous historical phenomena of the same genus. And yet the entire history of Europe—from the consolidation of the Roman Empire to its fall, from feudalization to the birth of communal civilization, from the establishment of the common Latin intellectual language to the vernacularization of communication (and back to a common new language?); from the development of an early universalistic legal grammar to the nationalization of law and back to its 'Europeanization'; from the original kinship ties to the Christian cross-territorial community and back to the religious membership retrenchment of Orthodox and Protestant reforms—is a continuous process of geographical and membership space retrenchment/differentiation and expansion/integration. I find it fascinating to view the richness of this history through the prisms of 'exit option', 'boundary building' and 'political structuring', and I find it just as fascinating to interpret the much more recent process of European integration with these same intellectual tools.

CONTENTS

LIST OF FIGURES

LIST OF TABLES

LIST OF ABBREVIATIONS

AEBR	Association of European Border Regions
AER	Assembly of European Regions
ASEAN	Association of South East Asian Nations
CAP	Common Agricultural Policy
CCRE	Conseil des communes et des régions d'Europe
CEDRE	European Centre for Regional Development
CFI	Court of First Instance
CFSP	Common Energy Policy
C-SIS	Central Schengen Information System
ECB	European Central Bank
ECJ	European Court of Justice
ECSC	European Coal and Steel Community
ECU	European Currency Unit
EDC	European Defence Community
EEA	European Economic Area
EEC	European Economic Community
EEP	Experience Exchange Programme
EMS	European Monetary System
EP	European Parliament
EPC	European Political Cooperation
EPU	European Payment Union
ERDF	European Regional Development Fund
ERIT	European Regions of Industrial Tradition
ETUC	European Trade Union Congress
EU	European Union
FAO	Food and Agricultural Organization
GATT	General Agreement on Tariffs and Trade
GD	General Directorates
IEM	Internal Energy Market
IGC	Intergovernmental Conferences
IMP	Integrated Mediterranean Programmes
N-SIS	National Schengen Information System
NUTS	Nomenclature of Territorial Units of Statistics
OECD	Organization for Economic Cooperation and Development
QMV	Qualified Majority Voting

SEA	Single European Act
TABD	Trans-Atlantic Business Dialogue
TCE	Treaty establishing a Constitution for Europe
TEC/EC	Treaty of European Community
TEU	Treaty of the European Union
VAT	Value Added Tax
WEU	Western European Union
WTO	World Trade Organization

1

A Theory of Exit Options, Boundary Building, and Political Structuring

Introduction

When referring to the modern form of the state, it is usual to recall the threefold Weberian definition of any political formation, where this is conceived as a (*a*) hierarchically structured organization for the maintenance of order; (*b*) within a defined geographical area; and (*c*) through the use and the threat of physical coercion.[1] This definition emphasizes the features of a bounded space, of an internally organized community, and of external strategies of demarcation through signals of possession or through physical defence against intruders. The Weberian formulation establishes a link between the strategies of demarcation of the external boundaries of the geographical space, on the one hand, and the differentiation of roles in the internal organization of the population occupying the space, on the other. On this view, the 'external territorial control' refers to the distinctions and differences in membership rights, privileges and obligations between natives and foreigners that are set up through the building of various kinds of boundaries, while 'internal political structure' refers to the institutional form and the legitimation principle of the relationship between rulers and their subjects.

The history of human organizations can be read as a series of repeated attempts to create territorial borders that correspond and coincide with systemic functional boundaries and which are in line with the consolidated socio-political hierarchies within the corresponding populations.[2] This same

---

[1] Weber, M., *Wirtschaft und Gesellschaft*, 2 vols. (Tübingen: Mohr, 1956 (1922)), 29–30. Throughout this book I will use the term 'political formation' to translate Weber's concept of *politische verbände* as I find the English translation of this concept as 'political group' inadequate and misleading.

[2] Rokkan, S., Urwin, D., Aerebrot, F. H., Malaba, P., and Sande, T., *Centre-Periphery Structures in Europe* (Frankfurt and New York: Campus Verlag, 1987), 17–18.

history can also be interpreted as the way in which political hierarchies have been shaped, reinforced, shaken, or destroyed by the success or lack of it in similar repeated attempts to limit the opportunities to transcend those same boundaries. Modern state making was a form of such a process, the success of which has led to its generalized imitation. The idea that the links between external territorial consolidation of a polity and its internal political structuring are significant is far from new. Indeed, it has a remarkable pedigree in political theory and historical research. Erasmus noted that: 'I am loth to suspect here what only too often, alas! has turned to be the truth: that the rumour of war with the Turks has been trumped up with the purpose of mulcting the Christian Population, so that being burned and crushed in all possible ways it might be all the more servile towards the tyranny of both kinds of princes' (ecclesiastical and secular).[3] Rousseau reminded us that 'war and conquest without and the encroachment of despotism within give each other mutual support. . . . Aggressive princes wage war at least as much on their subjects as on their enemies and the conquering nation is left no better off than the conquered'.[4] In a famous quote, Robert Seeley stated that 'the degree of political freedom within a state must reasonably be inversely proportional to the military and political pressures on its borders'.[5] Hintze alludes to this relationship when he argues that 'notwithstanding its heavy commitment in continental war, bureaucratic centralism did not develop in Britain because its isolation meant that it did not have to raise and administer a large standing army. Its strength was based upon the navy and navies do not shape the apparatus of government as do armies'; or when he argues that 'It is an admirable achievement of the French nation that it managed to develop militarism and administrative centralization within a parliamentary constitutional framework'.[6] Finer suggests that one cannot understand why French historians are so obsessed with the 'demon' of exit while the British are equally interested in the 'angel' of voice, without taking into account that France's borders were disputed up to the Second World War, whereas Britain's borders are more or less the same today as they were in 975.[7]

---

[3] 'Erasmus of Rotterdam', in M. M. Phillips (ed. and trans.), *The 'Adages' of Erasmus* (Cambridge: Cambridge University Press, 1536 (1964)), 347–8.

[4] Rousseau, J-. J., 'Judgement of saint Pierre's project for Perpetual peace', in S. Hoffman and D. P. Fidler (eds.), *Rousseau on International Relations* (Oxford: Clarendon Press, 1981 (1756)), 91.

[5] Quoted in Hintze, O., in G. Oestreich (ed.), *Soziologie und Geschichte Staat und Verfassung* (Goettingen: Vandenhoeck and Ruprecht, 1962), 366.

[6] Ibid., 415 and 428.

[7] Finer, S. E., 'State-building, state boundaries and border control: An essay on certain aspects of the first phase of state-building in Western Europe considered in the light of the Rokkan–Hirschman model', *Social Science Information*, 13 (1974), 79–126, 115.

However, this fundamental intuition is rarely spelled out with its full implications. This chapter is an attempt to remedy this, by elaborating more fully on the idea of a relationship between 'external territorial consolidation' and 'internal political structures'. My purpose is to develop a theoretical framework general enough to be applied to the consolidation of any type of political formation. I propose to start from the analytical discussion of the two key concepts of 'exit' ('entry') and 'boundary'. Building on these two, the following sections of the chapter focus on the three main process of internal consolidation: the formation of the centre and its internal hierarchy; the creation of loyalties and the formation of the system; the articulation of voice and the formation of specific political structures. All these concepts are pairs that point to actors' options and the corresponding macro features. 'Exit/entry', 'loyalty' and 'voice' are individual actor's behavioural choices or attitudes, while 'boundaries', 'system building', and 'political structuring' represent their corresponding macro and systemic counterparts.

The core of my argument is provisionally anticipated by the scheme in Figure 1.1, that suggests how the relationships between external boundary demarcation and internal structuring can be conceptualized for any type of political formation. Thus, the scheme may be read along any of the arrows indicated. We might be primarily interested in studying how the internal centre and its hierarchical order are shaped by the combined effect of the existing boundaries and of the exit options they allow. Alternatively, we can

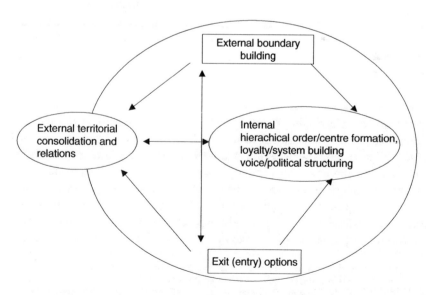

FIGURE 1.1. External boundary demarcation and internal political structuring

explore how the process of internal structuring of a territory is shaped by the strategy of boundary building and exit options of the internal hierarchical order. Similarly, both the boundary building and the availability of the exit options can be read as a function of the other processes. Independent and dependent variables are not fixed in this scheme. It merely signals the importance of the network of relationships between these factors when interpreting the external relations and domestic structuring of any political formation. This network of relationship is the object of the analytical discussion of this chapter.

As the terminology witnesses, here the impetus is provided by the work of Alfred O. Hirschman and Stein Rokkan, although I revise and adapt their views to my aims. Hirschman's 'Exit-Voice' paradigm constitutes a micro theory of individual behaviour facing organizational performance on a small scale; Rokkan develops a macro theory of the confinement and configuration of actors/resources in large-scale organization such as states. Hirschman's reasoning is primarily analytical; Rokkan's is primarily historical. While Hirschman describes structural profiles for individual choices, Rokkan privileges path dependencies in dynamic processes that constrain the same individual choices. The chapter explores how much can be gained by bridging the insights of these two great scholars.

Exit

Hirschman's key intuition is to conceive of exit and voice as alternative individual's reactions to the performance of the organizations and institutions that he/she belongs to. Hirschman establishes a negative association between the two—opportunities for exit reduce the need or willingness for voice, while their absence enhances them.[8] Exit and voice are thus analysed in their capacity to function as mechanisms of recovery in organizational performance. He originally thought that exit mechanisms were typical of economic transactions, while voice mechanisms were typical of political interactions, where the usual alternative to voice is acquiescence or indifference rather than exit. Exit is impersonal—it avoids costly face-to-face relationships; it is communicated indirectly via statistics. Voice, as an attempt to change an objectionable state of affairs rather than to escape from it, is not a private and secret act but requires the expression of critical opinions through personal involvement—it is direct and visible, and it exposes the 'voicer'.[9]

---

[8] Hirschman, A. O., *Exit, Voice, and Loyalty: Responses to Decline in Firms, Organizations, and States* (Cambridge, MA: Harvard University Press, 1970).

[9] Ibid., 15–16, 24. Hirschman concludes that in all organizations: 'for competition to work as a mechanism of recuperation from performance lapses, it is generally best to have

Although in successive writings Hirschman increasingly appraises the role of voice, in a first approximation, voice is viewed as a residual of exit. Those who do not exit are candidates for voice; voice feeds on either inelastic demand (i.e. slowness in exit when deterioration occurs), or on lack of opportunity for exit. Therefore, the role of voice increases as the opportunity for exit declines, to the point where, 'with exit wholly unavailable, voice must carry the entire burden of alerting management to its failing'.[10] Therefore, the choice of whether or not to voice will be made in light of the prospect for an effective use of exit. In other words, exit and voice are alternatives.[11] While in *Exit, Voice, and Loyalty*, Hirschman regarded exit as essentially costless when it was available, he later briefly discussed the potential costs of exit even in situations in which loyalty is absent.[12] Such costs, which are not evident in consumers' choices, become more obvious for interindustry transactions (trust, traditions, etc.) and are crucial in all forms of territorial exit.

This brief outline highlights the immense potential of Hirschman's concepts, and, at the same time, their limitations when applied outside and beyond the frame of reference of the modern territorial state, a frame which he takes for granted in his early work and only partially revises in its later studies. To apply his conceptualization to any historical form of organization (or, more precisely, to any form of political arena—see infra for this concept) some further developments and modification are necessary.

Hirschman's main reference point is always that of the individual and his/her exit opportunities within state organizations. In fact, he defines 'stateless' as a situation associated with the regular practice and possibility of physical

---

a mixture of *alert* and *inert* customers', with alert customers providing the information on the decline of the product; and the inert customer preventing this decline from having immediate and catastrophic effects with no possibility of recovery for the firm. He also applies the same reasoning to the state: 'Every state ... requires for its establishment and existence some limitations or *ceilings* on the extent of exit or of voice or of both. In other words, there are levels of exit (disintegration) and voice (disruption) beyond which it is impossible for an organization to exist as an organization. At the same time, an organization needs *minimal* or *floor* levels of exit and voice in order to receive the necessary feedback about its performance'; Hirschman, A. O., 'Exit, voice, and loyalty: further reflections and a survey of recent contributions', in A. O. Hirschman (ed.), *Essays in Trespassing. Economics to Politics and Beyond* (Cambridge: Cambridge University Press, 1981), 213–35, 224–5 (originally in *Social Science Information*, 13 (1974), 7–26). This line of Hirschman's reasoning is not directly relevant in this context.

[10] Hirschman, *Exit, Voice, and Loyalty*, 34.

[11] That those people who are less likely to exit are more likely to voice has some empirical underpinning. See Orbell, J. M. and Uno, T., 'A Theory of Neighbourhood Problem Solving: Political Action vs. Residential Mobility', *American Political Science Review*, 66 (1972), 471–89. His results suggest that differential distribution of exit options has a bearing also on the differential options of voice.

[12] In Hirschman, 'Exit, voice, and loyalty: further reflections', 222–3.

exit, and views this as the cause of the non-emergence of large, centralized societies with specialized state organs. That is, the availability of exit options prevents the formation of modern states, since this process depends on the limiting of those exits.[13] Even when he deals with exit from and voice for public goods, the question is whether to exit or to voice within state organizations. While exiting from an organization providing private goods terminates the relationship, in the case of public goods the member can stop being a producer but cannot stop being a consumer. Calculations therefore become more complex and involve evaluating the cost of voice from within (remaining a producer of public goods) or of voice from outside (exit public good producing organizations but continuing to voice about best public goods). The customer who exits public goods production cannot avoid caring about their quality as he/she is always subject to their consumption. Actually, he/she may be persuaded not to exit in order to prevent further deterioration of the product quality. Hirschman is rarely concerned with other units of exit than the individual member (firms, corporations, territories) because they imply exit from the state, something that he tends to see in the classic terms of migration and secession:[14] 'Exit is ordinarily unthinkable, though not always wholly impossible, from such primordial human groupings as family, tribe, church, and state.'[15]

The alternative between exit from within-state organizations, on the one hand, and migration and secession from the state, on the other hand, is too radical if we want to broaden the theoretical framework to include all forms of political formations and political arenas, including, therefore, political formations that are different from the national-welfare democratic state, preceding or following it. The current situation whereby economic transactions and new informatics and communication technologies are increasingly internationalized offers new opportunities for exit to goods, services, ideas, messages, fashions, etc. as well as to the corresponding organizational units for their production. Cultural homogeneity and economic control of the state's membership space can thus be consolidated only with difficulty given the current technologies of instant satellite communications, fax, network of computers, etc. In the light of this, it is interesting to apply Hirschman's conceptualization to the grey area of exit options that now lie between the two extreme and clear-cut cases: that is, to those exit options that mean

[13] Hirschman, 'Exit, Voice and the State', *World Politics*, 31 (1978), 90–107; reprinted in Hirschman, *Essays in Trespassing: Economics to Politics and Beyond*, 246–65, from which I quote 250–1.

[14] See Hirschman, 'Exit, Voice and the State', 249: 'The exit concept could, of course, be extended to cover cases of this sort. I shall, however, limit myself here to situations in which physical moving away of individuals or groups is an essential characteristic of the splitting up process'.

[15] Hirschman, *Exit, Voice, and Loyalty*, 79.

neither total withdrawal from organizational membership nor full territorial mobility (although they do depend on the increasing possibility of these options). These are thus 'partial' forms of exit, to be added to the 'total' forms.

In total exits—leaving a territory, seceding from a state, abandoning a membership organization, or stopping buying a good—everything is simultaneously withdrawn in one act. However, as pointed out above, we also need to conceive of 'partial exits'. Within certain governmental arenas there might exist or develop particular functional or spatial immunities into which the individual/corporation/group/territory can withdraw. Historically, an example of this is the 'sanctuary' exit, the fugitive who is safe at the altar of the church, or the Commune in the Middle Ages. There might also be a selective withholding of functions or duties de facto or on an institutional basis (military service, fiscal obligations, 'opting out'). This is not new either. Traditionally, certain regions were exempted from military services (Northern Ireland in the Second World War) or enjoyed extensive exception from taxation (e.g. Aragon as compared with Castilia in the Spanish Kingdom). Moreover, for a long time, various communes and provinces, and certain 'orders' or 'classes', enjoyed exemption from taxation as territorial or functional islands.

Table 1.1 presents a typology of exit opportunities based on the differences between public and private goods[16] and the distinctions between production

TABLE 1.1. *Types of exit and consequences*

	Private goods	Public goods
Production	Exit production of private goods:	Exit production of public goods:
	Relevant for internal political exchanges	Relevant for internal political exchanges: free riding and resource holder withholding
Consumption	Exit consumption of private goods:	Exit consumption of public goods:
	Impossible to transfer on territorial consumers the costs of the production of specific regulations, protections, allocations, etc.	Access to the production of alternative public goods outside the territory or de-territorialized
		Consequences for the territorialized political production

[16] In this context the distinction between 'public' and 'private' goods refers to the source of the production (public authorities versus private actors or taxation versus contract) rather than to the nature of the consumption (exclusiveness and publicity).

and consumption. The four boxes yielded by the cross-tabulation describe a wider set of exits than the total exits discussed above. Voluntary exit from the production of private goods (top-left cell) takes the temporary form of subtracting resources from the local production process, usually with the goal of exercising pressures on either social counterparts or public authorities. Strikes and lookouts are the most obvious forms. These (temporary) exits are significant for the outcomes of the within-territory political exchanges. They are aimed at improving one actor's terms of exchange by inflicting damages and reducing advantages to partners and political authorities.

Exit from the production of those public goods (top-right cell) that are based on voluntary participation also has considerable consequences for internal political exchanges as it can modify the balance of mobilization resources among politically relevant actors such as pressure groups, parties, and social movements. In many individual cases it takes the form of free riding. It can also take the form of (temporarily) withholding of resources necessary to establish negotiated orders between social partners and the political authority, in all those cases in which the participation of the social partners is necessary to establish and implement such agreements. Exit from the production of public goods based on compulsory participation—like taxation, duties, and obligations—is normally made very difficult by strong legal sanctions.[17]

The most interesting consequences are visible in the exit options from the consumption of private and public goods. Exit from the consumption of a given private good is the normal operating principle of the market. However, in a context in which the territorial economic boundaries are low and exit technology in the market and acquisition activities high (credit cards, mail order, e-commerce, de-territorialized service provision, etc.), exit from territorially produced and distributed private goods may have important repercussions on the 'political production' of a polity.[18] In principle the entire income generated on a given territory can be used by buying goods and services directly in different territories. This impinges on the capacity of the internal hierarchy to transfer the costs of production of territorially specific regulations, protections, allocations, jurisdictions and arbitrations—which are charged on the goods/services produced and distributed in the territory—on local and territorially confined consumers. In other words, it makes it impossible to charge local customers with those political costs within the

---

[17] Exiting from the production of a public good financed by general taxation is impossible even where one does not consume such good. Resorting to private schools and health care does not exempt one from financing these public services.

[18] I use this term in the sense given to it by Stoppino, M., *Potere e teoria politica* (Milano: Giuffré, 2001). See later for a more extensive discussion of it.

polity that can be avoided by selecting functional equivalent private goods produced under different (lower) production costs. This generates a situation of territorial institutional competition among different systems of political production.

Finally, the most unusual and challenging type of exit involves the capacity for individuals and their resources to withdraw (and to subtract themselves) from the consumption of particular public goods. In the ideal type model of the modern (nation-) state, this is unconceivable. One can decide not to vote, but cannot avoid consuming the decision of the elected officials, the security provided by the state, the credential control of professional orders and educational institutions, or the jurisdiction of territorial courts. Equally, one cannot opt out of the redistributive social obligations that are embedded into the national social security and welfare systems. The territorial sovereignty of the state is represented by its ability to exclude alternative authority sources over its territory and, therefore, alternative public goods. This is, however, exactly the field in which recent developments have started to change the picture and we should not rule out the possibility of various types of actors—individuals, organizations, firms and even territories—consuming public goods that are not produced in the territory without necessarily abandoning that territory physically. In particular, we need to acknowledge the growing possibility of accessing external resources in the forms of (*a*) external regulations, (*b*) external jurisdiction, and (*c*) external material allocations.

The possible consequences of the capacity to exit the consumption of territorial public goods are considerable. Access to alternative non- or extra-territorial public goods reduces the incentive to participate in the production of both voluntary and compulsory territorial public goods. Moreover, as with the exit from the consumption of private goods, the exit from the consumption of territorial public goods generates pressures on the territorial political production. This production increasingly needs to consider the preferences of those who are dissatisfied on account of being forced to continue to support the production of public goods that they do not consume. In short, exit from the consumption of private and public goods affects the extent to which the state can extract resources for building/maintaining territorial solidarities, and the extent to which the political system can spread such resources to its weaker and peripheral strata, sectors and territories.

Once the analytical possibility is acknowledged of opting out of the consumption of public goods without necessarily moving physically, a new set of behavioural options is opened up to domestic actors. Table 1.2 synthesizes these. In a situation of territorial closure, actors cannot exit from the state and their choices concern the possibility of withholding the resources they

TABLE 1.2. *Exits within, outside, and across territories*

Key actors	Inside territorial political units	Outside territorial political units	Across territorial political units
	Actors/resources **withholding**	Actors/resources **physical withdrawing**	Actors/resources **competition**
Territories	Fiscal, competence, administrative, and implementation resources	Secession	Access cross-territorial resources (material, regulative, and jurisdictional)
			Avoid unfavourable social obligations and public goods consumption
Individuals	Social hiding (tax evasion, black market and shadow economy, etc.), striking, disobeying, abstaining	Migration	As above
Resources	Investments, commodities, labour, skills	Delocation	As above
Aim	To extol the best term in internal political exchanges in terms of social obligations and public goods consumption	To escape territorial social obligations and public goods consumption	To selectively choose social obligations and alternative public goods consumption

control on a temporary basis. The aim is to inflict damages on and to reduce returns to other actors, so as to obtain the best terms in internal political exchanges in terms of social obligations and public goods consumption. The only alternative is a total exit option, by means of which actors withdraw themselves and the resources that they control, via secession, migration and delocation, with the aim of escaping their territorial social obligations and public goods consumption. The new possibility of consuming (regulative, jurisdictional and allocation) public goods across territorial units instead introduces a non-physical 'partial exit' that allows at least some margin for the selective choice of alternative social obligations. Resources are no longer necessarily withheld temporarily or withdrawn definitely, but can 'behave' as customers of competing public goods.

The final point of this section concerns the differential distribution of the opportunities to exit. Exit is an individual actor choice, but its cost varies and, therefore, not all actors have the same possibilities and opportunities for exit. This leaves open the possibility that the dissatisfied-mobiles—those who might exit—make the organization particularly sensitive to their needs, and, indeed, so much so that the organization tries to anticipate the course of action that will most likely prevent their exit. Moreover, the options of some will probably have impact on the options of the others, and exit choices may well provoke reactions of voice in those who do not possess or who do not want to use this option. Inequality of exit, together with its consequences for organizational performance, can thus also be seen as a source of conflict within a given organization. In many cases, how much exit is permitted from an organization is a controversial internal issue concerning the extent to which the organization can or should control its membership boundaries. Growing and unequally distributed exit options may be the basis for conflicts among those who want to restrict those options and those who want to open them up. The former realize that the options of the latter (*a*) are precluded to them; (*b*) increase the internal resources of the potential exiters beyond their capacity to voice; and, last but not least, (*c*) considerably reduce the resources and possibilities for the success of internal voice by materially subtracting the resources necessary for responding to it. For example, the quality of schooling in suburbs is affected when the richer and most highly educated citizens leave, not only because those schools lose the most likely vocal defenders of quality standards, but also because they may lose the material resources through which a certain qualitative standard was guaranteed to those who could not otherwise afford it.

At the abstract level, the discussion of the differential individual options for exit cannot progress any further. In concrete situations, the chances of exit are defined by specific mechanisms and techniques of boundary building, which are macro features of the system external to the individual's choice. Institutional barriers to exit are set at all levels of social organization and justified on various grounds, from improving efficiency to guaranteeing professional credentials, to defending useful social institutions, and even to stimulating voice in deteriorating, although recoverable organizations which would be prematurely destroyed through free exit. We therefore need to develop a theory of institutional boundary building, without which the discussion of the differential distribution of exit options remains fairly speculative. Boundaries define the configuration of the individual actors and resources 'locked in' a given territorial polity. Following the discussion so far, I define the process of 'locking in' as the obligation to consume territorial public goods in the forms of allocation, regulation, protection, jurisdiction and arbitration.

Boundary

Rokkan was strongly influenced by Hirschman's simple concepts, and he used the exit/voice paradigm to interpret different waves of European state formation since the sixteenth century. For him, exit was crucial for the resourceful set of cities and small territorial states in the Central European 'city-belt', which successfully resisted incorporation into broader territorial systems until the nineteenth century (see Chapter 2). Rokkan thus applies the exit paradigm to the formation of territorial units within Europe, to problematize the division of territories into 'units', and to problematize state boundaries (which Hirschman does not do). The exit-voice mechanism is primarily (but not exclusively, as will be shown below) applied to the study of territorial social systems, that is systems that are limited in their membership and codes of interaction within spatially identifiable boundaries. He uses the concept of boundary to unpack the historical formation of the 'state'.[19] The concept of 'boundary' can be seen as the macro equivalent of the individualistic concept of 'exit'. In fact, each choice for exit (or entry, of course) always implies the transcendence of some barrier and entry into some other entity. Exit is the transfer of a component part from one system to another. At the most general level, exit is always the crossing of an established boundary.

The English language has three terms to indicate a line of demarcation: 'frontier', 'border' and 'boundary'.[20] The term 'frontier' reflects the experience of the nation-state most directly, indicating the line where different jurisdictions meet, and it is characterized by the demarcations signals such as customs, police, and military personnel. The term 'border' also points to a territorial line of demarcation and the narrow zone around it. However, in American English, border is usually utilized to refer to international frontiers. 'Boundary' is regarded as the narrowest of the three, conveying the meaning of a line of demarcation, even if this is sometimes internal to the state. In short, the three terms can be regarded, and are often used, as synonymous. I will, however, follow an alternative line of reasoning, attributing to 'boundary' the broadest possible analytical meaning of indicating any demarcation line between territorial *or* membership groups (and this

---

[19] Rokkan, S., *State Formation, Nation Building, and Mass Politics in Europe. The theory of Stein Rokkan*, ed. P. Flora with S. Kuhnle and D. Urwin (Oxford: Oxford University Press, 1999), 343. He also outlines a distinction between 'primary exit' and 'secondary exit' (103). Primary exit refers to early innovation, while secondary exit refers to the concrete spreading of opportunities and alternatives for individuals.

[20] For a discussion of these three terms see Anderson, M., *Frontiers. Territory and State Formation in the Modern World* (Cambridge: Polity Press, 1996), 9–10.

would seem to be in line with Rokkan's usage, even though he never offered any clear definition of the term). On this view, the term *boundary* is used to indicate the focal point for the delimitation of a territory or of a group; in other words, boundaries identify both territorial groups *and* membership groups. For instance, an economic boundary defines an area of free market transactions (economic rights, property rights, exchange options, productive factors' mobility, common currency); a cultural boundary defines spaces characterized by the traits of the inhabitants membership group (national, ethnic, linguistic, racial, etc.); a politico-administrative boundary delimits the territory on the basis of the regulatory regimes (politico-social rights, education, labour market, etc.); a coercion or military boundary delimits the territory on the basis of the extraction-coercion agency and capacity. In this work, the term *border* will be used to indicate the actual physical frontier of historical states.

The crucial consequence of this definition is the following: a border can delimit a territory that is characterized by specific, distinctive and coinciding economic, cultural, administrative and coercion boundaries. On the contrary, a border can also define a territory whose boundaries are blurred, overlapping with those of other territories, and/or disjointed from one another.

In an individualistic perspective, exit is the act of transcending a boundary. All potential forms of mobility bring with them the constant threat of exit, as well as the development of pressures to contain movements within boundaries. The building of boundaries sets the costs and payoffs of barriers for various types of transactions across local communities, membership groups, organizations, and territorial entities. In this way, at the systemic macro level, boundaries 'lock in' crucial resources and actors within the system and determine the internal configuration of politically relevant resources. Boundaries are 'locking-in mechanisms' that increase the cost of exit and set differential incentives to stay within the system. These locking-in mechanisms can affect actors' economic interests and corresponding instrumental calculations when they impinge upon the material costs of exit. They can also affect actors' identities and solidarities (and the corresponding institutions) when they impinge upon the cultural costs of exit. They can, moreover, affect actors' safety and integrity when they impinge upon administrative, coercion and violent impositions. As a result, every strategy for the differential control of boundaries has consequences for the configuration of the political resources inside each territory/group. Through the concept of 'boundary' we can set up the linkage between strategies of external control and internal political developments, between the collectivization of territories (and groups) and the development of hierarchies for their defence.

In his historical and empirical work, Rokkan refers primarily to external territorial boundaries. However, he also extends this conceptualization to the internal political dynamics. For instance, his thresholds of legitimation, incorporation, representation and executive powers that any new non-established political movement has to overcome in the first democratization process are interpreted as barriers to entry, that is, they are viewed as internal boundaries. His map of Europe thus generates hypotheses about the interaction between external and internal boundary-building strategies. In other words, in his analysis, the policies pursued in controlling external transactions also affect the internal channelling of voice, that is, the way in which the threshold of legitimation, incorporation, representation and executive powers are overcome.

There is a striking correspondence between Rokkan's macro-level link between external boundary control and internal political structuring and Hirschman's micro-level relationship between exit options and propensity to voice. I will now clarify and elaborate on this linkage, adapting it to my purposes. First, however, a more thorough discussion of the concept of boundary is necessary, as was done with the concept of exit. The first step is to provide a general and low connotation definition of the concept. To the best of my knowledge, the concept of boundary in the sense that it is used here is not typical of Weberian terminology. Yet, boundary is the key element that defines a crucial dichotomy by Weber: that between 'open' and 'closed' social relationships.[21] Boundaries are those elements that determine the level of openness or closure of a social relationship: a social relationship is open towards the exterior 'if and in so far as, its system of orders does not deny participation to anyone who wishes and is actually in a position to do so'. On the contrary, a social relationship is closed towards the exterior 'so far as, according to its subjective meaning and its binding rules, participation of certain persons is excluded, limited or subject to restrictions', [. . .]. 'If the participants expect that the admission of others will lead to an improvement of their situations, an improvement in degree, in kind, in the security or the value of the satisfaction, their interests will be in keeping the relationship open. If, on the contrary, their expectations are of improving their positions by monopolistic tactics, their interest is in a closed relationship'. The 'subjective meaning' and its 'binding rules' are exactly what I define as boundaries here.

By setting the level of closure of a given social relationship, boundaries determine a clear distinction between the 'ins' and the 'outs', and this criterion of exclusion is based on unequal access to rewards, resources and opportunities, no matter what the basis for inequality is.[22] The closure practices which derive from boundary setting can develop along various criteria: lineage, property, education, credentials, power and force, status, race, ethnicity, gender, religion, language, etc., and on the basis of different rules or codes of closure. Only certain boundaries and their corresponding exclusion rules are backed by the legal apparatuses of the state. For instance, international borders can be interpreted as a set of boundaries that close the social relationships between insiders and outsiders, to the extent that they set the distinctions and differences in membership rights, privileges and obligations between the 'natives' and the 'foreigners'. Similarly, even the most fragile club sets distinctions and differences in the rights, privileges and obligations of members versus non-members.

Boundaries define collectivist and individualistic criteria of exclusion and closure.[23] Collectivist criteria of exclusion are directly responsible for the transmission of advantage to other members of the group (e.g. family descendants, lineage, caste, race, religion, ethnicity and state membership). Individualistic criteria (property, power, credentials, and achievements) are equally designed to protect advantages, but are less efficient than collectivist criteria in transmitting such advantages to the descendants or next generation of group members. In Western cultures a long-term tendency can be identified for the collectivist criteria of exclusion to be replaced by individualist criteria of exclusion.

The distinction between boundaries and associated closure rules and codes *within* a territorial system and boundaries and associated closure rules and codes *between* territorial systems reformulates the distinction made above between the demarcation of external boundaries of geographical space and the differentiation of roles in the internal organization of the population occupying this physical space. This formulation underlines more closely the relationship between the type of external boundaries and the means by which they are set up, on the one hand, and the same processes for internal boundaries, on the other. The differences among boundaries can be presented as five features:

1. *Nature*: The distinction here is between 'territorial' and 'functional' boundaries. In conditions of low socio-economic development, low technology, and sense-based communication, all sorts of social interactions are land-and distance-bound; they are thus territorial to a large extent.

---

[22] See Murphy, R., *Social Closure. The Theory of Monopolization and Exclusion* (Oxford: Clarendon Press, 1988), 46 for an elaboration of the concept of 'exclusion'. Closure theory is built up from the scattered elements drawn from the work of Weber and Marx.

[23] For this distinction see Parking, F., *Marxism and Class Theory. A Bourgeois Critique* (London: Tavistock, 1979).

Changes in technology, economy, and communication foster the development of patterns of interaction and of organizations that are increasingly non-spatial. These 'functional' organizations are non-spatial in the sense that they regroup people who are separated by distance and deprived of direct face-to-face interaction. The boundaries of these organizations are identified by the rules, norms, principles, roles and behaviours governing the identification of their members. Systems[24] whose membership is defined by spatially identifiable boundaries are territorial units. States are a special type of territorial unit. Nation-states are an even more specific variety of these. The differences between types of territorial units can be presented in terms of other features of their boundaries indicated below.

2. *Type*: This feature designates the type of input the boundary is meant to filter. Boundaries are of different types; they may filter emotional and affective relations, social rights or cultural messages. Territorial boundaries may screen and filter economic transactions, administrative regulations, legal jurisdictions. Functional boundaries may sort and protect credentials, lineage, property and so forth.

3. *Permeability*: The permeability of each boundary refers to the extent to which external entries and internal exits are screened, filtered and selected. Boundaries can be open or closed, high or low, to a greater or lesser extent, where these terms indicate the degree to which external inputs can penetrate through the boundary and internal elements can exit those same boundaries. Openness is normally associated with options and choices for the individual actor: to communicate and receive information, to know and to be known, to select her own membership affiliation, to enter and walk out of groups and organizations. Openness has costs for systems, units and organizations, as members and resources can easily abandon them when facing competitive pressures. Boundary closeness, too, entails costs, as boundary control structures and agencies consume energies and resources.

4. *Effectiveness*: This feature refers to the extent to which the boundary and its openness/closeness is regulated by decision-makers of the unit/system/organization. In other words, the extent to which the central hierarchy is able to control the entries and exits by intentionally varying the degree of permeability.

5. *Coincidence*: This characteristic refers to the level of overlapping that exists among different types of boundaries. Whether different types of

[24] Even if some of these concepts draw on elements of general system theory, in this context there is no need to accept the key GST idea that there must be some level of isomorphism among all systems—from sub-atomic particles to molecules, from cells to organs, from organisms to groups, from states to world organization—and that concepts and principles are transferable throughout the whole spectrum.

boundaries impinge on the social territory or membership group or, alternatively, are territorially or functionally 'disjointed' has crucial implications for the nature of the unit, system, organization or group. Most theories of social and political structuring—such as theories of social stratification, of intergroup conflict, of political behaviour, of nation-state development—assume that the degree of coincidence or overlapping that occurs between different types of boundaries is crucial, even if they do not use the concept of boundary.

Nature, type, permeability, effectiveness and *coincidence*[25] describe features covering the variations in empirical and historical boundaries. I will first concentrate on the type, permeability and coincidence of boundaries in specific connection with the external boundaries of territorial systems. I will deal with the effectiveness of boundaries further down, in the section dealing with central hierarchy formation and its 'political production' (see later).

Table 1.3 presents a scheme of the types of boundaries that distinguish membership according to different criteria. The table identifies four dimensions of boundary building among units in the force, culture, economic, and administrative domains. Alongside with territorial formations (city-states, nation-states, empires) defined by military and administrative boundaries, there are also cultural systems (religion, languages, national identities) and economic systems (trade networks, tariff unions, national or global economies), and politico-administrative systems defining functional regimes of rights, duties and obligations. Unfortunately, no terms allowing us to avoid the tedious repetition of expressions such as 'cultural boundary', 'economic boundary', administrative boundary, etc. have yet been established or accepted. However, even if no appropriate labels are as yet available,[26] it is important to keep these different boundaries as distinct as possible at the conceptual level.

---

[25] Another feature of boundaries is *degree of importance*: the degree to which the maintenance of the key goal or focal activity of the system depends on the efficiency of the boundary maintenance. For instance, in certain historical periods the focal activity of a territorial system can only be maintained if its military boundary is effective in screening the intrusion of an alternative military force. In different contexts or times, the capacity to exclude alternative legal jurisdiction can be the crucial capacity to maintain the system. See Strassoldo, R. and Bubert, R., 'The Boundary. An Overview of its Current Theoretical Status', in *Boundaries and Regions. Explorations in the Growth and Peace Potential of the Peripheries* (Trieste: Edizioni Lint, 1973), Proceedings of the conference 'Problems and Perspectives of Border Regions', 29–57, 49.

[26] Boundaries were conceptualized in a richer way in the Latin language than is the case in most of our 'national' languages now. Concepts such as *limes, terminus, confinum* and *finis* identified several different types of boundaries. This reflected the higher boundary differentiation of the Roman Empire in military, cultural, and citizenship terms.

TABLE 1.3. *Types of territorial boundaries*

	The boundary is defined in terms of:			
	Market transactions	Cultural traits	Politico-administrative claims	Force military/coercion claims
Processes that create and consolidate the surrounding limits of the territory	Market building	Nation building	Functional regime building	State building
Focal point for operationalization of the territory	Economic rights, property rights, exchange options, factors' mobility, common currency	Membership space characterized by the traits of the inhabitants (language, religion, ethnicity)	Political/social rights, regulatory systems (education, welfare, labour market)	Central repressive and extractive agencies

More specifically, then, the formation of economic boundaries and the building of markets have their focal point in the openness of transactions in a given geographical area and in the necessary correlates of property rights agreements, contracts enforceability, exchange options and factor mobility. Cultural boundaries instead define a membership space characterized by the 'traits' of the inhabitants (language, religion, ethnicity, national identity, etc.). Of course, in principle, we know that cultural identities are not necessarily concentrated geographically. However, what I am interested in here is the vast majority of historical cases in which some sort of territorial concentration defines and reinforces the cultural identity of the individuals by the continuous interaction that they undergo with their peers/equals in the geographical space they share. The politico-administrative boundaries identify those primarily legal boundaries that differentiate different functional regimes and regulatory systems such as educational systems, welfare regimes, labour markets institutions, courts' jurisdictions, etc. Finally, the 'force' boundaries define the geographical space within which a single central authority exercises its ultimate right to physically coerce the subjected population. Therefore, it can be concluded that the physical geographical border of the (modern) state, however important, is only one of several boundaries characterizing such entity.

Table 1.4[27] summarizes the exit options and boundary-building discussion developed so far for the different types of territorial boundaries. These boundaries define sets of cross-boundary transactions and sets of control measures. The (potential) units of these transactions and control in the different subsystems are goods and services, corporations, physical persons, messages, territories and even 'roles'. Potential exit options as well as boundary-building mechanisms can be identified for each subsystem As new 'technologies' for exit/entry develop, they generate pressures on existing boundaries. By the same token, new boundary-building mechanisms are also continuously invented. Along each of these territorial boundaries, the development of rules and codes of closure can set/reinforce boundaries, and their decline can remove/weaken them. For each dimension, then, exit options and boundary building interact.

Figure 1.2 cross-tabulates the permeability and coincidence of boundaries in order to identify the variations in the external consolidation of those territorial units that are of particular ideal-type significance for my argument. Dichotomizing permeability into low (closed or strong boundaries) and high

---

[27] The table is adapted from Rokkan, S., 'Entries, voices, exits: Towards a possible generalization of the Hirschman Model', *Social Science Information*, 13 (1974), 39–53, 43. I have added the line corresponding to the politico-administrative subsystems—which Rokkan sets together with the force-coercion subsystem—and I have added and moved items of exit units and boundary mechanisms.

TABLE 1.4. *Exit options and boundary building*

	Exit option units	Boundary building mechanisms
Economy	Goods	Embargoes
	Services	Tariffs/quantity restrictions
	Tourists	Labour-market controls
	Corporations	Credit/capital controls
	Investors	Nationalization of economy
	Customers	
Culture	Messages, news	Prohibition
	Styles, ideas	Censorship
	Fashion, fads	Loyalty-building rites/symbols
	Scribes, scientists	Control of socializing agencies
	Religious/ideological orders	Nationalization of culture
	Intellectuals	
	Missionaries	
Force/coercion/extraction	Soldiers, armies	Territorialization of defence
	Police	Territorialization of policing
	Spies	Borders control
	Underground movements	Territorial extraction system
	Organized crime	Restriction on residence
	Tax payers	Restrictions on travelling
Politico-administrative (functional regimes)	Voters	Protection of citizenship
	Candidates	National specific social rights
	Legal claimants (judges/cases)	Professional credential codes
	Substate governments	National jurisdiction
	Students	National educational
	Welfare recipients	Title system

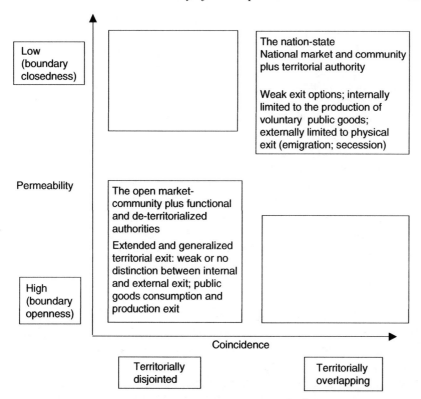

FIGURE 1.2. Characteristics of boundaries

(open or weak boundaries) and coincidence as 'disjointed boundaries' versus 'overlapping boundaries' a space of variation is created that defines two clear polar types—in the bottom-left corner and in the upper-right corner—and two mixed cases of difficult identification in the other two corners.

Both our daily experience and our historical memory lead us to clearly perceive a situation of extended, if not complete, territorial overlap and coincidence (the upper-right box of Figure 1.2). The modern European nation-state has successfully integrated the above mentioned boundary-building processes, so that it is characterized by boundaries that are simultaneously military, economic, cultural and functional. Thus, in crossing the border of one nation-state we cross all its different boundaries, moving under the rule of alternative extractive agencies, into a different economic market, a different cultural community, and a different set of functional regimes (educational, welfare, etc.). In this case, the correspondence between authority and territory is most pronounced and the scope and reach of the political production also tends to be wide and deep. This (territorial) coincidence of different type boundaries is the nation-state's distinctive trait—distinguishing it from earlier or different forms of *political formation*, as well as its legitimacy principle. The modern nation-state is based on a collectivist criterion of exclusion, aiming at monopolizing certain advantages for the members of the territorial group in various but coinciding functional areas where the rights and obligations of these are sharply distinguished from those of 'foreigners'. Interestingly, such type of state may be subject to a decline in this collectivist exclusion and to becoming more universalistic. The fact that different types of boundaries have tended to coincide in the age of the modern (nation-) state does not, in other words, means that they did so before or that they will necessarily continue to do so in the future. Boundary coincidence can therefore be seen as a specific historical phase or development.

The coincidence of different types of boundaries within a given territory also give rise to the neat distinction between the 'external relations' of a territorial unit and its internal role differentiation and political dynamics (and, therefore, to the distinction between 'international relations' and 'domestic politics' as academic disciplines). This distinction would appear to be the contingent historical result of a specific constellation: the case in which a strongly differentiated internal hierarchical order manages to control its external territorial and functional boundaries—and to correspondingly reduce exit options—so closely as to insulate domestic structuring processes from external influences and to make them relatively independent developments. At the same time, the internal hierarchical order presents itself as the single organizing principle of the internal domestic structuring and as the single autonomous centre for handling external relations. It therefore becomes possible to separate the study of the internal development of the domestic 'governmental arena', from the study of the anarchic 'natural arena' (see later) of external interactions. However, any historical deviation from this pure type of coinciding and mutually reinforcing cultural, economic and military administrative boundaries actually makes the distinction between 'foreign' and 'domestic' politics of limited, and sometimes even misleading, use.

Another reason why it is hard to conceive these boundaries as analytically distinct is that, while we can easily construct the ideal type of their coincidence—that is, the ideal type of the sovereign, unitary, autarchic and culturally homogeneous state—it is difficult to identify pure cases of disjointed boundaries. We can make a few examples. The primordial hunter-gatherer community did not possess a distinct territoriality and had primarily cultural boundaries, as kinship links imposed almost insurmountable barriers on externals in all fields. Again, those 'imperial' territorial hierarchies that encompassed different cultural groups and included several substantially closed market areas represented a pure force/coercion/extractive boundary. The Roman Empire had a clear perception of where its *limes*—its military borders—lay and where its *civitas*—Roman citizenship—ended. Furthermore, there were several additional intermediate borders between limes and civitas—for instance, the politico-administrative borders of those militarily subject populations that were left to run their internal matters according to their traditions and rules. Another example can be seen in the pure market boundaries that existed beyond political-administrative borders in those free-trade areas encompassing city networks, such as the Hanseatic League, within which the respect of basic economic rights was guaranteed across cultural, military, and politico-administrative borders.[28]

In the bottom-left quadrant of Figure 1.2 we find those cases of a polity whose boundaries are weak—where transcendence is thus easy and high— and do not coincide territorially and are not coterminous with each other. The ideal-type political formation described here may be part of a broader territorial defence and security community whose range will not necessarily coincide with that of the cultural membership group. Various administrative functional regimes which are not unique to this territory will impinge on it; it may also be fully economically integrated with other polities which are not necessarily the same as those with which a security defence is built, a cultural community is defined, or an administrative regime is shared. This is a situation in which territoriality has lost a considerable amount of its weight. On the same territory will impinge different and diversified authorities with a legitimate functional claim in different domains (military security, public order, market transaction, cultural identity, etc.). No one single authority should be able to claim an overriding sovereignty and the concept itself of sovereignty is deprived of its historical meaning. Authority tends to be de-territorialized, and to be based instead on functional area and competences.

These two clear-cut extreme cases serve as reference points for pre-nation-state polities, as well as for the kinds of changes that the nation-state undergoes. Some or all the boundaries may weaken and be lowered, allowing more frequent boundary transcendence by actors and resources, with a consequent impact on the type and scope of territorial political production. Boundaries may also tend to disjoin from each other, leading to potential competition between different kinds of territorial and functional authorities.

---

[28] The *van der dütschen hanse* league included about 200 cities between the middle of the fourteenth and the middle of the fifteenth centuries. It was based on specific economic agreements and mutual commercial advantages among the members. Although there was a long-term predominance of the Lubecca-led regional 'quarter', a political 'constitution' was never formalized. There were, however, rules of closure, discriminating against externals through the principal mechanism of the economic boycotting of their harbours.

While boundary lowering and growing exit/entry options directly affect the scope and reach of territorialized political production, boundary territorial disjoining directly affects the competition between alternative territorial authorities of different scope and in different domains.

We have no labels to indicate these situations of mismatch. There is no terminology for loosely bounded territories, that is for polities whose boundaries are disjointed and not overlapping and/or weak and highly permeable. We have some familiarity with the situation of areas and/or groups for which coercion and administrative territorial claims are not congruent with cultural identities: the various types of 'external', 'enclave' and 'interface' cultural peripheries.[29] It is, however, more difficult to conceive and label those situations in which economic and politico-administrative borders or economic and cultural borders do not coincide: in which politico-administrative rights and/or cultural identities are not territorially congruent with the economic rights and transactions.[30]

This discussion and theoretical revision of the key concepts of 'exit' and 'boundary' allow us to use them for the analysis of the overall process of consolidation of any territorial political formation. I start from the analysis of the role of the central territorial hierarchy, a category Hirschman does not treat and that seems to correspond to Rokkan's concept of 'centre formation'. Following this, I will examine an additional micro–macro parallel in the work of my two key authors: the concept of 'loyalty' in Hirschman and that of 'system building' in Rokkan. Finally, I will conclude the journey with a discussion of the third and final conceptual opposition: that between 'voice'—so far mentioned only in relation to exit—and of 'political structuring'.

Hierarchy and Centre Formation

The control of entry/exit choices via the setting of boundaries presupposes the existence of some central hierarchy of the political formation (Figure 1.1). The nature, role and strategy of this central organizational hierarchy are not dealt with explicitly in Hirschman's work. Hirschman sees the central hierarchy as a reactive entity that is more or less forced to respond to the

---

[29] For a discussion of the different types of cultural peripheries see Rokkan, S. and Urwin, D., *Economy, Territory, Identity. Politics of West European Peripheries* (London: Sage, 1983).

[30] Of course, Medieval thinking was more 'flexible' in terms of sub-systemic boundaries. For a rich series of examples of 'lack of coincidence' in the modern sense see Hintze, *Soziologie und Geschichte Staat und Verfassung*; and Gierke, O., *Political Theories of the Middle Age* (Cambridge: Cambridge University Press, 1988).

deterioration of its performance when it is alerted and stimulated by either exit or voice or both. However, the same original consolidation of a central hierarchy is dependent on the formations of some types of boundaries and on the limitation of some kind of exits/entries. Although theories of the original formation of territorial political units—or 'states' if we apply this term to every territorial unit[31]—do not resort to exit and boundary concepts, in my opinion they can easily and profitably be reformulated through such concepts.

In Carneiro's theory of early state formation,[32] warfare is the crucial mechanism. However, he contends that without some level of confinement of the actors, the formation of a political centre and of its hierarchy is unlikely. To describe this he uses the concept of 'environmental circumscription', meaning by this an area of circumscribed agricultural land. In conditions of no circumscription and of unlimited agricultural land (and of a low population) the effect of warfare tends to disperse the villages and keep them autonomous. There is no effective way of preventing the losers from fleeing to a distant part of the forest. With environmental circumscription (effectively no exit option), warfare tends to politically integrate the series of villages. States come into being where the availability of agricultural land is restricted, that is, in cases of ecological or environmental circumscription. If and when agricultural land is easily available, warfare leads to population migration, as means of subsistence can be found elsewhere. It is therefore competition for land that triggers warfare and the attempt at political subjugation that give rise to wide political units. A second condition is 'resource concentration'. In conditions of no or low environmental circumscription, the concentration of a particularly valuable agricultural resources works in the same way, as a kind of circumscription that increases competition for cultivable land. Therefore, resource concentration can be added to environmental circumscription as a factor leading to warfare and thus to political integration beyond the village level.

Third, Carneiro introduces a principle of population pressure and 'social circumscription'. The high density of the population in an area can produce effects on the people who live near the centre of the area. These effects are similar to the effects produced by environmental circumscription: it becomes difficult for villages in the core central area to escape war by moving away.

[31] Finer, S. E., *The History of Government From the Earliest Times*, 3 vols. (Oxford: Oxford University Press, 1997) follows this line: see Vol. 1, *Ancient Monarchies and Empires*, 3–15.

[32] See Carneiro, R. L., 'A Theory of the Origins of the State', *Science*, 169 (1970), 733–8; Carneiro, R. L., 'Political Expansion as an Expression of the Principle of Competitive Exclusion', in R. Cohen and E. R. Service (eds.), *Origins of the State* (Philadelphia: Institute for the Study of Human Issues, 1978), 205–23; Carneiro, R. L., 'The circumscription theory', *American Behavioral Scientist*, 31 (1988), 497–511.

Therefore, even in the absence of strong environmental circumscription, the effects of resource concentration and of population density may lead to warfare and its state-building effect. Finally, social circumscription refers to the fact that at some stage the new political unit meets other political units of equal political complexity and warfare capacity, and that these geographically circumscribe the spread of the new state.

All the conditions of confinement (or 'circumscription') that Carneiro regards as conducive to early state formation are conditions of 'no exit' based on physical and non-physical boundaries to migration and displacement. The inability of people and tribes to avoid the encroachment of the new centre represents the crucial fostering condition of state formation. The mechanisms that lead from environmental circumscription and/or resource concentration and/or population density/social circumscription to the likelihood of warfare and to state formation beyond the village, are mechanisms based on the formation of boundaries and on the confinement of exit options.

Service's theory of early state formation concentrates more heavily, instead, on the institutionalization of centralized leadership, on its legitimation principle and on role differentiation within the polity. Service gives primary importance to the way in which leadership becomes centralized and functionally differentiated into specialized political roles. In other words, his theory of institutionalized leadership tends to concentrate primarily on the internal integrative processes of state formation.[33] However, Carneiro and Service's theories are not alternative or in competition.[34] In the Weberian definition of the state with which this chapter begins, the linkage between the external consolidation of the state—the specific condition of environmental and social circumscription—and its internal structuring—the process of internal integration and differentiation—is implicit. In other words, the building of boundaries and the confinement of exit options normally result from the activities and the initiatives of a central political hierarchy that is actively engaged in the territorial consolidation of the political formation. At the same time, the same process of boundary building and exit confinement strengthen the internal hierarchy and contribute to the formation of the centre in the political unit. Increased political control is normally converted into a variety of policies in various domains. These may be meant to change the balance between private and public goods and consumption, for instance, by making resources available for investing in those areas that are necessary

[33] See Service, E. R., *Origins of the state and civilization: The process of cultural evolution* (New York: W.W. Norton, 1975); Service, E. R., 'Classical and Modern Theories of the Origins of Government', in Cohen and Service (eds.), *Origins of the State*, 21–34.

[34] This is the opinion, for instance, of Deflem, M., 'Warfare, political leadership and state formation. The case of the Zulu Kingdom, 1808–1879', *Ethnology*, 38 (1999), 371–91.

for economic development, welfare provisions, new skills development, or military investments.

The closedness of boundaries and the reduction of exit options generates processes which (*a*) increase political production in scope and reach, with an intensification in the production of rights in various spheres and a widening of the fields of reference; (*b*) trigger mechanisms of 'legitimation' of the central hierarchy; and (*c*) trigger mechanisms for the political structuring of the polity. The closedness of various types of boundaries of a polity normally increases its capacity for political control. This political control does not need to be authoritarian or totalitarian. Even poliarchic polities may have higher or lower levels of boundary closedness. Moreover, the scope, complexity and reach of the activities of the internal hierarchy—its *'political production'*, following the terminology developed by Mario Stoppino—[35]depend on the process of confinement that is implicit in boundary building and exit control.

To establish a clear relationship between the exit options and boundary building, on the one hand, and the 'political production' of the central hierarchy, on the other, requires some theoretical elaborations. A 'political arena' can be said to exist when at least some exit options are impossible or irrelevant, that is, when actors perceive themselves as locked into a network of mutual interaction. If exit is possible, then a social actor can escape the conflict, competitive, cooperative or negotiation social relationships with others.[36] Every political arena is, therefore, characterized by a certain degree of closure (no-exit), which, in principle, may be due physical or natural reasons. However, in every political arena, the unavoidable interactions between locked-in actors generate forms of political action aimed at obtaining the behavioural conformity of the other actors to one actor's will, values and goals. Political arenas can therefore be produced by extra-political dynamics (like mere physical confinement) but they generate political action as search and production of behavioural conformity.

Political arenas can be 'natural' arenas or 'governmental' arenas[37] according to the absence or presence of a special 'third' actor endowed with the monopoly in the production of behavioural conformity. In natural arenas— as, for instance, in the natural international arena—actors often find themselves in various situations of resource asymmetry. Attempts to influence other actors who are able to provide the goods and value that are sought after, take the form of promised recompenses or of threats of damages. These

---

[35] Stoppino, *Potere e teoria politica*. The discussion that follows is strongly influenced by the observations of this author on the concept of power and the nature of politics.

[36] I have discussed these types of relationships in Bartolini, S., 'Collusion, Competition and Democracy. Part 1', *Journal of Theoretical Politics*, 11 (1999), 435–70.

[37] See Stoppino, *Potere e teoria politica*. Other authors use the expression 'authority arena'.

possible actions define power relationships in which each actor aims to achieve maximum behavioural conformity from the other actors. In other words, in a natural political arena the guaranteed power attributed to each actor depends exclusively on its resources (economic, symbolic, violence) and their strategic use through a continuous process of conflict and negotiation. The outcomes of these conflicts and negotiations, however, are precarious and unstable and determine a situation of uncertainty (as to costs and advantages) and insecurity (as to physical integrity). Changes in the quantity of resources or in their strategic value can modify the established pacts. In conclusion, in a natural political arena, the behavioural conformity of the others is achieved temporarily. Such conformity is neither stabilized over time nor generalized and guaranteed with respects to the claims of all other existing or potential actors of the arena.

Unlike natural arenas—a field in which the power of each actor closely corresponds to the level and use of his/her own resources—a governmental arena is a field in which the power guaranteed to the social actors depends on the role and the function of a third actor (and its agents) located into the central hierarchical organization.[38] In other words, a governmental arena (any governmental arena, from the state to the professional order) is endowed with an actor and an institution specialized in the production of behavioural conformity. The guarantee of the behavioural conformity of the others takes the form of a right, titles, and capacities. That is, it takes the form of 'endowments' that confer on the actor concerned the stable and generalized behavioural conformity of the other actors (and, if necessary, the right to resort to the political authority to ensure such conformity), with respect to its right to exercise certain activities. In a governmental political arena, every guaranteed power/right/title represents the capacity to exercise an activity with respect to which the dispositions and attitudes to conformity of all the other member actors are fixed and stabilized in time (at least in the minimal sense of non-interference).

In this sense, the essential good produced by the central hierarchy is not any specific final value, but, rather, the stabilized and generalized conformity of the others towards the acquisition of that value.[39] The essential good produced by every governmental arena is thus the conformity of the others. If the 'political production' of a system is clearly based on a binding network of decisions and rules from which actors cannot escape, its essential feature is not represented by these binding decisions per se, but rather by the creation of a guaranteed multilateral conformity for a vast group of actors. Because political production generates this network of multilateral guaranteed con-

---

[38] Stoppino, M., 'Che cosa è la politica', *Quaderni di scienza politica*, 1 (1994), 1–34.
[39] Stoppino, *Potere e teoria politica*, 245.

formities for a plurality of actors, it makes it possible for them to engage in relevant social interactions as exchanges, competition, cooperation, negotiations, and limited conflict. There is, in fact, effective political production only to the extent that none of the actors concerned is free to endanger the stabilized and generalized conformity of the others.

In governmental arenas, there is a differentiation between the search for political authority and the search and defence of specific values, rights and titles. While in natural political arenas the conformity achieved through the use of the resources is a single case of conformity, *hic et nunc*, and a single exercise of power, in governmental arenas this is instead the capacity to exercise such power as this expands over time and extends over a plurality of actors. When political power guarantees the existence of stabilized and generalized behavioural conformity, the single actor does not need to accumulate personal power resources. It can search for others' conformity through the rights and titles distributed by the political hierarchy in the form of its due quota of conformity.

The public goods distributed through this specialized function may be wider or more restricted in type and scope in different cases and historical periods, but they normally include at least some protection (defence from others through coercive sanctions); arbitration (control and limitation of the conflicts between qualified actors); jurisdiction (guarantees about the compliance to commitments made by social actors and their respect of the services and performances promised and dues); regulation (definition of the rules of the game); allocation (direct allocation of goods, services, duties). It is implicit in what I have argued so far that the capacity, scope, and effectiveness of this production of public goods is crucially dependent on the control of the boundaries between the governmental arenas and other governmental arenas. The higher the control of the transaction across authority arenas, the more extensive and effective is, in principle, the capacity of the autonomous production of public goods and the higher the capacity of the internal hierarchy to stabilize and legitimize its domination position.

At this stage we can define the process of 'centre formation' more precisely as the process of transformation of natural political arenas into governmental political arenas. Centre formation implies locking in resources that are essential to widen the scope and reach of political production. In government arenas, a fundamental role in the closure of the field (and in the reduction of exit options) is played by the production of rights (in the form of titles, competencies, liberties, faculties, capacities, authority). These 'guaranteed rights' are organized into a network of binding orders that stabilize social interaction in a field. This makes it clear that in order to have a political production that distributes rights and titles, it is necessary to prevent the exit of those actors or resources over which those rights and titles can be exercised. Therefore, confinement through boundaries is essential to political production and to the generalization and stabilization of conformity. There can be no politics without confinement in this sense; there is no politics without a locking in of actors and resources.

The above mentioned is crucial for all those situations in which the reaching of the goals of an actor requires the conformity of other actors. If an actor does not need this conformity to achieve its own goals and values, its rationality consists in the best use of its resources. This distinction also clarifies the crucial difference—discussed above in reference to Table 1.2—that exists between the 'internal withholding' of resources *in* conflicts and negotiations and the 'eternal withdrawal' of the same resources *from* negotiations and conflicts. Negotiation is a communicative interaction in which actors make threats (emerging damages and declining advantages), promises (emerging gains and declining damages) and symbolic messages concerning facts and knowledge, values and beliefs, to obtain the most favourable terms of exchange. The symbolic element is best represented by that amount of persuasion by which the perceptions and the values of the other actor can be influenced. On this view, the parameters of a negotiation interaction depend on: the imbalances in the crucial resources (from domination to asymmetry, to equality): the extent to which the resource held by one actor is crucial for the other; and the height at which the boundaries are set for the possibility of exit of one actor or the other, that is, the presence of alternative courses of action to the negotiation itself. In the negotiation, the threat to withhold resources to increase damages and reduce advantages is always present. Whenever the communicative interaction is ineffective—result of the actors involved having incompatible evaluations of the relative strategic force of the resources available to them—interactions can become conflictual. In the conflict, the threat and the withholding become real (strike, lockouts, etc.).

The story is different with resource withdrawal, whether this be physical or functional. When the permanent withdrawal of crucial resources is a credible threat, the governmental feature of the arena tends to reduce. The scope and reach of political production declines, as the generalized and stabilized conformity of the others actors is no longer necessary for many goals and values and is therefore no longer guaranteed (for the non exiters) and no longer needed (for the exiters). The governmental arena can thus be said to dilute in the less authoritative environment of a natural arena—where the rationality of key actors is directed towards the best allocation and use of their own resources. In a situation in which withdrawal is a real opportunity, there is an incentive for key actors to seek their goals and values via the best allocation of their personal resources, rather than via the political exchanges and negotiations that guarantee the behavioural conformity of the other actors through the intervention of the political production of the central hierarchy. In other words, the conformity needed is no longer based on authoritative decisions binding 'locked-in' actors/resources, but on the actual equilibriums resulting from sheer asymmetric relationships among actors/resources.

Loyalty and System Building

Hirschman does not provide us with a positive definition of 'loyalty'. Loyalty is not a behavioural response different from exit and voice, a 'silence-non-exit'. Instead, it appears to be more of a psychological condition that mediates the relationships between exit and voice.[40] It is seen as something that can, to a certain extent, neutralize the tendency of quality-conscious customers and members to be the first to exit. 'Loyalty behaviour, as examined thus far, can be understood in terms of a generalized concept of penalty for exit'. The penalty may be directly imposed, but in most cases it is internalized: 'The applauded alert behaviour of the alerted consumer shifting to a better buy becomes disgraceful defection, desertion, and treason'.[41] In this sense, loyalty increases the cost of exit and may stimulate voice. Loyalty is an affective or emotional relationship to the organization or group that one belongs to, and makes it difficult (if not impossible) to contemplate the possibility of abandoning such a group or organization. In other words, loyalty seems to suspend the instrumental calculations that preside over the choice of exiting or non-exiting. Loyalty is thus a sort of 'internalized boundary'.

In macro models of Rokkan's work, the concept of loyalty corresponds closely to those mechanisms and structures forcing the components of the system to stay within it. In reference to territorial systems, rather than to individual choices, Rokkan interprets loyalty as those structures and processes of system maintenance represented by cultural integration, social sharing institutions, and participation rights.[42] Loyalty is therefore built upon the 'identity', 'solidarity', 'trust', and 'social capital' that exist among the members of a system (or group). All these concepts presuppose the creation of areas of equality within which instrumental calculations concerning material self-interest are suspended or considerably reduced by a shared system of norms. Rokkan's attention focuses on how the psychological individual properties derive and are reinforced by the historical processes

---

[40] Dowding, K., John, P., Mergoupis, T., and Van Vugt, M., 'Exit, Voice and Loyalty: Analytical and Empirical Developments', *European Journal of Political Research*, 37 (2000), 469–95, 477–88, underline this ambiguity of loyalty.

[41] Hirschman, *Exit, Voice, and Loyalty*, 79, 82–3, 98.

[42] Rokkan, S., *State Formation, Nation Building, and Mass Politics in Europe*, 100–1.

producing the perception of a shared and common destiny (mainly national identity in territorial groups), the legitimacy of sharing resources for mutual help and insurance, and the sharing of deliberation rights about collective decisions in the forms of political participation rights. Rokkan's concept of 'system building' can therefore be used to point to these processes of formation of identities/solidarities at the macro level.

The construction of boundaries of identity/solidarity is not an exclusively symbolic affair but is related to control over resources and social differentiation. Solidarity (and its absence) entails consequences for the allocation of resources and, above all, for the structuring of the entitlements of the members of the collectivity as against outsiders. Such entitlements refer to the different resources that are distributed within the collectivity, but also to access to public goods or to major institutional markets and arenas. Societies thus differ with respect to the kind of resources that are distributed in the name of the collectivity to its members; the nature of public goods that are instituted within them; the legal mode of this institution; the capacity to back the interests and ambitions of particular subgroups within a collectivity.

Giesen and Eisenstadt have suggested that there is an elective affinity between different cultural codes of collective identity, on the one hand, and structures of power and allocation, on the other.[43] They provide a typology of the symbolic codes of collective identity which is particularly useful for my line of reasoning, if interpreted in the light of the scope and reach of political production that different definitions of collective identities can sustain and afford. The core of all codes of collective identity is a distinction between 'we' and 'the others', and these authors discuss three such major codes: *primordiality*, *civility*, and *culture* (or *sacredness*).

Primordiality elements of collective identity focus on gender, generation, kinship, ethnicity, and race as bases for constructing and reinforcing the boundaries between inside and outside. This code of closure makes reference to original and unchangeable distinctions that are by definition exempted from communication and exchange, which cannot be changed by voluntary action, and which relate to 'nature' and as such provide a firm and stable basis that goes beyond the realm of voluntary actions and shifting involvements. The relationship of primordial collectivities to their environment is not missionary, since the others are not guilty of wrong choice—simply, they cannot be educated or convinced, converted or adopted. Primordial codes thus basically 'naturalize' the constitutive boundary between insiders and outsiders and they tend to be exempted from social definition or alteration. As a result, their boundaries cannot be moved or crossed. Indeed, the

---

[43] Eisenstadt, S. N. and Giesen, B., 'The Construction of Collective Identity', *Archives Européennes de Sociologie*, 36 (1995), 72–104.

complex rituals to cross these boundaries actually reinforce and reaffirm them. Following this, a territorial unit that coincides with a membership group identified by primordial codes has an embedded egalitarian tendency in the distribution of the entitlements, and it is compatible with a political production that packages a wide set of resources and public goods accessible to all members of the community independently of their personal resources (and denies such entitlements to the outsiders more easily).

The second major code of construction of collective identities—the civility code—is constructed on the basis of familiarity, with implicit rules of conduct, traditions and social routines that define and demarcate the boundary of the community. The routines, traditions, and institutional arrangements of a community are regarded as the core of its collective identity, the bases of which are the temporal continuity, the recurrence of social practices, and the constitution of the community. Tradition and collective civic rituals (the myths of the founder, particular persons, places and historical events, etc.) are also crucial. Very often, bonds are embedded in the constitutional practices of the public arena, and there are no special rituals of initiation, commitment or confession to demarcate the boundary. As a result, the boundary is more 'permeable'. The outsider can be accepted as a member of a civic community if he or she slowly begins to participate in local practices and institutional arrangements, and carefully avoids challenging any existing practices in the name of more universalistic values.

Civic codes, therefore, engender hierarchical distinctions between the bearers of traditions and the new members moving forwards the core of the community. They entail a tendency towards an unequal distribution of entitlements and towards the restricting of egalitarian distributions to particular spheres. They also foster differentiation between the 'public' and the 'private', the polity and the market, the rights to entitlements to public goods—which are restricted to members of the community—and access to trade and market exchanges—which is open to everybody and is identity-free. The range of public goods and entitlements, distributed to all members through political production is more restricted than in primordial communities. In my terminology, civility codes enable a higher differentiation of boundaries building and have a tendency towards less coinciding boundaries in different spheres.

The third code of collective identity definition—the cultural code—grounds the boundary between the other and us in a particular relation which links the collective subject to the sacred. It is a 'cultural' code in the sense that it shows a universalistic dynamic, whereby the collectivity is related to an eternal realm of the sacred and the sublime (god, reason, progress, rationality). The cultural ties of these collective identities imply a universalistic orientation and a missionary attitude towards the others, who are seen as 'inferior' and can be converted, adopt a superior culture, or simply modify their errors. Boundaries can be crossed by communication, education, and conversion, and, in principle, everyone is invited to do so, although the centre of the collectivity is protected from penetration through mechanisms of cultural stratification. That is to say, the cultural construction of collective identity is based on a privileged access to the sacred, to a divine mission, or to a particular representation of universal reason and progress, and the openness of this boundary is compensated by stratified access to the centre through rituals of initiation. This natural inclusive openness is linked to the capacity of this type of identity code to maintain a high level of inequality in entitlements among the members and a low level of collective political production.

Although most concrete types of collective identity are usually a mix of different symbolic codes with primordial, civility and cultural components, one of them usually tends to be predominant. My point, in conclusion, is that the primordial, civic and cultural codes can be ranged in terms of the difficulty of crossing the boundary, the barriers, and the costs of exit/entry. This is also reflected in the strength of the equality areas among the members that these codes define and, consequently, in the different scope and reach of the distribution of entitlements that is embedded into the code.

The Roman Empire and its Byzantine successor determined an expansion of the territorial group that made the internal primordial groups more heterogeneous. At the same time, mew membership groups developed in a way that made the territories more homogeneous: the expansion of the civic code of Roman citizenship and the cultural code of Christianity. This created an innovative dynamic between territorial and membership groups in the West and led to the possibility of defining differential boundaries as a result of which it was possible to enter the territorial group without entering the membership group, and to be member of a membership group without belonging to the territorial group.

On this view, the development of the nation-state overcame the early opposition between primordial and localized membership identities and broader civic and cultural-religious identities. In Europe, the national identify fostered by the new states intervened as an intermediary between the broad cultural and civic membership group (Christianity, Roman citizenship) and the small and localized primordial and civic identities. The 'nation' thus standardized and integrated localized civic/primordial identities, creating a broader set of civic identities, practices, and rules. At the same time, it also differentiated between and split internally, the broad non-territorial membership groups whose links were based on language, religion, and ethnicity.

In a discussion focusing on the process of territorial system building, the central issues are not identity/solidarity as such, but rather the process through which they are expanded (or retrenched) to become coterminous with a particular territorial political formation. Identities/solidarities tend to be higher and to increase with the level of closure and the stability of a community, so that territorial and/or membership groups that are very open to the entry and the exit of components and members accumulate less identity/solidarity than those that are closed and stable.[44] However, identity can have 'bridging' effects, widening the scope of solidarity and collective identity, as well as 'bounding' effects, that is, excluding and segregating effects. Where identity/solidarity is limited to very small groups—the family can be taken as an extreme case—this may well produce results as an efficient family business, but it may also produce corruption, familism, and nepotism.[45] Beyond the family circle, the bonds of solidarity and the scope of trust identify different-sized communities: neighbouring village, city, region, nation. These broader communities too present the ambivalent dynamic of 'bridging' and 'excluding'. The main trust of Weber's work on the Protestant ethic[46] was that it widened the scope of trust and confidence developing a common identity that went beyond the narrow circle of family members and neighbouring people. In this sense, the national identity is a form of 'widening' to the extent that it is capable of activating and sustaining forms of solidarity and trust that go beyond the narrow circle of known people and of face-to-face relationships and extends to often vast territorial communities. But it is also a form of 'narrowing' to the extent that it retrenches from previous broader religious, linguistic, or cultural communities.

National identity, social sharing solidarities, and political identities are forms of 'enlargement' of cultural ties. They do not accumulate more easily in narrowly defined contexts, on account of the intensity of interactions among the members of limited and stable groups.[47] Quite the contrary, they tend to bridge diverse communities within a territory and as such require the support and assistance of highly formalized institutions and organizations such as the educational system, the welfare state and the institutionalization of political rights. The close association between specific codes of

---

[44] On 'social capital' see Coleman, J., *Foundations of Social Theory* (Cambridge: Cambridge University Press, 1990), 302–19. He considers social capital as a property of the structure of social relationships—as an attribute of groups, organizations and communities, not of individuals. This is rather surprising in view of his prevalently individualistic and rationalistic approach.

[45] Which tends to became 'amoral' under certain conditions. See Banfield, E. C., *The Moral Basis of a Backward Society* (Glencoe: The Free Press, 1958); and, for a critique, Pizzorno, A., 'Amoral familism and Historical Marginality', *International Review of Community Development*, 15 (1966), 55–66.

[46] Weber, M., *Gesammelte Aufsätze zur Religionssoziologie* (Tübingen: J. C. B. Mohr, 1920), Vol. 1, Chapters 1 and 2.

[47] Coleman's view of 'social capital' is that it is inherently higher the more confined the social group. See Coleman, *Foundations of Social Theory*, 302–19.

identity and entitlements concretely associated to them through institutions can therefore represent the process of system building. System building creates those ties by which internal conflict management can be handled without continuously jeopardizing the maintenance of the polity. To define system building we can focus on individual cultural and psychological elements or we can focus, at the macro level, more on institutions and rights: the national symbols and the nationalization of culture through education and linguistic standardization; the development of social rights and social insurance institutions as 'welfare states'; the spreading of political participation rights and the overcoming of democratization thresholds. Every process of boundary change in the sphere of community building redefines membership groups characterized by different endowments of identity/solidarity. That is, different national societies are endowed with different stocks of identity/solidarity and can be differentially affected by those processes of redefining membership groups that are associated with the expanding scope of the division of labour and of social interactions beyond the boundaries of the nation-state.

Voice and Political Structuring

So far I have defined exit/entry, boundary building and central hierarchy as identifying the 'centre formation', and loyalty and identity as being related to system building. I will now discuss the third key individualistic concept, 'voice', and its macro level correspondent, 'political structuring', more thoroughly.

As discussed earlier, in the absence of material and cultural negative sanctions to exit, voice is normally more costly than exit. Hirschman describes only one case in which the cost imbalance in favour of exit is redressed: 'expressive' voice. Under certain conditions, voice can be perceived as an end and as an enjoyable activity, a benefit and a rewarding experience, rather than as a cost. This is particularly the case with public goods, when voice can become less costly than is normally thought or expected and may well have 'an occasional edge over exit'.[48] Beyond this particular case, the conditions holding over the resort to voice when exit is available depend upon : (*a*) the extent to which members are willing to trade off the certainty of exit against the uncertainties of an improvement in the deteriorated product via voice; (*b*) the estimate that members make of their ability to influence the organization; and (*c*) the presence of loyalty mechanisms and expressive motivations which may lower the cost of voice. Hirschman

[48] Hirschman, 'Exit, voice, and loyalty: further reflections and a survey of recent contribution', 217.

suggests that the range of voice options 'depends also on the general readiness of a population to complain and on the invention of such institutions and mechanisms as can communicate complaints cheaply and effectively',[49] but he does not develop this point any further. Institutions do not play a significant role in his picture, presumably because, within the individualist perspective, institutions themselves require voice to begin with, in order to be built.

Where Hirschman comes closest to facing the issue of the passing from an individualized voice to a collective and structured voice is in his recasting of the events leading to the collapse of the GDR.[50] When, as in this case, exit is advocated collectively and is not only practised individually, it becomes a form of voice and the two become intertwined. It is surprising, however, that Hirschman finds this association or transformation of exit into voice as problematic and puzzling in relation to his earlier schemes. He discusses how exit usually 'ignites' voice, but it was in fact rather the lack of individual exit that ignited voice in the GDR events. Too many people wanted to exit at the same time and, as a result, they realized that their individual expectations could not be fulfilled without collective action.

However, it is oversimplistic to think that voice activity is created more or less automatically because of the absence of exit options. A direct relationship of this kind may be analytically convincing for individual choice situations; at the macro level, however, individual voice needs political structures to express itself. Consequently, I will use the label 'political structuring' to point to the formation of those institutional channels, political organizations, and networks of relationships that allow for individual voice to achieve systemic relevance. We need a theory of political structuring which is sufficiently general and abstract in its language and theoretical linkages to encompass these processes in large-scale territories. For this, the concept of voice as it is handled by Hirschman needs to be reworked to make it more robust, taking it from the sphere of individual inclinations and calculations for voice to that of the 'structuring', aggregation and collectivization of these. This can still be done using the notion of the costs of voice and exit, but it should be pointed out at this stage that these costs can be lowered not only through loyalty mechanisms (as pointed out in the system building section) but also through institutional features, just as exit costs can be increased by both loyalty and various types of boundaries. Summing up, not only do loyalty/identity contribute towards redressing the cost imbalance favourable to exit in a purely individualistic perspective, but also institutions.

[49] Hirschman, *Exit, Voice, and Loyalty*, 43.
[50] Hirschman, 'Exit, Voice, and the Fate of the GDR', *World Politics*, 45 (1993), 173–202.

The first step towards making the concept of voice more robust is to strengthen the connection between it and exit. In theory, voice may be paralysed by the exit of the potentially most vocal. However, as the collapse of the GDR shows, exit can also foster voice, if the proper channels are available. Those who cannot exit may become vocal about their lack of opportunity to do so, but also about the indirect costs of other people's exit. Hirschman argues that exit only damages the possibility of responding through voice in the micro and macro terms spelled out above: for the individual—for whom exit opportunity lowers the interest in voice—and for the whole organization—for which exit choices lower the level or quality of overall voice. In other words, he does not conceive of 'voice against exit'. In the GDR example, the mass exodus contributed to the voice of the East Germans who did not want to exit but to stay (*wir bleiben hier*). Hirschman interprets this process via the concept of loyalty: those untrammelled by feelings of loyalty will be prone to exit, while the others will resort to voice. In the case of the GDR, however, there seemed to be two vocal groups: (*a*) those who were loyal and did not want to exit; and (*b*) and those who had less loyalty feelings, would have liked to exit, could not do so, and felt negatively affected by the exit of the others.

Let us spell out this point more fully. Let us assume that those actors who can move, fully or partially—vote by walking away, exit jurisdictions, leaving compulsory group membership for voluntary functional 'clubs', etc.—will do so whenever they perceive that a more convenient option is available. The exit of those who are mobile will have consequences on the polity's capacity for political production; that is, on the provision of public goods to the non-exiters. If the non-exiters do not perceive the relationship between the exit of those who are mobile and the deterioration of the political production for those who are not,[51] the differential distribution of exit options will have no direct effect on voice. If, on the contrary, this relationship is perceived, how might the non-exiters react?

In economic models, these people are irrelevant. Loyal consumers have no alternative behavioural options. The only carriers of competitive sanctions are the exiters. Economics-based theories of market interactions, of party competition, and, more generally, of every social interaction process suggest that, in the long run, exiters will bring benefits to non-exiters too, because their defection pushes the organization to improve the quality of its output. However, in an extended model that includes voice options, the non-exiters can react to their ineffectiveness as 'economic' agent through their resources as citizens. They can protest, organize pressure, and withhold the

---

[51] If, for instance, they are convinced by the argument that the spreading of exit options is beneficial to everybody in the long run.

resources under their control. That is, they can seek the intervention of the central hierarchy to generate new forms of behavioural conformity. It is therefore possible that the differentiation of exit options (resulting from lowered boundaries) generates voice against exit if and when the latter is perceived to deteriorate the quality and quantity of public goods provision for the non-exiters. So if, at the level of the individual, voice is an alternative choice to exit, at the systemic level voice and exit can be closely related one to the other.

The second step of this revision of voice concerns its relationships with institutions. For the individual, the cost and effectiveness of voice depends to a large extent on the level of structuring of organizations, movements and channels for the expression of complaints. Voice cannot simply be seen as a rhapsody of individuals' words—even if this may temper a population's desire for action. To be effective in large-scale organizations, voice needs to be structured; it requires some organization plus some symbolic elaboration of the collective goal. If it is not structured, it is unlikely to be heard, and it cannot extend beyond highly motivated and resourceful individuals.[52] At the macro level, therefore, voice corresponds to the creation of channels through which consumers of both private and public goods can communicate their complaints, and the creation of political arrangements by which the deterioration of the organization's performance cannot only be brought to its attention, but can also be modified. Voice mechanisms can be viewed as 'structures' that ensure a regular supply of information from component parts about the conditions affecting the functioning of the system. Political structuring is the articulation, mobilization and organization of individual voice and the setting up of arrangements for consent and redress. That is, the institutionalization of voice is the result of repeated experiences of non-exit options and ineffective individual complaints.

Providing that some original hierarchical authority exists, the process of political structuring progresses along two dimensions: *voice structuring*—the mobilization, and organization of individual voice; and *institutional differentiation*—the development of arrangements of consent and redress. 'Voice structuring' points to the political articulation of the community; 'institutional differentiation' indicates the role and function differentiation of the central hierarchy of the governmental area. The incentive to structure any governmental arena internally (including the territorial systems I concentrate on in this book) is a function of (*a*) their external closure; (*b*) their internal system building (identity and equality areas building); and (*c*) the scope and

---

[52] The empirical literature on political participation has shown that institutions actually lower the cost of voice. See in particular Verba, S., Nie, N. H. and Kim, J., *Participation and Political Equality. A Seven Nation Comparison* (Cambridge: Cambridge University Press, 1978).

reach of the internal hierarchy's political production. In the context of this work I will not dedicate much space to institutional differentiation, discussing it only briefly (see later). My main focus will instead be that of the structuring of voice.

The third step in expanding the concept of individual voice to the macro level involves identifying the mechanisms that link individual actors' choices to the corresponding systemic macro structures. This means answering the following question: how does the closedness of a governmental arena (exit/ entry control and boundary building) and its system building, foster the internal political structuring? Three mechanisms operating this linkage can be signalled: (*a*) the politicizing of the internal closure rules and codes; (*b*) the 'convertibility' of different types of resources; and (*c*) the consolidation of systemic patterns of interaction. In the following sections I explain why.

External Closure and Politicizing of the Internal Closure Rules and Codes

Strengthening external territorial boundaries in one or more of the subsystems implies developing internal exclusion roles and codes. Within each territorial unit the development of this kind of internal rules and codes of closure starts from a de facto exclusion based on unequal access to rewards, resources and opportunities (lineage, property, education, credential, power and force, status, race, ethnicity, gender, religion, language, etc.). The process moves forward through the recognition and legitimation of these criteria of exclusion as these are operated by the protection, regulation, jurisdiction, allocation and arbitration policies of the hierarchical order. As a result, the political structuring within each authority arena (and particularly in those of a territorial type), takes place by politicizing some closure rules and practices and by representing and organizing interests around the defence of or the challenges to the monopolization of certain positions. The more the boundaries of the governmental arena tend to coincide, the fewer exit options there are, and the more pressure there is for internal closure rule politicization.

The inspiration for these ideas comes from Simmel and Coser's work on the social structure and overlapping membership.[53] According to this theory, the higher the frequency and the degree of disjointed membership there is—in the sense that the social agent acts within different social contexts—the more likely it is that none of these social contexts will be dominant. Individuals take different social roles, some of which may even imply competing and contradictory tasks, activities, expectations and values. There is little chance that individuals will show the same combination of roles and

---

[53] Simmel, G., *Conflict and the Web of Group-Affiliations* (New York: Free Press, 1955); Coser, L. A., *The Functions of Social Conflict* (London: Routledge, 1956).

group membership, since these roles (in the family, employment, friendship, communication and leisure), their relative stratarchic position (education, property, income, class, religion, ethnic, power, etc.), and their socio-functional nature (consumer, taxpayers, voter, citizen) tend to differentiate.

At the opposite end of the scale, there are fewer socially significant categories and they are characterized by mutually exclusive membership. A high proportion of agents act in one main category or social group, which tends to be exclusive. At the same time, in the stratarchic social system these people belong to highly correlated, if not entirely coincident, layers of social stratification in educational, property, class, etc. terms, and the closedness of each membership group does not allow for any differentiation of socio-economic chances and functional roles. The hypothesis is that, this situation generates and exacerbates conflicts among self-containing social groups, whose non-overlapping and reinforcing membership facilitates common values and perceptions and makes intergroup information exchanges difficult. These closed groups tend to claim a much higher involvement of their members in some collective aspiration or design.

This basic mechanism which links patterns of social interaction to the likelihood of contentious collective action and social conflict, has also been applied to the formation of cleavages. It is only in conditions of strong social boundaries, and the consequent no-exit options of a given social group, that the political structuring of that group can take place. So, for the working class, for example, the high exit options of the US experience, and indeed of all immigrant societies, led to their being little incentive to structure the organizational voice.[54] That is to say, if individual members have easy exit options (being replaced by new immigrants, or high geographical and social mobility) they are not inclined to engage in organized action. On the contrary, if one or more lifetimes of closed social boundaries are experienced (in the case where there is no intergenerational mobility), then no individual exit option is viewed as possible, and only collective solutions are perceived as feasible. Moreover, the closedness of a social position also reinforces the loyalty element to the other members of the group. The more closed the 'class' position is, the more likely it is to give birth to organizational voice.[55]

In low-mobility and high-status organized societies, the social boundaries among social groups and classes may be so high and institutionally

[54] This thesis was formulated by Sombart, W., 'Studien zur Entwicklungsgeschichte des nordamerikanischen Proletariats', *Archiv für Sozialwissenschaft und Sozialpolitik*, 21 (1905): 210–36, 308–46, and 556–611. It is discussed in depth in Lipset, S. M. and Marks, G., *It did not happen here. Why Socialism Failed in the United States* (New York and London: W. W. Norton, 2000), 125–65.

[55] Lipset, S. M., 'Radicalism or Reformism: The Sources of Working Class Politics', *International Political Science Review*, 77 (1983), 1–18.

reinforced that exit options are unthinkable; this reinforces cultural solidarity in the closed group and fosters the overcoming of individualistic options as against collective voice choices. In the past, law sanctioned some of these differentiations among social groups as institutionalized inequalities. In modern industrial societies, however, these institutionalized inequalities have been progressively substituted by social and market inequalities that do not have any legal upholding but which are still characterized by specific subgroups' values and patterns of behaviour. In general, then, social stratification studies can be defined as studies of the rigidity of the within-state system of social boundaries.[56]

This general thesis can be reformulated using my specific terminology and applied to the perspective presented in this work: the easier are the social exits from a group affiliation, the less likely is the political structuring of strong group identities, ideologies and collective action. That is, the easier it is for individuals to exit from the social milieu and/or group, the fewer resources are retained within such a group, and the less likely it is a collective action by the group as a result of the free-riding activities of those who expect to exit. The logic here is the same as that illustrated for the state. The exit (or the exit possibility) of some depresses the voice and resources of those remaining and tends, therefore, to weaken their potential for collective action. In conclusion, the more closed the group affiliation, the more likely the politicization of the closure rules in a global ideological way.

The mechanism that links the macro feature of the rigidity of boundaries to individual behaviours and choices is described by social psychologists by contrasting interpersonal versus intergroup behaviour.[57] On this view, an interaction between individuals is defined as 'interpersonal' when it is fully determined by their interpersonal relationship and individual characteristics, and is not affected by the social groups or categories to which they respectively belong. Conversely, an interaction is defined as 'intergroup' when it is fully determined by the individuals' respective membership in social groups or categories, and it is not affected by their interpersonal relationships. What is important here is that where intergroup conflict is intense, it is more likely that the individuals will react towards each other as a function of their respective group membership, rather then in terms of their individual characteristics or interindividual relationships.

---

[56] On the permeability of social stratification systems, see the inspiring ideal types developed by Svelastoga, K., *Social Differentiation* (New York: David McKay, 1965).

[57] Here I am referring to the 'realistic group conflict theory' as outlined by Tajfel and Turner, rephrased with the language of exit/voice. See Tajfel, H. and Turner, J., 'An integrative theory of intergroup conflict', in W. Austin and A. Worchel (eds.), *The Social Psychology of Intergroup Relations* (California: Brooks/Cole, 1979), 33–47.

A second important distinction concerns the individuals' beliefs systems and distinguishes between 'social mobility' versus 'social change' beliefs. 'Social mobility' beliefs rest on the perception of society as flexible and permeable, and on the perception that it is possible (through talent, hard work, good luck, or some other means) to move individually up the social ladder. On the contrary, 'social change' beliefs correspond to the perception that the structure of relations between social groups in society is characterized by marked stratification, making it impossible or very difficult for individuals to exit an unsatisfactory, underprivileged or stigmatized group membership. To use the jargon of this book, these beliefs systems concern the openness of the social relationships in which the individual is embedded.

One would also expect there to be a marked correlation between the degree of objective stratification rigidity and limited exit options in a social system and the social diffusion and intensity of the belief system of 'social change'. The individual perception of the difficulty of moving from one group to the other fosters intergroup behaviour and within-group loyalty. In other words, individual chances of social exit are related to systems of beliefs that have a causal function in shifting social behaviour towards members of outgroups between the poles of interpersonal and intergroup behaviour. I could re-phrase this by describing it as a movement from the pole of unstructured interpersonal behaviour to the pole of structured intergroup behaviour. Using my terminology, boundary removal among stratified social groups, less institutionalized relationships, more exit options and corresponding social mobility beliefs, all lead to greater in-group variability of behaviour towards members of the out-group, to less intergroup behaviour, and to less and more difficult political structuring of such behaviour. On the contrary, 'social change' belief system is likely to reflect either an existing and marked social stratification or an intense intergroup conflict of interests or both. As a consequence, the nearer the members of a group are to the 'social change' extreme of the belief systems continuum and the 'intergroup' extreme of the behavioural continuum, the more uniformity they will show in their behaviour towards members of the relevant out-group.

This approach links the social reality of the openness of life chances of individuals to their social behaviour through the mediation of socially shared beliefs systems. To the extent that the objective and subjective prohibitions on trespassing (exit) are weak, individual mobility strategies may be available, and in so far as individual mobility implies de-identification, it will tend to loosen the cohesiveness of the group. This weakening of the subjective attachment to the in-group among its members tends: (*a*) to blur the perception of distinct group interests corresponding to the distinct group identity; and (*b*) to create obstacles to mobilizing group members for collective action.

Within this perspective, the linkage between individual exit options and aggregate political structuring can be represented in the following way:

Group structure rigidity/permeability
(exit/entry and boundaries)

Rising of boundaries	Decline of boundaries
New technologies of locking in	New technologies of exit

Belief systems

Social change belief	Social mobility belief
Strengthening of in-group identity	Decline of in-group identity
Strengthening of in-group behavioural conformity	Decline of in-group behavioural conformity
Strengthening of intergroup conflict	Decline of intergroups conflict
More intergroup type relationships	More interpersonal type relationships

Political agency

Political structuring	Political destructuring

Resource Convertibility

The more the boundaries of a governmental arena are closed and coinciding, the more the resources within the system become 'convertible' or 'exchange-able' into each other. In closed systems, the demands and resources of the 'periphery' (cultural, economic and politico-administrative) are addressed to the centre and are converted into power resources at the centre. Similarly, social group identities and interest definitions are converted, if the system is closed, into elements of the central battle for control and power. If a system is open, the resources accumulated by territories, groups, individuals, etc., cannot be converted directly into centre, because actors can refuse to engage in a battle or confrontation over those resources. The centralization of resources and convertibility of various resources (authority, competencies and technical skills, group identity, organization, implementation capacity, control of key resources, political mobilization, votes) is possible only to the extent that the various boundaries are sufficiently closed to create a 'system', that is, to prevent actors from considering the option of not 'directing' their claims at the centre and of not 'converting' their resources into the power struggle at the centre.

The convertibility of resources takes places through 'political exchanges'. The central political hierarchy is interested in successful political exchanges involving politically relevant actors that control different kinds of resources that, in principle, can be temporarily withheld. The central authority's mon-opoly in the production of guaranteed rights through legislation and rule-making is normally used to promote and facilitate political exchanges.

However, not all resources can be controlled by normative decisions and for the successful formulation, first, and implementation, later, of policies, the search for the behavioural conformity of the actors involved may easily extend beyond the accepted sphere of normative decisions. In other words, nobody can coerce capitalists to invest or to innovate, labour to be disciplined and productive, institutional groups to comply with implementation requirements. Therefore, political exchanges are predicated upon, first, the central authority's credible threat to raise boundaries to further lock in resources and limit the sphere of autonomy of actors/resources potentially unwilling to exchange and, second, on the non-availability of alternatives strategies for the actors concerned. Under these conditions, the declining returns or the growing costs of non-cooperation (or of conflict) can be used to foster the political exchanges.

The centralized political exchanges at the heart of the system, approximate negotiation among equal actors, even if one of them is governmental and is thus in principle endowed with the formal power to coerce.[58] The willingness of actors to engage in negotiated agreements about public policy depends, first of all, on the availability or not of unilateral alternatives (either in the status quo or in the consumption of alternative public policies). If the possibility of unilateral exit from the cooperation exists, this is the most fundamental bargaining power; in fact it is the condition for the bargaining itself. Actors with poor unilateral alternatives to the agreement have weak bargaining power and must therefore make concessions and accept compromises. The boundary-building process in cultural, economic, political and military/coercion domain strongly confines the availability of these unilateral alternatives.

The second element that fosters cooperation and exchanges is the threat of unfavourable alternative coalitions among other actors. If alternative coalitions are possible, then each actor must compare the value of cooperation and exchange not only to its own unilateral alternatives (if they are available), but also to the alternative coalitions that the other actors may form and join (e.g. for business, that trade unions and governments agree to legislate). Generally speaking, the possibility of striking alternative coalitions increases the bargaining power of the potential coalition members with respect to those who are excluded or deprived of this chance and who are therefore faced with the possibility of exclusion and with the implied costs of this. The threats of exclusion may generate stronger pressure on recalcitrant

[58] On negotiation I am influenced by the perspective outlined in Scharpf, F., *Games Real Actors Play. Actor-Centered Institutionalism in Policy Research* (Boulder, CO: Westview Press, 1997). See the excellent synthesis of negotiation theory in Moravcsik, A., *The Choice for Europe. Social Purpose and state Power from Messina to Maastricht* (Ithaca, NY: Cornell University Press, 1998), 62–5.

partners than the threat determined by the absence of agreement, and may lead an actor to accept an agreement which is worse than the solution that it would gain through a unilateral alternative (withdrawal).

To conclude, closed (relatively not permeable) boundaries that coincide in different spheres and impinge on the same territory (*a*) reduce the unilateral alternatives of withdrawal, because they make it impossible to consume alternative public policies, to appeal to alternative jurisdictions, or to access external resources; (*b*) maximize the sphere of convertibility of resources for internal political exchanges; and (*c*) allow alternative coalitions to be available and to exercise pressure towards cooperation. These elements foster the formation of political structures and of political agents within them, particularly when negotiations and exchanges are repeated over time.

Systemic Interaction

Political structuring is an interactive process resulting from the systemic interaction (conflictual, cooperative, competitive, negotiation) of parts and elements that perceive the impossibility of exiting from the system. In a governmental arena, structures are shaped by the progressive formation of front lines and of political alliances between groups of political entrepreneurs, corporate interests organizations, social groups, political movements, and organizations. The pre-existing alliances of the in-groups shape the possibilities for the alliances of the out-groups. Every incoming new actor will thus be constrained to locate itself within a set of pre-existing alignments and alliances.

This process reduces and shrinks the space for alternative alliances and counter-alliances. In this situation, the development of political structures produces rising performances and a 'path-dependent' stabilization of behavioural patterns. In other words, external closure tends to favour a system of internal rules. At the same time, actors accumulate experience and develop specific competencies within the institutional framework and also personal interests. Values and identities are also defined during this process of structuring.

In addition, issue linkage is fostered. The closer the boundaries of a system, the more likely the broadening of the range of issues on which internal political exchanges impinge. Actors may have varying preference intensities across different issues and they also have asymmetrical preferences on different issues. If negotiations involve several linked issues, and some trust and learning is generated, mutual concessions and side payments are possible. Coinciding boundaries are particularly crucial from this point of view. The fact that the centre of the system can successfully count on the locking in of cultural as well as economic, administrative and coercion resources greatly enlarge issue linkage and the policy packages that can satisfy a larger group of actors.[59]

Internal learning, trust generation, and the internal redefinition of interests are a function of the accepted or acknowledged impossibility of exiting from the institutional structure. This process is mutual in the sense that, once external boundaries are closed, internal groups redefine their position, interests and values as a function of their being locked into the system and of therefore being obliged to interact with other, similarly locked-in actors. External closure defines and imposes a systemic interaction which itself defines identities and interests in terms of the compelling and compulsory relationships among internal groups.

Exit/Entry, Boundary Building and Political Structuring

I have so far argued that the circumscription of exit via boundary building fosters the development of systemic structures of political negotiation via the three mechanisms of 'politicizing of the internal closure rules and codes', 'resource convertibility', and 'systemic interaction'. In a situation of low boundaries and generalized and costless exit, there are few incentives for political structuring. Internal closure rules are thus less likely to become contentious because their exclusionary clauses are of modest importance. The convertibility of resource is low because many actors have unilateral alternatives to withdraw from centralized political exchanges. Systemic interactions are weak because issues in different domains cannot be linked and actors do not experience the rising performances and the stabilization of behavioural patterns associated with the systemness of their interactions. Political interactions tend, as a result, to slide towards a natural arena type.

In situations where there are high and frequent opportunities for exit, it is likely that the organizational hierarchy will find it easier to resist, evade, and postpone the development of mechanisms for responding to whatever voice is left. Under these circumstances, the political production of the governmental arena is limited, since the scope of generalized and stabilized behavioural conformities is restricted to widely shared and elementary public goods. The political production is not driven by forms of political decision-making, but by the central hierarchy's guess about subjects' responses as to

[59] Note that it is not unusual for linked concessions to create external losers that may react. Issue-linkage is more likely, therefore, if gains and losses are internal to the same group, or when benefits are internalized and costs are imposed on diffuse, unorganized or non-represented groups. The role of votes as a resource in domestic politics is crucial precisely because it ensures that politics is not simply a series of transfers of costs to unorganized, diffuse groups like tax payers, consumers, etc.

who provides the best deal in terms of the desired quality and quantity of public good production. In the most extreme case, it may become irrelevant to ascertain preferences through a political process based on some form of voice, which becomes difficult to channel, organize and discipline as a result. There is less need to convince the rulers to change their minds and policies, and no complex procedural techniques develop to weight and combine the preferences of the affected, as these are more effectively revealed by their withdrawing and/or moving to the other arenas whose government package best satisfies their preferences. Consequently, rather than having a given and predefined population and a central hierarchy that tries to adjust its policies to the population's preferences, governments can decide policies in order to attract consumers. Following in this approach, central hierarchies compete by offering their services of governing so as to attract the greatest number of buyers in the form of taxpayers.[60] The 'full-exit' world is, therefore, a world without voice.

The historical plausibility of the full and generalized exit options model[61] is irrelevant in this context.[62] Its function is to offer an extreme analytical picture of the internal political structuring implications of the absence of the closure rule and boundaries. At the opposite side of the spectrum, the total closure of all the main territorial boundaries leaves voice as the only mechanism available for within-system communication. Yet the sheer amount of resources that need to be concentrated by the internal hierarchy to maintain the total closure of the boundaries generates considerable asymmetries be-

---

[60] A theoretical formulation of this situation was originally developed by Tiebout, C., 'A Pure Theory of Local Expenditure', *Journal of Political Economy*, 64 (1956), 416–24 concerning local government expenditures and tax levels. Friedman proposes a model in which state policies are affected exclusively by the decisions taken by potential taxpayers about where they are to be taxed, rather than by other processes of political decision-making. Friedman, D., 'A Theory of the Size and Shape of Nations', *Journal of Political Economy*, 85 (1977), 59–77.

[61] The 'full exit model' is sometimes regarded as 'preferable', and it becomes a normative model, as in the work of the anarcho-capitalists. See Rothbard, M., *Man, Economy and State*, 2 vols. (Princeton, NJ: Van Nostrand, 1962). Here, voice is seen as 'rent-seeking', and policies aiming to secure specific results are viewed as prone to becoming the target of rent-seeking activities even if they may not have been initiated this way. See Streit, M. E., 'The Economic Constitution of the European Community: From "Rome" to "Maastricht"', *European Law Journal*, 1 (1995), 5–30, for an example of this logic applied to a critique of the EU development.

[62] See Goldberg, E., 'Borders, Boundaries, Taxes and States in the Medieval Islamic World' (University of Washington: unpublished paper without date) for an interesting application of this logic to state borders and state consolidation in the Medieval Islamic world. The historical application of the model is, however, quite implausible. The model assumes that there are kings on one side, and mobile merchants on the other. In fact, the largest contribution made then to royal revenues came from the land and not from tax on trade. Therefore, it was far more important to obtain and increase land control to maximize revenues.

tween its resources and those of other politically relevant actors. An extensive political production is possible, but the resource imbalance makes it unrealistic to conceive of the central hierarchy as one actor among others, endowed with special but limited 'conformity oriented' resources. In this situation, voice mechanisms are more likely to be manipulated than to be effective.

Between the polar types of a total autarchic political formation and of the full exit boundaryless model, a mix of voice and exit mechanisms seems to be necessary to ensure some responsiveness from central political hierarchies. The effectiveness of voice is best guaranteed by some element of exit, which in turn prevents the manipulation/suppression of the former. At the same time, some elements of voice guarantee the persistence of exit rights. In the Western experience, the mix of exit and voice has varied from case to case and historically. The Western nation-state is characterized by a specific model of boundary differentiation: clear-cut military and administrative boundaries and a more or less open flow of persons, goods, and information on the cultural and economic fronts.

In Table 1.5 the two main components of political structuring—voice structuring and institutional differentiation—are summarized briefly. As mentioned above, my attention has concentrated on political structuring as voice structuring, while institutional differentiation has been left to one side because it is less important for it and it has also been investigated more extensively by the literature. Here, I mention only the two principles of institutional differentiation that are relevant for my discussion related to the European Union (EU). The first type is bureaucratic, and is characterized

TABLE 1.5. *Socio-political inputs and institutional threshold of political structuring*

Political structuring	Territorial versus group conflict management	
Voice structuring	Individual voice	Protest, petition
	Aggregate voice	Tumults, mobs, revolts
	Collective voice	Collective action, movements
	Organized voice	Membership in corporate and political organizations
Institutional differentiation (democratization)	Mechanisms of voluntary listening	Legitimation
	Guarantee or right to be heard	Incorporation
	Arrangements of consent, redress, and modification	Representation
	Actual imposition of outcomes	Executive access

by regulation by 'experts' or by people whose major qualification is that of having some specific knowledge. The holders of the governmental arena control may supervise these experts, but not the clients to whom they provide their services. The bureaucratic ideal type emphasizes 'rational' computational allocation and decision-making and belittles allocation and decision-making through 'representatives' and organs of self-government. The second type of institutional differentiation of governmental arenas is that of 'institutional democratization'. In this 'representative' or 'public' type, the principles at least of protection, arbitration, jurisdiction, regulation and allocation are established by the public deliberation of 'representatives' of various types of constituencies, whose powers are defined by procedural principles and rules (such as one-person-one-vote; majority decision; appointment and revocability of executives).

For within-state developments of the modern era, the precise timing of voice structuring and institutional democratization has been crucial. The starting point is that of a polity which is neither institutionally democratized nor politically structured (in the modern sense); from this point, some polities advanced along the path of institutional democratization long before voice was extensively and effectively structured at the mass level (Britain and also France); in contrast, other polities can be strongly structured from the political point of view, but non-institutionally democratized (Germany, Norway, Sweden).[63]

Figures 1.3 and 1.4 concisely represent the relationship established between external boundary building, exit options, and the internal political structuring of every governmental arena. Following the curve of Figure 1.3 from the upper-left corner down to the bottom-right, we can see the conditions of political structuring. These early boundary building that come about through the formation of a new governmental arena increases the cost of exit of the internal membership group. The early boundaries may develop in a limited domain. For instance, the early efforts at territorial state formation in Europe in the late fifteenth and early sixteenth centuries developed mainly through the strengthening of the force-coercion boundaries, while in cultural, economic and politico-administrative terms a variety of internal and cross-border boundaries continued to exist.

When the central hierarchy of a governmental arena strengthens its territorial control by raising new boundaries for goods, persons, messages, rights, credentials, etc., in new functional areas and makes them progressively coin-

---

[63] Dahl's two dimensions of 'inclusiveness' and 'liberalization' have inspired this table. See Dahl, R. A., *Polyarchy. Participation and Opposition* (New Haven and London: Yale University Press, 1971). However, my concept of voice structuring goes beyond that of pure electoral inclusiveness. Dahl's concept of 'liberalization' refers to a specific, although crucial, aspect of 'institutional democratization'.

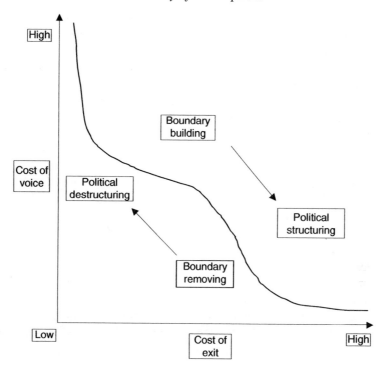

FIGURE 1.3. Costs of exit and voice in governmental arenas

cide with the territorial space, then the cost of exit rises considerably. Early boundary building does not significantly reduce the cost of voice. The same process of boundary consolidation implies boundary insecurity, external pressure, internal voice repression, and the invocation of abstract ideals of authority legitimation and therefore voice-indifferent ideologies (competence, the nation, class, efficiency). When external boundaries are consolidated, economic interest differentiation, cultural diversities and institutional privileges engender processes of internal political structuring which considerably lower the cost of voice while at the same time increase the cost of exit to the extent that the process strengthens expressive solidarities and collective ties.

If we read the curve in Figure 1.3 from the bottom-right to the top-left corners, the opposite process is described. Removing or lowering boundaries—as a deliberate choice or as a result of new exit technologies—lowers the cost of exit in the cultural, economic, and politico-administrative spheres. While the individual cost of voice may not increase immediately, however, it does increase when the growing exit begins to unlock actors and resources, to reduce the resource convertibility, the systemness of interactions, and the capacity to politicize the internal closure rules and codes. These processes tend to destructure the existing structures of voice organization. Lacking the appropriate resource control, opposition and conflicts find it difficult to structure at the central level. It becomes less crucial to be able to compete at the centre of the governmental arena if there are fewer resources to be distributed there and if generalized and stabilized behavioural conformity can no longer be imposed from there.[64]

We can see the same process at work in Figure 1.4, where the role of the political production of protection, regulation, jurisdiction, allocation and arbitration of the governmental arena is highlighted. The external functional boundaries of the polity lock actors/resources in a more comprehensive and extensive way than would be possible with a mere military/coercion boundary. The political production is also responsible for the production, reproduction and defence of the institutionalization of internal membership groups' differences. Finally, it is also the key element in the production of guaranteed behavioural conformity for all the titles and rights of the actors within the system, and it contributes therefore to the political structuring of their conflicts and oppositions. In other words, if boundary building/removing is a general and abstract concept for all forms of territorial and social circumscription, political production represents its empirical manifestation

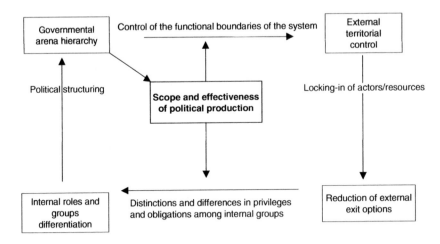

FIGURE 1.4. Political production, boundary building and exit options

---

[64] I discuss these effects on the competitive drives of parties in Bartolini, S., 'Collusion, Competition and Democracy. Part 1 and 2', *Journal of Theoretical Politics*, 11 (1999), 435–70; 12 (2000), 33–65; and Bartolini, S., 'Notes on the macro-constellation of party rise, consolidation and decline' (Haifa: 19–22 May 1997), Conference on 'Structural and behavioural aspects of democratic development'.

in concrete policies that delimit, consolidate, generalize, and stabilize the titles, endowments and rights that materialize the boundaries.

Although in Figure 1.4, political production appears to be the main factor affecting external territorial control, exit options, internal differentiation, and political structuring, the relationship between the former and the latter, in fact, is one of reciprocal strengthening or weakening. This is because every further increase in the control of the various boundaries of the system makes new room available for the extended political production of rights and titles to stabilize the behaviour of internal politically relevant actors. In addition, political structuring is itself a factor that can produce (and historically did produce) increased pressures that widen the scope of political production, particularly in the field of regulation and allocation. So, if we read Figure 1.4 clockwise from left to right we can imagine it as describing the process of internal political structuring of a territorially consolidated polity. However, we can also consider the same figure as having negative signs, starting from a decline (not an increase) in the control of the systemic boundaries, a corresponding decline in the external territorial control, an unlocking of politically relevant actors and resources, and an increase in their opportunity to exit from the territorial political production. This affects the internal differentiation of the polity and leads to an internal destructuring of alliances, oppositions and political organization, accompanied by a reduced scope and reach of the political production of public policies (and of extended and generalized behavioural conformity).

Figures 1.3 and 1.4 and this chapter as a whole argue that any modification of the territorial boundary control and of the corresponding configuration of actors/resources locked in the same territory has direct and significant implications for the polity's political production and any possible internal structuring. Just as closure and structuring are theoretically linked, so are exit and destructuring. This, then, is the nucleus of a theory of boundary building and political structuring, and exit-options and political destructuring. However, it is not only for existing units that different functional boundaries are raised or lowered. Boundaries are moved to higher, more encompassing territorial and membership groups or may be narrowed down to retrenched ones. Any attempts at new boundary building at higher or lower levels may thus derive from the incapacity of the authorities to defend those boundaries at that level.

Conclusions: The Micro–Macro Framework

The aim of this chapter is to delineate a theory of political structuring in the changing conditions of territorial confinement. Using Hirschman and

TABLE 1.6. *The micro–macro concepts*

Individual		Key concepts	Systemic
Individual actor's choice to subtract herself	**Exit**	**Centre formation**	Control of the transcendence of systemic boundaries
Individual actor's cultural and solidarity ties increasing the cost of exit	**Loyalty**	**System building**	Structures and processes of system maintenance through collective identities, solidarity ties and institutions, and participation rights
Individual propensity to political participation	**Voice**	**Political structuring**	Within system structuring of channels and organizations for political representation

Rokkan's work, I establish a correspondence between micro-individual choices and the corresponding systemic processes. Table 1.6 summarizes this micro–macro correspondence.

The decision to exit is an individual choice that can be actively induced, totally foreclosed, or charged with different costs, depending on the boundaries that are set. Therefore, the capacity to control the transcendence of boundaries corresponds, at the systemic level, to individual exit choices. This capacity is the hallmark of 'centre formation'.

Individual loyalty represents the psychological and emotional ties that mediate between exit and voice, increasing the cost of the former. At the systemic level, this corresponds to the structures and processes of system maintenance through collective identities, solidarity ties and participation rights. This is labelled 'system formation' as distinct from centre formation. The establishment of a centre does not necessarily entail or require the development of those areas of social, cultural and political equality that set additional boundaries to the polity and define the broader or narrower scope of its legitimate collectivized deliberations.

Voice is the individual propensity to political participation. At the systemic level, voice requires the structuring of channels and political organizations for representation. The latter lowers the cost of voice for individual actors as they normally provide institutional rules and infrastructural support for its expression. This set of channels and organizations represent the 'political structuring' of the polity. In short, individual exit, loyalty, and voice correspond to the macro feature of centre formation, system building and political structuring.

This framework is general enough to be applied to different territorial political formations. The nation-state is a historically (and geographically?) specific configuration of this framework. However, the framework also helps to conceptualize political formations that are different from the nation-state because they are characterized by a different configuration of boundaries and exit and a different scope of political production of the centre, of system building and of political structuring. The framework can be adopted to characterize pre-nation-state polities as well as to understand post-nation-state polities.

The following steps of this book substantiate this framework empirically. In the next chapter this is done by recasting the history of European nation-state formation at a number of critical junctures. Following this, the framework will be applied to the process of European integration. Here, I will analyse the new centre formation at the EU level, the boundary-redrawing implied by its political production, the configuration of actors/resources locked into the new territorial system, and the prospects of system building and political structuring in this new polity.

2

Structuring Europe:
The Experience of the 'Nation-State'

Introduction: Large-Scale Territorial
Differentiation and Retrenchment

In this chapter the analytical scheme developed in Chapter 1 is applied to the experience of the formation of the European system of states. This is re-examined in the light of the processes of military, economic, administrative, and cultural retrenchment/expansion at critical historical junctures story. The recasting is selective in that it emphasizes how the processes of boundary control in various spheres contributed to the specific and historically unique constellation of political structuring in the Western experience. The latter is interpreted as an historical process during which different types of boundaries reinforcing each other progressively separated European polities.

By its zenith, the Roman Empire had built a strong military and administrative centre for the control of large territories, and ruled a vast network of military and commercial cities around the Mediterranean. The Empire thus became the vehicle by which new membership groups based on a major script religion, Roman citizenship, and a common elite language developed and spread. Separate organizational structures for these spheres were generated with resources of their own: armies, administrative consulates, the church, and new networks of cultural and economic centres. The Empire, therefore, created a vast territorial space and also contributed to the development of broader membership spaces. That is to say, the mobility of these armies, the security of the trading routes, and the common administrative and high culture language all contributed to the breaking down of established local cultural boundaries. At the same time, the Empire established complex rules for demarcating and delimiting the membership space of Roman citizenship. The later development of the community of baptized Christians had an even stronger impact on membership space redefinition.[1] So, within the expanding empire, the internal physical and geographical boundaries began to lose importance, and were, at the same time, replaced by the stronger membership boundaries of the Roman citizenship and ritual community. While the territories were increasingly open to all sorts of transactions, the core organizations were closely bound through strict rules of initiation.

When the Empire collapsed it did so in terms of its military and then also its administrative structure, while the city network remained in place, as did the Christian church and the tradition of long-distance communication via a common language. Indeed, much of the economic and cultural infrastructure remained intact, and was even reinforced on the cultural dimension as a result of the fight against Islam. Following the collapse of the Western Roman Empire, the first move towards territorial reintegration was the formation of the Frankish kingdom in the eighth century. While Charlemagne managed to regroup major areas of the former Western Roman Empire, this first 'European' empire was split into kingdoms soon after his death (Treaty of Verdun 843): a Western kingdom, a Germanic kingdom and the middle kingdom of Lotharingia. This division into three entities triggered the dialectics of centrifugal and centripetal movements that were subsequently dominated by the problem of internal authority consolidation and external boundary control. The territorial accretion of a successful monarch necessitated a delegation of power to local authorities capable of exercising such power by proxy. Even if the Court and the King moved peripatetically through the territory and lacked a central seat, the problem was generated of how to keep these local representatives under control, and prevent them from establishing their own competing kingdom as a result of their local delegated power basis.[2] The monarch's solution was to appoint trusted individuals to do this job. However, this solution was frequently unsatisfactory and unstable as vassals and barons were continuously tempted to resist royal power, and, often with external support, to substitute themselves to the monarch.

In an era of limited technological development, early barriers to exit were mainly geographical. The geography of Europe, and in particular its mountainous Pyrenean, Alpine, and Carpathian chains, established from the beginning a high integration threshold for all attempts at political unification and helped to keep sizable exit options open, even in the case of minor territorial units. Particularly on the east side, the sheer breath of the spaces

---

[1] The development of these confraternities contributed to cutting across long-lasting kinship ties, helping the development of Christianity as a cross-territorial religion based on individual membership through participation in the rite of communion. See Weber, M., *Wirtschaft und Gesellschaft* (Tübingen: Mohr, 1956 (1922)), 102–3 and 532–4.

[2] On the political structure of Feudalism see Finer, S. E., *The History of Government From the Earliest Times*, 3 vols. (Oxford: Oxford University Press, 1997), Vol. 1, 855–934.

involved, prevented Western-originated forces from integrating the east, and made its own endogenous integration difficult other than in the form of large-scale empires.

The main expression of politico-administrative retrenchment was feudalism, as it took the form of the rising power of intermediary power-holder controlling resources in the primary economy and, later on, in the administrative, judicial, and coercion domains. Of course, feudality could come and go, and the feudal lord could defy his sovereign through change of lordship. Indeed, the specific characteristic of feudalism was that political allegiance was divorced from territoriality.[3] In Medieval Europe, individuals, groups or corporate bodies could establish power relationships over other individuals, groups or bodies irrespective of their physical location. An ideal example of this was the case of the *Connétable de Richemond*, the French hood and strong-arm commander leading the armies of Charles VII, who turned out to be none other than the Earl of Richmond. 'As such he was under certain obligation of obedience to his liege lord, Henry VI of England: but as heir-apparent to the fief of Brittany he was also under certain obligations to the king of France'.[4] Similarly, the clerical orders and the Catholic Roman Church exerted special jurisdictional powers over their members irrespective of their domicile. In general, however, changes in lordship were both frequent and of little significance for the whole system, except, perhaps, when a particular geographical location made these changes to be perceived as a gain or loss of a peripheral province, or when particular timing—for instance during a lord war—made such a change momentous for the fate of any one lord.

Together with feudalization, a further step in the differentiation of boundaries was the development of networks of cities with more or less autonomous status. The ancient city and its Middle Age successors had developed strong boundaries for the differential control of different types of transactions. The city exerted strict control over its membership space, while, at the same time, keeping its territorial borders relatively open to the export and import of people, goods, and ideas.[5] Local alliances of lineage ritually expressed through the institution of the common meal and the common hearth defined a membership space with strong cultural boundaries, but left open other kinds of transactions through the territorial space. As time

---

[3] See Gierke, O., *Political Theories of the Middle Age* (Cambridge: Cambridge University Press, 1988 (1900)).

[4] Finer, S. E., 'State-building, state boundaries and border control: An essay on certain aspects of the first phase of state-building in Western Europe considered in the light of the Rokkan-Hirschman model', *Social Science Information*, 13 (1974), 79.

[5] This intuition can be found in the classic work of Fustel de Coulanges, N. D., *La cité antique* (Paris: Hachette, 1957).

went by, open geographical spaces of economic transaction undermined the membership claim to pre-eminent right of control over the territory.

Even if the idea and ideals of a universal (Roman) citizenship and (Christian) ritual community survived the collapse of the remnants of the Roman Empire, the early Middle Ages can be defined as a period in which both geographical and membership spaces underwent retrenchment and 'disjointedness' (i.e. progressive lack of coincidence). Geographical space were defined by boundaries that could be crossed with relative ease as a trader, missionary, labourer, or traveller; membership spaces, on the other hand, were characterized by cultural boundaries that were far more difficult to penetrate. As a result, the correspondence between geographical military-administrative spaces and new significant membership groups started to diverge and this divergence began to be institutionalized. This retrenchment/differentiation took place along all four dimensions of the boundary control of territorial spaces discussed in Chapter 1.[6] In the *coercion* dimension, fragmented and mercenary armies tried to monopolize physical coercion to defend narrower territorial borders. In the *economic* dimension, barter, exchange, common currency and credit institutions progressively separated territorial markets. In the *cultural* dimensions, churches and schools, priests, schoolteachers, scribes, and scientists developed distinct cultural identities and symbolic myths. Finally, in the *administrative* domain, bureaucrats and politicians contributed to a differentiation of a variety of administrative regimes for the definition of various types of citizenships. These retrenchment processes first occurred in military and administrative terms; next, in economic terms, and, finally, also in cultural terms (i.e. the schisms in Christianity and the differentiation of vernacular linguistic standards).

These processes can be defined as 'retrenchments' if the point of reference is the large imperial territorial spaces and membership communities of the past. However, they can be regarded as processes of 'enlargement' and as the constitution of a broader territorial and membership community if the point of reference is the acute atomization of the first centuries following the

---

[6] Rokkan distinguishes three dimensions of differentiation in the development of large-scale territorial systems: military-administrative, economic, and cultural differentiation. Rokkan, S., 'Cities, states, nations: A dimensional model for the study of contrasts in development', in S. Rokkan and S. Eisenstadt (eds.), *Building States and Nations*, 2 vols. (Beverly Hills, CA: Sage, 1973); and Rokkan, S., 'Dimensions of State Formation and Nation-Building: A Possible Paradigm for Research on Variations within Europe', in C. Tilly (ed.), *The Formation of Nation State in Western Europe* (Princeton, NJ: Princeton University Press, 1975), 562–601. As mentioned in Chapter 1, I prefer to keep the four dimensions of differentiation and boundary building separate, distinguishing the force-coercion-extraction boundary and differentiation domain, from the politico-administrative one. In my opinion, the four-fold typology of boundaries becomes necessary when dealing with the late or post-nation-state developments. In reality, Rokkan also speaks of four dimensions at times. See his four dimension polygons.

collapse of the Empire. The early formation of territorial states in Europe can therefore be seen as a retrenchment from former more unified and encompassing entities, and, at the same time, as an expansion of extremely localized Middle Age territorial and membership groups. In the following sections of this chapter, I discuss how the retrenchment/enlargement processes along the four dimensions interacted with each other and contributed to the eventual specific form of political structuring of the European nation-state. I do so by identifying five critical junctures that analytically separate the phases of 'state building', 'capitalist development', 'nation building', 'democratization' and 'social sharing'. These phases represent respectively the formation and consolidation of coercion, economic, cultural and politico-administrative boundaries.

State Building (Force-Coercion)

The most crucial step of retrenchment along the territorial force-coercion dimension was first the progressive military and then administrative consolidation of the smaller territorial units as sovereign states. The process of central government power consolidation and state building was a process of subsystem administrative differentiation (since military, tax, juridical and economic subsystems were not initially well differentiated) and of accumulation of the central control of these subsystems. In this way, the force-military and administrative boundaries were made progressively coincidental. In early state building, these processes took a long time to implement because the low differentiation of the subsystems prevented the conquering centre from using military forces, judicial instruments, tax revenues, and economic levies, these being recruited and armed, administered, and collected by the local nobles or magnates. The low functional differentiation of the subsystems proved an obstacle as it provided peripheral territories, nobles and magnates, communes, competing kingdoms, etc., with enough control of the resources to threaten and actually implement exit in a strong sense—when they seceded— or in a weak sense—when they accepted the formal authority of the king in exchange for concessions which in fact reinforced their local position and autonomy. This long-term process of functional differentiation and centre accretion can be described in power, juridical, symbolic, and systemic terms.

In *power terms*, the process centres on the accumulation of resources and means.[7] Some centres of political power tended to widen their spatial reach

---

[7] See Dahl, R. A., 'The concept of power', *Behavioral Science*, 2 (1957), 201–15. He adds the dimensions of 'effectiveness' (the probability of an order being executed) and of 'scope' for the analysis of power.

over a given territory against other centres disputing that control. This was achieved by reducing or eliminating the latter's capacity to initiate autonomous military enterprises, guarantee law and order, and extort resources from the local populations. The fundamental resource in this process was generally military force.[8] Herz uses the concepts of 'impermeability' or 'impenetrability' to define the modern state, and defines its nature through the metaphor of the 'hard shell' of fortification that encircled its territory.[9] Although the idea that a system of territorial states based on the power of a prince would defend peace better than the Holy Roman Empire and its emperor was already widespread in the high Middle Ages, the territorial state could not prevail until medieval units of impermeability—the knight in his castle and the city within its walls—were eradicated. It was war technology that modified the balance of power here, since gunpowder has a major impact on the units of protection and security, and infantry and artillery proved superior to old style weapons. 'The large-area state came finally to occupy the place that the castle or fortified town had previously had as a unit of impenetrability'.[10] To achieve definitive consolidation all the independent fortifications within the new territorial unit needed to be eliminated, with new fortresses being erected along the line encircling its territory.

Initially, resources for the territorial consolidation of the new centres were minimal: some tenuous rights and some material basis, the former being difficult to 'cash' without the latter. At a certain stage, however, an imbalance of resources in favour of the new centre allowed it to impose its will over peripheral powers. The accretion of rights and resources impacted upon the political style of the peripheral elites, the masters of the local subsystems. These last first tried to defeat the prince by cutting him back to size. When it became clear that the prince's resources base was too large in material and juridical terms to be destroyed, local elites tend to acquiesce in the reduction of their own subsystem and to compensate for this by ensuring control of the use of the prince's resources. That is, they negotiated submission in exchange for a local control over the now formally accepted prince's resources and competences. In my terminology, they negotiated over renouncing exit in exchange for the institutionalization of internal rules of closure that would guarantee them privileged access to certain types of resources.

In *juridical terms*, centre accretion means the creation and monopolization of new legal techniques. The territorial aggrandizement of the state owed

---

[8] On the role of war and military force in state formation see Tilly, C., *Coercion, Capital and European States. AD 990–1992* (Cambridge: Blackwell, 1990).

[9] Herz, J. H., 'The Rise and Demise of the Territorial State', *World Politics*, 4 (1957), 473–93; reprinted in Herz, J. H., *The Nation State and the Crisis of World Politics. Essays on international politics in the twentieth century* (New York: David McKay, 1997), 99–123.

[10] Ibid., 104.

more than it is usually acknowledged to legal techniques. Territory was frequently acquired and lost by various means throughout the whole period of state formation, but power and military conquest was not necessarily the most frequent and/or safe means. Inheritance, purchase, marriage, and feudal interventions in the successions of vassals were an equally if not more important means of acquisition for the expanding king and his kingdom. Feudal law provided many opportunities for the intercession of the overlord and for his acquisition of new rights; for instance, the right to intervene in a disputed secession to a fief, the right to arrange the marriage of his heirs, or the right to extend royal jurisdiction via judicial appeals and Royal Court decisions.[11]

New legal theories and techniques expanded in three distinct directions the role of the prince as *rex* to the expenses of his role as *dominus*: (*a*) his right to adjudicate began to encroach upon, and ultimately extruded, that of other private persons. As the distinction between law-finding and lawmaking was as thin then as it is today, this eventually implied the power to make law by ordinances, decrees or declarations; (*b*) his duty to maintain peace began to encroach upon, and finally extruded, the private person's right to levy forces, make wars and, eventually, to possess arms; and (*c*) his right to extract men, materials and money from his subjects began to undercut similar rights of private persons until it finally became his monopoly. These *regalia* (rights pertaining to him/her in his capacity as *rex*) extended cumulatively and blended together. Externally this process was complemented by the exclusion of every limitation previously imposed by either the Emperor or the Papacy.

Finally, the juridical aspects of centre formation extended to a more complex institutional development. In the early phase, states were still a set of governmental practices that were relatively unstandardized, discontinuous, and unconnected, and in which logics and resources of different types (often strictly personal) played a decisive role. Governmental prerogatives, initially quite simple and narrow, were extended in a uniform way to regions that functioned according to a multiplicity of local jurisdictions and of administrative settings. Disputes concerning the law represent a significant normative aspect of territorial consolidation, and later on, reference to the law, the reinterpretation of old legal institute and principles, and the definition of new ones perform a particularly important function in state practice.[12] In fact, in the Western experience, law extended progressively from its two universal functions (the distribution of propriety control over material means and the repression of deviating and antisocial behaviours) to the

---

[11] Finer, *The History of Government*, Vol. 1, 93.

[12] For a variety of examples of this point see Poggi, G., *La vicenda dello stato moderno. Profilo sociologico* (Bologna, Italy: Il Mulino, 1978); and Poggi, G., *The State. Its Nature, Development and Prospects* (Stanford, CA: Stanford University Press, 1991).

establishing of the instances that oversee the distribution and management of political power. The state resorted to a secular juridical knowledge that was normative, and normative innovations served to organize the personnel, the material resources and the capacities through which the state operated. Therefore, the interpretation of these norms became a fundamental way to orient and control these same operations of the state.

In *symbolic terms*, centre accretion took the form of rationalization and legitimation. In order to justify their ambitions to military strengthening, the territorial lords were obliged to institute and maintain durable 'peace' over large territories. They also swore oaths with groups and collective bodies and, sometimes, they also oversaw the tutelage of various subordinate groups, and these commitments were often celebrated through solemn and sacred ceremonies. The construction of the European states was accompanied by a discourse that took order, security, peace, and protection against risks as its ongoing themes. For instance, the recollection, albeit remote, of the Roman imperial experience inspired and legitimized several attempts to constitute wider and more durable political entities than those that had managed to survive the great migrations and the breakdown of the Carolingian empire. The possession of the title of 'king' was an enormous symbolic resource for the dynastic groups that controlled the territories around the Ile de France. Finally, the attribution of abstract goals to the state was essential to its legitimation. The state operates concretely through a multiplicity of changing individuals and groups, whose actions reflect different, and sometime contrasting, conceptions of its ends and means. The state progressively presented itself and came to be conceived as an entity destined to transcend the physical existence of several generations, to which concrete ends can be assigned.

Finally, in *systemic terms*, centre formation leads to an increasing delineatedness of boundaries. At the beginning, system boundaries were diffuse, and it was difficult to say where one master system ended and another began. The military, judicial, economic, and taxation functions merged and overlaid each other and were handled by a myriad of subsystems that are supervised loosely, and often only nominally, by the master. In the final system, instead, the boundaries are spatially definite, the functions sharply differentiated, and the structures specialized and tightly articulated by the master system. The modern idea of 'border' as a precise linear separation between two contiguous spaces with different orders has slowly developed over the idea of a *marca* or of a *frontiera*; that is, a vaguely delimited area in which a slow and complex transition from one jurisdiction to another takes place, and for which sophisticated technical knowledge and competences are necessary to handle the territory.

Power, juridical, symbolic and systemic aspects of centre accretion always implied the acquisition and extension of territory. However, while acquisition is a necessary condition, it is not a distinctive feature. What in reality made the state 'new' was much more the processes of boundary control and internal penetration than the mere acquisition of territory. Rights over a territory and its population were easier to acquire than to preserve as the latter required the successful extrusion of counterclaimants within or outside the territory. As a witness to this time, Machiavelli was so aware of this that his *Il principe* devotes more attention to how princedoms have to be kept and consolidated than to how they can be acquired. This dual theory of power-acquisition versus power-consolidation reflects the modernity of his thinking, but also reflects the changes in the conception of power entailed by the emergence of a certain type of state in which the goal of mere external defence became more closely linked to the control of internal counterclaimants. To achieve this, it was not territory as such that was needed, but its internal penetration by the new central hierarchy.

The crucial turning point for this mutual process of external consolidation and internal penetration of the new state was the 'Westphalia system'. After the end of the Thirty Years war and the Westphalia Peace, the Medieval remnant of permeability—when, for instance, outside powers allied with internal factions against their prince—began to disappear. The new order saw declining external interferences and more exclusive internal jurisdictions. This transition was particularly evident in the core German territories of the Holy Roman Empire. Here, for all practical purposes the Westphalia Treaty had conferred independence to the princes of the Empire, without, however, fully abolishing the old feudal structure of obligations, jurisdictions, allegiances, duty of membership and complex decision-making mechanisms.[13] It is not surprising that the most sophisticated argument about 'sovereignty' was developed in this area, where the discrepancy between the claim of actual (state) control and the claims of legitimate imperial control were more obviously at odds.

As 'political adviser' to the Duke of Hanover, Leibniz developed a strong argument supporting the actual independence of all those rulers who were formally subject to the Emperor, defining the actual capacity to rule as 'sovereignty' and distinguishing it from the 'majesty' of the Emperor.[14] Majesty, in his view, consisted in a number of jurisdictions that conferred the right to demand obedience and involved duties of fealty, but this was not sovereignty because it did not involve the actual power to constrain subjects on their territories. Since this real power was now in the hands of the prince, the power of the emperor to enforce his authority rested on his means of war.

---

[13] Herz, 'The Rise and Demise of the Territorial State', 105.
[14] In the famous Leibniz, G. W., 'Entretien de Philarete et D'Eugene', in A. F. de Careil (ed.), *Oeuvres de Leibniz* (Paris: Firmin Didot Freres, 1865 (1677)), Vol. 6, 343–408.

Therefore, all the rulers of impermeable territories whose resistance could be curbed only via force were, irrespective of their status and formal attributes, actually sovereign. This capacity in turn differentiated sovereign princes from those who were such only in nominal terms because they lacked the military capacity to defend their territory (as was the case of many papal princes). In other words, given that territoriality as effective garrisoning was defined as the new principle of sovereignty, the superior in law had no other means (as court decisions, for instance) other than coercion to enforce claims against the real territorial ruler. The de facto condition of territorial impenetrability was thus legitimized as the basis of sovereignty.

The new system brought about a relative stabilization of the political units. While losses of territory were still frequent, the complete annihilation of states as independent units through war and conquest became increasingly rare.[15] However, equally important, if not more so, was the new principle of non-interference. After the Westphalia Treaty, governments ceased to directly support religiously likeminded communities across the borders when they were in conflict with their own state. This mutual recognition of respective sovereignty in religious matters (as well as in others) meant that the dominant elites of each territorial state were willing to renounce certain political goals of aggrandizement in exchange for an increased internal control over their own state. Exploiting this relative freedom from external interferences, the ruling elites began to point their attention inwards, towards imposing their sovereignty onto their internal societies. The safety and security of their internal domination was thus strengthened in exchange for a limitation in the search for external security through war.

The Westphalia international agreement thus modified the balance of power between territorial authorities, on the one hand, and confessional groups and universalistic hierarchies, on the other, in favour of the first and limiting the exit options of the second. The *internal* sovereignty of the modern state was therefore mainly the result of the *external* consolidation of its borders in terms of military-administrative, economic and cultural transactions. The relationship between these two factors was crucial. Under the new conditions, the behaviour of states and their dynastic rulers was no longer constrained internally, as, once the medieval idea of broader membership spaces in the form of a *res publica Christiana* had lost its hold, no principle of public law remained. The full autonomy of the new state supported the monopoly of the internal power on a virtually infinite number of

---

[15] That the disappearance of the states was regarded as exceptional is witnessed by the strong impression and perception of illegitimacy with which contemporaries judged and recriminated, for instance, the Napoleonic restructuring of the established system of territoriality, the destruction of one of the oldest political units, Venice, or the partition of Poland.

matters. With the development of the modern sovereign state, exit further diminished; at times, borders became so clearly demarcated and heavily patrolled that individuals who wanted to leave against the state wishes had to take high risks.

If, externally, the new aspiring state needed to control borders against the centrifugal forces of exit, internally, it tended to expand its rights over the population in scope, effectiveness and universality. This led to the creation of the extraction/coercion cycle that was so disruptive for many polities: war and defence required money, which was raised by taxing territories and groups, ad the latter required voice in estates, assemblies, Cortes, or courts. If they were denied this, they could resort to exit through tax revolt or even secession as in the case of Portugal and Catalonia from the Kingdom of Spain. In this vicious circle, in order to rise the taxes which were necessary to sustain the army defending the border, the centre had to coerce, for which it needed an army.[16]

This growing boundary control had different costs, and these influenced decisively the structuring of internal voice. The French–British contrast, or, more generally, the British–Continental contrast, or, even more broadly, the Anglo-Saxon–continental contrast (including, in this case, the ex-British colonies which, from the USA to New Zealand all developed in conditions of low external pressure) suggest the hypothesis that the territories and centres that were less subject to the problem of exit as a result of geographical circumscription and military security were more willing to yield to pressure for the form of voice available at the time. In England by 1328 the kingdom possessed one central assembly as expressing voice, the composition of which remained more or less fixed, and whose consent for taxation and high court role were recognized. While there were conflicts and setbacks, the issue remained an issue of voice not of exit, and several parliaments expressed their dissatisfaction with the poor performance of the kingdom (particularly after 1603). The exit that existed consisted in the temporary withholding of taxes and of military personnel. In contrast, in France, the Estate General failed as a voice institution, were rarely achieving kingdom-wide representation, infrequently granting taxes, and never functioning as a law court (a different assembly, the parliament, was the sovereign court).[17]

On the Continent, and in particular in its core Holy Roman Empire area, exit opportunities remained very high, and the process of state formation

---

[16] The 'coercion-extraction' cycle and predicament is central to Finer's work on state formation. See 'State-building, state boundaries and border control' and *The History of Government*. It is also the central dichotomy in Tilly's work, *Coercion, Capital and European States*.

[17] For a French–English comparison in this light see Finer, *The History of Government*, Vol. 3, 1308–57.

largely influenced by military resources.[18] Decisive for this area was, first, the military balance between the centre and peripheral territories that the centre tried to incorporate/control. Equally important were, second, the resources external to its own border that the territory willing to exit could mobilize— notably from another master system. Finally, also crucial was the military balance between the master systems, as this could allow a peripheral territory to exit master systems and become a master system in its own right (a buffer system, as, for example, Savoy and Switzerland between France and the Habsburgs).

Given this situation on the continent, it is not surprising that the emergence of new states proved earlier, stronger and most durable if they were located at the periphery of the old empire, while the lands stretching from Italy to Germany through the alpine Swiss cantons, to the cities at the mouth of the river Rhine, remained fragmented and dispersed until the nineteenth century. According to Rokkan's view, it was far easier to develop effective core areas at the edges of the city-belt territories of the old empire, where centres could be built with less competition and could achieve command of the resources in the peripheral areas that were far removed from the cities in the central trade-belt. In this case, the acquisition of new territories and the control of the territorial borders and the firm locking-in of people and resources was made easier by the low or inexistent exit options of the under-lords and territories. Peripheries here tended to be external, rather than interface territories among different master systems. The first successful attempts at modern state-building on the edges of the old empire took place on the coastal plains to the west and to the north, in France, England, and Scandinavia, and later on also in Spain. The second wave of successful centre-building took place on the landward side, basically on the east side of the central trading city-belt: first the Hapsburgs, with their core area in Austria; then the Eastern march of the German Empire (Poland), next Sweden and finally, and decisively, Prussia.

In contrast, the heartland of the old Western Empire was constellated by cities located on a broad trade route belt stretching from the Mediterranean to the east, as well as to the west of the Alps, northwards to the Rhine and the Danube. This 'city-belt' was at the same time the stronghold of the Roman Catholic Church, with a high density of cathedrals, monasteries, and ecclesiastical principalities. The resurrection of the Holy Roman Empire under the leadership of the four German tribes did not help to unify the territory.

---

[18] Hintze was the first to clearly emphasize the relevance of the distinction between the core around the Frankish empire and the peripheral areas of British islands, Scandinavia, Castile, Naples–Sicily and territories east of Germany for the comparative study of European political development. Hintze, O., *Soziologie und Geschichte Staat und Verfassung*, ed. G. Oestreich (Goettingen: Vandenhoeck and Ruprecht, 1962).

The emperors were prey to shifting electoral alliances; many were figure-heads, and the best and the strongest expended their energies in quarrels with the Pope and the Italian cities. The extraordinary density of established cultural, religious, and economic centres within this territory made it difficult for any one of them to accumulate enough resources to become more powerful than the others. Indeed, in a situation of this kind, any accumulation of power means and resources that were viewed as threatening to a neighbour, were easily contrasted by the forming of alternative, power-balancing alliances. There was no geographical core area in this region for the development of a strong territorial system, and it became instead the scenario for endless onslaughts, countermoves and attempts to reorganize during the centuries from Charlemagne to Bismarck. First the French monarchs gradually did manage to take over the old Lotharingian–Burgundian buffer zone from Provence to Flanders and to incorporate typical trade cities such as Avignon, Aix and Lyon. In the wake of the French Revolution, Napoleon moved across the middle belt both north and south of the Alps and set in motion a series of attempts at unification that ended with the successes of the Prussians and the Piedmontese in the 1870s.

As well as the early difficulties discussed by Rokkan, state building in the city-belt faced additional problems. First, attempts at state building by latecomers were faced with interests and resources of the early-consolidated states, which viewed any new latecomer centre accretions as a threat. A second reason is that late 'conquest centres' had to deal with pre-existing political structures and institutions that were far more sophisticated and deep-rooted than those that the Austrian Hapsburgs, the kings of Spain, of France, not to speak of England, had had to contend with. Latecomers had to deal with more functionally differentiated systems. The more contested nature of latecomers territorial expansion and the more complex pre-existing political structures and institutions of the conquered territories led to deeper and rootless efforts to impose internal control and penetration, often resulting into a suppression of traditional pluralism and of early voice channels. This particularly applies to the Piedmontese and Prussian centre formation and subsequent drives of territorial expansion.

In the city-belt, the alternative to this late-contested pattern was the formation of a defensive confederacy of equals among the cities characterized by the lack of a dominant centre. Thus, the key cities to the north of the Alps managed to establish a defence league, and gradually built up the Swiss confederation. Similar leagues born along the Rhine and across the Baltic and the North Sea (the Hanse) never managed to consolidate as sovereign territorial formations. The Spanish and Austrian Hapsburgs' encroachment on the city-belt from both west and east, and their attempt to control the crucial territories to the mouth of the Rhine for some time, triggered the next successful effort of consociational federation: the United Provinces of the Netherlands.[19]

To the east, before the First World War the borders of the region were defined by three empires: the Ottoman, Austro-Hungarian, and Russian dominions. When these empires collapsed just before the war (Ottoman) and after it (the other two), the new peace architects created new states or reconstructed old ones invoking the principle of self-determination. The twelve states which emerged were all non-homogeneous from the ethnical and/or religious point of view. Poland included large German minorities; Romania included a significant number of Hungarians within its borders; Czechoslovakia comprised two Slav nationalities and a large German minority. The new state of Yugoslavia was made up of at least seven nationalities, while a considerable group of 'Yugoslavs' was excluded from the new state. It therefore comes as no surprise that the inter-wars years were characterized by ethnic tensions and conflicts: rivalry between the Lithuanians and Poles, Czechs and Hungarians, Hungarians and Romanians, Hungarians and Austrians, Hungarians and Yugoslavs; Yugoslavs and Austrians; Yugoslavs and Italians; Italians and Austrians; Bulgarians and Yugoslavs; Bulgarians and Romanians; Germans, Poles and Czechs; Russians and Rumanians, Poles, and the three Baltic peoples. It was only as a result of the Second World War and its consequences that stability of borders in this region was achieved, lasting until the collapse of the Soviet state. The imposition of Soviet rule on Central and Eastern Europe created a sharp east/west division and an impenetrable border that was as strong as, if not stronger than, the division created by the Turkish invasions of the fifteenth and seventeenth centuries.

The historical contestedness of territorial consolidation for single polities influenced their level of 'stateness' decisively, that is, the extractive, regulative and repressive potential that each state holds vis-à-vis the society. This accumulation of resources was primarily the result of the pattern of state formation. If consolidated boundaries and a legal order clearly predated the formation of a strong central bureaucracy, then the repressive powers of the state were more likely to remain weak and relatively independent of the requests and direct control of the central hierarchy. If the consolidation of the state's basic institutions were uncontested or only relatively so, then the pressure for a centralized administration of the repressive apparatus tended to be weaker and the legal tradition to be less state-centred. If the creation and consolidation of the state structures was early enough and did not involve processes of large scale political mobilization or violent popular

[19] Daalder, H., 'On Building Consociational Nations: the Case of the Netherlands and Switzerland', *International Social Science Journal*, 23 (1971), 355–70.

resistance, then the state's apparatuses were likely to be less politicized and its repressive means to be more responsible to local judicial bodies. If central bureaucracy never consolidated, or it consolidated after representative institutions have been introduced, then the state apparatus did not constitute an available resource for the repression of newcomers. Obviously, the opposite conclusions apply under opposite circumstances.[20]

For an evaluation of the levels of 'stateness' that result, the ideal-type experience of a few well-known countries (generally France versus Britain versus Prussia) may in this case be somewhat misleading;[21] it is thus more fruitful to break the concept up into a number of constitutive dimensions[22] and to compare individual cases along each of them, going on to reconstruct their overall relative position later. Elsewhere, I have attempted an evaluation of Western state stateness via the operationalization of the different dimensions of (*a*) creation of the organization for the mobilization of resources: bureaucracy and tax burden; (*b*) external consolidation of the territory: army; (*c*) maintenance of internal order: police and judiciary; and (*d*) state activism in regulatory activities and in economic and social interventionism.[23]

Comparing the level of 'stateness', as indicated by the extractive, repressive and economic steering capacity of the state,[24] with the contestedness of the

---

[20] Here, I am reformulating theses that have been widely discussed in the literature of state formation and political development. See the articles in Tilly, *The Formation of Nation State*, in particular Bayley, D. H., 'The Police and Political Development in Europe', 328–79, who shows how the basic characters of the state apparatus were shaped long before the beginning of the industrial conflict; Daalder, H., 'Paths Towards State Formation in Europe: Democratization, Bureacratization and Politicization', in H. E. Chehabi and A. Stephan (eds.), *Politics, Society, and Democracy. Comparative Studies* (Boulder, CO: Westview Press, 1995), 113–30; Dahl, R. A., *Poliarchy, Participation and Opposition* (New Haven and London: Yale University Press, 1971), 48–9.

[21] See Birnbaum, P., *State and Collective Action: The European experience* (Cambridge: Cambridge University Press, 1988) for an ideal-type discussion of stateness.

[22] A decomposition strategy overcomes the critique that the characterization of the stateness of political processes at the macro level does not take into account possible cross-sector variations within a given state. See Atkinson, M. M. and Coleman, W. G., 'Strong States and Weak States. Sectoral Policy Networks in Advanced Capitalist Economies', *British Journal of Political Science*, 19 (1989), 47–67, 49.

[23] The combining of these different dimensions into a single 'stateness' indicator is documented in Bartolini, S., *The Political Mobilization of the European Left 1860–1980. The Class Cleavage* (Cambridge: Cambridge University Press, 2000), 313–20, Table 7.2, 318. Mann, M., *The sources of social power*, Vol. 2 (Cambridge: Cambridge University Press, 1993), 358–95 provides several tables of data about the 'size' of the state and discusses to some extent this dimension for European major powers only. Standardized data about these dimensions can be found in Flora, P. et al., *State Economy and Society in Western Europe 1815–1975. A Data Handbook in Two volumes*, Vol. 1. *The Growth of Mass Democracies and Welfare State* (Frankfurt: Campus Verlag; London: Macmillan Press; Chicago: St. James Press 1983).

[24] It seems to me that what I call here 'stateness' corresponds to the general concept of 'coercion' as used by Tilly, C., *Coercion, Capital and European States*, 19–20.

TABLE 2.1. *Modalities of state formation in Europe*

		Contestedness of boundary consolidation				
		Never fully consolidated	Early consolidation with little tension and resistance	Early consolidation against considerable resistance	Late and gradual consolidation	Late and violent consolidation
Stateness	Low	Switzerland	Sweden Denmark		Norway	
	Medium		Britain		Netherlands	Ireland Finland
	High			France (Austria)	Belgium	Italy Germany (Prussia) Austria

modalities of state formation in Table 2.1, it emerges that the countries which never consolidated as a unitary state (Switzerland), those of early and un-challenged consolidation (United Kingdom, Sweden, Denmark), and those of late and gradual consolidation (the Netherlands and Norway) are all low-or medium-stateness countries, the only minor exception to these being Belgium. The countries with early consolidation, but with considerable re-sistance, and those of late and violent consolidation all tend to be high-stateness countries, also because they were deeply involved in nineteenth century continental warfare. Finland and Ireland are the exceptions in this group, both having low-stateness in the context of a late and violent consoli-dation. These peripheries of large empires (the British and the Russian) had state structures and resources that were largely externally imported (and later withdrawn) rather than internally generated.

Capitalism Development (Economy)

At approximately the time of early territorial state formation, a new driving force began to operate toward boundary loosening, rather than boundary strengthening: the emergence of capitalism as a world force, contributing toward the reduction of physical distances, increase in economic interde-pendence, and cutting of long-lasting barriers.

The politico-administrative and military retrenchment following the col-lapse of the (Western) Roman Empire made contract enforcement uncertain or impossible, with a sharp decline in long-distance trade and exchanges. The rebirth of trade, starting with the beginning of the new millennium and accelerating rapidly thereafter, was based on several factors, among which was most important the development of new forms of trust based either on individual or family reputation mechanisms—which enabled future exchange to be based on information about past conduct—or on a community's reputation mechanisms—with cities or corporations taking collective responsibility for their citizens/members' behaviour. These forms of collective responsibility started to decline by the late thirteenth century, and were progressively substituted by various alternative legal procedures that reintroduced the principle of individual legal responsibility. According to one view, such decline mainly reflected the economy of scale, made possible by the population increase,[25] the emerging states' attempt to undermine the 'spontaneous' operating of the market and community institutions in order to increase state fiscal revenues,[26] the erosion of the efficiency and reliability of these community institutions and mechanisms due to the increase in trade and commerce and the growth of the size of merchants' community.[27] In the late Middle Ages, 'royal licenses of immunity' increasingly freed individuals from being persecuted for any debt except those that they had personally incurred. For the individual, this enabled an exit from smaller communities' collective duties, while it generated a new dependency on the political production of the enlarged states concerning the enforceability of individual responsibilities.

The relationship between state consolidation and capitalist development was complex and tangled. On the one hand, state formation was accompanied by the strengthening and progressive coincidence of various types of boundaries over extended territorial units while capitalist development was a powerful drive to boundary transcendence in the economic sphere. On the other hand, however, the reliability of contractual commitments due to the rationalization of administrative activities and the material security resulting from the progressive monopolization of coercion means, helped the development of capitalism, and the progressive integration of local markets into a broader national one.

Paradoxically, in early modern Europe, states and capitalism seemed to develop according to different preconditions and prerequisites. While early states developed along the west and (later) east periphery of the Central European belt of trading cities and microstates, early capitalism was stronger

[25] North, D. C. and Thomas, R. P., *The Rise of the Western World* (Cambridge: Cambridge University Press, 1973).

[26] Benson, B., 'The Spontaneous Evolution of Commercial Law', *Southern Economic Journal*, 55 (1989), 644–61.

[27] Greif, A., 'Interpersonal Exchanges and the Origin of Markets. From the Community Responsibility System to Individual Legal Responsibility in Pre-modern Europe', in M. Aoki and Y. Hayami (eds.), *Communities and Markets* (Oxford: Oxford University Press, 2001), Chapter 2.

in this central area. Thus, the most highly developed market forces and infrastructures of merchant capitalism flourished in the area of low hierarchical control from Central Italy to the Flanders. By contrast, the most developed state hierarchical infrastructures consolidated in the relatively poorer and also culturally peripheral areas, and were often heavily indebted with the city-belt lending institutions. It would appear that states needed a periphery with low economic resources to expand territorially, while capitalism needed an environment of low stateness and economic openness to flourish.[28]

Three centuries later the picture was completely different, having witnessed a relative weakening of the stateless area and a continuing military and economic strengthening of the surrounding territorial states.[29] With the expansion of state economic functions, the integration of the local market, and the re-orientation of the main commercial trade routes across the oceans, the stateless aspect of the city network proved to be a blessing, with the growing costs of security, military weakness, and the low market integration. From 1600 onwards, the costs of the stateless market grew, particularly because in those areas where relatively large territorial states had been founded, mercantilism, national protectionism, and the formation of internal market boundaries enormously damaged the commercial activities of the stateless trading cities. That is, state operations were crucially important in triggering a nationalization and territorialization of capitalism. This can be seen in various areas and, in particular, in the area of *market* formation, *currency* development, and *capital and credit* rationalization.

Market Formation

The market is a *geographical space*, extended to a greater or lesser extent according to technology of communication and conditions of safety, in which the exchanges present a certain number of regularities and follow a

---

[28] Burch, K., 'The 'properties' of the state system and global capitalism', in S. Rosow, N. Inayatullah and M. Rupert (eds.), *The Global Economy as Political Space* (Boulder, CO: Lynne Rienner, 1994), 37–59 deals with the relationship between state and capitalism, and, in particular, with the substitution of landed property income with mobile property income in the seventeenth and eighteenth centuries. According to the author, 'Prior to 1700, there was no distinction between the state system and capitalism: a bifurcated understanding of real and mobile property was not yet institutionalized. Property meant, primarily, real, landed property' (47). This overlooks early capitalist developments outside the large territorial states and long before that date. In the Italian city-states of the 14th–15th centuries, real and mobile property were clearly understood as 'bifurcated'.

[29] Tilly suggests two reasons for this decline: 'commercialization and capital accumulation in larger states such as England and France reduced the war-making advantages of the small mercantile states and second, war expanded in scale and cost, partly as a function of the increased ability of the larger states to milk their economies, or their colonies, to pay for armed forces.' Tilly, *Coercion, Capital and European States*, 190.

certain number of rules, while the latter are guaranteed more or less effectively by different sorts of sanctions. Markets pre-existed state formation and
continued to resist the constraints through which states tried to discipline
them. However, regular and safe exchanges were dependent on the expect-
ation that barter be honoured, and this required some sort of overall authority for it to be ensued. In this sense, the establishment of extended markets
was enabled by the state. It is possible that the commercial flourishing of the
city-belt was facilitated by the low taxation resulting from the weak central
political hierarchy. However, in the long run, the absence of a central
standardizing and market integrating force meant that tariffs and customs
barriers were more numerous, pervasive, and higher than in the early-state
areas.

In this phase one can distinguish three spatial definitions and three modalities of market organization: (*a*) the *village or rural area market*, with
exchanges among peasant and artisan producers; (*b*) the *city market*, in
which exchanges among city consumers and producers and exchanges between the city and countryside combine; and (*c*) the *long-distance trade and
exchange*, which connected spaces characterized by distant and different
cultures and political dominations.[30] The village modality developed within
the rural seigniorial system; the city modality within the cities and the
countryside surrounding them; the long-distance modality rested instead on
a network of trading cities with wide horizons and relative independence.
While each of these modalities was in communication with the others, they all
had their own rules and systems of functioning which they tried to safeguard.
With the coming of the modern age, the state would try to use these to its own
advantage, playing on their divisions, stimulating and also confiscating at
least a part of their profits, and finally setting itself as the guardian of their
rule of functioning. This led to a fourth and new spatial organization of the
market which borrowed elements from each of the three previous modalities,
but presented itself as a higher and superior form: the *national market*.

For labour, goods and services, the national market defined itself against
the local, village or city markets, with the disappearance of previous internal
barriers to entry/exit in the cities (corporations) as well as in the countryside,
and their transposition to the borders of the state. These redefinitions of
market boundaries developed their own ideological underpinning. Between
the seventeenth and eighteenth centuries, the members of corporations who
escaped these ties and established themselves as independent workers, merchants and artisans often moved to the periphery of the major trading

---

[30] See Aymard, M. and Postel-Vinay, G., 'L'Etat et les marchés', in B. Théret (ed.),
L'Etat la finance et le social. Souveraineté nationale et construction européenne (Paris: La
découverte, 1995), 351–69.

centres, in order to be less exposed to the judicial pursuit of their authorities. These exits were accompanied by the development of new arguments to refute the accusation that, outside the order of the corporation, the quality of work would no longer be protected or guaranteed. These arguments[31] referred to the freedom of choice of job, the freedom of choice of buyers, and the quality and price advantages engendered by competition among producers of the same good.[32] Via these justifications, merchant activities acquired their own dignity and developed an autonomous set of ethical rules which were independent of those of the dominant community of their fellow workers.

The labour market first organized in a given region as a result of the complex combination of permanents jobs, normally reserved to the local workers, and of many temporary and fluctuating activities ensured to a large extent by a mobile population coming from surrounding countryside. Local and long-distance markets of manpower thus coexisted for a long time responding to different rules and needs. Industrialization utilized these circuits of recruitment but, in doing so, also generated a form of 'sesentarization' of this same manpower towards the end of the nineteenth and beginning of the twentieth century. This led to a nationalization of the labour market.

For goods and services, the costs and the possibilities to exit/entry were shaped as a function of financial needs and also of a new 'economic policy'. The customs policies alternate between periods of high protectionism and period of liberalization of the exchanges. The core countries had a freer choice and could mix in variable proportions the measures aimed at protecting their internal market and those aimed at assuring for or imposing on others, the freedom of their trade.

Currency

The identification between state and currency goes back to the origins of the former. Every Greek city-state had its own currency, while the Roman domination was accompanied by a systematic effort to extend a unique system of currency to the totality of the empire. Due to the persistence of

---

[31] Using an idiosyncratic vocabulary, Boltanski, L. and Chiapello, E., *Le Nouvel esprit du capitalisme* (Paris: Gallimard, 1999), 626–29 label these justifications *'cités'*.

[32] These arguments developed before economics formulated the theoretical rationalization of competition and of its unintended beneficial effects. Mandeville, B., *The Fable of the Bees* (Edinburgh: Printed for W. Gray and W. Peter, 1755) was probably the first to posit the existence of unintentional consequences of intentional human actions and the idea that even private vices can contribute to public happiness. Smith was not ready to accept the latter idea and in his moral writings accused Mandeville of an inverted moralism. See A. Smith, 'The Theory of Moral Sentiments', in *Works and Correspondence of Adam Smith*, Vol. 1 (Oxford: Oxford University Press, 1976 (1764)), 308–14.

local currencies necessary to the local market, there were limitations on this policy. All the same, the Roman currency was valid throughout the empire and in numerous of its neighbouring states. The generalization of the seigniorial system and the political fragmentation of the Middle Ages made currency differentiation to prevail in the following centuries. New states, for sure, issued their own currency, but they were unable to enforce a monopoly of currency issuing, and it took several centuries to reduce and eliminate alternative currencies over the same territory. Central power holders managed to reduce the role of these local currencies—normally coins in bronze or copper—by refusing them as ways of paying taxes, to the advantage of the pieces in gold or silver utilized by richer merchants and the public organizations. However, at the same time, states had to accept the circulation over their territories of currencies issued abroad, utilized by merchants and individuals in relation to their credibility and prestige. The most sought after currencies were those of the big commercial metropolises, Florence, Venice and Genoa. Only with the arrival of American silver did Spain, among the big monarchies, manage to impose its own pieces.

In a second stage, a greater coherence in the currency system was achieved by the alignment of the currencies of various states to a few reference currencies, such as the ottoman *sultanino* of the sixteenth century, which had more or less the same value of the Venetian *sequin* or the Hungarian *ducat*. By the sixteenth century the first international account currencies had appeared. With respect to these, the value of the various other currencies varied as a function of their intrinsic value and their appreciation on the long-distance exchange markets. These currencies—such as the *ecu* of the Besançon Plaisance fair—were private currencies, invented and controlled by a small merchant aristocracy and bankers.

The importance of this dual market of 'international' (real pieces and change currencies) complicated the efforts of the different states to become masters within their own territories of currency circulation, and therefore to impose a nominal value different from their intrinsic value on the coins they issued. It was not until these states began to replace metal coins with paper currency that they were able to develop methods of control and regulate the volume of currency mass and to fix the rate of interest and exchange.[33]

Capital and Credit

Kings and their administrators understood early on that the state required revenue was most effectively obtained by promoting mobile rather than

---

[33] This summary of European currency history is based on Aymard and Postel-Vinay, *L'Etat et les marchés*.

landed property, and that the expanding capitalist enterprises and fluid resources benefited from stable institutional orders.[34] In early modern Europe the evolution of the capital and credit markets tended to be organized at different geographical levels, none of them corresponding with state territories. Cosmopolitan capital and credit markets linked commercial centres via circuits of short-term credit and of capital transfer by compensation of debts, first bilateral with bill of exchange, then multilateral with the fairs of exchange. Local capital and credit markets had a small range and allowed the circulation of local savings in the form of usury loans, and of anticipated buying and selling contracts of promissory note with settlement of annuity.[35] It was the public demand, with its massive and irregular character (often due to wars), that modified these markets and their rules continuously.

In the sixteenth century the Spanish monarchy innovated a new system in its territories: the issuing of titles that were guaranteed by their future revenues— the *juros*—whose value varied in inverse relation to the rate of interest and in direct relation to the confidence that was placed in the state's capacity to pay those interests.[36] New financial instruments (the English 'consols', the French 'life annuity' (*rentes viagères* or *tontines*) and new institutions (bourses, stock exchanges) were developed in the eighteenth century. While still in the seventeenth century the French and Spanish monarchies depended on a small number of large secured creditors, able and willing to run high risks in the short-term in the hope of making big profits in the longer term, in the following century they managed progressively to address a much higher number of creditors spread over the territory. Monarchies therefore tended to open up the local savings markets that had been closed until then, contributing in this way to the first unification of national markets of public credit.

This increased resort to an internal credit market did not, however, allow states to free themselves completely from the resources collected outside their borders. The borrowing of the large states contributed to the creation of a European international market. States thus fostered markets that financed their consolidation, and they also increasingly intervened directly, even militarily, to enforce the respect of engagements taken by peripheral states (e.g. in Mexico, China, and the Ottoman Empire).

The continuous deplorable state of royal revenues provided the main incentive to promote new institutions and companies, once the conviction had been formed that borrowing, even if it was costly, was preferable to

---

[34] 'With the development and acknowledgment of mobile property, capitalism became a system of fluid exchange, moving beyond its grounded agrarian dimension.' Burch, *The 'Properties' of the State System and Global Capitalism*, 48.

[35] Aymard and Postel-Vinay, *L'Etat et les marchés*, 358.

[36] This system had been inaugurated by the Italian cities in the fourteenth and fifteenth centuries already, through the institutions called *'luoghi del monte'*.

monetary manipulations that risked blocking the country and its sovereign from accessing any further external credit. The formation of central banks during the seventeenth century (the Dutch central bank in 1605, the Bank of England in 1694, the failed attempt to set up a French central bank in 1719), where different interdependent currencies were valid (of the state, of other states, and of private actors) was a move towards collective rationalization through the creation of a last-resort lender and regulator of the monetary market. In Britain, the Crown created new companies and promoted the existing ones, it granted charters, patents, monopolies and other benefits to companies to stimulate production and value commodities and to develop a national economic and institutional infrastructure. The English and Dutch joint stock companies dating back to the early 1450s, grew in importance by the early 1550s, and became extremely important by 1650. These companies received a monopoly concession in exchange for conducting activities on behalf of the state and for bearing most of the investment risks. In return, the state earned revenue by taxing imported goods and their consumption use. The intertwined nature of politics and the economy in this phase can be witnessed in the intimate connection of these companies with statecraft and foreign policy. For example, Queen Elizabeth I knighted pirates for their merits in appropriating the wealth of others, while Louis XIV formed 'devil's brigades' to extract taxes at home. In all these cases, more funds became available for further domestic institutional building and restructuring, for infrastructural development and for international competition, often involving military campaigns.

As the largest capital borrowers, state treasuries had a strong interest in 'marshalling' capital markets to their advantage, and they used their regulatory power to this end. Rulers used rights over mobile property to service competition with other states; they turned to joint-stock companies to satisfy political needs; they used trading and holding companies to foster colonial aspirations; they financed military and infrastructural developments via the credit that was extended by the newly created central banks. All the sectors that the early state had had to subcontract to private individuals and enterprises were later on progressively transferred under its direct management. From this point of view, even the industrialization of the nineteenth century was perceived from the beginning as a means to foster the economic and military power of the state, which became even more actively engaged in fostering endogenous economic development.

Conclusion

In the early modern age, the alliances and leagues of the Central European city-belt were an alternative outcome of economic integration through low levels of stateness, restricted jurisdictions and relatively open free-trade areas. This option was, however, crushed by the sheer military power of the nascent large-scale territorial states and their colonial discoveries and resources. The latter's were a crucial discontinuity that ended the Central European experiment of a stateless form of economic cooperation without any centralized authority building. Only the territories of the Netherlands and Switzerland reproduced this federative territorial pattern in their relatively belated state building.

Claiming that capitalism and statecraft moved along parallel lines means that capitalism was 'nationalized' to a large extent. From this point of view, the opposition between the boundary-building operation of the rising state and the boundary-removing pushes of capitalism described at the beginning of this section is probably exaggerated. The potentials of a capitalist cross-territorial market remained fundamentally subordinated to the imperatives of 'high politics', as embodied by the state system. In reality, the close parallels in the periodization of the rise both of the nation-state and of capital to world hegemony is paradoxical from this point of view, but probably not accidental. The complexity of the interaction between military-administrative and economic boundary building does not allow for a clear-cut definition of the dominant process. Wallerstein's model of peripheralization assigns primacy to development in the economic sphere, positing a hierarchy of economic centres and defining peripheries as territories depending on these rich centres. The processes of the rise of the bureaucratic state, the reformation, and nationalism are analysed as reactions to the decisive changes brought about by the world economy with the opening up of the ocean trade routes in the sixteenth century.[37] Against the interpretative paradigm of economic peripheralization, other scholars[38] assert the primacy of the state and its military-administrative apparatus and argue that long-distance trade was of only limited importance in this period: what really

---

[37] Wallerstein, I., *The Modern World System*, 2 vols. (New York: Academic Press, 1974/ 1980). Wallerstein distinguishes between four zones generated by the emerging of the early European world economy: a *dominant core* (moving northwards from Spain to the Netherlands and later on including England: regions with the highest concentration of secondary-tertiary activities whose population's welfare depended primarily on the trading products brought in from distant peripheries); *long-distance peripheries* depending on the core (Latin America, Eastern Europe, etc.); *semi-peripheries* dominated by cities in decline (Italy, the French Midi, and, increasingly, Spain); and *external areas* laying beyond the reach of the network of long-distance trade (notably Japan and China until well into the nineteenth century).

[38] See Anderson, P., *Lineages of the Absolutist State* (London: New Left Books, 1974); Finer, S. E., 'State-building, state boundaries and border control', 79–126; and Tilly, C., *Coercion, Capital and European States*.

mattered was the consolidation of the control system in the immediate hinterland conquered by each centre.[39]

International economic competition among states did not decline with industrialization, although the latter strengthened the internal autonomization of 'society', understood as a sphere of economic actions rejecting any interferences from, or tutelage by the state.[40] With respect to this emerging 'society', the state should guarantee the credibility of commitment and respect of the contract, but should not interfere in property rights or individual economic activities. This separation between economics and the state was typical of the nineteenth-century liberal thinking, which tried to render the market and capitalism a driving force of openness once more.[41] This corresponded to real developments of internal interest differentiation. Economic activities and transactions had become society's prime mover and most dynamic element. The increasingly complex and dynamic economic processes became progressively more important in relation to the political relationships on which they were originally grounded.[42] However, it should be pointed out that the liberalization phase failed, in fact, as a result of the ideological force of nationalism and the power of persistent state rivalries. Following the end of the Second World War, the project of making capitalism a force of boundary openness and boundary removal revived with the GATT and the revitalization of free trade ideology. This has opened up a

[39] Rokkan, S. et al., cite a telling example of how border control can determine the 'economic' peripheralization of areas across borders and their re-orientation to the centre as economic peripheries of the latter. For centuries, the absence of a canal connection between the Rhone and the Rhine, and between both of these and the Seine, prejudiced the system of heavy-freight canal connecting Europe. A Rhone–Rhine canal would have constituted an important and attractive alternative—also during the railways period—to the routes running over the Alps. However, notwithstanding the obvious economic advantages for the region and European overall trade, the administrative authorities in Paris were not favourable towards a transportation system which would have brought Eastern France closer to the Rhineland axis, and allowed the traffic going from north to south to bypass Paris. It is clear that in this case geopolitical concerns were of paramount importance for Paris. See Rokkan, S., Urwin, D., Aerebrot, F. H., Malaba, P., and Sande, T., *Centre-Periphery Structures in Europe* (Frankfurt–New York: Campus Verlag, 1987), 40.

[40] Sartori G., 'Politica', in *Elementi di teoria politica* (Bologna, Italy: Il Mulino, 1990), 195–216, 200–3.

[41] For the thesis that the period between 1879 and 1914 was characterized by the most open and interdependent international economy even as compared with the present situation, see Hirst, P. and Thompson, G., *Globalisation in Question* (Cambridge: Polity Press, 1996) in particular Chapter 2.

[42] Habermas goes as far as to say that 'the administrative state depends on taxes, while the market economy relies on legal guarantee, political regulations and infrastructural provisions. [. . .] The immense political success of the nation-state can partly be explained by the fact that the modern state, that is, the tandem of bureaucracy and capitalism, has turned out to be the most effective vehicle for accelerating social modernization'. Habermas, J., 'The European Nation State. Its Achievements and Its limitations. On the Past and Future of Sovereignty and Citizenship', *Ratio Juris*, 9 (1996), 125–37, 126.

new phase of state loss in its control over capitalism—which was no longer a national, but increasingly an international force—and over actors who no longer needed a close connection with the state.

However, the ongoing internal autonomizing of the sphere of economic contractual activities was also intimately linked to cultural developments within the state: to its cultural nationalization, with a progressive expansion of the spheres of cultural, social and political equality among its citizens. Thus, the increasingly autonomous sphere of contractual and economic activities was framed and legitimized within these new and self-reinforcing 'national'— rather than merely state—boundaries. The extended socio-economic inter-actions and practices at the territorial level of the state were therefore accom-panied and made possible by the nationalization of the subjects in cultural, political and social terms. The next three sections deal with the three crucial processes of loyalty creation and system building that transformed the 'state' into the 'nation-state': nation building, democratization, and social sharing.

Nation Building (Cultural Retrenchment/Expansion)

For a long time the relationship between rulers and the ruled within the state was based on simple relations of power, myth, and the defence of property and physical security. Nation building was the third crucial process of European development that further developed and differentiated the bound-aries of the state on the cultural front.

The formation of the 'nation' can be defined as the establishment of direct vertical contacts between the elites and ever-larger sectors of the peripheral territorial population, as well as the development of a 'national community' whose horizontal exchange concerned not only goods but also symbols. Technically, this was realized through religious and linguistic standardiza-tion, conscript armies, school and education, the mass media, the spread of myths and feelings of national identity. Thus, under this label are regrouped those system characteristics which pertain to the 'cultural homogeneity' of any given society. Such cultural homogeneity is in many ways an essential ingredient for the spread of a nationwide appeal to cross-local conflicts of an economic and functional type, and it has both a vertical and a horizontal dimension. The horizontal dimension includes those elements of cultural non-homogeneity which separate segments of the society characterized by any clear religious, ethnic, linguistic and other types of cultural/identity differences. Each segment is composed of both mass and elite groups. The vertical dimension refers to the developments of links between the masses and the elites that are available only under certain conditions of the spread of education and of mediated communication.

Nation building should therefore be seen as an additional crucial step in the retrenchment/expansion of membership spaces. National identity was a retrenchment with respect to the previous, more encompassing unifying forces of Latin as intellectual mean of exchange and Christianity as a community. On the other hand, national identity was an expansionary and inclusive definition of new membership groups that went far beyond the localized territorial identities, dialects, rites, myths and symbols. On the cultural front, this long-term process of retrenchment/expansion took the form of a redefinition of European membership spaces through the processes of linguistic vernacularization, religious divisions and, more generally, national identity enforcement. Therefore, although the emphasis of national cultural distinctiveness is a nineteenth-century process, the foundations and preconditions for a more or less extensive nationalization of the masses were laid down long before this, through the linguistic and religious fragmentation of the European membership spaces.

During the Middle Ages, a set of vernacular languages slowly consolidated from the large variety of flourishing vernacular literatures. These languages were enriched and enhanced by intellectual groups—epitomized by the great symbolic figures such as Dante, Shakespeare or Luther—raising both their status and their expressive capacity. This process progressively broke down the European intellectual unity that had formed around Latin as the single intellectual and scientific language. Further decisive developments in this field came with the invention of the printing and the religious division of the Reformation, which severed any remaining connection with the Greek and the Roman traditions. The mass reproduction of messages in these vernaculars and the widening access to them led to the possibility of reaching new strata, progressively differentiated and separated the national standards of communication, and increased the intellectual fragmentation of European elites. At the same time, it also placed a considerable limitation on the mobility of cultural messages, fashions, ideas, etc., and made possible to limit cultural exit by confining communication within the limits of a particular vernacular. 'Gutenberg created an essential technology for the building of nations'.[43] The Reformation, the printing press, the development of 'national literatures' and, finally, the school system tied the subject to the territory culturally.

The Reformation led, of course, to the most dramatic cultural division of Europe since the collapse of the Empire. It went well beyond a break with the Roman Church on matters of theological doctrine: it strengthened the cultural distinctiveness of each territory and in the Protestant North it integrated priests within the bureaucratic structure of the state. As a result, it reinforced the elements of loyalty, reducing further the possibilities of exit. In other

---

[43] Rokkan, S. et al., *Centre-Periphery Structures*, 57.

words, the Reformation accentuated the cultural significance of the borders between territories, and frequently combined, in a self-reinforcing drive, religious differentiation with linguistic differentiation.

The Protestant/Catholic dividing line was important as, on the whole, we find that in those countries where the Protestant reform produced an early 'nationalization' of the territorial culture, processes of mobilization from below into mass politics were also fostered. On the one hand, the close relationship between the state and church reduced the potential for a state-church conflict. On the other hand, the early development of literacy in Protestant countries—required and legitimated by the need to access directly the sacred texts—aided and encouraged the mobilization of the lower strata into mass politics. On the contrary, in Catholic territories, the supranational nature and approach of the church tended to favour mobilization from above by the Catholic hierarchies: the lateness in the spread of literacy made the mobilization from below of the lower classes more difficult, and conflicts over the control of the educational system led to the mobilization of the church against the state.[44]

In Latin Europe, the dominant Catholic church (in conflict with nation-building liberal elites over the defence of its vested interests) managed more or less successfully to establish itself as an alternative agency in competition with the state regarding the control of the allegiance of the masses. Minority opposition Catholicism—of the Dutch type—urging the separation of the (Protestant) church from the state and opposing the established elites, was more of an anti-establishment movement and maintained considerable control over lower class groups. Even Lutheranism and Calvinism were aligned with vested authorities and interests more in some countries than in others. For Lutheranism, this was more the case in Prussia-Germany than in Switzerland, where it was more radical and modernist, while in Sweden it provided instead the basis for both an official national state religion and a fundamentalist opposition. Calvinism was more anti-establishment and nonconformist in some countries than in others, depending on its relationship with the dominant elites and on whether there were stronger links with vested interests and the elites, or with the lower classes.[45] In conclusion, not only was the type

---

[44] On these themes see Ruffini, F., *Relazioni stato chiesa* (Bologna, Italy: Il Mulino, 1974). Religious pluralism as such was important, independently of the religion in question. It often provided the basis for political resistance against the elites, forcing the limitation of the state power in certain spheres and affirming the legitimacy of corporate powers and rights. This aspect is not treated aside in this work.

[45] Mommsen, H., 'Zur Problem der vergleichenden Behandlung nationaler Arbeitbewegungen am Beispiel Ost- und Sudostmitteleuropas', *Internationale Wissenschaftliche Korrespondenz*, 15 (1979), 31–4; van der Linden, M., 'The National Integration of European Working Classes (1871–1914)', *International Review of Social History*, 33 (1988), 285–331.

of religion and the extent of the political significance of religious identity important, but also the position that churches and religious groups occupied within each national system of conflicts and oppositions.

These religious differences were crucial because they produced considerable variations in the early cultural homogenization of the different state populations. In addition, they later on influenced the battle for the control of the most effective system of nation building: education, and the creation of a nationwide network of communications to link individuals horizontally (as groups and communities previously separated into physically and communicatively confined territories) and vertically (with the elites).

The educational systems and the other efforts that were made to implement a national linguistic unification were based on a synthesis between vernacular languages and the dominant elites/court language replacing Latin. The goal of the 'nationalization' of the educational system was to equalize basic cognitive capacities such as those of writing and reading across the population as a whole. Generally speaking, the spread of cognitive capacities resulted in a growing number of individuals that could be reached by a wider range of sources of messages, through a larger number of channels of communication, and with potentially longer exposure to them. Contrary to the process of urbanization and industrialization, literacy development could be more easily fostered by the state if it was deliberately pursued through cultural agencies and/or by state bureaucracy.[46] Almost all European states built unified and compulsory public educational systems, issued legislation to extend the duties of schooling (only later this was formulated as a right), and entered in conflict with competing control agencies (churches and local elites) over the mastery of the curricula.

Different nation builders pursued cognitive mobilization with different intensity. There are differences in literacy levels between Protestant and Catholic countries, although the fit is not perfect. Earlier and higher levels of literacy are apparent in Scandinavia, followed by Switzerland and Germany and, very close behind them, Finland. At the other extreme, we find high levels of illiteracy in France, Austria and Belgium, and even higher in Spain, Portugal and Italy. Notwithstanding the deviant cases of Ireland and England, Wales and Scotland,[47] the difference between predominantly

[46] Contrary to what is suggested by modernization theory sequences, the cognitive mobilization of European citizens preceded economic modernization (industrialization and urbanization). The experience of other parts of the world is reversed: urbanization processes predate literacy developments. See Flora, P., 'Historical Processes of Social Mobilisation: Urbanisation and Literacy 1850–1965', in Eisenstadt and Rokkan, *Building States and Nations*, Vol. 1, 227.

[47] The levels of illiteracy in England, Wales and Scotland were far higher than in the other Protestant countries between 1870 and 1900, and not much different from those of the Catholic ones. Ireland, although still characterized by relatively high levels of illiteracy

Protestant and religiously mixed countries, on the one hand, and homogeneously Catholic, on the other, is striking. The standard interpretation of this phenomenon takes its lead from the classic theses of Max Weber about Protestantism as the Christian religion with the strongest national language written tradition and, therefore, with the strongest incentive to literacy development among believers and the national population at large. This is confirmed both by the early introduction of schemes of compulsory national primary education in Protestant countries, and also by the more informal role played by Protestant churches in giving incentives to the spread of reading and writing capacities, a feature which is absent in Catholic countries.

Thus, for instance, compulsory education schemes were introduced in Prussia as early as 1763; in Denmark, as early as 1814 (up to seven years of age but for only three days per week; in 1849, this was increased to six days); in Norway, between 1848 and 1889; in Sweden, between 1842 and 1848, and there the parliament introduced six years of elementary education for all children in 1878. Parishes were responsible for setting and financing elementary school to teach writing, reading and arithmetic. However, even before this time, the teaching of Luther's catechism pushed parishes to enforce educational requirements for marriages and other social occasions. In Finland, legislative thresholds of this type cannot be identified, given that the country did not become independent until the twentieth century, but it has been reported that already in the first hundred years after the Reformation, the Lutheran church made the ability to read a prerequisite for enjoying certain civil rights as well as for marriage. Similar forms of incentives are to be found in the history of Sweden, Norway, Denmark and even Scotland.[48]

The differences in literacy rates between Southern Catholic countries—such as Italy before national unity, Spain and Portugal—and the Northern Catholic countries—France, Austria, Belgium and Ireland—can be interpreted via the push that communal self-government gave as an extra incentive to literacy development or the international status and geo-position of the country.[49] For countries at the centre of the European system of interstate relationships and concerned with self-defence and self-assertion, there was stronger pressure to develop efficient bureaucratic machines (both military and civil).[50] Compulsory education was thus aimed at increasing the

in 1870 (25.8 per cent), recuperated rapidly: by 1910 the estimates made of its illiterate population showed levels that were among the lowest in Europe.

[48] See Cipolla, C., *Literacy and Development in the West* (London: Penguin Books, 1969); and Harvey, G.-J., *Storia dell'alfabetizzazione occidentale*, 3 vols. (Bologna, Italy: Il Mulino, 1989).

[49] Flora, 'Historical Processes of Social Mobilisation', 230

[50] For Ireland the accelerated literacy development at the end of the nineteenth century can be interpreted as part of the struggle for national independence and cultural

skills of citizens in the market, technical matters, and political involvement. However, in my view, its most significant aspect was, in fact, not technical. Education was aimed at fostering the feelings and emotions of individual and collective identification with the nation and the central political authorities embodying its destiny, which were often in conflict and competition with other kinds of symbols, such as those located in the churches, and the local and peripheral cultures and elites.

This process of cultural homogenization and nation building was never peaceful, completed, comprehensive or uniform. Not only was there a varying degree of ethno-linguistic-religious non-homogeneity produced by the consolidation of military-administrative boundary in the 'buffer' peripheries at the edges of the central city-belt and in the 'external' peripheries at the border of states. There was also the fact that different routes were taken to shape national identities. The most common model for this was that of bureaucratic incorporation, leading to the rise of territorial and civic political nations. This was usually led by the aristocratic elites from a lateral community, by using a strong state to incorporate the lower strata and outlying areas. If the unit was sovereign and independent, it did not require a liberation from alien rule, but a transformation of its political system and its cultural self-definition. If, on the contrary, there was a colonial legacy of high dependency on a dominant imperial centre, a new cultural identity needed to be forged, and this was linked to the same formation of the new political unit and its liberation from foreign rule (as in Ireland and Finland). In other cases, the process of vernacular mobilization was more important for the creation of ethnic and genealogical political nations. The intelligentsias and some middle strata that were excluded from a vertical community created nations from below using cultural resources (ethno-history, language, ethnic religion, customs, etc.) to mobilize other strata into an active 'politicized nation' (as in Norway).

It is debatable whether these different routes implied two ideal type models of nation formation: one with a predominant *civility* content (historical territory, legal-political community, equality of members, common civic culture and ideology) and one with a prevalent *primordial* content (genealogy rather than territory, common descent; vernacular culture, language and customs; common traditions).[51] I find it more important to focus on the importance of the timing between the process of state consolidation of military-administrative boundaries, on the one hand, and the consolidation

self-expression. See MacElligot, T. J., *Education in Ireland* (Dublin: Institute of Public Administration, 1966).

[51] Smith, A. D., *National Identity* (London: Penguin Books, 1991), 8–15, speaks of 'civic-territorial' and 'ethnic-genealogical' models.

of state cultural boundaries, on the other; that is, the timing between state formation and nation formation. Attention paid to timing enables us to avoid understanding nation building as a process of enforcement from above by the deliberate imposition of a 'modern' or 'modernizing' state on a traditional society. While this was to a considerable degree the experience of the early territorially consolidated states, it could not certainly have been the model of the latecomers. In the cases of late state building, and particularly when the three processes of state building, nation building and internal democratic structuring were coincident (Germany and Italy are the most notable cases), cultural nationalism slid more easily into a political weapon for the further strengthening and affirmation of state autonomy, international legitimacy and internal cohesion.

In fact, there is an important relation between the way in which the constituent properties of a polity are defined and the internal political order on which the polity itself can be organized. Contrary to 'civility' codes of identity definition, 'primordial' or 'cultural' codes[52] are politically 'empty'. That is, the reality that they represent can be pursued and defended in all kinds of political orders; the goals and values that are in principle embedded in their definition can be fulfilled by any kind of regime and political formula. In brief, race, culture, ethnicity, religion and even class represent constituent units that are independent from any type of political regime. Indeed, precisely as a result of their emphasis on collective identities and values, tends to underscore individual liberation and self-fulfilment in favour of the individual's insertion in broader units which are in principle compatible with whatever institutional order.[53] In these cases, it is more likely that nation building will take authoritarian forms. Thus, contrary to early comers, the latecomers state building elites could not base their claim on a de facto pre-existing territorial sovereignty and engage in the nationalizing of the subject populations. They were more likely to voice their claim to a territorial state by invoking abstract primordial and cultural legitimizing principles. So, there is, in my opinion, a considerable relationship between the earliness-lateness and contestedness of centre formation, the concepts and principles invoked and used for its legitimation and 'nationalization', and the political forms of its internal structuring.

To temper the understanding of nation building as mere familiarization and enforced inculcation, one should carefully consider the experiences of Switzerland and the Netherlands, which differ significantly to the latter idea. Here, the basic constituent units were neither individual emancipation nor

---

[52] See Chapter 1 for the discussion of these codes.
[53] See Lepsius, R., 'The Nation and Nationalism in Germany', *Social Research*, 52 (1985), 43–64 for this point and a discussion with reference to the German experience.

the collective abstract ideal, but community life and association coalition according to principles of territorial and sometimes of functional groups subsidiary. Both these countries entered the nineteenth century without a strong central power, a standing army, a national bureaucracy, and a national educational system, and with a political culture of localism and entrenched pluralism. For a long time, no nationwide public authority existed, nor was there a clear process whereby people could transfer their commitment and loyalty from smaller villages or petty principalities to the larger/central political system. Only if one defines nationality more in terms of at least some consciousness of togetherness, rather than as an exclusive transfer of loyalty to a new state, could signs of an incipient nationhood be found, at least among the leading political strata of Swiss and Dutch society.[54] In these cases it would be difficult to point to one social group, or one political centre, or one legal institution that might be regarded as the chief nation-building force. In neither case, then, is the model of a centrally enforced and inculcated national identity working.

In conclusion, throughout the European state system the modalities of nation building were different in timing, constitutive ideational elements and degree of enforcement and inculcation from the centre. At the same time, all the different models can be regarded as contributing to the same process of cultural boundary building. This was far easier where it could rely on homogeneous primordial or cultural (religious) identities, and was more complex and protracted in ethno-linguistic and religiously divided territories. However, the development of education added to ethno-linguistic and religious standardization, generating a new emphasis on the cultural distinctiveness of the territory and, in particular, of the state territory. It thus brought about an area of cultural equality among 'nationals' that transcended primordial and culturally localized identities, when it was not directly reinforced by them. On the whole, this process corresponded to the building of a new cultural boundary and the underlying aim was to make it coterminous with the existing military, administrative, and economic boundary of the state. It was also a fundamental precondition to the generation of a new form of allegiance between the territorial state and its dominant elites and its citizens/subjects. Nation building was therefore a further limitation of the exit option—a way of strengthening loyalties, as a means by which to strengthen sovereignty.

---

[54] Daalder, 'On building consociational nations', 358–9. However, in the Netherlands, the lower barriers to social mobility, the more pervasive centralization that occurred under Napoleonic rule, and the more accentuated international insecurity and involvement allowed particularism to be more easily and earlier broken than in Switzerland; it also made federalism less viable as it was less culturally embedded, and rendered Dutch national identity more integrated than in Switzerland.

In a typical feudal lord–man relationship, a man could have as many lords as he held land, manors or offices. In the newly consolidating state, the relationship linked the prince to the subject in a more exclusive way, as the inhabitant of a delimited area. The strengthening of this demarcation led to the need to define more accurately the set of rights and obligations which were valid for the membership group. To the extent that the new membership group was culturally defined and coincided with the territorial group, this also required the specification of the rights embodied by this membership vis-à-vis the non-residents, the external. These had to be institutionally defined, and this usually took the form of the institutionalization of deliberation rights and of mutual social sharing. The nation was, indeed, the key to modern democracy and the welfare state, and democracy came to be identified and operated within areas of considerable cultural homogeneity or within areas whose cultural non-homogeneity was publicly declared and acknowledged within some broader unifying political identity.

Democratization

The fourth crucial phase of the political development of the modern European state was its internal liberalization and democratization. Here, I will not stress the differences between liberalization (constitutionalism, limited government, and executive responsibility towards the legislature) and democratization (the spread of the political rights of participation) and I will use the term 'democratization' for both processes. My goal is to emphasize (a) the general significance of this phase and (b) to show how the cross-European variation in democratization is related to processes of state formation, capitalist development, and nation building.

Democratization was a process of internal voice structuring in externally consolidated and relatively closed territorial systems, whose military, economic, and cultural boundaries had already tended to stabilize. The growing political production of the centre and the reduction of exit options fostered an internal political mobilization of resources, a legitimation of internal conflicts, and the institutionalization of domestic political exchanges under the mediation of political authorities. With mutually reinforcing cultural loyalties, economic boundaries, military-diplomatic defences, and administrative differentiated regimes, a deterioration in state outputs tended to produce a loss of loyalty if voice was not available. Thus, increasingly, the problem became one of representation and voice structures in exchange for 'legitimacy' and 'support'. Correspondingly, the conflicts about boundary strengthening and loosening had consequences for the structuring of political alliances and institutions within each territory.[55]

Conflicts over the demarcation of boundaries and their stiffness or looseness reflected oppositions of interest among the social groups controlling different resources within each territory. The processes of state building, nation formation, and capitalist development shaped the definition of these interests and identities. In each of the domains different inwardly oriented groups of resource-holders developed. In the political-administrative domain there was a differentiation between dynastic groups, the bureaucratic personnel, and increasingly the elective political elites; in the economy, merchant and industrial capitalism accentuated the differentiation in interests of the commercial, industrial, and financial bourgeoisie from landed elites; in the cultural domain, educated elites in schools and universities, and a larger 'communication class' controlling communication networks differentiated from the early cultural agencies of the church and ethno-linguistic communities. Counterclaimants, too, developed on each of these fronts: peasants and working class movements as opponents of landed interests and capital; countercultural movement for religious, ethnic or linguistic distinctiveness defence; and oppositional elites and institutional pressure groups in the politico-administrative domain.

The variations in the specific model of internal political structuring were a result of the interaction between stateness—resulting from the state-building historical process; the level of economic interest differentiation—resulting from capitalist development and industrialization; and the cultural homogeneity/ heterogeneity of the population—resulting from nation building:

1. *Stateness* determined the extractive and coercion resources of the state builders and influenced their willingness to yield to voice;
2. The level of *socio-economic differentiation* of dominant interests determined their cohesion and their need/willingness to ally with the state builders;
3. The *cultural homogeneity* of the environment influenced the lines along which functional versus cultural conflicts interacted and contributed to the structuring of political demands and organizations.[56]

---

[55] 'Democratic regimes proved more stable in countries where a national identity developed hand-in-hand with revolutionary struggles for civil liberties within existing territorial states, while democracies turned out to be less stable wherever national movements and Wars of Liberation against a foreign enemy had first to create borders for the nascent national state'. Habermas, J., 'The European Nation State', 128.

[56] I have applied this model of interaction between state building, nation building and economic interest differentiation in my work about the mobilization of the class cleavage. Bartolini, *The Political Mobilization of the European Left*. In this section I rely on the historical analysis and the empirical material provided there in Chapter 7, where the reader can find a precise operationalization of the variables.

The democratization of pre-existing state structures took the form of a political structuring of socio-political movements in the corporate channels of interest representation, in the politico-electoral channel of the parties and political movement formation, and in the territorial channel of centre–periphery relations. There was a strong variation in the extent to which these new actors came to perceive the existing political system as legitimate and feel that they could pursue and achieve their goals and values within the existing framework of state and political institutions. The attitudinal orientation of these groups was concretely shaped by the learning experience deriving from the responses offered by the dominant groups and established elite, when facing their demands.

Institutional Democratization

These variables can be linked into explanatory hypotheses concerning the levels of institutional 'openness' of the European states towards new claimants' demands and organizational efforts. Four aspects are crucial here. The first is the extent to which demands made by the new political movements were met by the established elites and institutions resorting to non-political means of confrontation; that is, by resorting to direct legal and administrative repression and harassment. This refers to the extent and efficacy with which the 'state', as an administrative and policing machine, was used against internal opposition and contestation. The second important aspect is the extent to which the institutional regime was 'liberalized'; that is, the extent to which the resources of power and influence available in the administrative and bureaucratic machinery of the state, or in the social and market relationships of the society, were balanced by the resources of parliamentary influence and negotiation based on electoral weight. The parliamentarization of the executive opened up a new structure of opportunity, allowing oppositional movements to concentrate some of their resources and efforts on the direct influence of the executive, rather than in non-parliamentary confrontation arenas. The third aspect refers to the obstacles set up to impede the fair electoral and parliamentary representation of the new movements. Even liberalized regimes—not to mention authoritarian constitutional monarchies—resisted with differing style and vigour the full transformation of the opposition movement's electoral force into parliamentary influence by various mechanisms of delayed and low enfranchisement, electoral misrepresentation, and other means which restricted the electoral potential of the movement. Finally, the fourth aspect concerns the obstacles that were placed against the direct accession of non-establishment parties to executive responsibilities.

Stateness and repression, responsible government, fair representation, and *executive power access* are often linked and interrelated into a syndrome.

They are also linked to these enfranchisement patterns and to cleavage structures and the crystallization of political group alliances. The state tradition and role in the process of political modernization has been linked to the alliances among social groups leading to liberal, authoritarian or totalitarian outcomes,[57] to the onset of revolutions,[58] to the process of social group formation,[59] and to collective action.[60] The contestedness of the process of state formation and its end result in terms of 'stateness' made available potential resources which were not, however, necessarily used or directed against the opening up of channels of voice structuring and political representation of new claimants. That is, the 'stateness' of a polity represented a set of resources to which established and dominant groups could resort in their attempt to obstruct the structuring of voice. The dominant groups' calculations of the cost of internal repression or tolerance depended, most importantly, on the availability of the means of repression. Thus, in a situation of low stateness dominant groups could hardly embark on a repressive strategy based on the state, while high stateness made such a repressive strategy available, but in no way mandatory. In conclusion, a connection between state resource availability and repressive political outcomes can certainly be made, but other factors also played an intervening role.

In fact, the calculations of the cost of repression/toleration also had an economic and political dimension, too. Could the dominant economic interests be defended within a political climate of toleration? Politically, could such toleration allow the dominant political elites to retain their security of tenure and their hold on the polity? In this case the issue was whether the dominant elite and circles (king, bureaucracy, upper classes) were sufficiently united to pursue a repressive course of action or not. Whenever toleration was perceived as endangering not only the economic interests of the dominant classes but the existence of the political power position of the dominant rulers, then the cost of toleration were high. On the other side, even the severity of the economic challenge depended on the homogeneity of economic interests, as indicated by the differentiation of dominant economic groups. In this case, the thrust of the argument is that the more advanced the capitalist development and industrialization, the higher the differentiation of

[57] Barrington Moore, J. Jr., *Social Origins of Dictatorship and Democracy. Lord and Peasants in the Making of the Modern World* (Boston, MA: Beacon Press, 1966).

[58] Skocpol, T., *States and Social Revolutions. A Comparative Analysis of France, Russia and China* (Cambridge: Cambridge University Press, 1979).

[59] Katznelson, I., 'Working-Class Formation and the State: Nineteenth-Century England in American Perspective', in P. B. Evans, D. Rueschemeyer and T. Skocpol (eds.), *Bringing the State Back In* (Cambridge: Cambridge University Press, 1985), 257–84.

[60] Birnbaum, P., *State and Collective Action: The European Experience* (Cambridge: Cambridge University Press, 1988); Birnbaum, P. and Badie, B., *Sociologie de l'Etat* (Paris: Grasset, 1982), 189–90.

urban commercial and industrial interests versus the rural ones, and, therefore, the less likely a common and uniform dominant group perception of the economic challenge.

We can, therefore, interpret the easiness of institutionalization of voice as a function of (*a*) the stateness of the polity and (*b*) the level of internal differentiation of dominant economic interests. In Table 2.2, these two dimensions are charted together with the timing of parliamentarization and the level of voice repression and administrative harassing. Considering the cohesion levels of dominant interests (and therefore the likelihood that they will agree on supporting a repression strategy) in capitalist and industrial development countries with strong industrial and commercial interests, political repression in the late nineteenth to the early twentieth centuries tended to be low with one exception: Germany. For the countries where rural interests tended to be still predominant, two groups emerge. On the one hand, Finland, Austria, France and Italy showed a relatively high and frequent resort to repressive measures; on the other, this was not the case in the three Scandinavian countries, where, notwithstanding the overwhelming weight of rural interests (represented, however, not by large landowners, but by a large class of independent small farmers), no heavy repressive response was waged against opposition movements in the 1890–1930 period.

The level of voice repression before the First World War is only partially related to the liberalization of the regime. In the eight cases where we find relative toleration, six are parliamentary regimes, although the French and Italian parliamentary regimes exercised considerable repression over their internal oppositions. On the other hand, Denmark and Sweden still had constitutional monarchies which strongly resisted liberalization but in which the level of internal repression was low for most of the period under

TABLE 2.2. *Stateness, economic interest differentiation, institutional democratization, and voice repression*

		Stateness	
		Low	High
Economic interests differentiation	Low	Denmak, Sweden *Ireland, Norway**	*France*, **Italy** **Austria**, **Finland**
	High	*United Kingdom* *Switzerland* *Netherlands*	**Germany** *Belgium*

Italic font: comparative early parliamentarization of the executive (* for domestic matters only).
Bold font: comparative high level of voice repression.

scrutiny. Stateness is thus a much better predictor of the level of repression of early voice than either the level of differentiation of economic interests or the liberalization of the regime. Of the five countries that had strong state resources at their disposal, four turn out to have directed them largely against internal opposition.[61] Belgium is the only case of a country with relatively high state resources whose political elite did not systematically resort to them to meet the claims of newcomers. Of the eight countries classified as having low or modest stateness, only Finland presents a pre-1918 history of strong political movement repression.[62]

Combining these different dimensions, the understanding of the variation improves and stateness emerges as the crucial necessary condition for a voice-repressive strategy. Whenever high state resources were available to an established political elite, they were used against newcomers. The exception of Belgium can be explained by the combination of its early liberalization and high internal differentiation of interests between rural and urban interests. On the other hand, countries like Denmark and Sweden, even if they had a conservative and autocratic political structure and a predominance of rural interests, could under no circumstances afford a confrontation strategy against newcomers for their sheer lack of resources.[63]

As a result, the level of voice-repression tended to be higher: (a) the higher the stateness of the polity, since this made the means available; (b) the lower the internal differentiation of dominant interests, since this made their perception of a common threat and their agreement on a common response more likely; and (c) the lower the parliamentarization of the regime, since this defined the limits on the utilization of these resources and also offered some possible alternatives of control. In contrast, repression was minimal in countries with little stateness, high interest differentiation and an early parliamentarization of government (United Kingdom, Switzerland, and the Netherlands). In Austria, low interest differentiation and dynastic autocratic regimes combined to perceive the challenges of the opposition as intolerable

[61] Italy and France have probably the worst record in terms of casualties determined by the army and police repression of strikes and political demonstrations. See Goldstein, R. L., *Political Repression in the Nineteenth Century* (London: Croom Helm, 1983).

[62] This was Russian imported. The Russians inhibited the development of an autonomous Finnish state to such an extent that when their rule collapsed, Finland was left with practically no state but, rather, with a typical 'praetorian' society within which armed groups and political organizations fought directly one against the other. On the 'pretorian society' see Huntington, S. P., *Political Order in Changing Societies* (New Haven, CT: Yale University Press, 1968), 95.

[63] The indecision of the Swedish Crown and dynastic circles on whether to yield to the Norwegian request for parliamentarization, first, and independence, later, is a good example of this. A repressive reaction was considered at length and was probably the preferred option, but considerations about affordable costs predominated in which the low resources of the Swedish state were probably the most crucial aspect.

and the high stateness of the polity lowered the costs of repression. In autocratic regimes with low stateness (Denmark, Sweden, and Finland (or Norway, although this had an earlier liberalization)), repression could be exercised systematically only if it rested on external resources (Finland), but was too costly if attempted on the basis of the scanty internal repressive means of the state. France, Italy and Germany are more problematic cases. In the first two, high stateness combines with early liberalization and with a weak interest differentiation towards a considerable level of repression. In Germany, instead, a higher interest differentiation (concentrated, however, outside politically dominant Prussia) combines with high stateness and no liberalization towards a high repression strategy.

We can understand these developments within the framework of exit options and boundary building by arguing that in Central Europe the suppression of territorial exit (secession) and the assertion of the right to control the movement of people and commodities across borders required such a concentration of effort and authority that this led to the crushing of voice. Outside this core area, external border controls were easier and a better balance between exit control and voice channelling was achieved.

Political Mobilization

The structuring of voice occurred not only as a result of institutional liberalization, but also took place through wide processes of competitive mass mobilization. Citizens were progressively mobilized in various non-political spheres: by capitalism and industrialization in the economic sphere, through media such as exchange and money; through the extension of market, geographical and labour mobility; through the imposition of tariffs, credit and capital procedures and techniques, and through the availability of services and goods. Citizens were also mobilized by the military and administrative machine of the state, as soldiers, and as subjects of administrative agencies, through travelling and residential restrictions and/or liberalization. Moreover, they were mobilized culturally through scripts and other mass media into ideological, religious, and ethno-linguistic movements by the socializing agencies of the nationally dominant culture, as well as by dissident intellectuals, missionaries and messages, news, etc.[64]

Specific 'political' forms of mobilization[65] occurred along functional and territorial axes. Along the functional axis, it crystallized into the formation of

---

[64] On the relationship between political and other types of mobilization see Nettl, P. J., *Political Mobilisation* (New York: Basic Books, 1967), 115–22.

[65] Initial political mobilization was not necessarily monopolized by new actors such as political parties and interest organizations. Governments, state bureaucracy, charismatic leadership, etc. were also capable of engendering political, and even strictly electoral,

different types of politico-electoral movements and of different types of corporate interest groups and associations. Along the territorial axis, mobilization resulted in the politicization of territorial distinctiveness and in a more or less accentuated peripheral resistance to the established centres. This centre–periphery structuring sometimes took the form of political movements, but could also take on the form of institutional arrangements for the territorial resolution of conflict (federalized polities). Functional conflict resolutions and territorial conflict resolutions interacted, giving rise to the European variation of political structuring forms and institutions.

This process can be summarized in a set of analytical steps. The macro processes of modernization (monetarization, urbanization, secularization, cultural standardization, industrialization, administrative control, and centralization) generated the initial oppositions due to differences of interest and/or *Weltanschauung*. Once the centralization of the political decision-making was established within a territory, these opposition lines crystallized into conflicts over public policy. This led to the emergence *of alliances of political entrepreneurs* who acted to mobilize support for one set of policies against others. These politico-organizational entrepreneurs made choices concerning the strategy of mobilization (action through and reliance on pre-established community and other association networks versus action through and reliance on the development of purpose-specific membership organizations) and the arena for the confrontation (aggregation of votes/members for political/electoral contest versus direct extra-parliamentary action (strikes, pressure through public demonstrations, revolt, revolution, etc.)). Complex political structures thus resulted from the interaction between the forming of specific political organizations for the mobilization of the vote and the forming of mass organizations in the channel of corporate interest representation.

In his general classification of historical conflicts, Rokkan[66] simplifies the analysis by concentrating on the broad fronts of conflict in national histories. He distinguishes four critical cleavages, each of which is broadly viewed as being the consequences of two kinds of revolutions: the national and the industrial. The processes of formation of the nation-state provide the potential for two basic conflict lines: (*a*) the dominant cultural group and the nation-builder elites versus the ethnically, linguistic, or religiously distinctive

mobilization. On the extent and conditions to and in which parties successfully monopolized this role vis-à-vis other agencies see Daalder, H., 'Parties, Elites, and Political Development in Western Europe', in LaPalombara, J. and Weiner, M. (eds.), *Political Parties and Political Development* (Princeton, NJ: Princeton University Press, 1966), 43–77.

[66] Much of Rokkan's work was devoted to cleavage formation. The classic reference is 'Nation Building, Cleavage Formation and the Structuring of Mass Politics', in S. Rokkan (ed.), *Citizens Elections Parties* (Oslo: Universitetsforlaget, 1970), 72–144.

subjected population; and (*b*) the attempt by the nation-state to centralize, standardize, and mobilize versus the Church and its traditional encroachments and privileges in society. The Industrial Revolution also produced two lines of conflict: (*a*) the first between the predominantly rural landed interests and the emerging classes of commercial and industrial entrepreneurs; and (*b*) the second between the owning classes and the tenants and workers, thereby splitting the urban milieu.

The age of Reformation and counter-Reformation marked the climax of the conflicts between the centre and the periphery. The result of these conflicts was generally to strengthen and consolidate the territorial boundaries, as well as the linked issue of the cultural and religious identity of the state within these boundaries. In those new polities resulting from national secessions, similar conflicts were postponed and re-emerged only later in the nineteenth century. The colossal political mobilization which occurred during the French Revolution, and its spread with the Napoleonic wars, determined the emergence of the conflict between the mobilization efforts of the state—with its need for system support and legitimacy—and the resistance of the Church. Here, the key issue rapidly became that of the control over the growing mass education and welfare provisions. The structural conditions triggering the urban-rural and class economic conflict developed later on, resulting from the growth in world trade and industrial production during the nineteenth century. These developments initiated conflicts between the landed and urban interests regarding tariff problems. These were, in turn, linked to issues of maintaining acquired status versus recognizing achievement, and they later split the urban front along issues of labour as a commodity, working conditions and contractual relationships. These conflict lines were not necessarily translated into politics everywhere, however, and, indeed, their strength depended on their contextual situations.

This consolidation of alliances between political entrepreneurs, organizations, social groups and cultural movements shaped the cleavage structure of European polities during the hundred years or so between the middle of the nineteenth and twentieth centuries. Cleavage lines were forms of *closure of social relationships*[67] that defined new membership groups within state territories in reference to their centre of decision-making. Social differences or interest differences *as such* did not automatically produce the respective cleavage, but rather the nature and intensity of the emotions and reactions which accompanied membership in these groups, and the kinds of social and political bonds which organizationally united the individuals who belonged

---

[67] For the theoretical definition of a 'cleavage' see Bartolini, S. and P. Mair, *Identity, Competition and Electoral Availability. The Stabilization of the European Electorates 1885–1985* (Cambridge: Cambridge University Press, 1990), 213–20.

to them. Once achieved, these positions became firmly established, and it was the endurance of this entrenched position in group terms that allowed the perception of a cleavage to become stable over and above the individuals involved, and to create a specific cultural background and a varying propensity to collective action.

However, while these new forms of 'national' new political alignments gained force and spread over the territory, they also interacted continuously with persisting elements of territorial distinctiveness that tended to resist and fragment the nationalization of cleavage lines. Although the dominant tendency over the previous two centuries had been for politics to switch from being based primarily on territorial identities and institutions to being based primarily on cultural and functional differences within each territory, territorial conflicts and alignments continued to cut across the nationalization drive of function-based conflicts with varying levels of intensity. Functional cleavages were not easily spread over a territory, even when the external boundaries of this last tended to be closed. The alternative between forms of representation based on cultural and territorial distinctiveness and allegiances, on the one hand, and those based on functional-economic interests, on the other, did not always and necessarily result in the predominance of the latter. Territorial representation imposed limits on the capacities and possibilities for party conflicts within the localities and tended to reduce or transform politics into a question of external representation of the whole community. In contrast, the functional/economic emphasis implied and reflected a type of alliance which crossed local geographical units and undermined the established leadership structure within the community, introducing elements of direct interest conflict into it.

Moreover, territorial and cultural defence need not be linked together as they tend to be in Rokkan's work. There might be strong forms of territorial representation without there being any cultural defence—as the example from France and the USA in the nineteenth and early twentieth centuries show—just as a cultural defence mobilization cutting across territory and nationalizing politics might well exist without any strong territorial basis—as the experience of minority Catholicism in the Netherlands and Germany exemplifies—and, finally, a cultural defence might well be guaranteed *through* territorial defence—as the Swiss Catholic cantons experience exemplifies. Thus, in certain circumstances, and namely in those of new and vast areas of territorial integration, functional interests may be trapped within an uneasy surrounding environment in which, both cultural and territorial defence combine to make it difficult to appeal to functional identities across territories and cultural traits.

At the same time, the cleavages themselves were *social relationships* that implied a level of *external closure* that was progressively reinforced by their behavioural and organizational dimension. Cleavage lines rested on a differential distribution of resources and on social positions from which it was relatively difficult to exit. Although the exit opportunities could be further reduced by the development of sanctions related to the normative and organizational dimension of the cleavage, it is clear that without some sort of structural impediment to exit, it was difficult for cleavage lines to crystallize. The relation of people to the social basis of a cleavage were defined by attributes which it was more or less difficult to change individually and which, therefore, often required group or collective effort. In this sense, it should be noted that there is an important difference between functional cleavages, on the one hand, and other cleavages—which can develop on the basis of ethno-linguistic or peripheral communities or even on religious identity—on the other. Class conditions are social stigmata that can be modified by individual social mobility or by emigration. Ethnic or religious identities are based on characteristics that instead lead more easily to a closed relationship. This difference, in turn, helps to explain why the latter cleavages show such an impressive capacity to survive over time and to encapsulate their respective communities.

It is not possible to give a detailed account of the variations in the development of national political structures in this context. It is, however, useful to chart the sources of variation in political structuring within which the specific historical experiences of the European polities can be arranged. I do so through four maps that outline, so to speak, the property space of political structuring outcomes. The first map in Table 2.3 analytically distinguishes the three main channels of political structure formation: the electoral, the corporate, and the territorial. It defines for each channel the main actors, the principles on which their interactions were structured, the resources controlled in each channel, and the type of conflict and oppositions predominating in it. The comparative question underlining the table concerns the specific balance and relative weight among the channels that characterize each polity and historical period. The structuring of a polity could be dominated by territorial alternatives, corporate interest intermediations or by centralized politico-ideological conflicts, or by a specific but different mix of these channels.

The second map in Figure 2.1 represents the social inputs for political structuring and it allows the possible alliances among social groups and political movements to be identified. If social positions are easily converted into political awareness and collective action, the main social groups tend towards self-representation, and in the Figure 2.1 their squares would tend to coincide with the ellipses representing political movements. The peasant world would thus organize into an agrarian party; the aristocracy, the landowners, and the dynastic bureaucratic interests instead would organize

TABLE 2.3. *A map of political structuring variations by channels*

	Electoral Channel	Corporate channel	Territorial channel
Actors	Mass citizenry	Resource-holder organizations	Territorial governments
	Formal electoral equality	Inequality in resource distribution	Inequality in resource distribution (size, competences, etc.)
	Structuring of electoral alternatives	Structuring of interest articulation	Structuring of territorial representation (federalized/unitary, supranational/ intergovernmental)
	System of parties	System of corporate groups	System of interterritorial bargaining
Resources	Give and withdraw electoral support, loyalty, legitimacy	Capacity to control and withhold key resources (labour, commodities, investments, etc.)	Capacity to block-delay decision-making process
	Capacity of citizens to activate moral commitment of other citizens		Capacity to delay, withhold policy implementation
	Capacities of political elites to achieve and command citizens' electoral support, loyalty, legitimacy		
Conflicts	Ideological oppositions	Group conflict management/resolution	Territorial conflicts

for a conservative defence of their position; the bourgeoisie would express its vision of society through a liberal party; and the working class would set up a socialist movement.

This perfect coupling is not realistic, however—even in a historical context in which socio-economic interests tend to predominate. The representation of agrarian interests and society (the upper side of my social group square) against external forces can predominate over the internal division of the agrarian population, and peasants and landowners may find their position very close in the defence of common interests. On the other side of the square, the working class and the bourgeoisie, both of which represent industrial society, can share interests and forms of representation for quite a while in an early phase. If we read the figure along the axis that opposes the established

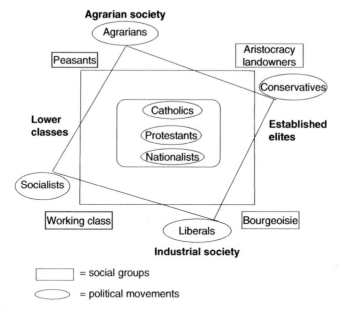

FIGURE 2.1. A map of political structuring variations in socio-political inputs

social and political elites to the lower classes, common interests can exist between parts of the peasantry and the working class movement, on the one hand, and between the bourgeoisie, the landowners, and aristocratic interests, on the other. Clearly, the picture becomes more complicated if, in the process of political mobilization, forces act with no clear relation to the main agricultural or urban, established or emancipationist social groupings. Denominational, nationalist, and territorial mobilizations had few clear social references and were able to drain support from all the most important social groups.

In fact, in the third map in Table 2.4 a cultural-territorial variation is represented. If the cultural infrastructure of the polity was characterized by high national cultural standardization and homogeneity, the socio-political alliances of Figure 2.1 tended to prevail within the context of a unitary and centralized state. If, on the contrary, the cultural infrastructure was highly heterogeneous, socio-functional groups and conflicts intertwined with territorial and cultural ones. If cultural heterogeneity had a clear territorial dimension, this generated either secessionist pushes or territorial arrangements of conflicts (federalization) that fragmented and weakened the socio-political oppositions. If instead, the cultural heterogeneity had no clear territorial dimension, then there was no other possible strategy than its suppression or 'pillarization' into social segments.

TABLE 2.4. *A map of political structuring variations in cultural-territorial outcomes*

	relative homogeneity	→	unitary nation-state
cultural infrastructure			
		→	it has a territorial dimension	secession
			federalization (territorial units)
	strong heterogeneity		
		→	it does not have a territorial dimension	suppression
			pillarization (social units)

These processes eventually affected the organizational dimension, which is charted in Table 2.5. Political organizations active in all three channels could be more or less divided along cultural lines (*culturally segmented*); more or less territorially centralized depending on the level of national integration as opposed to the persistence of territorial organizational autonomy (*territorial centralization*). Political structuring could also be more or less 'pluralist' depending on the level of ideological competition among different organizations in the same field, distinguishing simple cleavage structures versus multiple cleavage structures, two-party systems versus multi-party fragmentation; peak associations versus a pluralist fragmentation of interest organization (*organizational fragmentation*). Finally, organizations and movements active in the different channels (parties, pressure groups, territorial movements and governments) could be strongly interlocked across the channels or be highly independent and deprived of solid linkages to each other (*organizational interlocking*).

Charts and maps cannot compensate for a detailed historical reconstruction of each polity development but they can help to organize evidence and generate hypotheses about the implications of one aspect for the others. By combining the three channels distinction with the model of socio-political inputs and with the variation in territorial and cultural defence, and, finally, by linking these together into a map of resulting organizational outcomes we find that there is considerable potential to describe the national models of European political structuring. In turn, as argued above, the status of each case along these dimensions can be effectively accounted for by the specific historical sequencing of its experience of state formation, capitalist development and industrialization, nation building and institutional democratization.

TABLE 2.5. *A map of political structuring variations in organizational forms*

Territorial centralization	**Cultural segmentation**		
	Segmented	Integrated	Interlocked
Centralized		Unified	Separate
Decentralized	Fragmented		**Organizational interlocking**

Patterns of organizational structuring

Organizational fragmentation

Social Sharing

The fifth historical developmental process of the European nation-state was the forming and enlarging of systems of mutual assurance among the members of the territorial group. These systems extended to the nation principles of social sharing previously applied exclusively within smaller membership groups characterized by more direct face-to-face relationship and emotional ties: family and kinship groups, confraternities, workplace mates, and corporations. Social sharing institutionalized solidarity in terms of social rights linked to the status of citizens and members of the national group.

The French Revolution, the myth of the nation, and the idea of popular representation progressively strengthened the claim of the state as the dominant form of political organization, to the extent that all these processes therein strengthened the control over its various boundaries. However, these developments only partially modified its basic functions and core activities: rising and controlling armed forces, taxing and print money, enforcing national law, protecting property and ensuring physical security. It was, then, at the end of the nineteenth century—and the following two world wars—that a more complex system of mutual obligations between rulers and ruled came into being. The new forms of political mobilization of the enfranchised groups, the accentuation of interstate rivalries, and the challenge of the Russian Revolution combined to make the legitimation problems of the conservative and liberal elites more acute, and to foster an expansion of the functions and goals of the nation-state and a corresponding increase in the quantity and scope of application of its political production. An alternative interpretation to this view suggests that this expansion of regulatory and allocative political production resulted primarily from the long-term functional needs of capitalist accumulation. Whether causal emphasis is laid on the legitimation needs of (mainly non-elective) political elites or on the problem pressure determined by industrialization and capitalist accumulation,[68] the consequence was the same: that regulatory and allocation policies expanded considerably.

[68] As examples of the first line of interpretation see Heclo, H., *Modern Social Policy in Britain and Sweden* (New Haven and London: Yale University Press, 1974); and Alber, J., 'Government Responses to the Challenge of Unemployment: The Development of Unemployment Insurance in Western Europe', in P. Flora and A. J. Heidenheimer (eds.), *The Development of Welfare States in Europe and America* (New Brunswick: Transaction Books, 1981), 151–83. For the second line of interpretation see Cutright, P., 'Political Structure, Economic Development and National Security Programs', *American Journal of Sociology*, 70 (1966), 537–50; and Wilensky, H., *The Welfare State and Equality* (Berkeley, CA: University of California Press, 1975). No reference is necessary here to the many variations of these two main interpretative frameworks.

In pre-industrial societies, elements of civic, social and political duties and rights were not absent, but were closely tied to each others. Even social rights—whose origin lay in local communities' and functional associations' membership—formed part of this same non-differentiated system.[69] They derived directly from the individual's social status, and it was this that determined the kind of justice an individual could access. Social status was the yardstick not only of social and economic inequality, but also of civil and political inequality. With some localized exceptions in the medieval city-states, there was no general principle of citizen equality to generate tensions with actual social and economic inequality. At the end of the eighteenth century, however, the old system of integrated rights and duties connected with belonging to a city or to a corporation was dismantled by the new process of geographical centralizing of the administrative functions of the state, and by the new contractual relationship that had become prevalent in the market. This meant the dissolution of the traditional integrated institutions of citizenship, whose different elements each went their own way. The whole machine that had granted access to the institutions from which citizenship derived, thus dissolved and had to be entirely reformulated.[70] The introduction of the first forms of compulsory primary education—justified not as an individual need, but rather as a social duty—can be viewed as the first sign of this new reformulation and of the reintegration of social rights into the notion of citizenship. Marshall has probably underscored the extent to which elements of modern nationalized social citizenship had already developed in nineteenth century continental Europe and in autocratic, not capitalist advanced regimes. Denmark, for example, had introduced compulsory primary education in the first few decades of the nineteenth century, and autocratic Germany and Austria were the forerunners of social insurance development in the latter half.[71] However, Marshall makes clearly the

[69] For the transition from early to contemporary social rights see Marshall, T. H., *Class, Citizenship and Social Development* (New York: Anchor Books, 1965) and in particular 'Citizenship and Social Class', 71–134.

[70] Marshall sees the British Poor Law—a relief for those defeated in the competition—as the best example of the expulsion of social rights from the citizenship status. Marshall, 'Citizenship and Social Class', 79–90.

[71] For the comparative timing of welfare state development in Europe see Flora, P. and Alber, J., 'Modernization, Democratization, and the Development of the Welfare State in Western Europe', in Flora and Heidenheimer, *The Development of Welfare States in Europe and America*, 37–80; Alber, J., *Vom Armenhaus zum Wohlfahrtsstaat. Analysen zur Entwicklung der Sozialversicherung in Westeuropa* (Frankfurt: Campus Verlag, 1982); and Flora, P., 'Wachstum zu Grenzen. Stabilisierung durch Wandel. Zur Historischen Lage der entwickelten Wohlfahrtsstaaten Westeuropas', in M. Kaase (ed.), *Analysen zu Theorie und Empirie demokratischer Regierungsweise* (Opladen: Westdeutscher Verlag, 1986), 27–39.

point that the new social citizenship was a new 'status' attributed to those who were full members of a community on grounds of equality.[72]

The new international constellation brought about by the end of the Second World War in Europe was crucial to the further development of this new social citizenship. First, the nuclear balance and terror meant that borders ceased to be an issue in Europe, and actually deprived all European states of any significant and independent foreign policy. This prevented the cultural definition of the nation from generating new tensions in the state system deriving from the lack of coincidence between civic citizenship and cultural communities. Second, the Cold-War divide created a confrontation/ competition among different social systems, propelling the search for support to the capitalist system. Third, under these circumstances, it was possible to free the implicit universalistic principle underlying the constitutional state from the imperatives of power politics at the international level, as well as from the language of national interests. It was the first time in the history of Europe that such a positive conjunction managed to prevent the more threatening side of the nation concept and ideal—its ethno-cultural definition and implications—from being used. This configuration of favourable factors thus allowed social citizenship to expand and the class conflicts to be considerably 'pacified' through the expansion of the national welfare state.

The welfare state became closely entwined in the fabric of society. It considerably enhanced the use of law and regulation to bring a growing number of societal processes under authoritative legal constraints, and to simultaneously expand state functions towards the provision of social infrastructures and benefits—a development that was only possible within the framework of the capitalist, national, and later democratic state. It required the bureaucratic machinery and technical extractive capacities that the modern state provided; it required the resources that capitalism, industrialization and the dominant world economic position of Europe offered; it required the enlarged and cross-local areas of equality and solidarity that the nation provided; finally, it required the mechanisms of legitimate political decision-making in which numbers could be waged against resources. The considerable national differentiation in timing, quantitative coverage, patterns of spending and institutional settings of the epoch-making development of social rights are outside the scope of this brief description.[73] It is more important here to underline the capacity of the welfare state to set new

---

[72] Marshall, *Citizenship and Social Class*, 84.

[73] For the timing variation see references in fn. 71. For the typologies of institutional variation see Esping-Anderson, G., *The Three Worlds of Welfare Capitalism* (Cambridge: Polity Press, 1990); and Ferrera, M., *Modelli di solidarietà. Politica e riforme sociali nelle democrazie* (Bologna, Italy: Il Mulino,1993).

boundaries, define new membership groups, and become a source of new political structuring.

The welfare state acted as an anchor to stabilize national political systems by harnessing people's life chances to the state-national institutions, via the creation of explicit entitlements to (a modicum of) material resources.[74] The development of forms of social insurance was an institutional breakthrough in the history of the European nation-state, because it changed the management of social risks—from the previous occasional, residual and discretional interventions that were granted to people with low social status and often considered as undeserving, to standardized benefits distributed in an impartial and automatic form based on precisely defined rights and obligations of citizens possessing certain requirements. The key trait of this new social insurance was that it was *compulsory*, based on the obligatory membership of wide categories of people. This meant that risks could be shared across wide populations, leading to three main advantages: (*a*) a less costly protection per actual beneficiary; (*b*) the possibility of charging 'contributions' (i.e. flat rate or proportional payments) rather than 'premiums' (i.e. payments differentiated on the basis of individual risk profiles, as private insurances normally require); and (*c*) the possibility of granting special treatment (low contributions or minimum benefits) to categories of disadvantaged members. Consequently, compulsory social insurance, as opposed to private and/or voluntary insurance, produced redistributive effects that were not only horizontal—from the non-damaged to the damaged, as in all insurance schemes—but also vertical—from higher to lower incomes.

Given these characteristics, the social sharing institutions contributed to a further process of external closure and internal structuring of the nation-state. The development of national social security schemes represented both a further consolidation of the 'external boundary' to the nation-state because the complex regulatory component of this administrative system reduced mobility. The adoption of the 'pay-go' system of pension financing—whereby the contributions paid by the active generation are immediately used to finance the benefits paid to the inactive—implied an intergenerational contract according to which the next generation was unable to exit the system without provoking a major crisis in the pension benefits of the currently inactive. Nationals were also 'locked in' to the system because of accumulated and non-exportable benefits. The latter increased the contentiousness of national politics on these issues, on the one hand, but also the sense of loyalty

[74] Ferrera, M., 'European Integration and National Social Sovereignty: Changing Boundaries, New Structuring?', *Comparative Political Studies*, 36 (2003), 611–52. This article is the best analysis of welfare state institution development in a Rokkanian perspective (structuring) and a Hirschman perspective (exit). In the following pages I rely on Ferrera's presentation of the welfare state.

towards the national variant of the welfare state, on the other. Non-nationals, in fact, found it difficult to enter the membership spaces of insurance schemes because of contributive cumulating, transferability, etc., which were closely guarded by the regulative hands of each nation-state.

The welfare state did also create new membership spaces. In contrast to civic and political rights, which were extended downwards, social rights were expanded upwards, from lower to higher incomes and from manual to non-manual occupations. The patterns of extension were different in Britain and Scandinavia, in continental Europe and Latin Europe, but in all cases the schemes rested on a 'nation-wide' pooling of risks and standardized rules (even if according to occupation).

The development of the social insurance schemes was also a crucial element contributing to the internal political structuring of all the European nation-states. The Northern Europe welfare states reinforced the state penetration of civil society and enhanced the latter's loyalty to the state and the nation. In many continental countries, social sharing remained characterized by less 'stateness' and structured on the basis of pre-existing social and cultural differentiations (pillars, religious denominations, territorial institutions, and professional groups). In Southern Europe, a complex set of factors contributed to an unusual fragmentation: regional differences, economic backwardness, state–church conflict, and ideological polarization. However, in all cases the new institutions and policies soon became the object of voice activities: voice for entry, by those social groups which requested that benefits be extended to them, or voice against entry, by those social groups which wanted to stay out of state-run schemes because they viewed themselves as self-reliant.

These factors contributed to the novelty of the forms of capital control in the most recent phase of welfare state development, since the end of the Second World War. The confinement of the operations of capital abroad was an old concern of the state, and various phases of opening and closing had alternated. The French Revolution and the Napoleonic wars repealed the 'liberalization' of the 1750s. The two world wars repealed the new openings that had been operating since the 1860s. There were continuous fears and worries about the consequence (for social reform, namely) of an excessive mobility of capital, in contrast with the traditional non-mobile wealth of land, buildings and labour. Positive appreciations were also made, however, about such mobility, viewed as a safeguard against absolutist traditions and the arbitrariness of government.[75]

---

[75] The diversion of passions through interest from aggressive behaviours towards a search for personal advantage was often seen as an additional and unintended positive effect. See Hirschman, A. O., *The Passions and the Interests. Political Arguments for Capitalism before its Triumph* (Princeton, NJ: Princeton University Press, 1977).

In the post Second World War period, the bounding of capital relied for the first time on the consolidation of an alliance among anti-capitalist social groups, bureaucratic elites, and political elected officials. The class cleavage, the expansion of the public bureaucracies, and the professionalization of elected political elites thus combined to shape the last phase of capital mobility containment. Organized social groups actively sought to develop social rights and were interested in being recognized by political and bureaucratic elites as representative spokespeople of their constituencies. Elected political elites were increasingly subjugated to the responsive logic of electoral politics for their survival in power. Public bureaucracies had an interest in their continued alimentation and growth, and supported an active state intervention that legitimized their expertise and state-centric vision. All in all, the alliance among these forces was fundamental to the shaping of the 'cage' for capital mobility and for making capital nationally 'responsible' and dependent. An exchange of the type reproduced in Figure 2.2 developed among these three main set of actors: support was given, legitimacy was achieved, and tenure of power was guaranteed in exchange for politico-administrative boundary building which limited market-capital mobility.[76]

This objective convergence of interests was the window of opportunity that allowed the development and the growth of welfare states between the First World War and the 1970s. In particular, it allowed the national differentiation of welfare states, as national responses were not constrained by any consideration of international competitiveness thanks to the degree of control that was successfully exercised on capital over the territory. The cost of this was borne by capital in general and by certain sectors of capital in particular, and by consumers and taxpayers, in a cultural climate in which the definition of an individual as 'consumer' was subordinated to his/her definition as family member, worker, voter and citizen.

Conclusions: The Political Structuring of the European Nation-State

Summing up five centuries of European history in a few pages is a daring exercise. It can, perhaps, be justified by the goal of clarifying a single central idea: that the nation-state is a historical configuration of highly coinciding and mutually reinforcing boundaries to the transcendence of cultural symbols and messages, economic interactions, administrative regimes and physical coercion.

---

[76] It goes without saying that certain capitalist sectors and groups also benefited from these boundary buildings, exploiting monopolistic opportunities and regulatory defences.

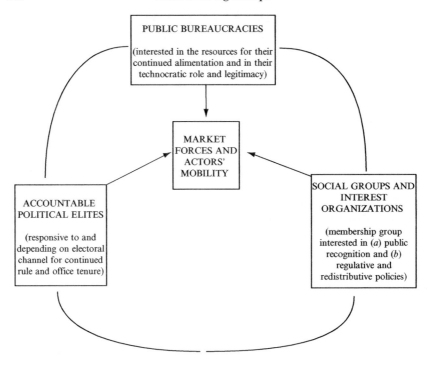

FIGURE 2.2. Capital constraining alliance within the democratic nation-state

To recapitulate, the new forces of capitalism developed and operated within the pre-existing framework of ethnic communities and states frequently involved in rivalry and warfare. The rise of, first, merchant, and then financial and industrial capitalism intensified these rivalries, while war, in turn, cemented both the state and its dominant ethnic population into territorial and legally unified nations. Close links were often forged between the operations of capital and the rise of particular nations: 'Trade sharpened the sense of national difference, and provided economic content for national conflicts, . . . equally the rising national sentiment of the bourgeoisie gave a new edge to their competitive drive overseas'.[77] Therefore, capital provided the economic instruments of the modern state, but, at the same time, the framework of ethnically based states and their loyalties often dictated the direction of trade and competition between merchants and (later) industrialists. Thus, the state and the nation progressively 'locked' capital within the territorial institutions whose legitimacy depended, on the one hand, on the principles of sharp differentiation of its citizens from the 'foreigners', and, on

[77] Smith, *National Identity*, 166–8.

the other, on the progressive removal of within-population status and in-equality boundaries so that the latter would result equally undifferentiated from each other internally. The nation-state thus produced a measure of internal homogenization and eventually came to represent an 'equality area'. Trade and capitalist rivalries, wars and national identities served each other, and in this process of mutual reinforcement the potential mobility of cap-ital—its implicit boundary-removing nature—ended up being bounded by the ties formed by the areas of cultural solidarity represented by the nation and by the legitimacy of the sovereign bureaucratic state.

The dominant processes remained those of progressive coincidence and mutual reinforcement of the administrative-military, cultural and economic boundaries. Different phases of the state, first, and then nation building reinforced different kinds of borders. The intense phase of war-making brought about what Hintze defined as the *sovereign warlike state*, as repre-sented above all by the absolutist states of the Frankish empire. The intense trade rivalry that began with mercantilist policies in the seventeenth century and which had blossomed fully by the nineteenth century created the *closed commercial state*. The codifications of Roman law in the eighteenth and nineteenth centuries, offered the basis for the model of the *liberal constitu-tional state*, which, while emphasizing constitutionalism and personal free-dom, was both the product and the protector of a legal order. The *national state* of the nineteenth and twentieth centuries emphasized, instead, the idea of a national community. No longer was the state simply an organization for domination; rather, citizens identified with it and participated in it.[78] Each phase of development left some vestiges of the past in the more recent functions: the *sovereign warlike state* has left the defence of community and order; the *closed commercial state* left the attention to the economic prosperity and a focus on the economic internal resources as weapons in international trade competition and international power; the *liberal consti-tutional state* has left the rights and procedure to defend individual economic freedom, first, and, later on, other freedoms; the *national state* has left the national community and identity, and the correlated contractual nature of the state.

I have presented the five crucial processes of nation-state consolidation in Europe as consecutive and neatly separated. Obviously, this was in order to describe it more clearly. In general, a good case can be made for the historical precedence of the centre-formation process in military and administrative terms and for the development of capitalism. However, European state formation was not technically terminated until the First World War, and

---

[78] See Page, C. E., 'The Political Origins of Self-Government and Bureaucracy: Otto Hintze's Conceptual Map of Europe', *Political Studies*, 38 (1990), 39–55, 52.

even after this date territorial borders remained highly contested, changing in the east and around the historical city-belt. Similarly, the timing of capitalist development and its level was uneven along the West-East and North-South dimensions of European territory. However, the early consolidation of large-scale territorial states and their territorialization of trade and capital—which had originally flourished in the city-belt—were fundamental discontinuities that set the stage for largely imitative successive developments. The other three processes of nation building, democratization and social sharing are more closely linked and overlapping, so that to distinguish one from the other is analytically useful but historically difficult.

This 'coincidence' of the various boundaries is what has brought about our common sense perception of what a state-society should be and how it should work. This coincidence produces a collectivity of human beings that share a common understanding about what is important in their lives (identities); mostly interact with each other inside this collectivity through social and economic practices and activities; share rules and have ways of deciding how to regulate their lives in common. It is this coincidence that allowed the creation of powerful political agencies of mobilization.

In Figure 2.3, I represent the process of nation-state formation and consolidation through three fundamental 'triangles'. The figure should not be read as a temporal sequence: different nation-states followed different temporal trajectories and, in addition, there were continuous interactions between the three main processes of *centre-formation, system building*, and *political structuring*; and, continuous interaction within each of these three spheres.

Centre formation could not stabilize, consolidate, and broaden its scope without there being some processes of system building. The latter allowed the state to rest on more solid grounds than those based only on coercion. In the system-building sphere, the production and reproduction of the symbols of *national identity*, the development of *social sharing institutions*, and the institutionalization of *political participation rights* reinforced the centre formation in a cultural and administrative dimension. They also legitimized decision rules to tighten or loosen the control of exit options for relevant actors/resources. Similarly, the building of extensive cultural, social and political equality areas strengthened the territorial loyalties and solidarities. The latter were crucial for democratic political structuring through the internal differentiation of the population along ideological, corporate and territorial lines, without engendering the survival of the nation-state itself.

Within each sphere, interactions are also evident. In the centre formation sphere, the internal hierarchy was able to widen the scope and reach of its monopolistic production of behavioural conformity in various and expanding domains through its continuous efforts to control external boundaries

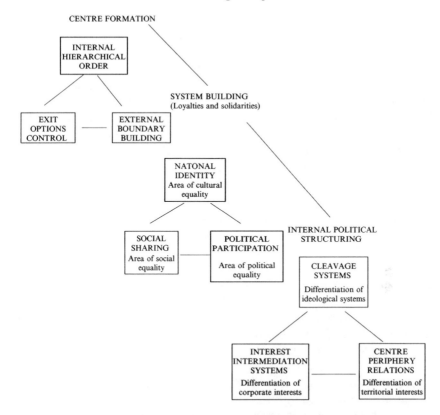

FIGURE 2.3. The analytical triangles of 'nation-state' political structuring

and to make membership groups progressively correspond with territorial groups. Within the system-building process, a self-reinforcing circle developed between the strengthening of national identities and the welfare institutions of social sharing, and between the former two and the principles of political participation to decision-making.

Given that the complex cultural infrastructure of Europe was resilient over time, the more economic interdependencies were to grow the more cultural differences were to become more important.[79] The problem was not the level or the distribution of inequalities, but rather the extent to which these inequalities coincided with cultural differentiation. For this reason the process of system building is the key differentiating feature of the European nation-state experience. Only in such a system could the development of direct relationships with the centre produce the transformation of territorial

[79] Gellner, E., *Nations and Nationalism* (Oxford: Basil Blackwell, 1983) makes this point in his interpretation of nationalism as a result of industrialization.

into functional conflicts and the transformation of cultural conflicts into predominantly economic ones. Conflicts of a functional nature required a 'culturally homogeneous environment' that avoided the cultural segmentation of groups and allowed their organizational unification and centralization.[80] Even more important, system-building processes work as a shield in so far as they allow socio-economic conflicts—kept as separate as possible from territorial and cultural conflicts—to be handled by democratic political institutions and allow for political exchanges and redistributive deals within the existing political community without endangering its own survival.

The third 'triangle' of nation-state development concerns the modalities of political structuring more directly. Centre–periphery relations, corporate group intermediation, and cleavage systems constitute the main structuring processes and their concrete outcomes determine different balances between them. Although in every political system all of them are present, their different combinations yielded different structures of predominance. If ideological cleavages are the dominant form of political structuring, they tend to subordinate centre–periphery relations and corporate intermediation structures. In this case, interest groups align clearly with electoral-political movements and often remain in a dependant or interlocking relationship with them. This often means that they are organizationally fragmented along ideological lines. Even centre–periphery relationships can be considerably subordinated to political-ideological conflicts, and the solution of territorial issues and conflicts can be dealt with through and within mass electoral organizations and the central democratic institutions. In such a situation, corporatist and territorial arrangements are undermined by pure partisan politics. Pure 'unitarism' is, therefore, based on a predominance of cleavage system and interest intermediation alignments that undermine and weaken territorial structuring. On the contrary, when the centre–periphery dimension is the dominant principle of structuring, the territorial subsidiary that shapes the polity tends to subordinate and weaken centralized interest intermediation and cleavage structures, and the cross local alliances of a partisan or corporate nature are undermined by pure territorial politics.

If the central idea of this chapter—that domestic political structures are historically grounded in specific configurations of economic, cultural, administrative and coercion confinement of actors and actions—is right, then we can expect that political developments affecting the boundary configuration of the nation-state will also affect the domestic forms of its political structures. The European integration is clearly a development that directly affects

---

[80] See Schumpter, J. A., 'Social Classes in an Ethnically Homogeneous Environment', in J. A. Schumpter (ed.), *Imperialism and Social Classes* (New York: Augustus N. Kelly, 1951).

the boundaries of the nation-state and we can reasonably expect long-term influences on the latter's internal political structures. Before getting to this, however, we need to devote attention to the specific features of the new centre which is consolidating at the European level. The following chapter is devoted to this inquiry.

3

Centre Formation in the European Union

It is often maintained that the history of nation-state political structuring discussed in Chapter 2 is not relevant when one deals with the process of European integration, given that the EU is a special case, a unique development, and a *sui generis* process. Therefore, according to this view, not much can be learned from its historical antecedents. Contrary to this idea, I claim that (*a*) the experience of nation-state formation offers a useful analytical framework for a theory of regional integration; (*b*) the elements of the nation-state that are regarded as absent in the European polity were not 'given' preconditions *of* the nation-state, but were, instead, constructed historically *by* the nation-state; and (*c*) the problems and the fate of the EU cannot be studied adequately without considering the historical legacies of its ingredients: the nation-states.

In this chapter and the next, I will discuss the special features of the EU centre formation and system building according to the scheme developed in Chapters 1 and 2, which is summarized in Figure 3.1. In this chapter, I discuss the process of the new centre formation considering its territorial enlargement, competence accretion, and institutional differentiation. In Chapter 4, I discuss the specific set of boundary building and removing that is associated with the activities of the EU.

The Historical Constellation

The second half of the twentieth century witnessed, on the one hand, the 'golden age' of the national-democratic-welfare state, and, on the other, the progressive opening up of a new phase of boundary redefinition in all functional spheres that, by the latter quarter of the century, had become the dominant trend. Already the late nineteenth and the first half of the twentieth century—although progressively dominated by warfare and economic protectionism—had offered examples of the declining importance of certain

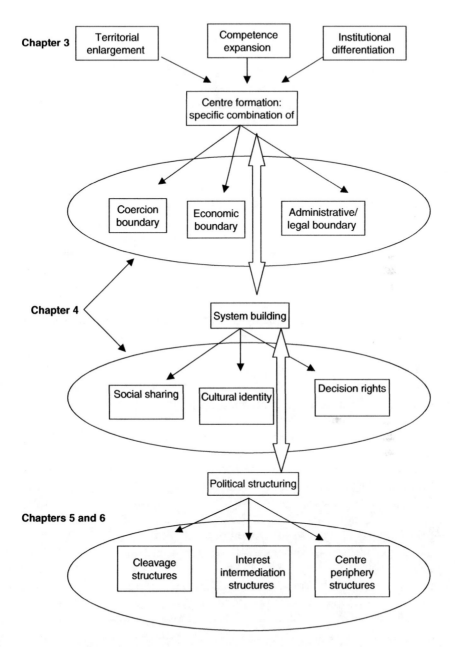

FIGURE 3.1. The framework of analysis chapter by chapter

state boundaries. Most of these concerned the military/coercive/protection boundaries of the state and cast doubt on its viability as a defensive unit.[1] Before the Industrial Revolution the territorial state was largely self-contained from the economic point of view. Although starving fortresses into surrender had once been common, this could not be done to entire nations, and economic blockades never forced states into surrender. With the Industrial Revolution, countries grew increasingly dependent upon imports and this meant that they could prosper only by controlling areas that were much larger than their territory. The economic warfare of the twentieth century showed that state boundaries could be substantially penetrated by the totalizing nature of war and that the successful defence of territory no longer required a pure military demarcation, but a broader than territorial strategy.

Strategic bombing airfare, first, and eventually nuclear warfare could defeat an enemy by directing military action not at its borders, but at the core 'soft' interior of the population, bypassing all territorial defences and foreshadowing the end of significance of frontiers and the demise of the traditional conception of non-permeability and defensibility, as well as the distinction between lawful combatants and the civilian population. With nuclear weapons and their long-distance control, this process was completed and whatever remained of the capacity of the state to control its military boundaries, and to claim a capacity to shield and protect the local civilian population disappeared.

The cultural 'capsule' of the state had also become more permeable by the late nineteenth century. Traditionally, dynastic rulers and governments had fought each other with little ideological involvement on the part of the larger masses. The revolutionary propaganda of the French Revolution changed this situation quite fundamentally, but new ideas—while spreading more rapidly—still needed bayonets and canons in order to impose themselves and be imposed. Fundamentally responsible for the new phenomena of rapid state boundary penetration were the new technologies for spreading messages and fashions which emerged in the late nineteenth and early twentieth centuries. Nations were now becoming more susceptible to undermining from within, through the subversion of loyalties, through the fomenting of internal challenges to the unity of the territorial state, and through the undermining of the morale of the population. Marxism and Bolshevism proved powerful cross-national revolutionary ideologies, undermining the claims of the state to internal ideological coherence, particularly in critical war situations. Fascism and Nazism also followed similar paths of

---

[1] Herz gives an excellent account of the factors of military openings and I rely on his work in the following pages. See Herz, J. H., 'The Rise and Demise of the Territorial State', *World Politics* 4 (1957), 473–93.

ideological and political penetration. More recently, religious fundamentalism as well as the democratic credos have been exported to an extent and with an intensity that would have been difficult to imagine in the past. The easiness with which movements of ideas penetrate state boundaries—whether as the result of subtle penetration tactics, powerful popular movements, or institutional efforts of existing hegemonic states and international organizations—shows the growing difficulty of controlling a nation culturally, or of guaranteeing its allegiance.[2]

After the Second World War, the economic and military constellation was restructured in a direction that bypassed the European system of nation-states. The stop placed on the German attempt to dominate Europe formally reintroduced the old system of European states. However, the post-war international order was dominated by two states that were external to the core European system of states: the USA and USSR. The Cold War justified the USSR securing a part of the European system of states as a buffer zone, and the US keeping a strong military presence in the other part. Thus, a Western Bloc replaced the earlier European core of states. The US strategic view was that the oceans no longer acted as an effective barrier to protect the USA. New weapons and transport technologies having made the USA vulnerable as an island off the coast of the Eurasian heartland, the US felt necessary to establish alliances eastwards and westwards in both the Atlantic and the Pacific. Summing up, the Cold War and the NATO involved a new international constellation with a transfer of sovereignty that encapsulated the historical European state rivalries into two regional subsystems (Western and Eastern), both of which were integrated within larger blocs (Atlantic and Soviet). This modified the Western European state system and provided a general framework for integration based on (*a*) the effective cutting-off of the Eastern part of the state system and a clear definition of the European Eastern border (that had never before been established); (*b*) the division of Germany; (*c*) the Western feelings of a threat from the east; and (*d*) the US security-based interests in Western Europe.

Like the military situation, monetary Western integration was also organized along Atlantic lines. The establishing of an international monetary order required integrative mechanisms that would facilitate the interchange among the many local money systems, and this was achieved with the Bretton Woods system (1944). In the 1950s, the European ran a distinctly regional monetary system (the European Payment Union, EPU), although it was backed by the USA. By 1958, convertibility was set up and fixed, and stable exchanges followed. Bretton Woods evolved into a system in which convertibility was

---

[2] It goes without saying that not all states are equally penetrable from the military and ideological point of view. Despite this, all of them have become more penetrable.

successfully displaced by the USA, and this hegemonic power was thus formally freed of all balance of payments constraints. The USA could float its debt abroad without paying any interest, with the privilege of being completely free of any external discipline. It has been argued that the European allies accepted this US monetary irresponsibility in the 1960s and 1970s in exchange for the free ride they were given in the defence field, where they successfully resisted any US attempt at burden sharing.

The combination of several events (the end of the Bretton Woods agreements, the dollar convertibility abandoned in 1971, the oil crises, the dollar revaluation and devaluation throughout the 1970s and 1980s, the off-shore financial markets developments, the technological innovations in the economic exit, the growing importance of multinational corporations) opened up a new phase at the end of 1970s. In this, the monetary integration of Western Europe found itself progressively unable to rely on US currency and economic guarantees. Since the dollar fluctuations were related to US deficit spending in order to finance global defence without increasing taxes, West European countries tried to remedy this in order to avoid becoming the victims of the world consequences of the US quest for security by attempting an 'Europeanization' of the monetary field. European monetary integration has thus been a major target of the EU since the late 1970s, and has led to the building of specific institutions to europeanize monetary relations: the currency snake and the European Monetary System (EMS) tried to limit the floating of European currencies with each other and to coordinate macroeconomic policies.

A further radical change in the military dimension of the post-War constellation occurred as a result of the collapse of the Soviet regime and of those regimes of the Soviet-influenced buffer zone.[3] The dismantling of the security barriers between Eastern and Western Europe following the end of the Cold War added the economically stagnating areas of Eastern Europe to the integration project, which was also further complicated by the fact that the end of the USSR hegemony in the east generated a process of state fragmentation in some areas. The EU members, who were finding security integration very difficult, still regarded North Atlantic Treaty Organization NATO as necessary, however.[4] It may be suggested that the recent developments of the

---

[3] Up to the 1960s, the economic performance (and even its superiority) of the Communist collective and planned economy was a hotly debated issue in the West. Only by the 1970s did it become increasingly clear that the collectivized economy was not able to match the performance of capitalist economies in the long run. Hobsbawn rightly regards this point as very important for understanding the general political climate of that period: Hobsbawn, E. J., *Ages of Extremes. The Short Twentieth Century 1914–1991* (London: Penguin Books, 1994), 257–86.

[4] Mjoset, L., *Western European Integration. An historical perspective extended into the 1990s* (Oslo: Arena, 1996); and Mjoset, L., 'The Historical Meaning of Europeanisation' (Oslo: Arena, 1997), Working Paper, no. 24, includes a discussion of the historical picture I briefly allude to in this section.

twenty-first century—mainly related to new US strategic doctrines concerning its relationship with the Muslim world and international anti-terrorist security—are also straining the military Atlantic integration, in which case, both the historical pillars of the Atlantic integration—the military and the monetary—would have become obsolete.

In short, the West European experience of regional integration developed in a historical constellation in which military/security and monetary matters were de facto integrated into an Atlantic—that is non-European—context. Western European integration had started at the precise moment at which the USA began to support the reconstruction of the area as a buffer zone to contain the USSR. The crucial security and monetary integration was however left out of the project, and was organized between the trans-Atlantic partners under US leadership. So it was the Cold War that eventually provided the framework for the overcoming of the internal divisions and tensions among the continental West European states. However, this overcoming occurred mainly if not exclusively in the field of trade and policy coordination, while money and security issues remained an Atlantic integration problem. The US (interested in integrating West Germany into the Western bloc) saw the EU as part of the anti-Soviet bloc, although separate from its military (NATO) and from its monetary arms (the dollar area).

The end of the dollar era and of the Cold War could produce a declining demand for European integration, since Western Europe was no longer submitted to a direct military threat. At the same time, however, these changes also reopened the issue of Eastern Europe boundary definition and national relations, with the implication that the EU could take on a more active role in foreign and international affairs in Eastern Europe. On the economic front, once the Cold War was over, the importance of Western European economic and monetary integration ceased to be significant from the point of view of the international balance. It signalled an end to the period during which the USA had suspended, for political stability reasons, their economic competition towards Western Europe, accepting negative balances of payments and economic privileges in trade relationships. It also ended the period in which military protection had been extended to Western Europe at low cost and with limited compensations. In brief, then, the USA was now dealing with Western Europe being less embarrassed by geopolitical and geomilitary considerations concerning the crucial role of this area.

In conclusion, the general constellation of the Western European system of states in the second half of the twentieth century was characterized by a monetary and security integration which was 'Atlantic', as it was mainly built up through the dominating role of the USA in the international context of the Cold War. Early European integration mainly concentrated on trade and policy coordination under this Atlantic umbrella. Progressively, however, monetary and then security Atlantic integration have become less reliable and more costly for Western European states. The Maastricht Treaty, more than any other before it, has symbolized the attempt to Europeanize the fields of money and security which had been dominated until then by Atlantic integration.

Centre Formation

At the beginning of the twenty-first century, the EU[5] and its three pillars constitute the historical evolution of several international agreements originally aimed at to managing together a set of economic resources of strategic interest (CECA 1952; Euratom 1958) and a regulatory framework to create a common internal market (CEE 1958) through the pooling of some powers and capacities of the member states into central and supranational institutions. In the initial project, 'common policies' were almost inexistent, with

---

[5] In this text I will refer to the 'Union' and 'Community' to indicate the entire set of institutions and integration process within which member states are involved. Reference to specific treaties will be made when necessary. This radical simplification is necessary given the complexity of the various treaty relations and their frequently changing labels. The original three treaties were the European Coal and Steel Community Treaty (ECSC; in force from July 1952 to July 2002), the European Atomic Energy Community Treaty (Euratom) and the European Economic Community Treaty (EEC), jointly entering into force in January 1958. In July 1967, the institutions of these three treaties were unified (*Merger Treaty*), but their juridical personality was kept separate, justifying the resort that was made to the term *Communities*. A major following modification (leaving aside the treaty changes implied by the accession of new member states) occurred in July 1987 with the *Single European Act* (SEA) concerning the measures for the achievement of the internal markets. The Maastricht Treaty or Treaty of the European Union (TEU, entered into force November 1993), created what is usually called the 'European Union' (EU). This treaty relabelled the EEC as the European Community (EC) and added the two new areas of intergovernmental cooperation—Justice and Home Affairs and Foreign and Security Policy. Some simplification was introduced by the Amsterdam Treaty modifications of the TEU. With the sacrifice of some legal subtlety, the consolidated version of the treaties can now be regarded as composed of two treaties: the Treaty of the *European Community* (with juridical personality), and the Treaty of the *European Union* (without juridical personality), the first basically referring to the EEC Rome Treaty and to its modifications, and the second to the Maastricht Treaty of the European Union and to its modifications. The same Amsterdam Treaty also transferred some competences of the EU Justice and Home Affairs section into the EC, and the former 'pillar' was relabelled 'Police and Judicial' cooperation. With the Nice Treaty (in force since February 2003) the EU and the EC Treaties have been merged into one consolidated version. The Treaty Establishing a Constitution for Europe (TCE) was approved by the European Council in June 2004 and is currently under ratification by the member states. It integrates the different treaties into a single text, attributes to the EU a single juridical personality, and innovates the institutional framework, the institutions and the voting procedures in several ways. Some of these innovations are referred to in the text and footnotes, when appropriate for the argument of the chapter.

the exception of the two areas of competition and agriculture. The historical development witnessed four sets of changes:

1. Continuous enlargement to new members, with no cases of withdrawal.
2. Treaty revisions: the Single European Act (SEA) in 1986; the Treaty of the European Union, or Maastricht Treaty in 1992; the Amsterdam Treaty in 1997; the Nice Treaty 2001, and the currently under ratification Treaty Establishing a European Constitution (2004).
3. A number of crucial non-treaty steps: the 1966 Luxembourg compromise to postpone the deadline for the introduction of Qualified Majority Voting (QMV) and the unanimity required to amend Commission legislation; the post-1974 progressive institutionalization of the European Council (recognized in the 1992 Treaty of the EU); the monetary policies of the 1970s to minimize the effects of currency movements (the 'snake' in 1972, the SME in 1978, the EMU); the solution of the British Budgetary Question in 1984.
4. The transformations of the EU taking places in period of no treaty revisions, and in particular: the competence expansions; the judicial review and the progressive 'constitutionalization' of the treaties via the jurisprudence of the European Court of Justice (ECJ); crucial policy innovations (for instance, in the Common Agricultural Policy (CAP) and other areas); the strategies of public and private actors' involvement (interest groups, regions and other relevant actors).

These dates highlight different phases of 'treaty activism': almost thirty years of treaty minor changes (1957–86) and then about twenty years of incessant treaty revisions (1987–2004).

The ultimate motives for creating the EU remain open to debate: steps to increase the international status and position of Europe; an attempt to avoid war and to ensure peace and stability; the search for a modernization of national economies; the reaching of the market size to rival competing trading blocks; or a subset of these goals. However, all of them can be referred to the common perception of the inadequacy of European states to function as a self-sufficient capsule for economic and military competition.

The basic kernel of today's EU is the set of policies concerning the forming of a 'common', 'single' or 'internal' market. This core is represented by the four freedoms of movement for goods, people, capital, and services, institutionalized into the EU treaties provisions through norms that require member states to guarantee formally these freedoms, to remove restrictions on them, and to harmonize (or to approximate) those laws that indirectly constitute barriers to them. The additional elements to this core have been more flexible, and have allowed for some treaty-based (after Maastricht) differentiation (social policy, Schengen, EMU, country-specific protocols on exemptions, etc.). The kernel of the common market, on the contrary, has witnessed limited differentiation, taking the form of some delays in the implementation of common measures due to specific national problems. In short, while nation-states based their strength on their capacity to control the level of boundaries transcendence, the new EU centre bases its credibility and legitimacy on its capacity to guarantee the effective lowering of economic boundaries among member states.

The predominant interpretation of this institutional dynamic suggests that over time member states progressively endowed the supranational institutions with enforcement mechanisms in order to protect themselves from the negative consequences of the cheating of other states. The supranational institutions used these enforcement mechanisms to act on their mandates to foster the 'European interest', defined as the expansion of their own institutional and policy competences. Thus, the Commission was required to prosecute violations of European law before the ECJ, and used its control over infringement proceedings as a means of pressure to broaden and shift the scope of European provisions. The ECJ was required to solve European legal disputes but it also used its authority as ultimate interpreter of European law to build a system of enforcement that eventually aimed at protecting individuals from the possible negative consequences of the state's cheating the treaties. The European Parliament (EP) was set up as a consultative body, but broadened its institutional competences and differentiated its institutional and political internal structure to become a legislative assembly in a widening set of areas.

Through this historical process, the EU has acquired an unusual set of features. It was born out of international treaties, but it cannot be regarded as an international organization. It has built the most impressive network of external representation at the European, intercontinental, and even global level. At the European level there are relationships with international organizations such as the Western European Union, NATO and the Council of Europe. At the interregional level, the EU engages in dialogue diplomacy with other regional integration organizations such as the Association of South East Nations (ASEAN), the Gulf Cooperation Council (GCC) and Mercosur, and it also plays an active role in inter continental dialogues such as the Europe–Asia and Europe–Africa summits. At the global level, the EU has the status of an observer in most UN bodies, belongs to the G8 circle, has a considerable share in the creation of the World Trade Organization (WTO), is a member of the Food and Agricultural Organization (FAO), and has a special status in the Organization for Economic Cooperation and Development (OECD). Finally, the EU has delegations in more than 120 non-member states. This dense network is most unusual for an international organization and reveals the EU's ambitions to be an international actor in its own right.

The EU not only has foreign delegations, but also a foreign economic policy; it can impose economic sanctions, participate in peacekeeping missions, and it has also a small military intervention force. However, it does not have any military force, defence policy or foreign policy. It does not even have any clearly defined borders, if one considers the special arrangements that exist with certain non-member countries (with the European Ecomomic Area (EEA) when it existed, with Norway more recently), and even the possibilities of the functional contracting-out of member countries form crucial areas of foreign and home affairs cooperation.

Its inwards-looking nature is also quite extraordinary in the literal sense of the term. The EU institutions have a relatively small bureaucracy, limited administrative resources, no police to enforce decisions or to punish non-conformity, and no control whatsoever over the means of physical coercion within the territory on which it impinges. The exclusion of coercion for the enforcement of any internal behavioural conformity is regarded as a constitutive feature of the EU, which makes it different from any previous attempt at unification and integration. However, coercion is not the only way to create dependency. If it is true that centres can no longer be created and sustained through coercion, it is equally true that centre formation and the dependencies that this creates can no longer be resisted with force, either. The costs of unilateral withdrawal for recalcitrant members seem to have grown exponentially.

Notwithstanding the frequent improper use of the term 'constitutionalization' (see later on this point), the EU has no constitution and different parts of the treaties fall under different review and revisions procedures at the EU level and within each of the member states. At the same time, the EU legislation (directives and regulations) is recognized by the member states as superior to their own national legislations and as directly applicable within their territories to individuals and all legal entities. In this sense, there is no question that the EU is an institutional system that allocates values within a defined community of individuals.

The EU administers a considerable budget that is higher than the national budget of several of its member states. It rules about the internal market and issues a single currency. However, although the financial resources available are fixed by one of the EU institutions and can, in principle, be expanded according to needs, these have been defined either as transfers from member sates or as a proportion of parameters external to the EU institutions themselves (levies on imports, percentages of EU Value Added Tax, etc.). That is, the EU has no power to decide about and directly collect taxes from citizens or firms.

The EU has no 'government', understood as a single visible centre of political authority. Yet the EU can impose considerable economic sanctions on both member states and internal actors, just as it can impose political sanctions on member states (e.g. the sanction on Austria). The EU calls elections for a parliament that is directly elected by the member countries' citizens, which no other 'non-state' organization has ever been able to do. Despite this, the EU lacks political organizations capable of articulating a public opinion. Its main institutions have little or no direct or indirect political responsibility before the representatives of EU citizens' (Central Bank, Court of Justice), or have a very limited direct political responsibility (the Commission in front of the European Parliament), or have an indirect and 'segmental' responsibility (the Council, whose members are not collectively, but individually responsible to national parliaments).

The EU promotes a set of interrelated public policies. These can be listed at every moment in time.[6] However, it is difficult to precisely delimit and define these policies, even if they are all linked through reference to treaty goals. In other words, the EU makes references to clear-cut goals of integration ('an ever-closer union') that can change in quantity and quality according to needs, and with the exclusion of a few policies that come clearly under its competence, there is no competence division among the various levels. At the same time, the EU has limited and mainly ex-post powers to control policy implementation. Further, it has no or very limited competencies in fields such as welfare, education, culture and political rights, and it cannot even define its own citizenship, that results from decisions taken by member states. Therefore, the EU has almost no powers in the definitions of those equality areas that are crucial to the creation of loyalties and to 'system building'. Beyond the four fundamental economic freedoms, there is no concept of a political community based on citizenship rights and obligations.

This cursory list of features makes it clear that both, the central hierarchical structure of the EU and its various boundaries are very difficult to define, are subject to widely diverging interpretations, and are rapidly and continuously changing. In the following sections I will highlight the considerable peculiarities of the new centre formation as it emerged in the 1990s, after the Maastricht and Amsterdam treaties.

---

[6] A tentative list would currently include in the first pillar: CAP; External Trade; Competition; Monetary (common currency); Social and Territorial Cohesion; Fishing Policy; Mediterranean policy; Environment; Immigration; Transport; Telecommunications; Research; Social (limited). In the second pillar: Common Foreign Policy. In the third pillar: Justice and Home Affairs Policies.

Territorial Expansion and Weak Territoriality

The most visible element of the new centre accretion is its rapid and colossal territorial/population expansion. In May 2004 the EU totalled a population of about 450 million people and a surface of about four million square kilometres. In half a century, the number of countries adhering to it has quadrupled, the population is roughly twice today's total population of the original six members, and the territorial surface is now almost four times the original surface. Further expansions are planned and no clear-cut closure of the territorial border of the EU has so far been defined. While the sheer number of people and surfaces now administered may imply qualitative changes in the scope of the central activities, what is even more important is the possibility that a growing number of constitutive units (the member states) may broaden the latitude of action of the central institutions.

This impressive, rapid, and unprecedented territorial enlargement (see Table 3.1) is characterized by a weak principle of territoriality, which reveals itself through a variety of aspects. The first element of this territorial weakness pertains to the continuous enlargement itself. The membership of the EU has not only changed constantly, but it is also unclear in what direction future enlargements might extend. Towards the east and south-east, the EU lacks a clear-cut geographical external boundary (i.e. oceans, continent); at the same time, it seems impossible, so far at least, to identify any defining properties of the existing territories and populations to establish which further territories and populations can (or should) or cannot (or should not) be incorporated: democracy, respect for human rights, level of economic development are all 'aterritorial' features and conditions for admittance that can be achieved by any polity at some point in time. Christianity or any other even vague and ambiguous historical or cultural legacy seem unable to discriminate among potential candidates, and would be widely disputed internally if an attempt was made to use them as rules of closure. So, the EU project is territorially open-ended, and even if nobody believes, it can be expanded indefinitely, it seems impossible to define the limits of this potential extension in positive terms.

The weakness of territoriality is also evidenced by the fact that the territories of the member states do not clearly define the territoriality of the EU in the sense of a uniform legality. To begin with, the territorial scope of the different Communities and treaties is different. The three early communities (ECSC, EURATOM, EEC) had a different territorial scope: the broadest geographical scope was that of Euratom, applying to the entire territory of all member states with selected exceptions for Danish and United Kingdom territories (Faeroe Islands and Greenland, British sovereign zones in Cyprus,

TABLE 3.1. *Territorial and population expansion*

Members	1958	1973	1981	1986	1995	2004
	France	Denmark	Greece	Spain	Austria	Czech Republic
	Belgium	United Kingdom		Portugal	Sweden	Cyprus
	Germany	Ireland			Finland	Slovakia
	Italy					Slovenia
	Netherlands					Hungary
	Luxembourg					Poland
						Lithuania
						Estonia
						Leetoni
						Malta
New members	6	3	1	2	3	10
Total members	6	9	10	12	15	25
New members' population	172,300	63,300	9,640	47,180	21,260	74,200
Total population	172,300	251,480	269,820	317,000	366,080*	453,700
New members' surface	1,168,326	355,800	131,960	597,170	979,783*	738,234
Total surface	1,168,326	1,524,126	1,656,086	2,253,256	3,232,991*	3,971,225

Based on nearest census population. Population (in thousands); Territory in Km².
*Adding territory/population of the ex-DDR.

and partial application to the Channel Islands and the Isle of Man). The geographical scope of the EEC Treaty was more limited, applying to the entire territory of the member states but indicating a special position for Overseas countries and territories (which were exempted from most EEC law). The territorial scope of the ECSC (due to expire on the 23 July 2002) was even narrower, as it applied to the 'European territories of the member states', therefore excluding territories which are not European from a geographical point of view. Similar territorial differences can be found throughout all the treaties.[7] These differences can be regarded as minor, as they involve small proportions of the populations, but they do point to the fact that the definition of the EU territory is not in the hands of the EU itself. The territorial scope of EU law can be changed unilaterally by a member state, by excluding and including their non-core territories or by giving independence or incorporating territory (the reunification of Germany changed both its population and territory and required no legal approval by EU institutions; but this can be regarded as a special case).

Next to these explicit and treaty-based territorial exclusions, there are many other forms of differentiated territorial legality. This territorial differentiation, which legal scholars identify with the term 'flexibility',[8] has occurred in areas and topics as diverse as economic and monetary union, social policy, the control of the borders, asylum, immigration and refugees, many aspects of external trading relations, in policy implementation including the internal market, consumer and environmental policy.[9] In other words, there have been and there still are important opt-outs based on unwillingness or inability in the area of social policy, in the communitarization of Schengen agreements through the Treaty of Amsterdam, and in the monetary integration.

Facing these important differentiations, the possibility for a group of states to go ahead with 'closer cooperation' ventures in fields that are not

---

[7] For a detailed account see Ziller, J., 'Flexibility in the Geographical Scope of EU Law', in G. De Búrca and J. Scott (eds.), *Constitutional Change in the EU. From Uniformity to Flexibility?* (Oxford and Portland: Hart Publishing, 2000), 113–31.

[8] I prefer the term 'differentiation' used by Tuytschaever, F., *Differentiation in European Union Law* (Oxford: Hart Publishing, 1999). For the widespread resort to the term 'flexibility' see De Búrca and Scott, *Constitutional Change in the EU*.

[9] I do not include the temporary derogations for new member states or those forms of discretion in implementation exemplified by the Directive on Integrated Pollution Prevention and Control (Council Directive 96/61/EC, 1996) in this list of elements of weak territoriality. These are indeed forms of 'flexibility', but should not be regarded as forms of territorial 'differentiation' of the same kind as those discussed in the text. See for these forms of flexibility De Búrca, G., 'Differentiation within the Core: The Case of Common Market'; and Scott, J., 'Flexibility, "Proceduralization", and Environmental Governance in the EU', in De Búrca and Scott, *Constitutional Change in the EU*, 133–71 and 259–80 respectively.

envisaged by the treaties has been accepted since Maastricht, provided that certain general compatibilities are respected (introduced in the Amsterdam Treaty, Art. 43 EU Treaty). The closer cooperation provisions are aimed at allowing those member states which want to go ahead to do so within the framework of the treaties, as this framework does not prohibit or exclude members from pursuing closer cooperation outside the framework of EU law (including the European Commission (EC) law). The treaty institutionalization of rules for closer cooperation has derived from the perception of the risk that new instances of intergovernmental cooperation outside the treaties could create parallel cooperations competing with the common institutional framework of the treaties.[10] The rules can, however, also be read as limiting what they define. While Amsterdam's closer cooperation has in principle made certain aspects of differentiation constitutionally possible and acceptable, these rules circumscribe and constrain the type, forms and levels of internal differentiation that can be enacted in the EU context. For example, Art. 43 forbids any closer cooperation that affects the *acquis communautaire*—that is, it excludes closer cooperation that would affect the competences, rights, obligations, and interests of non-participants. Art. 11 EC also excludes cooperation that affects Community policies. These criteria set high boundaries on cooperation and would appear difficult to satisfy.[11]

The weak territoriality of the EU has yet a further dimension. From the beginning, the member countries were, and have remained, embedded in a large number of different types of international treaties. The EU treaties did not terminate, incorporate or exclude any pre-existing bilateral and multilateral treaty; did not stop new agreements and treaties from being made among a subset of the members of the EU (even on matters related to the EEC treaties); and did not prevent new agreements and treaties from being made by member states with third non-member countries.[12] The complexity and richness of the web of treaties of which the EU and its member states form part is so dense, that it defeats any precise typological exercise. There are at least five dimensions that differentiate these international treaties and agreements.

---

[10] See Kortenberg, H. (pseudonym), 'Closer Cooperation in the Treaty of Amsterdam', *Common Market Law Review*, 35 (1998), 833–54 for the expression of this concern by an internal observer.

[11] See Gaia, G., 'How Flexible is Flexibility under the Amsterdam Treaty?', *Common Market Law Review*, 35 (1998), 855–70; Ehlermann, C.-D., 'Differentiation, Flexibility, Closer Cooperation: The New provisions of the Amsterdam Treaty', *European Law Journal*, 4 (1998), 246–70.

[12] For the pre-existing and parallel web of commitments of the member states see Wallace, H., 'Whose Europe is it anyway? The 1998 Stein Rokkan Lecture', *European Journal of Political Research*, 35 (1999), 287–306.

First, one can distinguish these agreements by the level of *EU inclusiveness*, distinguishing between those that include only a subset of EU member states as opposed to those that include all of them. As an example of the former one could mention the Benelux Economic Union Treaty, the Franco-German Elysée Treaty, Schengen, and the Good Friday Agreement between the United Kingdom and Ireland. The most conspicuous example of the second would be the West European Union. However, both categories can be *inter se* or *cum tertiis*—that is, limited to EU member states, as in the examples above, or including non-member states. Agreements that include some member states and some non-member states are exemplified by the NATO, the Central Rhine and Rhine Protection Commission, the Nordic Cooperation, the Cooperation between Schengen and Norway-Iceland, and transfrontier agreements (river resources, cultural and educational issues). Agreements that include all the member states plus other non-member states are the Council of Europe, the UN conventions, and the WTO. Additional classification criteria should distinguish those agreements whose membership is closed, which have therefore been reserved from the beginning for some member states, from those open to all willing participants, as well as bi-or tri-lateral agreements from multilateral ones. Cross-cutting all these dimensions, each of which is subdivided by the others, we gain a clear sense of the complexity of this web of international agreements and of the complexity of claims that impinge upon the territory of the EU's members.

The treaties do not make any references to limitations in this field as these would appear as a radical curtailment of state sovereignty in treaty-making capacity. The issue is, rather, whether it is possible to envisage a set of constraints deriving from the existing treaties to conclude international agreements at the discretion of states, preventing them from entering into conflict with the EU legal framework. In legal terms, the principle of the primacy of EC law could be invoked, since this suggests an incompatibility between substantive international agreements and EU law. Similarly, the doctrine of 'pre-emption', which is most clearly expressed in external commercial policy, suggests that the state treaty-making competence is pre-empted in the fields of specific Commission competence.[13] In addition, the principle of subsidiarity can also be seen as limiting the discretion to adopt acts affecting earlier international agreements or to preclude future agreements. Finally, as far as treaties among a subset of member states are

---

[13] This principle created a particularly controversial case in external transport policy, in which 'open sky' agreements between member states and the USA have been challenged with infringement procedures by the Commission, which argues that this was a field of its competence under the Transport Title of the EC Treaty.

concerned, the Amsterdam 'closer cooperation' framework places further limitations on this possibility (see earlier).[14]

These potential constraints may become more effective in time, but the cooperation among EU member states outside the framework of the EU is likely to continue. It has one fundamental advantage: using the instruments of international law, states remain in control of both the negotiation and the implementation of agreements. Viewed in this light, a drive towards centre accretion would correspond, first, to the declining number and importance of *inter-se* cooperation among member states outside the framework of EU law; that is, states should find intergovernmental cooperation less attractive than cooperation within the framework of European law. Second it should also correspond to a decline in the number of bi-or multilateral agreements *cum tertiis* to which some member states do not adhere, particularly if these are closed (i.e. if they exclude the participation of others), if they affect areas close to EU competences, and if they are functionally rather than regionally justified. Politically, this would lead to a situation in which the power of the states to conclude international agreements on matters of EU competence (or on any matter) would be progressively removed.

Competence Accretion

The EU has not stopped broadening the scope of its competencies and interventions. While most of its policies remain of a regulatory type—as was originally intended—inroads have also been made into interstate distributive policies (according to the *juste retour* principle, such as the CAP or the ESPRIT programme for high tech R&D, SOCRATES and others), and even interstate redistributive policies (such as the structural funds expenditures). While these new policy responsibilities have been formalized in the treaties, in most cases the Commission had already penetrated a given policy area before an explicit treaty recognition of its competence. Héritier has documented the various techniques of competence accretion used by central supranational actors, the Commission, but also the Parliament and the ECJ.[15] These institutions have moved in the interstices, if not in the vacuum, determined by unclear structures of responsibility and have exploited this overall uncertainty to expand and overcome vetoes.

---

[14] These legal solutions are discussed by De Witte, B., 'Old Fashioned Flexibility: International agreements between member states of the European Union', in De Búrca and Scott, *Constitutional Change in the EU*, 31–58, 41–57.

[15] See Héritier, A., 'The European Polity, Deadlock and Development', in C. Joerges and E. Vos (eds.), *EU Committees: Social Regulation, Law and Politics* (Oxford: Hart Publishing, 1999), 273–80.

The first strong push towards competence expansion is the continuous redefinition of external territorial boundaries and acquisition of new members. The negotiations and deals for the enlargements often give the centre a chance to redefine and expand its competences. When new members enter the EU, policies can be redefined if the new member define policy conditions for its entry (e.g. when Finland joined the structural funds, programmes were extended to include polar regions), or if the existing members establish specific conditions for their acceptance of the new members (for example, Italy and Greece requesting an Integrated Mediterranean Programme when Portugal, Spain and Greece entered). Even the reform of decisional rules (often implied by new territorial enlargements) can help policy expansion, as, for instance, with the Social Protocol in Maastricht, allowing QMV with the opt-out of Great Britain.

A second powerful drive towards competence expansion has been the constant institutional competition between the Commission, the Council, the Parliament, and the ECJ, all trying to enhance their institutional position and powers by stretching their competences to the limit. A clear example of this was the way the Commission widened telecommunication policy, using Art. 90.3 to bypass the Council,[16] or when it developed an environmental policy without any legal mandate to do so. The EP has also often used widely appealing public attention policies (threat to public health, immigration, etc.) to do the same. A third mechanism of policy accretion has been the capacity of the centre institutions to accommodate interest in various ways. Compensation can be offered in other fields to those who perceive themselves as losers in a given field through package deals. Postponing compliance in order to gain the support of opponents can also smoothen the diversity of interest orientations. Partial exit may be allowed when single elements of a policy programme are made optional for some members.

Héritier describes a fourth important mechanism of competence accretion as the strategy of 'bottom-up circumventing': in this case, the Commission can build up support within associations and corporate groups before starting legislation or instead of legislating. For example, it was important to build networks of supportive actors of a subnational (regions) or corporate nature, before initiating a new policy action in the field of structural/cohesion funds, as well as telecommunications. The Council would later find it difficult to go against national social actors already involved in the process and already having found some consensual ground. A fifth 'technique' of

---

[16] Documented by Schneider, V., 'Institutional Reform in Telecommunications: the European Union in Transnational Policy Diffusion', in M. G. Cowles, J. Caporaso and T. Risse (eds.), *Transforming Europe: Europeanization and Domestic Change* (Ithaca, NY: Cornell University Press, 2001), 60–78; and Natalicchi, G., *Wiring Europe: Reshaping the European telecommunications régime* (Boulder, CO: Rowman & Littlefield, 2001).

competence accretion has been the resort to a general and sometimes vague 'framework legislation' used to 'test' reactions and to put a foot in the door. In this approach, the general directive does not specify the costs of decisions, leaving these to the implementation phase, and typically it will subsequently call for more specific action that was not originally envisaged (a strategy which has been used very clearly in environmental policy and telecommunication policy, but also in social policy).

Finally, several techniques have been used to overcome and circumvent specific member state opposition. Measures previously dealt with, according to the principle of unanimity may be transferred to areas subject to the QMV, as when the Commission decided to deal with contractual labour market issues under the Health and Safety article of the EC Treaty. Together with this strategy of decision rule domain switching, there has been that of 'experts' insulation': networks of national experts who are insulated from any public and political debate, deal with technically complicated matters, and their solutions are later presented to the Council, which lacks the full knowledge and competence to handle these. In other cases, the Commission has exploited regulatory competition among member states to the advantage of the accretion of its political role. Competition among the member states to adopt the regulatory framework coming closest to their own has allowed the centre a latitude of action to choose the one which best fits its own interests and future plans. It has also been suggested that the extensive and supranational powers for patrolling the creation of the single market has allowed the Commission to use its institutional role of defender of free circulation as a legal basis to extend its competences.

This expansion probably occurred for many reasons, but two institutional elements have fostered it in particular. First, in the treaties, the legal definition of the competences of the EU presents several ambiguities. On the one hand, Community competences are described substantially and precisely in the various treaty articles. These lists represent a transfer of specific and enumerated powers. On the other hand, in Art. 100 the powers of legal harmonization are defined and laid down 'functionally', through the definition of goals such as 'creating a functioning common market'. Finally, Art. 235 declares that if the Community action is required in an area that is not envisaged by a treaty, the Council can decide unanimously, following a proposal by the Commission and after consulting the Parliament, on any necessary and suitable measures that need to be taken.[17] This combination of 'treaty enumerated powers' and of 'functional needs' that may require special action have given the Commission considerable room for manoeuvre.

---

[17] See Joerges, C., 'Taking the Law Seriously: On Political Science and the Role of Law in the Process of European Integration', *European Law Journal*, 2 (1996), 105–35, 113.

Second, until the late 1980s, the willingness of the ECJ—the body that was meant to check the techniques of competence accretion enumerated before— to accept the expansion of legislative powers that were justified exclusively by their goals (i.e. by being required and necessary although going beyond the sphere of enumerated competencies) could be interpreted as reflecting the Court's endorsement of the unanimous agreement among the member states.[18] However, with the introduction of the qualified majority rule for the measures concerning the realization of the internal market and the extension of majority rule in the Maastricht Treaty, this argument no longer holds. By the mid-1990s, the conclusion that 'the ECJ has conspicuously failed to generate any confidence in its ability to put effective checks on the jurisdictional appetite of the Brussels' lawmaking apparatus' was entirely justified.[19]

In fact, since Maastricht, the Commission's competences expansion has led scholars to wonder about the potential limits of this progressive broad-ening.[20] Complaints and decentralization requests have increased and limi-tations have been placed on the role of the Commission in a number of areas.[21] For example, the 'subsidiarity clause' was inserted into the main body of the treaty, rather than in the preamble, where it would have remained a non-binding provision, so as to make it justiciable before the ECJ. The wording of the clause was, however, imprecise—and even ambigu-ous (see infra on Subsidiarity)—and the Edinburgh Council adopted guide-lines for the application of the principle in December 1992, instructing the Commission to justify every proposal that it sent to the Council in terms of the subsidiarity principle. These guidelines were subsequently incorporated into the Amsterdam Treaty as a legally binding protocol. A second sign of backlash in the field of Commission's competences can also be identified in the growing budgetary constraints. Germany in particular, facing the costs of reunification, made clear the unwillingness to increase its financial contribu-tion. More generally, fiscal austerity among the contributing countries (in-cluding the stability clauses) made the economic environment unfriendly to any further growth of the budget, notwithstanding the costs of the imminent

[18] Weiler, J. H. H., 'Journey to an Unknown Destination: A Retrospective and Pro-spective of the European Court of Justice in the Arena of Political Integration', *Journal of Common Market Studies*, 31 (1993), 417–46.

[19] Weiler J. H. H., 'A Quiet Revolution. The European Court of Justice and Its Interlocutors', *Comparative Political Studies*, 26 (1994), 510–34, 532.

[20] See Pollack, M. A., 'Creeping Competence: The Expanding Agenda of the European Community', *Journal of Public Policy*, 14 (1994), 95–145; Dehousse, R., 'Community Competences: Are There Limits to Growth?', in R. Dehousse (ed.), *Europe After Maas-tricht. An Ever Closer Union?* (München: Law Books in Europe/C H. Beck, 1994), 103–25.

[21] See for a list Pollack, M. A., 'The End of Creeping Competence? EU Policy-Making Since Maastricht', *Journal of Common Market Studies*, 38 (2000), 519–38.

enlargements. Finally, the Berlin European Council in March 1999 decided that the budget would not increase any further until 2006.

The interpretation of these developments in the 1990s is that member states were openly resisting any further centralization. In every process there are phases of growth, stagnation, and even withdrawal, and if the post-Maastricht period can be seen as one of stagnation, it was certainly not one of withdrawal, as none of the acquired competences has been re-nationalized or otherwise withdrawn from the central institutions. In fact, during the period of expansion the EU developed all sorts of new statistical, accounting and economic information and techniques which go well beyond those traditionally provided by the nation-states and which both justify, and legitimize its technical competence—a technical competence that is not available at the level of the state and which is likely to become more important in the future. In addition, notwithstanding budgetary limitations, the policy regulatory output of the EU does not show any sign of decline.[22] Finally, (see later for a discussion) the wording of the treaty clause on subsidiarity is so ambiguous that in a different political and economic phase it could also be used or interpreted in such a way as to further expand the competencies of the Commission and the Parliament. There is no reason therefore—pending the *incognita* of the consequences of the enlargement to the ten new members from Central-Eastern Europe—to declare the long-term tendency to a centre competence accretion in the EU as over.

Bureaucratic Development

The bureaucracy of the central institutions is relatively small: in 1995, the Commission had about 19,800 functionaries; the Parliament had at its disposal approximately 3,900 functionaries and the Courts (ECJ, CFI, CoA) about 1,300; about 2,400 national functionaries surround the Council(s). Finally, about 660 functionaries work for the Committees (Regions, Social and Economic) and about 500 for the joint services. Altogether this makes for a central bureaucracy of about 28,000 functionaries.[23] This total stood at approximately 6,500 in 1958. One should keep in mind, however, that this bureaucracy is almost exclusively 'central' and dedicated to 'policy formulation', that it has no decentralized offices of territorial control, and no tasks of policy implementation or direct control. Notwithstanding its limited size, however, the EU bureaucratic infrastructure presents some characteristics of

---

[22] For data on directives, regulations, and decisions issues since in the Maastricht Treaty, Pollack, M. A., 'The End of Creeping Competence? EU Policy-Making Since Maastricht', *Journal of Common Market Studies*, 38 (2000), 529.

[23] Page, E. C., *People Who Run Europe* (Oxford: Clarendon Press, 1997), 23–8.

large-scale administrative organizations. It is worth pointing out that it is so far the only structure that successfully establishes cross-national effective networks. This can be seen in its Brussels headquarters, but also in its networking with national bureaucratic subsectors.

The Commission is no longer the small agency as in the early years and the General Directorates (GD) are no longer organizational subsections of this small agency, but rather quasi ministries. This highlights a process of institutional differentiation that is typical of national bureaucracies which usually makes the bureaucratic process more difficult to direct politically, and more resilient in its practices and performance, and even its goals. There are considerable traces of institutional fragmentation. In many sectors, the contacts and relationships among different institutions proliferate. Each GD has connections and contacts with corresponding working groups in the Council, and both have connections and contacts with the corresponding parliamentary commission functionaries. All three also have contacts and connections with a series of interests, organizations, experts, etc., in the same field. These networks have been called 'epistemic communities', underlining the development not only of common view, but also of a sort of sectoral *esprit de corps*.[24]

The EU bureaucracy tends to have a missionary and goal-oriented view of its role.[25] The selection procedures tend to emphasize a commitment and adhesion to the goals of growing integration. To begin with the commissioners and their cabinets, the appointment procedures are unlikely to select personnel and staff who are uncommitted to the EU's development or excessively receptive to national indications. The mutual acceptance principle (by members state authorities), which is institutionalized for the commissioner and implicit for other high functionaries, is powerful because no agreement among states would ever be achieved for the appointment of this personnel if a different principle was upheld. Any personnel selection at the higher level of the European administration—which is subject to some direct or indirect control and influence by nation-states—is paradoxically but necessarily oriented towards the selection of personnel inclined to the defence of the 'general' interests of the EU, which can hardly be defined in any other way than the general interests of its central institutions. This 'pull factor' in selection combines with the 'push factor' that tends to orient towards Brussels and the European institutions those functionaries whose interests and

---

[24] See Richardson, J., 'Actor Based Models of National and EC Policy-Making: Policy Communities, Issue Networks and Advocacy Coalitions', in H. Kassim and A. Menon (eds.), *The EU and National Industrial Policy* (London: Routledge, 1996), 26–51.

[25] Shore, C. and Block, A., 'The European Communities and the Construction of Europe', *Anthropology Today*, 8 (1992), 10–12; and Page, *People Who Run Europe*, 39 and 135.

preferences tend already to be biased towards the integration process, and the role of supranational institutions in it. Given these recruitment features, the orientation towards the integration of the officials of the EU is more in line with a socialization perspective that posits that preferences, attitudes and interests be endogenously shaped and remoulded by the institutional setting within which the official works, rather than by a principal-agent model, by which officials act as member state agents.[26] For the national negotiator officials involved in the Council working groups, the longer their experience of socialization in these groups, the more supranational their basic orientation.[27] Senior officials of the Commission thus tend to be inclined towards supranationalism to begin with, and to support the ideal of a European public interest superior to that of private or government interests.[28]

Attention should not be focused exclusively on the central administrative institutions and their personnel, but also on the ' Europe of administrators', linking national as well as European bureaucracies. The administrative machinery of the EU also includes supranational secretariats, organizations, and committees that, even if originally formed to represent national or subnational or even wider interests, develop their own perceptions, orientations, and interests overtime. The careers and resources of these institutions and people are dependent upon the continued and further expansion of the integrative tasks they are required to carry on. From this point of view, the fact that they may be nominated and even controlled or monitored by national actors is not decisive. They can easily develop an *esprit de corps* and a vision of their necessary function, internalizing ideas and goals that cannot be simply reduced to those of their national authorities. Moreover, their success in dealing with certain problems in the circumscribed areas of their competence may help them to increase resources and capacities to extend their intervention beyond the areas originally assigned to them and the goals of national authorities, and to see this as legitimate. This feature is usually viewed from two different perspectives: as a sign of Commission activism and of (sometimes) supranational dynamism or as a technical problem of coherent policy coordination across administrative units.

The development of horizontal administrative linkages between European and national administrative experts is most clearly perceptible with the court system, with its division of labour among national courts and judicial insti-

[26] See Trondal, J., 'Re-socializing Civil Servants: The Transformative Powers of EU Institutions', *Acta Politica*, 39 (2004), 4–30.

[27] Beyers, J., 'How Supranational is Supranationalism. National and European Socialization of Negotiators in the Council of Ministers', *Acta Politica*, 33 (1998), 378–408.

[28] Hooghe, L., 'Images of Europe: Orientation to European Integration among Senior Officials of the Commission', *British Journal of Political Science*, 29 (1999), 345–67.

tutions and the ECJ (see later). Parliaments, on the contrary, have been much slower to develop horizontal administrative cooperation with European institutions and, in particular, the EP. Since the 1990s, considerable efforts have been made to discuss internal reforms (specialized committees, scrutiny, etc.) to admit national European and MPs into these specialized committees and working groups and to develop initiatives to meet members of parliamentary committees dealing with similar matters at national and European level. This generates the need for a specialized administration in order to deal with the routine of these contacts and to increase horizontal contacts between national and European parliaments administrative officials. However, even in the Council, a tendency towards the development of a specialized administrative infrastructure with considerable influence has been noted. The various European Councils consist of a myriad of specialized formations and the Council of Foreign Affair ministers—to which a coordination function has been attributed—cannot handle this role effectively. The Council of Minister relies heavily on preparatory work by the Committee of Permanent Representatives (COREPER), which, for its part, it is often inclined to ratify choices made in specialized Council Working Group.[29] Matters agreed at the COREPER appear on the EU Council agenda as 'items A' and are generally approved without any discussion. They represent 70–75 per cent of the decisions taken by the Council.[30] That is, a large majority of EU decisions are taken at a bureaucratic level (even if they are formally adopted by the Council). Moreover, each type of Council tends therefore to act autonomously, and the European Council has neither the time nor the resources to oversee this impressive machinery. Therefore, unless the issue acquires a high political visibility, there is a fairly high chance that a consensus will also emerge because the Permanent Representatives regard the search for a compromise as their primary normal function.

Integration has led to cross-national *sectoral cooperation* among specialists of any given area. A growing number of national bureaucrats are involved in developing and applying Community policies. The interactions between national and Community bureaucrats are manifold: expert groups deliberately set up by the Commission to test national governments reactions, EU Council working groups, intergovernmental committees mandated to monitor implementation. In each national bureaucratic department, specialized desks and offices have been created to deal with European affairs. Dehousse sees these as the development of a growing number of agencies that constitute

---

[29] On this point see Gonzalez Sanchez, E., 'La négociacion des décisions communautaires par les functionnaires nationaux: les groupes de Travail du Conseil', *Revue Française d'Administration Publique*, 63 (1992), 391–99.

[30] See Quermonne, J.-L., *Le système politique européen* (Paris: Montchrestien, 1994), 56.

a system of networks bringing together national and Community officials with responsibility for a given area.[31]

Some of the most centralized states have tried to balance this centrifugal drive by setting up bodies that are responsible for coordinating all their Community policy (in France and Britain, for instance); the influence of these seems to be low and declining, compared with the technical ministries.[32] A comparative study of policy coordination has shown that in six of the then twelve members of the EU (Germany, Italy, Spain, Portugal, Greece, Luxembourg) no arbitration mechanism existed that was capable of settling the conflict between specialized departments effectively.[33] At the same time, this vast cooperation enterprise has fostered functional differentiations within the state apparatuses themselves, encouraging the creation of networks to link executive agencies, judicial bodies, and, more recently, the legislatures of member states and the EU: 'the fragmentation of decision-making promotes the development of European regulations, which legitimize and cement the existence of autonomous functioning, specialized networks'.[34]

The interpretation of this tendency is that the process of integration and the relationship with the EU tend to empower state subsystems via cooperation among technical, low-partisan experts. Dehousse's point is that, given the essential role of national public administrations in decision-making at the European level, the EU offers them the possibility to communicate and negotiate in a very congenial atmosphere, insulated from publicity and parliamentary scrutiny. As a result, the innovation of EU policies and procedures normally strengthen their prerogatives as national bureaucracies.

The Community cannot do without the assistance of national bureaucracies and needs to guide the activities of those bureaucracies. In doing so, it has accentuated the fragmentation of the nation-state. Even if it is true that some of these administrations lose part of their autonomy in this process, as decisions are no longer taken unilaterally, this fragmentation enhances their possibility to intervene, while protecting them from direct partisan intervention or national parliamentary scrutiny. Bureaucracies are, in this way, given opportunities to evade parliamentary control mechanisms at the national level. The development of functional networks across national borders also fosters the formation of transnational functional governance: 'Transnational administrative cooperation has fed the growth of Community competence,

[31] Dehousse, R., 'European Integration and the Nation State', in M. Rhodes, P. Heywood and V. Wright (eds.), *Developments in West European Politics* (London: Macmillan, 1997), 37–56, 41.

[32] See Lequesne, C., *Paris-Bruxelles: Comment se fait la politique européenne de la France* (Paris: Presses de la Fondation Nationale de Sciences Politiques, 1993).

[33] Siedentopf, M. and Ziller, J., *Making European Policies Work* (London: Sage, 1988); Ziller, J., *Administrations Comparées* (Paris: Montchrestien, 1993), 43.

[34] Dehousse, 'European Integration and the Nation State', 52.

judicial cooperation, has ensured the acceptance of the European court's bold jurisprudence, and the slowness with which parliaments have reacted, has contributed to the depoliticization of European public policies'.[35] To date, these interconnections between national and European techno-bureaucracies have attracted less attention than they deserve.[36]

Centrally Administered Legal System

The most important aspect of centre accretion has probably occurred in the legal field, taking the form of the development of legal system that is both administered and interpreted centrally. Within the architecture of the EU, the role of the ECJ was to avoid the risk of the selective application of the treaties, and this implied that the role of the Court was twofold: first, it was to be the supreme interpreter of the treaties and would therefore control the conformity of the national and European legislation to them; second, it was to ensure the uniform application of such law across the EU. The article concerning the ECJ in the Treaty of Rome indicates that the founders wanted it to interact primarily with other Community bodies and the member states. Art. 169 and Art. 170 made for claims of noncompliance with Community obligations to be brought against member states by the Commission or other member states. In addition, Art.173 gave the Court additional jurisdiction over a variety of issues brought against the Commission and the Council by member states, the Commission, the Council and specific individuals who had been subject to a Council or a Commission decision addressing them directly.

Through a series of autonomous interpretative decisions, the Court transformed European law from a system of public international law into a system of law similar to that of constitutional federal states. Disputes about the violations of the treaties obligations[37] were thus not restricted to the

---

[35] Ibid., 53.

[36] 'Once there were those who worried about the supranational features of European integration. It is time to worry about infranationalism—a complex network of middle level national administrators, Community administrators and an array of private bodies with unequal and unfair access to a process with huge social and economic consequences to every day life....' Weiler, J. H. H., *To be a European Citizen—Eros and Civilization* (Madison, WI: International Institute, Spring 1998), Working Paper on European Studies, 39.

[37] In the creation of the market, the main issue was the distinction between those non-tariff barriers representing a trade distortion through illegitimate practices aiming at favouring national producers, and the legitimate interests to the social, health, cultural and environmental protection that member states could continue to pursue. Inevitably, whether under the harmonization principle or the mutual recognition principle, the subtle boundary between illegitimate distortions and legitimate interest protection was to be left to the ECJ jurisdictional activity.

interstate level, but were shifted to the national courts and involved domestic parties. The elaborate system of judicial review integrating national courts with the ECJ began to extend beyond Community law, to check the compatibility of national law with Community law. These decisions transformed the treaties from a previously horizontal 'set of legal arrangements binding upon sovereign states into a legal regime vertically integrated which confers judicially enforceable rights and obligations on all legal persons and private and public entities within the Union territory'.[38] This passage from the original horizontal scope to the vertical dimension highlights the EU's transformation from an intergovernmental organization governed by international law into a system of legal adjudication founded on the principle of the hierarchy of the sources. In this sense it is often referred to as the process of 'constitutionalization' of the treaties (see infra). The main phases of the institutionalization are normally identified by the ECJ's formulation of a number of 'doctrines'[39] in its jurisdictional activity that have not been challenged by other national or European bodies.

During the period 1962–79, the ECJ secured the principles of 'supremacy' and 'direct effect'. According to the first (Costa *v*. ENEL, Case 6/64, 1964 ECR 585), in any conflict between EU legislation and national legislation the former must be given primacy. Moreover, for the ECJ, every EC rule in force renders automatically inapplicable the conflicting provision of national law (Simmenthal, ECJ 1978). The doctrine of supremacy prohibits public authorities from relying on national law to justify their failure to comply with EC law. The doctrine of direct effect (Van Gend en Loos *v*. Nederlandse Administratie der Belastigen, Case 26/62, 1963) allows private individuals or companies to report member states or other public authorities for not abiding by obligations foreseen by the treaties or for not adequately transposing the legislation of the EU into national legislation. In this way, the EC law confers onto individuals legal rights that public authorities must respect and

[38] Stone, A. and Caporaso, J., 'From Free Trade to Supranational Polity: The European Court and Integration', in W. Sandholtz and A. Stone (eds.), *European Integration and Supranational Governance* (Oxford: Oxford University Press, 1998), 92–133, 118.

[39] Most countries have a vast literature on these doctrines and their legal implications. I have used the following, mainly English language, sources. Weiler, J. H. H., 'The Community System. The Dual Character of Supranationalism', *Yearbook of European Law*, 1 (1981), 268–306; Weiler J. H. H., *Il sistema comunitario europeo. Struttura giuridica e processo politico* (Bologna, Italy: Il Mulino, 1985); Weiler, J. H. H., 'The Transformation of Europe', *Yale Law Journal*, 50 (1991), 2403–83; Caporaso, A., 'From Free Trade to Supranational Polity. The European Court and Integration' (Berkeley, CA: November 1996), Paper at the conference 'Supranational Governance: The Institutionalization of the European Union'; Weiler, 'A Quiet Revolution', 510–34. Slaughter, W., Stone, A., and Weiler, J. H. H. (eds.), *The European Court and the National Courts—Doctrine and Jurisprudence: Legal Change in its Social Context* (Oxford: Hart Publishing, 1998); Stone, A., *Governing with judges. Constitutional politics in Europe* (Oxford: Oxford University Press, 2000).

be protected by national courts. While 'regulations' were originally the only class of Euro-rules that the member states meant to be directly applicable in national law, the ECJ found that certain treaty provisions and the class of secondary legislation—the directives—could be directly effective and should therefore be directly enforced by national judges. This doctrine empowers individuals and companies to sue governments and other public authorities either for their lack of conformity to the obligations contained in the treaties or regulations, or for not properly transposing the provisions of directives into national law.

Since the 1980s, there has been a second wave of institutionalization regarding the centralized administration of the legal system through which the ECJ supplied national courts with enhanced means of guaranteeing the effectiveness of EC law. The doctrine of indirect effect (in Von Colson, ECJ 1984 and Marleasing, ECJ 1990) set the principle that national judges must interpret national rules as if they were in conformity to EU law. Even if a directive has not yet been transposed or has been inaccurately transposed into national law, national judges are authorized to interpret the national law in conformity with the directive. In other words, this doctrine authorizes national judges to rewrite the national law so as to be able to apply the EU law when appropriate national legislation is missing or incorrect. Finally, with the doctrine of governmental liability (Francovich, ECJ 1991)—or the doctrine of the responsibility of the state—the ECJ stated that a national court can consider a member state responsible for the damages encountered by private entities as a result of a lack of transposition or of a failure to properly implement the directive. As a result, the member state is required to compensate the individual for their losses. In this case national judges become agents of the ECJ.

The principle operationalizing for the centralization of the jurisdictional function has been Art. 177, the force of which became evident only later on. According to this article, when the EC law is relevant to the settlement of a legal dispute in a national court, the presiding judge may—and in some cases he/she must—ask the ECJ for a correct interpretation of that law. The national judge then applies this interpretation, or preliminary ruling, to decide the case. Lower national courts can refer such questions for a preliminary ruling at their discretion. Art. 177 was designed to ensure the uniform application of Community law across the national jurisdictions. This procedure was probably designed to help the national courts understand and come to terms with the nature and content of EC law and to apply it correctly. Over time, the process of legal centralization has been strengthened by the interaction that occurs between private litigants, national judges, and the ECJ working within the framework provided by Art. 177. In this system of legal recourse, European citizens realize their treaty-embedded rights before national courts, while the latter refer disputes concerning European law to the ECJ; the latter interprets the relevant EU provisions in a preliminary ruling; finally, the national courts then use this ECJ interpretation to decide the case. In most instances, this system results in the enforcement of European law against national law and administrators.[40] The effectiveness of the EU legal system depends critically on the willingness of the national judges to refer disputes about EC law to the ECJ and to settle those disputes in conformity with the Court's case law.[41]

Virtually all the important domains concerning the obligation of member states to dismantle barriers to free movement within the EU territory are governed by the judicially constructed rules of the ECJ, while member states are required to justify the permanence of barriers on public interest grounds. In turn, the Court interprets these latter justifications in terms of the EU's rather than the member states' priorities. On the contrary, the ECJ is very much less effective in creating new rules or coordinative norms with which to regulate the problems common to all member states, in constructing of EU legal regimes to replace national ones, and in constructing institutional arrangements and norms to modify, extend, correct, restrain and counteract the operation of the market. This is, possibly, unavoidable, given the functional role of the ECJ in reference to treaties. It is, however, a fact that interpretative innovations of the ECJ decisions to date have been mainly oriented towards removing internal boundaries rather than devising or strengthening new external boundaries.

So, we can at this point say that, with the support of state organs (the lower national courts) an EU legally-derived organ (the ECJ) has come to constitute the EU as a legal order different from that of the nation-states, which is rooted and located autonomously somewhere other than in the state(s) themselves. In other words, this EU institution pulled itself up by its own bootstraps, asserting a new supranational order and electing itself as its

---

[40] Stone, A. and Brunell, T. L., 'Constructing a Supranational Constitution. Dispute Resolution and Governance in the European Community', *American Political Science Review*, 92 (1988), 63–81; and Stone, A. and Brunell, T. L., 'The European Court and the National Courts: A Statistical Analysis of Preliminary References, 1961–95', *Journal of European Public Policy*, 5 (1998), 66–97, document the extraordinary expansion of EC law into new areas. In the 1970s more than half these references concerned the free movement of goods and agriculture. In the 1990s, these fell to only 27 per cent, while new areas such as environmental protection, commercial policy and competition became more important.

[41] Not all national courts have shown the same willingness to accept this situation. There are few British references, and often British judges invoke the right to interpret directives themselves without reference to the ECJ. See Golub, J., 'The Politics of Judicial Discretion: Rethinking the Interaction between National Courts and the European Court of Justice', *West European Politics*, 19 (1996), 360–85. The comparative paucity of British references is likely to be the judicial expression of the country's lack of enthusiasm or sympathy for integration. The author argues that this evidence should lead to a revision of the general idea that national judges have generally been cooperative.

sovereign legal interpreter. In political terms this is no novelty, as any de facto claim to sovereignty is a discontinuity rooted into the control of force or some other key resource. In this case, the fascinating point is that the institutionalization of the European legal system has come about largely as a result of the activities of the judicial institutions themselves.[42] The peculiarity of this development is such that legal scholars have resorted to the term 'integration by law'.[43]

Several reasons are advanced to explain the successful and unchallenged 'revolutionary' role of the ECJ. First, it is difficult to counter the ECJ jurisprudence within the institutional context of the EU. To refuse to comply with requires the complicity of national courts and it can lead to a very risky level of internal and external tensions and conflicts. It is possible to revise the treaties, but this requires a unanimity which is very unlikely to come into being.[44] Second, the resistance of national higher courts towards the role played by the ECJ has been largely overcome thanks to the competition between the lower and higher courts to enhance their influence and prestige

---

[42] It has also generated some justified criticism by legal scholars against political and social scientists for not having paid adequate attention to this development. See Shapiro, M. and Stone, A., 'The New Constitutional Politics of Europe', *Comparative Political Studies*, 26 (1994), 397–429.

[43] The meanings of this expression are, however, different. In a first understanding of the term, 'Integration by law' can simply be used to underline the special contribution that law has made to the construction of the EU as the development of a constitutional charter of the participating states, whose character and properties make it different from state laws and also from international private and public law. In a second version, the term points to the specific density of 'juridification' at the European level, which makes it very different from contingent cooperation among states, on the one hand, and from international organizations and regimes, on the other. In a third version, 'integration by law' underlines the peculiarity of the Community 'legal system', in the sense that it is deprived of both state-like sanctions and the legitimacy of a constituent process and body. In yet another and stronger version, 'integration by law' points to the autonomy of legal developments from the will of nation-states and to the autonomous *causal* role of legal order in promoting integration. Weiler speaks of the 'systemic evolution of Europe' as the result of 'the self-created and internally sustained power of law': Weiler, 'The Transformation of Europe', 2428. For a discussion of legal theories about European integration see Joerges, 'Taking the Law Seriously'; Burley, A.-M. and Mattli, W., 'Europe before the Court: a political theory of legal integration', *International Organization*, 47 (1993), 41–76; Stone and Brunell, 'Constructing a Supranational Constitution'.

[44] Note, however, that member states overturned the ECJ rulings with secondary legislation in the case of the exportability of supplementary pensions rights and the exclusion of EU migrants from particular social security benefits. This left them vulnerable to judicial overrule on the basis of the treaties. However, in this case, a migrant with this precise claim failed to convince the ECJ, which chose to legitimate the linking of particular benefits to permanent residence within the granting community, regardless of the discriminatory effects that this would have on migrants. See Conant, L., 'Contested Boundaries. Citizens, States, and Supranational Belonging in the European Union', in J. Migdal (ed.), *Boundaries and Belonging: States and Societies in the Struggle to Shape Identities and Local Practices* (Cambridge: Cambridge University Press, 2004), 284–317.

vis-à-vis each other. Particularly the continental lower judiciary, with a record and tradition of marginal participation in the lawmaking, has been attracted by the challenge of a more prominent role than previously envisaged or allowed by its hierarchical national superiors, and which is instead foreseen by the European lawmaking process. In addition, institutional rules prevent national politicians from sanctioning either national courts or the European Court. In this field, the institutional alliance between lower national courts and the European court, together with the support of academic circles and of the national judicial corporations was a factor of success. Finally, an additional element is that the ECJ activism that took place up to the mid-1980s occurred in a context of weakness of the other institutions. The European Council was only beginning to become institutionalized; the Parliament was still marginal; disagreements among member states were rife. The ECJ stepped in this vacuum. It is likely that, as counterbalancing powers are strengthened, the role of the ECJ will be correspondingly muted.[45] However, the European legal system is already laid down, and is likely to prove difficult to reverse this state of affairs to any significant degree.

The long-term implications of this development are also widely debated, and, in particular, the extent to which the centralized administration of the legal system will bring about a movement of unwanted and unforeseen expansion into other domain. The claim for jurisdiction by the ECJ in market-making matters does not necessarily put into question or endanger the continuing sovereignty of the nation-state as regards the remaining areas of territorial jurisdiction. As Walker says, 'To the extent that such questioning does take place, it tends to derive from a confusion between and conflation of comprehensive sovereignty (legislative *Kompetenz-Kompetenz*) and interpretative autonomy (judicial *Kompetenz-Kompetenz*) and a consequential exaggeration of the significance of the ECJ's power to determine the boundaries of its own jurisdiction. To be sure, interpretative autonomy may be deployed in a controversially extensive manner, it may even on some views be abused, but an interpretation of functionally limited text, however expansive, remains an act circumscribed by an acknowledgment of boundaries within the terms set by a particular interpretative community, rather than a licence to expand jurisdiction indefinitely'.[46]

However, the most important question is not the actual extent of jurisdiction, but rather the direction and domain of such expansion due to the current institutional design and treaty content. This issue will be dealt with

[45] See Alter, K. J., 'The European Court's Political Power', *West European Politics*, 19 (1996), 458–87.

[46] Walker, N., 'Late Sovereignty in the European Union', in N. Walker (ed.), *Sovereignty in Transition* (Oxford: Hart Publishing, 2003), 3–32.

more accurately later on, when I discuss the current economic, cultural, and administrative and coercion boundaries of the EU system. It is, however, difficult to agree with the conclusion expressed in the previous paragraph when we consider the continuous debate within the Court on the definition of what is a 'service' or a 'good', and the possibility, in theory, to expand the list of the latter to encompass almost all nationally produced public goods. As the 'public' nature of a good is clearly the result of a historical definition via contending interest and political conflicts, the more or less circumscribed nature of the interpretative activities of the ECJ in the future is equally subject to the political environment (think, for instance, about the crucial definition/classification of health provisions and of pension schemes, whose outcome is profoundly affecting the fabric of national welfare states; see Chapter 4).[47]

From the point of view of this work, the most essential characteristic of the institutionalization of a centrally administered legal system is its impact on the customers of sovereignty: citizens, interests, and the substate territorial communities. With respect to this we can say that, first, the setting up of an autonomous and superior European legal order has considerably reinforced the internal engine of boundary removal among the member states, now constitutionally defined and defended. Second, the ECJ has made the EC law usable by individuals, businesses, interest groups, firms, and territorial authorities for them to obtain policy outcomes that might otherwise be impossible, or more costly, if they were to be achieved through national legislation or political pressure. It has given individuals, corporations and interests access to jurisdictional resources outside the framework of the member state where they locate. Thus, these doctrines have made it possible to directly consume non-national public goods, which, as a result, are no longer provided monopolistically by the nation-state or territorially anchored to it. Private litigants can request national judges to enforce EC law by setting aside national law, that is, to exit from the national adjudication system and the territorial jurisdiction without moving physically. This access to an external (with respect to the nation-state) adjudication body and the possibility of subtracting oneself from the national authorities in many important fields of economic activity is likely to feed back into the interest and ideological orientations of affected groups and individuals and to resonate on the internal political structuring of the nation-state.

---

[47] Not to mention fundamental rights as one of the most interesting possible future developments. In this area the opportunities for the Court to set precedents and to expand its sphere of activities depend on the inclusion of such rights into the treaties, as envisaged by the Treaty Establishing an European Constitution.

Competence Distribution

The member states sitting in the Council, the Union's institutions, and even key political groups disagree about three fundamental aspects concerning the institutional design of the EU:

1. Which policies should be dealt with by the EU (enlargement, deepening, etc.);
2. Which institution or institutions should deal with these policies;
3. Which decisional rules should be adopted by these institutions to these policies.

As these differences in preferences change over time and over topic, the institutional and procedural framework of the EU is continuously revised by new Intergovernmental Conferences (IGC) agreements and compromises. The competences of the EU are treaty enumerated and are decided by unanimous agreement among member states. However, as already described above, there are various ways in which the Commission, and even the Parliament, can foster the redefinition and expansion of these competences before they come to be formally enumerated in the treaties and various principles of legal interpretation by which the ECJ can achieve substantial similar effects. As a result, the competence distribution within each treaty configuration is contentious due to the plurality of decisional rules and to the complex definition of the legal statuses of acts. There is, first, the *vertical* division of competence within the nation-states and the EU. Within those areas dealt with by the EU's institutions there is also a considerable *horizontal* institutional competition between the Commission, the Council, and the Parliament concerning the definition of the legal status of the acts, the decision rules to be applied, and the role of the ECJ.

Vertical Competence Division

A momentous peculiarity of the EU treaties is their failure to institutionalize any clear-cut division of competencies between the EU and the nation-states. The historical treaties do not use the federal solution of itemizing those competencies that pertain to the EU, those which are jointly exercised, and those which are left to the exclusive competence of the member states. In this respect, the Treaty establishing an European Constitution (TCE)—if and when approved—innovates. It tries to clarify the vertical competence distribution by distinguishing the exclusive competence of the EU, the concurring competences EU-member states, and the three areas of the promotion and coordination of economic and employment policies, of definition of a common foreign policy, and of coordination, support and complement to the action of the member states. It states that any competence not explicitly attributed to the European level must remain at the national one. Note, however, that the treaty does not provide any new form of 'constitutional' protection for the member states' competences different from the consent of their respective 'governments'. Actually, it introduces new forms of 'flexibility' in the extension of the EU powers within the field of the EU objectives and also in the revision of the EU competence (Art. IV-7bis), making it easier for a unanimous Council to modify them. In this sense, the TCE is in line with the previous tradition, as it continues to define the defence of nation-states' competences as exclusively based on the agreement among their governments in the Council.

This ambiguity in vertical competence distribution has probably resulted from the continued desire to make it clear that the EU was not a 'confederal' or 'federal' state, but something *less* than these. However, with the expansion of economic and economic-related regulations (and with the creation of the second and third pillars), it has become clear that the market-making competencies of the EU are tending to cover a growing set of additional domains for regulation, as the EU's government expands its interventions and the economy becomes more integrated. This has, as a result, triggered renewed debates about the vertical distribution of competencies. Paradoxically, in fact, this unwillingness to clearly adopt a federal-type list dividing the competences, in order to show that no federalism was envisaged, ends up by exacerbating the question of vertical competence distribution.

The ultimate authority for resolving issues of competence attribution is the Council, which, in its treaty-making capacity, is unbounded by internal mechanisms, rules and procedures.[48] However, any important revision of the treaties is subject to the unanimity principle and to its inherent high internal decisional costs, which have been expressly devised (and accepted) to reduce the potential external risks of the decisions.[49] Moreover, national governmental leaders making decisions about competences find it hard to avoid making concessions to other EU institutional bodies or to other actors that control substantial resources (the Commission and the Parliament for example, but also the complex network of institutions and interests around the social dialogue, the regional funds, etc.). This increases the complexity of the decision-making to an enormous extent—even when there are clear and

---

[48] Although it is externally constrained by the ratification of its own national parliaments or referendum majorities when this is constitutionally required.

[49] On the balance between decisional costs and external risks of decisions see Buchanan, J. M. and Tullock, G., *The Calculus of Consent: Logical Foundation of Constitutional Democracy* (Ann Arbor, MI: University of Michigan Press, 1962); and Sartori, G., 'Tecniche decisionali e sistema dei comitati', *Rivista Italiana di Scienza Politica*, 4 (1974), 5–42.

precise goals involved—given that the Council needs to take these concessions into account.[50] In other words, at this stage of integration, the question
of competence distribution cannot be handled from a purely intergovernmental point of view.[51]

The decision to insert the general principle of 'subsidiarity' into the treaties
shows the difficulty of the Council in handling the vertical division of
competences. The history of this concept becomes useful to discuss and
evaluate its effectiveness and viability. Subsidiarity is linked to the history
of political structuring in that it attributes a strong and institutionalized role
to structures that are recognized in their autonomous sphere of competence.[52] Within the context of the European state formation, subsidiarity
points to a natural priority or prevalence of the rights of 'natural' membership groups (the family, the ethnic, or religious group), of interest intermediation structures (corporations, professional associations), and of peripheral
structures (cities, local governments) over the two principles of centralized
and unitary rule: absolutist and plebiscitarian rule, and their most typical
means, dynastic bureaucracy, on the one hand, and mass electoral politics,
on the other. The concept of subsidiarity contrast the general principle of
pluralism (by which people aggregate on the basis of their individualistic
preferences and options) in so far as it always requires and implies a high
level of institutional defence and preservation of spheres of autonomy and
self-determination for specific and identified groups or institutions. Finally,
note also, that, historically, subsidiarity was advocated by Althusious to
defend the right of the city-states within the empire, by the social philosophy
of Proudhom to defend the rights of declining social groups threatened by

With specific reference to federal systems see Scharpf, F. W., 'The joint decision trap:
Lessons from German federalism and European integration', *Public Administration*, 66
(1988), 239–78.

[50] On the procedural complexity and on the possibility and implications of choosing
among several procedures see Jupille, J., *Procedural Politics. Issues, influence, and institutional choice in the European Union* (New York: Cambridge University Press, 2004).

[51] This is described very well by Ruggie, J. G., 'Territoriality and Beyond: problematiz-
ing modernity in international relations', *International Organization*, 47 (1993), 138–74:
'That is to say, it is increasingly difficult to visualize the conduct of international politics
among community members, and to a considerable measure even domestic politics, as
though it took place from a starting point of twelve (or fifteen) separate, single, fixed
viewpoints. Nor can models of strategic interaction do justice to this particular feature of
the EC, since the collectivity of members as a singularity, in addition to the central
apparatus of the EC, has become party to the strategic interaction game. To put it
differently, the constitutive process whereby each of the twelve defines its own identity—
and identities are logically before preferences—increasingly endogenize the existence of the
other eleven'.

[52] For a review of 'subsidiarity' in different constitutional settings see Rinella, A., Coen,
L., and Scarciglia, R. (eds.), *Sussidiarietà e ordinamenti costituzionali. Esperienze a con-
fronto* (Padova, Italy: Cedam, 1999).

modernization; by the Catholic church to defend its privileges and rights from the secularizing and modernizing ambitions of the nation builders. In all these examples subsidiarity was understood and consciously pursued as the attempt by groups to 'institutionalize' their rights and competences when they were challenged.[53]

Within the complex cultural and institutional infrastructure of Europe, the principle of subsidiarity could have been defended on two solid grounds. First, it could be advocated as a means for protecting the diversity in Europe as a value and as a resource in itself. The protection of distinctiveness as a value in itself focuses on the protection of local cultures, traditions, and institutions; these should not be subjected to external standardization or to excessive uniformity, because they represent longstanding and embedded cultural traditions and solidarity links among people. In a second and slightly different mode, subsidiarity could have been invoked for the defence of differentiated solutions at the institutional and cultural level. These should be preserved because this differentiation is one of Europe's resources, an experimental laboratory for different solutions to common problems, in which cross-territorial comparisons, learning, and competition among different experiences can eventually help to identify the most adequate solutions to specific problems via spontaneous imitation-adaptation.

The Council, eventually, stole the fashionable concept of 'subsidiarity' out of its historically pregnant meaning and adopted none of the two possible ways to use it in connection with the protection of the European diversity. The principle of subsidiarity was eventually legitimized with the economic jargon of efficiency and achievement, turning it effectively into the negation of itself. The formalization of the principle of 'subsidiarity' took, in fact, the following form:

In areas which do not fall within its exclusive competence, the Community shall take action, in accordance with the principle of subsidiarity, only if and in so far as the objectives of the proposed action cannot be sufficiently achieved by the member states and can, therefore, by reason of the scale or effects of the proposed action, be better achieved by the Community. (Art. 5, European Community Treaty)

It is then specified as follows:

For any proposed Community legislation, . . . the reasons for concluding that a Community objective can be better achieved by the Community must be substantiated by

---

[53] On this concept see the interesting articles by Endo, K., 'The Principle of Subsidiarity: From Johannes Althusius to Jacques Delors', *The Hokkaido Law Review*, 44 (1994), 2063–1966; and Endo, K., 'Subsidiarity & its Enemies: To what extent is Sovereignty Contested in the mixed Commonwealth of Europe?' (Florence: European University Institute, 2001), Working Paper European Forum Series, no. 24.

qualitative or, whenever possible, qualitative indicators. (Protocol No. 30 of the European Community Treaty)

This formulation of subsidiarity in the Amsterdam treaty aimed at setting clearer boundaries to the expansion of the activities of the Community. However, it does not cut back the regulatory powers already accumulated by the EU on the basis of the treaties, the EU's legislation, and the ECJ case law. Second, the references to efficiency and performance in the text (leaving aside the unfortunate reference to 'indicators') runs against any definition of spheres of *guaranteed* autonomy for subcommunity entities. Finally, even if the text refers to efficiency and cost-benefit analysis more than to entrenched rights of autonomy, it offers no clear guidelines to allocate sovereignty to the levels. The principle that whatever is most efficiently done at any given level should be done at that level is so general and vague that it could, in principle, be accepted by a centralized hierarchy as a bureaucracy or even an army.[54] The standards for deciding about the 'efficiency' of decisions—leaving aside the issue that 'efficiency' depends on a prior value judgement about the desirability of preserving diversity versus ensuring uniformity—are so unclear that the text is unlikely to offer any guidance for making judgements about assigning authority to the EU or the national states. The ECJ, when asked to adjudicate specific cases in relation to this article, will therefore be left pretty alone in setting boundaries and modifying them. In case of a Court favourable to the expansion of the EU's powers to intervene, and of a Council unable or unwilling to agree on its limitation, the subsidiarity text could be actively used to further expand the competencies of the EU.[55]

More generally, one could argue that the EU treaties (including the future TCE, in my opinion) lack any reference to the protection of the European peoples/states as opposed to the European governments. We know that many decisions taken by QMV in the Council can substantially modify powers and competencies and usually be treaty ratified later.[56] The revision of the treaty defined competencies is the domain of IGC and of unanimity

---

[54] Shapiro, M., 'Subsidiarity as a Legal Standard for the European Union' (Florence: European University Institute, 2000), Conference Paper.

[55] The Treaty Establishing a European Constitution (TCE) will improve the operational definition of the principle of subsidiarity by giving to the national parliaments, for the first time, the possibility to express opinions on whenever they think that the principle of subsidiarity is violated.

[56] The rules for QMV envisaged in the TCE ask for a double majority in terms both of the member states and the percentage of the EU population. Art. I-24 refers to 55 per cent of the Council members votes, with at least fifteen countries that represent at least 65 per cent of the EU's population (the percentage of Council members' votes is increased to 75 per cent when the Council does not decides on proposals coming from the Commission or from the Ministry of Foreign Affairs of the EU). This is an important change. For the first time, even if in a mild form, a treaty includes a reference to the European people—and not exclusively to European governments—as a source of decision power.

voting. These treaty changes are subject to very different ratification procedures, from simple majority in national parliament, to optional and compulsory referenda, and these ratifications procedures are nationally determined and not set up by the EU treaties. Beyond this, it is assumed that the protection of the European people is guaranteed by the veto powers of their national governments. However, veto powers protect the governments from the decisions they do not want to accept, but poorly protect the European people from the decisions their governments take (or could take) unanimously. The role of member states qua community of citizens could be protected much more and far beyond the formal treaty prescriptions that assign decisional power to the governments in the Council.[57]

Horizontal Competence Division

While the judicial power has come to be clearly defined within the EU, the distinction between the legislative and executive powers between the Council, the Commission and the Parliament is very far from being so.[58] It is hard to reach any clear understanding of the relationship between these powers and the institutions. This question was not important during the early phase. After the failure of the politicized profile of the first Commission's president Walter Hallstein in the clash with De Gaulle, the Commission maintained a very low profile for a long time, concentrating on establishing contacts with a large set of groups of interests and non-governmental organizations[59] and resorting to soft policy instruments (rules, recommendations, guidelines, and sheer practices) sufficient to condition economic and social interests.[60] Since Delors' activism, however, the question of the division between legislative and executive functions has become more significant, although it has remained unclear.

Even in its phases of activism, the Commission cannot be defined as the 'executive' of the EU. It has some of the features of an executive: (*a*) an administrative bureaucracy to prepare decisions and to monitor their implementation and enforcement; (*b*) a principle of political responsibility to the

[57] 'Ce sont donc des prérogatives d'Etat qui sont protégées par le vote unanime et non l'attachement des peuples à des intérêts ou des systèmes particuliers': Salesse, Y., 'Institutions européennes, déficit démocratique et interêt général', in L. Cartelier, et al., *Critique de la raison communautaire* (Paris: Economica, 1996), 35–68, 56.

[58] For a general appreciation see Lenaerts, K., 'Some Reflections on the Separation of Powers in the European Community', *Common Market Law Review*, 28 (1991) 11–35.

[59] See Mazey, S. and Richardson, J., 'Interest Groups in the European Community', in J. Richardson (ed.), *Pressure Groups* (Oxford: Oxford University Press, 1994), 191–213.

[60] These 'soft laws' have continued to remain an important component of the Commission activity; see Snyder, F., 'Soft law and Institutional Practice in the European Community', in S. Martin (ed.), *The Construction of Europe. Essays in Honour of Emile Noël* (Dordrecht: Kluwer, 1993), 197–225.

EP, which can dismiss it with a two-thirds censure vote; (*c*) it is, like all national executives, appointed by a different body (the European Council); (*d*) it does not decide but presents decisions to other bodies, as national executives do; and (*e*) it does not always have the legislative initiative, and, indeed, no national executive has such a monopoly. The fundamental difference between national executives and the Commission resides in (*a*) the latter's lack of 'constitutional competences' concerning the institutional architecture; and (*b*) its exclusion from vast areas of EU's decisions in the II and III pillars.[61]

Sometimes, the Council is envisaged as a second state-based legislative chamber, reacting to legislation initiated by the Commission, and sometimes as a branch of the dual EU executive. It functions as a legislative branch in those areas where it is charged with the final approval of the legislative initiatives of the Commission. Similarly, it has typical legislative powers to both initiate and conclude constitutional revisions. Contrary to national legislative bodies, however, there are considerable limitations on its formal right to initiate legislation in several areas. Seen as an executive, the Council(s) is even more atypical. First, it lacks an adequate bureaucratic infrastructure to process the heavy burden of administrative preparation of the decisions. Second, it is not appointed by a different body. Third, it does not refer to any other body for final decision in several areas. Fourth, its composition is fixed and made up by ex-officio members, rendering it politically non responsible as a body to any other body (individual members are responsible, but the Council as such is not). Fifth, the co-decision procedure implying the search for agreement with the EP resembles the legislative *navette* of symmetrical bicameral systems more than any other known executive-legislative relationship. It is, however, undeniable that the Council(s) is both, the executive and legislative of the second and third pillar.

Even the most recent institutional changes concerning the selection of the President of the Commission highlights more of a competition than a division of powers. Since Amsterdam, the EP has nominated the President by approving (or rejecting) the person designated by the Council.[62] This new

---

[61] The French doctrine and practice of *domaine reservé* in dual executives cannot be used to rationalize the enormous limitations on the Commission role with respect to the Council in the second and third pillar. See Blondel, J., 'Formation, life and responsibility of the European Executive' (Siena: CIRCaP, 2000) Occasional Paper 7. On the contrary, the idea of '*domaine reservé*' could be discussed in conjunction with those areas of Community competence where Commission's acts do not require the consent and approval of the Council and the Parliament.

[62] In the past the governments simply agreed over the appointment of the President of the Commission. Since Maastricht the parliament has had to be consulted. The TCE foresees that the European Council proposes the President to the European Parliament that approves by majority voting.

situation corresponds more closely to a division of selection power between the Council and the Parliament: they are both associated in the process of choosing of the President in an act of 'bicameral competence'. This may reinforce the impression that the President of the Commission is the head of the European Executive, resulting from the agreement of its two main legislative bodies. However, this change has also been accompanied by the Council's new power to appoint the High Representative for Foreign and Security Policy (who is also the Secretary General of the Council), thereby increasing the confusion of roles and competencies between the latter and the President of the Commission, who is in charge of many areas of foreign commercial relations. The Foreign Policy minister of the EU, while exercising his/her mandate in the name of the Council alone, has competencies and resources that are stronger and broader than those of the commissioners responsible for the external 'economic' relations. While recognizing the supranational nature of the first pillar by agreeing to lower its control over the President of the Commission, the Council has developed a new position through which to control other domains more thoroughly and with less dependence on the Commission. But this new institutional differentiation within the Council infrastructure also overlaps with some delicate dossiers of the first pillar too.

In this area, the pending reforms of the TCE are ambivalent. The treaty foresees the change from the rotating six months presidency of the Council to an individual presidency (that is, not a member state presidency), elected by the Council by qualified majority for two and a half years, renewable once and incompatible with other key institutional national roles. It also foresees the creation of the Ministry of Foreign Affairs of the EU, appointed by the Council with the agreement of the President of the Commission, functioning as vice-president of the Commission itself, and combining the functions of the High representative for Common Foreign and Security Policy with those of the commissioner for External relations. It seems to me that neither of these two changes goes in the direction of clarifying or strengthening the division between legislative and executive functions. If anything, the contrary seems to be true.

Therefore, the issue of executive-legislative relations and of 'executive responsibility' is immaterial in the EU at the present moment. Whereas there can be no doubt about the nature of the EP as a pure legislative assembly—and it is only the extension of its power that is discussed with respect to the Council and Commission—the definition of the Commission-Council relationship in terms of an executive-legislative relationship is impossible, just as it is impossible to squeeze the two institutions into the concept of 'dual executive', given their non-residual legislative capacity. In conclusion, the set of central institutions are differentiated according to the area of decision and the decisional procedure, and at the overall EU level, neither one or the other clearly predominates, nor is there an extra-institutional structure to harmonize their relationships (such as cross-national political parties would be).

It has been argued that the EU is a form of mixed rule where powers (and competences) are not, and should not, be divided according to executive-legislative functions, but between the 'stakeholders' in the system (states, parties, technocrats, commercial interests, and so on and so forth) which tend to organize as 'estates' did in pre-democratized Europe. These 'stakeholders' get together in varying combinations according to the tasks and the pattern of collaboration needed to fulfil these.[63] In other words, the EU institutional system is not based on an organic division of powers, but on a specific institutionally-defined equilibrium between the representations of different interests.[64] Even if one accepts this interpretation without entering into its critical discussion,[65] it still holds true that we need to examine the conse-quences of an institutional design in which executive-legislative relations are undifferentiated, considering that the Western world took two centuries to conceptualize the advantages of some sort of separation of powers, and to make it operational.

The most obvious short-term consequence of this is that, a very high level of institutional competition is embedded and unavoidable in the system. This can be seen in the vagary of the agenda setting, in the instrumental approach adopted towards the decisional rules, and in the complexity of the policy process.

The EU does not have a 'political agenda' as such. It is the competition that is intrinsic to the fragmented institutional setting that decides the agenda. The IGC, in its treaty-making power, is the overall agenda setter in so far as it defines the 'goals' of the EU. In the second and third pillars of the EU, the European Council and the other Councils clearly set the agenda. In the first pillar, the power of initiative of the Commission gives it the role of agenda setter within the frameworks of the goals decided and, sometimes, as we have seen, beyond these. It is, however, acknowledged by most observers that the Council, and particularly the European Council, increasingly also defines more detailed issues, thereby substantially, if not formally, encroach-

[63] Majone, G., *Regulating Europe* (London: Routledge,1996).

[64] Lenaerts, K. and Verhoeven, A., 'Institutional balance as a guarantee of democ-racy in EU governance', in R. Dehousse and C. Joerges (eds.), *Good Governance in Europe's Integrated Market* (Oxford: Oxford University Press, 2002), 43.

[65] I only note that 'estates' were highly institutionalized, while it is hard to identify the institutional locus of 'technocrats', 'commercial interest' and the like in the institutional structure of the EU.

ing on the power of the Commission. The EP's increased powers have also made it a co-setter of the agenda in certain areas. Even a cursory overview of the competence expansion shows that this agenda is sometimes dominated by events—like any national agenda—sometimes decided by the Council, sometimes the result of the capacity of the Commission to exploit the differences and oppositions between private and public actors and institutions, and sometimes dictated by the capacity of the Parliament to negotiate its support in exchange for policy initiatives. In this situation, the main central institutions and specialized agencies of the bureaucracies tend to solve the disputes about competencies and decisional roles by exploiting conflicts of interests and among interests to appropriate new resources, spheres of competences, and powers at the cost of other institutions.

The plurality and complexity of decisional procedures constitute the main feature and, at the same time, the battlefield of this institutional competition. It is customary to oppose two polar types of decisional procedures within the EU: the communitarian method—characterized by the monopoly of the Commission in legislative initiatives, the frequent use of QMV in the Council, the co-decisional role of the EP, and the uniformity of interpretation and implementation guaranteed by the ECJ jurisprudence—and the intergovernmental method—characterized by the absence of the right of legislative initiative of the Commission (but in a few sectors in which this is shared with the Council), the prevalent if not general use of the unanimity vote, the consultative role of Parliament, and the limited or absence of Court intervention. Two principles have also been laid down legitimizing the two methods: the communitarian method would represent the principle that the general interest of the EU is better served when all its institutions can exercise their different competencies in the production of the legislative output without any particular guarantee being attributed to any privileged interest. The intergovernmental method is, instead, based on the assumption that the general interest of the EU is better served when the interest of each single member state is protected.

Between these two poles, however, a series of mixed decisional procedures exists. The historical development of the activities of the EU is characterized by the constant move of issues and competences along this continuum, with the transferral of a sector of decision from the intergovernmental towards the communitarian method of decision, and vice versa. The intermediate space between the pure communitarian and intergovernmental methods is constellated by a set of complex and different decision procedures. The treaties' provisions, for instance, do not allow the procedures used by governments in their consultation and development of common positions to be clearly classified, so, while the Council can adopt up to twenty-five different legislative procedures, the Commission and its committee structure can use seven.[66] Only specialist lawyers and trained functionaries can follow the complexities of these different procedures and predict the politico-institutional implications of their differences.

The EP can be involved in decision-making with a 'co-decision' role which makes it de facto a co-legislator, and the list of matters subject to this communitarian procedure has been considerably expanded since the Maastricht Treaty. The early mechanism of parliamentary 'consultation' is still applied to agricultural policy and some other cases. The 'cooperation' procedure—where the EP can propose amendments but cannot overcome the opposition of the unanimity of the Council—applies to some decisions of the Economic and Monetary Union. The procedure that requires the Parliament's 'assent' implies that the Parliament can reject but not amend proposals presented by the Council and the Commission and this also applies today to agreement of accession of new states, to some international economic agreements, to issues of European citizenship, to the European Central Bank (ECB) mission, and to the Structural and Cohesion funds. There are, in addition, some other special procedures that pertain, for instance, to the approving of uniform electoral law (in which the EP also has the right of legislative initiative), and to the approving of the budget (in which the Council and the Parliament share roles and functions of a different kind).

The variety of decisional procedures has become increasingly complicated over time and it reflects the ongoing competition among institutions and the changing balance of power among them.[67] This is also shown in the growing contention over the definition of the legal bases of the EU's acts. The legal bases of each Community act, indicated in its beginning section, vary from sector to sector according to the content of the act and following the treaties dispositions. They define which among the many decisional procedures must be followed for its enactment, the majority required in the Council (unanimity, qualified and simple), the role of the EP (consultation, cooperation, co-decision, assent), and the eventual competence of the ECJ. To state, for instance, that rules concerning the trading of garbage belong to environmental protection rather than to free circulation of goods implies that the pure consultation procedure, rather than the cooperation procedure, be adopted. In other words, the definition of the legal bases of acts also establishes the balance of institutional power within the EU institutional setting, and is not surprising that it has become a contentious matter over time in which the role

---

[66] For a good synthetic summary see Hix, S., *The Political System of the European Union* (New York: St Martin's Press, 1999), 43.

[67] The TCE proposes to simplify the system of the legal acts of the EU reducing their number radically to only six: laws, framework laws, regulations, decisions, recommendations, and opinions.

played by the ECJ has increased considerably. For example, until the Maastricht Treaty, the EP did not have the power to appeal the Court against the legitimacy of the acts of other institutions. The ECJ has nullified acts vitiated by wrong legal base several times, and, in doing so, it has slowly modified the position of the Parliament in this area. In 1990, the Court recognized the possibility for the EP to initiate legal action for annulment and for failure to act against other institutions violating its own institutional prerogatives. The Maastricht Treaty formalized this power to appeal, while the Nice Treaty has taken it further, recognizing the EP's control of legitimacy (via appeal to the ECJ) over all acts of the EU. Thus, the EP can now jurisdictionally defend its own institutional prerogatives.

More generally, the different procedures concerning the role of the Parliament constitute an excellent example of institutional competition, to the extent that the changing role of one institution modifies the role of the others. Under the cooperation procedure (the predecessor of the co-decision procedure), the EP could only win over the Council if it managed to convince the Commission to support its amendments. Under the co-decision procedure, the Commission's opinion still matters, but ultimately the EP can reject a text regardless of its position. The Commission's proposals are subject to a bargaining between the Council and the EP, which are jointly responsible for legislative outcomes. Therefore, the co-decision procedure has at least the potential to marginalize the Commission. As a result, the Commission has resorted to new tactics to maintain its monopoly over legislative initiation: it can suggest and pass amendments on to the EP, which introduces them as EP amendments. Alternatively, under the co-decision procedure the Commission could side with the Council more often and more openly, although so far this has rarely happened. Finally, the Commission can more often revise its proposals in line with the EP's proposals.[68] Even the relationships between the EP and the Council are modified. The Council can act as a unitary and disciplined body, striking a deal at an early stage and putting aside national differences during the negotiations. If this does not happen, the co-decision procedure tends to foster competition between different alliances of member

---

[68] 'An illustrative example was the 1994 directive on open network provision voice telephony. The EP's conciliation delegation insisted on stronger consumer protection provisions, as well as lighter "comitology" procedures, then were offered by the Commission. The Council refused to budge on either issue in conciliation. Bangemann urged the EP to accept the directive, arguing that it was the best hope for liberalization in the sector. He also insisted that there was no chance of the Commission issuing a revised text that better suited the EP's wishes. However, after the directive was rejected by the EP's plenary (379 to 45 with 13 abstentions), Bangemann's bluff was exposed and the Commission introduced a new legislative proposal which was more in line with EP demands'; cited in Peterson, J., 'States, Societies and the European Union', *West European Politics*, 20 (1997), 1–24, 16.

states in connection with factions in the EP. When the largest factions of the EP manage to produce a cleavage among the Council's members, then broader political issues and alliances can become incorporated into the process of decision-making.

Finally, even the policy formation process reflects the high interinstitution competition that is alimented by the absence of a separation of powers. In the policy formation, there is an extremely complex set of linkages between the Council, the Commission and the EP, each surrounded by a rich network of committees. As the initiator of the legislation, the Commission uses a large network of consultative 'preparatory committees' (about 700) of experts and consultants from nation-states and interest groups (and, in some cases, regions). These committees are created, financed and presided over by the Commission's personnel. Once the Commission's proposal has been officially presented, accompanied by the opinion or/and amendments of the EP, the negotiation begins with the machine of the Council(s), with their main (about twenty) sector groups by policy area. The COREPER attributes the text to one of the approximately 270 permanent or ad hoc committees, working groups or specialized groups, in which the Commission usually participates. These structures are networks of experts from the national administrations. Once the new norm (regulation, directive or decision) has been formally adopted, the next phase takes the form of the regulation activity by the Commission within the range of executive competencies delegated by the Council. This also implies the mobilization of a large set of consultative, regulative and management committees.

The fusion and diffusion of legislative and executive powers and roles have, over time, contributed decisively to the erratic formation of the agenda, to the increasing complexity of the policy formulation process, and to the diversification and contentiousness of the legal bases and decisional rules of EU acts.

Unusual 'Constitutionalization'

Politicians, the media and even scholars increasingly use the term 'constitutionalization' and 'constitution' in reference to the treaties.[69] The term 'constitutionalization' originated from the international relations and international law scholarship milieu, referring mainly to the operation through which the ECJ created the European legal system discussed supra. 'Constitutionalization' therefore refers to the process by which the treaties of the EU

---

[69] Early on the Court of Justice has pointed to the EC Treaty as the 'constitutional charter of the European Community' in one of its cases (Case 294/83, Les Verts *v.* European Parliament).

(the EC Treaty in particular) have evolved from an arrangement binding only on states into a regime of judicially enforceable rights and obligations on all legal persons and entities.[70] It consists in the elimination of those discretionary elements concerning the EU as an international legal order and in the process of creating interpretative, application and behavioural uniformities through the activities of the ECJ, the national courts, and the treaty and secondary legislation texts. This has implied that what was initially conceived as a multipartite treaty has been progressively transformed into a constitutional document and basic law; that the ECJ has evolved into a Constitutional Court; that direct effects can be produced not only by treaty provisions, but also by regulations, directives and decisions under certain circumstances; that, as a consequence of direct effect and supremacy, the treaties are now part of the legal order of each member state and are applied by national courts. Community law is thus operative within the legal order of member states, and by this, it is argued, that the EU has transformed into a 'constitutional' legal order.[71]

However radically innovative this transformation might appear from an international law point of view, historians of domestic political institutions and of political thought are likely to find the labels of 'constitutionalization' and 'constitution' rather too audacious. A more detailed discussion of this point may help to clarify a few of the features of the EU constitutionalism/constitution that are strikingly unusual. Traditionally, on both sides of the Atlantic, constitutionalization and constitutionalism has indicated the idea of 'limited government'.[72] These terms referred to a set of principles aimed at limiting and circumscribing the previously unbounded and unconstrained powers of absolute monarchs.[73] And, indeed, the people that agitated throughout Europe asking for a 'constitution' between 1830–31 and 1848 wanted exactly some guarantees against the abuse and the arbitrariness of power; they wanted government limited by some general principles. The goal was thus to 'legalize' power by offering a special protection to specific liberties of the governed, and this is the substantive meaning of the term in the tradition that rests on the *Federalist* (1787–88), the *French Declaration of*

---

[70] Jupille, J. and Caporaso, J. A., 'Institutionalism and the European Union: Beyond Comparative Politics and International Relations', *International Review of Political Science*, 2 (1999), 429–44, 440.

[71] See for instance Craig, P., 'Constitutions, Constitutionalism, and the European Union', *European Law Journal*, 7 (2001), 125–50.

[72] For a review of this history see Sartori, G., 'Constitutionalism. A preliminary Discussion', *American Political Science Review*, 56 (1962), 853–64.

[73] These principles were generally 'written' but not always so, as the English case shows. At the same time, a great deal of what could be called the British constitution is in a written form (Magna Charta, Confirmation Acts, Habeas Corpus Act, Bill of Right, Mutiny Act, Toleration Act, Act of Settlement and others) although it is not formalized into a single written document.

Rights (1789), and the classic systematization of constitutional thinking by Benjamin Constant in his *Cours de Politique Constitutionnelle* of 1818–20.[74]

In legal terms, limited government and the limiting of arbitrary power were achieved (leaving aside here the political conditions that permitted this) through the varying combinations of three basic techniques: the bill of rights; judicial (and constitutional) review and control; and the vertical and horizontal separation of powers. In the Philadelphia constitution-making, the separation of powers took a radical direction, with a vertical separation of powers between the federal centre and the federated states, and a horizontal separation of powers among the central institutions of the Congress, the Presidency and the Supreme Court.[75] In the European experiences, the pre-existence of a centralized absolutist tradition and of strong executives meant that the division of power principle was mainly institutionalized in the balances between central institutions (mainly governments and parliaments), while the territorial vertical division of powers was historically less important (with the exception of Switzerland).[76]

I have argued above that a specific feature of the EU institutional architecture is the lack of a clear-cut separation of power and competencies between the EU and the member states and among the EU's central institutions, the European Council, Parliament and Commission. Government is not much 'limited' by the separation of competences.

Bill of rights were absent from the early treaties. The closest reference to something of this sort are in Arts. 6–7 of the EU Treaty where it is stated that the EU is founded on 'the principles of liberty, democracy, respect for human rights and fundamental freedoms, and the rule of law'. It is also interesting to underline the unusual disjunction between the fundamental rights, dealt with in a general way in Arts. 6–7 of the EU Treaty, and the European citizenship, regulated by the EC Treaty. It is true that the absence of a bill of rights in the

---

[74] Therefore, constitution/constitutionalism refer to specific forms of political power containment, not to the formal aspects of writing a proper constitution, regulating those matters that are more fundamental than others, attributing to a text the special status of a primary law source, or shielding such a text from transformation through the requirement of stringent amendment procedures. Elster, J., 'Ways of Constitution-Making', in A. Hadenius (ed.), *Democracy's Victory and Crisis* (Cambridge: Cambridge University Press, 1999), 123–42, follows this latter line. Using this criteria, however, the Soviet Constitutions were as 'constitutional' as all the others.

[75] See Fabbrini, S., 'Transatlantic Constitutionalism: Comparing the United States and the European Union', *European Journal of Political Research*, 43 (2004), 547–69. The rights to be protected (the Bill of Rights) were added later with the first ten amendments approved by the two chambers of Congress in 1789 and finally approved by the states in 1791. The amendments have increased to twenty-seven since then.

[76] This also explains why competition in the USA developed mainly along institutional lines, between federal and state institutions and between central federal institutions, while in Europe competition was more based on central political alignments between majorities and oppositions, political parties, and, in general, centralized political actors.

EU treaties has not prevented the ECJ from making references to them. In 1959, the ECJ declared itself as to be incompetent to deal with cases involving human rights, while in 1969 it stated that it had a duty to ensure that EU legislation was in line with human rights. In 1989, it went on to announce that it was competent to evaluate the legislation of member states with respect to the violation of such rights. This progressive involvement with human or fundamental rights was driven by the doctrine of supremacy. The obvious inconsistency between EU law supremacy and the national protection of fundamental rights pushed the ECJ into becoming increasingly active in its explicit references to those human rights, since it believed that otherwise there was a risk that the EU legislation would be nullified when judged as incompatible with the fundamental right recognized and guaranteed by the constitutions of the member states. This activism on the part of the ECJ, however, is obliged to make reference to rights listed in documents other than the treaties, which remain non 'constitutional' as far as the dimension of fundamental rights protection is concerned.

From 1999 onwards, an ad hoc Convention elaborated a Chart of Fundamental Rights, fixing a number of principles drawn from the treaties, the directives, the Community regulations and the jurisprudence of the ECJ, and at the Nice summit of 7 December 2000 this Chart was solemnly 'proclaimed' and signed by the presidents of the EP, the Commission, and the Council. Finally, the TCE proposes to give binding value to the Chart, inserting it in the second part of the 'European Constitution'. Even before its insertion into the TCE, the potential long-term unintended consequences of the Chart were object of debate.[77] Were its binding nature to be confirmed by the ratification of the European Constitution Treaty, these consequences could become more momentous. Of course, these fundamental rights do not protect people on the EU's territory under any circumstance, as it happens with national fundamental rights. The European fundamental rights apply to European institutions and member states only to the extent they apply European law.[78] Yet, it is the case that the final approval of the TCE would be a step in the direction of the EU fundamental right protection and that the likely unintended consequence could go beyond the original intentions (as it has happened so often with the ECJ activities).

[77] See Engel, C., 'The European Chart of Fundamental Rights', *European Law Journal*, 7 (2001), 151–70.

[78] Ziller, J., *La nuova costituzione europea* (Bologna, Italy: Il Mulino, 2003), 21. For example, the Charter declares the right to life and explicitly prohibits death penalty. Yet, the Union does not have penal courts, and it is unlikely that this European fundamental right could be invoked to declare 'unconstitutional' a death penalty decided by a national penal court. Of course, the resort to death penalty can be used as a criteria for deciding about new member countries accession or about sanctions against existing member. This, however, is a political criteria having nothing to do with constitutional protection.

Finally, the strongest sense of 'constitutionalization' refers to the trans-formation of the European legal system operated by the ECJ jurisprudence mentioned above. However, this judicial review is limited in scope as it does not concern all aspects of the treaties but only a subset of them: the core (first pillar) activities of the EU. Moreover, an additional non-trivial limitation should be added: constitutionalization is mainly limited to judicial review, judicial review is limited in scope to certain domains, *and* in such domains constitutional review is limited to a set of pre-defined goals.[79] This latter limitation requires further elaboration.

Constitutions define, at one and the same time, basic rights and duties, the procedures for selecting those who are allowed to take decisions, and the procedures for taking those decisions. As far as the substantive goals of the decisions are concerned, constitutions are normally salient or not very detailed. Most of their provisions are devoted to defining those areas in which the freedom of political decisions is constrained by higher principles. Outside these constraints, in fields where it is legitimate to do something, constitutions say little that is very specific about the actual content of what has to be done. Every area that is not constitutionally protected is, in principle, subject to political decision-making. In other words, constitutions define certain protected areas, and are procedurally oriented and goal inde-pendent in all others.

The EU treaties define institutions and procedures for taking decisions, but they are largely devoted to a list of substantive goals in specific policy areas aiming fundamentally at the formation of a common market on a continental scale. They include a large set of substantive goals, whose imple-mentation has, at this point, its own constitutional defence (in the ECJ). The areas where the EU has no competences are not defended or precluded by constitutional boundaries, but are defined negatively by mere omission. Paradoxically, the original definition of the Communities as having the target of a common market implied a very broad (rather than a very narrow) perspective on Community activities. Everything depended on what was defined as 'common market', and this was not specified precisely in the treaties. The definition was therefore left to political and intergovernmental agreements and no other means could be used to defend other institutions or actors from what the national governments could decide by unanimity.

---

[79] Therefore, in my opinion, to describe the EU as a confederal institutional arrange-ment and a federal legal arrangement (Weiler, J. H. H., 'Federalism without Constitution-alism: Europe's Sonderweg', in K. Nicolaidis and R. Howse (eds.), *The Federal Vision. Legitimacy and Levels of Government in the United States and the European Union* (Oxford: Oxford University Press, 2001), 54–70, 58) seems to go too far. The legal arrangement is federal only in so far as the building of the market is concerned, and this should be sufficient at least to qualify this 'federalism'.

Constitutionalizing the treaties has therefore meant constitutionalizing certain specific goals. In this sense, the constitutionalization of the treaties has 'frozen' certain specific goals by shielding them from political redefinition. This situation is normal for a goal-oriented international organization. However, it cannot be labelled a constitutionalization process without manipulating of the meaning of the term unduly. That is, a judicial protection of the market is both too 'unlimited'—as the sphere of what a market is cannot be defined precisely—and too limited—as it predefines a substantive goal—to be the sole basis of a 'constitution' or a 'constitutionalization' process.

In conclusion, what is called 'constitutionalization' has been limited so far to judicial review, to the area of market transactions and related issues, and to specific predefined goals in this area. The treaties were not devised as a constitution, and they did not therefore include those features that are typical of these, and included many elements that are not. We have now a constitutional court for a non-constitutional text. Private and public actors have been constitutionally empowered, but only with respect to a predefined set of goals. At the least, it can be claimed that this is an 'unbalanced' form of constitutionalization. In terms of the specific aim of this work, the 'constitutionalization' concerns the internal boundary-removing role of the EU, while it has probably a negative impact on its external boundary-setting capacity.

The nature of treaty constitutionalization is not only a terminological issue, although words usually carry a strong ideological weight. The key problem is that in defining the peculiarities of the EU central institutional order, the term 'constitutionalization' creates confusion over what these peculiarities are. The unbalanced 'constitutionalization' that we see in the case of the EU is an exceptional developmental particularity for international treaties, and has rightly been underlined as such by international law scholars. However, when we examine the process from the point of view of the formation and consolidation of the new European central hierarchy, its particularity is not 'constitutionalization', but, on the contrary, a very clear lack of this. There is a noticeable lack of clear provisions for limited government, there is no vertical or horizontal separation of powers, and, finally, only a weak net of protections for citizens exist in areas other than those of their capacities as economic agents.

Uncertain Legitimation

The analysis of legitimacy as the likelihood that 'collectivized' decisions—taken by somebody for somebody else—will be abided by the somebody else in question even if the decisions are disliked and costly, has proven to be empirically elusive. In this theoretical connotation, legitimacy manifests its crucial role only in extreme situations and, usually, can only be evaluated ex-post. For this reason, most of the debates about 'legitimacy' concentrate on a more manageable definition that understands legitimacy as the principles and procedures through which it can be rationally argued that collectivized decisions must be accepted by those who have not participated in them, or, while participating, have not had their preference satisfied. This latter definition is amenable to a debate about legitimacy in the absence of hard evidence about the likelihood of obedience.

Two solid consequences derive from this. First, legitimacy is unnecessary and immaterial whenever decisions are not collectivized; that is, when the actors concerned and affected are left with exit options—with the possibility to avoid the application and consequences of the decisions. Second, legitimacy is equally unnecessary and immaterial when decisions are based on the direct participation of the actors that are concerned and affected, that is, when collectivized decisions are, in fact, collective decisions. The most extreme case of this is when decisions are unanimous and actors have an effective veto power on disliked decisions. In short, legitimacy problems emerge only in conditions of no exit or no unanimity.

That said, one could stop any debate on legitimacy and the EU. The EU does not require any additional legitimacy beyond that indirectly offered by the voluntary consent of the member states and the ratification processes of their national parliaments. To the extent that the EU is based on the voluntary agreement of member states to participate, it leaves a constant option to exit open for all members, it allows partial exits, opt outs, variable geometries and the like, it resorts on many issue to unanimity voting and/or to mechanism of disproportionate weights, so legitimacy is immaterial within the EU and there is little need to discuss it. The EU does not lack legitimacy; it is not insufficiently legitimate. It is simply *alegitimate* in the sense that the problem is irrelevant to its decision-making.

This being the case, the need for legitimacy and the jargon of legitimacy should be used only by those actors and institutions that aim at widening the scope of the collectivized decisions within the EU that are not based on the exit options and/or the unanimous consent of the affected and concerned actors. It is no coincidence that it is the Commission that often resorts to this conceptual tool and jargon: the concern that it has expressed over the problem of popular knowledge and interest and popular identification with the EU (the last and clearest example of this being the White Book on Governance), its continuous attempts to shape a popular perception of the EU (from the Tindemans report to the rising rhetoric of the 'citizens of Europe', of 'Europe of the people'), the emphasis that it places on educational exchange programmes, its project to rewrite the history(ies) of Europe, to assist 'European' media, and even the successfully steeling of the Council of Europe's twelve-starred emblem in order to use it first as the official logo and then as the official flag , etc. All this can be interpreted and explained as the understandable need of the supranational hierarchy to sustain and advertise its legitimacy, in order to increase its collectivized political production and to limit the exit options and veto powers of the signing member states.

However, reference to only the needs of the central techno-bureaucracy to have its role and scope of action accepted cannot entirely account for the success with which the 'legitimacy' rhetoric has spread across all the European milieus, media and experts. Three other developments have helped this issue to gain a wider public forum. First, the spreading of QMV in the Council(s) is obviously transforming genuinely collective decisions (under unanimity) into collectivized decisions that some member states have to accept even if they do not support them. Second, the transformation of the EP from a consultative body composed of national delegations into a directly elected assembly with growing legislative powers in several fields has also broadened the scope of legitimacy issues. Third, even the 'constitutionalization' process discussed in the previous section and the role of the ECJ has widened the area of decisions for which the issue of legitimacy is relevant. In all these three cases, decisions are no longer unanimous and exit options are tending to be progressively reduced. At this stage, legitimacy issues have indeed become legitimate.

Taking the lead from this conclusion, a position argues that legitimacy problems can only be solved by 'democratizing' the EU, via the introduction of political electoral responsibility for those who take decisions. This implies an extensive reform of the institutional architecture of the EU and has triggered a debate about which reforms would be more capable of strengthening the political responsibility of the European elites and, thereby, the legitimacy of their choices. There is also a growing debate about both the feasibility and the desirability of political representation and political responsibility within the EU, a debate that often touches on the theoretical issue of the possibility of supranational democracy. I do not intend here to examine the challenges of this debate. More simply I would accept that 'political legitimacy' can only be achieved via electoral political responsibility of the top executive and legislative deciders, and, independently of whether this is possible, desirable, or necessary, I agree with the 'democratic deficit' school that, from an observational point of view, such legitimacy simply does not exist at the European level. This conclusion also cuts the debate short and leaves the field wide open to constitutional engineers and their proposals. At the factual level, we are left to conclude that there are some good reasons for believing that mere intergovernmental indirect legitimacy—if we want to label it like this—is likely to be insufficient to face recent developments, while the (national-type) political legitimacy is simply non-existing, even judging by the softest standards.

There is, however, a third line of reasoning about the legitimacy of and in the EU which is intermediate between the thesis of its irrelevance and that of its deficit. According to this line, the above-mentioned factual conclusion does not mean that EU activities are deprived of legitimacy. As legitimacy is not necessarily electoral political legitimacy, it is claimed that other forms of legitimacy that are specific to its own architecture exist in the EU. Since these activities are sustained by this 'different kind' of legitimacy, they should be viewed as legitimate in reference to new standards and criteria.

The origin of this 'alternative' view of legitimacy was national. Governance theory is a search for new procedures and institutional settings that guarantee interested and affected parties the chance to participate in relevant sectoral decision processes.[80] Originally, governance structures and procedures were presented as capable of improving the effectiveness of policy implementation, by limiting the capacity of resource controllers to boycott or otherwise impede successful policy implementation. They were envisaged as functioning only in limited and sectoral policy areas, remote from the broader concerns of public opinion. Slowly, however, the widening of their scope and range has rendered them less interstitial, and over time they have been presented as a new principle of legitimacy, with the arguments that the involvement of the interested and affected actors is a source of legitimacy. From here, the argument has developed to suggest that these structures and procedures are, indeed, a form of 'political legitimacy' of its own, and that the decisions stemming from them are the most legitimate that can be achieved in the sectoral domain. Finally, a further shift of the reasoning concludes that traditional forms of political democracy heavily—although never exclusively—anchored to the partisan-electoral-legislative process can be effectively substituted by these new structures and procedures in various decisional fields.

Sharpf has followed this line of argument more thoroughly than others, proposing the distinction between 'input-oriented' and 'output-oriented' legitimacy. This distinction was initially expressed in the following terms: output-oriented legitimacy is based on the maximization of common welfare and in the fair allocation of the costs and benefits of decisions; it depends on negotiations and exchange; it is based on the intrinsic quality of the outcome for all parties. Input-oriented legitimacy instead involves the democratic accountability of decision-makers and is, in principle, procedural, that is, it is unrelated to any costs and benefits calculation by the parties.[81]

---

[80] For a review of the origins of governance theory see Mayntz, R., 'Politische Steuerung: Aufstieg, Niedergang und Transformation einer Theorie', in K. V. Bayme and C. Ogge (eds.), *Politische Theorien in der Ära der Transformation* (Opladen: Westdeutscher Verlag, 1996), 148–68.

[81] In Scharpf, F. W., *Demokratietheorie zwischen Utopie und Anpassung* (Konstanz: Universitätsverlag, 1970).

Scharpf has extended the distinction between 'input' and 'output' legitimacy to the EU.[82] He suggests that not all policies require input-oriented legitimacy. Only thick identities and the majority principle can lead to social and/or spatial redistribution decisions that would not otherwise be acceptable. The EU does not enjoy this kind of identity and its institutions cannot sustain a legitimacy based on inputs and on decision-making by majority rules of citizens or even countries. However, more restricted and narrow range problems and issues like those of regulatory policies can be based on output-oriented, efficiency-based legitimacy, even if they have a legitimation force which is more limited and contingent than that of the majority democracy based on identity. Legitimacy by outputs is based on less demanding preconditions, it can tolerate multiple identities, has a more limited scope, and is based on 'interests' rather than 'identities'—and as 'interests' are supposed to be highly negotiable, there is no need to assume the existence of a high level of solidarity in the group. All interests have to be taken into consideration in the definition of the 'public interest', while making sure that the costs and benefits of the decisions in the name of the public interest are distributed on the basis of acceptable norms of distributive justice. 'Government for the people' (as legitimacy by outputs is called) bases its legitimacy on the capacity to solve collective decision problems that have a long-term rather than punctual decisional structures, and are multifunctional rather than narrowly specialized.

Scharpf mentions four types of mechanisms that can be used either alone, or in conjunction to sustain the legitimacy determined by the outputs. The first is classic 'electoral responsibility' that Scharpf, however, does not consider as a mechanism to express, transmit and channel the preferences of citizens on public policies, but rather as the 'infrastructure of political accountability'. The distinction is subtle—so subtle that it is difficult to grasp. Given, however, that at the EU level those who take the most important decisions do not have any direct electoral responsibility, we do not need to pursue this point any further. The second mechanism for output-oriented legitimacy is 'corporatist and intergovernmental agreements': negotiated agreements concerning macroeconomic management and or the determination and control of rule application in certain domains. The third mechanism is that of the resort made to independent expertise: to remove some policy choices from the control of elected officials and central bureaucracies and giving such control to independent bodies of 'experts', insulated from public debates and electoral accountability. The fourth 'mechanism' is based on 'public policy pluralist networks', and it involves a largely informal

---

[82] I refer here to Scharpf, F. W., *Governing Europe. Effective and Democratic?* (Oxford: Oxford University Press, 1999), Chapter 1.

process of exchange of information and critical appraisal of different options with an open access (not restricted to major representative organizations) to concerned interests that contribute to the elaboration of public policies. In short, corporatist negotiated orders, independent experts, agencies and networks of concerned actors may generate a special kind of legitimacy for the EU acts based on the output quality of the process.

This framework is sophisticated, but, on close inspection does not manage to meet the challenge that the concept of legitimacy poses. Let's start from the basis of the argument. The point that 'output legitimacy' is less demanding and requires a thinner identity basis because the scope of its decision is limited and restricted is self-defeating. Output legitimacy is bounded in scope because it excludes those issues that would require identity and solidarity to be successfully solved through 'input legitimacy' from the decision-making process. If, however, the scope of decisions is limited to what the actors themselves regard as 'decidable', then output legitimacy can be said to exist simply because it avoids those decisions for which legitimacy is normally required, and only deals with those issues that require the specific consensus and agreement of the sides concerned. This is not 'another' or 'different' or 'lower' legitimacy; it is simply generalized consensus and agreement, which is what is necessary for decisions to be taken when there is an absence of legitimacy.

The logic of 'corporatist and inter-governmental agreements' rightly points to an 'output-based legitimacy'. However, this mechanism is open to two interpretations: (*a*) the decisions stemming from these agreements are legitimate because the actors concerned have all been consulted/involved (and are more likely to adhere rather than to boycott); or (*b*) the decisions so reached are legitimate because they are more 'effective', that is, they achieve the goals better and more frequently than those decisions that are arrived at without corporatist negotiation. If the 'output legitimacy' of these negotiated agreements derives from the involvement of all the affected partners—the first interpretation—then the legitimacy arrived at is based on a special 'input' rather than on output: the input of affected interest controlling key resources rather than the input of all citizenry under conditions of political equality. Even in this case decisions are legitimated by the input, even if this input is different from that of majoritarian decision-making in legislative assemblies. Even more important, if the specificity of this legitimacy is the participation of all (or almost all?) the affected interests, the need for legitimacy is actually reduced, as we have seen in the elementary rule that the more inclusive the input, the less necessary any legitimacy of the output.

If the 'output legitimacy' of these negotiated agreements derives from their effectiveness in reaching the goals—the second interpretation—in what way does the effectiveness of the policies increases their legitimacy in the eyes of those who have not taken part in defining of the goals? One needs to postulate that, the goals of these arrangements being accepted and appreciated by the public, the gain in effectiveness obtained by corporatists/intergovernmental agreements will produce legitimacy. But again, if the goals are accepted and appreciated, the problem of legitimacy is already resolved *ex ante*.

Independent expertise and bodies of 'experts' form the third typical mechanism and source of output-oriented legitimacy. Competence is a well-established principle of authority and source of legitimacy. It is based on the recognition of strong asymmetries of knowledge and experience and on the acceptance of the requirements that stratify access to the credentials for them.[83] Competence aims to achieve 'efficient' decisions (as different from effective implementation). We all prefer the decisions concerning the safety of our sea journeys to be taken by the ship's captain, rather than by majority decisions of the passengers or by negotiations among representatives of the officers, crew and paying travellers. However, the competence principle applies well, and is indeed 'legitimated', in matters where individual values and interests are easily generalizable (as is the interest to survive, be healthy, be safe, etc.) and which, as such, are 'pre-defined'. It is far less acceptable in those areas where the public interest is more difficult to define and the individual is regarded as the best judge of its own interests and values.[84] Majone takes the radical view that in the sphere of technically complex 'efficiency issues', the delegation of decision-making powers to independent experts is justified and does not require any further legitimation, and that 'efficiency' for certain issues is more important than democracy. On this view, competence, expertise, procedural rationality, transparency, accountability by results, etc. are sufficient to legitimize the EU and to justify the delegation of necessary powers.[85]

This elegant formulation only circumvents the problem of who should 'legitimately' decide which are the efficiency issues, what they are and how they should be decided. It is likely that people have different opinions about these matters, and, in certain critical circumstances, that these may become very intense preferences. The solution not to investigate these preferences and to insulate efficiency debates among experts from any political pressure

---

[83] Note, incidentally, that even in the most obvious cases of generalizable public interests the credentials of competence and the mechanisms to access those credentials can be challenged and rejected.

[84] Dahl calls this principle 'personal choice'; Dahl, R. A., *After the Revolution? Authority in a Good Society* (New Haven, CT: Yale University Press, 1970), 8.

[85] Majone, G., *Regulating Europe* (London: Routledge, 1996); Majone, G., 'Europe's "Democratic Deficit": The Question of Standards', *European Law Journal*, 4 (1998), 5–28; Majone, G., 'The Regulatory State and its Legitimacy Problems', *West European Politics*, 22 (1999), 1–24.

may well be an excellent idea—although it is not a new one. It may also work in favourable times and circumstances. However, it has nothing to do with legitimacy as defined above. This line of argument assumes that some issues, given their technicality or complexity, are surrounded by some sort of general consensus on the goals to be achieved and by the incompetence about the means to do so, and that this general consensus (about efficiency, for instance) can be reached without asking anybody about it. By assuming that preferences do not need to be ascertained, the political predicament at the heart of the legitimacy issue disappears and loses relevance. As such, the competence/efficiency formula is a sophisticated removal and avoidance of the legitimacy problem, not a different solution to it.

The fourth 'mechanism' is that of the 'public policy pluralist networks'.[86] The legitimizing aspect of policy networks is deemed to be that of associational pluralism and the process of deliberation and public discussions that allow 'generalizable interests' to be defined consensually. Scharpf notes that public policy networks tend to describe the informal interaction models that precede, accompany or follow formal decisions rather than the formal institutions of decision-making. The argument rests on the idea that network interactions eventually improve the quality of public policy choices. In my opinion, however, it is not clear and specified how these networks contribute to the output legitimacy of the eventual political decisions in the eyes of the public and beyond the scope of those who participate in them.

In conclusion, if output legitimacy is meant to generate the support of those affected and concerned actors who directly or indirectly participate or who are consulted by corporatist negotiations, independent bodies and public networks, then we do not need to abuse the concept of legitimacy to understand what is, quite simply, specific consent. If the output-oriented legitimacy extends from concerned and participating interests to broader publics, then the proposition is tenable. It is not clear, however, how the mechanisms discussed above can achieve this extension. The little we know about general public appreciation and reaction to the outputs of the EU leaves some room for doubt about this kind of legitimacy, and the frantic abuse of this term in relation to the EU points in the same sceptical direction.

In Table 3.2 I summarize the various principles of legitimation discussed above. For each of them there is a principle of input legitimacy based on who is allowed to take part in the decision, and there is also a principle of output legitimacy. Note that, for the sake of simplifying the table, I have decided to put the 'umpire' source of legitimacy together with the 'competence' source

---

[86] For an assessment of the importance of 'networks' and of 'network governance' within the EU see Kohler-Koch, B. and Eising, R. (eds.), *The Transformation of Governance in the EU* (London: Routledge, 1999), in particular the introduction by the editors, 3–13.

TABLE 3.2. *Legitimacy sources for decisions under no exit option and no unanimity requirement*

	Political responsibility	Corporatist orders	Independent bodies/ authorities Umpires/judges	Policy networks
General legitimizing principle	Political equality	Control of resources	Competence	Participatory deliberation
Input legitimizing principle	Participation of all citizens	Participation of relevant affected, concerned 'interests'	Participation of experts, litigants auditors	Open participation of affected concerned and interested actors?
Output legitimizing principle	Electoral victory	Effectiveness of implementation	Efficiency, impartiality, optimality of solutions with respect to predefined goals	Quality of solutions through deliberative selection of generalizable interests*
Resources exchanged	Vote, mobilization capacity	Implementation and enforcement resources	Technical and procedural, competence, information	Diversity of ideas/interests
Decision mechanism	Voting and majorities	Negotiation/deals	Majority and deliberative	Deliberative
Conditions	Some level, of socio-cultural equality, homogeneity, solidarity	Elites representing cohesive entities. (Consociationalism, neocorporatism, intergovernmentalism)	Strong asymmetry of knowledge Existence of rules external to the umpire Stratified access to requirements and credentials	Difficult to define
Limits	Excludes non negotiable issues	Excludes non-organized general interest	Requires predefined general interests	Difficult to define

*As opposed to egotistic equilibriums or institutional power impositions.

of legitimacy. There would be, however, good reasons for separating the two: while umpire legitimacy can only be accepted by making reference to pre-existing rules whose interpretation may be contentious but whose content cannot be changed in the case under discussion, competence legitimacy is not linked to rules, but it is based on recognized substantive expertise credentials which are applied to specific concrete choice situations.

All these legitimation principles, mechanisms and decisional techniques are operational at the national level and they complement each other in different functional areas. In no way do national democracies rest on the principle of electoral legitimacy alone.[87] What makes the (national) political legitimacy particular, however, is not the concomitant and parallel existence of these various principles and mechanisms, but, rather, the centralized convertibility of the resources that each of them exchange. As argued in Chapter 1, votes (and the principle of political equality) can be weighted against the control of implementation and enforcement resources of the relevant organized interest, and the latter against the former. Expertise and procedural competence, and genuine deliberation fora also play a role in specific functional areas that are predefined by other decisional principles and spill over their effect even outside them. The holders of different kinds of resources, the politicians and the voters, the bureaucrats and the interest representatives, the experts and the judges, continuously exchange their respective assets in a situation in which, ultimately, none of them can subtract itself from the collectivized decisions that fundamentally rest on the principle of political equality. These 'sovereign' political decisions are, therefore, not the essence of democracy, not are they the only source of legitimacy, but rather the guarantee of the convertibility of a plurality of resources and legitimacy principles.

From the point of view of sociological analysis it makes little sense to defend the normative model of political legitimacy for the EU and my presentation should not be read as such. This model is unlikely to be applicable to the EU and may even be damaging to its own activity. The point is convincingly that the national standards of political legitimacy are too high and inappropriate for the EU, which should be evaluated by the standards of other international organizations.[88] It is likely also that the distrust and mutual horizontal control among the member states and the competition between authorities in a composite polity represent powerful sources of inter-

---

[87] Stein Rokkan make this point crystal clear even in the title of one of his most interesting papers: Rokkan, Stein. 1975: 'Votes Count, Resources Decide': Refleksjoner over Territorialitet vs. funksjonalitet i Norsk og Europeisk politikk. In (eds) Ottar Dahl, Edvard Bull, Gordon Hølmemark, Per Maurseth og Knut Mykland. Makt og Motiv: *Et festskrift til Jens Arup Seip* 1905–11. Oktober. 1975. Gyldendal Norsk Forlag. Oslo.

[88] Héritier, A., 'Elements of democratic legitimation in Europe: an alternative perspective', *Journal of European Public Policy*, 6 (1999), 269–82.

elite control (which is not legitimacy, of course), or that transparency and access to information have to be considered as legitimizing aspects of the EU.[89] Yet, none of this makes a convincing case for the existence of 'alternative' or 'different' forms of legitimacy in the definition of the goals and major decisions of the EU.

In the context of the current EU institutional architecture, it is difficult to identify any other sources of legitimacy than the direct borrowing of national legitimacy through the governments' representatives. In the absence of a non-territorial source of political legitimacy, the other sources of legitimacy are self-referential. Decisions based on relevant actors participation, on independent authority impartiality, on policy networks and on techno-bureaucratic technical expertise, can hardly generate a different and new type of legitimacy for those outside the narrow circles of the participants to these processes. Past political formations have managed to survive under conditions of enlightened administration on behalf of passive and uninformed publics, in cooperation with affected interests. In these cases, the problem always was, and still is, how to enlarge the scope and reach of the political production of these polities in relation to the ambitions of their rulers and to the problem pressure of environmental circumstances. To abuse the concept of legitimacy generates the risk of miscalculating the extent to which true legitimacy surrounds the European institutions and their decisions. This miscalculation may lead to the overestimating of the capacity of the EU to overcome major economic and security crises—if and when they will emerge—particularly if it supports the idea that 'the area of effective European action may still continue to expand as agreement is reached on additional purposes and means of European action'.[90]

Conclusions

In this chapter, the centre accretion at the supranational level has been characterized by a particular combination of features. Extraordinary territorial expansion and legal centralization has been accompanied by continuous competence accretion—which has been very fast considering the relatively short time span over which it has occurred—and by the considerable integration of the national and supranational techno-bureaucratic infrastructure. These typical centre-formation features have developed

[89] Héritier, A., 'Composite Democracy in Europe: the role of transparency and access to information', *Journal of European Public Policy*, 10 (2003), 814–33.

[90] Scharpf, F., 'Democratic Legitimacy under Conditions of Regulatory Competition. Why Europe differs from the United States' (Madrid: Istituto Juan March, 2000), Working Paper 145, 20.

together with a persisting weak territoriality, an unclear competence attribution in vertical and horizontal senses, a partial constitutional empowerment of the subjects qua economic agents, and uncertain legitimacy sources. Although the techno-bureaucratic central elites are engaged in attempts to establish direct links with the European ordinary people, this configuration points to an 'elite consolidation',[91] resulting from an alliance and integration between national rulers (the national governments, the MPs) and the supranational techno-bureaucratic centre builders (in the Commission, the Court, the European Central Bank). The alliance between these actors is based on cooperation towards reaching shared goals, but also on institutional competition and mutual controls that take the form of persistent fused powers, unclear competence distributions, and weak legitimacy sources. Any attempt to separate the powers, distribute the competencies, and strengthen more direct forms of legitimacy more clearly, would probably upset the interelite form of control on which this consolidation has rested to date.

In Chapter 4, I will have a closer look at the political production of the new centre. This review will be selective and driven by the theoretical concern spelled out in the Chapter 1 in terms of boundary building/removing. I will focus on the main activities and policies of the EU interpreting them in the light of their capacity to remove internal boundaries and to set external boundaries to the new enlarged system.

---

[91] I borrow this term from te Brake, W., *Making History: Ordinary People in European Politics, 1500–1700* (Berkeley, CA: University of California Press, 1997).

4

The Political Production of the EU: Boundary Building and Boundary Removing

Introduction: Negative and Positive Integration Versus Boundary Building and Removing

In the light of the particularities of the new centre formation, I now turn to the analysis of its political production. The focus of this chapter is not on the content of this production per se, but, rather, on its significance for the general process of confinement of actors and resources within the new system. As argued in Chapters 1 and 2, every process of centre formation is also characterized by the setting of new external territorial boundaries and by the removal of internal boundaries. The political production of the EU will be examined in this perspective. First, however, I qualify the relationship between the boundary terminology and the widespread 'positive/negative' integration terminology.

The terms *'boundary building'* and *'boundary removing'* resemble the widely accepted terms of *'negative integration'* and *'positive integration'* introduced by Sharpf.[1] Negative integration, or 'market-making' integration, refers to those measures and policies that aim to increase the integration of markets through the elimination of restraints on trade and the distortions of competition, and which are almost exclusively concerned with the civic rights to enter into contracts. Positive integration, or 'market-correcting' integration,[2] refers to those measures and policies aimed at shaping the working of the

---

[1] Scharpf, F. W., 'Negative and positive integration in the political economy of European welfare states', in G. Marks, F. W. Scharpf, P. C. Schmitter, and W. Streek (eds.), *Governance in the European Union* (Sage: London, 1996), 15–39. The theme of 'negative' versus 'positive integration' is systematized and generalized in Scharpf, F., *Governing Europe. Effective and Democratic?* (Oxford: Oxford University Press, 1999), 43–83.

[2] Strictly speaking, 'negative integration' and 'market making' are synonymous, while 'positive integration' and 'market correcting' are not. Positive integration measures can actually be market making. See ibid., 45. This distinction is not crucial for the argument of this section.

market, that aim positively at social goals and regional imbalances, that concern the content and outcomes of contracts. Positive and negative policies of integration can be regarded as a specific EU-related case of the more abstract and general boundary-building and -removing conceptualization. However—leaving aside the evaluative overtones of the positive/negative terms and their excessive reference to the market (other types of boundaries deserve attention that are not included within the category of 'market correction')—I prefer the boundary terminology for two important theoretical reasons.

First, positive and negative integration seem to suggest two mutually exclusive classes, with legislation and policies falling into either one or the other category. On the contrary, setting boundaries means setting rules of exclusion (and inclusion); removing boundaries means the opposite, de-differentiating between groups and territories with inclusive standardizations. For a process of territorial integration involving two levels—the EU and the nation-state—the boundary language conveys the idea that at one and the same time, the process dismantles internal boundaries while setting external ones. What is boundary building at the EU enlarged level is, by the same token, boundary removing at the national system level and vice versa. For instance, the development of a European basic welfare ('positive integration') would be boundary building for external purposes (exclusionary), and boundary removing among nation-states, given the dismantling of national exclusionary rules. Monetary integration ('negative integration'?) removes the most important economic boundary of the nation-state, but the Euro and the Central Bank system set a powerful new external boundary. Competition policy (negative integration) equally removes cross-state economic boundaries but it is not associated with any setting of a European-wide boundary that can be used to discriminate the rights, privileges, and entitlements of the internals versus the externals. The European Court of Justice (ECJ) decisions concerning gender inequalities in hiring, salary, firing, retirement, and leave of absence ('positive integration') set a common external boundary on the European labour market standardizing the rights and duties of its members as opposed to outsiders, but they also remove internal boundaries and de-differentiate the labour markets of the member countries.

Second, positive and negative integration refers to policymaking actions and does not directly evoke the consequences for actors' structures of opportunity in a general theory of system confinement. The boundary language evokes different patterns of 'locking in' or 'opting out' options for the relevant actors and resources involved. Boundary closure and boundary transcendence in various domains relate more directly to the strategies of different actors/resources endowed with differential capacity and interest orientation towards the transcendence/closure of these boundaries. Therefore, the boundary terminology is more appropriate for a study dealing with the impact of integration on political agency and political structures at the European and national level.

In the sections of this chapter, I first discuss the two crucial and clear-cut boundaries of the economy/market and coercion. Following this, I discuss the setting of those cultural and administrative boundaries that most directly affect the system building; that is, that foster system maintenance by generating loyalty and reducing exit via the consolidation of a shared system of norms that compel the components of the system to stay within it beyond their mere instrumental and selfish calculations. According to the theoretical discussion in Chapter 1 and to the historical reconstruction of the nation-state experience in Chapter 2, the political production of the EU relevant for system building is organized into three sections, devoted respectively to the issue of European 'identity', 'participation rights', and 'social solidarity and sharing'. The concluding section summarizes the specific configuration of the different boundaries of the EU.

The Economic Boundary

The objective of European integration was the formation of a common market among the member states by removing obstacles to trade. This required fostering effective competition by allowing the free circulation of goods, services and productive factors (labour and capital). This, in turn, required the harmonization, or the mutual acceptance, of various regulative regimes impinging upon this free circulation. Eventually, the problem of a common steering for the macroeconomic policies also emerged. We can regroup the economic activities of the EU under these four headings: establishing a custom union; fostering effective competition by allowing the free circulation of productive factors; fostering the harmonization of regulative regimes functional to the previous two goals; steering macroeconomic policies.

Creating the Market

The abolition of internal custom rights was effective by 1968.The common external customs were originally set at the medium level of the four custom territories then comprising the Community (Benelux counting as one).[3] The

---

[3] The founders of the Community believed that the economic advantages of the custom union would be so clear as to overcome the political, sentimental and cultural resistances. See Tovias, A., 'A Survey of the Theory of Economic Integration', in H. J. Michelmann and P. Soldatos (eds.), *European Integration. Theories and Approaches* (Lanham, MD:

custom union also required the definition of common commercial policies for third countries. Common external tariffs and a common commercial policy were powerful tools to use in international political economy. However, their scope was limited internally by the difficult agreements among the members, and was constrained externally by the EU integration in the General Agreement on Tariffs and Trade (GATT) and World Trade Organization (WTO) international regulations, which were expanding to a growing number of areas and goods. The European commercial policy remained confined to the relationship between the regional custom union and world free-trade agreements, to the special relationships existing between the EU and certain developing countries (ex-colonies, Mediterranean), and to the relationships with the new potential candidates. The custom union therefore removed tariff obstacles to trade within the EU, but proved rather a weak new external boundary and a feeble basis for an external commercial policy dictated by the discriminatory interests of its member states.

However, the elimination of tariffs and quota had, by the 1980s, still given rise to only a limited economic and market integration. Paradoxically the 1960s and 1970s had seen both, the early attempts at common market formation and the very interventionist role of the European states to regulate the national markets. So, by the 1980s, the EEC was largely confined to the Common Agricultural Policy (CAP; see later), the iron and steel sector, and to some protectionism at the European level (the Multi-Fibre agreement), and notwithstanding the custom union the European markets remained largely fragmented by a number of commercial boundaries. New pressures for integration were generated by the economic stagnation, the concern about the competitiveness of European firms, and the worsening position of the European countries in international trade.[4] The emphasis thus shifted to checking the internal mixed economies and attacking the market implications of national regulations in the key areas of competition policy, technical standards, regulations, and supervision of financial institutions.

University Press of America, 1994), 57–76, 62. In contrast, economic theory argued that customs unions were set up for political, sentimental or cultural reasons, while being economically 'irrational' because of costly trade diversion. See Viner, J., *The Customs Union Issue* (London: Steven and Son, 1959; Johnson, H., 1965), 'An economic theory of protection, tariff bargaining and the formation of customs unions', *Journal of Political Economy*, 73 (1965), 256–83; Cooper, C. and Massell, B., 'A New Look at Customs Unions Theory', *Economic Journal*, 75 (1965), 742–47.

[4] For an excellent summary, Tsoukalis, L. and Rhodes, M., 'Economic Integration and the Nation State', in M. Rhodes, P. Heywood and V. Wright (eds.), *Developments in West European Politics* (London: Macmillan, 1997), 19–36, in particular 21. For data on the deterioration see Faugère, J.-P., *Economie européenne* (Paris: Presses de Science Po et Dalloz, 1999), 29–39.

The approximately 300 measures of the Single European Act (SEA) were aimed at freeing the forces of competition by removing the more complex and subtle obstacles to trade and by making effective (by 1 January 1993) the free circulation of all goods, services, capital and labour.[5] This required the removal of *physical* obstacles related to the stopping of goods at borders for their statistical data collection, Value Added Tax (VAT) application in the country of destination, transport licences control, etc.; the removal of *technical* obstacles related to norms aiming at quality, health, sanitary and safety control, fostered by passing from a strategy of 'harmonization' and common regulation to that of 'mutual recognition' of different countries' regulations;[6] the removal of obstacles deriving from *discrimination in the public markets* privileging the national offer to that of foreign producers (energy, water, transport, telecommunications, etc.); the removal of obstacles to the *free movement of peoples and capitals*.

The logic of the 'internal market' of 1987 differs from that of the 'common market' of 1957. The European market was no longer conceived as a means to connect consumers and producers beyond national borders within established productive structures. It instead became a tool to modify the productive structures themselves, in order to improve their competitiveness to better face the world market. The example of the complex implications of the free circulation of capital[7] gives an idea of what impressive operation of economic boundary removal across the member states was inaugurated by the new integration steps going beyond the abolition of tariffs and quota obstacles to trade. The typology of capital flows to be liberalized included (*a*) commercial credits accompanying trade and exchanges; (*b*) direct investments associated to the freedom of location; (*c*) personal capital movement (linked to the free movement of people); (*d*) flaws linked to the formation of a large European stock market (shares, bonds, obligations); and (*e*) short-term capital moving from one currency to the others. The free movement of financial services

---

[5] The SEA also introduced a qualified majority instead of unanimity for Council decisions in a number of fields (free circulation of capital, services, transport policy, cohesion and research).

[6] The Rome Treaty (Art. 28, ex Art. 30) prohibited all measures whose effect was equivalent to quantitative restrictions. The early solution was to fix regulations at the EU level that were valid for each state. In 1979, the ECJ (Chassis de Dijon, 1979) ruled on the 'mutual recognition' of the validity of foreign norms and regulations. Mutual recognition means that nation-states have to accept the regulations of other states as equivalent to their own. It is estimated that in 1996 about 20 per cent to 30 per cent of goods passing the internal EU frontiers were submitted to harmonized regulations, while the remaining exchanges came under the procedure of mutual recognition. Faugère, *Economie europé-enne*, 43.

[7] Foreseen by the Rome Treaty, re-launched by the directives of 1986–87, established on the 1 January 1990 (Art. 67 of the Rome Treaty; Art. 73*b* Maastricht Treaty; Art. 56 after Amsterdam).

implied that the financial institutions of a member state could open subsid-
iaries and offer services in another country under the surveillance of the
country of origin (not of the country of operation).[8]

At the operational level, the four market-making freedoms were accompanied by a renewed activism by the Commission in the field of Competition
Policy, directed against cartels, restricted agreements, abuse of dominant
position, and any other agreement that might prevent, distort or restrict
trade. In the early treaties, the behaviours fouling competition were sanc-
tionable, while the structural modifications of the market were not. Competence in this latter area came into being only in 1989, with the Merger
Regulation, after sixteen years of heated debate. As a result, the EU now
checks a priori the concentrations and mergers of large firms and corporations against the regulations concerning the emergence of non-competitive
structures.[9]

The Commission strategy for a more rigorous and consistent competition
policy focused first on cartels and anti-dumping, and later on state aids. The
Commission's monitoring of state aids[10] to big and small firms[11] is characterized by a high level of technical complexity and potentially high levels
of political discretion and contentiousness.[12] This complexity is due to the
actual definition of a 'sate aid'. Aids come in the form of government grants,

---

[8] The freedom of financial service is fundamentally different from the freedom of
location and establishment. The latter put firms into competition on the basis of common
and identical national rules. The freedom of offering financial services subjects the financial
institution to the regulation of the country of origin, and therefore to different regulation
than its competitors on the state territory. The difference is between competition among
firms under a single 'national' regulatory framework, and competition among different
regulatory frameworks. There are, however, measures to prevent 'wild' competition in the
name of the 'general interest' of the guesting country and minimal harmonization of rules
of prudence.

[9] See McGowan, L. and Wilks, S., 'The first supra-national policy in the European
Union: Competition Policy', *European Journal of Political Research*, 28 (1995), 141–69.

[10] The treaty has separate provisions of review and monitoring of state aids, derogating
from the general infringement procedures. The evaluation of state aids' compatibility with
the common market is performed by the Commission that decides on their adoption,
revision or abolition. The treaty distinguishes between 'existing' and 'new' aids and it
introduces a complicated but potentially robust monitoring process. See Lavdas, K. and
Mendrinou, M., 'Competition policy and institutional politics in the European Community: State aid control to small business promotion', *European Journal of Political Research*, 28 (1995), 171–201, 184.

[11] The introduction in 1992 of the first detailed guidelines on national subsidies to small
businesses partially reversed a tradition of minimal intervention in this area. The vast
majority of enterprises in Europe comprises small firms. Firms with less than 100 employees represent between 40 per cent and 70 per cent of total employment and 99.3 per cent of
the total number of Community firms. Micro-enterprises with fewer than ten employees
represent 91.3 per cent of all enterprises.

[12] See Smith, M. P., 'Integration in Small Steps: The European Commission and
Member-State Aids to Industry', *West European Politics*, 19 (1996), 563–82.

interests subsidies, research and development assistance, tax credits, exemptions and deferments, reductions in social insurance contributions, state equity participation, and loan guarantees. The Commission must obtain full information about the terms and purposes of aids: whether the aid is directed towards an economically disadvantaged region, is for research and development, is aimed at rescuing and/or restructuring an enterprise in financial difficulty or at helping to expand a strong enterprise in a dynamic sector, is a general business incentives or is to be used in a sector experiencing structural decline, or is to cover the operating losses of an individual enterprise. Not all state aids are viewed as illegal and the policy requires that each individual scheme be evaluated. In other words, the Commission must decide whether the aid meets legitimate goals or generates competitive advantages, and can make exceptions for aids to low income areas, to promote projects of common European interest, to remedy a serious disturbance in the economy of a member state, or when they do not adversely affect trading conditions. The ECJ case law in this area has become important for both members states and interested third parties.[13] The 'direct effect' doctrine provides for an action against the legality of an aid granted by a member state to be brought before the national courts.[14] Notwithstanding the efforts of the Commission, progress has been limited in the field of public procurement. Enforcement powers and the resort to the ECJ to make sure that national transpositions of Community public procurement directives create legal rights for aggrieved firms has not produced the expected effects, mainly because private actors have been reluctant to file complaints against states in this field.[15]

The independence of the Commission in this area is very high: it is not obliged to seek the approval of the Council or to be concerned by the EP; it must, however, consult the Advisory Committee on Restrictive Practices and Monopolies and the Advisory Committee on Mergers (both comprising officials appointed by member states), although it is not bound by their

[13] The Court uses the market investor's principle to judge cases, ascertaining whether a private investor would have behaved in the same way as the state (for instance, to give money to a sound firm with strong growth perspectives). If not, the case requires further investigation. The decision can become very complex, given the special arrangements that are allowed for particular sectors, like coal and steel (which fall under the competence of the Council), sector arrangements in agriculture, fisheries, textiles and clothing, synthetic fibres, automobiles and shipbuilding, assisted low income areas, and the German Eastern Länder (to facilitate transition to the market economy and privatization project).

[14] Lavdas, K. and Mendrinou, M., 'Competition policy and institutional politics in the European Community', 178. Note that the ECJ soon became overloaded with an increasing number of competition cases, and felt compelled to propose the creation of another Court, the Court of First Instance (CFI), charged with dealing with all appeals against Commission competition decisions.

[15] See Smith, P. M., 'States and Liberalization: Single Market Competition and its Limits', *Journal of European Public Policy*, 8 (2001), 519–40.

advice. Regulation 17 (1962), which instituted the Directorate General IV (Competition), also equipped the Commission with substantial powers for achieving its own goals: its agents can inquire and seize copies of relevant firms and companies documentation, can charge penalty payments, can impose fines as high as 10 per cent of the yearly business in question; and can hold a general inquiry into a sector area. In this policy domain the Commission is a federal agency whose powers are much stronger than anything that would be accorded to it today if the regulation had to be agreed *ab initio*.[16]

Competition policy therefore extended from the monitoring of firms and business behaviours to the monitoring of governments' conduct in their public markets and in their industrial aids and distributive policies, in the sense that the latter could be considered as affecting free competition within the enlarged market.[17] It is worth noting that for a long time the Commission industrial policy, aiming at the economy of scale that would have strengthened the European industries as against US and other giants, was somehow at odds with competition policy. The old strategy of the EEC was of a neo-mercantile style: the European economy could be promoted to international competition with the consolidation of a large and united market as a base for a reduced number of European companies. This was evident in the series of technology promotion and collaboration programmes (ESPRIT on information technology; BRITE on materials; RACE on telecommunications; EUREKA on high technology europrojects, high definition television, semiconductors, etc.). Other large-scale state-funded programmes included the European Space Agency and the heavily subsidized Airbus Consortium. However, this approach was increasingly undermined by globalization and by a growing cooperation between European and US firms in every field.[18] The new neoliberal environment of the 1980s fostered a widespread acceptance of the idea that more competition would in itself allow a number of diverse problems to be solved, including those of economy of scale and international competitiveness. On this view, to the extent that large scale was desirable, rationalization would be achieved with more competition and anti-trust should therefore be strong.

It is debatable to what extent governments were aware of the implications of this further step in economic integration. Paradoxically, the Commission's

---

[16] This is the opinion of Goyder, D. G., *Competition Law in the EEC* (Oxford: Clarendon, 1988), 36.

[17] On state aids see Lavdas, K. and Mendrinou, M., 'Competition policy and institutional politics in the European Community', 171–201.

[18] This has also given rise to a rivalry between GD III and GD IV, i.e., between competition policy and industrial policy, as the former can and will continue to be challenged on the basis of economic, industrial and political considerations.

use of its monitoring powers resulted from its making a virtue of the Council refusal in 1966 to adopt a regulation governing state aids in the Community. The unwillingness or inability of member states to offer a general regulatory framework for subsidization also allowed the ECJ to increase the latitude of its interpretation of the basic articles. The Commission and the Court, therefore, progressively refined the legal instruments and criteria of evaluation at their disposal and applied the treaty provisions expansively, with unforeseen implications. The ensuring of equal opportunities for competition thus curtailed national government controls without setting any comparable controls at the EU level, and the implications of this situation became evident only at a later stage. Until the end of the 1980s, the 'dormant' potential of the treaty provisions had made economic boundary removal slow, and subject to considerable national veto power and flexibility. However, in an extensive interpretation, competition and free circulation policies could be extended to almost all areas of activity for which an economic dimension can be identified (see later in the chapter for further implications of these principles). There are various principles for exception in the treaties that have proved quite flexible and responsive to the prevalent political and intellectual climate. On the whole, however, free circulation and competition policies are the kernel of the atomic engine of the integration process, an engine that it is quite difficult, even for the Council, to switch off or even to cool down.

The progressive focusing by the Commission (and the ECJ) on this wider range of 'obstacles' has radically modified the balance between internal boundary removing and external boundary setting. Unlike internal customs/quota abolition and external customs/quota setting (via commercial policy goals), none of the categories of obstacles to trade and fair competition mentioned above has had any implications for external boundary setting. That is to say, these policies opened European economies towards the international market as much as (if not more than) it opened them with respect to each other. In addition, also the main market-flanking policies of the EU differ sharply in the ways in which they achieve market integration and in the ways in which they set external economic boundaries in the process of removing the internal ones.

Agriculture, transport, environment, energy, and communication policies differ in terms of their levels of 'institutionalization', that is, in their levels of inclusion in comprehensive and formal policy frameworks, of more or less a precise legal treaty basis, and, eventually, of their 'communitarization'. However—from my point of view—these policies differ primarily in terms of the tension they express between the goals of perfecting the internal market and unfolding competition by removing boundaries, on the one hand, and the goal of achieving specifically aimed public goods by creating new external boundaries, on the other. The CAP is the extreme example of the creation of a European market (i.e. removing internal boundaries) by setting a very high external boundary and being formally exempted from competition policy. Transport and environmental policies are located instead in an intermediate position, with a more perceptible tension existing between the goal of achieving positive public goods and that of fostering the market via accrued competition. Energy and communication policies are located at the opposite extreme of market-making policies that open up national markets via accrued competition without setting external boundaries and defending specific political goals.

The CAP is a mix of a boundary-removing policy destined to eliminate the obstacles to a common agricultural market and of a strong external boundary-building policy. Together with its primary market goal, the CAP has specific policy goals that are politically defined and which explicitly foresee derogation from the basic guidelines of the entire EC Treaty (Art. 33 TEC): to improve agricultural productivity, to guarantee the life chances of farmers, to guarantee the stability of the supply, etc. To reconcile the free circulation of agricultural produce with the other policy goals, prices and aids are fixed by sector independently of the member state. As a result, obstacles to free movement are abolished by subventions and aids for everybody.[19] The CAP is thus a system of external protection of the market, which works through an increase in the prices of imported produces to guarantee the income of European farmers against the fluctuations of the international market, even if the principle of Community preference foresees exceptions through special agreements (Lomé, Mediterranean agreements). Together with this protection of the internal market, there is also an external system of incentives for the export of surpluses through subventions, which is—not surprisingly—highly disputed. The CAP functions as an interventionist and protectionist policy with a rich financial endowment and a colossal body of legal and jurisprudential work[20] that sets a high external territorial boundary to the EU against international competitors.

Contrary to agricultural policy, transport and environmental policies are not exempted from the competition rules, but are also characterized by attempts to achieve specific results, which are not necessarily market produced. Transport policy, in particular, is an interesting example of the difficulty of combining effective market competition and positive public goals in

[19] For a description of the original mechanisms and the reforms of the PAC see Faugère, *Economie européenne*, 182–99.

[20] At the beginning of the twenty-first century 45 per cent of the Union budget finances the CAP; about 4,100 normative acts constitute Community law in this area, that is, about 80 per cent of all Community law; since 1958 a third of the judgements pronounced by the ECJ have concerned the CAP.

the architecture of the EU.[21] The treaty legal bases set out the Community action to remove protectionist barriers and discriminatory practices that favour national vectors, firms and industries in the field of public and private transport (while identifying the possible exceptions motivated by public needs, as in non-profitable services to insular areas) by (*a*) increasing inframode competition among several firms within each type of transport (air, road, rail, and maritime); and by (*b*) increasing intermode competition, making different types of transport competitive with each other. However, together with the enhancement of competition, goals are also set up supporting a change in the current equilibrium among the types of transport in favour of mainly train, maritime, and river transports against others (mainly road).

Fostering inframode competition by dismantling the complex set of rules within each transport mode that allow the public provider to act in a monopolistic regime, opening the field to a plurality of competitors, liberalizing the public services of air, rail, road, maritime transport and harbour management are all goals that are consistent with the general competition-fostering model of the Commission activities.[22] The goal of intermode competition, however, brings about more complex considerations regarding market correction and market failure. The level of public subsidies given to the different types of transport needs to be evaluated and disciplined, and the social costs associated with its negative externalities to be attributed to each mode. Finally, the goal of intermode equilibration and shifts in favour of one mode as against another are even more difficult and complex.

The 'white' and 'green' papers by the Commission are full of suggestions and good policy prescriptions referring to the most environmental friendly and less energy consuming modes, to the negative externalities and social costs of the road transport in terms of health, security (accidents), quality of life, flora and fauna, artistic and cultural patrimony, consumption of physical space, acoustic pollution, damaging emission, traffic congestion, space occupation, and the indirect effects of traffic on the efficiency of economic activities in general. To foster the creation of a desirable European transport network, the Commission financially supports common interest projects, co-finances feasibility studies, and offers guarantees to cover loans,

---

[21] See Tebaldi, M., 'La politica dei trasporti', in S. Fabbrini and F. Morata (eds.), *L'Unione Europea. Le politiche pubbliche* (Roma-Bari: Editori Laterza, 2002), 193–221.

[22] The degree of success of this varies considerably, the most successful being in the field of air transport, and the least in rail, maritime and road transports. See the articles in Héritier, A. (ed.), *Differential Europe. The European Union Impact on National Policy Making* (Lanham, MD: Rowman & Littlefield Publishers, 2001); Héritier, A., *Policy Making and Diversity in Europe. Escaping Deadlocks* (Cambridge: Cambridge University Press, 1998).

favourable rates of interest and, in some cases, even limited direct loans.[23] However, the Commission does not have any particular instrument with which to really favour an intermode equilibration because such policy requires non-market positive advantages for one mode as against another, and, clearly, fostering competition as such does not offer any real guarantee of actually achieving the goal of reducing road transport to the advantage of other types. From this, in the absence of any strong support by the Council, derives the Commission's surreptitious attempts to justify such goals through technical and efficiency reasoning.

It is likely that the Commission milieus also expected to be able to pursue public good goals in the field of environmental policy, despite the weakness of the treaty legal basis for this. In need of an economic rationale to promote initiatives in this field, the Commission adopted environmental protection measures arguing that these were necessary to prevent national policies from altering the functioning of the common market. Between 1965 and 1973, when the first environmental plan was adopted, the Community passed measures regulating the emission of polluting gas, the classification of dangerous substances and several other regulations for other domains as well. Between 1972 and 1986, three Action Programmes were approved as non-binding documents. The most important step was the directive on the 'environmental impact evaluation' in 1985. The SEA (Title VII Art. 130r, 130s and 130t) introduced the legal basis for environmental policy, listing the goals of the conservation, protection, and improvement of environmental quality, human health, and a rational use of resources. It also introduced qualified majority voting for a number of areas of intervention linked to the single market formation. (Art. 95 ex Art. 100A).[24] In addition, it authorized member states to adopt environmental protection measures that could be more stringent than those of the Community. Following on the heels of this, there was a period of intense Community production in the area of environmental protection.

By 1992, the environmental policy was strategically redefined with a progressive abandonment of the regulative approach (criticized for too much standardization and for weakening international competitiveness) with resort being made to mutual recognition based on minimal harmonization and delegation to the states of the approval of the products.[25] This led to a policy based on market instruments and incentives and on voluntary meas-

---

[23] Some financial support is devoted to specific projects; other funds are within the Structural Funds, and in particular the European Fund for Regional Development.

[24] And with Amsterdam the co-decision procedure was extended to all environmental decisions.

[25] On the abandoning of the regulative approach in this and other domains see Héritier, A., Hill, C. and Mingers, S., *Ringing the Changes in Europe. Regulatory competition and the transformation of the state: Britain, France, Germany* (Berlin and New York: W. de Gruyter, 1996).

ures aimed at achieving results via the spontaneous adhesion of actors to public goals. Although the cases of very high risk continued to be regulated, other instruments began to predominate: fiscal dissuasion, voluntary measures to internalize environmental costs without losing competitiveness, measures to spread information, education, professional training, financial assistance for activities favouring environmental quality.[26] Ecological labelling and environmental audit are the most direct results of this new philosophy, according to which environmental protection is transformed into a factor of competitiveness. The slowing down of the regulative approach and the sizing down of environmental policy is the object of very heated debate, and the results promoted by the school of 'no regulation but incentives' are doubtful. Judging by the depression of the environmental milieus, these last are merely ideological and not concrete. These self-regulation measures do not seem to have produced anything more than symbolic results.

Finally, energy and telecommunication policies were never intended to be anything other than a spreading of the internal market and of competition policy in delicate areas of previously highly regulated and monopolistic sectors.[27] By 1988, the Commission had extended the internal market concept to include the energy sector, with a series of proposals for creating an Internal Energy Market (IEM). It also sought to achieve formal competence in energy matters to formulate a Common Energy Policy (CEP), going beyond the deregulatory nature of the IEM. At the beginning, the Commission lost the struggle to achieve formal competence through the drafting of a specific chapter in the treaty. At the same time, the ECJ supported the IEM orientation by ruling that electricity was to be considered a good rather than a public service, which, of course, brought energy under the competition law. Telecommunications were not explicitly mentioned in the treaty, and action in this field was based on their progressive incorporation into competition law, resulting in one of the liberalization-privatization success stories. By 1999, the liberalization was complete. Indeed, the first directive of the Commission in 1988 was issued without resorting to the approval of the Council of Ministers. Since then up to the most recent directive in 2001, which summarizes all the previous ones, the Commission has often followed this direct and autonomous procedure. The reason for this success is probably that by the 1970s–80s the technological gap with the USA and Japan was so clear that no state could dream of dealing with it individually, and it is also likely that US liberalization exported competition from the national to the international market.

[26] See the Molitor Report of 1995.

[27] My references are drawn from Matlary, J. H., *Energy Policy in the European Union* (London, Macmillan, 1977); Natalicchi, G., *Wiring Europe: reshaping the European telecommunication regime* (Boulder, CO: Rowman & Littlefield, 2001).

Managing the Economy: The Macroeconomic Policies

Policies driven by the need to establish an open and liberalized market set
weak boundaries for a European market. In an area of open trade and
undistorted competition, the boundaries of a market are mainly controlled
and manipulated by the instrument of macroeconomic policies: *monetary
policy* (monetary mass control, rates of interest, and rates of change); *budget
policy* as fiscal and taxation policy; *employment or occupation policy*.

Employment policy was inaugurated with the Amsterdam Treaty in 1997
and with the following extraordinary Luxembourg summit. The legal bases
for occupation policy are in Arts. 2–3 of the EC Treaty, and include the
promotion of a high level of employment as one of the primary goals of the
EU. Title VIII Art. 125–130 defines the goals and the general principles
inspiring the Community action in this regard. Art. 128 specifies the procedure for common decisions to achieve a coordination of national policies
and Community surveillance on occupational policy results. In this area, the
Council decides on the proposals of the Commission by QMV, in consultation with the Parliament, the Socio-Economic Committee, the Committee
of Regions and the Committee for Employment (created at Amsterdam).
Employment policy can hardly be considered a 'policy' at the EU level,
however. Forms of mutual surveillance are simply meant to bring pressure
to bear on member states whose performance in terms of occupation policies
are bad to adopt and imitate those solutions that have proved effective in
other countries, without resorting to legislation and binding decisions. There
are a few special financed activities (Adapt, Employment, Equal, Horizon,
Integra, Now) but the Community strategy is basically oriented towards the
creation of institutional comparison and the identification and definition of
(presumed) good practices. The strategy here is centred on a set of goals
defined as 'occupability', 'entrepreneurship', 'adaptability' and 'equal opportunity'. Notwithstanding the insistence in presenting these activities as
innovative, there is little that could qualify them as instruments for managing the European economy.

Fiscal and Budget Policy
Fiscal policy is the distribution of the costs of political production through
direct and indirect taxes and social contributions. The EU does not have a
fiscal policy in the sense that it does not have any taxation power or control
over its budgetary resources; it does have a fiscal policy in the sense that the
project of the common market was perceived from the beginning as closely
related to the harmonization of the member states' fiscal policies. The component of fiscal policy complementary to the creation of the market is far

more in line with the standard operating mode of the EU than fiscal and budget management in view of other goals.

The EU 1998 budget,[28] amounting to €92,596 billion, lies between the total national budget of Finland and that of Denmark. It corresponds to €250.6 per inhabitant and to €0.68 per day per inhabitant. Comparing the Community budget and the public spending of nation-states, the latter devote about 2.2 per cent of their public expenditures to the EU. In the first years of the Community, its tiny budget was almost exclusively devoted to the ECSC. Even with the beginning of the European social funds in 1961 and of the CAP, the financial means of the Community remained very low, respectively at 0.04 and 0.11 per cent of the Community GDP. In 1969, the budget reached 0.48 per cent of the GDP and in 1970, 0.74 per cent. In this year the CAP represented 87 per cent of the total expenditure; in 1980 it represented 68 per cent of the budget, with 65.4 in 1984, 63.3 in 1987, 62.1 in 1988, and 45.4 percent in 2001. In all this time, in absolute terms the budget reserved for agriculture has not diminished. The increase in the overall budget has concerned the funds destined to structural interventions, which rose from 15.1 to 40.5 millions from 1988 to 1999. That is, the budget devoted to structural funds has actually multiplied by five between 1988 and 1999 if computed in euros (in real terms it has multiplied by four). In 2001, 43 per cent of the approximately €95 billion budget was used for the CAP, 30 per cent for the cohesion funds, 3.5 per cent for research, 7 per cent for foreign activities and cooperation, 11 per cent for expenditures for pre-adhesion and enlargement, and 4.5 per cent for the costs of the administration. Overall, the EU budget is less than the figure of 1.27 per cent of the EU GDP that is often referred to. In the 1990s, the average real percentage stood at about 0.95 per cent.

The Commission has no autonomous fiscal power. Before 1971, the states covered the expenses of the Community by direct transfer. Since then, the income of the EU has become independent. That is to say, the new sources have a Community legal base and a European nature, even if they are still collected by the state administrations, which receive a proportion of them as compensation for their services. In terms of revenue, the agricultural customs have declined over time with respect to the customs resulting from the common external tariffs. At the present time, agricultural customs total 2 per cent of the entries, and external tariff customs about 15 per cent. In the 1980s, the VAT percentage (introduced in 1979) became the most important own means of the EU and it now represents 36 per cent of the budget. Its growth was interrupted by the 1988 reform, introducing the fourth resource, or resource on the GDP, which had risen to more than the VAT

---

[28] On the EU budget and budgetary policy see Colom, J., '*La politica finanziaria*', in Fabbrini and Morata, *L'Unione Europea. Le politiche pubbliche*, 306–35.

income by 1998. The Council is exclusively competent for the Community resources, with the Parliament playing only a consultative role. The fear of a continuous increase in the budget has led the Council to fix a maximum ceiling, expressed as a percentage of the European (not national) GDP.

These figures and institutional set up make it clear that budgetary policy of the EU cannot have any significant effects on the economy and the economic cycle. In fact, the EU's fiscal policy is mainly interpreted in terms of its capacity to standardize, harmonize, and make convergent the fiscal policies of the member states in view of abolishing fiscal barriers to free trade and competition. States free to pursue different direct, indirect and social contributions fiscal strategies can manipulate the costs of factors and de facto raise fiscal barriers. Moreover, the liberalization of capital flaw may produce the transfer of savings from one country to another to take advantage of a more favourable fiscal regime. This can produce a loss of fiscal income for the state and a loss of activity for financial intermediation. The transfer of profits from one institution to a foreign institution produces consequences on the revenues of the national financial firms and of the state. In addition, before the EMU, 'relocation' could be accompanied by monetary consequences on the rate of exchange among currencies. The taxation regime of profits and savings was therefore strategic in a context of capital flaw liberalization. However, the goal of convergence towards an overall average common level of taxation has been difficult and contested. The overall tax weight ranges from about 50 per cent of the GDP in Sweden and Denmark, to about 35 per cent of Ireland and Great Britain.

The legal foundations of the EU's fiscal policy (Arts. 90, 91, 92 and 93 EC) state the principle of equal fiscal treatment for goods and services that are similar within the territory of the EC, forbid fiscal charges for protecting national productions and fiscal compensations for sustaining exports towards other member states, suggest the harmonization of indirect taxes, and require the unanimity of the Council after a proposal by the Commission and consultation with the Parliament (and of the Social and Economic Committee) for any decisions involving the harmonization of national fiscal policies.

The harmonization of the main indirect taxation (VAT) was essential in order to make this taxation neutral with respect to trade within the Community, and to correctly measure the contribution capacity of individual member states to the EU budget.[29] This process of harmonization was politically difficult and technically complex, being necessary to identify which transactions were common references to all countries, and to give Community

---

[29] On tax harmonization I rely on the account by Genschel, P., *Steuerharmonisierung und Steuerwettbewerb in der Europäischen Union* (Frankfurt am Main and New York: Campus, 2002).

definitions of all the key concepts necessary for computing VAT. Eventually, this allowed fiscal controls to be abolished at the frontiers, thereby fostering the free movement of goods, and since 1993, private citizens have been able to buy goods in different countries, paying local levels of VAT, with no further taxation needing to be paid on return to their home country.[30]

On the contrary, direct taxation—about 13.7 per cent of the European GDP—is not subject to any coordination or harmonization. The EU's policy is instead limited to marginal intervention concerning specific cases of double taxation or lack of taxation. The most important problem remains the taxation on the capital returns of people who reside in member states other than those where their income is generated. The Commission argued and documented that this lack of harmonization fostered a shift in taxation from capital to labour, the development of special fiscal regimes for the low taxation of foreign investments, and a negative effect on economic competition for those countries that have no such special systems.[31] From the 1989 Scrivener regulation proposal[32] to the set of measures aimed at hindering harmful competition (Communication of 5 November 1997)[33] the Commission has continued to exercise pressures for harmonization with very limited results. Similar problems concern the fiscal regime for firms and companies. The provisional decision is that in 2005 all harmful fiscal regimes should be dismantled, but the Council has reserved the final word on this. The situation is even more problematic for social contributions, the most important of the obligatory contributions and which correspond to about 15 per cent of the EU GDP. National variations are enormous, with the maximum level in France, about 19 per cent, and the minimum in Denmark, at 1.7 per cent of the GDP. Strictly speaking they are not part of the fiscal regime and so no

---

[30] Indirect taxation includes special taxes on mass consumption goods, imposed by member states for public health, environmental protection or energy saving. Since 1993, some important taxes of this type have been subject to a common regime: tobacco, alcohol, and mineral oil. Moreover, minimal levels of excise have been defined, leaving the maximum level open to the discretion of the member state.

[31] *The fiscal policy of the EU* (Brussels: Commission, 1996).

[32] The project supported the harmonization of taxation by suggesting a relatively modest source taxation (initially 15 per cent, subsequently 10 per cent). The solution was a compromise between the German solution, where the taxpayers declare these revenues, and the French solution, where the banks and the financial companies (and in general those that pay the revenue of the savings) declare the gains of the saver. The opposition of some countries (notably Luxembourg where savings and capital gains are not taxed and savings are secret) led to the abandonment of the Scrivener project and, since then, harmonization has progressed through the lowering of taxation on the revenues of savings.

[33] This suggested two solutions for member states within which the formation of capital earnings took place: (*a*) that all information on earning should be provided to the state of residence of the investor, so that the state of residence could compute its income; (*b*) that a minimal tax of 20 per cent should be applied to be given to the state of residence of the investor.

harmonization is foreseen. In this sector, the only action that has been taken by the Commission has been towards the coordination of national regimes, mainly to solve the problems of contributions for those workers who move from one country to another for professional reasons. The rules of unanimity in this area have produced frequent vetoes by national governments.

Unquestionably, the EU fiscal policies have so far been mainly seen and presented in the perspective of the 'non-distorsivity' of national fiscal regimes, rather than as instruments of macroeconomic management.

Monetary Policy

The pressure towards setting up monetary policies derived from the failure of the dollar-based international monetary system to stabilize international trade, and from the growing mobility of capital at the international level. The growth of the inter-European trade made exchange rate stability a condition of economic cooperation. Moreover, the progressive loosening of capital mobility controls and financial integration were making it impossible for member states to maintain the autonomy of their monetary policy, and, at the same time, the stability of the changes. European countries tried to contain the resulting monetary instability through various attempts at monetary policies coordination. Through the Werner report on monetary union, first, the 1972 European monetary snake, second, and, finally, the 1978 SME[34] integration moved from the microeconomy of the markets to the macroeconomy of monetary and budgetary policies.[35] Slowly, it became clear that stable inter-EU exchange rates were a goal that required further politically-driven integration.

From 1979 on, the European monetary system managed to resolve internal tensions with periodic realignments that accounted for inflation differentials. However there remained the problem of the fundamental asymmetry that was related to the central role of the German Mark (DM). Germany's low inflation and economic weight made the DM the de facto monetary standard. Only Germany set its monetary policy independently: the other countries had either to adjust to German policy, to devalue or to leave the system. Till the beginning of the 1990s, the other main economies kept a certain level of autonomy over their monetary policy, either by refusing to integrate their

---

[34] The SME was not integrated into the treaties and it was made up of monetary rules that were presented as parallel to the market integration. Note also that the SME was the first step towards an 'opting out' possibility: the adhesion to the zone of fixed exchange rates was not, in fact, obligatory.

[35] For the various predecessors of the EMU, its preparation and phases see the account by Morata, F., 'La banca centrale Europea', in S. Fabbrini (ed.), *L'Unione Europea. Le istituzioni e gli attori di un sistema sovranazionale* (Roma-Bari: Editori Laterza, 2002), 200–26.

currency into the European system and allowing it to fluctuate (Great Britain) or by keeping a strong control on the changes by reducing the free movement of capitals (Italy and France). By the early 1990s, the conversion of a core group of EU states to a anti-inflationary discipline as a dominant macroeconomic goal was the precondition for the acceptance of the Monetary Union (EMU). Next to this neoliberal consensus, the political context also included the growing perception that the US economy was profiting from the dominant position of the dollar in the international monetary system. Finally, the issue of German unification helped to soften German opposition. With the Maastricht Treaty, in 1992, a common currency was planned together with major and crucial breakthroughs into macroeconomic policy.[36]

The overall goal of monetary union was the full liberalization of capital circulation, the full integration of financial markets, the total and irreversible convertibility of currencies, and, eventually, their substitution with a single currency. The corollary of this was that the free movement of capital and fixed parity were incompatible with independent macroeconomic policies of member states. Under the EMU regime, monetary sovereignty passed to the independent European Central Bank (ECB), while the budget policies stayed under national sovereignty. However, the use of the public debt by national authorities to cover a budget deficit is now regulated within the limits of 3 per cent of the GNP. On paper, countries that break this rule are penalized through an automatic system of fines, whose maximum can reach 0.5 per cent of the GNP, and the only ground for avoiding these sanctions is a grave recession (with a loss of more than 2 per cent of the GNP). To set these into motion, a majority of 2/3 must be reached in the Council. Additional convergence conditions involve the overall public debt, and the rate of inflation and of interest. The impossibility of financing the deficits by money production implies that in order to obtain a softening of the monetary policy the undisciplined country either exercises pressures on the others and on the ECB, or it exits the EMS in order to finance its debt, determining a crisis of confidence in the system. A final possibility is that it asks for solidarity with redistributive effects.

The EMU and the delegation of monetary regulation to an independent Central Bank are based on a number of assumptions. The first is the macroeconomic irrelevance of unemployment, to be dealt with through structural reforms of the labour market; the second is the macroeconomic nature of inflation; the third is the abdication of national governments' macroeconomic

---

[36] The solution is usually presented as a colossal deal: the French gained a commitment and a precise schedule; the Germans gained the assurance that the system would be set up in the same way as their BBK; the British and Danes were allowed to opt out; and the Southern regions obtained greater distribution resources.

regulation; the fourth is the limitation of national freedom in budgetary politics under the 'stability pact'. the fifth is the need for member countries to run budget surpluses in order to gain the financial flexibility necessary to face a recession without breaking the rules of the pact if they want to avoid its sanction system.

Unlike the USA, where a broad set of political goals are linked by the activities of the Federal Reserve, including economic growth, employment or other goals (and where the federal state combines monetary with budgetary and fiscal instruments of regulation), the main goal of the EMU and of the ECB has been predefined as 'price stability', and, operationally, the control of the rate of interest and the monetary mass as a function of that stability.[37] Neither the treaty nor the attached protocols defined 'price stability', however, and the ECB itself defined this as a rate of inflation going no higher than 2 per cent. It should be added that the independence of the new European Central Bank is higher than is usually accepted at the national level, as its institutional architecture departs from all norms of political accountability.[38]

The setting of a common currency and the eradication of local currencies is the main economic boundary for any new territorial political formation. In this case, there is a perfect correspondence between internal boundary removal and concomitant external boundary setting for market activities. In monetary policy, the transfer of power to the 'federal' level is complete and the monetary subsystem is fully 'federalist'. The power given to the ECB and the European System of Central Banks is directly operational and there is no intermediation for what concerns the currency. The cohesion of the common currency system and the bank system is so high and strong as to coincide with an absolute 'unity'. The Central Bank's position is characterized by precise goals defined by the 'constitution', specific and exclusive powers to reach such goals, and operational tools at its disposal. In the monetary field, all powers are transferred in an exclusive way, which does not happen even for the exercise of exclusive normative powers of the Commission, for which the states keep the competence over subordinate implementation. In monetary policy, the instruments of action find immediate and full coincidence in the juridical and in the operational structures, as currency has an immediate impact on the individual spheres of action. The operational acts of monetary policy are constraining, and immediately productive of direct effects. The

---

[37] The proposal to broaden the goals of the EMU to include the support to sustainable growth and to high levels of employment was discussed and rejected during the Convention preparing the TCE.

[38] For a review of current and historical practices of Central Bank independence in several European countries see Elgie, R., 'Democratic Accountability and Central Bank Independence: Historical and Contemporary, National and European Perspectives', *West European Politics*, 21 (1998), 53–76.

direct implication and effectiveness of these monetary decisions makes concrete the perfect identity between the juridical and economic orders. The direct relationship between citizens and the federal state is guaranteed by the function of the currency itself. In other words, the common currency is more 'centralized' than the legal administration, for which, subordinate state implementation is necessary.[39]

However, this powerful boundary setting is only partially operational in the EU. The EMU has transformed national economic disequilibria into European economic disequilibria and, at the same time, it has eliminated national mechanisms of regulation (of the rates of exchange and interest and of the currency supply). However, none of these mechanisms has been restored at the European level. The pre-defined (and self-defined) goals of the ECB limit the possibility of using this new strong boundary for the achievement of any specific—internal or external—goal beyond that of price stability. In particular, any possible economic demand or supply shocks (trade deficits resulting from the growing preferences of consumers for goods coming from partner countries, or any significant differences in the productivity of different partner countries) that could be adjusted with soft mechanisms of the national monetary, budget, fiscal or income policies before the EMU, will have to be met with the harsher mechanisms of recession and employment adjustment (unemployment, mobility of labour and flexibility of salaries).

This is even more the case given that other 'European' mechanisms of adjustment are simply not available. As discussed above, no European fiscal and budget instruments for adjustment and stabilization are available, and neither are there any European 'welfare' compensation mechanisms (see later). In the USA, the federal budget is estimated as being able to absorb up to 40 per cent of the regional effects of a shock.[40] To achieve something similar within the EU, the MacDougall Report estimated that it would be necessary to raise the EU budget to 5–7 per cent of the European GDP.[41] According to another expert opinion, a European budget of about 2 per cent of the GDP of the EU would be sufficient to reduce the impact of a regional shock of about 20 per cent. The resources to be added to the current 1.2 per cent budget could simply be transferred from the national level, without a net increase of the fiscal charge on European tax-payers being

---

[39] See Predieri, A., *Euro, poliarchie democratiche e mercati monetari* (Torino: Giappichelli, 1998), 340–42.

[40] See Sala, X., Martin, I. and Sachs, G., 'Fiscal Federalism and Optimum Currency Areas', in M. Canzoneri, V. Grilli and P. Masson (eds.), *Establishing a Central Bank: Issues in Europe and Lessons from the United States* (Cambridge: Cambridge University Press, 1992), 195–219.

[41] MacDougall et al., *Report of the Study Group on the Role of Public Finance in European Integration* (Luxembourg: 1977).

necessary.[42] To function as an effective 'translation' of this crucial economic boundary from the national to the European borders, the EMU needed the system of economic-territorial policies of the EU to be reconfigured as to be capable of compensating for the loss of the role of national macroeconomic policies. It required stabilization mechanisms covering the entire EU through a net transfer of resources towards regions particularly affected by negative shocks. This has not happened so far.

As a result, it is clear that in its current form the EMU is not capable of governing the internationalization of the European economies or to setting the limits of the scale economies sought and of the volume and directions of commercial transactions. This instrument has been created at the cost of radically limiting any macroeconomic management of the European economy. It is governed by a limited range of predefined goals and cannot be used to establish any economic growth plans or for any other politically defined goals or, more generally, for any goals with a longer-term perspective. Neither can the EMU be used to reintroduce a level of closure of the European economies that is coherent and useful for the desired structure of the European system. Even in this case, it would seem that the mutual distrust among member states on which all EU institutions rest, and the overwhelming concern to avoid free riding has contributed to shape an extremely narrow straitjacket of mutual checks and impediments. The EMU thus looks more like a rigid system for disciplining member states' behaviours rather than like an instrument functional to the common EU interests and economic hegemony.

In conclusion, there are two fundamental asymmetries in the economic boundaries of the EU. The first and paramount asymmetry concerns the level of institutionalization. Monetary policy is delegated to a supranational organism, the ECB with great powers, autonomy, no political responsibility, and pre-defined and pre-decided goals and decisions that are directly effective and operational in the currency domain. Competition policy and the related market-making policies are to a considerable degree in the hands of the Commission's autonomous action, but are made operational only through the ECJ case law in cooperation with national judges. Fiscal, budget and occupational policies are left up to the single member states. As a consequence of this asymmetry, a second asymmetry emerges in the incapacity of the EU to react to economic shocks resulting from the heterogeneity of socio-economic and productive structures. While these differences may require very different macroeconomic conjuncture policies, the EU monetary policy prescribes a single and unitary macroeconomic policy provided for in

[42] Praussello, F., 'La stabilità dell'Unione Monetaria Europea in presenza di squilibri regionali', *Storia Politica Società*, 1 (1999), 63–9.

the stability pact (deficit, debt, inflation, rates of interests) and the EU lacks any alternative non-monetary instruments (fiscal, budget, welfare), which would in any case presumably be regarded as violating the centralized policies of competition, anti-aids, etc.

The Coercion Boundary

Coercion, as the ultimate instrument to ensure compliance, has an external and internal dimension. Foreign and military policies ensure the behavioural conformity of other states or groups and individuals outside the territory, whereas policing and other internal policies guarantee order and security within the territory. None of these goals was envisaged in the integration project. Both have been institutionalized recently as special pillars of the EU, separate from its economic dimension.

The 'External Dimension'

The Common Foreign and Security Policy of the Union (CFSP), formally institutionalized in 1992 by the Maastricht Treaty, has its roots in the failure of the European Defence Community (EDC) in 1954, the following revital-isation of the Western European Union (WEU), and the European Political Cooperation (EPC). The EPC was only an informal mechanism of voluntary consultation/cooperation which was framed within a legal document of the Community only with the SEA. The Maastricht Treaty established the second pillar of the CFSP and introduced some majoritarian elements into the formulation of this policy. Qualified majority decisions were envisaged for only some aspects of implementation of common actions. The Maastricht Treaty included for the first time the military aspects of security and esta-blished a formal link between the EU and the WEU in two non-legally binding Annex declarations. In these, the will was reaffirmed to strengthen the WEU as an armed branch of the EU, to partially integrate the national military structures, and to coordinate defence policies to arrive at a common defence policy. The acceleration of the CFSP development was fostered by the coincidence of a set of new external conditions, including the end of Cold War, the German unification, the Gulf War, and the dissolution of the Yugoslav state.

The Amsterdam Treaty in 1997 did not radically modify this institutional setting. The issue of majority decisions was left unsolved. The Council decides by qualified majority when it adopts 'common actions', 'common positions', their implementation, and decisions on the basis of a common strategy. However, if a member state invokes reasons of national interest the issue is referred to the European Council so that the latter can take its decision by unanimous vote. There was some progress between 1998–99, as a result of the more firmly integrationist British position under Tony Blair's premiership and of the Kosovo war in spring 1999, which made the need of a military intervention force clear. At the European Council of Helsinki (December 1999) the resistance of some members (the military dimension has been opposed particularly by the British, Dutch and Danish, who prefer the NATO to retain its dominant role) made it impossible to envisage an European army but the decision was taken to develop a military voluntary cooperation by 2003 to allow the deployment of a force of 50–60,000 soldiers for one year to carry out missions foreseen by the Petersburg Declaration and not foreseen by the NATO. Other important Helsinki decisions concerned non-military cooperation. The Nice Treaty's most important decision in this area was to provide for the creation of the permanent structure of the Military Committee and military staff, and the adoption of the list of the military units made available by each member state. No substantive changes have been made concerning the issue of qualified majority voting versus unanimity.

The goals of the CFSP are, however, ambitious (TEU, Art. 11): to defend common values, fundamental interests, independence and integrity of the EU; to strengthen security and keep peace in conformity with the UN Chart, the principle of the Helsinki Final Act and the Paris Chart; to promote international cooperation; to develop and consolidate democracy, the rule of law, human rights and fundamental liberties. For this ambitious list of goals, the EU Council defines *common strategies* of intervention in those sectors in which member states have important collective interests, and it fixes the goals, the means to be deployed, and the length of the intervention. Common strategies become concrete with the adoption of *common actions*, binding member state behaviour and directed towards specific situations requiring operational interventions; and *common positions*, which define the EU's general position or approach on specific or general issues. All this is framed within the principle of *systemic cooperation*, requiring constant consultation among member states on whatever question is relevant for EU interests. Member states are also committed to coordinate their behaviour in international bodies (such as the Security Council of the UN, where France and the United Kingdom are expected to defend the interests of the EU).

In the institutional architecture of the CFSP, the European Council is the most important institutional actor. After this comes the Council of Ministers of Foreign Affairs and other related foreign matters (defence, trade, economy). More recently, two politico-military institutions—the Political and Security Committee and the High Representative for Foreign Policy (who is also the General Secretary of the Council)—were set up permanently. The Commission has four Directory General (DG) dealing with foreign affairs: for enlargement; for trade concerned with external economic relations; for development; and for external relations. The Commission also has more than 100 delegations representing a kind of EU embassy of the foreign countries. The Commission has the right to make policy proposals, but does not have the sole right of policy initiative, nor is it charged with policy implementation. The EP has the right to be informed and consulted, ask questions, make recommendations, and hold an annual debate on foreign and security policies. It is involved in the decision-making only indirectly, to the extent that some of the major agreements made by the EU concerning associations, cooperation, etc. have budgetary implications that it must approve.[43]

This progress in policy institutionalization point to a growing awareness and willingness of the member states to set those military and security boundaries essential to a unitary action in these areas more clearly. However, in terms of actual achievements, the capacity of member states to converge on common positions remains very limited. The complex intergovernmental mediation tends to produces only declamatory interventions. Even declamatory unity is often lacking.

In this context it is sufficient to recall the many failures, which contrast sharply with the few and modest achievements.[44] Starting from the 1970s and moving through chronologically, the European governments' reaction to the fourth Arab–Israeli war in 1972 was deeply divided. The response to the Soviet Union's invasion of Afghanistan was more unitary. The attitude towards the 1979 Iran Islamic revolution was not satisfactory on account of the slowness of the response. In line with the greater capacity to react to Cold War issues, the Polish state of emergency power in 1981 generated a quicker response, as well as some sanctions. In 1980, the Venice declaration recognizing Palestinian rights to a homeland increased the differentiation with US positions. In 1982, the support to Britain in the Falkland war overcame the close relations by some Southern member states with Argentina. In 1984–85, the political and economic cooperation with countries of Central America again became a field of differentiation with the USA. In

[43] Regelsberger, E., 'The institutional setup and functioning of EPC/CFSP', in E. Regelsberger, P. de Schoutheete de Tervarent and W. Wessels (eds.), *Foreign Policy of the European Union: From EPC to CFSP and beyond* (Boulde, CO: Lynne Rienier Publishers, 1997), 67–84.

[44] My references are Soetendorp, B., *Foreign Policy in the European Union: Theory, history and practice* (Longman: London, 1999); Eliassen, K. A. (ed.), *Foreign and Security Policy in the European Union* (Sage: London, 1998; Holland, M. (ed.), *Common Foreign and Security Policy: The Records and Reforms* (Pinter: London, 1997); Knodt, M. and S. Princeu (eds.), *Understanding the European Union's External Relations* (London: Routledge, 2003).

1985–86, the apartheid policy in South Africa led to European economic sanctions being taken. In general, in the 1980s the east-west block relationship represented an area of growing differentiation with the USA, with the EU trying to mediate against the confrontational policies of President Reagan. In the Gulf War (January–March 1991), however, the EU was unable to find any common ground on which to act, although it tried to present a common front at the beginning of the crisis. Later, during the conflict, only France and Great Britain contributed significantly to the war. In ex-Yugoslavia the EU was unable to impose either a ceasefire, mediate or to force the parts to accept a solution of the crisis based on the idea of a Balkan confederation of independent states. Eventually, in November 1991, the EU was forced to stand back and let the UN and the US to intervene. At Maastricht, in that same December 1991, these failures were used to emphasize the need for a special pillar to define and implement a common security and foreign policy. Art. J1 committed member states to abstain from taking any unilateral action that might go against the EU's common interests or detract from its effectiveness in the handling of international relations issues. Only a few days later, however, Germany unilaterally recognized the independence of Slovenia and Croatia (23 December), going against the views and hopes of the other members. Since then, there have been several periods of more or less open tension with the USA on military issues, the Middle East and the far Middle East, but these have divided European countries more often than united them. The last and most obvious divisions became clear in the second Gulf War in 2003, which possibly generated the highest level of differentiation regarding the positions of EU member countries, including, this time, even the new members who were to join the EU in 2004.

It is argued that the ongoing process of consultation, cooperation, and information spreading has contributed to building a socialization process as a result of which differences have been considerably reduced (and trust increased), while, at the same time, the awareness of the impossibility for single states to pursue autonomous international actions has increased. Yet, despite this considerable policy *institutionalization* and a degree of policy *convergence*, the ability of the EU member states to *act together* on foreign and military issues is virtually non-existent. In the operational field, the relationship between the EU, the WEU and NATO are problematic,[45] and,

---

[45] The WEU was created by the Brussels Treaty of March 1948 between France, Britain and the Benelux countries. The treaty was modified in 1954 to accept Italy and Germany and remained a dormant organization during the Cold War. For the EU-WEU relationships see Ham P. van, 'The EU and WEU: From Cooperation to Common Defence?', in G. Edwards and P. Pijpers (eds.), *The Politics of European Treaty Reform* (London: Pinter, 1997), 305–25. For the more recent developments towards the merging of many aspects of the WEU operational activities within the Security and defence policy of the EU see the

to date, joint action has not been very effective. For example, the WEU did not help to coordinate Western Europe military, humanitarian and rescue operations in former Yugoslavia and Rwanda. In Yugoslavia and Albania, the EU acted more in a humanitarian assistance capacity than otherwise, tending to prefer non-military operations, and it never deployed combat land troops, but only police contingents.

As a military arm of the EU, however, the WEU was a very singular organization. Entry in the EC-EU did not entail or require membership in the WEU and vice versa. Denmark and Ireland have never become full members of the WEU and together with the last three newcomers (Sweden, Austria, Finland) have observer status. Ten Central and Eastern European countries have obtained associate status and partnership since 1995, which allows them to participate in the Permanent Council and working group meetings. Turkey and Norway are associate members, while they do not belong to the EU. In other words, the relationships between the EU and the WEU (and, one could add, NATO) always were based on 'variable geometry'. Depending on the topic under discussion, the WEU met with its (ten) full members, with associate members (now six), with observers (now five) or associated partners (now seven). In its varying capacity the WEU has at times included all EU states, all NATO states and the Central European and Baltic countries, although, obviously, only the ten full member states are covered by the security guarantee of Art. 5 involving military support in the case of attack. From an operational point of view, the WEU never had a standing command structure comparable to that of NATO, and the formation of Eurocorps and their use in the framework of WEU-NATO relationships remain an unresolved issues.

The most recent developments have brought about a gradual merge between the EU second pillar and the WEU. The document annexed to the Maastricht Treaty on EU-WEU relations envisaged mutual information and 'cross-participation'. In 1993, for symbolic reasons, the WEU moved its secretariat to Brussels and reduced the term of its presidency (previously lasting one year) to six months. The document annexed to the Amsterdam Treaty envisaged 'integration' between the EU and the WEU and already made the latter the operational harm of the EU initiatives in the defence field. With the Nice IGC and the Marseille Council meeting of the WEU (November 2000) the operational capabilites of the WEU were almost entirely transferred to the European Defence and Security Policy. At the time, the WEU still exists as a residual institution concerning the core military alliance

decision taken at Marseille Council meeting of the WEU, 13 November 2000, in M. Rutten (ed.), *From St. Malo to Nice. European defence: core documents* (Paris: Institute for Security Studies, 2001) Western European Union Chaillot Papers 47, *www.isseu.org*, 147.

clause of art. 5 that only concerns the ten full members. In this sense, the variable geometry of the WEU (members, associate, partners and observers) has ceased and has been transferred to the EU.[46] The very complex relations between the EDSP, the WEU (in its residual military guarantee) and the NATO, contribute to the difficult definition of the military boundary of the EU.

In any discussion on the chances of developing a foreign and military EU policy a close look at the list of differences in geopolitical interests, military autonomy, atomic arms control, extra-European traditional linkages, etc. may well lead to the conclusion that cooperation in these areas is extremely unlikely. The objection that can be made against this argument is that a divergence of interests originally existed in almost all areas of policy integration and this did not impede the integration progresses. All the same, it can be argued that the pooling of military means differs significantly to other forms of supranational pooling. In order for this kind of pooling to be set up, the EU would need to perceive a common threat, sense of vulnerability, and interests to defend. However, in response to this latter point, it can also be pointed out that a military capacity is not aimed only at responding to security and military threats, since geopolitical and economic interest diplomacy too, require elements of credibility as a military power to avoid being involved in intractable international crises in which abstention is impossible and intervention is not credible. Therefore, if the EU has no real external menace, it has a problem of international credibility as an economic diplomatic power, to the extent that its economic foreign policy depends on the consolidation of some degree of military credibility. At the same time, however, military and defence remain special fields of cooperation because the creation of a military central bureaucracy and an instrument for military intervention is the most tangible sign of a new centre formation. Historically, once a new military centre is created, it can at some point be used for internal purposes, too. Therefore, any reluctance or enthusiasm to accept a centralized instrument of foreign policy credibility should be understood considering (*a*) the objective differences in foreign, defence and military interests, goals, and priorities; (*b*) the objective external threats as an EU-wide security problem; (*c*) the needs for external credibility as backing for trading and economic diplomacy; and (*d*) the internal fears, mistrust, and resistance against a military centre-building process.

A combined analysis of these four components suggests that, at the moment, objective interest differentiations and internal fears prevail over weak objective external threats and credibility needs. The Cold War was an over-

---

[46] In the pending TCE, there are provisions related to the 'solidarity clause' and to the option of a permanent structured cooperation in the security realm (Art. I-40(6)).

whelming threat that helped to subsume national interests and perceptions under the NATO umbrella making a cooperative attitude mandatory, and when it ended, an enlarged Europe was left no longer facing such a strong common threat. Even in its current situation of crisis, NATO remains the most integrated Western institution in the defence and security realm, while the European countries face a variety of new 'risks' that affect them to varying degrees of intensity. The potential instability of the Russia/CIS region, the Middle East, Central Asia, and the Southern Mediterranean, the proliferation of missile technology and weapons of mass destruction, international terrorism, secessions and partitions of states, and religious, ethnic and border disputes, are risks and challenges that very differently affect the member states, pushing them to pursue their own calculations about costs and benefits of cooperation and defection.

Pooling Internal Coercion

There are considerable historical variations among countries and types of regimes in their strategies for controlling territorial movements and residence, unlawful behaviours, border patrolling, and the direction of this patrolling—inwards-oriented towards controlling exits, or outwards-oriented towards controlling entries. In this field, boundary-building activities witness a constant trade-off: for exit control, there is the advantage of removing indigent, dangerous or troublesome populations versus the cost of losing valuable human resources (skills, intellectuals, professionals); for entry control, there is the alternative advantage of gaining valuable human resources versus the costs of integrating newcomers into the local population. The control of internal behaviours was handled as a domestic affair within the nation-state, and was left to international bilateral or multilateral agreements for those illegal behaviours that had an international scope or for those people who had moved outside the territory where they were actually wanted.

European integration has facilitated and fostered internal mobility. Since the Rome Treaty was signed, the number of border crossings is believed to have increased 20-fold. In the 1990s, movements across the borders of Germany accounted for 864 million people; the figure is over 291 million for France, while the figures for Spain, the Netherlands and Italy were in the order of 120–35 million. From the total of these figures, it is estimated that 1,200 million people annually cross the internal frontiers within the Schengen area by land, sea, and air.[47] This internal mobility goes hand in hand with a

---

[47] Foucher, M., 'The Geopolitics of European Frontiers', in M. Anderson and E. Bort (eds.), *The Frontiers of Europe* (London: Pinter, 1998), 235–50.

growing pressure for entry via immigration within the member states of the EU. In contrast, emigration has been reduced to small niches of highly qualified and skilled manpower.

Immigration and crime control issues could have been left to nation-state policies to handle if it had not been for the implementation in the mid 1980s of the principle of the free circulation of the people within the EU. This required the progressive abolition of border controls on citizens of EU member states, and the effect became immediately apparent in national immigration, asylum and visa policies, and the national control of crime, triggering off a very clear spill-over effect. The twofold problem of external entry into the territories of the EU (immigration, visa, asylum) and of internal crossing of the borders of member states (crime monitoring, penal code, extradition) finds a correspondence in the legal framework of the EU, which distinguishes between 'internal frontiers' (among member countries) and 'external borders' (with non-member countries).[48] In this area, progress towards the integration of the control resources of member states have been particularly rapid over the last twenty years. They are a perfect example of the mechanism that sets a close relationship between internal boundary removal and (the need for) external boundary consolidation.

The institutionalization of this policy domain[49] started outside the EU institutions. In 1985, the Schengen countries—Germany, France, and the Benelux—decided to start the process of abolishing frontier controls. The suppression of police patrols on internal frontiers led to a corresponding increase in the control of foreigners at those frontiers of the member states that were also external EU borders. In the late 1980s, the twelve agreed on two conventions developed by the meetings of the ministers responsible for internal national security (the Trevi group). The first concerned the criteria for identifying the state responsible for filing and processing the asylum request and whose decision is valid for all the others states (Dublin Convention, 15 June 1990); the second text anticipated a common policy for awarding visa, was supposed to be signed in 1991, but was blocked by a bilateral problem between Spain and the United Kingdom. In the area of immigration, the first actions were oriented towards a narrowing of the differences among the national legislation through information, coordination and consultation at the EU level. From 1985 on, a relative uniformity of national legislations was gradually introduced, concerning the position and treatment of the 'foreigners'. As this took place, more formal mechanisms were also progressively added to coordinate national responses, and immigration

---

[48] Even if this difference does not exist in the German text, in which the same term *grenze* is used for both types of frontiers.

[49] See Delgado, L., 'La politica dell'immigrazione', in Fabbrini and Morata, *L'Unione Europea. Le politiche pubbliche*, 249–75.

entered to form part of the EU's agenda, coming under the umbrella of cooperation in Justice and Home Affairs at Maastricht, understood as part of the policies inherent to internal security.[50] The policy areas included in this additional pillar were, in fact, wide-ranging: immigration policy; policy concerning the entry and residence of non-Community citizens; asylum policy; rules for crossing the external borders of member states and the corresponding controls; the fight against drugs and international fraud; judicial cooperation in the civil and penal law fields, customs cooperation; police cooperation against terrorism; international criminality.

The Amsterdam Treaty incorporated the Schengen *acquis* into the EU, with the additional goals of creating a space of liberty, security and justice through free circulation and adequate measures of border control, asylum, immigration and visas (Art. 2). This required the acceleration of harmonization. Visa policy was excluded from the third pillar and some of its aspects communitarized: the specification of the country where citizens are requested to obtain a visa in order to enter the EU, and the adoption of a uniform model of visa.[51] The third pillar was thus divided into two sections: Title IV on 'visas, asylum and immigration' and Title VI on police and judicial cooperation on penal matters. The issues included in Title IV are subject to communitarization following different timings and levels. This means that, after communitarization, the Council-Commission will be able to adopt communitarian legal instruments, regulations and directives, the ECJ will be able to intervene to interpret the specific Title, and the Parliament will probably be more extensively involved in cooperation.[52] The Nice Treaty did not produce any significant changes in this area (although it did explicitly allow for reinforced cooperation). During the policy institutionalization, membership widened from the early small core group to all member states except the United Kingdom and Ireland, whose intention to keep the control of their frontiers was confirmed in their request for special exemption (together with Denmark) on the chapter of the free movement of people foreseen by the Amsterdam Treaty.[53]

The introduction onto the agenda of the issues of internal security and the control of coercion boundaries across member states and towards the extra-EU world is a fundamental novelty in the evolution of integration. The

---

[50] Walker, N., 'The New Frontiers of European Policing', in M. Anderson and E. Bort (eds.), *The Frontiers of Europe* (London: Pinter, 1998), 165–86.

[51] The need to harmonize the areas of visa and asylum policies was probably one of the most obvious, given the enormous cross-country differences. Without a common visa and asylum policy, immigrants would soon discover where best to enter, and be free to move within the borderless territory of the EU later.

[52] The Schengen agreements were considered to offer weak jurisdictional guarantees and have also raised doubts about the safeguarding of human rights.

[53] Walker, *The New Frontiers of European Policing*, 165–86.

measures adopted by national governments in this area are now subject to an EU institutional arena of decision-making, even if this is predominantly intergovernmental. The Commission moved very rapidly, creating the new General Directorate for Justice and Home Affairs. Although the effectiveness of the Justice and Home Affairs cooperation has be questioned for those cases in which decisions require unanimity and/or are not binding,[54] the traditional functions of border-crossing controls have moved rapidly from being the exclusive competence of member states to being an intergovernmental policy, and, finally, at least in part, an area of Community competence. There are many implications to this transfer of competence in principle,[55] of which a few significant examples can be drawn from the early Schengen negotiations. The Netherlands and the United Kingdom, for example, do not oblige citizens to identify themselves, and those countries with compulsory identification rules were pressurizing them into adopting more rigid identification procedures. The right of owning hunting weapons was virtually unchecked in France, while it was rigidly controlled in Germany and the Netherlands: either the latter would have to relax their laws, or the former would have to tighten theirs. Eventually, the French and Belgians tightened up their regulations. In the field of drugs policies, the Netherlands had less repressive regulations and higher levels of discretion in law enforcement. In the negotiations, all countries made pressures on the Netherlands, which eventually made a few (modest) concessions.[56]

Regarding external border controls, the free movement of people within the EU territory has led to drastic changes. In fact, at each external EU border—which is, of course, also a member state frontier—those individuals who, although admissible on the territory of the entering state, are not admissible in the territory of other member states, will have to be identified (and, in case, not admitted, sent back, or even imprisoned). As external EU control is exercised by the border state in the name of the other states too,

---

[54] Delgado, *La politica dell'immigrazione*, 265.

[55] The 'institutionalization of Schengen' is a case of competence expansion via an 'external' intergovernmental strategy and has set up a model for deepening cooperation without passing through the procedures of unanimous or majority voting. The technical-juridical modalities of this kind of institutionalization are both complex and ingenious. The European Council authorized the states undersigning the agreement to start a reinforced cooperation between themselves with exactly the same content of the so-called Schengen *acquis*. Schengen is, therefore, the first example of reinforced cooperation and flexibility.

[56] On the Schengen negotiations see Kapteyn, P., *The Stateless Market. The European Dilemma of Integration and Civilization* (London: Routledge, 1996), 71–91. This useful work is biased by the assumption that the Dutch (and the Danish) have a higher moral sensitivity than other countries and that the adaptation of their legislation to the European level marks a decline in civilization.

this has consequences for the national judiciary activities. It is not a direct challenge to the territorial monopoly of such activities, but rather an extension of duties to incorporate into one country the requests of others. Officials of a country will thus be acting according to the rules of another (in addition to their own rules). It may happen, therefore, that they are obliged to stop individuals who are either not wanted on the soil of their country, or who are wanted for offences and charges which are not illegal in the officials' own country.

In a frontierless EU, other areas affected concern crime prevention and control. Persons otherwise subject to national control are now free to move across Europe and to decide where to settle, operate, etc. The freedoms of the market have also increased the exit options for organized crime, which can step from one jurisdiction to another, and so evade national standards of prosecution and also set up its operational headquarters in the most convenient geographical location. In the Schengen negotiations, the crucial issue was how to reduce the potential for crime mobility that open borders would facilitate and encourage. The still considerable differences between European judicial prevention and repression systems (in the scope of the powers that the police and the judiciary have and in the limits to their action) opens up opportunities for organized crime and problems for crime control that make necessary further European level integration in this area.

In order to fight organized criminality and clandestine immigration, a system of EU policing is essential. Each state has to make available its own information about a certain number of aspects that are strategic for the control of the territory: people wanted; cars, arms, banknotes, documents stolen or falsified; etc. These data need to be centralized and made accessible to all the member states police and investigating judiciary. The central data bank of Schengen (C-SIS: Central Schengen Information System) located in Strasbourg and connected with a national counterpart in each state (National Schengen Information System: N-SIS) has been set up to document all European police bodies in real time. As well as accrued cooperation, however, the Schengen *acquis* also concerns the state's claim to the monopoly of the control of illegality over its own territory. For example, if the German police stop a French car during a control, they can directly access the necessary data without needing to ask the French authorities for it. Again, the police forces of a member country can continue its investigative activities into another member of the borderless space without needing any prior authorization. Where it is not possible to inform the national authorities in time, it can continue to pursue across the border a fugitive taken in the very act.

A further implication of Schengen for the coercion boundary of the EU member states concerns the issue of extradition, and, more generally, the issue of which country should prosecute a given crime. Developments in judicial cooperation in this field constitute an important departure from the traditional jurisdiction principle of nineteenth century territorial sovereignty, according to which a crime should be prosecuted in the country where it was committed.[57] The increasing amount of trade and mobility has resulted in a growing number of crimes being committed in more than one country, and a growing number of criminals being prosecuted in more than one country. To date, agreements in this area have been based on common-sense cooperation measures aimed at reducing the advantages to criminality. However, the problem of jurisdiction based on the differences between judicial systems remains open. To stop criminal inflow—attracting crime and criminal activities—a country with less harsh measures of punishment (for instance, for drug related crimes, or mafia association repression) has an interest to send criminals back to their home country for trial, asserting that its own judicial system does not apply to foreigners. In a similar vein, and again in order to stop crime and criminals' mobility, the citizens of a country in which punishment is less harsh for a given crime should be judged according to the territoriality principle for the crime committed in the country with harsher measures of punishment. It is hard, however, to imagine the judges of each country to decide, case by case, whether a person should be prosecuted at home or in the local country according to a comparative judgement concerning the harshness of punishment. In the absence of any penal law integration, trial mobility might be a solution but this would also require some sort of general rule about who and where it is legitimate to prosecute—according to the nationality of the citizen or to the country of capture.

In conclusion, states need to share important information for security and to lose the right of monopoly over intelligence activities and the use of force in their own territory. In addition, the effective management and policing of external borders depends on national authority cooperation and trust in the police, administrative and judicial authorities of other member states. This is likely to strengthen cooperation and relationship in yet another network of infranational bureaucracies, those linked to intelligence, police and the prosecuting judiciary (see above in Chapter 3 on infranational bureaucratic networks).

The field of Justice and Home Affairs is, therefore, particularly rich in implications for the traditional nation-state control of the coercion boundary. In this area, the activity of internal boundary removing generates strong pressures for the development and strengthening of new external boundaries

---

[57] On this set of issues see Longo, F. (ed.), *The European Union and the Challenge of Transnational Organized Crime. Towards a Common Police and Judicial Approach* (Milano: Giuffré, 2002).

in a very clear way. However, the setting of new external boundaries and the control of internal mobility from the criminal point of view necessarily push towards either a strong harmonization of the penal codes, policing and judicial practices for both foreigners and European citizens or to the acceptance of the intrusion into the national system of practices, controls and activities by other states' agencies. The indirect consequences of this modification of the state control structures should not be underestimated. The state and judicial systems at the national level have entered a phase of profound change and necessary adaptation in a number of very delicate fields.

System Building: Cultural Identity, Political Rights and Social Sharing

In this section I look at EU political production in the perspective of 'system building'; namely in its capacity to create and/or to extend at the European level those links that historically secure the allegiance of the ruled to rulers. A 'system' is built when a membership group is created coterminously with the territorial group. A membership group is defined as a group characterized by 'citizenship' properties in a sociological sense: the participation of an individual within the normative system of a group. In this non-legal sense, citizenship is the degree to which a person can control her/his destiny by acting within the group and represents the proportions of her/his life problems that can be solved within such a normative system. This, in turn, depends on the degree to which the group generates solidarity among its members, owns the institutions to resolve the problems of those members, and offers them a degree of influence in the group's government.[58] Therefore, citizenship involves a combination of the three fundamental elements of *identity*, *rights*, and *decision power*.

Citizenship is a boundary-defining property for which some degree of closure is indeed necessary to define the group members as opposed to the outsiders, externals or foreigners. The extent to which a citizenship/membership group is coterminous with a territorial group is subject to historical and geographical variation. In Chapters 1 and 2, I underlined the fact that every territorial hierarchy also tends to transform the territorial population under its domination into a membership group, and that the European experience of nation-state formation is characterized very largely by its insistence on and success in this endeavour. We can look at the EU in the same vein. Some scholars think that the elements of a membership group are bound to develop

---

[58] I modify the definition by Stinchcombe, stressing the element of solidarity that he underscores; Stinchcombe, A., 'Social Structure and Politics', in F. I. Greenstein and N. W. Polsby (eds.), *Handbook of Political Science* (Reading, MA: Addison-Wesley, 1975), Vol. 3, 557–622, 602.

with the strengthening of integration.[59] Others deem system building to be utterly unnecessary (if not detrimental) for a political formation like the EU. In this section, however, the question is not whether the EU does or does not require system building, but rather the factual question of what actual political formation the EU is depending on how much system building characterizes it. To this end, I discuss the three key areas of (*a*) the creation of an area of cultural equality via a layer of European identity; (*b*) the achievement of political participation rights of a distinct European type; and (*c*) the policies and institutions for the sharing of social risks.

Cultural Identity

The EU makes it easier to penetrate the different territorial groups without entering the respective national membership groups. In the enlarged European territorial group, the internal membership groups become more heterogeneous necessarily. The issue is thus whether there are any opportunities to expand membership that make the enlarged territorial group more homogeneous via the construction of a new cultural boundary establishing a demarcation between insiders and outsiders, strangers and familiars.[60]

The construction of a cultural boundary necessarily entails a process of inclusion and exclusion. This requires the designation of the differences between insiders and outsiders, members and non-members. The attribute of similarity among the members as against the strangers generates the construction of a layer of equality among the insiders, fostering forms of identification, trust and solidarity. The demarcation of membership realms also presupposes symbolic codes of distinction that allow these difference to be recognized. In turn, the designation of these differences generates problems for any attempt at crossing the boundaries. Eventually, the entire process entails consequences for the allocation of resources and, above all, for the structuring of the entitlements of the members of the collectivity as against outsiders. A close relationship also exists between the 'symbolic codes of distinction' and social and political rights, as the former are related to the type of resources that are shared in the name of the collectivity among its members, the nature of public goods that are instituted within them, and the legal mode of this institution.

---

[59] See Haas, E. B., *Beyond the Nation-State: Functionalism and International Organization* (Stanford: Stanford University Press, 1964), 49–50; Ake, C., *A Theory of Political Integration* (Homewood, Il.: Dorsey Press, 1967).

[60] I follow the approach taken by Barth, F. (ed.), *Ethnic Groups and Boundaries. The Social Organization of Cultural Difference* (Oslo: Universitetsforlaget, 1969); Eisenstadt, S. N. and Giesen, B., 'The construction of collective identity', *Archives Européens de Sociologie*, 36 (1995), 72–104.

In Chapter 1, I discussed the pure types of *primordiality, civility*, and *cultural* codes of inclusion/exclusion, ranking them in terms of the difficulty of crossing the boundary and of the costs of exit. In Chapter 2, I argued that the European nation-state inserted itself as an intermediate layer between broad non-territorial membership groups of a cultural type (such as Christianity) and localized primordial and civic identities. In the process of nation formation, the state (*a*) standardized the localized identities, creating a broader set of civic practices, rules, traditions and familiarities; and (*b*) differentiated broad non-territorial membership groups (language, religion, ethnic).

It is impossible to identify common elements of primordiality in the complex ethno-linguistic infrastructure of Europe. Linguistic fragmentation remains an insurmountable obstacle to any mass level symbolic interaction. In the experience of nation-state formation, linguistic territorial fragmentation and the absence of a single linguistic standard sometimes persisted for centuries after the centre formation.[61] It was quite possible to build up a standard that was intelligible at the elite level across the entire territory and leave the lower strata of the population communicating over shorter distances in only their inherited oral dialects.[62] However, on the one hand, all current European languages have strong written standards and literary glories, are institutionally defended, and are used for long distance communication; on the other, the English language, as the new standard that is intelligible at the elite level, is not European distinctive. It is spreading to local populations, it is not imposed through the EU, but, on the contrary, it penetrates local national communities through thousands of common life experiences (mass media, new electronic communications, manuals and instructions for mass consumption goods, university texts). It also happens to be the language of two EU member states, and, at the same time, it is the language of the main non-European power centre, the USA. Indeed, its spread owes more to its already being an external global standard than to its being a European-specific one.[63]

The early cultural code at the roots of the definition of Europe in the Middle Ages, Christianity, has not overcome its historical division and has no European hierarchy; it is no longer a specific characteristic of this part of

---

[61] For the extensive linguistic fragmentation of France still in the nineteenth century see Weber, E., *Peasants into Frenchmen. The Modernization of Rural France 1870–1914* (London: Chatto & Windus, 1979).

[62] Rokkan, S., ed. P. Flora with S. Kuhnle and D. Urwin, *State Formation, Nation Building, and Mass Politics in Europe. The theory of Stein Rokkan* (Oxford: Oxford University Press, 1999), n. 27, 356.

[63] This is why Sidentop's idea of establishing English as official language of the EU in order to foster a successful European federation is not convincing. See Siedentop, L., *Democracy in Europe* (London: Allen Lane, 2000).

the world, and it is becoming less important for large sectors of the European population. A strong reference to the Christian tradition in the Unions Treaties (as discussed at the European Convention in 2003–4) would represent a cultural code setting strong boundaries with respect to Islamic religion countries, but it would also generate internal tensions and exclusions with respect to the large immigrant groups professing different religions. The EU is unlikely to be able to make strong and clear references to such (or other) broad 'cultural code' of demarcation. Finally, it is also very difficult for a European 'cultural' code of identity to now be based on some sort of feeling of civilization superiority and missionary goal, as was the case during the colonial era.

The difficulty of identifying broader than national codes of identification and exclusion combines with the strong resilience of national identities. These cannot be 'europeanized' in the sense that they cannot be 'de-nationalized'. The issue is how much room do they leave (room no longer claimed by the nation-state) for a new layer of European identity. National identities are made up of the three elements of primordial, cultural, and civility codes combined in different proportions. Those elements of cultural 'Europeanization' that exist are perceived differently according to the mix of primordial, cultural and civic elements defining each national identity. Moreover, the way in which these European cultural elements are defined may have considerable impact on the redefinition of the national identities themselves.

Some countries define the national membership group in terms of innate traits of primordial group, of the *jus sanguinis*, of belonging to an ethno-cultural community. Other countries define nationals in terms of their acquired traits: born on the territory, the *jus soli*, in political-legal terms. Moreover, and independently of how nationals are defined, different countries define the cultural obligations associated with the status of national differently. In some countries, these obligations may require a strong inculcation and familiarization process that ensures that all members are assimilated into a single dominant cultural model. Alternatively, the cultural obligations of national membership status may dispense with this strong assimilation, and members can have the possibility to define themselves and to be accepted as nationals while adhering to a different set of cultural models and subnational identities. Tilly has defined these two modalities respectively as 'exclusive', the former, and 'inclusive', the latter.[64] Koopmans and Kriesi[65] have cleverly cross-tabulated the two dichotomies of 'innate'

[64] Tilly, C., 'Citizenship, Identity and Social History', *International Review of Social History*, 40 (1995), 1–17.

[65] Koopmans, R. and Kriesi, H., 'Citoyenneté, identité nationale et mobilisation de l'extrême droite. Une comparaison entre la France, l'Allemagne, les Pays-Bas et la Suisse', in P. Birnbaum (ed.), *Sociologie des nationalismes* (Paris: Presses Universitaires de France, 1997), 295–324.

and 'acquired' and of 'exclusive' and 'inclusive', coming to the typology indicated below in Table 4.1, to which they also add a set of convincing exemplary cases.

If primordial elements are divisive, if broader than national cultural codes are not available, and national identities are unlikely to be 'Europeanized' even in the long term, the EU can at most be characterized by an attempt to build civility codes of identities by reutilizing new practices and rituals in a European sphere of communication and identification with key values and institutions. The definition of the 'European' (Union) membership group can thus only rest on acquired rights and traits. It will also have to be of an 'inclusive' type, based on the acceptance of a plurality of cultural codes of identities and obligations recognized as such. The pressure for a harmonization of immigration law and practices within the EU has tended indeed to favour an inclusive and pluralist definition of European nationals. However, changes towards a more inclusive and acquired legal-political definition of citizenship are likely to engender different reactions depending on the historical bases of each national model.

A civility code of identity for the EU population could, in principle, develop unintentionally: for example, a supranational EU-identity could evolve from the practice of cooperation in specific areas and specific tasks (epistemic communities, international networks, etc.). One branch of the literature suggests that supranational extensive interactions and bargaining, like those that now take place daily in the EU arenas, are capable of slowly creating meanings and identities out of repeated practices, mutual learning, trust development, etc.[66] Frequent interactions and discussions of common

TABLE 4.1. *Types of definition of the national membership group*

		Cultural obligations	
		Exclusive	Inclusive
	Innate	Germany	Switzerland
Traits			
	Acquired	France	Netherlands

Source: Koopmans and Kriesi, 'Citoyenneté, identité nationale et mobilisation de l'extrême droite'.

---

[66] See Checkel, J. T., 'Why Comply? Social Learning and European Identity Change', *International Organization*, 55 (2001), 553–88; Risse, T. and Sikkink, K., 'The Socialization of Human Rights Norms into Domestic Practices: Introduction', in T. Risse, S. C. Ropp and K. Sikkink (eds.), *The Power of Human Rights: International Norms and Domestic Change* (Cambridge: Cambridge University Press, 1999), 1–38; Schimmelfennig, F.,

problems may also progressively generate a spillover of widely shared democratic norms, orientations, and practices from domestic politics into the supranational (and international) level.

The attempt to foster the development of a civility code of identity for European citizens is, to a certain extent, intentionally pursued by the Commission and the EU using cultural, media, and educational policies. These elite-driven attempts are justified by the need to legitimize the rule of the EU centre and to restrain interest-oriented behaviours by inducing forms of behaviour that are trust and obligation-oriented. At the symbolic level the debates about the various regimes that constitute the EU refer with increasing frequency to 'non-EU nationals', '*extra-communautaire*', 'third countries', and 'non-member states'. In these regimes, these categories are defined with increasing precision and this process is gradually 'constructing' some sort of definition of the 'European'.

The Commission's interest in educational policies has grown consistently, culminating with the foundation of a specific Directorate General (XXII) in the late 1980s.[67] However, from the beginning, there have been conflicts between the Commission and member states on educational issues. In 1973–74, the Commission's Janne Report proposing some 'harmonization' of national education practices and policies generated a firm refusal by the education ministers of the states. Following initiatives met with a more or less equal lack of interest and enthusiasm. However, in the end, the Maastricht Treaty institutionalized the European educational dimension (Art. 149–50, TEC),[68] although the Commission's limited inroads into educational matters were, as usual, legitimized in terms of socio-functional rather than socio-identity aspects.[69] Education is thus seen as flanking the labour market, as a means to standardize educational credentials, supply the skills necessary for advanced and specialized tasks, raise the number of people

'International Socialization in the New Europe: Rational Action in an Institutional Environment', *European Journal of International Relations*, 6 (2000), 109–39; Schimmelfennig, F., 'Liberal Norms, Rhetorical Action, and the Enlargement of the EU', *International Organization*, 55 (2001), 47–80.

[67] For a survey of the legal norms and aspects see McMahon, J. A., *Education and Culture in EC Law* (London: Athlone Press,1995). For the policy aspects I rely on Ryba, R., 'Towards a European Dimension in Education: Intention and Reality in European Community Policy and Practice', *Comparative Educational Review*, 36 (1992), 10–24; Field, J., *European Dimensions. Education, Training and the European Union* (London: Kingsley, 1998); Moschonas, A., *Education and Training in the European Union* (Aldershot: Ashgate, 1988).

[68] See Lenaerts, K., 'Education in European Community Law after "Maastricht" ', *Common Market Law Review*, 31 (1994), 7–41.

[69] Nevola, G., 'Education and Political Socialization between National Identity and European Citizenship', in M. Haller (ed.), *The Making of the European Union. Contributions of the Social Sciences* (Berlin: Springer Verlag, 2000), 331–59, 339.

receiving higher education, improve the competitiveness of the systems, increase job opportunities, etc. Even the goal of spreading linguistic knowledge is mainly technically justified, rather than culturally legitimized.[70] In addition, not many resources have been made available for educational policy beyond the technically motivated programmes ERASMUS, SOCRATES, LEONARDO, COMINIUS, LINGUA, COMETT, YES, and these programmes do not regard the primary school level, which is, in fact, the key one.

In addition to educational, the cultural policy of the EU is identified with the defence of national and subnational cultures as opposed to freedom of exchange in the market, as can be seen, for instance, in the national quota of broadcasting in France and Ireland. This cultural policy thus takes the form of 'cultural exception', where the word 'exception' refers to the fact that the rules and the rulings (of the ECJ) that are normally applied to cultural products are based on competition law and differentiate very little between books, art treasures, movies, etc. and other types of commodities.[71] In short, while this cultural policy protects national cultures from market forces, it has no implications for a wide EU cultural boundary definition.

In reality, a 'cultural policy' is probably no longer possible in the third millennium, as the technologies of cultural exit are so highly developed as to make any attempt at cultural bounding impossible. In addition, cultural boundaries are no longer specific, as cultural exchange is enabled through the removal of other boundaries (mobility, exchange). Very little can be done in the way of enforcing a clear project of familiarization and inculcation of European identities through symbols, myths, celebratory events, school textbooks, and curricula engineering. The EU as such achieves visibility only indirectly, via the functional-instrumental approach to higher education and skills requirements.

However, even if a more proactive educational and cultural policy were to be accepted by national governments, the civility codes of a potential European layer of identity are limited. The 'shareable' European history and memory that are often alluded to can be read in several ways, some of which are actually divisive. There are specific patterns of historical development, different from those of the rest of the world, that produced the idea of 'modernity' and modern society. There is also a set of fairly isomorphic

---

[70] On the entangling between cultural policy and economic integration see Weatherill, S., 'Finding Space for Closer Cooperation in the Field of Culture', in G. De Búrca and J. Scott (eds.), *Constitutional Change in the EU. From Uniformity to Flexibility?* (Oxford and Portland: Hart Publishing, 2000), 237–57.

[71] See McMahon, J. A., 'The Protection of Cultures', in M. Anderson and E. Bort (eds.), *The Frontiers of Europe* (London: Pinter, 1998), 205–21, which analyses a number of interesting ECJ sentences in this area, namely the VbVB &VBBB versus Commission (1962) and Commission versus Italy (1968) cases.

constitutional values, principles and institutions leading to a typically European mix of citizens' duties and rights as a result of a mix of liberal, solidarity and republican ingredients. The distinctiveness of these aspects is, however, debatable and it is likely to be perceived only within relatively small elite groups. These elements seem unlikely to generate significant additions to the extremely complex cultural infrastructure and diversity of Europe, as none defines clear criteria of distinction and difference between 'us' and the 'others'.[72]

If the identity layer is very 'thin', what are the consequences? In Figure 4.1 Cederman's useful representation of identity types, which is in line with my own conceptualization, is reproduced.[73] The vertical dimension indicates the thickness of the cultural identity, while the horizontal dimension identifies the level of closure and exclusion/inclusion of the interaction processes within a territorial group. Thick identities involve not only a strong emotional commitment, but also a comprehensive functional scope covering many cultural aspects of private life. Thin identities are limited to communication within the public sphere. Moving from A to B, a group expands its scope of interaction with other groups, and, at the same time, necessarily reduces the identity thickness of the resulting enlarged group. The trade-off is that

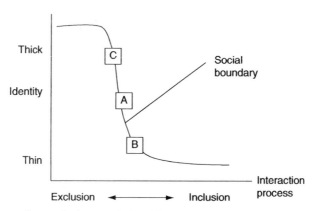

Source: Cederman, *Political Boundaries and Identity Tradeoffs*.

FIGURE 4.1. Thickness and inclusiveness of cultural identities

[72] For a more positive view of the 'identity building' capacity of the EU see Laffan, B., 'The European Union and its Institutions as 'Identity Builders' (Florence: European University Institute, 2000), IDNET Conference 'Eurpeanisation and Multiple Identities', 9–10 June.

[73] Cederman, L.-E., 'Political Boundaries and Identity Tradeoffs', in L.-E. Cederman (ed.), *Constructing Europe's Identity. The External Dimension* (Boulder, CO: Lynne Rienner, 2001), 1–32.

inclusion can only be obtained at the cost of dilution of identity. Moving from A to C, the group thickens its identity and the inevitable side effect of this will be exclusion.

The shape of the boundary curve indicates the nature of the trade-off. The sharper and more abrupt the boundary drop, the more dramatic the loss of thickness beyond some level of inclusion is. If the line is smooth, the boundary effect is minor (its total absence is represented by a horizontal line) and inclusion does not bring about any identity losses. Given that European integration generates a higher density of socio-economic transactions and cultural interactions, this should bring about a thinner identity depending on the shape of the cultural boundary curve. We can conceptualize different situations in this frame without necessarily referring to the development of a positive European identity. Considering that the European process looks quite open, we can question at which level of higher inclusion in cultural transactions will make the cultural identity of Europeans so thin as to dilute the actual value of such a concept. On the other hand, a thicker identity for Europe may be defined so narrowly as to exclude people and entire countries.

A certain level of cultural identity may, of course, exist without materializing in the common decision-making institutional and political production. For example, Mazzini indicated Scandinavia among the eleven nation-states of Europe, a Scandinavian monarchy was discussed several times in the nineteenth century, and supranational 'Nordic' organizations were attempted and failed several times in the twentieth century, but eventually the 'Scandinavian' identity never resulted in a demand for a Scandinavia Union and was important only for the cooperation between nationally organized movements (socialist, for instance) and institutions.[74] On the other hand, multinational state political identities can be endangered by an overactive role of the state in social engineering that they are unwilling or unable to sustain. This was the case of the political modernization phase of the Habsburg Empire before the First World War; it also describes very well the growing intercommunity tensions in post-Second World War Belgium. However, even in a classic case of historically built national identity such as the British case, which is seen as developing between the Union Treaty (1707) and the accession of Queen Victoria, it can be claimed that this identity rested on a light impact of the state on civil society and was mainly a 'state' identity that was externally oriented towards the Empire and defence. The potential power of Parliament and government over society was not really activated

---

[74] See Stråth, B., 'Scandinavian Identity: A Mythical Reality', in N. A. Sørensen (ed.), *European Identities. Cultural Diversity and Integration in Europe since 1700* (Odense: Odense University Press, 1995), 37–58.

until the modernizing post-war Labour government, first, and the Conservative revolution of the 1980s, later, which used state power to actively transform civil society. It is in these activities that, according to McCrone,[75] the roots of the crisis of the British multinational state lies.

We can distinguish several different relationships between thickness of identity, interaction levels, and scope and reach of the EU political production.[76] If one starts from a thick conception of national identity and from a strong association between it and the nation-state, the conclusion is that there will be a sharp fall in the level of identifications beyond a certain level of interaction and that this breaking point is already evident at the national level. In this case, the very negative trade-off between inclusion and identity formation not only rules out identifications at a higher than national level, but also the level of inclusion already achieved must be contained and the scope of action of the EU limited to that reduced set of policies that are compatible and can be sustained by the very thin identification elements of the community. Whether decided on at the intergovernmental or supranational level, the scope and reach of the EU political production must, as a result, remain in line with its sharply reduced identification bases. Otherwise, tensions cannot be avoided and they may take the form of nationalistic reactions and/or even revive thick subnational identities, sometimes over-emphasizing on some 'primordialistic' element.

A second perspective shares the assumption of the first, that interactions enlargement and identity building must coincide in order to allow extensive political production by the EU centre. However, contrary to the first perspective, it assumes that a thick identity can be built at the European level, although beyond the European level the same effect of a sharp drop of identification processes is predicted. In this perspective, the resilience of national identities with respect to the European identity may be deplored.

A third possible approach puts forwards the constructivists view, while foreseeing retention of the nation-state as identification locus for many areas and processes. The trade-off exists, but the shape of the curve and the boundary profiles may differ from issue area to issue area and the curves are subject to social construction. In other words, retention and suppression tendencies with respect to the national identities may vary on the basis of the prevalent 'discourse' that dominates policy debates, which can therefore modify the slopes of the boundaries. In this case, the possibility of EU political production is conditioned by the parallel development of convincing

[75] McCrone, D., *British Supranational Identities: A Scottish Perspective*, in Sørensen, *European Identities*, 59–74.

[76] Here, I have been inspired by Cederman's classification of European identity conceptions, revising it for my own purposes and, in particular, linking it to the problem of the scope and reach of the EU political production, which is my main perspective in this work.

and legitimizing discourses. Tensions only arise when advanced integration policies are pursued without this kind of ideational underpinning.

The last perspective represents the extreme position of the denial of any trade-off in cultural terms. It views national identification as a thin and malleable identity and sees the swing of interaction level and processes at the cultural level away from the nation-state, towards the European level and even towards the global level, towards a fully global identity, as non-problematic and welcome. On this view, Europe tends to be seen as a step towards a globalizing tendency, ultimately creating a world community, in which there is no exclusion dilemma and no inherent trade-off between levels of cultural interactions and thickness or dilution of identities. Therefore, no constraining conditions should be set for the political production of the EU, except those imposed by political circumstances and efficiency calculations.

Lastly, should one be worried by the thin cultural identity elements in the continuously expanding policies and populations of the EU? From the point of view of the theoretical framework adopted in this book, the level of system building of a political formation (and within it, therefore, the level of identity and solidarity ties of the membership group) is crucial to determine the scope of political production particularly in the area of social sharing and the decisional rules that can be accepted as legitimate. In the European nation-state, the spheres of identity and solidarity, the social sharing institutions and participation and decision rights are intimately linked and support each other. Without some element of system building, the equalization of participation rights, the structuring of political conflicts, and their resolution through electoral institutions is impossible, in the sense that it is not accepted as legitimate. Thus, the elements of system building are the foundations for the suspension of pure instrumental calculations in the distribution of benefits and entitlements between peoples, groups and territories within the same political formation. System building legitimates the otherwise irrational idea that a large group of people take decisions on a vast range of delicate issues by resorting to some principle for ascertaining and summing up the preferences of individuals, groups, or territories. Therefore, the level of system building at the EU level is intimately linked to the level of political production that can be carried out at that level. If correspondingly high levels of system building do not support a high level of political production, this is likely to create tensions that should normally take the form of radical requests for exit options.

Cultural identifications are probably additive. It is likely that a layer of European civility code of identity can be added to the national and regional ones. However, if the European identity is doomed to remain a very 'thin' identity, then one should draw conclusions *first* about the scope, reach, and level of its political production, and *then* about the type of decisional mechanisms it can sustain and accept as legitimate. The problem is, therefore, not the level of the EU system building, but the type, reach, and scope of political production that it can safely sustain and legitimate.

Participation Rights

Large-scale territorial groups with high interactions and exchanges can probably define their membership predominantly in terms of acquired rights and duties, that is, in terms of legal citizenship. We should, therefore, turn our attention to these rights within the EU, beyond those of an economic nature related to the internal market and the four freedoms. Note that the free movement of goods, capital and services is not, strictly speaking, an EU right, as they apply to anyone whose economic activities falls within the scope of EC law, and do not rest or depend on EU's citizenship. On the contrary, the free movement of people rests on member states' nationality, even if it can be extended to other states' nationals by international agreements.[77]

Art. 8.1 of the Maastricht Treaty set up a EU citizenship (now Art. 17–22 CE). This is an 'indirect' citizenship as every individual who is a national of one of the member states is a citizen of the EU. Each country thus remains master of the definition of European citizenship as a function of its own history and geography and, in particular, of its colonial past. For instance, the Eskimos of Greenland were Europeans, before they renounced to this by referendum, while the *ressortissants* of the Commonwealth come in an intermediate position. The EU therefore has no competence in the definition of European citizenship and all states are obliged to accept the definition of nationality given by other member states.

For the many immigrants from ex-colonial territories who enjoyed a number of freedoms and rights (for instance, circulation) inherited from the colonial past, this has led to the loss of status and rights with respect to other Europeans who were before simply foreigners. Non-EU citizens resident in a member state do not enjoy freedom of movement within the EU and if they stay more than three months in a country other from that where they reside, they are subject to the regulations concerning foreigners. The introduction of the category of the 'Europeans' has thus undoubtedly widened the gap between '*communautaires*' and '*extra-communautaires*'.

European citizenship is therefore accompanied by a restriction of access conditions and restrictions to the status of the new migrants: asylum seekers,

---

[77] Kadelback, S., 'Union Citizenship' (New York: New York University, 2003), Jean Monnet Programme, Working Paper 9, 16. This is an excellent review of the legal intricacies of the Union's citizenship.

relatives in mixed marriages, temporary workers, students, and illegal immigrants. In order to deal with these, a number of intra-law situations non homogeneous throughout the territory have come into force: provisional statuses, humanitarian *permis de séjour, contracts de sous-traitance.*[78] European citizenship therefore defines a series of concentric circles associated with different rights and obligations. At the centre of these circles are the European nationals of each territory. The definition of these is not always clear and simple as many ex-colonial states (France, United Kingdom, Spain, Portugal, Netherlands) have bilateral agreements with their ex-colonial territories that often include clauses concerning access to the nationality of the ex-colonial power. In other cases, openings in the mobility of labour have been established in favour of countries that are not members of the EU (Norway and the Nordic countries labour market).

A second circle is formed by the European citizens residing in another member country territory; they are excluded from some public administration positions,[79] are exempted from military service duties, and cannot vote at national political elections. For the rest, they enjoy pretty much the same rights as the national residents in terms of freedom of circulation, residence, work and economic enterprise. Those European citizens who do not reside on the EU's territory constitute a third circle of European citizenship. The fourth circle is represented by those non-European EU citizens who reside within the territory of the EU. They do not enjoy intra-European rights and, as mentioned before, in some cases the status of residents is seen as a regression in relation to the rights previously granted to them within the nation-state.[80] In a fifth circle one may include, although there are some significant legal differences, those non-Community citizens who are also non-residents, the refugees and asylum seekers.

The second fundamental area of equality that forms part of the definition of a membership group is 'political' and indicates the rights of political participation and decision. These are rights that pertain to the first two groups identified above: the approximately 370 million Europeans (before enlargement) and, particularly, the approximately 5.5 million Europeans residing in member countries that are not their own. About 13 million non-EU foreigners who reside regularly within the EU are excluded from these rights.

[78] See Soysal, Y. N., *Limits of Citizenship. Migrants and Postnational Membership in Europe* (Chicago: University of Chicago Press, 1994).
[79] Access to public employment is guaranteed in the Union with the exception of those employments that imply the exercise of public power and national sovereignty (police, army, top civil service positions).
[80] For a discussion of extra-Community versus European differences see Wihtol de Wenden, C., *La citoyenneté européenne* (Paris: Presses de la Fondation Nationale de Sciences Politiques, 1997).

The list of specifically 'European' political rights is, in fact, relatively meagre. The fundamental political freedom of speech and association are granted within the EU on the basis of the national provisions and are, to all intents and purposes, national rather than European rights. The same argument applies to the nationals' right to vote in European elections. Given the extension of the EP's powers since its foundation, this additional voting right offers some decisional power to the voters, even if this can be exercised with respect to only a circumscribed set of issues. However, is it debatable whether this right is a specific European right or whether it is simply an application of national political rights. Voters and candidates are not mobile in Europe, and the voting/candidacy right for national elections are still locked into the national systems.

The 'portability' of voting/candidacy rights is limited to local and European elections. Every EU citizen residing in a member state that is not from the one she/he comes from has the right to vote and be elected to European and municipal elections. The first right was already operational in the European elections of 1994, while the second was postponed until the year 2000. The specific European element of this right lies in the fact that the electorate is no longer 'national' in the sense that it includes non-national members of the EU. Therefore, voting in the European/local elections is a European right only to the extent that it concerns the portability of this right into the territory of another member country.[81]

The portability of voting/candidacy rights for local municipal elections has been justified in several countries by referring to the administrative ('*gestion-naire*' in French) character of these as opposed to the political character of national elections, to which the principle of nationality still applies. Moreover, in several countries, local election voting rights were already recognized for certain groups of non-national and non-EU immigrants. In those countries where this was not the case, immigrant organizations feared that this recognition of political rights to Europeans risked postponing the debate on the right to vote and the eligibility of non-European foreigners.

The actual use of these portable political rights is very limited. In the first EP elections in which the right was recognized, in 1994, only 3 per cent of the EU residents in a member state different from their country of origin was asked to be registered on the electoral lists: 1 per cent in Greece; 5 per

[81] In several countries the establishing of the local political rights for Union citizens has led to specific constitutional amendments. The most interesting debate on this question was in France because here local elections have an explicitly 'national' political dimension to the extent that municipal councillors participated in the election of the Senate, exercising this function 'in the name of the French people'. For this reason the constitutional law of 25/6/95 exluded EU citizens from the functions of mayor and participation in the designation of the electoral college which elects the Senate members. (Art. 88, para. 3, French Constitution).

cent in Belgium; 4.4 in France; 3.7 per cent in Germany; 10.5 per cent in Luxembourg; 13.5 per cent in Spain; 25 per cent in Denmark and 2 per cent in Portugal. The real level of participation of European citizens living abroad was therefore minuscule: about 50,000 voters used this right in Germany and 47,500 in France.

Another specific 'European' right is that of petition. Every European citizen has the right to petition in front of the EP (Art. 8*d*). Already Art. 128 of the internal rules of the EP recognized the right to present, either individually or collectively, questions and complaints to the EP. Finally, the Union Treaty recognizes for EU citizens the right to address the new institution of the 'mediator'. This mediator is nominated by the EP for a five-year period; it is independent from all the other EU institutions and it cannot be revoked during the mandate. Its function is to provide the citizen with non-jurisdictional protection concerning the cases of bad administration that emanate from the bodies of the EU, with the exclusion of the ECJ. Where the mediator considers a complaint to be valid, an inquiry can be set up whose results are transmitted to the institution concerned and to the EP. In 1995, Mr Soderman from Finland was appointed the first mediator for the EU and in eight months he received 537 complaints, of which 436 were handled. In addition to the petition and appeal right, the Amsterdam Treaty also introduced a right to information and access to documents in possession of the EU institutions (with important exceptions concerning preparatory documents and member states consent in fields such as public security, defence, foreign affairs, economic policies). Finally, one can add to this list the right of European citizens to be protected and assisted, in countries where her/his own state is not represented, by the diplomatic institutions of other member states under the same conditions of the nationals of that member state.[82]

The list of the specific rights that constitute the European political citizenship ends here.[83] In principle, the portability of voting and candidacy rights linked to residence opens up the boundaries of the nation-state, allowing non-nationals to enter its political community. However, the exclusion from national elections, the absence of European referendum rights, and the sheer quantitative insignificance of those exercising these rights makes it difficult to view these phenomena as reaching any significant level of importance. It is also interesting to note that the treaties do not make reference to any specific

[82] This right is significant for tourists and businesspersons, particularly if one considers that in 1995 there were only five states in the world where all EU member states were directly represented. However, the concrete application of this right is uncertain and it is regarded as ineffective. Kadelback, 'Union Citizenship', 28–31.

[83] Among the general European rights there is the right not to be discriminated on grounds of nationality. This equal treatment right is here dealt with in relation to the market freedoms (see earlier) and to the social right (see later).

Restructuring Europe

European duty for EU citizens parallel to their rights. Clearly, EU citizens do not pay European taxes and are not requested military duties, but the treaties do not even mention, and the EU does not expect, any duty of loyalty or solidarity among its citizens (notwithstanding its symbol of flag, anthem, etc.).

Social Sharing

Social protection and social sharing represent a set of institutional provisions aimed at *socializing the risks* and *institutionalizing the solidarity* among the members of a territorial group.[84] With the formation of a single integrated European market, to what extent are citizens' social risks socialized and solidarity among members institutionalized at that level? In the Rome Treaty a few hints to social policy existed in reference to migrant workers, equal pay for women and men, 'harmonization of national security systems' (never seriously considered), the fostering of a dialogue between labour and capital, and some regional policy.[85] The first important step was the 1408/71 Regulation, which inaugurated a supranational regime to specify the conditions under which benefits matured into a national system could be converted and exported into the system of another member state. The regime aimed to ensure that the exit options opened up by the common market be matched by corresponding entry options, unhampered by administrative impediments. A new phase was set off by ten directives on social policy passed by the Council between 1975 and 1980 as part of the Social Action Programme (started in 1974). Three of these directives dealt with employment protection (minimum rights of workers affected by the restructuring of enterprise); three concerned the equal treatment of women and men (equal pay, equal opportunity in hiring, and working conditions) and led to important changes in the national legislation in this case; the last four dealt with workplace and health safety. By the arrival of Delors in the mid-1980s, the aims of the Social Action Programme had been defeated by heavy British and business opposition.

In 1988, the European Trade Union Congress (ETUC) presented a 'Community Charter of Social Rights' leading to European-level collective bargaining and workers' co-determination as legally binding and enforceable.[86]

---

[84] Ferrera, M., *Modelli di solidarietà* (Bologna, Italy: Il Mulino, 1993), 349.

[85] For the early history of EU social policy see Liebfried, S. and Pierson, P., 'Social Policy', in H. Wallace and W. Wallace (eds.), *Policy Making in the European Union* (Oxford: Oxford University Press,1996), 185–208.

[86] The Charter included a list of fundamental rights of the workers, including the right to work in a member state chosen by them; the right to an equitable salary; the right to better working and life conditions; the right to the protection of health and security in the

The following year the Commission drafted the 'Action Programme', including measures to implement the Charter. In December 1989 (Strasbourg Summit), after strong British opposition, a deal was negotiated according to which eleven countries adopted a non-binding soft version of the Charter, amended of all the contentious issues (right to strike, right to a 'decent wage', etc.). This version of the Charter did not give the Commission any new mandate to legislate. On the contrary, it included references to the limits of its power as defined by the Treaties, and its sections mentioned the need for each right to be enforced in accordance with national practices. Given the Charter's weak substance and legal status, the future rested on the Commission's new 'Action programme'. This proposed forty-seven measures for the following thirteen years; twelve of which corresponded to points included in the Charter programme. Only twenty-eight measures were to create binding legislation, the other nineteen measures being presented in the form of 'reports', 'opinion', 'memorandums', and the like. The programme encountered wide opposition from various governments,[87] and eventually Great Britain did not sign the final document, even if it participated in the discussions to water it down. Interestingly, then, the British government was here given the chance to shape a policy for which it had previously declared that it would not adhere, in a case of 'exit *after* voice' and continued 'voice *after* exit'. This 'opt-out' imposed limitations on the policies that could be adopted by the eleven, since the social obligations and costs imposed on the firms of the adhering countries would generate competitive advantages to British firms continuing to enjoy unlimited access to the EU market.[88]

The social protocol attached to the Maastricht Treaty extended majority voting to a range of subjects beyond health and safety (introduced in the SEA), thereby improving the chances of the measures of the action programme being passed into law.[89] The substance of the agreement was limited

---

working place; the right of men and women to equal treatment; the right to protection for children and adolescents; the right of elderly persons to decent life conditions; the right to improvement in the professional and social integration of handicapped people; the right to information, consultation and participation; the right to associate and negotiate collectively; the right to social protection according to the modalities of each member state; and the right to the professional training.

[87] See Addison, J. T. and Siebert, W. S., 'The Social Charter of the European Community: Evolution and Controversies', *Industrial and Labor Relations Review*, 44 (1991), 597–625; Teague, P. and Grahal, J., 'The European Community Social Charter and Labour Market Regulation', *Journal of Public Policy*, 11 (1991), 207–232; Streek, W., 'European Social Policy after Maastricht: The "Social Dialogue" and "Subsidiarity" ', *Economic and Industrial Democracy*, 15 (1994), 151–77, 161.

[88] See Silvia, S., 'The Social Charter of the European Community: A Defeat for European Labour', *Industrial and Labor Relations Review*, 44 (1991), 624–43.

[89] Majority voting was extended to the areas of: (*a*) improving working environment to protect workers' safety and health; (*b*) working conditions; (*c*) information and

to the implementation of the 1989 Social Charter. The treaty also introduced the so-called 'Social Dialogue' into the EU decision-making machinery. The European peak associations of labour and business (ETUC and UNICE) were given the right to participate in social policymaking. The Protocol stated that the Commission should consult management and labour on policies and proposals, that the parties of the social dialogue may inform the Commission of their direct agreement, and that such agreements may be then implemented by labour and management at the national level directly, or be approved by the Council on the Commission's recommendation.

In concrete, the aim was to devolve responsibility for public policy to business and labour, giving to their agreement and direct consultation a quasi public status and setting the possible precedents for a tripartite 'corporatist' policymaking at the European level. The social dialogue was an attempt at political structuring by the Commission (thereby overcoming the resistance of business). It could also increase its power towards the Council, as measures agreed upon by the parties would be more difficult to reject. It would be able to curb the tendency of business and labour to influence directly national governments, and to strengthen their European level organizations. By widening the scope of bipartite cooperation, the Social Dialogue would also be able to crate the conditions for an industrial relation system at the European level, and to help European social policy go beyond the narrow limits of the Treaties.

However, one should also consider the following destructuring elements. A footnote to Art. 118*b* (2) stated that any agreement achieved at the Community level by labour and capital did not create an obligation for nation-states to amend their legislation to apply it. Therefore, effective direct implementation rested on the national force of the organizations. This implied that the agreements could be unevenly implemented and made peak organizations disinclined towards setting them up. Finally, the reluctance of the employer association (UNICE) was fostered (*a*) by its capacity to fall back on its best option of no regulation in the case of a non-cooperative outcome of negotiations; (*b*) by the inability of the Commission to threaten unilateral legislation in the case of no agreement; and (*c*) by the Commission's limited capacity to produce inducements in other areas to influence negotiations and to make exchanges and concessions to achieve the compliance of the parties.

consultation of workers; (*d*) gender equality; (*e*) integration of persons excluded from the labour market. The protocol also specified the areas that continued to require a unanimous vote (social security and the protection of workers; protection of workers where the employment contract is terminated; representation and collective defence of the interests of workers, including co-determination), and those that were definitely excluded (wage setting, right of association and right to strike and of lock-outs).

The Amsterdam Treaty incorporated the Social Protocol of Maastricht (now signed by all fifteen members), made the Commission responsible for the task of coordinating and stimulating employment-oriented policies (the content of the 1997 Luxembourg Process), and marginally modified the areas of majority voting, unanimity, and those that were definitely excluded.

In general, those areas of legislative reforms (gender provisions; health and safety of work) where the Rome Treaty and the SEA allowed for the direct intervention of the Commission (and the ECJ) and qualified majority voting in the Council led to a rise and a spread in standards. Direct legislation and ECJ decisions have often required national reforms and adaptations. In these fields, business has fewer chances of exit and it could not refuse to participate as regulatory action could have been taken even without it. In the other sections of the 1989 Social Charter and Maastricht Social Protocol, achievements have, however, been by far less obvious. The opposition of countries and interests was fortified by a decision structure offering them the possibility to opt-out (for countries) or to refuse to cooperate (for interests).[90]

A second component of EU social sharing is represented by the general policies that fall under the label of 'cohesion policies'. The structural funds associated with these policies are redistributive macrosocial policies, as opposed to the regulative microsocial policies of the Social Chart. These four funds are:[91]

1. The European Regional Development Fund for productive investments, local infrastructures, the development of small and medium firms, and education, health and research in the least developed regions;
2. The Cohesion Funds (added by the Maastricht Treaty) to help poorer counties (Greece, Spain, Ireland, and Portugal) to face the integrated market by investing in the infrastructures of transport and in the protection of the environment;
3. The European Social Fund to co-finance actions in the areas of professional training and aid to employment;
4. The European Funds of *'orientation'* and *'garantie agricole'*, to help transform and develop agrarian structures.

Action was first taken in the mid-1970s and a policy with some degree of autonomy dates by the first reform in 1979. It was in this period that Italy and Ireland negotiated regional support in exchange for participation in the monetary system (SME). By 1984, the Commission's margin of discretion increased with the beginning of the Integrative Mediterranean

---

[90] See the interpretation by Streek, 'European Social Policy after Maastricht', 156–7.
[91] Strictly speaking structural funds include only Regional Development funds and Cohesion funds.

Programmes (IMP) to compensate Greece, France and Italy for the entry of the two new Southern countries (Spain and Portugal).[92] The 1988 reform of the structural funds with its five new broad objectives was the result of a compromise between the more and less developed states for the latter group to accept the conditions of moving towards the single market and, later on, the single currency. The reform also formalized the process of closer cooperation between the Commission and the competent public authorities in each member state 'designated by the central government' to participate in all phases of the planning. This meant involving territorial bodies more closely in the process of formulating and implementing the Community's financial projects, although under the close control of the national authorities. The Maastricht 1993 reform was negotiated in terms of more cohesion funds (for Spain, Greece, Portugal and Ireland) in exchange for monetary union and led to the doubling of the structural funds through the creation of the specific cohesion fund. The result was the recognition of economic cohesion and solidarity as one of the chief goals of the EU (Art. 2).

The Amsterdam Treaty marks the beginning of the reform of the structural funds in view of enlargement.[93] The adhesion of ten new members increases the overall population by about 30 per cent, the territory by 34 per cent, the GDP by 9 per cent, and the average per inhabitant income fell by 16 per cent. The principle underpinning the Agenda 2000 was that the enlargement should be financed through the existing cohesion policies by internal budget reforms, at no additional cost. Spain, Greece, and Portugal insisted on keeping Cohesion funds for the Euro countries too, and in the Nice Treaty Spain managed to maintain the principle of unanimity in the distribution of such funds up to 2007. The new policy of cohesion for the 2000–6 period emphasizes three goals: (*a*) underdeveloped regions (GDP pro capita lower than 75 per cent the Community average); (*b*) regions affected by structural changes; and (*c*) human resources development.

Structural funds are used as an aid and indemnity for the victims of the market, defined either as geographical areas or as social categories (long-term unemployed, young people looking for a job). They are run in cooperation with national states and local governments; they complement, but do not substitute, national aids, and they are based on the logic of 'objectives'

---

[92] In 1986 the adhesion of Spain and Portugal increased the economic imbalances among the member states. At that time the Spain and Greece GDP by inhabitant was 74.8 and 54.3 per cent of the Union's average (while Ireland and Portugal were in the middle).

[93] Bollen, F., 'The Reform of EU Structural Funds: 10 Questions on the Magnitude and Direction of Reforms' (Maastricht: Institut Européen d'Administration Publique, 1999), Eipascope.

and multiannual planning.[94] In the period 1994–99, the structural funds distributed about 150 thousand million ecus and in the period 2000–6 this sum will amount to about €180 thousand million. They represent the only visible redistributive policies of the EU that are not based on the principle of 'fair return' (Table 4.2). The redistribution is characterized by a predominantly territorial dimension and it is therefore only indirectly 'social'. Redistributive spending has much of the time been conceived as an element of wider negotiations and used as a side payment to compensate some economically less advanced member state for their acceptance of some major advancement in economic and market integration. Finally, their overall scope in quantitative terms, although significant for some countries, should not be overestimated. In the 1990s, the total budget of the EU amounted to rather more than 1 per cent of the members' GDP and the structural and cohesion funds represented roughly 30 per cent of the EU budget. Their overall budget therefore amounted to about 0.30 per cent of the European GDP. The large literature dealing with these policies[95] is thus due more to

TABLE 4.2. *Overall structural funds*

Country	1994–9 (in million ecus)	2000–6 (in million euros at 1999 prices)
Belgium	2,096	1,829
Denmark	843	745
Germany	21,724	28,156
Greece	15,131	20,961
Spain	34,443	43,087
France	14,938	14,620
Ireland	6,103	3,088
Italy	21,646	28,484
Luxembourg	104	78
Netherlands	2,615	2,635
Austria	1,574	1,473
Portugal	15,038	19,029
Finland	1,652	1,836
Sweden	1,377	1,908
United Kingdom	13,155	15,635
Total EU	153,038	183,564

Source: European Commission, GD Regional and Cohesion Policy.

[94] For the list and the inclusion criteria up to 1997 see Faugère, *Economie européenne*, 166.

[95] See the wide range of references in Hooghe, L. (ed.), *Cohesion Policy and European Integration* (Oxford: Clarendon Press, 1996); Keating, M. and Loughlin, J. (eds.), *The*

their institutionally empowering role than to their redistributive and social sharing features. Structural funds have been regarded as a key element of the development as a system in which authority and influence in the formulation and implementation of policies are fragmented through different levels of government (territorial, national, Community).

In conclusion, direct social sharing policies within the EU amount to:

1. *Labour market regulation*: the bulk of Community regulative action concerning workers' protection at the end of the working contract, collective firing, the organization of the working day, the protection of atypical forms of work, maternity leave, part-time.
2. *Promotion of occupation and employment*: policies for employment training, support to employment on a local basis.
3. *Equality of treatment and opportunity*: probably the field in which there has been the most consistent and important impact, with a wide set of regulatory decisions and of corresponding ECJ interventions.
4. *European regulation of workers' collective rights*: the firm, company or enterprise committees.
5. *Interests intermediation between trade unions organizations and business associations at the EU level*: the Social Dialogue.
6. *Fight against discrimination*: directives against ethnic discrimination; the European agency against racism and xenophobia; norms about the insertion of the disabled (the early idea of action against poverty was largely abandoned after 1994).
7. *The social dimension of the cohesion policy*: territorial distribution, programmes against unemployment and fostering employment.

The overall scope of European social 'spending' is clearly marginal. In the 1990s, Western nations spent between one third (the Netherlands) and one fifth (Switzerland) of their GDP on social spending, and the EU average was probably above 30 per cent of the national GDPs. A rough comparison suggests that EU policies with a 'social' dimension together involved, at most, 1 percent of national social policy expenditures. That is, for every euro spent by the EU, €100 is spent by national governments. And hardly all 'structural' spending can be defined as 'social policy'. The comparison is very rough but the discrepancy of the relationship between EU and national welfare state spending is clear.

In the first six domains, action is almost exclusively regulative. Only the cohesion policy has a clear redistributive dimension. Given the impossibility

Political Economy of Regionalism (London: Frank Cass, 1997); Balme, R. (ed.), *Les politiques du néoregionalisme* (Paris: Economica, 1996).

of expanding social welfare (and spending) by 'adding' EU protections to the national ones, EU social citizenship can only take the form of regulative enhancements of the 'portability' of national social rights to match the mobility resulting from market integration. Originally, the migration of workers led to a coordination in social protection and the establishment of social funds to promote labour mobility and retraining. However, the extension of mobility from the employed to the non-economically active (pensioners, students, etc.), from industrial workers to qualified white-collars, self-employed and professionals may add pressures for the definition of a European social citizenship as some minimum social rights in terms of eligibility criteria, length and levels of benefits.[96] So far, however, neither the regulative nor the redistributive European social policy is able to define any visible or significant relevant layer of European social citizenship. Social policies resulting from territorial disparities are unlikely to maintain their original scope with Eastern enlargement. Social sharing is likely to remain a national feature essentially.

European Integration and National Social Sharing

In addition to the direct EU regulative and distributive social policy there is one important indirect impact of EU *non*-social policy on *national* social policies: namely, the intersection that comes into being between the free circulation principles and competition policy, on the one hand, and national social sharing rules and institutions characterized by a monopoly of management and delivery of services, both in their forms of cash payments and reimbursement and of direct delivery of services, on the other. Competition law is applicable to all firms and some softening is foreseen only for firms dealing with general interest services. The Treaties do not define what is a firm and the ECJ has adopted an extensive definition (in the Hoefner Case, C-41/90 of 23.4.1991), implying that a firm is any entity that exercises an economic activity. The ECJ has been asked to pronounce on the question whether national social protection institutions are firms, whether they exercise an economic activity, whether this activity is submitted to competition law, and, eventually, whether their monopolistic position implies an abuse of dominant position.[97]

---

[96] Flora, P., 'The national Welfare State and European Integration', in L. Moreno (ed.), *Social Exchange and Welfare Development* (Madrid: CSIC, 1993), 11–22, 19–20.

[97] Dehousse argues that the ECJ plays a role similar to that of national constitutional courts when dealing with the compatibility of legislation with the constitutional text; Dehousse, R., *The European Court of Justice. The Politics of Judicial Integration* (New York: St Martin's Press, 1998), 205.

It is useful to outline in some detail the evolution of the ECJ jurisprudence in this domain.[98] In 1993, in a case (Poucet and Pistre Cases, C-159; 160/91, 17 February 1993) concerning the refusal by two French citizens to pay their social security *cotisations* to the *Caisses* managing health and old age insurance, and asking for the freedom to be insured by private insurances of their own choice, the ECJ ruled that these first pillar regimes of social protections should not be regarded as enterprises, and, therefore, the activities exercised by these *Caisses* should not be submitted to competition law as they pursued a *social goal* and rested on the *principle of solidarity*. The social goal was that of insuring individuals against risks such as sickness, old age, etc. irrespective of their economic capacity, and by the absence of profitable aims. To specify the 'principle of solidarity', the Court made reference to a number of arguments: (*a*) contributions are not tuned to health, age, etc., but in proportion to income; (*b*) services offered are the same for all beneficiaries; (*c*) there is no risk selection and redistribution takes places among those who need and those who do not; (*d*) rights which are not linked to any payment (as in old age pensions) exist; and (*e*) in the old age regime, solidarity takes the form of pensions for retired people financed by the payments of the active population.

Shortly after this judgment, the Court was asked to deal with complementary (voluntary or obligatory) social insurance regimes set up by law or by collective agreements among social partners. In the Coreva Case (C-244/94, 16.11.1995), insurance companies disputed the monopoly granted by French law to a *Caisses de securité sociale* managing a complementary old age pension scheme. In this case, for the first time, the ECJ considered an organization running a supplementary and voluntary social protection regime as a firm, and stated that the monopoly guaranteed by law was against competition law. Even in this case, the principle of solidarity was invoked, but applying the same defining principles of solidarity mentioned above, the ECJ concluded that in this case coverage was not compulsory, voluntary affiliation was a condition for solidarity, and the sharing of the risks was not considered enough to grant exclusion from competition law.

In the Albany Case (C-67/1996), Dutch employers wanted to exit from affiliation in the second pillar industry insurance schemes instituted and designed by collective agreements establishing compulsory and publicly regulated funds run by social partners, and go for group policies with private insurance companies. The ECJ ruled for the status quo, while admitting its anti-competitive nature. The ECJ restated that pension funds exercise an economic activity in competition with insurances and are therefore firms.

---

[98] See Bosco, A., 'Vers une remise en cause des systèmes nationaux de protecion sociale' (Paris: Notre Europe, 2000), Problématiques européennes no. 7.

However, the compulsory nature of affiliation conferred onto them by public authority can be justified as constituting an exception to competition law concerning enterprises of general economic interest. In order to do so, the ECJ uses the terminology of special social missions of general interest or enterprises that are 'instruments of economic and social policy'. The Albany ruling was regarded as an exception to the 'opening' attitude of the ECJ towards second pillar insurance schemes. In the same year, in a case similar to the Poucet and Pistre (Garcia Case: C-238/94 26.3. 1996) the ECJ reiterated that social security regimes must be compulsory for the principle of solidarity to be invoked to shield them from the competence of competition law.

Three other important decisions were taken in 1999 concerning the complementary regimes for old age pensions set up by social partners. The question was whether social partners can organize solidarity within a group of wage earners and whether the state can acknowledge this capacity. In this case the ECJ was very careful. First, it recognized and mentioned the existence in the treaties of other goals beyond competition, referring to the social protection principles mentioned in Arts. 2 and 3 TEC. In addition, the ECJ made specific reference to the article of the treaty concerning social dialogue and to the agreement on social policy signed by the social partners and annexed to the Maastricht Treaty and finally included in the Amsterdam Treaty. In other words, the ECJ made reference to the existence not only of national social protection legislation, but also to the social goals mentioned within the treaties themselves. The Court's conclusion was that collective agreements between social partners should not be subject to competition law, and the same applies to the national laws which makes affiliation compulsory to these sector pension funds at the request of the social partners.

In conclusion, the ECJ has so far excluded the application of competition law to first pillar compulsory social protection regimes, while, on the contrary, the management of complementary and voluntary regimes is subject to competition law. To decide these cases the ECJ has referred to the general principle of the pursuit of social goals and the existence of a solidarity element, that is, the sharing of risks which necessarily implies a single regime excluding competition.

Another strong tension exists between national social protection policies and the principles of free circulation of people, services and goods. Exceptions in this domain can only be justified by overriding reasons of a 'general interest'. To make viable the free movement of persons, the already mentioned Regulation 1408/71 had set four basic principles to guarantee the 'portability' of some social rights: (*a*) equal treatment of all EC nationals; (*b*) the cumulability of insurance periods; (*c*) the exportability of benefits; and (*d*) the applicability of a single legislation (the *lex loci laboris*).[99] Art. 4 excluded 'social assistance' from the scope of the coordination envisaged. The basic idea was that the free movement of workers required the portability of work-related entitlements, but not those social rights that were unrelated to work or to contributions more clearly associated with concepts of need and related to national solidarity conceptions. The use of service abroad was also regulated. Art. 22 stated that the national social security regime must reimburse the person having received medical treatment abroad up to the national cost, provided that a preliminary authorization is obtained. In 1972, in the Frilli Case, the ECJ ruling gave those social assistance minima linked to social citizenship (e.g. social pensions) to non-nationals. Another ruling in 1987 (the Giletti Case) went further, making these benefits exportable from the country of payment to that of new residence.[100] The Council reacted with a new regulation in 1992 (no. 1247), which included a list of benefits subject to limited coordination and that can be consumed in the territory only if the holder is a legal resident. The issue has thus become one of residence for social assistance, and the member states have some space to define this, even if the ECJ has recently entered in such area (for instance, in the Swaddling and Martinez Sala Cases).

Another closely related issue is the more or less extensive definition of goods and services whose freedom of circulation must be guaranteed. Medical services and health care, as well as medicaments, are at the core of the jurisprudence discussing the extent to which the principle of free circulation of services can break the public monopoly in the delivery of certain services. The Court has established that the free movement of services could not be invoked to avoid the duty to subscribe to compulsory health insurances, but it has not yet expressed its opinion in the area of compulsory additional and integrative regimes. Health care and insurance are the most crucial areas because, contrary to old age pensions and invalidity and unemployment benefits, for instance, they have stronger 'market' characteristics and are fragmented into many providers and markets (e.g. medical instruments, pharmaceuticals, doctors in private practice, etc.). Moreover, this is the area in which some national political forces more clearly aim at transforming

[99] The portability of social rights within the Union has clear limits. Integrative pensions (second pillar pensions) cannot be transferred, giving rise to negative consequences for the intra-European mobility particularly of skilled workers. Moreover, there has been an explosion of means-tested services and there are considerable limitations in their portability. The status of migrating workers is recognized only for regular contracts and typical employment, while for 'a-typical' employment there is no access to non-contributive services. Non-active persons remain outside the field of application of these regulations altogether.

[100] The case concerned the French authorities' refusal to pay a means-tested pension to an Italian migrant who returned home.

these services into private goods. The distinction between health care as a redistribution and solidarity institution, and health care as an economic enterprise is, clearly, subtle and politically sensitive.

In two cases (Schumacher Case, C-215/87, *Commission against Germany* C-62/90, 8.4.92), the ECJ stated that medicaments should be considered as goods. Therefore, their free circulation concerned producing firms as well as individuals buying them for personal use. As far as health care and medical services are concerned, in the jointly decided Luisi and Carbone Cases (C-286/82 and 26/83), the ECJ affirmed that the freedom of services delivery includes the freedom of consumers to enjoy the service in a different member state, while Art. 60 of the EEC Treaty meant this liberty to be applied to those who deliver services, and not to those who consume them. The Grogan Case (C-159/90, 4.10.91) confirmed this orientation in a particularly delicate case. An Irish Court asked the European Court whether abortion should to be considered as a health care service and whether a state that does not deliver (and indeed, prohibits) such care could also prohibit the diffusion of information concerning the availability of that service in other member states.

In the Decker and Kohll Cases (C-120/95; C-156/96), in order to decide whether the obligation of a preliminary authorization for the reimbursement of medical treatment obtained abroad was an obstacle to the exchange of goods and services, the ECJ was obliged to discuss the general principles of free circulation as they refer to social security. The ECJ judged that a Luxembourg rule stating that health care obtained abroad can only be reimbursed if a preliminary authorization is demanded and obtained was incompatible with Community law. By viewing prior authorization as an unjustified impediment, the decision has substantiated the principle of free choice in the place of treatment for European citizens (as in the case for national systems, where citizens are free to choose where to be treated) and the freedom of circulation of European patients. In both these cases, the ECJ took into consideration the financial implications for the resident's social security system. The final opinion was in favour of defending free movement because it appeared that the reimbursement of a pair of spectacles, in the Decker Case, and the reimbursement of orthodontic treatment, in the Kohll Case, had no significant effect on the finances of the national security system.[101] In the Smits-Peerbooms Case (July 2001), the Court included hospital services within the same free circulation scope, but added that the need to preserve the financial balance of medical and hospital systems that are open to all justifies a restriction such as that provided for under the

---

[101] Palm, W. and Nickless, J., 'Access to Healthcare in the European Union: The Consequences of the Kohll and Decker judgements', *Eurohealth*, 7 (2001), 13–22.

system of prior authorization. It added, however, that such administrative authorization must be based on criteria that are made public, objective, and non-discriminatory.[102]

In these various rulings, medical care is, therefore, viewed as service by the treaties and every consumer of medical services can buy them freely within the EU. The ECJ has thus designed new rights for European citizens, although it is not clear whether these are citizens' or consumers' rights. For the social cover of health care, this situation creates a dual system. On the one hand, Regulation 1408/71 integrates the patient with prior authorization into the social protection system where she/he receives medical treatment *as if she were insured with it*, given that costs are settled between the two social protection systems according to the tariffs of the state where the treatment was delivered. Mobile persons thus become temporary 'members' of the host country health care system. In contrast, patients without prior authorization claim the coverage of their home country's social protection system when returning into it *as if they had received the treatment there*, given that reimbursement is made according to the conditions and tariffs applicable in the state of residence (not of treatment). One national health system thus 'exports' patients (and citizens), in much the same way as they are sometimes exported into the private sector when, for instance, long waiting lists exist in the public one; another health system 'imports' patients. From both perspectives, these rulings open up forms of exit from the consumption of nationally delivered public goods.

These principles have so far concerned a limited number of cases: high technology and specialized treatments; claimants from border areas and from social groups that are well informed and competent about service quality.[103] This notwithstanding, the interaction between national social sharing systems, competition law and the market free movements has been growing, with an accumulation of constraints being placed on national social policy connected with European market integration.[104]

---

[102] Vandenbroucke, F., 'The EU and Social Protection: What Should the European Convention Propose' (Cologne: Max Plank Institute for the Study of Societies, 2002), occasional paper, 17 June.

[103] For quantitative information see McKee, M., 'The Influence of European Law on National Health Policy', *Journal of European Social Policy*, 6 (1996), 263–86; Coheur A., Lewalle, H., Palm, W. and Nickless, J., 'Implications de la jurisprudence récente concernant la coordination des systèmes de protection contre le risque maladie' (Bruxelles: Rapport de la Direction Générale des Affairs Sociales de la Commission Européenne, 2000), 178; Hermesse, J. J., 'L'ouverture des frontières aux patients. Les conséquences économiques', in *Actes du Colloque 'Soins sans frontières dans l'Union Européenne?'* (Luxembourg, 1998), 53–63.

[104] By 1994, the ECJ had offered more than 300 decisions on social security coordination and more than 100 on other social policy matters. Liebfried and Pierson, 'Social Policy', 194. On the general relationship between economic integration and the social

In their golden age national social transfer and social service systems excluded non-nationals (by 'nationality' or strong residential requirements) and locked nationals firmly in as compulsory members. Conflict and divisions were purely internal, concerning within territory groups' fights for inclusion and exclusion. Since after the Great Depression and the Second World War, the boundaries of markets largely coincided with those of the national state and with the social policy constituencies, national welfare state systems were able to develop in relative isolation from one another. When second pillar or supplementary insurances became viable, some groups started to subscribe to them in order to add supplementary benefits to their state-based schemes. Governments therefore had to decide the level of closure of these supplementary schemes: compulsory or voluntary, public or private. The British Conservative government, for instance, in 1958 started with public supplementary schemes from which workers could contract out into non-public funds. In the 1980s Thatcher relied on this early opening to promote the privatization of these supplementary schemes. In contrast to the British approach, the Social Democrats in Sweden and in other Nordic countries successfully resisted pressure to open up, and supplementary schemes remained state-run and compulsory. Continental countries (like Germany) followed the path of contractual supplementary schemes run by the social partners, while in France the *régimes supplementaires* were compulsory and fragmented.[105] The process of European integration has slowly started to modify the status quo of national social security systems, and this is leading to an unsuspected growing number of implications.[106]

The first of these implications has to do with the control exercised by the state over the beneficiaries of its social services. In compliance with the freedom of movement, member states can no longer limit their social benefits to their citizens. More precisely, member states no longer enjoy the exclusive right to administer the claims of migrants to welfare benefits and must accept that the decision concerning the status of a social services beneficiary (e.g. to be sick) can be carried out by the bureaucratic agencies of other member states. The jurisdictional control of these rights has been largely transferred to the supranational centre-administered Court system.

A second implication concerns the territorial principle: member states can no longer insist that their social service benefits apply to their territory

integration see Ferrara, M., 'Los dilemas de la Europa social', in S. Munoz Machado, J. Luis Garcia Delgado and L. Gonzales Seara (eds.), *Las Estructuras del Bienestar en Europa* (Madrid: Escuela Libre Editorial, 2000), 421–33.

[105] See Ferrera, *Modelli di solidarietà*; Esping-Andersen, J., *The Three Worlds of Welfare Capitalism* (Cambridge: Polity Press, 1990).

[106] See in particular Liebfried, S. and Pierson, P., *European Social Policy Between Fragmentation and Integration* (Washington, DC: Brookings, 1996).

and must be consumed there. Benefits paid by each state have become portable across the whole market and people insured in a national system can increasingly shop around and consume the services offered by other EU systems (e.g. in health care). This affects the monopolistic provision of public goods: patients, for instance, can exit the consumption of national public goods (health care services and medicaments), consuming extra-territorial public goods.

A third implication is that member states are less able than in the past to prevent other social policy systems from competing directly on their territory with their regimes. In the field of supplementary insurance, foreign providers of benefits have access to the national system. In addition, the internal market increasingly challenges the line dividing public and private spheres. In the long run, any welfare policy deliberately shaped to prevent the consumption of private welfare goods runs counter to the 'constitutionalized' market freedoms.

A fourth crucial implication concerns the fiscal and financial viability of national welfare systems and their redistributive function.[107] The import and export of non-citizen patients and citizens' consumptions abroad has implications for the costs of services. In health care, the ECJ has ruled on the mobility of patients without challenging the sovereign right of the state to compel its citizens into compulsory public insurance. This may impact on cost-containing strategies at the national level, challenge the logic of functioning of services resting on in-kind provisions, and strengthen the position of private providers. The fact that the EU's direct and indirect effects on 'national' social spending are not accompanied by EU fiscal responsibility creates a potential area of friction between the (EU) level of legislative and judicial competence and the (national) level of fiscal competence.[108] Potentially the biggest challenge to national welfare sovereignty is, indeed, to the principle of compulsory membership within public schemes for state nationals (or residents). Competition law and the four freedoms are slowly beginning to undermine the state's capacity to prevent, through compulsory and universal social schemes, the freedom of choice of well-off and low-risk individuals, since, clearly, the division in basic, supplementary and private

---

[107] On this point see Ferrera, M., 'European Integration and National Social Sovereignty: Changing Boundaries, New Structuring?', *Comparative Political Studies*, 36 (2003), 611–52. In this section I am much indebted to this author, since he addresses these issues within the Rokkanian and Hirschmanian frameworks of exit/entry options and boundary building/removing in line with my approach.

[108] On the important problem of the tension that has been created between the fiscal and legislative functions of different 'levels' of government (central, regional, local, and European) see Alber, J., 'Il ripensamento del welfare state', *Rivista Italiana di Scienza Politica*, 27 (1997), 49–99; Alber, J., 'A Framework for the comparative study of social services', *Journal of European Social Policy*, 2 (1995), 131–49.

insurance schemes opens up exit opportunities for affluent consumers and middle class individuals. If they are not kept in the public schemes through a mix of coercion and generosity, the coverage of the public social sharing may gradually become residual, reducing its financial viability and its redistributive function.

Finally—and most importantly from my point of view—there are implications for the features of national political structuring. It is doubtful whether, in the long term, it is possible to institutionalize social sharing and solidarity at a territorial level other than that of the market. Individuals do not participate voluntarily in the transfer and regulatory policies generating costs that can be avoided. Similarly, local communities cannot be expected to implement policies that reduce their competitiveness in a wide and integrated economic system. If social services are subsidized with local taxes, citizens from outside cannot be discriminated against, and the EU law forces local institutions to charge the same prices, then a potential tendency is developed to shop for services. In an integrated market, either social policy is made at a level that is coterminous with the market, or local communities and constituencies end up providing welfare to 'strangers'. Within the nation-state, broad cultural solidarities avoid the visibility of the costs and relate conflicts inherent in this situation. At the enlarged EU level, however, these cultural bonds seem to be too weak to suspend instrumental calculations. As the building of the national welfare state was the subject of internal voice and contestation, contributing to the establishment of political alignments and alliances, its external restructuring via quantitatively relevant exits/entries may generate the reorientation of interests and voice activities in this domain. The consequences of this may well also imply a change in the orientation of sectors of the European population towards nationally provided public goods, with implications for political agencies such as interest organizations, parties and subnational governments. The extent to which these developments may affect the centre-periphery relations, the interest intermediation system, and the cleavage system in member countries will be the specific topic of the following chapters.

Conclusions: The Boundary Configuration of the EU

Any new political formation is defined in terms of the institutional configuration of the central hierarchy and of its internal and external boundaries. These were the topics of the Chapters 2 and 3. The institutional structure of the new centre shows various familiar features—(*a*) territorial expansion; (*b*) competence accretion; (*c*) legal centralization; (*d*) bureaucratic infrastructural development—and important particularities—(*a*) weak territoriality;

(*b*) lack of a vertical (national versus European centres) and horizontal (across EU institutions) division of power; (*c*) 'constitutionalization' of pre-defined policy goals; and (*d*) invocation of different non-hierarchical legit-imation principles. In terms of internal/external boundary configuration, the EU integration is a process of selective boundary de-differentiation, because boundaries are removed and therefore member systems are made less differ-entiated. It is selective because not all the major system boundaries are removed equally and contemporarily.

The clearest difference between the European state and the EU boundary setting process lies in the different consolidation timing. For early European states, the intense and continuous warfare meant that only coercion was ultimately capable of controlling the territories, whose actual control was achieved long before any other internal boundaries were removed, and, in particular, long before a standardized internal market or national commu-nity was created. For instance, the development of uniform national, penal, and civic codes was advocated in doctrinaire terms only during the Enlight-enment and progressed very slowly. The right to engage in work activity that could be freely chosen had to overcome the rigid guild systems and corpo-ratist protections, and the right to decide where to reside freely within the state territory continued to be strongly limited for long periods. In addition, the lack of linguistic standardization persisted for a long time. During the eighteenth and nineteenth centuries all states were 'regulatory states', engaged in policies of regulatory standardization across their territories in the fields of educational credentials, weights and all sorts of other measures, taxation, work conditions, etc. to remove those obstacles that fragmented the market and made military operations inefficient.[109]

In the EU experience , the regulatory standardization phase of the new centre has preceded actual territorial control. It was, indeed, the declining importance of territorial boundaries as military and high-politics borders that allowed integration to take place in the form of the removal of system boundaries among different regulatory systems. Internal economic barriers were removed first, and a centralization of the legal system followed, to defend this economic integration. Given the new centre's lack of any terri-torial control, internal boundary removal proceeded at a much higher speed and scope than external boundary setting. Therefore, territorial formal bor-ders no longer coincide with economic, cultural, and politico-administrative boundaries in a series of significant areas. As a result, the EU produces a

---

[109] A visit to the science and technology museums of the main European capitals shows the widespread 'regulatory' nature of the eighteenth and nineteenth centuries states. To regard the 'regulatory state' as a new type or phase is, therefore, mere oblivion. An intense regulatory phase is typical of the periods of territorial consolidation of enlarged polities, when control is extended beyond the mere military reach.

progressive disjoining and lack of coincidence of the previously highly coterminous economic, cultural, coercion, and politico-administrative boundaries
of the nation-states.

Even in the economic field we find a different situation. In certain areas,
the removal of internal boundaries has been accompanied by the setting up of
new European-wide external boundaries with the capacity of the new centre
to control their transcendence. This is most obvious in the customs, tariffs,
and quota areas, in the agricultural field, and in monetary policy. In other
sectors—such as competition law, anti-state aides, and mobility of capital—
internal boundaries have been successfully removed without any new external boundaries being set up to separate the new system from the broader
international environment, and without the formation of an agency with the
capacity to regulate the levels of boundary crossing and transcendence. In
other economic sectors, however, boundaries have been left largely un-
touched, as in the fiscal field, for instance. In this configuration, certain
economic activities and policies are still confined within the nation-state's
formal control; others are confined within new EU strong external boundaries; and others form part of a more general 'global' openness.

This differential distribution of economic boundary control is probably
responsible for the relative ineffectiveness of the EU in its macroeconomic
management of internal goals and external hegemonic interests. The theory
suggesting that the nation-state has ceased to be an efficient economic
manager and can only provide those public and social services, at the lowest
possible cost, which international capital deems to be necessary and essential,[110] applies very well to the set of European small- and medium-sized
states and national economies. It is less applicable to the USA, however,
whose huge internal market, low trade dependency, and high currency international status, grant considerable control over most of its macroeconomic
policies. While the European countries taken individually are more trade
open (as the imports plus exports over national product) than Japan and the
USA, the EU is sufficiently 'big' (about 25 per cent trade openness) to oppose
global pressures when this is considered necessary, and to pursue political
goals in the trade, social, and environmental domains through modalities
that are not in the reach of its member states. However, if the scale of the
European economy in principle allows options that are not open to national
governments to be considered, the problem remains that this kind of options
are not realized within the framework of the existing decisional structures of
the EU. The EU, for instance, is not a sufficiently large fiscal actor to engage
in macroeconomic management, and its central institutions are not able to

---

[110] See Ohmae, K., *The Borderless World* (London: Collins, 1990); Reic, R. B.,
The World of Nations (New York: Vintage, 1992).

create complementary policies of a non-monetary nature to support such management (employment, taxation, labour market, etc.).

In the field of legal integration, the ECJ has contributed actively and efficiently to the removal of EU internal market boundaries. It has been asked to define the nature of quantitative restrictions on imports as well as that of other measures that were equally discriminatory. It has been crucial in defining which exceptions can be made to free movement on the basis of public morality, public security, health, and cultural patrimony. More generally, almost all areas of boundary removing are governed by rules that have been interpreted by the Court, including that powerful boundary removal generated by the principle of the mutual recognition of equivalent national regulative standards and conformity requirements. In the future, the implication of the ECJ doctrines and adjudication traditions could extend to a growing number of fields, or, alternatively, be confined.[111] For instance, no public service domain can, in principle, be exempted from the logic of competition law, and defending the freedom of circulation has implications that are so potentially far-reaching as to be almost impossible to foresee.[112] However, the Court cannot effectively enforce external boundaries that are not incorporated in the treaty competences by judicial review.

In the coercion domain, boundary building shows an unusual development. On the one hand, no military external boundary of the EU can be identified, and the level of integration of the military hierarchies is considerably hampered by the 'variable geometry' of military alliances of member states. On the other, home affair cooperation, internal policing, external visa, immigration and asylum control, and the sharing and centralization of crimes and criminal control have progressed at a considerable speed in only a decade. The current renewed problems of internal-external security may foster further integration in this area.

While the centre consolidates economic and legal integration, it does not create a 'system'. The area of system building highlights limited activities of boundary removal, weak external boundary setting and strong state claims of control. This is also the area in which negative trade-off are most evident. While normative structures increasingly regulate the contacts and interdependency exchanges among people across states, the growing set of mutual practices and recognitions is not accompanied by a corresponding develop-

[111] Actually, the activism of the ECJ seems to have attenuated in the most recent years. See the last chapter of Dehousse, *The European Court of Justice*. However, none of the most innovative doctrines of the Court has been challenged or refused.

[112] Expansion into neighbouring areas from its historical mission to integrate national economies and markets can be justified by the links that relate economic integration with other sector policies. Dehousse, R., 'Constitutional Reforms in the European Community: Are There Alternatives to the Majoritarian Avenue?', *West European Politics*, 18 (1995), 118–36, 125.

ment in common purposes or visions beyond the elite level. The cultural systems, as groups of shared meanings and symbols, remain highly territorialized, while the European external cultural boundaries remain vaguely defined and institutionalized to a limited extent.[113] While national participation and decision rights cannot be exercised effectively in those areas where policies are either exclusively, predominantly or even concurrently under EU responsibility, and the centre of decision-making is no longer the state centre but the EU centre, genuine European participation and decision rights are scanty. The regulative and redistributive social sharing at the EU level is naturally very limited and new 'social rights' at this level result from the ECJ application of mobility and competition principles to the national social sharing systems. European rights that facilitate mobility have eroded the importance of territory and nationality as criteria for inclusion in national membership groups enjoying equal treatment with respect to employment, residence, social welfare benefits, and taxation. They are now more 'consumers' rights (of social transfers and services) than 'social rights'. As such, while they extend individual options, they also tend to undermine and destructure the principles on which national social sharing have been built upon historically. Moreover, the frequent 'cheating' of nation-states in this area shows the long-lasting lack of broader commitment to the development of a transnational European society.[114] The broad ECJ judicial interpretation has created rights that national governments never intended to honour, and it has extended these rights to groups of beneficiaries that national governments certainly intended to exclude, to the extent that many legal entitlements entail financial costs while benefiting individuals who cannot even contribute to the re-election of national governments.

The explanation of the specific shaping of boundaries of the EU described in this chapter can stress either institutional or political elements. The institutional explanation focuses on the relationship between the institutional structure of the new centre and its strategy of boundary control. The structural imbalance in favour of the removal of internal boundaries as opposed to the setting of new enlarged external boundaries in general, and more

---

[113] The EU is a 'negative community' in which there is an agreement on common practices and rights, but no definition of common purposes. Kratochwil, F., 'Of system, boundaries, and territoriality. An inquiry into the formation of the state system', *World Politics*, 39 (1986–87), 27–52, 33.

[114] Nation-states have often cheated concerning mobility rights for 'public service'; have tried try to limit, until 1990, the residence rights to those who were active, excluding the non-active; have tried to restrict access to national welfare provisions; have shaped their legislation in such a way as to preempt ECJ interventions. On this see Conant, L., 'Contested Boundaries. Citizens, States, and Supranational Belonging in the European Union', in J. Migdal (ed.), *Boundaries and Belonging: States and Societies in the Struggle to Shape Identities and Local Practices* (Cambridge: Cambridge University Press, 2004), 284–317.

specifically the weaknesses of system building boundaries, is embedded in the high level of intergovernmental consensus required by the nature of EU institutional design. The need to reach an agreement within the Council, the mutual advantages that these agreements need to identify, the difficulty of determining any particular situation which might be preferable to the status quo for all countries or for a sufficient number of them (even leaving aside the veto power of one single country, still possible in several areas), and the ideological, economic and institutional design differences among states make it extremely difficult to stipulate common regulatory agreements at the EU level.[115]

At the same time, the fundamental lack of trust among members and the emphasis on avoiding free riding and cheating has made for a treaty structure that is oriented towards specific goal attainment and anti-infringement rules in the field of common market creation. The 'constitutionalization' of economic rights connected to the market operated by the ECJ has raised the core economic constitution to the level of supreme law with respect to which every other orientation by the member states, as well as by other European bodies, has to be evaluated. To limit cheating and free riding, the member states have set a very tight straitjacket for themselves, making it extremely difficult the consolidation of new boundaries of the EU. Within the existing institutional design, most policies can be seen more as instruments to discipline members than as tools to foster their interests against non-members. The same dynamics of member states self-disciplining through internal boundary removal that is not accompanied by any external boundary setting can be observed in several fields that have been discussed in this chapter (the most conspicuous example being monetary integration).[116]

The conclusion that certain options available within the new 'scale' of the European economy have not been adopted, and that most 'policies' are inwardly oriented towards the disciplining of internal members, then may suggest a more 'political' interpretation. It may thus be argued that this specific construction of differential boundary transcendence was carried out in order to free European political elites from the growing constraints

---

[115] Scharpf has investigated the specific relationship between the configuration of the central EU hierarchy's decision rules and its resulting strategy of boundary control in great details. See Scharpf, F., 'The joint decision trap: Lessons from German federalism and European integration', *Public Administration*, 66 (1988), 239–78; Scharpf, 'Negative and positive integration'; Scharpf, *Governing Europe*.

[116] Adrienne Héritier expresses a more positive opinion about the capacity of the EU to implement market correcting measures, particularly in liberalized network industries and public service sectors. See 'Market Integration and Social Cohesion: the politics of public services in European regulation', *Journal of European Public Policy*, 8 (2001), 825–52; and 'Containing Negative Integration', in R. Mayntz and W. Streek (eds.), *Die Reformierbarkeit der Demokratie. Innovationen und Blockaden* (Frankfurt am Main: Campus Verlag, 2003), 101–21.

of their internal national, democratic, and welfare states. These political elites find it easier and preferable to agree on external constraints that 'objectify' the need for internal discipline. More precisely, the setting of a core economic constitution as an external constraint was a way by which to externalize the pressure for domestic change and reform and, at the same time, to externalize the political costs of economic rationalization. As a result, they have—so far—managed to shield the internal sources of their support and legitimacy from the costs of measures based on 'economic rationality'.

In this latter perspective, the current configuration of boundary building and removing can be read as deriving mainly from the absence at the EU level of those counterforces which, in the history of the nation-state, made for a progressive territorial containment of economic rationality within the shell of national, social and political rights. To put it differently, the current boundary configuration is typical of a political formation in which the standardization of the internal market regulation and the centralization of the jurisdictional activities have developed before and without the centralization of political power (as a result of the institutional intergovernmental structure) and the creation of political structures and agencies.

A wider discussion of the interconnection between the 'institutional' and 'political' interpretation of the EU requires a more thorough investigation of the consequences of this on political agencies and structures at both the EU and national level. The next chapters deal with the political consequences that this specific configuration of boundary control and transcendence has for the corresponding configuration of 'exit options' and 'locking in' of resources' and actors' inside each territory. These consequences may extend far beyond the original intentions or current wishes of the main architects, entrepreneurs, and financers of the new centre: the nation-states' political elites.

5

Political Structuring in Loosely Bounded Territories: Territorial and Corporate Structures

Introduction: Three Structures of Political Representation: Territorial, Corporate and Electoral

Political structuring rests on the process of individual voice articulation, mobilization, and organization through different channels and agencies. Structuring implies the development of intermediate bodies and organizational networks of political and social movements linking citizens to interest groups and political organizations into broad political alliances 'vertebrating' the polity. Structuring, finally, also points to the stabilization of patterns of interaction by the creation of rules and norms of behaviour, coalitions among sets of actors, and the development of interorganizational linkages.[1]

In Chapters 1 and 2 the consolidation of internal political structures was presented as a process of internal differentiation of externally consolidated territorial units, resting on the progressive *coincidence* of economic, military, administrative and cultural boundaries that 'locked' actors and resources into binding political exchanges within the territorial borders of the state. Three main political structures were singled out as main avenues for conflict management: the structure of centre–periphery relations, the structure of

---

[1] The term 'structure' does not identify physical objects, but the property of the relations among parts in a system or subsystem. Ferrera gives the following definition of 'structuring': 'the ... stabilization of ... patterns of interaction and institutional-organizational forms through the creation of specific coalitions among actors, of increasingly articulated and codified rules and norms of behaviour, and the establishment of inter-organizational links', Ferrera, M., *The Boundaries of Welfare. European Integration and the New Spatial Politics of Solidarity* (Oxford: Oxford University Press, forthcoming). Morlino uses the term 'anchoring' in a similar vein; Morlino, L., *Democracy between Consolidation and Crisis. Parties, Groups and Citizens in Southern Europe* (Oxford: Oxford University Press, 1997), 338–45. See also Easton, D., *The Analysis of Political Structure* (New York: Routledge, 1990), Chapter 3.

corporate interest intermediation, and the structure of cleavage alignments. Of these three, the territorial and the corporate are very long-lasting, going back to the assemblies of the feudal systems and to the representative bodies of the Middle Ages based on orders, corporations, territories, estates, curia, etc. Both structures have survived into modern times: modern forms of territorial representation and conflict management take the form of federal principles and institutions and of other types of institutionalized local-regional autonomy; modern corporate representation takes the form of dense organizational mobilization of the resource controllers: labour, capital, trade, professions, etc.

The comparative literature has discussed the extent to which the organizational infrastructure of the resource controllers presents 'pluralist', 'neo-corporatist' or 'etatist' features, with neo-corporatist organizations of interests resembling the old-type corporatism.[2] For my purposes, I reserve the term of 'corporate structure', 'corporate representation' and 'corporate channel' for all forms of interest intermediation,[3] irrespective of the specific mode of their organization.

Old types of centre–periphery structures have, instead, been more affected by the processes of modernization. In the old forms of territorial representation, territorial entities were the natural focus for the external representation of the local community, whose internal divisions were either suppressed or treated as irrelevant.[4] However, the localistic ties, on which external territorial representation rested, became progressively dysfunctional to the effective structuring of voice, and were insufficient to satisfy the progressive internal differentiation of interests produced by socio-economic modernization within the local community. The nationwide and centralized polity began to necessitate cross-local linkages based on other kinds of affinities than those of a purely territorial nature. Eventually, the development of cross-local alliances of a 'functional' nature among different section/groups became more important than the forms of territorial external representation.

The survival and persistence of early forms of territorial and corporate representation during the period of prevailing absolutist rule is a key element

---

[2] To the extent that they are based on (*a*) one interest organization per functional sector; (*b*) de facto compulsory (or quasi-compulsory) membership for all units (farms, firms, agencies, individuals); (*c*) clear hierarchies of organizations, and no competition among those organizations; (*d*) provisions for recognition or licensing by the state; (*e*) granting of monopoly of sector representation in the deliberative bodies of the state. See Schmitter, P., 'Still the century of Corporatism?', *Review of Politics*, 36 (1974), 85–93; Schmitter, P. and Lehmbruch, G. (eds.), *Trends Towards Corporatist Intermediation* (London: Sage, 1979).

[3] Rokkan, S., 'I voti contano le risorse decidono', *Rivista Italiana di Scienza Politica*, 5 (1975), 167–76.

[4] Tarrow, S., *Between center and periphery: grassroots politicians in Italy and France* (New Haven, CT: Yale University Press, 1977), 55.

to the following slow and smooth development of the modern, mainly politico-electoral forms of 'democratic' political representation. Indeed, where absolutist rule eradicated or weakened the early forms of pluralism, the following developments towards inclusive electoral democracy was severely hampered and delayed.[5] Notwithstanding this developmental link, political modernization is associated with the progressive overcoming of these early forms by politico-electoral structures of representation. The electoral or plebiscitarian forms of representation are thus based on a formal political equality within territorially defined membership groups, by decisions reached by some sort of aggregation of equally weighted preferences, and on the dominant role played by specific political organizations specialized in channelling and aggregating those preferences as votes: the political parties.

The integration of these three main structures of political representation was difficult to achieve. In principle, and in their pure form, the three are, in fact, incompatible. If territorial external representation were to dominate, little room would be left to express conflicts of interest, *Weltanschauung*, and identity that either transcend the local community or divide it internally. For the supporters of the pure corporatist state, no further room is left for ideological conflicts cutting across the lines of the (recognized and licensed) system of interests once representation is organized along them. No other principle of representation capable of undermining the corporative negotiated outcomes is acceptable.[6] Finally, in a radical majoritarian view of representation—the Rousseau tradition—corporate and territorial interests are perceived as sectional and illegitimate interferences in the formation of the majority's will be based on the principle of one person, one value, one vote.

The development of modern European political parties guaranteed an equilibrium between these channels, given that their long arms extended across all three forms of representation and made their combination viable. In other words, parties provided political personnel that made for 'electoral mobilizers', 'interest articulators', and 'peripheral political elite' to overlap. They did so by providing a single hierarchical order to organize from within various spheres of representation activity and to iron out the tensions that emerged from their relationships. In addition, the within-party hierarchy and

---

[5] Rokkan S., 'Nation Building, Cleavage Formation and the Structuring of Mass Politics', in S. Rokkan (ed.), *Citizens Elections Parties* (Oslo: Universitetsforlaget, 1970), 72–144; Daalder, H., 'Paths Towards State Formation in Europe: Democratization, Bureacratization and Politicization', in H. E. Chehabi and A. Stephan (eds.), *Politics, Society, and Democracy. Comparative Studies* (Boulder, CO: Westview Press, 1995), 113–30.

[6] On this point see the exhaustive analysis of the historical 'corporatist' theories of society and state in Ornaghi, L., *Stato e corporazione. Storia di una dottrina nella crisi del sistema politico contemporaneo* (Milano: Giuffré, 1984).

the interparty pattern of competition were 'exported', penetrating local politics as well as corporate alignments, and provided the general organizational principle promoting the symmetry of the territorial, corporate and electoral subsystems. Political parties thus represented ideological-organizational alliances between economic and/or cultural agencies in the centre and local leaders and movements in the different peripheries.

The EU policymaking process is divorced from the territorially-based institutions for political representation and legitimation and from the membership spaces of collective identities. It impacts directly upon nation-states' boundaries (*a*) by removing boundaries among them; (*b*) by building new common external boundaries; (*c*) by differentiating new internal functional regimes; and it impacts indirectly (*d*) by effecting state capacities to set new types of boundaries; (*e*) by imposing substantive constraints on national policies in various domains; and (*f*) by redefining group interests and identities. If the domestic political structuring was based upon the declining opportunity for exit determined by the external consolidation of the boundaries of the democratic, welfare, and national state, what happens to these political structures when boundary redrawing opens up new exit opportunities for individuals, groups, firms, and even territories? How does the new pattern of integration among loosely bounded territories—whose functional boundaries do not coincide with borders—influence the structures of national corporate, territorial and politico-electoral representation? One aspect of the problem concerns the possibility of forming new European political structures; the second concerns the effect that integration has on established national political structures. This problem can be further divided into three subquestions, guiding this chapter and the next:

1. To what extent is the loosening of state boundaries likely to foster the *rebirth of territorial politics and territorial representation* as opposed to the traditional forms of nationwide functional representation?
2. To what extent does the imbalance between market-making forces and market-controlling political decision at the European level push for a *redefinition of national interest group internal cohesion and political allegiance*?
3. What is the impact of these processes on the *political alignments of European electorates and party systems*, and how will it shape new social and political oppositions?

This chapter focuses on the first two questions, discussing the extent to which the boundary redrawing implied by the integration process—discussed in Chapters 3 and 4—generates new, territorially enlarged and higher-level centre–periphery and interest intermediation structures, and/or impacts on the existing national ones. Chapter 6, will discuss the same questions for the politico-electoral structures.

Centre–Periphery Structures

Centre–Periphery Relations in Nation-State Formation

Once the forms of pre-modern territorial representation were superseded by functional and cross-local systems of cleavages and interest articulation, the relations between the political 'centre' of the state and the subnational territories were set up via institutional arrangements going from a maximum of federalist decentralization to a maximum of unitary centralization, and by political arrangements involving a specific mix of partisan, bureaucratic and 'local notables' linkages. However, the process of modernization triggered by the British industrial revolution and by the French political revolution did not completely obliterate the older territorial distinctiveness on which the boundaries of the nation-states were superimposed.

During the nineteenth and early twentieth century it was felt that modernization implied a process of progressive integration, eliminating the territorial distinctiveness that was based on cultural and economic distances, differences, and dependencies. Either new and more homogeneous states were to be formed (by secession and aggregation), or the modernization process would progressively attenuate the territorial concentration of distinctive features and/or their political significance. Even the new nineteenth century federal constitutions (Canada and Germany) and the federal solution advocated for Italy and Spain were pictured as a uniform (albeit not unitary) system of government, with limited concessions being made to territorial distinctiveness (the Quebec system of civil law, the Bavarian state tradition—further eroded by the German Weimer constitution—the distinctive arrangements for the Basque provinces in Spain). Even if complete uniformity was never attained within the nation-state, the general trend was towards the denial, non-recognition, or softening of territorial distinctiveness. After the Second World War, forms of autonomous arrangements were extended to Wales, Northern Ireland, the Italian special status border and island regions, and a variety of European islands (Greenland, the Faeroes, the Alund islands, the Azores, the Canaries, Corsica).[7]

This trend towards territorial standardization was based on the belief that the rise of the national, democratic and welfare state was incompatible with the continuing historical rights of previously independent territories and with the recognition of distinctiveness as a collective right. The 'nation' implied a unitary identity as opposed to the multiple identity required by

---

[7] See Keating, M., 'Asymmetrical Government: Multinational States in an Integrating Europe', *Publius: The Journal of Federalism*, 29 (1998), 71–86 for a full list of these experiences.

the persistence of this distinctiveness. In addition, liberal democracy was based on an individualistic principle of representation organized through non-territorial (or cross-territorial) collective identities (cleavage systems and functional interests), and even the welfare and education policies were devised to break down particularistic identities on the basis of the principle of individual social equality. In fact, those cases mentioned above where a relative autonomy was recognized can all be viewed as small-scale exceptions, with no major implications for the structure of the state.

The consolidation of the state system determined the forming of the various kinds of European peripheries according to their geopolitical, geo-cultural and geoeconomic position with respect to the new state geography. The European state and nation building was not only a process of integration and unification of disparate and different territories, economies and societies; it also implied the disintegration or the division of previously integrated territories, economies and societies. When cultural identities were strong, this created minorities on both sides of the new border. Border groups, economies and societies had, therefore, to face a reorientation towards national centres around the new cores of political decision, production and exchange. Their linkages with the older economies and societies were necessarily and progressively cut, and their claims redirected accordingly.

The interaction between various types of boundaries also made for various types of peripheries. Military-administrative centres—with their chanceller-ies, ministries, courts, legislative bodies, etc.—did not necessarily coincide with economic centres—with the headquarters of major trading and indus-trial companies, stock exchanges, banking insurance, etc.—or with cultural centres—with their religious and/or linguistic distinctiveness, universities, theatres, publishing houses, etc. Territories that were culturally peripheral with respect to the dominant state centre were not necessarily economic peripheries, just as economic peripheralized territories were not necessarily culturally distinctive with respect to the dominant cultural centre. Cultural peripheralization was almost exclusively the result of the reinforcement of military-administrative boundaries, which cut across pre-existing areas of cultural homogeneity as defined mainly in ethno-linguistic and religious terms. Economic peripheralization was mainly the result of the changes in the dominant trade routes. The East-West Southern axis through the Medi-terranean civilizations was dominant until the Roman Empire began to decline and Islam to conquest various territories. The dominant trade route switched progressively northward, along the Rhine valley and the Alps from Central Italy to the Hanseatic League in the North Sea and the Baltic, and its dominant position lasted until the sixteenth century. Later, the transoceanic trade route, crossing Western Europe and the world oceans, led to the relative decline of the transalpine route.

The interaction between these various processes of centre building and peripheralization resulted in territorial structures that were more or less 'monocephalic' or 'polycephalic', where most polycephality was typical of the Central European city-belt of the ex-Holy Roman Empire. On the contrary, during the sixteenth to the eighteenth centuries the dominant administrative centres within territories to the east and west of the medieval trade-route belt continued to strengthen: London, Paris, and Madrid on the Atlantic side, and Vienna, Munich, Berlin, Stockholm, and Copenhagen on the landward side. These centres controlled vast peripheries and accumulated large military and administrative, as well as cultural and economic, resources.

The complexity of the interaction between military-administrative, cultural and economic boundary building does not allow us to make any clear-cut distinction as to which process was dominant in defining the internal differentiation of territories. Immanuel Wallerstein[8] has developed a model of centre–periphery relationships that assigns primacy to development in the economy sphere, posits a hierarchy of economic centres and defines peripheries as territories depending on these rich urban centres. He makes a distinction between four zones generated by the emerging of the early European world economy: *the dominant core* of regions (moving northward from Spain to the Netherlands and later England) with the highest concentration of secondary-tertiary activities and whose population's welfare depended primarily on trading products transported from distant peripheries; *long-distance peripheries* dependent on the core (Latin America, Eastern Europe); *semi-peripheries* dominated by cities in decline (Italy, the French Midi, increasingly Spain); *external areas* beyond the reach of the network of long-distance trade (notably Japan and China until well into the nineteenth century). In his view, the administrative and cultural hierarchies, the rise of the bureaucratic nation-state, the Reformation, etc., can be analysed as reactions to decisive changes brought about by the world economy with the opening up of the ocean trade routes in the sixteenth century.

Against this interpretative paradigm of centre–periphery formation, scholars like Anderson and Finer[9] have asserted the primacy of the state and its military-administrative apparatus. They argue that long-distance trade was of only limited importance in this period, and that what really mattered was the consolidation of the control system in the immediate conquered hinterland of each centre. This points out to the importance of

---

[8] Wallerstein, I., *The Modern World System*, 3 vols. (New York: Academic Press, 1974/ 1980).

[9] See Anderson, P., *Lineages of the Absolutist State* (London: New Left Books, 1974); and Finer, S. E., *The History of Government From the Earliest Times*, 3 vols. (Oxford: Oxford University Press, 1997).

different centres for theories of centre–periphery relations. Rokkan underlines the importance of the interaction between horizontal (territorial) and
vertical (membership) peripheralization in the three domains of cultural,
economic and politico-administrative systems for the monocephalic or polycephalic territorial structures that came about as a result. As an example of
the interaction that determined the peripheralization of areas across the
borders and the administrative boundaries, and their reorientation to the
centres, he mentions the important gap in the system of heavy-freight canal
connecting Europe. For instance, a canal connection between the Rhone and
the Rhine, and between both of these and the Seine, would have constituted
an important and attractive alternative—also during the railway period—to
the routes over the Alps. However, notwithstanding obvious economic advantages for the region and European trade overall, the administrative
authorities in Paris were always reluctant to invest in a transport system
that would have brought Eastern France closer to the Rhineland axis and
allowed the North-South traffic to bypass Paris. Geopolitical issues can thus
be said to have concerned military and administrative authorities in Paris to
an important extent.[10] In conclusion, although large-scale switches in the
main trade routes might have determined the *systemic* peripheralization of
certain areas within the world economy, internal economic, cultural and
politico-administrative peripheries were mainly the result of the structuring
of the modern nation-state and of its capacity to limit the exit options of
territories as well as of individuals and resources. These conflicts over the
demarcation of boundaries, and their stiffness or looseness, clearly reflected
oppositions and differences of interest among social groups controlling the
resources in different domains: in the economy, the commercial, industrial,
financial bourgeoisie that controlled capital, commodities, and services; in
culture, the educated elites in the churches, universities and schools, media
and networks that controlled message-codes; in the politico-administrative
domain, the political and military-administrative elites that controlled rule-
making and personnel. However, in the democratization process, territorial
and peripheral claims were less legitimate and less acceptable than functional
interest representation, given their inherent challenge to the control of the
central political elite. This is why, with only a few exceptions, nineteenth and
twentieth century politics was largely about individual rights and collective
cross-local social movements and why it tended to regard the peripheral
mobilization of resources as threatening.

   These powerful trends notwithstanding, democratization showed that
territorial distinctiveness remained an ongoing element of politics in Europe.

---

[10] Cf. Rokkan, S., Urwin, D., Aerebrot, F. H., Malaba, P., and Sande, T., *Centre–
Periphery Structures in Europe* (Frankfurt: Campus Verlag, 1987), 40.

In the late 1960s and 1970s, following a further expansion of the bureaucratic state into welfare, industrial and economic policies, a clash emerged between the classic top-down model of government and the new demands of local management, often voiced by new mobilized actors within the regions. The central political elite responded with a variety of programmes promoting devolution and regionalization (Belgium, Italy, France, Spain—failed attempts in Britain). More recently, from the late 1980s on, a further wave of territorial representation demands seems to have emerged together with new forms of territorial politics.

This new wave differs in many ways from previous historical phases and examples of peripheral resistance:

1. It is often based on a new form of 'nationalism' or cultural identity that no longer aims at the establishment of its own independent statehood, but rather to a revision in the form of the state so that it provides new forms of local autonomy. It is 'autonomist' rather than 'separatist'; it recognizes the possibility, or even the desirability, of dual or multiple identities; it tends to concentrate more on the issues, problems and practices of self-awareness and self-organization than on lineage distinctive cultural models; it is more often the territorial community that seeks the social and cultural categorization and institutionalization of its distinctiveness than the state.[11]

2. It develops in the context of the creation of new centres and new types of centres in the international environment. The relationship between centre and periphery is no longer based on the dyadic relationship between the state and the regional distinctive community. Therefore, it can no longer be only or exclusively dealt with within the nation-state through policy concessions or administrative reforms.

3. It is developed through new forms of local political mobilization. These do not always or necessarily take the form of new political organizations and movements. Rather, they are based on less well-organized and for-malized networks of local alliances, often cutting across the historical cross-local organizations of mobilization into the central national state (parties and interest organizations).

4. It is based on a new perception of the institutional competition among territories for the acquisition of resources that are no longer controlled exclusively by the state centre. This implies the perception of communality of interests and problem-pressures among territories that are neither territorially contiguous nor necessarily part of the same state.

---

[11] Smith, A. D., *National Identity* (London: Penguin Books, 1991), 138–9; Allardt, E., 'Prerequisites and Consequences of Ethnic Mobilization in Modern Society', *Scandinavian Political Studies*, 3 (1980), 1–20.

5. It is likely to create new types of constitutional and political strain within the nation-state because of the different attitudes of the substate territorial elites participating in suprastate integration processes.

This section concerns the possible changing nature of centres and peripheries in this new context as compared with the historical peripheries in Europe. The core theoretical questions can be summarized in the following terms. The historical peripheries of a cultural, economic or politico-administrative nature were the result of the process of territorial, cultural and economic retrenchment associated with the formation of the nation-state and national economy. The closure of boundaries for various types of transactions (goods, messages, peoples, capital) to which the formation of the European system of states gave rise actually determined the forming and strengthening of new centres and the peripheralization of other territories. What has happened to the historical peripheries in the phase of territorial, cultural and economic expansion and opening resulting from European integration? Is this associated with a redefinition of centres and peripheries? Will other and different peripheries be created? On the basis of which resource-imbalances can new peripheralization occur in a loosely bounded territoriality such as that generated by the EU? What opportunities and costs have been produced for different types of territories by the multiplication and differentiation of centres at the EU level?

The Territorial Dimension of European Integration

The original integration project was not meant to have any direct impact on either individual citizens of the member states or on their subnational territories. Yet, just as the 'constitutionalization' revolution of the ECJ created rights and duties for individual national actors, so the EU policies have, since the 1980s, created new legal and material opportunity structures for subnational territories and governments. In particular, the EU (*a*) has made available access to extra-national material resources; (*b*) has created new legal frameworks and institutions for subnational governments' action; (*c*) has fostered a transborder mobilization of the latter; and (*d*) has fostered new local force reactions and coalitions.

Access to EU Resources

As argued above, historically nation-states have prevented open territorial competition based on the differentiation of regulatory regimes, invoking more often principles of national unity and solidarity to argue for territorial transfers. Moreover, the hidden redistribution induced by national budgets has always been more important than publicly admitted. Budget-induced interregional transfers can be large. According to a recent study, in 1993 the seven richest regions of France, Germany, Portugal, Italy, Spain, Sweden, and United Kingdom (Ile de France, Hamburg, Lisbon & V.T., Lombardy, Madrid, Stockholm and the South-East of the United Kingdom), which represent 16 per cent of their overall population and 19 per cent of their GDP, financed 54 billion ECU of budget-induced interregional transfers. This is equal to 6 per cent of their regional GDP and 1.1 per cent of the total GDP of the countries. In these seven countries, the 29 net contributing regions, with 55 per cent of the population and 64 per cent of the total GDP, financed 128 billion ECU, that is, 4 per cent of their regional GDP and 3 per cent of the total GDP of the countries.[12] National public funds therefore play a very significant role in cohesion processes, transferring huge amounts of money from richer to poorer regions, more than twice the amount of the national contributions of these countries to the budget of the EU, and inducing a large hidden reduction of within-country interregional disparities. Applying the result of the above-mentioned study to the remaining member states, these transfers represent something like more than twenty times the European budget of the structural funds.

The fact that the hidden transfer mechanisms work at the national level within Europe produce the paradoxical result that equal regions (in terms of the GDP) are not treated equally by their respective national budgets. So, the richest regions of Spain, such as Catalonia, are financing poorer Spanish regions despite the fact that they have the same GDP per capita as the Midi Pyrénées or Lorraine, both financed indirectly by the French budget. In fact, the more a tax system is decentralized, the less the system redistributes between populations and areas. The EU is a very decentralized public finance space, contrary to the USA, where the federal budget induces huge transfers between states, reducing interregional income disparities between 23 per cent and 28 per cent.[13] In other words, European national borders limit interregional transfers.

---

[12] A number of sophisticated studies deal with the extent to which public expenditures generated by obligatory contributions across the regions of a country are redistributed in expenditures across the same regions by providing an involuntary but significant interregional transfer. See Wishlade, F. et al., *Economic and Social Cohesion in the European Union: The Impact of Member States' own Policies* (Glasgow/Paris: EPRC/OEIL, 1996); and Davezies, L., 'Interregional Transfers from Central Government Budgets in European Countries. A Fragmented Cohesion Process?' (Florence: European University Institute, 1997), Conference on 'Territorial Politics in Europe. A Zero-Sum Game?'; Davezies, L., 'Un essai de mesure de la contribution des budgets des pays membres à la cohésion européenne', *Economie et Prévision*, 2/3 (1999), no. 138–9.

[13] See MacDougall Report (1977).

Contrary to the prevalent hidden nature of national budget-induced territorial redistribution, in the mid-1970s the EU started an open policy of
territorial redistribution.[14] At the beginning, the regional programme was
simply an interstate transfer mechanism, functioning as a side-payment to
induce states to cooperate in market integration. The European Regional
Development Fund (ERDF) was created in 1975 after the entry of the United
Kingdom, which would have otherwise been a large net contributor to the
Community. By the mid-1980s it had become an interstate compensation
mechanism for the countries of the Mediterranean and for Ireland. Eligible
regions were determined by national governments, since the Commission had
little information and statistics on the regions (it started to collect them only
in the late 1970s). The policy process was, in general, so strictly controlled by
the member state that it was unlikely it could produce regional mobilization.

In 1979 and 1984, several reforms increased the allocation discretion of the
Commission. The eligibility of the regions was based on Community criteria
referring to the GDP and unemployment levels, with greater emphasis placed
on programmes than on projects. Although the favourable conditions in the
mid-1980s produced a leap forwards in cohesion policy, the 1988 reform
became necessary when a number of states demanded compensation for their
assent to the single market programme, which was regarded as more advantageous for the core areas. Later on, the objectives 1, 2 and 5b of the regional
funds used scarcity of population as a distribution criterion in order to satisfy
claims of the Northern member countries. The definition of 'regions' and of
the disparities to be reduced are, however, still not clear; neither the treaties,
nor the structural funds relations, nor the Commission documents provide a
definition of region. The only official tables, the NUTS (Nomenclature of
territorial units of statistics), give three levels of territorial entities to which
units seem to be arbitrarily assigned.

The regional policy was characterized by a growing tension between policy
rationale (to concentrate funds to maximize effectiveness) and political
rationale (to distribute them widely to reduce opposition, by allowing each
member state to be given a share of the funds). Sometimes, this was a
problematic additional burden on national budgets, due to the rule requiring
national and regional governments to match any European amounts they
received in equal measure from their own budget, so that, in fact, large

---

[14] On regional policy see the references in Chapter 4, fn. 95 and Hooghe, L. and
Keating, M., 'The Politics of European Union Regional Policy', *Journal of European
Public Policy*, 1 (1994), 367–39; Hooghe, L., 'EU Cohesion Policy and Competing Models
of European Capitalism', *Journal of Common Market Studies*, 36 (1998), 457–77; Borzel,
T., *States and Regions in the European Union. Institutional Adaptation in Germany and
Spain* (Cambridge: Cambridge University Press, 2002); Onzelman, T. and Knods, M.
(eds.), *Regionales Europa—Europaesierte Regionen* (Frankfurt: Campus Verlag, 2002).

amounts of regional aid remained unspent: 20 millions ecus in 1996, almost a one year's financing. However, the policy was, overall, a success, making a considerable amounts of material funds unlikely to be raised otherwise available to a number of regions. In the middle of the 90s, the structural funds (ERDF, ESF and EAG) accounted for about one-third of the EU budget. By 1999, the two instruments of cohesion policy—structural and cohesion funds—distributed yearly 35.7 per cent of the EC budget, a bit less than 0.5 per cent of the EU GDP, annually. The Commission has declared that these funds manage to reduce immediate income inequalities in the EU by 5 per cent, as compared with 3 per cent in the 1989–93 period.[15]

Forty per cent of the population has been touched by structural funds in Spain, Portugal, Greece, Ireland, and parts of United Kingdom, Belgium, East Germany, Italy and Luxembourg. The role played by of the national centre in running these programmes varied according to the degree of decentralization and regionalization of the member state. Notwithstanding the strong intermediary role played by the nation-state here, this was a real novelty. For the first time since the consolidation of the European states, substate territories have access to material resources made available by a non-state source.

In addition, the same period is also characterized by a growing ability of subnational governments to access the material resources of the international financial markets. The 1990s have seen a booming of regional and city bonds and the large international credit-rating agencies have started to differentiate the credit worthiness of subnational institutions. The result of this is that different subnational governments may be able to find the monetary resources necessary to finance local investments in the international market, although they will be obliged to pay different rates of interest depending on their credit worthiness. Finally, subnational governments' credit ratings are no longer restricted to a lower level than their respective national governments. A very credit-worthy local authority may thus be able to obtain a stronger rating than its own country. It is, therefore, likely that only those regions that give very solid guarantees of paying back would access international financial market easily and cheaply. This notwithstanding, it remains true that in the last quarter of the century, subnational governments have obtained growing access to material resources that have been made available outside the scope of the nation-state.

Institution Building

The EU and the Commission have also played an important role of institution building with regard to subnational territories, and this has probably

---

[15] CEC, *Report on Economic and Social Cohesion* (1999), 98.

been the most important. The EU policies have fostered the decentralization trend in most EU countries, and the structural and cohesion funds have prompted even the most centralized states such as the United Kingdom, Greece, Portugal, and Ireland to create entities at the regional level for the implementation of EU regional policy. These policies have thus increased regional capacities to deal with territorial problems and to manage policies of local economic development in terms of economic and organizational resources. The EU has contributed not only with resources, but has also provided the legal framework incentives and a set of new legal and financial tools for regions to work with. In short, the EU has played an institution-building role for subnational regional strengthening.

The partnership between the Commission and national and regional governments is the chief institutional innovation of the structural funds. The Commission has tried to use these funds as a political means to establish linkages with subnational authorities and actors. Various rationales supported structural funds, in general, and the principle of partnership, in particular: the efficiency and effectiveness of the market in backward areas; solidarity to those that are losing as a result of the single market; democratization of decision-making by involving a wider range of societal and public actors; innovation in governance due to the non-hierarchical coordination and mobilization of indigenous forces. However, some political reasons were also tied to this: the Commission viewed partnership and structural funds as a way of legitimizing its role in relation to regional actors, and of undermining that of states. In the late 1980s, the Commission and Delors wanted to increase the subnational input into the structural programming and to encourage a European-wide system of territorial relations in which subnational authorities would play an influential role. Partnership also implies, however, a certain amount of competition between the national and subnational levels. By the mid-1990s, this project had lost out to an approach that viewed the involvement of subnational authorities as a function of specific policymaking needs, and not for the sake of participation.[16] All the same, EU partnership projects have provided regional and local actors with some good opportunities to challenge national governments on particular issues, and also to reinforce their domestic position (in Britain and Spain particularly, but also elsewhere).

In addition to fostering 'decentralization' and supporting 'partnership', the EU has shaped the development of a new set of legal and financial tools for the regions.[17] The Outline Convention of Frontier Cooperation, signed in

---

[16] Hooghe, L., 'The Structural Funds and Competing Models of European Capitalism' (Florence, European University Institute, 1997), Conference on 'Territorial Politics in Europe. A Zero-Sum Game?', 13.

[17] See Borras-Alomar, S., 'Interregional Cooperation in Europe during the Eighties and Early Nineties', in N. A. Sørensen (ed.), *European Identities. Cultural Diversity and*

1980 under the auspices of the Council of Europe, established legal tools for cross-border cooperation; the INTERREG programme was established in 1990 with the goal of fostering the creation of cross-border links of cooperation; INTERREG II gave priority to projects that included the establishment of shared administrative structures of regional/local levels of government. Other EU instruments did not refer specifically to cross-border cooperation, but did enhance it: SPRINT and STRIDE are Research and Development programmes aiming at the establishment of networks across diverse European aspects concerning technological innovation, technology transfer, technology dissemination, etc. The 'Innovation Development Planning Group', a consultant group in this field, has always emphasized the importance of information flow about the possibilities and difficulties for cross-border cooperation; LACE, the European Centre for the Study of Cross-border Cooperation in collaboration with the Association of European Border Regions, coordinates the pooling of experiences, information, and precise documentation on the topic.

The Experience Exchange Programme (EEP) is yet another instrument for regional cooperation established by the Commission and addressed to local and regional authorities in charge of different subjects related to economic development. The programme is discussed annually and implemented in close cooperation with the Assembly of European Regions (AER) and the European Centre for Regional Development (CEDRE). In 1988, at the beginning of the new five-year structural fund plan, the Commission created the Consultative Committee of Local and Regional Authorities to strengthen the relationships with these local governments.

There has also been an explicit fostering of the representation of subnational territories. The Council of European Municipalities (CCE), funded in 1951, was transformed in 1984 into the '*Conseil des communes et des regions d'Europe*' (CCRE) to stimulate regional engagement. In 1985, however, the regions set up the CRE (*Conseil des regions d'Europe*) as a separate regional representation organization. This changed its name to the AER in 1987, and gradually widened its membership to cover the whole of the EU territory. It also formulated a large set of regional demands in the run-up to Maastricht (see later).

Other regional interest organizations have been created on a functional basis and their specialization contrasts with the general and broad regional interests represented by the AER. For instance, the Lille-based ERIT (European regions of industrial tradition), created in 1984, aims at integrating the

Integration in Europe since 1700 (Odense: Odense University Press, 1995), 127–46; Borras-Alomar, S., Christiansen, T. and Rodriguez-Pose, A., 'Towards a "Europe of Region"? Visions and Reality from a Critical Perspective', *Regional Politics & Policy*, 4 (1994), 1–27.

interests of this kind of regions; the AEBR (Association of European Border Regions) was established in 1971 to promote the mechanisms and funds allocation for specific activities of a cross-border nature; the Conference of Maritime Peripheral Regions of the EC, founded in 1973 and located at Rennes had similar goals. Finally, a wide range of regional representation and information offices opened up in Brussels.[18]

The most important new institutions are the treaty-based ones. In the intergovernmental debate of 1989–90, the German Länder advanced four main requests to their government, which were largely debated within the Assembly of European Regions. The first was to entrench the subsidiarity principle in the amendments of the treaties. The second request was to have a right to access the Council of Ministers when dealing with issues and policies that came under the exclusive competence of the Länder according to the German constitution. The third request was to establish a regional organ at the European level, and the fourth was to grant regional governments the right to directly appeal to the ECJ. In the negotiations leading to the Maastricht Treaty, the German government supported the first two demands and refused to endorse the third, considering that it undermined its exclusive competence in foreign affairs.[19] The Belgian government, on the contrary, endorsed the request for a regional body at the EU level on behalf of its regions.[20] Two of the four requests were accepted: the access to Council of Ministers and the creation of a Committee of the Region (Art. 198 Treaty on European Union), with representatives appointed by member states and divided between local and regional interests.[21] On the contrary, the right to appeal to the ECJ was not accepted and the subsidiarity principle was referred only to member state versus EU relationships, ruling out the region as a better 'level' of government for some policy areas.

Unsurprisingly, Europe's most autonomous regions, in Germany and Belgium, led this debate. However, the German solution that the Länder

---

[18] On these see Marks, G., Nielsen, F. Ray, L. and Salk, J. E., 'Competencies, Cracks, and Conflicts. Regional Mobilization in Europe', *Comparative Political Studies*, 29 (1996), 164–92.

[19] Jeffery, C., 'Towards a "Third Level" in Europe? The German Länder in the European Union', *Political Studies*, 44 (1996), 253–66.

[20] The Belgian constitution already acknowledged the competence of its two communities for international relations, treaties, etc. See Hooghe, L., 'Belgian Federalism and the European Community', in B. Jones and M. Keating (eds.), *The European Union and the Regions* (Oxford: Claredon Press, 1995), 135–65.

[21] On the Committee of Regions see Van der Knaap, P., 'The Committee of the Regions: The Outset of a "Europe of the Regions"?', *Regional Politics and Policy*, 4 (1994), 86–100; Christiansen, T., 'Second Thoughts: The Committee of Regions after its First Year', in R. Dehousse and T. Christiansen (eds.), *What Model for the Committee of the Regions? Past Experiences and Future Prospects* (Florence: European University Institute, 1995), European Forum Working Papers, no. 92, 34–64.

take responsibility for the implementation of European Directives in exchange for sharing power in the formulation of the national negotiation position, has tended to generalize to other states such as Spain, Austria, Belgium and Italy. In Germany, this solution was originally opposed by the government and it was only finally brought round to it by the fact that the federal government was dependent on the Bundesrat for the ratification of the Maastricht Treaty.[22]

In conclusion, the amount of formal and informal, binding and non-binding, representative and functional institution building promoted around subnational governments has been indeed impressive over the last two decades of the century. A variety of channels for this are available, some of which cluster around the initiatives of the Commission, a few—much weaker—cluster around the initiatives of the EP, others around those of the Council, and yet others around the national ones. These are ways by which subnational authorities can be involved in European decision-making and informally influence it. Also, clearly, institutionalized channels are more effective than non-institutionalized and consultation channels. However, opportunities to use all types of channels are unevenly distributed, so that, even here, there are privileged actors: regions as against other local authorities; regions that are better institutionalized; resource rich regions, rather than poor ones.

Finally, it is clear that through all these new institutions and channels opposition to or subnational mobilization against the EU is unlikely, if not impossible. On the one hand, most subnational non-secessionist groups support a federal-type EU and tend to have shared interests. On the other, anti-European subnational actors have to bypass high barriers of institutional exclusion (for most informal channels), and the organizational costs of coordinating the dispersed pockets of territorially, culturally and ideologically disparate parties. They are thus almost necessarily obliged to rely on national arenas and channels.

Transfrontier Mobilization

The material resources and inducements of institution building have resulted in a growing number of substate territorial cooperative experiences across the national borders of EU member states and between EU members and non-EU neighbouring states.[23] Transfrontier relations among local and

---

[22] See Schmidt, V. A. and Scharpf, F., 'Europeanization and Domestic Structural Change: A Question of Fit?' (Florence: European University Institute, 2001), Conference on 'Europeanization and domestic change'.

[23] Hooghe, L., 'Subnational Mobilization in the European Union', *West European Politics*, 18 (1995), 175–98 is a good summary.

regional governments actually predate the structural funds and the new regional policy of the Commission.[24] The first forms of this kind of cooperation originated in the early 1950s in the upper Rhine region, comprising Alsace, Baden-Württemberg, and Basel, as part of a movement towards Franco-German reconciliation. The Regio Basiliensis originated as a result of the lack of expansion space for the economy of the Basel region, and it was aimed at assessing the labour market requirements for a wide region including Southern Alsace in France and the south-west corner of Baden-Württemberg in Germany. Another cooperation among frontier towns in the Strasbourg region (Strasbourg, Kehl, Mulhouse, Freiburg) was established in the mid-1970s. The commissions for the Strasbourg and Basel transfrontier cooperation areas discussed projects concerning universities, transport— Basel airport located in France, the upper Rhine high-speed rail link, and a second Rhine bridge at Strasbourg—transfrontier investments and transfrontier labour commuting, the banking sector, and the tourism and leisure transfrontier business in the Black Forest. Frequently, the consultative committees of central and local government officials developed working parties in which private sector interests participated. Interest in the work of these commissions increased as a result of involvement in the EC programme, Interreg, and by the dismantling of frontier controls along the Rhine.

There are parallel developments leading to a growing transfrontier mutual dependency in other regions. On the French-Spanish border, Spanish investments were increasingly made in the French Basque Country, and Spanish tourism moved massively towards the Pyrenées Atlantiques. Frontier towns such as Hendaye in the south-west corner of France and Inun, the Spanish town immediately across the frontier, were heavily oriented towards activities that depended entirely on the frontier transport services, customs, police, and goods that were not easily available or were differentially priced across the frontier. There were some reactions to this in the French side, as inhabitants felt rather intimidated by the entrepreneurial dynamism of the Spanish side. On the Italian-French border the consultative group Alpazur was created, although it was not very active until 1992 (with the exception of its establishing a transfrontier natural park). In April 1991, Menton and Ventimiglia signed a protocol establishing cooperative ventures and in the following years a number of them were set up, including a university institute in medical biotechnology, a joint industrial zone, a waste disposal plant, and a master plan for urban development covering both municipalities.

---

[24] For details about these early forms of cooperation see Anderson, M., *Frontiers. Territory and State Formation in the Modern World* (Cambridge: Polity Press, 1996), 120–5.

Some of these transfrontier cooperations have enjoyed early recognition and a degree of political influence—as, for instance, the 'Argegalb' (1973), stretching from the Tyrol and Bavaria in the north to Lombardy in the south and Croatia in the east, and including the Swiss canton of Graubünden, and 'Euregio' on the Dutch-German frontier. Others found more difficult to be recognized by national and European institutions, as, for instance, was the case of the 'Community of the Pirenées' (1983)—which links three French regions, Aquitaine, Midi-Pirenées and Languedoc-Roussillon, and four autonomous Spanish regions, the Basque Country, Navarre, Aragon, Catalonia with the Principality of Andorra. The French government has been particularly reluctant to accept this cooperation, refusing most of the Community projects that requested Interreg Programme support.

Another field of early transfrontier cooperation was pollution. The polluting of the Rhine by the potash mines of Alsace was the object of cooperative projects among the regions and communes concerned across the border, sometimes supporting their governments' projects (Netherlands, Federal Republic of Germany, France and Luxembourg), but more often opposing them. Since EU environmental policy has set high standards, particularly for water pollution, transfrontier cooperation between local and regional authorities has helped to alert to incidents of transfrontier pollution, although it has had to overcome the differences in the legal systems and regulatory regimes, and the clash of major national interests (such as the location of nuclear power stations) to do so. This is why the capacity of these transfrontier coalitions to impose solutions to local problems on unwilling national governments is limited.

These transfrontier consultative and cooperative institutions were justified to overcome the segmenting effect of borders in problem-solving. But the cultural climate within which these experiences take place, plus the new single market institutions, are in many cases redrawing spatial hierarchies in a way that is different from the historically predominant pattern within the nation-state. To take examples from the most extreme case of centralized France, its historical monocephalic territorial structure is affected when, for instance, a city like Lyon is 'liberated' by its rather peripheral position within France and its constrained economic space. There local administrators have begun to perceive the city as one of the crossroads of Europe, rather than as a French periphery. Similarly, people from Montpellier may prefer to fly from Barcelona, people from Lyon from Brussels, Strasbourg from Frankfurt, rather than going to Paris to do so as has always been done. In the Savoy, the Turin savings banks attract those French businesspersons who are disaffected with the French banking system, overly centred on the capital.

Cooperation has evolved from the problem-solving framework of providing coordinated public services on both sides of a national border (infrastructure, cross-border commuting, civilian protection, disaster control, environmental issues) towards a more comprehensive framework that comprises the general economic development of these frontier regions, usually at the periphery of the national economic structure. More importantly, the basis for cooperation has also evolved from cross-border physical contiguity, to broader geographical principles and, finally, to functional and structural characteristics.[25]

The above cases of the Upper Rhine Area, the Community of the Pyrenees, the Euroregio, and the Argealp, as well as the 'Alpe Adria'—the 1978 Working Group of the Eastern Alps including four Italian and five Austrian regions, Bavaria, Slovenia and Croatia, five Hungarian provinces and the Ticino Canton—and the 1982 'Cotrao'—Working Groups of the Regions and Cantons of the Western Alps—are all clear cases of cross-border cooperation.

On the contrary, the 1989 'Arc Atlantique' cooperation of twenty-six regions,[26] within the context of the Conference of Peripheral Maritime Regions of the EC, is not based on common border problems, but on the similarity of the geographical characteristics, and on strong periphery awareness within the broader European context. The same applies to the 'Route des Hautes Technologies' created in 1990 and later called the 'Mediterranean Arc', that includes Catalonia, Valencia, Languedoc-Roussillon, Midi-Pirénnées, Provence-Cote d'Azur, Liguria, Piedmont, and Lombardy. Finally, a third type of cooperation is defined by structural similarity, rather than by common border problems or by geographical similarity. The 'Four Motors of Europe' group (Lombardy, Rhones-Alpes, Catalonia, Baden-Württenberg) is certainly not based on peripherality, but rather on a similarity of industrial structures.

New regional cooperation has therefore evolved from the problem-solving framework of how to provide coordinated public services on both sides of a national frontier towards a more comprehensive approach that comprises the general economic development of regions that are often at the periphery of the national economic structure. In addition, the bases for these experiences of regional cooperation have evolved from a physical continuity or some geographical principle to some sort of functional or structural characteristic.

---

[25] Borras-Alomar, 'Interregional Cooperation in Europe during the Eighties and Early Nineties'; Borras-Alomar, Christiansen and Rodriguez-Pose, 'Towards a 'Europe of Regions'?'

[26] Highlands, Donegal, Dumfries & Galloway (Wales), Somerset, Dorsel, Devon, Cornwall (UK); Basse Normandie, Bretagne, Pays de la Loire, Poitou, Charentes, Aquitaine (France); Basque countries, Cantabria, Asturias, Galicia, Andalusia (Spain); Norte Centro, Lisboa & Val de Tejo, Alentejo, Algarve (Portugal).

This 'mobilization' of cooperation experiences has taken place under the auspices and supporting role of both the national and the European centres. That is, supraregional centres fostered the mobilization of the regional economic and social potentials.[27] Notwithstanding this, the structural changes affecting the role of substate regional territories are numerous and conspicuous and should not be underestimated, particularly if one keeps in mind the historical obsession of the European continental nation-state with any sign of territorial autonomy or exit opportunity. These structural changes concern all the regions, but the new resources, institutions and fora may generate very different interests and opinions, and not necessarily—and maybe very improbably—a general 'regional' view or a general increase in regional power. While regional alliances continue to develop along common economic or infrastructural interests, and subnational territorial units try to establish their institutional position vis-à-vis the EU and national governments, the prospects of a harmonious 'Regional Europe' are non-existent given the potential conflicts of interests among the regions and areas and given the enormous differences in resources among them. Moreover, the relevance of territory and territoriality in Europe and new forms of territorial politics are not necessarily restricted to a regionalized Europe.[28] Where regions across borders come into closer contact with each other and gain access to new partners and new sources of funding, this does not eliminate the differences and conflicts among them and groups of them. Instances of meaningful, interregional alliances go hand in hand with a growing trend towards 'territorial competition' for inwards investment and Community funds in the internal and global financial market.[29]

New Territorial Coalitions

The fourth important element of the new territorial dimension of politics is its potential capacity to forge new types of territorial coalitions among social and political actors. Access to new types of extra-state material resources (the EU and the international financial market), access to new extra-state regulatory frameworks and institutions, and corresponding new forms of

---

[27] See Wright, V., 'Relations intergouvernementales et gouvernement régional en Europe: réflexions d'un sceptique', in P. LeGalès and C. Lequesne (eds.), *Les paradoxes des régions en Europe* (Paris: La découverte, 1997), 47–55.

[28] For a critique of the 'Europe of Regions' myth, see Christiansen, T., 'Interests, Institutions, Identities. The Territorial Politics of the "New Europe" ', in N. A. Sorensen (ed.), *European Identities. Cultural Diversity and Integration in Europe since 1700* (Odense: Odense University Press, 1995), 241–55, esp. 241–5.

[29] Borras-Alomar, Christiansen and Rodriguez-Pose, 'Towards a "Europe of Region"?', 22–3.

territorial governments mobilization across the borders and at the EU level can foster the development of new types of territorial coalitions.

The uncertainties produced by economic integration has allowed the relevant social forces and interests to express their concerns about the possible impact of EU measures on regional and local economic structures. These uncertainties generate demands by local socio-economic actors for regional action to identify the areas affected by these changes and to take appropriate measures to respond with regional structural adjustments. At the same time, regional governments have become more active in gathering together private and public forces with a view to competing in the wider international context of economic allocation, trying to make themselves an attractive location for investments. Regions that are culturally distinctive attempt to develop at the ideological and practical level a model of regionalism in which their cultural distinctiveness is considered as giving them a competitive advantage within EU integration and the new economic internationalization trends. The reference point has thus changed from the central state to the international (EU and world) arenas.[30]

Michael Keating has argued that the emphasis on territorial competition may foster regional 'developmental coalitions' defined as broad and place-based interclass coalitions of political, economic and social actors devoted to the economic development in specific locations. These coalitions may include locally based business interests, regional and local bureaucracies, as well as locally based national bureaucrats, and neighbourhood and social movements.[31] Keating's concept and analysis stresses the 'developmental' goal, while in my perspective the most important element is the tendency to enhance the unified external territorial representation of local interests as against their internal functional differentiation. Actually, internal social differentiation must be muted in order to foster an external territorial unification of interests.

The muting of internal interest differentiation in order to enhance external collective requests rests on a mechanism of cognitive and evaluative learning during the negotiations among subnational actors or actors at the

---

[30] Pierson, P. and Leibfried, S., 'Multi-tiered Institutions and the Making of Social Policy', in S. Leibfried and P. Pierson (eds.), *European Social Policy: Between Fragmentation and Integration* (Washington, DC: Brooking, 1995), 28–30, suggest that given the considerable importance of the territorial dimension in integration and the enhanced mobility of capital, economic interests may fragment along territorial rather than class lines.

[31] Keating, M., 'The Political Economy of Regionalism', in M. Keating and J. Loughlin (eds.), *The Political Economy of Regionalism* (London: Frank Cass, 1997), 17–40, esp. 32–4; Keating, M., 'The New Regionalism. Territorial Competition and Political Restructuring in Western Europe', in L. Andersson and T. Blom (eds.), *Sustainability and Development. On the Future of Small Society in a Dynamic Economy* (Karlstad: Karlstad University, 1998), 30–50.

subnational level. These local negotiations require actors to be autonomous in setting and modifying their goals. The model of interaction is generally less adversarial than at the national level, and some reciprocal recognition and definition of similarity of interests can develop more easily. The search for agreement over specific local solutions implies a declining dependency of local actors' on, and weakening linkages with, cross-local encompassing national organizations. This, however, generates problems for the national coordination of local representatives: that is, between local and national trade unions, local and national employers, local and national politicians, etc. In other words, the recognition of a common 'local' interest generates negotiation environments that may well weaken the vertical and cross-local relationships between local actors and the national ones. It may, therefore, tend to balkanize interest representation at the local level, increasing the needs and requests of local autonomy, redefining the hierarchical relationships within the national organization.

Sceptical views about the possibilities of regional coalitions argue that it is impossible for unions and tripartite negotiated orders to function in regional economies without the national power resources that guaranteed these in the past, the support of nationally legislated functional regimes, or some sort of regional coercion power capable of providing the public support required to establish stable non-voluntaristic and binding agreement among social actors.[32] This scepticism refers, however, to classic state neo-corporatism. Indeed, it is perfectly true to say that the possibility of territorially differentiated local coalitions undermines associational monopoly and interassociational hierarchy, and fragments interests (see later), contributing to the decomposition of national-level corporatism and to the difficulty of resurrecting it supranationally. This scepticism, in other words, focuses on the balance of power among different actors in these local coalitions. But regional developmental coalitions originate from what they contribute to: the recognition that in the integration process the organizational domain of every interest group is bound to be narrower than the relevant market is. For the perspective of this work, what matters is that alliances among functionally differentiated territorial actors (labour, trade and employers, local banking, local political elite) are able and likely to produce: (*a*) the muting of within local territory functional conflicts to the advantage of local coalitions; and (*b*) a corresponding declining organizational unity of cross-local (national) functional organizations (interest groups and parties).

---

[32] See Streek, W. and Schmitter, P., 'From National Corporatism to Transnational Pluralism: Organized Interests in the Single European Market', *Polity and Society*, 19 (1991), 133–64.

Local coalitions can develop in order to foster the territorial assets of cultural distinctiveness, strong local institutions or economic strength. However, they can also defend weak territories that lack cultural distinctiveness, institutional strength and economic resources. The latter can organize voice against exit, that is, it can resist and oppose those differentiation processes that benefit the better endowed territories. This opposition can take the form of alliances with the central elite in a centralist strategy, as well as that of a social dumping strategy.

Within-State Territorial Differentiation

The EU-generated 'external' resources and institutional settings for subnational territories contribute to and combine with two other structural changes to redefine the relationship between the centre and subnational territories: (*a*) a reassessment of the optimal scale of operation of infrastructural power; and (*b*) a tendency towards accrued territorial competition.

Changing Scale of Operation of 'Infrastructural Power'

Once the state's political production expands over time to provide centrally organized services (the welfare state, the educational system, credential control, etc.), the basis of its legitimacy extends and, at the same time, depends increasingly on this capacity. In this process, the state bureaucracy and the political elite place a distance between themselves and the dominant social elite, longer constituting an expression of their 'despotic' power. However, this autonomy and legitimacy also depends increasingly on this newly created 'infrastructural power', as the capacity to continue to efficiently deliver those goods, services and rules that cannot be provided in other ways.[33] At this stage, the state is subject to the challenge and competition of other organizations that prove or are thought to be able to deliver the same goods (services, protection, and rules). In other words, the changing basis of legitimacy of the contemporary state—from pure domination to performance of functional duties—exposed it to the risk of a functional decline with respect to other forms of production of these same goods by other types of organizations. This challenge has proven more intense in the realm of specific functional regimes defining the administrative-political boundary of the state: the defence of property rights with increasingly mobile property, environmental protection, skill credentials, social protection, etc. This has generated pressures for the reallocation of infrastructural power to substate

---

[33] The distinction between 'despotic' and 'infrastructural' power is made by Mann, M., 'The Autonomous Power of the State: its origins, mechanisms and results', *European Journal of Sociology*, 25 (1984), 185–213.

communities as well as to above-state new communities or international organizations.

This phenomenon, to a certain extent, is enhanced by the 'devaluation' of space as a result of technological developments in the communication and transport systems. The traditional location scheme according to which investments tend to be located as near as possible to one of the three sources of 'capital', 'market' or 'raw materials' no longer applies. In this sense, the process of reproduction of economic peripherality is severed as greater opportunities to locate resources without the constraints of pre-existing resource concentration emerge.

Moreover, technological change and international division of labour in advanced industrial countries are thought to bring about a declining import-ance of asset specificity, that is, of the value of an asset that is strongly connected to a specific use.[34] Specific assets are not easy to substitute and their exchange requires a high transaction cost and high economies of scale, while non-specific assets like financial products are just the opposite. A predominantly specific asset economy requires political hierarchy guarantee-ing those complex conditions of price efficiency and markets availability more than a non-specific asset economy. Therefore, depending on the tech-nological features, different economic processes may have different efficient or ideal political scales. If and when, with technological change and goods differentiation, the scale of the political structure becomes suboptimal because the existing political arrangements for the regulation of production, exchange, and consumption are inadequate for the asset type and the public goods required, then pressures for a new political scale may emerge, which reflect the altered requirement for political production. In this perspective, different political units (like the state) are more or less efficient in regulating, fostering, and controlling certain economic activities.

Nation-states experience problems in providing the traditional 'regulatory', 'distributive' and 'redistributive' public goods in a growing number of areas.[35] For some important areas of the regulatory framework of the market and economic activities, only international or cross-national regulations are effective. Distributive activities (through state-controlled and state-sponsored production and distribution, nationalized industries, public services, public finance and subsidies) and redistributive policies (health and welfare services, employment policies, environmental policy) are affected by the increasingly difficult task of defining which sectors are strategic, by the inter-national and regional agreements, and by the international competitiveness

[34] Cerny, P. G., 'Globalization and the changing logic of collective action', *Inter-national Organization*, 49 (1995), 595–625.

[35] The classic distinction by Lowi, T., 'American Business, Public Policy, Case Studies and Political Theory', *World Politics*, 16 (1964), 677–715.

and the favourable climate for international capital. This increasing divergence between the scale of infrastructural power for market activities and the scale of action of the state has generated interests, ideas and debates about the most ideal and efficient political scale.

Territorial Competition
When economic boundaries are lowered or removed, mobile factors can more easily move from one jurisdiction to others according to the social costs and regulatory burdens imposed upon them. The thinness of European-wide market regulations forces governments to adapt their economic and social policies following the requirements of European and international competitiveness. National competitiveness becomes more important, and national programmes and regimes are exposed to competition that can no longer be contained at the national level. As discussed in the Chapter 4, the pressure for competitive de-and re-regulation has led to already visible result in: (*a*) the shifting of taxation from mobile to immobile factors; (*b*) the shifting of the financing of the welfare state from employers' contributions to general tax revenues; (*c*) the limitation of state aids and subsidies to domestic industries for employment protection; (*d*) the pushes towards the privatization of previously nationalized industries that protected sectors of the labour force; (*e*) the constraints on public borrowing and the overall public deficit; and (*f*) the rising autonomy of central banks, no longer allowed to extend credit to governments.

The process of market opening at the European and global levels makes governments less able and willing to invest resources into programmes of territorial redistribution for backward regions. In order to foster national competitiveness, governments are inclined to divert resources focusing more attention on the most dynamic sectors and territories and on those activities that promote growth. In other words, there has been a certain amount of change in the priority of territorial politics: from redressing within-state territorial imbalances to fostering territorial endogenous resources and to promoting national competitiveness,[36] and from territorial to sector intervention.[37]

However, even if territorial politics is increasingly dominated by the competitive pursuit of economic development and growth, this does not entail the reduction of the territory to a pure set of exchange relationships based on instrumental calculations. Territorial collective identities, institutional

---

[36] Governments could behave as strategic oligopolists, creating advantages in the resource endowment that take on the form of a infrastructural supply. See Porter, M., *Competitive Advantage of Nations* (London: Macmillan, 1990).

[37] Keating, 'The Political Economy of Regionalism', 27.

strength, cooperation traditions, etc. can all provide the basis for forms of cooperation in the production of public goods and investments in the future. They can not only help to overcome external diseconomies of competition, but also create local conditions that, relying on historical traditions and the endogenous resources of a cultural, institutional, or social nature, may favour the adaptation and response of specific local territories. Local territorial identities may also find new pushes in these developments, as a reaction of local defence.

More precisely, the possibility of, growing territorial competition depends on:

1) The territorial mobility of factors (goods, firms, individuals, investments, taxpayers), which creates a potential demand. If there are no mobile factors, then there is no competition, in the sense that there are no customers to compete for. However, non- (or less-) mobile factors also play a role, to the extent that they are asked to bear the costs (or advantages) of the choices of mobile factors.
2) The territorial differentiation of the public goods production, which creates a supply. Territorial competition is mainly competition through the supply of different kinds, levels or qualities of public goods (transports, labour market, loans, etc.). If the supply is not differentiated, there is no incentive to change the territorial location. Inevitably, there are wide differences in the capacities of subnational territories to differentiate their public good supply. The lower the local resources and the stronger the central hierarchical control of the public goods supply, the less possible a differentiation is.

Historically, the European obsession with exit options led to measures limiting internal territorial competition as potentially explosive for both internal cohesion and international equilibrium. On the contrary, in the USA, for over two centuries, the history of federalism—and of horizontal relations among states and local governments—has been based on competition for economic growth, greatly intensified by the ease of incorporating new states, by the proliferating and fragmenting of local governments within both new and existing states, and by the decentralized tax system. While the Washington centre thinks in macroeconomic terms or in industrial sector terms and is less concerned with where business firms locate, pay taxes, and hire labour, state and local government officials view the economy spatially and think territorially.[38] The relative importance of the vertical state-society dimension (state policies and competition among social interests) versus the

---

[38] Sbragia, A., *Debt Wish. Entrepreneurial Cities, US Federalism, and Economic Development* (Pittsburgh: University of Pittsburgh Press, 1996), 218.

horizontal interstate territorial dimension (competition among territorial units for economic development and resources) depends on the model of state and nation building. Within the EU open market and open territorial structure, territorial competition is less bounded than it was within the nation-state structure and more likely to resemble the US experience.

However, the EU–US experiences differ in one crucial respect. In the EU, the elimination of explicit obstacles to trade, the harmonization of regulations that would otherwise segment the market, and the increase in mobility of labour, services, and capital may lead to divergence in both economic structure and growth rates of different regions, rather than to convergence in factor prices, economic structure and growth rates. The EU states and regions will become more specialized (as in the USA) and they will therefore become more vulnerable to regional-specific shocks. At the same time, however, they will be unable to respond with counter-cyclical monetary or exchange rate policy and will also tend to have immobile fiscal policy (see Chapter 4; in the environment of high factor mobility, shocks tend to have permanent effects on output and therefore to immobilize fiscal policy). In the USA, the heavily federalized fiscal system offers a partial solution to regional stabilization. In the EU, unless there is a considerable institutional change, this leverage is absent and problems of regional economic imbalance may be exacerbated.[39]

In this context of accrued territorial competition without any federalized mechanisms to counteract regional shocks, processes of substate territorial differentiation are likely to develop. These differentiations will mainly affect the politico-administrative boundaries, taking the form of a regulative differentiation of previously nationalized functional regimes. We can hypothesize the tendency towards a subnational level territorial differentiation of new forms of social protection, labour market regulation, and educational systems. This may involve the retrenchment of social solidarity towards more restricted territorial entities, and the weakening of national integration may also reduce the possibilities for nationwide solidarity and redistribution. The underlying logic of this aspect of territorial differentiation is that the higher the systemic interdependence (the boundaries of the social division of labour), the higher the need for localized forms of social integration (the community solidarity bonds). Once the borders of nation-states, now deprived of their high economic and military-diplomatic relevance, are increasingly perceived as boundaries of functional administrative regimes, only national identity and solidarity can justify their homogeneity through

---

[39] On this thesis see Krugman, P., 'Lessons of Massachusetts for EMU', in F. Torres and F. Giavazzi (eds.), *Adjustment and Growth in the European Monetary Union* (Cambridge: Cambridge University Press, 1993), 241–61.

the national territory. That is, in an integrated market, why should distant and disparate territories of the same nation-state share the same labour market regulations, educational system, social protection institutions, rather than differentiate them according to their specific needs and problems, and, maybe, share them with similar territories across the borders?

In conclusion, three factors push towards subnational particularism.[40] The first factor fostering territorial differentiation is the new logic of competition of the internal market, which tends to create a new aggregation of territorial and sector interests and to help the re-emergence of old cleavages between centres and peripheries of production and trade (e.g. economic axes such as those of the Renan region, Catalonia, the French Midi, Padania, Carinthia). The various social groups operating within these types of territorial areas tend to perceive a convergence in their interests and policy needs. Looking for more efficient forms of competition with respect to other territorial areas, these groups will thus develop common interests towards institutional arrangements (welfare, fiscal, labour market, education, etc.) that do not penalize them in the competitive game. These social groups are also likely to manifest a growing interest in localized functional regimes in the above-mentioned fields that are efficient, flexible and territorially circumscribed to them, that is, deprived of extensive redistributive dispersions. Moreover, the internal market allow to surface old and new backward territories that are incapable of keeping up with economic modernization. The imbalances in national budgets and the growing fiscal opposition of strong social groups might also challenge the traditional national redistributive circuits and mechanisms, contributing to a new dynamic of infra-European differentiation between development and underdevelopment. This may contribute to new territorial tensions along the axis of the national standardization of functional regimes versus their territorial differentiation.

The second factor that may contribute to territorial differentiation is the regional policy at the EU level and, more generally, the process of EU regionalization referred to in the previous sections. One of the indirect effects of the socio-economic cohesion policies is to strengthen subnational identities and to set incentives for the formation, including the cultural level, of territorially narrower risk-community and solidarity areas. The third factor contributing to territorial differentiation is the changing logic of national political competition. The dealignment of traditional cleavages and forms of political control and the disappearance of anti-system oppositions in Europe may determine an opening of the politico-electoral markets that offers new

---

[40] Ferrera lists these factors in reference to the welfare state, but, as argued in this chapter, they also apply to other functional spheres. See Ferrera, M., *Modelli di solidarietà. Politica e riforme sociali nelle democrazie* (Bologna, Italy: Il Mulino, 1993), 297–303.

spaces to political competition impinging upon the defence of interests of local type and nature, either through the mobilization of new issues or through the re-activation of the old territorial and also socio-economic cleavages (urban–rural, for instance). We should also mention here the potential interest and advantage available to political entrepreneurs to exploit the theme of particularistic solidarity (very visible in Belgium, Italy, and Catalonia, for instance).

I continue to use the rather general term of 'territories' because these potentials for substate differentiation are not limited to 'regional' governments. It has been rightly underlined that even cities and macro-urban areas may develop the above-mentioned strategies to increase sensitivity to territory as sites of investment and living by active training policies; participation in development companies; actively aiming to improve the environment to attract companies, investments, and privileged social groups or even to play the social dumping card (low wages, low taxation).[41] The important point to stress, however, is that these opportunities should not be seen as favouring or empowering one level of government versus another: the regions versus the state or the cities versus the regions or the states, or even all forms of substate government versus the former. New opportunities will not affect all regions and/or cities in the same way and direction, but will produce differentiation *among* substate territories. So we can expect the differentiation between winning and loosing regions, territories and cities, depending on those factors that determine different outcomes.

In conclusion, processes of integration and interdependence have made state borders more permeable; states have, to a large extent, changed their nature from territorial entities to regulatory systems; there is a high level of disengagement between state and territory leading to a greater emphasis on the non-territorial aspects of statehood. As a result, divisions within the state have been highlighted and the possibility for internal differentiation increased.

Conclusion: European Integration and Substate Territorial Interests' Redefinition

In the history of European centre–peripheries relations, the larger the number of different political options available to the periphery, the higher the resources that can be converted into political pressures upon the centre.

---

[41] On inter-urban competition in a global economy see Harvey, D., *The Urbanization of Capital* (Oxford: Basil Blackwell, 1985). Patrick Le Galès considers cities to be more important than regions, although he recognizes that there is no global phenomenon of a political role of the cities; Le Gales, P. and Harding, A., 'Cities and States in Europe', *West European Politics*, 21 (1998), 120–45; Le Gales, P., *European cities: social conflicts and governance* (Oxford: Oxford University Press, 2002).

However, the presence of these opportunities has often also been a liability, for granting degrees of local autonomy in cultural, administrative or economic matters may increase the willingness of the distinctive territory to transform into an independent state, or, worse, to incorporate within a neighbouring state. This has lead the centre to react with greater inflexibility and has inhibited its will to devolve. Ultimately, it was the centre's control over territorial coercion and economic exchanges that functioned as a threat to directly or indirectly curb or control the demands of subnational territories. At the same time, the development of large-scale identity and solidarity and the partisan integration of local and central political elites functioned as powerful mechanisms of system building, which prevented those parts from exiting. The integrated market reduces the economic controls and inducements available for national centres, and the absence of external threats within the EU makes difficult to justify and legitimate threats or the use of force. In perspective, only cultural and political integration mechanisms are likely to disincline peripheral territories from relating to the centre in the purely instrumental terms of cost/benefit analysis.

In a context of loosening boundaries, interface peripheries have an advantage over external peripheries given the existence of alternative and supportive cultural centres (where exit can be facilitated by a supportive external cultural centre). Territorial spaces that are subject to one national politico-administrative centre, but are fully integrated into a broader than national space of market transactions, have greater resources to convert into political pressures. They may also find alternative resources from those offered by the centre in terms of transfers and access to international capital markets (i.e. exit based on supportive external economic centres). Territorial spaces with a strong institutional autonomy and where alternative administrative borders compete in different functional areas—cross-border cooperation, functional regimes within the EU, etc.—can access external regulative and jurisdiction resources (i.e. exit is based on the supportive external administrative centres of the EU).

The sources of variation in the substate territorial responses to the new constellation can therefore be usefully represented as resulting from the four structural features of each territory represented in Figure 5.1. These structural features are associated with different degrees of control (or lack of control) of key resources, and result in different options along the dimension of exit from national territorial obligations and degree of revisionism in the relationship with the existing state, as indicated in Figure 5.2. *Geopolitical resources* derive from the historical status of the territory as an external, enclave, interface or 'failed-centre' territory, also entailing the territory's

capacity and experiences of cross-border cooperation and alliance mak
Finally, they include its relationship with the new EU centre. *Cultura.*
distinctiveness resources are embodied in a rich ethno-history, as a significant
source of cultural power and a focus of cultural politicization. Communities
able to boast such histories have a competitive advantage over others
where that history is scanty or doubtful. In this second case, intellectuals
and politicians 'must recover a sufficiently large quantity of communal
history to convince their own members that they have an illustrious past,
and they must authenticate it sufficiently to convince sceptical outsiders
of its merits'.[42] *Economic resources* concentrated in the territory include
the classic assets of economic development, external trade, and access to
non-state capital and labour markets. Finally, the *political-institutional*
resources include the institutional (competencies and policymaking capacities, autonomous fiscal imposition, existing differentiation of functional
subsystems), and the political (level of partisan integration of the local
political class into the national cleavage system; regionalization of the
party system, density of regional political, social, and economic institutions)
capabilities of local government.[43]

It is not surprising to find that the subnational territories' presence
and representation in Brussels is usually a function of their cultural

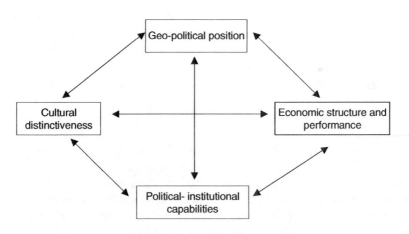

FIGURE 5.1. Sources of variation in territorial opportunity structures

---

[42] Smith, *National identity*, 164.
[43] Keating indicates seven dimensions of resources. See Keating, M., 'Les Régions
constituent-elles un niveau de gouvernement en Europe?', in P. LeGalès and G. Lequesne
(eds.), *Les paradoxes des régions en Europe*, 33–5.

distinctiveness and local politico-administrative autonomy. These types of territories are the first to exploit the opportunity to play off the antagonism between the national and the European politico-administrative centres. Nor is it surprising that cross-border cooperation experiences currently reflect the geopolitical position of a territory, with most of these experiences being concentrated along the lines of the cultural/administrative boundary mismatch of interface peripheries—for instance, along the Lotharingian-Burgundian line (or the east cultural periphery line that will soon come into being with the EU enlargement).

The interaction between the levels of these resource endowments helps to identify the most likely outcomes for revising the existing relationship with the centre in terms of territorial options. Separatist and 'irredentist' requests versus requests for the 're-centralization' of administrative regimes and resource distribution represent the two opposite extremes of this relationship. In the intermediate space, revisionism may range from redistributive requests for larger shares of state resources, to demands for autonomy in functional regime differentiation, to demands for increased supranational integration and cooperation.

The argument in this section has been that European integration is likely to foster processes of substate territorial differentiation, generate accrued substate territorial competition and a renewed awareness of it, and, finally, also contribute towards a rebirth of (substate) territorially-based politics in Europe. However, the analysis of the empirical variation in substate territorial responses requires to link the new opportunities to the actual configuration of structural resources, likely demands, and outcomes. On the basis of the scheme in Figure 5.2 we can formulate some hypotheses about this variation in territorial differentiation, which can be tested with the appropriate data. This demands systematic and solid fact-finding and comparative data accumulation on the within-state territorial differentiation of interests, institutions, policies, economic and cultural resources. That is, we need *territorialized* data on the socio-demographic and economic structure, but also on cross-territory linkages and fluxes (external regional trade figures; regional foreign trade dependency), and political administrative data and synopses about local government structures, competencies, fiscal revenues, resort to ECJ, resort to national courts against national governments, institutional territorialization of administrative regimes in the fields of economic district management, labour market training, credit practice differentiation, salary differentials, welfare and educational regulations, opportunities for and experiences of cross-border cooperation. Finally, we need some political data about party system regional distinctiveness, European versus national election differences, regional parties, and centre-peripheral relationships within the structure of nationally-based parties.

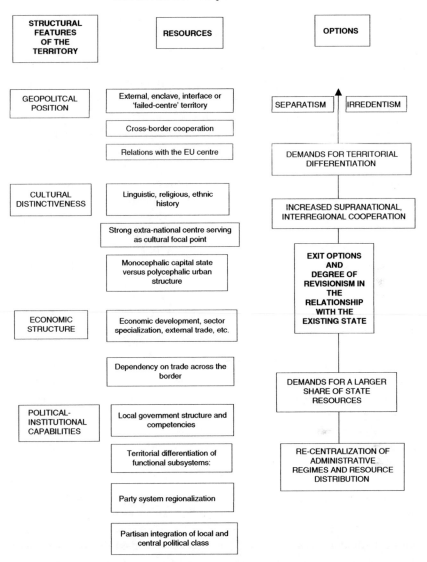

FIGURE 5.2. A map of substate territories' structures of opportunity

Corporate Structures

In a (neo)-functionalist perspective, the integration process affects identities and interests by producing a shifted focus of loyalties, expectations and political action towards the newly formed centre. European integration should eventually produce a 'restructuring' at the transnational level of societal interests, with a parallel impact on the forms of corporate interests representation. The contrary view is that the firm control kept by the nation-states will ensure that interest formation, aggregation, and representation takes place at the national level, supported by persisting national loyalties and identities, on the one hand, and by the institutions and procedures of democratic decision-making, on the other. Those adaptations that are needed as a result of economic integration will be nationally assisted, preventing those changes that have an excessive disruptive potential for national interests. In this section, I discuss the alternative between supranational structuring and the persistence of national structures of interest intermediation.

Interest Intermediation in the Union

At the national level, interest intermediation and representation developed into a more or less institutionalized system of a small set of highly inclusive and centralized groups. This institutionalization was based on a number of conditions.[44] It rested on the presence of an interventionist state and of a rather oligopolistic and/or regulated market. At the institutional level, it required the European predominant type of parliamentary democracy with fused and centralized powers, weak centre–periphery structures, and few institutional veto powers. At the political level, it required party government and peak association leadership. At the ideological level, it required a mutual recognition and consensus among interested representatives—namely, unions, and trade and employers' associations—on the main values to be sought. In short—according to the interpretative framework of this work— the institutionalization of the systems of interest intermediation and of policy formation/implementation required a high capacity for territorial confinement of the actors involved and a high capacity for independent political production by the political elites. This favoured the development of peak associations of the main economic interests, making negotiation around the key economic variables possible.

The EU model is not like this. Most observers define it as very pluralistic, lacking the conditions for a highly institutionalized system of interest intermediation or of policy formation.[45] The European representation of interests

---

[44] See Fabbrini, S., 'Il "policy making" dell'Unione Europea in prospettiva comparata', in S. Fabbrini and F. Morata (eds.), *L'Unione Europea. Le politiche pubbliche* (Roma-Bari: Editori Laterza, 2002), 336–66, especially 354–5.

[45] Schmitter and Streek, 'From national corporatism to transnational pluralism: Organized interests in the single european market'; Gabel, M., *Interests and Integration. Market Liberalization, Public Opinion, and European Union* (Ann Arbor, MI: University of Michigan Press, 1998).

is organizationally fragmented, with many groups of a relatively small size, which are less hierarchical and less integrated than the national ones, with peak associations having very low control over national affiliates, and with high intergroup competition. None of the early EU federal organizations had direct membership. Sector lobbies tend to be more important than peak associations and their number exploded in hundred sector organizations.[46]

It is generally acknowledged that the access of functional interests to the EU institutions is fairly open and easy, sometimes more open and easier than at the national level. The Commission eagerly recognizes those interest groups and each Directorate surrounds itself with standing, advisory, management committees based on their representatives. The same goes for the Council and, more recently, for the Parliament. As a result, the representation of interests at the EU level takes place in hundreds of committees. However, the interaction among these interest groups and EU institutions and their role in policy formulation and implementation is not institutionalized beyond this relatively easy access. The aim of the Economic and Social Committee was to institutionalize the representation of sector interests, but it failed to constitute a significant arena or even a forum for concrete discussion.[47] Its members are not selected by the different interests organizations themselves, but are appointed by the national governments and approved by the Council of Ministers. They do actually reflect some balance among employers, workers, and other interests and have ties with the various organizations of those interests. However, they serve officially as individuals, and not as group representatives.

The direct access and representation of interest organizations necessarily implies fragmentation and specialization. The process is one of pluralistic participation in policymaking, particularly since the growing activity of the Commission in the areas of environment, social policy, research, and development have extended the set of interest organizations involved. By the late 1980s and early 1990s, the EU had witnessed an explosion of interest representation in Brussels, with lobbyists and organizations, regional associations, umbrella organizations of member states, and even big companies being positioned in Belgium. In that period, some changes also took place in the prevailing modes of interest representation. The progressive extension of majority voting in the post-SEA Council made interest organizations more

[46] There are some differences among countries concerning the degree to which 'lobbying' is spontaneous or nationally coordinated and channelled. In France the coordination of EU-related interests is centrally located, in the hands of the *Secrétariat Général du Comité Interministériel*, who reports to the Prime Minister. In Belgium and the Netherlands, on the contrary, actors prefer to take sector issues directly to Brussels.

[47] On the ESC, see Smismans, S., 'The European Economic and Social Committee: Towards Deliberative Democracy via a Functional Assembly', European Integration online Papers, 2000, 4, 12.

attentive to influencing the policy formulation process at an early stage, given that obstructing decisions via their national government in the Council was sometimes too costly and less effective. The growing powers of the EP also made it more attractive for some public interest groups to approach this institution. However, reviewing these developments, the experts conclude that the explosive growth in interest representation has meant that 'increasing issue specific coalitions are brought together', that 'the EU institutions even contribute to the proliferation of interest group organizations', and that 'the present extension of trans-European political network, and their pluralistic differentiation which accompanies disintegration of long established national networks contribute to a fragmentation of public policy'.[48]

Notwithstanding the active attempt made by the Commission to offer recognition, material, and symbolic support to public interest groups (environmental, fighting poverty, consumers, feminist, migrant, human rights, etc.),[49] most interest groups active in the extended committee system are industrial and commercial. According to an estimate made in the early 1990s, about 50 per cent of groups were in this area; about 20 per cent were in the agricultural field; 20 per cent in the services, and only 5 per cent in the domain of environmental interests, consumers, trade unions, etc.[50] The fact that the system of interest representation in the EU is more favourable to functional interests than to public interests organizations comes as no surprise and requires no special explanation. The same situation occurs at the national level as a result of a colossal disparity of resources between the two types of organizations and the more acute problems inherent to the representativeness of the public interests groups.

This structural imbalance is simply worsened in the EU by the fact that public interest organizations are active in domains and policy areas that have no, or only weak, or recent legal bases in the treaties. Moreover, the capacity

[48] Kohler-Kock, B., 'Changing Patterns of Interest Intermediation in the European Union', *Government and Opposition*, 29 (1994), 166–80, 175 and 179. See also Eisling, R., 'Multilevel Governance and Business Interest in the European Union', *Governance*, 17 (2004), 211–45.

[49] For these efforts and the material resources devoted to them see Pollack, M., 'Representing Diffuse Interests in the EC Policy Making', *Journal of European Public Policy*, 4 (1997), 572–90. For more detailed information see Rucht, D., 'Think Globally, Act Locally? Needs, Forms and Problems of Cross-National Cooperation Among Environmental Groups', in J. D. Liefferink, P. D. Lowe and M. P. J. Mol (eds.), *European Integration and Environmental Policy* (London: Belhaven Press, 1993), 75–95; Eberwein, W. D., *Die Politik Humanitärer Helfe: Im Spannungsfeld von Macht und Moral* (Berlin: WZB, 1997), Discussion Paper no. 97, 301; Mazey, S., 'L'Union Européenne et les droits des femmes'; and Giugni, M. and Passy, F., 'Le champ politique de l'immigration en Europe', both in R. Balme, D. Chabanet and V. Wright (eds.), *L'action collective en Europe* (Paris: Presses de Sciences Po., 2002), 405–32 and 433–60.

[50] Mazey, S. and Richardson, J., 'Interest Groups in the European Community', in J. Richardson (ed.), *Pressure Groups* (Oxford: Oxford University Press, 1994), 191–213.

of this type of group to remain active in a cross-national environment for the long periods taken over policy decisions and implementation is probably lower than in a national environment. The most important difference, however, is that, at the EU level, public interest groups do not control any resources whose withdrawal or withholding can generate serious problems for either the effectiveness of public policy implementation or the electoral survival of political elite. The exchange that takes place between public interest groups and EU institutions is not based on any real threat of declining returns or increasing costs for the latter when no attention is given to the demands of the former. Only the perception of weak legitimacy by the EU elite in the Council, Commission and Parliament justifies their attention, which, therefore, is grounded on a 'benevolent' attitude.

Finally, the literature does not point to any trend toward reduced access for overly specialized interests, in order to simplify the structure of participation and to avoid overload from an excessively fragmented and lobbyist style input; there is no trend toward fewer and more 'representative' actors; nor is there a trend toward a more stable and formalized pattern of interaction.[51] Therefore, the early expectations that interest organization would organize on a scale coterminous with supranational legislation and that these groups would act as lobbyists for Brussels before their national governments were incorrect.[52] In conclusion, the EU offers an open and pluralistic arena for the 'incorporation' of fragmented and specialized sector interests, but no institutionalized system of interest intermediation in policy formulation. This is consonant with the institutional structure of the EU and its particularities, as discussed in Chapters 3 and 4.

This open and pluralistic environment (which is therefore poorly 'structured') derives, first, from the 'constitutional' polycentrism of the EU and its weak partisanship. To the unitary powers and procedures of the European nation-state, derived from the 'parliamentarization' of previously autocratic/bureaucratic decisional bodies, corresponds, in the EU, the absence of any single and unified executive, and the divided but overlapping powers of different institutions, the complicated mechanisms of member states control, the slow and complex procedures, the different legal bases and decisional procedures of different policy domains, the autonomy of the 'constitutional' review powers of the ECJ. To the centralization of the European nation-states corresponds, in the EU, the strong centre–periphery institutionalization of intergovernmental decision-making. To the strong partisanship of

[51] Andersen, S. S. and Eliassen, K. A., 'EU lobbying: The new research agenda', *European Journal of Political Research*, 27 (1995), 427–41, 434.
[52] Streek and Schmitter, 'From National Corporatism to Transnational Pluralism', summarize in the introduction the role early integration theory assigned to the development of interest groups at the EU level.

political alignments and to the high integration and considerable overlapping of party and interest groups personnel typical of the party government model, corresponds, in the EU, the lack of horizontal and vertical integration of both types of elite. This weak and deliberately de-emphasized partisanship fosters a 'technicalization' of potential conflicts and an 'efficiency' formulation of problems, going beyond the specific technical content of the issues. The direct access by interest groups to the consultation and decision centres is thus deprived of partisan orientations and, therefore, of incentives towards aggregation.

At the same time, other peculiarities of this centre formation make the attempt to incorporate interest groups and to allow them to participate actively a necessary and important asset. The market-making objectives of the Commission require the incorporation of the market actors in the decision-making process. The Commission has only a limited policy-monitoring capacity, and the general problem of the quality of implementation and of avoiding partial, distorted, or non-implementation pushes it to involve the relevant interests so as to check and limit these implementation problems. European institutions, and the Commission in particular, have limited personnel to obtain the necessary information for the policy process. The independent search for such information over the immense and differentiated territory of the EU is long and costly, and it requires a numerous and competent technical bureaucracy that is not available. As a result, this role of information gathering is left to the input of relevant interests and any information/control deficit is handled by involving them in many various types and levels of committees. The contribution made by interest groups is usually that of offering information of a technical nature, which is essential to the Commission in order for it to build its case against any potential resistance by other bodies and institutions. The presence of multiple sources of legitimacy and the absence of an overarching principle of political legitimacy increases the need for 'social legitimacy' of the decisional process. The support for the policies by those actors that are concerned and/affected by them is crucial given the lack of any other procedural legitimation. 'Social legitimacy', in the sense of consensus coalitions of social actors, is thus a crucial asset for the Commission to overcome and bypass the opposition of national representatives' to specific developments and policies.

Therefore, EU institutions allow for participation and distribute influence in exchange for information and support. This situation has become the ideological flag of the new 'governance' theory and practice. It is, however, also the normal situation of every 'weak state' (or 'low stateness') and non-partisan process, in which the role of providing input in terms not only of requests but also of information is necessarily left to the interested actors. In this sense, the open, pluralist, fragmented, and consensual model of interest incorporation is the default result of a structural weakness of both the central bureaucracy (autonomous information gathering and technical evaluation) and of partisan structures (preference identification and aggregation). In this light, the institutionalization of interest intermediation structures is extremely unlikely, for lack of sustaining conditions.

While acknowledging the negative impact of the institutional and cultural context, authors investigating the causes of this situation, have also underlined organizational weakness very strongly. In particular they underline the specific disabilities of labour (different political orientations, national divisions), which have fostered a tendency to seek national or intergovernmental solutions to their problems, and the absence of the representation of business interests as employers, in contrast to their requests as producers (protection, regulation or deregulation of their product markets). By refusing to organize and delegate powers to peak organizations to enter into binding agreements with counterparts, business and employers are able to constrain European institutions into ineffectiveness. That is, business has prevented the centralization of the regulatory capacity 'by simply refusing to build those organizations necessary to them to be able to make the binding commitments at the central level'.[53]

Overstressing the liability of labour and the unwillingness of business to cooperate suggests that the power and legitimacy of the Commission to structure interest intermediation could be generated from below, through the support of functional groups. This interpretation implicitly suggests that the disciplining of interests could be achieved by their own organizational capacity, creating those decisional structures meant to 'build' interests by limiting their free exit opportunities. This interpretative line echoes the idea of a 'societal corporatism', that is, a corporatism that is embedded in the society rather than fostered by the state. In my opinion, highly institutionalized interest intermediation structures (neo-corporatist structures, if one prefers) did not historically emerge as a consequence of peak organizations; rather, the latter emerged because they were fostered by the capacity of the central state bureaucratic and political decision-making processes to lock in territorially relevant resource controllers and to force them to accept centralized political exchange for which peak associations were necessary.[54] In fact, trade unions found it equally difficult to organize at the national level, and business associations had the same interest to defect at the national level. They were eventually forced or bribed into centralized negotiated orders by the pressure of elective political elites and by their threat to legislate

---

[53] Streek and Schmitter, 'From National Corporatism to Transnational Pluralism', 142–3.

[54] For the European trade unions the supporting evidence is discussed in Bartolini, S., *The Class Cleavage. The Electoral Mobilization of the European Left 1880–1980* (Cambridge: Cambridge University Press, 2000), Chapter 6.

anyway. The level of boundary closure—typical of the nation-state and untypical of the EU—allowed obstruction to be sanctioned and curbed. In the absence of territorial coercing-bribing political agencies, the centralization of political exchanges and the acceptance of binding decisions are unlikely and the costs of peak organization formation are unworthy to be borne. As a result, the centralization/ institutionalization of interest representation is highly problematic.

The institutional design of the new supranational centre is a sufficient explanation of the non-viability of a European institutionalized system of interest intermediation.[55] Certain institutional developments might help to remedy this (strengthening the Economic and Social Committee and cross-country institutions like the European Works Council), but the actors that shape the EU policies (Council, Commission, Court of Justice) do not fit comfortably into any understanding of 'corporatism', and the latter cannot be based on 'voluntary' cooperation among social forces. It is therefore more likely to see flexible corporatism arrangements being withdrawn at a level *below* the national, as subnational tripartite mechanisms of meso-corporatism.[56]

The trade unions, as one of the key actor of every institutionalized system of interest intermediation, have most consistently tried to organize at the EU level. A closer look at their experience is useful. With the relaunching of European market integration in the mid-1980s, both the political capital of the unions—rooted in the nation-state representation mechanisms—and their industrial strength—rooted in national market relations—came under challenge. The joining of the EU single market with world trade and capital liberalization began to undermine the national negotiated arrangements concerning wages, employment, working conditions, social benefits, and industrial relations. In this new contest, all the attempts made by national unions to improve their associates' conditions of contract came up against the constraints of international competitiveness in the specific market of the national enterprises. This meant that unless achievements made by the unions encompass all the competing companies in the relevant product market at least in Europe, these achievements could not be sustained. However, notwithstanding this clear predicament, it has proven difficult to

[55] Schmitter and Streek recognize this when they conclude that the EU was never granted the 'organizational design capacities necessary to reshape powerful interest organizations rooted in civil society'. Streek and Schmitter, 'From National Corporatism to Transnational Pluralism'. Streek makes a clearer reference to the EU institutional design in Streek, W., 'Neo-Voluntarism: A New European Social Policy Regime?', *European Law Journal*, 1 (1995), 31–59.

[56] This is convincingly argued by Pelinka, A., 'The (In)Compatibility of Corporatism and Federalism: Austrial Social Partnership and the EU', *West European Politics*, 22 (1999), 116–29, 124.

structure at the European level. So, although the European Trade Unions Confederation (ETUC) was established in 1973 with seventeen national confederations and ten European industry committees representing national industry unions, after more than twenty years, in 1996 (it included twenty-one countries, with many non-EU members), it remained a loose umbrella association, with a small secretariat in Brussels, no capacity to influence affiliates' policies or mobilize industrial force, and with no effective power on the part of its sector components to constrain employers into a European-wide collective bargaining or agreement.

From the outset, there have been two alternatives concerning the level at which to operate: to strengthen European organization to develop a supra-national trade unionism coexistent with the new market boundary, or to cling to the nation-state in line with a tradition of national TU protectionism and indifference towards Europe. There were also two alternatives con-cerning the predominant political strategy: to seek a special relation of incorporation with the national or EU central institutions and bureaucracy, de-emphasizing the partisan profile and accepting the techno-bureaucratic management of issues of concern, or to go for a more militant and partisan alliance with the national or European sympathetic parties. Each of these alternatives had obvious liabilities, and considerable disagreement sur-rounded their discussion and choice. Since at the EU level the unions had few resources to exchange with elective representatives and non-elective bureaucracies, an alliance between the unions and EU administration and politicians could only rest on a benevolent attitude of the latter. At the same time, even if the political elites could be pressurized at the national level, they were likely to be blocked into a free-rider problem at the European level. Consequently, consistent support could only be offered by a set of sympa-thetic governments in power at the same time. So the strategy of alliance with the new centre builders of Brussels was based on weak resources, while the strategy of pressuring the national elites faced external institutional con-straints in EU decision-making.

The choice of counteracting borderless competition with transnational labour's solidarity took quite a long time to consolidate. It was the profound organizational changes introduced in the 1991 ETUC congress—increasing the resources and autonomy of the Secretariat, abolishing the veto powers of national confederations, and broadening the use of qualified majority voting—and the 31 October agreement eventually included in the Maastricht Treaty that marked the change in the course of European unions and witnessed their ambition to transform the ETUC into a Confederation with the capacity to conduct European-wide collective bargaining. However, the opposition or the ambivalent position of the German and Nordic unions to this new orientation led, in 1993, to a compromise on European collective bargaining restricting the latitude for autonomous action by the ETUC secretariat, diluting majority voting, and reconsolidating the 'intergovernmentalist' features of the ETUC.[57]

The results of TU activities could be summarized as follows at the end of the 1990s. In the *market dimension*, TU have been weakened at the national level without any development of countervailing agreements at the EU level being achieved. The tendency towards the decentralization of much of the bargaining, with a broad shift from sector to company and especially plant-level bargaining, is more damaging within the open EU context than at the national level. The threat for national unions is thus greatest when employers can play plants off against one another cross-nationally. The European Industry Committees are busy in the areas of (*a*) sector-level social dialogue, sponsored and largely financed by the EU, where unions and employees exchange views and information and sometimes jointly try to influence the EU legislation; (*b*) the building of (Euro-)Works Councils (with Commission funds, again) as cross-national meetings of plant representatives; and (*c*) the exploration of possible future cross-national sector and firm-level collective bargaining. It is legitimate to ask what the future of these initiatives might be when the EU will no longer finance them. The European Working Council directive has encouraged employers to negotiate information and consultation arrangements for transnational companies, but the ETUC's aim to bargain collectively has lacked Commission support and willingness on the part of employers. In conclusion, 'unless trade unions become capable of countervailing capital exit threats and manage to underpin their demands by transborder mass mobilization (either seizing the right voluntarily, or by legal reform) their bargaining position will remain inferior'.[58] Notwithstanding this, there is as yet not much evidence that the single market has led to a widespread de-regulation of national industrial relations and collective bargaining. It seems that, so far, the weakening of the unions' position is more due to the restrictive EMU requirements in public spending and deficits, the convergence process, tax competition, and fiscal dumping than the growth of cross-border relocation or the restructuring of companies in the single market.

In the *social dimension* (see Chapter 4), achievements have been attained on issues of the social protection of employees and the collective

---

[57] Turner attributes this minimal cooperation more to actors' choices than to structural causes. In particular, he underlines the fact that the opposition of the CGT to the EU and the concentration of the German Unions on Eastern Germany integration and the incorporation of east German workers have deprived the cross-national efforts of two crucial pillars. Turner, L., 'Beyond National Unionism? Cross-National Labor Collaboration in the European Community' (Berlin: WZB, 1993), Working Paper, 1, 93–203.

[58] Dolvik, J. E., 'Redrawing Boundaries of Solidarity? ETUC, social dialogue and the Europeanization of trade unions in the 1990s', (Oslo: Arena, 1997), Report no. 5, 56–58.

representation and defence of workers. Social policy legislation is, however, limited to implementing the remaining blocked directives of the 1989 Action Programme. With the 'social dialogue', employers and labour organizations were granted a consultative and co-regulative role in social policy, and the opportunity to substitute pending EC/EU legislation with European agreements that eventually would become binding law. The practical use of the Maastricht social agreement is so far limited, restricting the regulatory role of the Community to that of providing framework regulations that define broad objectives, minimum standards and procedures, while allowing great leeway and flexibility in implementation at the national level.

At the *organizational level* the ETUC has expanded steadily in terms of both occupations and territories represented (despite the long-term exclusion of the French CGT). However, the degree of vertical integration is limited, while its focus falls mainly on horizontal coordination between nationally located social actors. There thus remains a high internal differentiation of goals between those affiliated unions wanting the ETUC to work as a representative of TU interests at the Commission and those wanting to promote TU cooperation throughout Europe; between affiliates motivated by the idea of European unification, and affiliates mainly interested in building up a European countervailing negotiation power; between affiliates supporting a growing integration, and those who are more sceptical; between affiliates supporting a confederal mode of negotiation and affiliates supporting a sector one. Organizational enlargements (to the south, the north, and the east) impact considerably on the internal dynamics of the ETUC. The complex problem of fostering collective identification and solidarity across lingual, cultural and institutional national diversities remains, and these internal differences have resulted into a paradoxical imbalance between considerable organization-building efforts and poor collective action in the market and the polity.

Rather than moving from collective action to organizational form, the ETUC has developed in the opposite direction, setting up its organizational structures before any capacity for collective action. Networking and institution building was handled by the representatives of already existing organizations and cross-national collaboration developed among top labour organizations that was not movement-driven.[59] To understand this one should first consider that the EU institutional design offers—as already discussed—few good reasons for collective action centralization. To overcome the logic of national membership is difficult due to the fact that the

---

[59] See Turner, L., 'The Europeanization of Labor: Structure before Action', *European Journal of Industrial Relations*, 2 (1996), 325–44. Ebbinghaus believes the opposition between national and European trajectories of structure versus action to be exaggerated. Ebbinghaus, B., 'Europe Through the Looking-Glass: Comparative and Multi-Level Perspectives', *Acta Sociologica*, 41 (1998), 301–13.

ETUC work is best organized as a lobby activity of political unionism, rather than as the development of collective bargaining and action at the EU level. To exercise collective action in the market requires far higher levels of membership solidarity than to pressure the (EU) institutions. In addition, transborder solidarity among interdependent European unions may be highly contentious, while the embedding of labour solidarity within national boundaries is an obstacle to Europeanization, even if this seems a rational and logical response to the openness of the European market.[60]

All the same, while unfriendly to collective action transnationalizing, the EU institutional setting gives its support to the incorporating of TU into its decision-making machinery. In particular, the willingness of the Commission to have trade unions as partners, combined with the inability of the ETUC to credibly threaten industrial conflict or to offer wage restraints and industrial peace, has helped to set institutional incentives for the redefinition of the unions' strategic interests in the direction of further ETUC (and EU) integration. In the end, the ETUC remains too dependent on the supporting role of the EU institutions and too committed to the general vision of the Commission,[61] allowing the specific form of EU centre formation to shape their style of activity. This alliance between central bureaucratic actors and social actors is a typical 'bismarckian' strategy of non-democratized regimes, where the flimsy bases of political legitimacy favour organizational consolidation and recognition of key social actors in exchange for support. The problem with the EU institutional design is that the Commission is in fact not able to deliver as much as it promises.

So, concerning interest groups activities at the EU level, we witness a series of apparently contradictory conclusions. First, given their number, activism and incorporation, EU interest groups are regarded as the most europeanized sector of political structures. Second however, these groups are unlikely to go beyond the pluralistic and fragmented structure and lobbyist style to generate a solid structure of institutionalized interest intermediation and policy formulation. Finally, third, scholars underline the fact that in facing these European difficulties, the main interest groups will remain linked to national arenas, as the states' veto power ensures them a continued monopoly of pressure group activities.[62] The first two conclusions can be easily

[60] Dolvik, J., 'Redrawing Boundaries of Solidarity', 33.

[61] Rosse and Martin note that 'groups that become unduly dependent upon contacts with and the resources of these institutions are almost certain to be tempted towards conversion experiences to the European ideal'. Rosse, G. and Martin, A., 'European Integration and the Europeanization of Labor' (Madrid: Instituto Juan March, 1988), Working Paper 126, 36.

[62] The conclusion of Streek, 'Neo-Voluntarism: A New European Social Policy Regime?'; and Kohler-Kock, 'Changing Patterns of Interest Intermediation in the European Union'.

reconciled. The EU empowers interest groups but only to the extent that they are or will become isomorphic with its institutional structure of separated and competing, fragmented, specialized, technical, and efficiency-driven bodies. The third conclusion is more controversial, as it largely depends on the degree and type of impact of the integration process on national interest intermediation structures and organizations.

Impact On National Patterns and Organizations of Interest Intermediation

Whatever the predominant pattern of EU-level interest intermediation, the indirect effects of integration produce changes in the modalities of interest intermediation at the national level and in the stability and cohesion of individual organizations. Changes in the predominant national interest intermediation structures are likely to occur whenever the national modalities of interest accommodation are in conflict with those prevalent in the same area at the European level. Interest intermediation at the EU and national levels are usually characterized by a predominantly 'corporatist', 'pluralist' or 'statist' idealtype model. According to Falkner,[63] these models hide important infra-state differences in sectors, areas and type of interests, and even at the EU level there is not one single 'pluralist' macro-system, but rather a plurality of sector-specific constellations. Therefore, the impact of European policies on interest intermediation structures will be more differentiated than is expected. Falkner proposes merging the policy network typology and the intermediation threefold typology into a single typology, to be applied at both EU and national levels to differentiate the sector systems of interest intermediation. She discusses the expected outcome in those cases in which different models of interest intermediation at the EU and national level meet in a given sector (see Table 5.1).

In this perspective, the EU-dominant mode influences the national one. When networks of the same kind operate at the member state and EU levels, no strong domestic impact is expected, while there is a high degree of potential destabilization of the national pattern when different types encounter. For instance, if a EU level statist cluster meets an issue network, policy community or corporatist policy community in a member state, the effect will always be to the detriment of the role of private interests. A pluralist issue network at the EU level will promote more openness for interest groups in a national statist cluster, will foster less participation for the private interests of a member state policy community or corporatist policy community. A EU policy community will influence national statist constellations and issue

[63] Falkner, G., 'Policy Networks in a Multi-level System: Converging Towards Moderate Diversity?', *West European Politics*, 23 (2000), 94–120.

TABLE 5.1. *Fit between EU and national interest intermediation patterns*

		European pattern			
		Statist cluster	Pluralist issue network	Policy community	Corporatist policy community
National pattern	Statist cluster	Reinforcing	X	X	X
	Pluralist issue network	X	Reinforcing	X	X
	Policy Community	X	X	Reinforcing	X
	Corporatist policy community	X	X	X	Reinforcing

Source: Falkner, 'Policy Networks in a Multilevel System'.

networks in the direction of greater participation by the societal actors, and a national corporatist policy community in the direction of less participation and cohesion by societal actors. A EU corporatist policy community will increase the chances for participation and co-decision in national statist clusters, policy networks and corporatist policy networks.

Although it is, in theory, possible for the EU interest intermediation pattern to be different in different sectors and policy areas, in practice the literature suggests few instances of EU 'corporatist policy community'.[64] The Table 5.1 could therefore be considerably simplified by getting rid of low frequency columns and cells. The fact is that while the administrative traditions of countries (and of infra-country sectors) vary in the way in which they deal with organized interests and incorporate them into the policy process, the EU pattern of policy formation and implementation is unified and homogeneous, even accounting for some sector variations. Moreover, in some European countries (France can be taken as a key example here) the process of policy formulation is insensitive to the affected interests as a result of political decision-making rules, institutions rules and traditions. On the contrary, the process of policy implementation is highly sensitive to affected interests, as a result of bureaucratic traditions and politico-bureaucratic implementation practices. In other countries (take Switzerland as the ideal example), the situation is the opposite: high policy formation sensitivity

---

[64] While there are examples of national corporatist policy communities challenged if not undermined by different types of European policymaking. See below in the text. For evidence about Sweden and Denmark in the field of labour law and industrial relations see Falkner, G. and Leiber, L., 'A Europeanization of Governance patterns in Smaller European Democracies' (Nashville, TN: 2003), VIII Biennial International Conference of the European Union Studies Association, 27–9 March.

accompanied by low policy implementation sensitivity. The rigid EU regulations leave little room to interest sensitivity in the implementation phase, which would amount to leaving up high implementation discretion to national governments. This tends to produce a loss of flexibility for interest accommodation in the implementation process in those countries that apply flexibility at that level. The consequence should be that interest would have to be taken into account in the EU policy formulation phase, so as to compensate for the impossibility or difficulty of adaptation of the policy implementation. This also implies that interest intermediation structures with high policy implementation sensitivity will find themselves in a more difficult situation than in countries where interests are more accustomed to taking part directly in the policy formulation process.

The indirect effects of integration are not, however, limited to the national predominant mode of interest intermediation, since they extend to the internal cohesion of established national interest organizations. National level interest organizations were built on specific conflict lines and alliance choices that helped to overcome a great variety of sector, territorial, skill, and other differences in view of the organizational economy of scale essential to fostering their *common* main interest. Employers, trade and labour associations, for instance, developed on the basis of the definition of common interests, overcoming many other sources of internal diverging interests and identifications. If these organizations are today naturally regarded as the bearer of a 'common' interest, it is only because they successfully internalized, reinterpreted, or simply suppressed the dysfunctional variety of other lines of interest differentiation within their constituency. If the boundaries defining the possible action of the relevant political actors and allies open up, then the traditional communality of interests and solidarity ties may be undermined by new options and opportunities. There is no reason to believe that these options and opportunities will be redistributed *between* interest groups rather than *within* them, and this could produce an internal differentiation and fragmentation of previously unified interest groups. Latent internal interest oppositions may surface, once the need and the possibility for common action and attitude towards the political production of the new centre fade away. In the following pages I present a few examples of this process of interest differentiation in areas where the indirect effects of integration seem to be clearer.

Welfare Policies

Over the past two decades, demands and attempts at welfare reforms have grown as a result of national (unemployment and public deficits, demographic stagnation and ageing, class and sector changes) and European (monetary integration parameters, encroachments of the ECJ case law on the national compulsory structures of pension and health care) pressures.[65] These pressures are likely to impact differently on national social sharing depending on their institutional structure. In the north, welfare policies reinforced the state's penetration of civil society and enhanced the latter's loyalty to the nation via materially substantial, organizationally efficient, and symbolically strong social sharing flows. In many continental countries, social sharing arrangements remained characterized by a much lower degree of 'stateness' and were structured in accordance with pre-existing social and/ or cultural differentiations ('pillarization', denominational, and occupational). In the South, the structuring of welfare institutions was faced with the challenges of economic backwardness, regional differentiation, harsh church-state conflict, ideological polarization and low administrative capacities, which fostered fragmented and 'clientelistic' dynamics.[66]

The impact of the EU boundary redrawing will be perceived differently across countries depending, in particular, on the division between basic and supplementary pillars and the mix of public and private provision. Where extensive national exit options already exist (Great Britain, for instance), the impact will be less significant. Where basic schemes are very important and supplementary schemes are so far marginal (e.g. pensions in Italy), these developments are not so important. The maximum and most destabilizing impact could be felt where second pillars are designed by analogy to the first (e.g. in the Scandinavian model).

The above-mentioned pressures are also likely to impact differently on different types of welfare programmes according to their more or less universal or selective nature. The middle classes see their role as that of contributors and financiers to selective programmes. On the contrary, they perceive themselves as beneficiaries of more universalistic schemes extending coverage and generous services beyond the poor, the helpless, the disadvantaged, the badly organized and the weakly mobilized. The level of public support of various social programmes is therefore related to their inclusiveness.[67]

---

[65] On the connection between national welfare states and European integration in terms of 'structuring/restructuring see Ferrera, *The Boundaries of Welfare*, on which I rely.

[66] Ferrera, *Modelli di solidarietà*; and Ferrera, 'European Integration and National Social Sovereignty'.

[67] See Flora, P., 'Wachstum zu Grenzen. Stabilizierung durch Wandel. Zur Historischen Lage der entwickelten Wohlfahrtsstaaten Westeuropas', in M. Kaase (ed.), *Analysen zu Theorie und Empirie demokratischer Regierungweise* (Opladen: Westdeutscher Verlag, 1986), 27–39; Esping-Anderson, G., *The Three Worlds of Welfare Capitalism* (Cambridge: Polity Press. 1990). For a critique of the view that the degree of inclusion of the middle classes is the key factor for the safeguarding and expansion of welfare programmes see Pierson, P., *Dismantling the Welfare State? Reagan, Thatcher and the Politics of Retrenchment* (Cambridge: Cambridge University Press, 1994). For a critique of the empirical basis

Country and programme variation combines with more general trends towards shifts in the financing of the welfare state from employers' contributions to general tax revenues, and with processes of the subnational differentiation of welfare provisions, including shifts in the financing of 'social services' from central to local government level.[68] For instance, in Belgium, the national welfare structure is being dismantled and replaced with subnational community schemes. In Italy, the National Health Service is increasingly being transformed into a system of health care regions as a result of the growing activism of some of the regional movements of the wealthiest regions (Lombardy, Veneto). In addition, some European regions are actively experimenting with cross-border cooperation between their welfare systems and there is a certain amount of active lobbying in Brussels by multinational enterprises to create a space for cross-border schemes reserved for their employees.

Finally, the ECJ defence of competition and market liberalization may further challenge the national principle of exclusivity (for basic schemes) and foster the development of a market regime for supplementary benefits (pension and health care in particular) which might well attract a critical mass of consumers. The new possibility of exit, even if granted, does not, however, mean automatic massive exit. But there is at least the possibility that a set of new options will be made available to the 'winners', with a strong incentive to opt out of public/national schemes (and voicing to be granted that option), leaving losers to fall on increasingly lean basic schemes and means-tested assistance. It is also likely that these opportunities will produce a differentiation of life-chance perceptions by different groups that were previously solidly united within the capsule of nationalized, compulsory, exclusive social insurance systems.[69]

Not only are countries, programmes, and substate territories affected differently; so are social groups. These pressures would appear to converge into the weakening of large-scale national social solidarity and national integration forces, and into the reduction of the capacity for nationwide redistribution. Both national social insurance systems and the associated social groups alignments have begun a process of unfreezing and opening up, with the emergence of new subnational, cross-national, functional and cross-functional interest coalitions. There is thus the possibility that a

of Pierson's conclusions see Albert, J., 'Il ripensamento del welfare state in Germania e negli Stati Uniti', *Rivista Italiana di Scienza Politica*, 27 (1997), 49–100.

[68] See Streek ,W., 'From Market Building to State-Building? Reflections on the Political Economy of European Social Policy', in Liebfried and Pierson (eds.), *European Social Policy*, 389–431.

[69] On this social differentiation see Ferrera, 'European Integration and National Social Sovereignty'.

parallel development will take place, matching new social protection institutions with new social cleavages. These processes could affect the internal cohesion of existing social and interest groups, according to the way in which their internal components are affected by these changes and the opportunities that they have to escape their costs or exploit their benefits.

Wage Policies

Similar pressures to 'destructure' national interest organizations emerge from the changes in income negotiation structures that are implicit in the EMU. There is widespread consensus that the EMU will bring about a change in wage-bargaining structures in many countries, forcing them to converge towards a similar model,[70] while there is less agreement on the direction of this general change. The institutional design of the EMU may require nothing less than the complete dismantling of income negotiation structures at the national level and a move towards bargaining decentralization at the company level,[71] or, less radically, a more decentralized wage bargaining in Europe as a whole.[72] If the Europeanization of wage negotiations at the supranational level is excluded, and the national level is weakened, the wage-bargaining decentralization (or even the re-centralization of income negotiations at the national-sector level) leaves ample room for internal divergence in the existing interest organization in this area.

A radical example of this tendency is visible in Austria, with the decline of centralized social partnership in the 1990s. The four major social partners agreed to drop price control (established by their Joint Commission's Subcommittee on Prices) and move to the observation of market tendencies, with a new subcommittee on international relations established for this purpose. Austria moved towards the European norm, and the internationalization of the labour market diminished the bargaining power of centralized labour. What is more important in this context is that this decline resulted in

[70] See Hall, P. A., 'Central Bank Independence and Coordinated Wage Bargaining: The Interaction in Germany and Europe', *German Politics and Society*, 31 (1994), 1–23; and Hall, P. A. and Franzese, R. J., 'Mixed Signals: Central Bank Independence, Coordinated Wage Bargaining, and European Monetary Union', *International Organization*, 52 (1998), 505–35.

[71] For an example of this radical position see Burda, M. C., 'European Labour Markets and Euro: How much flexibility do we really need?' (Berlin: European Network of Economic Policy Research Institutes, 2001), Working Paper.

[72] Martin, A., 'Wage Bargaining Under EMU: Europeanization, Re-Nationalization or Americanization?' (Boston, MA: Harvard University, Center for European Studies, 1999). A minority opinion suggests the opposite: that national governments may increase their control over wage development through a bargaining centralization at the sector level. See Pochet, P., 'The social consequences of EMU: An overview of National Debates', in P. Pochet and B. Vanhercke (eds.), *Social Challenges of Economic and Monetary Union* (Brussels: European University Press, 1998), 67–102.

a redistribution of wealth in favour of the employers' profits and 'in favour of those employees who are better prepared individually for the labour market.... The better prepared employees started to feel that they did not need organized labour any longer; and the less prepared employees got the feeling that their union had not the strength (or the intention) to work successfully for their interests'.[73]

Market Liberalization Policies

In Switzerland, a non-member country that closely follows EU policies in various fields, market liberalization policies have exacerbated interest differentiation within established interest organizations. The new anti-cartel law introduced in 1995 exemplifies very clearly the impact of Europeanization on domestic corporate politics by bringing to surface the latent divergences of interest in the employers' association between those oriented towards the export and external market—always very open—and those oriented towards the internal market—historically dominated either by cartel or by association defences. The active political engagement of the representatives of the export-oriented industry in favour of the anti-cartel law has 'meant a sort of 'de-salidarization' with respect to those economic sectors oriented towards the internal market, and one finds the same situation with respect to the reform of the agricultural policy.[74] The growing internal divisions have had a clear-cut and immediate political impact.

Recent research on Italy and Greece argues that EU policies of market liberalization and the European regulatory control of national policy instruments have resulted in business fragmentation and business participation in different policy-promoting or policy-opposing coalitions. These policies have produced a 'disentanglement' of interest politics from the previous state-partisan domination of representative networks. That is, they have created both an increasing autonomy of association activity from party-dominated and state-dominated networks, and an increasing interest fragmentation/differentiation.[75]

Extensive research comparing the impact of the EU economic policies on the German, British, and French Business Associations has investigated whether the emerging European transnational system of interest intermediation

[73] Pelinka, 'The (In)Compatibility of Corporatism and Federalism'.

[74] Mach, A., 'Quelles réponses politiques face à la globalisation et à la construction européenne? Illustration à partir de la loi suisse sur les cartels', *Swiss Political Science Review*, 4 (1998), 25–49, 40. The translation is mine.

[75] See Lanza, O. and Lavdas, K., 'The disentanglement of interest politics: Business associability, the parties and policy in Italy and Greece', *European Journal of Political Research*, 37 (2000), 203–35; and Lavdas, K., *The Europeanization of Greece: Interest politics and the crisis of integration* (London: Macmillan, 1997).

has any consequences for the national system of interest formation, aggregation and intermediation.[76] This research documents the extension of the new internal division generated by Commission initiatives (GD I Trade and III Industry) like the Trans-Atlantic Business Dialogue (TABD) launched in 1994 and recruiting leading businessmen and trans-atlantic leaders to discuss the elimination of non-tariff barriers to trade. The UNICE (European Business Association) and national interests associations were not happy about the results of the several meetings of US–EU businessmen and governmental officials (Seville, 1995; Chicago, 1996; Rome 1997). Those who led the 'dialogue' were not representatives of the European Business but of only a handful of companies, and a request was made to widen the dialogue to representatives of the UNICE and the national associations.

In fact, these new dynamics brought about by the TABD in the EU commercial policymaking process also created pressures for change in domestic business-government relations and also in the internal life of national business associations. Clearly, the Europeanization of business–government relations in the TABS alters the traditional privileged relationship between national associations and their government in external trade policy. This is because, by working together, companies and the Commission can present the member states with a negotiating strategy that has been 'pre-approved' by European industry, and this, therefore, makes the consultation process at the national level between national associations and government less important. Through this mechanism, large firms have been able to bypass both the national and the European associations, considerably weakening the role and position of national associations' leadership at the state and union levels. As the agenda and competencies of the TABD have expanded to include issues regarding the Euro–US position with respect to the WTO and OECD, large companies have devoted increasing resources to expertise in this area.

The new relationship between large firms and the European Commission thus challenges the dominant role of the national business associations (and member states) in the development of a common commercial policy. At the same time, it has also challenged the authority of the national associations as primary interlocutors in external trade matters. This does not mean that

---

[76] I refer to a number of papers: Cowles, M. G., 'German Big Business: Learning to Play the European Game', *German Politics and Society*, 14 (1996), 73–107; 'The Collective Action of Transatlantic Business: The Transatlantic Business Dialogue', American Political Science Association Meeting, August 1996; 'Organizing Industrial Coalitions. A Challenge for the Future', in H. Wallace and A. Young (eds.), *Participation and Policymaking in the European Union* (Oxford: Oxford University Press, 1997), 116–40; 'The TABD and Domestic Business-Government Relations', in M. G. Cowles, J. Caporaso and T. Risse (eds.), *Europeanization and Domestic Change* (Ithaca, NY: Cornell University Press, 2001), 159–79.

large firms are defecting from their national peak associations. The latter enjoy long-lasting historical legitimacy and maintain higher representativeness that is crucial in some areas of national policymaking. Still important is the power of member states over common commercial policy, and these can block transatlantic trade liberalization at that level, as France did in 1998, when it vetoed the establishment of a New Transatlantic Marketplace between Europe and the USA. However, the TABD is only one of the several occasions on which big firms can mobilize at the EU level to promote and participate in something that the national associations are less enthusiastic about, and this evidence can be seen in the light of the 'fit-misfit' between patterns of European and national involvement of interests in policymaking.[77] However, in a different light it may also be seen as example of a differentiation of national interest groups as a result of the emergence of old and latent conflicts within the peak organizations of business, trade, and even labour.

A further clear-cut case of national interest organizations' loss of unity and cohesion as a result of interest differentiation resulting from EU policies is in the field of electric energy liberalization in France and Germany.[78] In 1989, the member states' utilities companies set up a trade association in Brussels—Eurolectric—to defend their common interests. The French and German governments expressed their reservations against liberalization beyond the free transit of electricity across Europe. The Commission, realizing how much hostility there was to full liberalization, decided not to take any initiative under its competition law prerogatives. It submitted instead, in 1992, a first directive proposal subject to the approval of the Council and European Parliament. By 1995–6, sectors of the French government, potential energy supply competitors, some city councils, and the association of industrial electricity consumers (UNIDEN) began to show signs of impatience with the French national production and distribution monopoly (EDF). The EU negotiations revealed that the French model of electricity supply was no longer fully supported and that there were challenges and challengers to it. The most interesting aspect of the story is that when actors potentially favourable to the liberalization understood that the dynamics of the EU-initiated negotiations could be used as an instrument to break the constraints of the French electricity supply model, they began to call for reform in new and unprecedented ways. The Commission's plans and

---

[77] Schmidt V. A. and Scharpf, F., 'Europeanization and Domestic Structural Change: A Question of Fit?' (Florence: European University Institute, 1998), Conference on 'Europeanization and Domestic Change'.

[78] For details on this case see Eising, R. and Jabko, N., 'Moving Targets: Institutional Embeddedness and Domestic Politics in the Liberalization of EU Electricity Market', *Comparative Political Studies*, 34 (2001), 442–67.

pressures thus allowed industrial consumers and potential EDF competitors to voice concern and opposition that was previously left unspoken, when no opportunity for challenge was envisaged at the national level.

Contrary to the nationalized French structure the German electric supply is decentralized into a large number of public, private and mixed ownership firms whose activities are coordinated by contracts and associations. The sector is fragmented into some seven hundred municipal utilities among which three large regional utilities stand out, and it carries great political weight. The Länder and German political elites were very hesitant about proposals to introduce any competition, given the dispersed and fragmented structure of the electric energy delivery networks. The German government was also sceptical about the Commission's liberalizing plans but, gradually, the Ministry of Economics started to see the EU initiative as an opportunity to reform the system. The Federal Cartel Office gave its support to a liberalizing policy. The industrial energy producers, consumers and trade associations had been asking for cuts in energy costs.

Facing these pressures, the German Electric Utilities Association, including all the suppliers, tried to develop a unifying concept and a common platform, notwithstanding the fact that the anti-liberalizing internal agreement was not perfect. They cleverly tried to maintain the Association's organizational cohesion by asking for a reciprocity of market opening in the EU, underlining the discriminatory effects of the Commission's proposal on Germany's decentralized regime. However, the pressures for a reform in the EU negotiations and the position of the Ministry and its allies led to an erosion of consensus among the sector actors, produced major realignments in the domestic interest coalition, and impinged heavily upon the traditional cleavage lines within the sector. While the local utilities and their associations of municipal utilities ferociously opposed any kind of liberalization, the regional and larger utilities accepted it as a lesser evil, for they feared that the municipalities would be granted major exemptions from liberalization due to their linkages with political actors at the land and local level. They also ended up regarding the EU liberalization as an opportunity to undermine the municipalities' control over local supply areas. The opening of such local supply areas was unlikely to be achieved at the national level and, therefore, both the regional and the interconnected utilities demanded that the municipalities be included in the liberalization process. The new opportunities offered by the EU reform thus paved the way for a new division and new coalitions within the previously unified field of interests. The liberalizing pressure of the EU was supported by some national actors, it produced new exit opportunities from state-dominated regulation, and it eventually led to the internal interest differentiation within the association of all utilities.

In the agricultural field, strong external pressures and the Commission's commitment pushed towards a reform of the CAP, the cost of which was a major obstacle to the development of other EU's policies. In 1992, in the critical international situation created by the blocking of the GATT negotiations, the Commission managed to pass a long advocated reform. The reform revised the principles of agricultural support, lowering the guaranteed price levels and compensating them by direct aids to producers. In principle, the instruments introduced in 1992 have the same effect as the previous 'guaranteed prices' on the income of the different categories of concerned producers. They are calculated in such a way as to reproduce the previous distribution of support (with some minor regional variations). However, while support received through 'guaranteed prices' was particularly opaque, direct aids are calculated on the basis of the exploitation surface, and they are distributed every year in the form of a cheque to the producer.[79] This clear transparency, the high visibility and better individual attribution have transformed the debate in the professional milieus. The visibility of the disparities and inequalities generated by the new system has opened up issues of equity and social justice in the distribution of public support, particularly on the legitimacy of the principle that the biggest producers receive more support. In the French context, the authorities have changed their position radically. Experts' reports suggest the violent opposition to the reform of the *Féderation nationale des syndicats d'exploitation agricole* (FNSEA), but also that the big exporters (particularly of cereals) were favourable to it. Dealing with this new distribution of aid, the FNSEA was obliged to abandon its unitary rhetoric on the equality of conditions in the rural world, and to let emerge the considerable divergences of interest among the different components of the agrarian world.[80]

The PAC reform started a process of interest differentiation in the French agricultural world that had direct associational and political consequences.[81] In 1987, the reuniting of the left-wing trade unions of the rural world led to the creation of the *Conféderation Paysanne* (CP), whose representativity remained weak throughout the 1980s. However, the emergence of this new dimension in the public and political debate has strengthened the role and the legitimacy of the CP as an alternative actor. The new system of aids has also

[79] On the reform see Coleman, W. D. and Tangermann, S., 'The CAP reform, the Uruguay Round and the Commission', *Journal of Common Market Studies*, 37 (1999), 385–405.

[80] On the impact in France see Guyomard, H. and Maché, L. P., 'La réforme de la PAC. Une révolution ou un grand pas dans la bonne direction?', *Revue du Marché Commun et de l'Union Européenne*, no. 366 (1993), 222–36.

[81] On this interest differentiation see Roederer-Rynning, C., 'Farm Conflict in France and the Europeanization of Agricultural Policy', *West European Politics*, 25 (2002), 104–24, 120.

generated, as a side effect, a reopening of the debate about the ecological costs of certain types of agriculture. The more intensive farmers are those who obtain most of the public support and the new system has generated much debate about the introduction of a conditionality rule linking the distribution of aids to the resort to 'good' environmental practices.

Conclusion: European Integration and Interest Redefinition

This selective and exemplary evidence[82] would suggest focusing attention on the domestic processes of interest differentiation within long-established national interest groups.[83] It also suggests that exit opportunities opened up by EU policies tend to weaken the solidarity and interest ties of those same groups. On this ground, the argument of this section is that European integration seems to destructure national interest intermediation structures far more than it restructures them at its widened level.

Historical allies, part of the same interest group when regulative and distributive issues concern fights with other nationally-based groups, may become competitors with the opening of the market boundaries. In addition, the EU functions as an external focus and resource for sections of national interest groups that could never hope to break national interest blocks alone. The external pro-liberalizing role of the Commission prompts political actors to coalesce with these domestic challengers in favour of liberalization, and these coalitions acquire weight thanks to the EU-level leverage, which may enable them to win over entrenched interest groups. In other words, the agenda-setting role of the Commission makes possible cross-states alliances that *generate, reveal,* and *align* interests and potential interests that would normally be unable to coalesce cross-locally. Finally, these cases suggest that the study of structurally located interests is important, even if they do not necessarily motivate action at a given particular moment: they may do so when the structure of opportunity allows for that.

Interest associations are a product of the particular form of the nineteenth and twentieth century nation, democratic, and welfare state. National groups exercise pressure for protective and favourable legislation via two main

---

[82] The list of the cases can easily be expanded. For instance, national professional orders (lawyers, doctors, architects, engineers, etc.) have divided over the right of Community professionals to open a study and to exercise the profession in every member country (in line with the free circulation of services); sector associations (like leather good and textiles producers) divide internally between nationally rooted producers and producers that have delocalized some of their factories to third countries over EU special imports' customs.

[83] Along the lines followed by Eising, R. and Cini, M., 'Disintegration or Reconfiguration', Organized Interests in Western Europe', in P. Heywood, E. Jones and M. Rhodes (eds.), *Developments in West European Politics* (Basingstoke, Hampshire, and New York: Palgrave, 2002), 168–83.

TABLE 5.2. *Interest groups' strategies according to*
levels and types of decision-making

		Type of decision-making process	
		Techno-bureaucratic	Partisan
Level of decision-making	EU	Euro-techno-bureaucratic incorporation (participation, compliance, cooperation in policymaking/ implementation with the Commission and supporting agencies)	Euro-partisanship (increasing European political mobilization allying with the EP and supporting Europarties)
	National	Techno-bureaucratic (re-)nationalization (national monism to enhance national competitiveness)	Democratic (re-)nationalization (national level defence in alliance with Eurosceptical national parties and groups)

strategies: to go for political-partisan support for their demand (where their main resources are the potential control of votes and public opinion) or to attempt incorporation into the techno-bureaucratic decision-making of the state (where their main resources are information and implementation control). The EU level adds an important external resource/constraint onto this, and it complicates the matrix of strategic choices represented analytically in Table 5.2.[84] Each strategy requires and rests on different resources. National routes imply some opposition to the EU and a high degree of cooperation with the national partisan and/or bureaucratic organizations. European routes require support for the regulatory EU decision-making. Techno-bureaucratic incorporation strategies generally require low partisan profiles, high sector representativeness, and the control of information and implementation resources. Partisan strategies are instead based on a more open ideological fragmentation of interests and require the control of partisan assets such as membership votes and organizational support.[85] Although

---

[84] This table is inspired by Erne, R., 'Organized Labour—an actor of Euro-democratization, Euro-technocracy or re-nationalization? Trade-Union strategies concerning the European integration process', Ph.D. thesis (Florence: European University Institute, 2004); and Bennett, R. J., 'The Role of European Economic Integration on Business Associations: The UK Case', *West European Politics*, 20 (1997), 61–90.

[85] The links between interest groups and EP parties are weak and undermined by national alignments. See Panebianco, S., 'Relations between interest groups and party

large interest organizations may want to keep open more than one strategy, sector or subsector interests may find one or the other more convincing. It is likely that different interest organizations may end up being internally divided about which is the most useful and efficient.

Moreover, if the boundaries defining the possible action of relevant actors and allies open up, then the traditional communality of interests and solidarity ties within large national corporate groups may be undermined by new alignments. The EU boundary removal operations tend to internally divide interest groups among those who favour such openings and those who fear and oppose them. A mapping of groups combining the labour versus owners' social dimension with a sector dimension based on support for EU boundary-removing policies (supposing the public sectors and domestic producers to be the least supportive, followed, in ascending order, by agricultural sectors, multinational European producers (Eurochampions), financial services, and global producers) leads to considerable ambiguities in the location of class/sector groups.[86] Different social and sector groups are in favour of integration as boundary removal (deregulation, mutual recognition, competition, and free trade with minimal state intervention). The same applies if integration is identified with boundary building (growing regulation of the internal market and even the potential closure of such market). The public sector and domestic producers may be worried about more free market integration. Global producers and financial services appreciate free trade and the EMU, but may be worried about any development at the EU level of positive integration. Multinational European producers, competing in the Euromarket against third-country imports, may be more supportive of positive market integration at the EU level, with its implicit market closure protection. A 'reputation' location analysis of this kind suggests that the integration/independence dimension fosters intrasector alliances and oppositions that are different from the historically predominant intraclass alliances that have forged the main interest organizations at the national level. Put differently, this means that competing sector or subsector interests undermine cross-local wide functional alliances (as was the case with the national territorial interests described in the first part of the chapter).

groups in the European Union', in D. S. Bell and C. Lord (eds.), *Transnational Parties in the European Union* (Aldershot: Ashgate, 1998), 151–65; Wessels, B., 'European Parliament and Interest Groups', in R. Katz and B. Wessels (eds.), *The European Parliament, the National Parliaments, and European Integration* (Oxford: Oxford University Press, 1999), 105–28.

[86] See Hix, S., 'Dimensions and Alignments in European Union Politics: Cognitive Constraints and Partisan Responses', *European Journal of Political Research*, 35 (1998), 69–106.

This can lead to the surfacing of latent interest oppositions and to the consequent internal differentiation and fragmentation of previously unified interest groups, once the need for common action and attitudes towards antagonists and the state fades away. It can also result in new, once unthinkable, cross-local, in the sense of cross-state, alliances of interests. As the scope for protective legislation and rent-seeking at the EU level is limited, the scale and resources for efficient pressure activity are also different. Therefore, the activities of nationally based Eurogroups are unlikely to be politically embedded in the Europrocess as most of these peak associations divide into sectors, subsectors and within sectors and cannot easily reproduce the historically national unifying stance at the EU level.

Interest redefinition need not to be unduly exaggerated. National interest organizations have always rested on internal divergences that they iron out successfully. To overcome these, they rely on the historically accumulated capital of solidarity ties and ideological commitments that allow them to check the free-riding capacities of members and subsectors. Moreover, different national associations have different capacity to control the policy area that affects them at the domestic level, and to control domestic selective incentives that cannot find a substitute. Therefore corporate groups may *adapt* more or less successfully to the challenges originating from the shock of European boundary redrawing depending on (*a*) the within-group interest compatibility/differentiation; (*b*) the within-group strength of historical solidarity and identity ties; and (*c*) the group's capacity of domestic policy and selective incentives' control. Once the empirical parameters are known for different types of interests, the framework generates the most likely outcomes.

We can simplify the situation in which domestic consolidated interest organizations find themselves in the interest/identity/politics three-chotomy if and when they are affected by the processes of integration (see Table 5.3). Every impact that reproduces a situation of high interest compatibility and

TABLE 5.3. *The impact of integration and national groups' identities/interests*

		Interest compatibility within the group	
		High	Low
Identity and solidarity within the group and control of domestic policy and selective incentives	High	Persistence of national structuring Possible isoporphic European structuring	National interests (intermediation) destructuring
	Low	National interests (intermediation) destructuring	Likely national/ European restructuring

solidarity within the group is in line with historical national patterns, contributes to their persistence, and leaves open the possibility of supranational interest integration along similar and isomorphic lines to those prevalent at the nation-state level. On the opposite side, growing internal interest incompatibility accompanied by declining solidarity ties might lead to a profound restructuring with new infra- and inter-group alliances and coalitions shaped by attitudes towards the new centre political production. The mixed situations in which existing interest groups experience declining interest compatibility or declining solidarity ties are likely to generate only further interests' pluralization and fragmentation, a declining cohesion of national groups, and a destructuring of national patterns of interest intermediation, associated with a predominant lobbyist incorporation into the European techno-bureaucratic decision-making processes.

6

Electoral Representation in Loosely Bounded Territories: Mass Politics in the EU?

The shift in the location of institutional power related to European integration may be accompanied by a corresponding change in the direction of the efforts of mass politics.[1] As historically the rise of the state is associated with a transformation of collective action from localized to centralized, from spontaneous to planned, from reactive to proactive, from ephemeral to enduring,[2] the development of the European Union (EU) may produce changes in the forms of mass politics actions.

The classic literature on parties, party systems and voters' alignments is characterized by four main concerns. First, there is a *genetic* concern with the process by which social and cultural divisions are politicized into a set of oppositions and organizations during the phase of suffrage expansion and development of mass politics. Second, there is a *representation* concern with the extent to which elected political elites are representative of and responsive to the distribution of identities, interests, values and policy preferences of the voters and of public opinion in general. Third, there is an *alignment* concern with the extent to which simple or complex cleavages and issue dimensions relate to one another in the political space of competition, and shape the opportunities for alliances of outsiders and newcomers. Fourth, there is a concern with the *morphology* and format of the party system and how this affects the performance and the stability of the institutions.

When related to the process of integration, this simplified classification of studies translates into four main questions. From a genetic point of view, what are the chances that the EU territorial enlargement and institution building will generate new oppositions and new issue dimensions susceptible to becoming source of political conflict? From a representational point of view, are

---

[1] Marks, G. and McAdam, D., 'Social Movements and the Changing Structure of Political Opportunity in the European Union', *West European Politics*, 19 (1996), 249–78.

[2] Tilly, C., 'Major Forms of Collective Action in Western Europe, 1500–1975', *Theory and Society*, 3 (1976), 365–76.

established national and European political organizations representative of the values and interests of their national constituencies on specific EU issues? From an alignment point of view, how do European issues interact with the alliances and alignments that are predominant at the national level? From a morphological point of view, what consequences can we expect on the cohesion of national and European political organizations, on the format of national party systems, and on the viability of a EU-level party system?

The answers to these questions depend on which issues are considered to be 'European issues'. The latter can simply be defined in terms of 'pro' or 'against', of positive or negative *general orientation* towards the EU. Next to these general orientations there are more specific *constitutive issues* that pertain to 'membership' (the geographical and functional boundaries of the EU), 'competences' (what should be done at the EU level as opposed to other levels of government), and 'decision-making rules' (how collective decisions should be taken). Finally, European issues can also be identified as *isomorphic issues* that correspond to similarly structured national issues (economic interventionism versus neoliberalism, welfare, citizenship rights, immigration policy, law and order issues, etc.). In short, by integration issue we may mean a general and a specific orientation to the EU, specific constitutive issues concerning the nature of the polity, and even more specific isomorphic issues defining the nature of the policies.

European issues may in principle generate *internal party conflicts/splits*. As parties derive their historical cohesion from conflicts other than those concerning Europe, their members and leaders often have different European preferences. If these differences are pronounced, they may jeopardize the internal party unity. European issues may also generate *new anti-EU parties* that by campaigning make EU policies divisive issues. The addition of a European institutional arena like the EP generates problems of vertical and horizontal integration of parties across national boundaries and may occasion problems of *'fit' between national and European party system structure and alignments*. Finally, European issues may consolidate into the emergence of a new, salient, and stable issue dimension, generating *splits within the parties' national electorates*. Examining in depth these questions and potential consequences, in this chapter I deal with the relationship of European integration with mass electoral politics.

The Background of Electoral Instability and the Impact of European Integration

Since the mid-1970s the literature on parties and electoral behaviour has concentrated on evaluating the change in mass electoral alignments that followed the phase of cleavage systems freezing.[3] Individual level studies based on survey data accumulated substantial evidence on the declining impact of social-structural factors on the formation of electoral preferences, on important shifts in value orientations and on the emergence of new issues and concerns among the mass public. From this evidence these studies derived a new instability of traditional voting alignment and a new phase of political 'de-freezing'.[4] On the other hand, studies of aggregate electoral outcomes and of the overall balance of party support were more cautious in extrapolating voting changes from attitudinal changes, and more reluctant to conclude that a new phase had begun. They tended to emphasize behavioural continuity rather than change, suggesting that institutional incentives and/or specific shocks, and critical political junctures were necessary to mobilize the newly uprooted voters into different voting choices.[5]

In the 1990s the changes long documented at the level of individual political attitudes finally began to feed through to changes in the overall balance of party support, reconciling individual and aggregate developments. The 1990s differ from the 1970s–1980s considering three indicators of aggregate electoral change: turnout, electoral volatility, and the percentage of votes collected by 'new' parties founded since 1960 (Table 6.1). Average turnout levels have dropped consistently since the 1960s, but in the 1990s the decline generalizes—with three-fourth of the countries recording their lowest ever decade averages—and its magnitude amplifies. Between the 1950s and the 1980s, the average electoral volatility across Western European countries changed very little. In the 1990s, however, the average was 11.9 per cent, almost four points higher than that recorded in the 1960s and 1970s, and two points higher than in the previous decade. Finally, the average vote for 'new' parties (splinter groups are excluded) had grown since the 1960s, but in fact, in the last decade of the century almost a fourth of Western European voters cast their ballot for a party founded since the 1960s. The conclusion is that in the 1990s (*a*) fewer voters were willing to participate in elections than during any previous decades; (*b*) those voters who did participate were more willing to transfer their preferences between

[3] See Crewe, I. and Denver, D. (eds.), *Electoral Change in Western Democracies. Patterns and Sources of Electoral Volatility* (London: Croom Helm, 1985).

[4] Dalton, R., Flanagan, S. C. and Beck, P. A. (eds.), *Electoral Change in Advanced Industrial Democracies: Realignment or Dealignment?* (Princeton, NJ: Princeton University Press, 1984); Franklin, M. N., Mackie, T. and H. Valen (eds.), *Electoral Change: Responses to Evolving Social and Attitudinal Structures in Western Countries* (Cambridge: Cambridge University Press, 1992).

[5] Bartolini, S. and Mair, P., *Identity, Competition and Electoral Availability. The Stabilization of European Electorates, 1885–1985* (Cambridge: Cambridge University Press, 1990).

TABLE 6.1. *Mean levels of electoral participation,
electoral volatility, and vote for new parties*

	1950	1960	1970	1980	1990
Turnout	84.3	84.8	82.5	81.2	77.1
Volatility	8.1	7.1	8.9	9.6	11.9
Vote New Parties	—	4.4	9.1	14.4	22.4

Legend: Countries: Austria, Belgium, Denmark, Finland, France, Germany, Greece, Iceland, Ireland, Italy, Luxembourg, Netherlands, Norway, Portugal, Spain, Sweden, Switzerland, United Kingdom. In Greece 1950–1 elections are excluded; only one volatility value available in the 1970s; votes for new parties not included due to democratic breakdown in between the 1960s and 1970s. In Portugal and Spain vote for new parties not included due to democratic instauration in the mid-1970s.

Source: Gallagher, M., Laver, M. and Mair, P., *Representative Government in Modern Europe* (Boston, MA: McGraw Hill 2001), 3rd edn.; Mair, P., 'The Limited Impact of Europe on National Party Systems', *West European Politics*, 23 (2000), 27–51. Figures for Greece, Portugal and Spain in the 1950s, 1960s and 1970s are my own calculations. Malta is excluded. Therefore, mean decade figures are different from those in the main source.

parties than was the case before; and (*c*) support for new parties took off, strongly accelerating the steady upward trend since the 1970s.

An authoritative review of these data has recently argued that not much of this change can be attributed to the impact of EU issues. The increasing party system fragmentation is to a limited extent due to the issue of European integration as a small number of these new parties directly link to it. Moreover, these parties have tended to contest only European elections staying outside domestic politics. Considering the entire set of member countries' parties in 1999, only about 17 per cent of them are regarded as being strongly opposed to the EU[6] and they account for a much smaller percentage of votes. With few exceptions, parties clearly opposed to the EU are generally outside the mainstream of their respective party systems, and there is correlation between Eurosceptic positions and marginal position in the party system. Although a pro-and anti-European divide can sometimes be discerned, Europe 'has not made for new alliances or enmities'. One could add that there is sufficient evidence (see Finland, for instance) that when parties are incorporated into governmental coalitions they tend to soften their anti-Europeanism. Listing the more widespread changes in European party systems (fragmentation, decline of socialism, increasing public financial dependence, increasing association with the state, ideological convergence, coalition promiscuity, decline of traditional identities), this study concludes

---

[6] And this may be inflated if one considers a number of doubtful classifications of anti-EU parties like, for instance, the Italian National Alliance.

that none of them can plausibly be traced back to the direct impact of Europeanization and that neither the format nor the mechanics of the large majority of these systems was directly and significantly affected by the development of EU institutions and policies. European party systems are regarded as impervious to the influence of European integration.[7]

This would seem to be a foregone conclusion from the viewpoint of the average and aggregate effects. However, one feels uncomfortable with it when charting the extent to which European issues have influenced the electoral politics of the 1990s in several countries. Single-issue anti-EU parties are indeed few and they normally compete in European elections only. They are significant in only four countries. In Denmark the list includes the People's movement against the EU, and the June Movement to oppose the 92–93 referenda. In France the narrow 'yes' victory of the 1992 referendum on Maastricht was a galvanizing moment for Philippe de Villiers' movement against Maastricht (which had a follow-up in the de Villiers' candidacy in the 1995 presidential elections) and a left breakaway from the Socialists Party led by Jean-Pierre Chevènement. In Germany only the former leader of the Bavarian Citizen's Alliance party, Manfred Brunner, represents opposition to the EU. In the United Kingdom this list would include the tiny United Kingdom Independence Party.

However, explicit anti-EU positions are present in all member states via a number of parties that are neither specific anti-EU parties nor core-established parties and that are in someway at the periphery of the party system.[8] Green parties with a considerable anti-EU ideological component can be found in Austria, Finland, France, Ireland, Luxembourg, the Netherlands, Portugal, Sweden and the United Kingdom. Non-communist leftist parties with a similar orientation exist in Finland (Leftist Alliance), in Ireland (Democratic Left and Workers Party), in the Netherlands (Socialist Party), in Sweden (Left Party, ex-communists).[9] Communist parties with a clear and explicit critical view of the integration process are present in France, Greece, Portugal, and Germany (the Eastern-based Party of Democratic

[7] Mair, P., 'The Limited Impact of Europe on National Party Systems', *West European Politics*, 23 (2000), 27–51.

[8] But that can hardly be put together under the label of 'protest party' as Taggart does: Taggart, P., 'A Touchstone of Dissent: Euroscepticism in Contemporary Western European Party Systems', *European Journal of Political Research*, 33 (1998), 363–88. The author of this excellent review suggests distinguishing (*a*) single-issue Eurosceptical parties from (*b*) protest-based parties with Euroscepticism, from (*c*) established parties with a prevalent Eurosceptical position, from (*d*) Eurosceptical factions of existing parties which support the EU. I find the grouping of 'protest' parties too inclusive and I prefer to regroup non-core established parties by broad ideological orientation.

[9] Christensen, D. A., 'The Left-Wing Opposition in Denmark, Norway and Sweden: Cases of Euro-phobia?', *West European Politics*, 19 (1996), 525–46.

Socialists). The Spanish United Left and the Italian Rifondazione Comunista offers a qualified opposition and should probably be kept separate from the previous group. The most clearly expressed anti-EU feelings can be found in right-wing and nationalist parties in Austria (Freedom party), in Belgium (Flemish Block and National Front), in Denmark (Progress Party), in France (National Front), in Germany (the German People's Union and the Republicans), in Ireland (Sin Fein, recently more supportive), and in Italy (Northern League). One should finally add a small group of Protestant orthodox parties such as the Finnish Christian leagues, and the small Calvinists parties of the Netherlands (the Political Reformed Party, the Reformed Political League and the Reformed Political Federation). For the non-core leftists, communists, nationalists and far right, protest and populist, orthodox Christians and also, to a lesser extent, green parties, the anti-EU attitude can, however, hardly be regarded as the primary reason for their existence or source of electoral support. It is clearly an ideological addendum to a more general critique of the system.

Among the core and established parties, clear-cut anti-EU factions are more frequent in Northern Europe and particularly accentuated in Britain—where the two established parties are profoundly split while the Liberal Party and the Scottish Nationalist Party are somewhat more supportive[10]—in the Swedish Social Democrats and the Finnish Centre Party. In Portugal the right-wing Centre Social Democrats have recently moderated its opposition. In Italy, the right-wing National Alliance includes an important faction of anti-integrationists. Norway is a non-member state where the issue of EU entry deeply divides all established parties and there is therefore no need for it to be taken on board by single-issue or peripheral parties.

The impact of the EU issue dimension on the electorates can be observed directly only in cases of referenda on EU constitutional issues. Referenda are an ideal instrument for creating cross-party anti-integrationist alliances in the electorate by breaking up the predominant party alignments of voters. Between 1972 and September 2003 there were thirty-six such referenda in European countries following in successive waves the first widening of the EC in the 1970s, the ratification of the SEA in the 1980s, the ratification of the Maastricht and Amsterdam Treaties and the new member accession in the1990s, and, finally, the Nice Treaty and the Eastern enlargement.[11]

---

[10] Garry, J., 'The British Conservative Party: Divisions Over European Policy', *West European Politics*, 18 (1995), 170–89. By the early 1990s the European issues were the most potent division and policy polarizing divide. Tensions over Europe had contributed to Margaret Thatcher's downfall and have undermined the position of Major too.

[11] On the constitutional nature of these referendums, required or not, binding or not, see Hug, S., *Voices of Europe. Citizens, Referendums, and European Integration* (Lanham, MD: Rowman & Littlefield Publishers, 2002), Chapter 3.

The most significant examples concern France, Norway, Denmark, Finland, Sweden and Austria.

In Norway the 1972 and 1994 referenda on joining the EU were traumatic for the party system. The struggle over this issue was a centre–periphery conflict, with the centre heavily over-represented among the supporters. Research suggests that the Common Market was perceived as a very real threat to the values and interests of many Norwegians, and particularly to the social periphery.[12] The 1972 anti-EU mobilization was lived almost as a crusade and ad hoc organizations against the EC achieved a durable influence in Norwegian politics. To a whole cohort of young activists, students, trade unionists and many others, 'the people's' victory over the establishment remained the great political experience of their lives. Three very different opposing movements cooperated closely: the radical left, originally anti-NATO, the anti-Catholic orthodox Protestant, against the Catholic-dominated EC, and the representatives of the fishing and agricultural interests who feared competition from EC countries. The referenda turned into debates about styles of lives and urban and rural cultures. Everywhere anti-integrationists defended traditional lifestyles, criticizing interference from distant Brussels, creating a long-standing, credible and well-organized politically broad-based anti-EU umbrella.[13] In both 1972 and 1994 a complete substitution of the left–right alignment for the pro-anti-EU alignment occurred. The changing salience of the EU issue was accompanied by shifting political alignments and at the same time had consequences for the non-socialist cabinet, which resigned from office.

In Denmark in the successful 1972 adhesion referendum (63 per cent favourable) nearly all parties divided on integration. At the 1992 referendum on the Maastricht Treaty a majority of Danish politicians, representing most of the parties in parliament, was severely disavowed by a majority of Danish citizens unwilling to follow their advice. The conservative-led government that had accepted Maastricht suffered a parliamentary defeat (January 1993). The new referendum in 1993, based on Denmark's opting out of a number of policies (the EMU, the European defence policy, the European citizenship and other Home and Justice policies), yielded a positive result. But half of the social democrats did not follow the party's indication to vote 'yes'. The voters of the Conservative and Liberal Parties were more disciplined in supporting the 'yes'. The Progress Party opposition was followed by half to two-thirds of its voters. Two anti-EU parties that mobilize at European elections—the June Movement and People's Movement Against

---

[12] Hellevik, O., Gleditsch, N. P. and Ringdal K., 'The Common Market issue in Norway: A Conflict Between Centre and Periphery', *Journal of Peace Research*, 12 (1975), 37–53.

[13] Fizmaurice, J., 'The 1994 Referenda on EU Membership in Austria and Scandinavia: A Comparative Analysis', *Electoral Studies*, 14 (1995), 226–32, 230.

EC—obtained 25.5 per cent of votes in 1994 EP elections. Before the 1972, 1992 and 1993 referenda, the 'yes' parties collected respectively 90.2, 84.9 and 94.1 percent of the votes at national elections. The 'yes' vote was only 63.1, 49.3 and 56.8 per cent. After these shocks, continued divisions between and within parties led the Danish elite keeping the EU issue out of national elections. The March 1998 elections were held early (they were due in September) to limit the potential effect of the referendum on the Amsterdam Treaty in May 1998, and European issues were carefully kept out of the campaign by nearly all parties until just before the election.[14] In the 1999 EP elections over 35 per cent of the Danish voted for parties hostile to European integration. A third new right-wing anti-EU movement (the DF) joined the traditional anti-EU movements. The September 2000 referendum on the Euro reproduced the usual feature of citizens disavowing their party leaders.[15]

In Sweden, the EU referendum was less traumatic for the party system. The Moderate (conservative) and Liberal Parties were clearly committed to integration and the Euro, the Left Party and the Greens were very hostile and the Social Democratic Party had an internal sceptical faction. But contrary to the Norwegian experience, in 1994 the Swedish Social Democrats (SAP) managed to win a close referendum and to keep power. The key ingredients of this winning strategy were timing (first political elections then the referendum, so that an entire legislature was left to recover), internal management of the EU opposition faction (incorporation rather than isolation) and hard campaigning.[16] Nevertheless there was substantial internal factionalism in the SAP and only between 46 and 50 per cent of its voters are reported to have voted YES in the 1994 referendum (a level of discipline inferior to the Norwegian social democrats).[17] The Left and Green Parties—SAP's domestic allies—continued to be vociferously against membership and tried to use the EU issues against the Social Democrats. When in 1998 the Social Democrat minority cabinet formed an informal coalition with the Greens and the Left Party it was underlined that this alliance did not concern EU issues.

---

[14] See Bjugan, K., 'The 1998 Danish Parliamentary Election: Social Democrats muddle through to Victory', *West European Politics*, 22 (1999), 172–8; Haahr, J. H., 'European Integration and the Left in Britain and Denmark', *Journal of Common Market Studies*, 30 (1992), 77–100.

[15] In 2000 the main 'yes' parties—Venstre, Conservatives and SD—did not invest much in the campaign and failed to cooperate. The 'no' parties cooperated because they were not electoral rivals. See Qvortrup, M., 'The Danish Referendum on Euro Entry, September 2000', *Electoral Studies*, 21 (2002), 493–8.

[16] Aylott, N., 'Between Europe and Unity: The Case of the Swedish Social Democrats', *West European Politics*, 20 (1977), 119–36.

[17] The first estimate is by Bjørklund, T., 'The Nordic Referendums Concerning Membership in the EU', *Cooperation and Conflict*. 31 (1996), 11–36; the second estimate is by Johansson, K. M. and Raunio T., 'Partisan responses to Europe: Comparing Finnish and Swedish political parties', *European Journal of Political Research*, 39 (2001), 225–49, 234.

In Finland, where EU membership had hardly been discussed before the fall of the Berlin wall, it suddenly dominated the agenda from 1990. Fifty-seven percent of the Finns favoured membership in the October 1994 referendum. The peculiarity of Finland is that no party could be said to be anti-integration but none was unquestionably pro-EU either. The Centre (ex-Agrarian) Party, the Left Alliance and the Green League were the most divided, while the Swedish People's Party (SPP), the National Coalition and the Social Democrats were less so. Finnish parties, however, absorbed the EU issues into their overall policy profile while allowing internal differences.[18] In the European elections all parties—even the more pro-EU parties such as NC and SPP—avoided the issue, claiming that their ranks were open to all people, militants and politicians with both pro- and anti-EU attitudes, and actually nominating candidates with very different views on integration. This internalized tensions in an arena with less direct impact on the structure of the party and governmental system. The opponents of the EU had a choice between voting for these EU-critical candidates in established parties or supporting the new parties established on an anti-EU platform. As a result the single-issue anti-EU parties won only a combined 2.7 per cent of the votes.[19] In this case the lack of relationship between the level of Euroscepticism (43.1 per cent against in the 1994 referendum) and the level of support for anti-EU parties (2.7 per cent) can be explained by the clever strategy of the main Finnish parties of presenting a divided profile able to appeal to all groups. While in Sweden only 50 per cent of the Social Democrat voters, 41 per cent of the Christian Democrats, 45 per cent of the Centre Party, and 34 per cent of New Democracy voters followed their party line, in Finland the voters' discipline was better for the Social Democrats, the National Coalition and the SPP (respectively 75, 89, and 85 per cent of their supporters voting 'yes'). However, only 36 per cent of the Centre Party supporters voted the 'yes' indicated by the party leadership.[20]

As noted above, in France parties have long been divided on European integration. This was exacerbated by the 'non-required' 1992 referendum on the Maastricht Treaty, which led to a clear party-voters split. Internal breakaway occurred within the Gaullists (RPR), the centre-right (UDF) and the socialists (PS) for the 1994 elections, with dissidents presenting separate lists.

---

[18] Ibid., 245–6.

[19] On Finnish parties and their attitude to EU in general see Raunio, T., 'Facing the European Challenge: Finnish Parties Adjust to the Integration Process', *West European Politics*, 22 (1999), 138–59.

[20] According to Party documents data reported by Johansson and Raunio, 'Partisan responses to Europe'.

In 1994 the anti-EU Alternative Europe won 21.1 per cent of the votes. During the second half of the 1990s the former centrist UDF dissolved after three successive splits. This disintegration was a result of personality fights linked to two main issues: relationships with Le Pen and attitudes towards the EU.[21] In the 1999 elections the anti-integration list led by de Villiers and Pasqua emerged as the single biggest party of the right with thirteen seats. Weakened by the split in its leadership, the National Front lost from eleven to five seats. The opposition to the EU is cited as a possible vote motivation for NF. This was not the situation at the beginning,[22] but by 1997 Europe had become a major, if not the major, motive among certain voters for transferring their vote to the National Front.[23] In European elections, the vote for the established left and right parties (PCF, PS, UDF and RPR) declined from 50 per cent in 1979, to 40 per cent in 1984, to 28 per cent in 1989, to 24 per cent in 1994, to 23 per cent in 1999 of the registered electorate.[24]

In Ireland debates about Europe surrounding referenda are generally regarded as irrelevant for the party system, while in Austria and in Switzerland the impact is more visible. In Austria 66 per cent approved membership in the June 1994 referendum and only the Freedom Party campaigned against, although there is less clear evidence that this position contributed to the strengthening of this party. In Switzerland the 1990s debates and referenda about European Economic Area and bilateral agreement with the EU contributed considerably to the rising support of the extreme right that opposed Swiss participation. It won 9.3 per cent of the vote in the following federal elections of 1995, its highest score ever. Moreover, one of the bourgeois parties (CDC), by moving decidedly to the right and exploiting opposition to EEA and EU, won the elections improving its score and

---

[21] See Sauger, N., 'Les scissions de l'UDF. Unité et dissociations des partis, mécanismes de transformation de l'offre partisane', Ph.D. thesis (Paris: Institut d'Etudes Politiques, 2003), 99–141; see also Guoyomarch, A., 'The European Dynamics of Evolving Party Competition in France', *Parliamentary Affairs*, 48 (1995), 100–124.

[22] In the 1980s the EU was a very minor motivation factor for NF both in comparison with other parties and with other issues. In 1988, the then EC was mentioned as an important vote motivation for NF by 15 per cent of Le Pen voters, while it was by 29 per cent of the Right, 13 per cent of the Left and 22 per cent of the whole sample. In contrast, 'violence and security' and 'immigration' were mentioned by 55 per cent and 59 per cent of NF votes as against 38 per cent and 19 per cent of the right voters, 20 per cent and 13 per cent of the left voters and 31 per cent and 22 per cent of the whole sample. See CSA Exit Poll, 24 April 1988.

[23] This is documented in Cayrol, R., 'L'électeur face aux enjeux économiques, sociaux et européens', in P. Perrineau and C. Ysmal (eds.), *Le vote Surprise. Les élections législatives des 25 mai et 1er juin 1997* (Paris: Presses de la Fondation des Sciences Politiques, 1998), 94–118.

[24] In France the mobilization of the anti-treaty forces found strong institutional incentives in the protracted and visible institutional debates on constitutional revisions implied by the Maastricht Treaty. See the review by Stone, A., 'Ratifying Maastricht: France Debates European Union', *French Politics and Society*, 11 (1993), 70–88.

becoming for the first time the dominant party in the three most important cantons of the German Switzerland: Zurich, Berne and Argovie.

Should this evidence of anti-EU breakaway and factionalism, of anti-EU positions in party families, and of relevant party-voters differences be considered a 'limited' impact on national party systems? I think there are elements to keep the question open. In the European post-war electoral history there is no other single theme which has had similar large and standardizing effects across the European party system. There are good reasons, however, not to exaggerate this impact and not to take it at face value. It is not clear, for example, how much of the opposition to the EU is a mere reflection of national and domestic problems. Parties' anti-EU stands might merely reflect domestic strategies of differentiation from established parties. In addition, the fact that the traditional ideological position of parties in left–right terms gives us few clues to their attitude to the EU may be regarded as a sign of incompatibility of different protest attitudes. The ideological bases of Euroscepticism are so widely diverging as to make any coalition or alliance impossible except in negative terms. One can also interpret the weak relationship between the high levels of Euroscepticism and the electoral support of Eurosceptical parties as the usual asymmetry between general party identification and specific issue support. Even admitting the existence of widespread dissatisfaction that conflicts with the traditional left–right dimension, one can imagine that established parties can successfully manage this short-term fluctuation by depoliticizing the issue, by blurring clear-cut choices, by skilfully avoiding the involvement of the electorate at large on the matter, and by limiting the resort to direct democracy instruments that offer opportunities to access national politics to this widespread dissatisfaction. Established parties can also deflect tensions by offering opportunities for contestation to marginal domestic parties in the EU parliamentary arena, thus successfully shielding the national ones.

On the other hand, however, we should not exclude the possibility that there are some common elements in the strange amalgam of discontent across the traditional political spectrum for which the EU could indeed be a strong unifying catalyst. Given the enormous and growing visibility and the highly institutionalized nature of the EU, protest and anti-establishment stands, however ideologically disparate, might find in the anti-EU position a common denominator. Is it possible that the new right of '*Heimat*', the concern for national identity and independence, the fear of openness of frontiers to immigration, the insistence on the 'we versus the other', the defence of and the pride for national welfare, the orthodox Christian refusal of the mundaneness of the economic and technocratic elite, the peripheral fear of distant bureaucracies, have nothing to do with Europe and have nothing to do one with each other?

There are also some good reasons to believe that national established parties and elite are less able to meet these challenges than was the case when the frame of reference was that of more clearly bounded national territories. European integration is predicated upon the relinquishing of the nation-state control over many policy areas. This determines the muting of issues pertaining to those domains that are no longer under national control. National political elites are less proactive in dealing with the integration issues and in incorporating them within their programmatic profiles and competition. They tend often to collude, resorting to gag rules to expel from the political agenda those issues whose solutions are no longer under their direct control. They appear generally unwilling to shape their electoral competition and their competitive appeals to the electorate on such issues.[25] This situation opens broader spaces for those political movements and entrepreneurs who do not accept the responsibility for the systemic compatibility of the integration process and appeal to voters on nationalistic, protectionist, solidarity, and security issues, cemented by a common distrust of European integration and its anonymous, techno-bureaucratic and distal rule. This generates quite new and apparently surprising 'syncretic' political programmes, combining elements of different traditional ideologies as well as different sectors of the electorates previously regarded as unlikely. This new combination might be captured by the term 'populism', which has recently resurfaced in the European literature.[26]

These individual and aggregate level data suggest a situation of progressive detachment and disengagement, which could pave the way to potential processes of realignment along crucial new dimensions of competition. We need first discuss whether, and if so the extent to which, the European integration issues can be structured within the existing national and European alignments. We may then ask whether they have a potential for 'destructuring' these traditional alignments of the European electorates. We may finally investigate whether there is any possibility that these same issues trigger processes of realignment and of restructuring. These are complex questions to which a direct answer is probably impossible at this stage. They are, however, so important that they deserve running the risk of

[25] The most outspoken case of an explicit strategy of party collusion on EU issues is the Danish one. See Pedersen, M. N., 'Euro-parties and European Parties: New Arenas, new Challenges and New Strategies', in S. S. Andersen and K. A. Eliassen (eds.), *The European Union: How Democratic Is It?* (London: Sage, 1996), 15–40. He states that 'The process of political goal formulation has become extremely complicated after the so-called "national compromise", in which all parties but one participated. It is almost impossible to formulate a party specific platform on any EU-related issue without being accused of betraying this compromise' (34).

[26] On populism as 'syncretism' see Betz, H.-G., *Radical Right-Wing Populism in Western Europe* (New York: St Martin's Press, 1994); and Mény, Y. and Surel, Y., *Par le peuple, pour le peuple* (Paris: Fayard, 2000).

tentative conjectures and hypotheses. In the next sections I discuss those tensions generated (*a*) by the attitudes of national parties with respect to the European constitutive issues; (*b*) by the development of a two-level party system and the linkage between national and European electoral markets; and (*c*) by the potential emergence of a new salient issue dimension in European electorates related to the integration process.

National parties' attitudes towards the EU: 'geopolitical', 'partisan', 'genetic' and 'institutional' models

The attitudes of national political parties towards the integration process can be interpreted with four models. A *'geopolitical'* model assumes that support/ opposition is mainly determined by national specific features or geopolitical interests which result from entrenched cultural predispositions to be interpreted in the light of the specific pattern of state and nation formation: lateness and contestedness of the national unification, strength of the centre–periphery conflicts, level of historical cultural standardization/distinctiveness, international status, centralization of resources, and strength of the inherited traditions of representative institutions. In this case differences in support/opposition among national parties should be less significant than differences across nations.

An *'institutional'* model explains attitudes to the EU as a function of parties being in government or opposition at the national (and therefore European) level. This model suggests that parties in government are generally more supportive of EU integration than parties in opposition, and that those parties—whether governmental or oppositional at the national level— that belong to 'EU-level coalition' tend to be more pro-European.

A *'partisan'* model interprets orientation to the EU of national parties on the basis of the main dimension of competition prevalent at the national level, such as left–right, libertarian-authoritarian, materialist-post-materialists, etc. In this case, which is the opposite of the first model, the variation within European party family should be reduced, while variation among national parties should be much higher.

A *'genetic'* model interprets party orientation towards European integration as shaped by or related to their original national cleavage position. Mapping parties according to their genetic cleavage produces hypotheses about the levels of internal tensions that the integration process creates within them.

All of these ways of interpreting cross-party and cross-nation attitudes are to some degree convincing. The overall EU reluctance of Northern European countries points to the weight of their early cultural-Protestant national integration. In the importance that the theme of 'national independence' plays among the French and British elite one finds echoes of the two ex-colonial powers with a longstanding historical tradition of playing an important role on the international stage. In the generally supportive stand of the Italian and German political elite one can see the reaction to the late and stormy national unification of multicentred territories defeated in the Second World War. Similarly, in the general supportive attitudes of the political elite of the new Southern European members of Greece, Spain and Portugal one can identify a reaction to the peripherality of these countries in twentieth century international politics as well as the political peripherality of their lengthy non-democratic regimes.

An important 'institutional' factor can be identified in the attitudes of parties in new member countries if we compare their position before and after accession or when in government or opposition. The case of the Finnish and Scandinavian sceptical parties is probably the clearest; the Italian National Alliance and the Austrian Freedom Party are also conspicuous examples of 'government-induced' change in attitude.

The most thorough analyses, however, take either a 'partisan' or a 'genetic' line of interpretation. The partisan model finds support in the historical perspective. It is documented that during the cold war the EEC was generally supported by moderate and conservative forces and more or less vehemently opposed by the left. Once the Cold War was over, the argument has continued to be valid that a great number of communist, left-wing and even social democratic parties are afraid of market competition and also fear welfare retrenchment embedded in the boundary-removing logic of the integration project. In their works, Marks, Hooghe, and Wilson[27] interpret the more or less favourable orientation to the EU of national parties depending on their positioning on the socio-economic left–right cleavage and on the authoritarian-libertarian cleavage, or, in the second of the cited papers, with a GAL (Green, Alternative, Libertarian) versus TAN (Traditional, Authoritarian, Nationalist) opposition. Assuming that party families are significant categories to predict the position of individual parties, they validate their deductions by examining variations within each broad family.[28] They conclude that

---

[27] Marks, G. and Wilson, C., 'The Past and the Present. A Cleavage Theory of Party Responses to European Integration', *British Journal of Political Science* 30 (2000), 433–59; Marks, G., Wilson, C. and Ray, L., 'National Political Parties and European Integration', *American Journal of Political Science*, 46 (2002), 585–94 ; Hooghe, L., Marks, G. and Wilson, C., 'Does left/right structure party positions on European integration?', in G. Marks and M. R. Steenbergen (eds.), *European Integration and Political Conflict* (Cambridge: Cambridge University Press, 2004), 120–40.

[28] The positions of political parties towards European integration is based on the response of 299 country experts placing them on a seven point scale in 1984, 1988, 1992, 1996. See Ray, L., 'Measuring Party Orientations Towards European Integration: Results from an Expert Survey', *European Journal of Political Research*, 36 (1999), 283–306.

party families are important to characterize attitudes to the EU. There is more variation in support within each country than within each party family, which definitely weakens a geopolitical interpretation of support.

These works convincingly document the common elements of the parties on the TAN pole—nationalist, populist right-wing radical—as the most clearly defined group of Eurosceptical parties. They champion national sovereignty, and favour at most an intergovernmental EU with retention of the national veto; they want to curb the power of the EP; they reject a centralist and bureaucratic European superstate; they want to restore the supremacy of national law over European law; they consistently forge connections between the threat to national identity, 'foreignization' (*Uberfremdung*), immigrant criminality, political and social corruption; they are in general opposed to enlargement to the countries of Eastern Europe. Conservative parties with a 'TAN inclination' present similar features but to a lesser extent.

This approach, however, is less convincing when dealing with party families other than the TAN group and with the economic dimension of integration, as variation within the families presents too many elements of ambiguity. Left parties are generally regarded as afraid of market competition and welfare retrenchment, and to explain the growing social democratic support for integration[29] it is necessary to argue that this is seen as the only way to reconquering the market control lost at the national level. To explain the still considerable variation within the social democratic family, additional variables that refer to the party linkages with TU, the level of state spending, and the early/latecomer status of the country (which points to institutional and/or geopolitical aspects) are necessary. Within the denominational party family, most continental Catholic parties favour further integration, while Protestant parties are more reluctant to view positively what they sometimes see as a 'Roman church' hegemonized Europe (which points to a geopolitical dimension, rather than to a partisan one). In addition, even continental Catholic parties need to be divided into subcategories, with social Catholics being more supportive and right-wing Christian democrats less supportive (and growingly so). The very heterogeneous orientation of the liberal family is interpreted in reference to the three different historical cleavages it is generated by: the urban–rural cleavage in the case of the British and German liberals; the state–church cleavage for the liberal orientations in Italy, France, Spain, the Netherlands, and Belgium, and the historical centre–periphery cleavage for the Scandinavian (including Finnish), the Welsh and Scottish liberals. The urban liberals are the most supportive, while the

---

[29] See Ladrech, R., 'Social democratic parties and the EC integration', *European Journal of Political Research*, 24 (1993), 195–210.

agrarian liberals are the least supportive (following, in this case, what I call a genetic perspective). The majority of the Conservative parties are in favour of enhancing economic competition and free trade through the EU but many are also afraid of too much EU interference and regulation (the British Tories since Margaret Thatcher). Therefore, the conservative party family requires a crucial subdivision between neoliberal and nationalist conservative. Further distinctions are then discussed, adding groups such as 'Scandinavian conservatives' and 'post-authoritarian conservatives' (ND in Greece and AP in Spain).

A strict 'genetic' approach to map party orientation to the EU starts from an objective definition of the main EU features (centralization, bureaucratization, economicism as opposed to national and regional independence, resistance to market economy and globalization) and relate them to four historical domestic cleavages: economic left versus right (the right more supportive of markets); the centre versus periphery (the centre more supportive); the urban versus rural (urban groups more supportive); ecology versus growth (growth more supportive).[30] Detlef derives the expected position of parties on integration from the conflicting general predispositions based on genetic cleavage orientations. According to this logic, conservative parties should be generally pro-integration because their genetic orientation is pro-market, urban, and growth oriented. The Social Democrats' imprint is urban, favourable to growth but opposed to market and defensive of welfare and this should result in a general positive orientation with, however, strong internal tensions. Liberal parties will be more favourable to European integration when their historical origin is pro-market, urban and growth-oriented, but there will probably be strong internal tensions when the origin is not urban (as in Norway and Denmark). Left parties, being anti-market, ecological rather than growth-oriented and urban, will have a negative attitude, as will the greens; also the rural/centre parties will have a rather negative view.

Rather than proceeding by rigidly classifying parties as for or against, Detlef instead considers the degree of internal homogeneity of parties vis-à-vis the EU as deriving from the combination of their historical genetic cleavages. The rationale of this argument is that the level of internal party strife derives from inconsistencies resulting from historical multicleavage affiliation with different implications for the EU. This approach makes the source of the problem explicit: opposition lines that were historically bridged

---

[30] The best in this line is Detlef, J., 'Der Einfluss von Cleavage-Strukturen auf die Standpunkte der skandinavischen Parteien über den Beitritt zur Europäischen Union', *Politische Vierteljahresschrift*, 40 (1999), 565–90, which I take here as the reference example.

and integrated successfully at the national level by party organizations may become the source of internal problems in relation to the integration process. Positions, which are not contradictory in national politics, may become contradictory in reference to the EU. For instance, the combination of liberal pro-market and non-urban orientations, of anti-market, urban and growth orientations, of rural and right-wing orientations—all of which are compatible in different national settings—result in ambiguity and internal divisions when related to the specific content of the integration project (rural is negative and right-wing is positive, anti-market is negative and urban is positive, etc.). This truly genetic approach represents the most promising way to interpret party positioning.

In each of the four models one finds as much confirming as disconfirming evidence, however. A complex model taking into account the four dimensions of variations—the geopolitical position of the country, the national main competition dimensions and alignments, the party historical origin, and the party institutional responsibility—might fare better than any of the models alone. However, in geopolitical, institutional and partisan models the required specifications rapidly outweigh the generalizations when applied to within family variations. The further subdivisions based on specific explanations may be more or less convincing, but the overall plan to derive integration attitudes of parties from national geopolitical, institutional or partisan positioning crumbles as a result. The genetic approach is best in showing how the national historical alignments get reshuffled when taken as orientation bases for the integration. However, this approach requires that a definite and stable characterization be attributed to the EU (pro-market, pro-growth, pro-centralization, etc.) with respect to which the reaction of historically rooted parties can be interpreted.

In my view, these perceptive models show how difficult it is to interpret the alignment on the integration issues via national bases. Parties find it difficult to conceptualize an issue that may be read in different ways from the point of view of historical national political alignments (loss of national control versus supranational recovery of such control; economic options versus cultural roots; neoliberal orthodoxy versus bureaucratic and rules regulations etc.). Because the integration issue concerns the boundaries of the state, it is difficult to conceptualize it through those conflicts that originated within its closed territory. If the EU was a state-like bounded territory, the (national) alignments that concern the spread and scope of its political production could be reproduced within it. But as the integration process concerns precisely the degree to which internal and external boundaries will be kept or removed, the national historical alignments do not seem to be highly significant. The difficulty that the established parties experience in connecting the EU to their preferred dimension of national competition is not due to subjective incompetence. It is due to the objective incompatibility of those issues that pertain to territorial opening through expansion/integration with respect to those issues that pertain to the institutionalization of voice in economically and administratively closed and culturally homogeneous environments.

The Multilevel Party System

However, those national parties whose attitudes to Europe we cannot easily interpret do coalesce in European party families in the EU parliamentary arena. This is a sign of cross-country standardization in the party system landscape. To a certain extent the combining of parties in European party federation and parliamentary groups forces or constrains the original national position. On the face of it, the party families at the European level would seem to be largely based on left–right alignments and we should ask whether these main alignments are compatible with the orientation towards European constitutive issues.

Developmental Features

The birth of Europarties[31] suggests a number of developmental considerations. First, national parties have developed over a long period of time within non-democratized and non-parliamentarized institutional contexts. Even if excluded from effective decision-making power, they were the main avenue for the mobilization and representation of the claims of many social and political groups. This extra-parliamentary representative function is unlikely for Europarties. Key social actors today enjoy far more avenues of access to the EU decision-making centre than they enjoyed at the national level before representative government. With state representation in the Council, subnational territorial representation in the regional institutions, and corporate representation in the Brussels lobbying activities, it is less likely that political parties may be regarded by relevant interests as their privileged or preferred avenue of influence. The first conclusion is therefore that Europarties are the product of the institutional environment of the EU and have no hope of survival outside it. Their future development will be shaped by the EU institutional developments. If the EP enlarges its legislative powers, if majority decisions become more frequent, if censuring or supporting the Commission becomes more important, if selecting the position of the

---

[31] I use the shortcut of 'Europarties' to refer to both European party federations and European parliamentary groups whenever no distinction between the two is necessary.

Commission president becomes a reality, then European parties will have to develop those features that are required by the institutional structure.

Second, Europarties develop as a second layer with respect to the national ones, bringing about a multilevel party system. There is nothing extraordinary in this. True federal systems are an historical example of this type of two-level party system. Every national party system is a 'multilevel party system', with the national level as the 'master level'. Historically the national level became the master level either via organizational penetration from the centre to the periphery, opening branches, penetrating other organizations and elite groups, etc.; or via incorporation in coalition at the centre of locally entrenched elite and groups. Many parties were born in this second mode, as cross-local alliances of localized elite-mass linkages of a traditional type. The complex cultural infrastructure of Europe and the solid entrenchment of national parties clearly exclude the possibility of an organizational penetration from the EU level to the national one. Therefore, the possibility that European parties will develop is linked to a successful solution of the vertical and horizontal problems of cooperation related to the incorporation of peripheral (in this case, national) political elite into supranational coalition.

The third developmental consideration concerns the organization of the Europarties. Depending on the 'vertical distribution of power' parties may be classified as *hierarchical*, when power is concentrated at the top; *federally integrated*, when *each* level cooperates closely with the other; *federally autonomous*, when there is a limited cooperation but each level controls its own nominations, policies and elections campaigns; *stratarchic*, when there is almost no relation among levels; or even *confederal*, when lower levels control a weak centre.[32] Depending on the 'horizontal distribution of power', parties can be highly *unitary*, more or less *factionalized*, or of *indirect* type, when they are coalitions of independent functional sub-organizations with autonomous access to extra-party resources.[33] The stronger the territorial decentralization the weaker the role of central parties, and the more likely the case of split party systems or of multicentre parties. In strongly federalized and multilevel systems, the degree of autonomy of the levels is such that parties either confine themselves to one level alone, or are compelled to organize across separated levels of government. In general, organizing across several levels is likely to create centres of autonomy within party

[32] Wolinetz, S. B., 'Parties and Multilevel Systems of Governance: A Working Paper on Parties and Party Systems in the European Union and other multilevel systems of governance and the way in which they might develop' (Pittsburgh: 1999), Paper for the European Community Studies Association, 3–4.

[33] On the 'indirect' type of party see Duverger, M., *Les partis politiques* (Paris: Colin, 1967 (1951)); on the internal horizontal and vertical articulation of parties see Panebianco, A., *Modelli di partito. Organizzazione e potere nei partiti politici* (Bologna, Italy: Il Mulino, 1982).

organizations and push towards the *stratarchic* and *indirect* types. The likely incongruence among levels generates pressure for organizational adaptation in the structure of parties at both the national and supranational levels and increases the acuteness of various problems of coordination.

The fourth developmental consideration concerns the level of territorial segmentation of the European electoral market. It is argued that, although the same voters have now two arenas, European elections are fought on national issues and the so-called European party system is nothing more than the summation of national 'parts' that aggregate in federations and parliamentary groups for reasons that are not electoral reasons. Many national parties have had to strive for a long time to transform loose coalitions of local leadership groups into national organizations, and the nationalization of party politics required much time and effort.[34] Several contemporary party systems are still characterized by a high territorial segmentation of competition: the German CSU is a locally based system-party; the Parti Quebequois is a separatist party that plays no role at the federal level; the Spanish Convergencia Catalunia is the intermediate case of a locally based party playing politics at both regional and national level. Finally, national elections do not consist of direct competition among national parties, each local candidate or group of candidates competing with other individual candidates or groups of candidates from other parties. In short, electoral competition is always segmented territorially. The difference pertains to the perception of the degree of *vertical integration* or of *vertical split* of the competition. The European level competition is perceived neither as an integrated extension of the national one, nor as a separate competition on different issues.[35] The prospects of a European party system rest on either the integration with the national parties, or on the development of a split issue profile with respect to them. The current weak and artificial interlinkage between the national and European electoral markets is not due to territorial segmentation as such (the thesis that Europarties lack a common electorate to compete for), but to the fact that there is no common issue area or set around which

[34] Understood as a combination of (*a*) the spread of similar political organizations throughout the territory; (*b*) the convergence of the territorial levels of parties' electoral support; and (*c*) the uniformity of the electoral swing for individual parties as a result of their responding to political events and factors situated at the national (and not local) level. See Caramani, D., *The Nationalization of Politics: The Formation of National Electorates and Party Systems in Western Europe* (Cambridge: Cambridge University Press, 2004), 58–79.

[35] A review of the main concerns and findings of the literature about European elections up to the mid-1990s shows how unimportant they were considered in terms of electoral and European electoral market linkages. See Van der, Eijk, C., Franklin, M. and March, M., 'What Voters Teach Us About Europe-Wide Elections: What Europe-Wide Elections Teach Us about Voters', *Electoral Studies*, 15 (1996), 149–66.

national parties integrate vertically or, alternatively, 'split' and differentiate their competition.

Institutional Incentives and Disincentives

Although the development of the Europarties depends largely on the EU's institutional environment, this environment appears to be highly unfriendly to them. The list of the positive incentives is short and easily drawn up. The introduction of the direct elections in 1979 was the key institutional catalyst. It can be argued that the generalization of forms of PR for these elections is an institutional inducement to the consolidation of party parliamentary groups to the extent that it removes the destabilizing problem of the dispro-portionate impact of different national electoral systems on the composition of parliamentary groups.[36] The growing competencies of the EP can also be counted as an institutional incentive to formation and strengthening of the Europarties, although the mechanism is less clear. The recently acquired role in the selection of the Commission's President can also be added to the list. Membership in a main EP group is very important for single national delegations, as it allows them to obtain material resources, political advantages (positions in committees, presidencies, other positions within the EP), to avoid negative discrimination for delegations and individual MPs who are not members of a parliamentary group. According to one hypothesis, a large Europarty group increases its influence on the IGC negotiations and in general on the EU policy formulation (assuming that groups are homogeneous on those issues they wish to influence).

The list of negative incentives is, on the contrary, very long. First and foremost, the Europarties do not influence the choice of the EU 'executive(s)' and are not meant to systematically support them. The absence of a unitary executive and the lack of a clear-cut principle of responsible government means that the Europarties are 'unconstrained' by the discipline requirements for executive formation, composition, and tenure. In addition, Europarties do not enjoy sufficient policy power to make aggregation and discipline a worthwhile exercise for policy determination. Notwithstanding the considerable growth in formal influence since its early merely consultative role to the recent co-decision procedure, the EP and the Europarties have no 'constitutional' powers and bounded legislative powers.

---

[36] See the national contribution to different parliamentary groups in the 1979–84; 1984–89; 1989–94 and 1994–99 legislatures in Delwit, P. and De Waele, J.-M., 'Les élections européennes et l'évolution des groups politiques au Parlement européen', in M. Telò (ed.), *Démocratie et construction européenne* (Bruxelles: Editions de l'Université de Bruxelles, 1995), 277–91, 283–5.

Treaty norms that impose large majorities for the decision of the EP force major groups to coalesce (the minimum majority is 50 per cent plus one of the *members* of EP). It can be argued that the formation of ample majorities requires discipline and coordination and this has enhanced the role of the party groups.[37] However, these institutionally-forced large coalitions do not allow differentiation of voting choices if party groups want to avoid the incapacity to decide that would weaken the EP as a whole. The fact that on many essential issues the EP is obliged to pass legislation by an absolute majority of its members and the fact that no group approaches that threshold, and that no likely 'grand-left' or 'grand-right' alliance can do so either, obliges the socialist ESP and the Christian EPP to cooperate with the general goal of enhancing the role, the prestige and the power of the EP. This hinders the process of 'differentiation and identity formation'.[38] Even the need to support the overall institutional influence of the EP in the continuously evolving institutional architecture of the EU makes partisan alignments secondary. Other groups in the EP are freer to follow their ideological preferences without worrying about those institutional goals taken care of by the alliance between the European Socialist Party (ESP) and the European People's Party (EPP).

Additional factors make the institutional environment of Europarties difficult. The continuous membership enlargement destructures internal patterns of behaviour and alliance and undermines the institutionalization of the European party groups. It is difficult to strengthen in-group identity and behavioural conformity when the boundaries of the group are unclear, when exit/entry options are necessary, and therefore easy and frequent. The consolidation of parliamentary groups occurs mostly during the legislature— when their activities and composition are insulated from direct domestic influence—while election times create conditions for fragmentation as domestic factors can restructure the party composition and patterns of behaviour.[39] The European elections have distorting elements that do not foster the consolidation of parliamentary party groupings. Even after convergence towards generalized PR, fifteen countries elect their MPs with sixteen different electoral rules (the United Kingdom has two, one for Northern Ireland and one for the rest of the country). The differentiation of electoral laws affects the coherence and the structure of the EP parliamen-

[37] Bardi, L., 'Transnational Trends in European Parties and the 1994 Elections of the European Parliament', *Party Politics*, 2 (1996), 99–114, 103. On this 'institutional imperative see also Attinà, F., 'Democrazia, elezioni e partiti nell'Unione Europea', in F. Attinà and D. Velo (eds.), *Dalla Comunità all'Unione Europea* (Bari, Italy: Cacucci, 1994), 49–80.

[38] According to Ladrech, R., 'Parties in the European Parliament', in J. Gaffney (ed.), *Political Parties and the European Union* (London: Routledge, 1996), 291–307, 295.

[39] Bardi, 'Transnational Trends in European Parties', 104.

tary groups considerably, as modification of electoral results in one or more countries change disproportionately the ideological composition of the EP and the national composition of European party-groups. On the other hand, standardizing towards PR and abolishing correcting devices (such as national thresholds) to reduce national distortions have their own shortcomings. Large constituencies, over-representation of small countries, high proportionality, and higher volatility than in national elections (combined with low turnout) contribute to small parties (sometimes tiny parties) easily gaining access in some countries more easily than in others.[40]

A further negative institutional inducement is that Europarties have very limited resources to sanction and to discipline their members. Neither the parliamentary groups nor the parties' federations control EP candidate selection; only national parties do. There are no norms and institutions that allow the whipping of members of national delegations within a cross-national group. More precisely, while some sanctions on individual MPs exist, sanctions against national subgroups are impossible. The career and/or re-election of an MEP are not dependent on her/his vote, work and participation within the parliamentary group. Quite the contrary is true. Given that the ultimate decision is with national parties, engagement in national politics can be the best asset for an EP position, and lack of commitment towards the EP is not necessarily penalized by the national party. This situation is probably responsible for the level of absenteeism that characterizes the work of the EP. MEP participation is about 45 per cent for resolutions, 53 per cent for decision under cooperation, and 65 per cent for decisions under co-decision. In turn, this absenteeism forces an even higher level of vote conformity through the parliamentary groups due to the requirement that there be an absolute majority of members.

Finally, while the institutional environment forces Europarties to a high level of interfamily cooperation, the same environment exposes them to conspicuous problems of horizontal and vertical within-family coordination in collective action and free-riding containment.[41] Within each Europarty family, national delegations of parties in government can defect and exercise influence through the intergovernmental institutions and decision-making. Parties directly represented within the Council are unlikely to challenge that decision level, while parties with no Council presence are more willing to support supranational decision-makings when preferences there are more attuned to their own. As a result, in a context where sanctions against

---

[40] Schmitt, H., 'National Party Systems and the Policies of the European Union. First Results from the 1994 European Election Study' (Berlin: 26th IPSA World Congress, 1994), 21–25 August, 2.

[41] Pedersen, 'Euro-parties and European Parties', 15–40.

national subgroups are impossible the cohesion of the European party and parliamentary groups declines.[42]

The Strengthening of Europarties

To sum up, if we consider the lack of a representation demand from below and the decidedly unfavourable institutional environment, it is puzzling that scholarly literature suggests a slow but steady trend towards the strengthening of parliamentary groups and party federations. European parliamentary groups have a cohesion that is in no way comparable to that of national parties. Neither group consciousness nor group stability is high. So far, new groups composed of different parties have emerged at each election and old ones have disappeared. Splits and mergers are frequent, the mobility of individual members is high, and switching group affiliation and the arrival of brand new members upset and de-institutionalize the alliances and alignments that are created and strengthened during the legislature. Nevertheless, a number of studies have come to the conclusion that parliamentary parties show a growing degree of voting cohesiveness,[43] and research based on long-term roll-call analysis suggests a growing left–right alignment of coalitions and voting patterns.[44] These studies somehow underscore the fact that roll-call data concern only about 15 per cent of all deliberations in early legislatures and even after recent growth do not account for more than 30 per cent of them,[45] and that party group discipline is blurred by the above-mentioned institutionally induced 'parliament discipline'. However, under the assumption that the sample of roll-call vote is representative of all votes, these analyses suggest that the growing voting cohesion cannot entirely be explained by the institutional constraints and by the need of the Parliament to present cohesive stands in its confrontation with other EU institutions. It is instead interpreted as a sign of a growing left–right competition in voting behaviour and coalition making.[46]

---

[42] As in the election of Santer, when the socialist group discipline collapsed as a result of the Spanish, Danish and Irish social democrats voting for Santer against the ESP group line.

[43] See Bardi, L., ' Transnational Trends in European Parties'; Attinà, 'Democrazia, elezioni e partiti nell'Unione Europea'; Kreppel, A., 'Coalition formation in the European Parliament: From dogmatism to Pragmatism' (Catania, Italy: University of Catania, 1999) Workshop on 'Democrazia ed Elezioni nella Unione Europea', May.

[44] Hix, S., Kreppel, A. and Noury, A., 'The Party System in the European Parliament: Collusive or Competitive?', *Journal of Common Market Studies*, 41 (2003), 309–31.

[45] Roll-call votes are required for certain issues, like the approval of the Commission's President, or can be requested by a parliamentary group with at least thirty-two members.

[46] See Hix, S., 'Legislative Behaviour and Party Competition in European Parliament: An Application of Nominate to the EU', *Journal of Common Market Studies*, 39 (2001), 663–88; Hix, S. and Kreppel, A., 'From Grand Coalition to Left-Right Confrontation:

It is equally surprising that, notwithstanding the above-mentioned difficulties of within-group assimilation, there are many signs of an aggregation of national parties in a small number of groups. In spite of the high number of national parties gaining representation in the EP, the number of groups has remained fairly stable. The number of 'one-party groups' has not increased over time and the percentage of MEPs belonging to one party group has declined.[47] Therefore, it would seem that EP party groups have an astonishingly high capacity to incorporate new members.

In fact, only on the extreme right the difficulties of international cooperation among nationalist parties have made it difficult to strengthen a parliamentary group, while on the left and centre-right this tendency is evident. In 1984 the French National Front (FN) entered the EP with ten members and formed a fraction of the European right with the Italian Social Movement (MSI) and some delegates from minor right-wing parties from Greece and Ireland. At that time, only the FN was anti-immigration. In 1989, a number of other parties which had a strong anti-immigration focus entered the EP: the German Republikaner gained six candidates, the Lega Lombarda entered with two delegates, and the Belgian Vlaams Blok (VB) with one seat. Nevertheless, it proved impossible to form a common platform in the EP and only a technical group was formed with the Republikaner and VB, which neither the Northern League (LN) nor the MSI joined. Perhaps, it is the nationalism of these parties that makes them unwilling to cooperate. The VB upholds a historical claim to the Northern part of France where Flemish is the dominant language, that Le Pen rejects; the Republikaner supported South Tyrol claims expressed by the Freiheitliche Partei Sudtirols, while MSI rejects them. Moreover, strong ideological differences persist between regional nationalism (VB, LN) versus state nationalism (FN, Republikaner, MSI/AN) versus anti-immigration (FN, LN) versus conception and attitude to democracy.[48]

On the contrary, there is clearly an expansive logic of parliamentary groups on the left and centre-right. The growing competition between the EPP and the ESP brings about an expansive logic of incorporation into the main groups of small and unaffiliated national parties. Apparently the EPP and the ESP actively engage in reducing fragmentation and enlarging the size of the groups. On the left, the collapse of communism, the end of the Cold War, and the transformation of some communist parties has softened, if not eliminated, a historical cleavage, it has made more salient and visible a

Explaining the Shifting Structure of Party Competition in the European Parliament', *Comparative Political Studies*, 36 (2003), 75–96.

[47] See the data in Bardi, L., 'Transnational Trends in European Parties', 109.

[48] See Fennema, M. and Pollmann, C., 'Ideology of Anti-Immigrant Parties in the European Parliament', *Acta Politica*, 33 (1998), 111–33.

left–right divide in many European party systems, and has helped to strengthen the ESP group. The European United Left composed mainly of Italian and Spanish ex-communists has now disappeared, as several parties have shifted to the socialist group.[49] Even if the reasons for ESP convergence are nationally differentiated, the tendency to politico-ideological aggregation is evident.[50]

The most significant aggregation concerns, however, the centre-right. Since 1973, the enlargement to countries without Christian Democratic parties (with the exclusion of Austria) has threatened the identity of the European People's Party, based on the Christian parties of the EU founders (including France's MRP, at that time). In 1986, the admittance to the EPP of the Spanish Partido Popular (PP)—gathering what remained of Spanish Christian Democracy but also a large contingent from the former franquista right—generated much internal debate and moved the Christian Democratic Basque Party to resign in protest. Through the 1990s the exchanges among the centre-right forces of the EPP, of the European Democrats group, of the Liberal Democratic and Reformist (with the defection of Valery Giscard D'Estaing to the EPP), of the European Democratic Alliance of the Gaullists and the Fianna Fail, of the Union for Europe (including the Italian Forza Italia, the Irish Fianna Fail and the Portuguese CDS) suggest a growing awareness that a multigroup split was increasing the power of the socialists. The logic of these moves is that of an incipient parliamentary left–right alignment.

This 'aggregative logics' can be analysed looking at the interesting process by which the British Tory and Danish Conservatives joined the EPP group, dissolving their European Democrats group, as well as the example of the Italian Forza Italia. A long list of ideological and representative factors made this alliance unlikely and, indeed, unworkable. On the economic dimension the social Catholicism of many Christian parties (in, for example, Belgium, the Netherlands, Italy, and Austria) is at odds with the neo-liberalism free market ideology of the conservatives. The differences in social and agricultural policies are macroscopic. On the religious and values dimension one could hardly find a more difficult relationship than that between the secular (and Protestant) conservative parties and the Catholic profile of most EPP members. On the European integration dimension, again, it is difficult

---

[49] On the evolving attitude to the EU of communist and post-communist parties see the articles in J. Botella and L. Ramiro (eds.), *The Crisis of Communism and Party Change. The Evolution of West European Communist and Post-Communist Parties* (Barcelona: Institud de Ciencies Politiques i Social, 2003).

[50] For a detailed discussion of national motivations, see Notermans, T., 'Introduction', in T. Notermans (ed.), *Social democracy and monetary union* (New York and Oxford: Berghahn Books, 2001), 1–21.

to imagine a stronger opposition than that between the pro-integrationist views of many founding Catholic parties and the profound anti-integration and sceptical traditions of the British Tories and the other conservatives. On the political level it is difficult for those Christian parties with strong ties to Christian unions to accept the class-based anti-unionism of the conservatives, and for those Christian parties cooperating nationally with the socialists to accept the logic of anti-socialist right-wing coalitions.

Nevertheless, in spite of some internal dissents on both sides, this 'unholy' and unlikely combination took place. The Tories became allied members to the EPP in 1989, and reached full membership in 1997. A thorough analysis of this process[51] points to the factors that justified an instrumental alliance without ideological convergence: (*a*) the reinforced need for absolute majorities generated by the enhanced EP powers under the cooperation, assent and co-decision procedures; (*b*) the new sensitivity of the EPP to the problem of how to relate to conservative parties in view of the enlargement; (*c*) the conservatives' aim to end the evident isolation during the negotiation of the Maastricht Treaty; (*d*) the Christian democrats need to establish links with perspective governing parties (ND in Greece, PP in Spain), and to be represented in countries where otherwise the EPP had no representation; and (*e*) the common goal to maximize anti-ESP parliamentary influence and anxieties about socialist dominance in a moment when communist parties were approaching the ESP group. In short, politico-institutional imperatives of balancing forces and counting more within the EP won over the policy/ideological compatibility. In this sense a certain amount of 'systemness' of the EP party system seems to emerge.

However, these developments continue to be puzzling if one considers how difficult party alliances prove at the domestic level, in electoral and parliamentary institutions that offer an attractive prize to electoral size in the form of selection and control of executives and legislation. The strength of the above-mentioned political constraints in the institutionally unfriendly, relatively powerless, and politically invisible EP can only surprise. This alliance expansion logic has no visible perspective of electoral rewards in either European or national elections. The respective electorates remain uniformed about and unaware of these new alliances, and are not asked to ratify them.

The constraining power of such weak political incentives can only be justified by the equal or even greater weakness of the ideological constraints. The differences over the economic, religious and European dimensions can be overcome precisely because the EP is so irrelevant, invisible to public

---

[51] Johansson, K. M., *Transnational party alliances: Analysing the hard-won alliance between Conservatives and Christian Democrats in the European Parliament* (Lund: Lund University Press, 1997).

opinion, inconsequential for domestic alignments that no costs are foreseen in exchange for the advantages. Therefore, at the EU level and in the EP in particular, the low ideological intensity allows for compromises and alliances to be made that do not generate costs back home. In this sense the alliance between Northern conservatives and continental Catholics was an instrumental marriage made possible by the low visibility of the EP politics. It will therefore be strained only if and when the EP has real policymaking powers. The alliance and in general the expansive logic of European parliamentary groups is the result of the weakness of the EP, not a symptom of its strength.

Top-Down Institutionalization

These peculiar features of the Europarties are less puzzling, however, if we regard them as legitimizing devices that are institutionally assisted and dependent. There is in fact a tremendous push towards the top-down institutionalization of European extra-parliamentary parties, fostered jointly by the EU institutions and national party elites. The European Federations of parties have passed through different phases, from the early optimism of the 1970–79 period, to the stagnation between 1979 and 1989 (characterized by clear difficulties in drafting party manifestos and in low profile in campaigns), to the recent renaissance since1989, in connection with the drafting and ratification of the TEU. They remain weak institutions in membership, staff, finance, and internal organizational differentiation and structure.[52] Federations do not possess the internal organization to carry out policies decided by a leadership. The executive boards governing them are weak and mainly coordinate, advise, etc.[53]

It is unclear why national parties consider it important to add party federations to parliamentary groups and party leaders' summits. The argument put forward is that federations are necessary to coordinate party positions, are important during the negotiations accompanying the frequent IGCs, and offer large national parties in opposition—and thus excluded from intergovernmental negotiations—an opportunity to have a say on the agenda.[54] None of these reasons, however, make it compelling to add party federations in addition to parliamentary groups. The thesis that the renewed interest in party federations is due to the Eastern enlargement is more convincing. The federations offer a period of training and socialization, and

[52] Bardi, L., 'Transnational Party Federations, European Parliamentary Party Groups and the Building of Europarties', in R. Katz and P. Mair (eds.), *How Parties Organize: Change and Adaptation in Western Democracies* (London: Sage, 1994), 357–72.

[53] Ibid.

[54] Hix, S., 'The Transnational Party Federations', in J. Gaffney (ed.), *Political Parties and the European Union* (London: Routledge, 1996), 308–31, 319.

a way of integrating potential new parties before the accession of their country and their choice of a parliamentary group. Yet, even this helpful role cannot explain the growing emphasis on European political parties by the EU institutions and the national political elites alike.

The Treaty of the Political Union included a reference to political parties and a specific recognition of the party federations: 'Political parties at the European level are important as a factor for integration within the Union. They contribute to forming a European awareness and to expressing the political will of the citizens of the Union'. Since then Europarties have begun to seek more explicit public recognition, legalization, and public funding. The Amsterdam and Nice Treaties added the short but not unimportant sentence that the Council establishes the statute of the 'political parties at the European level' and the rules concerning their public financing (Art. 191). This formula was suggested by the EP Constitutional Affairs Committee's final report of 27 March 2000 in view of a vote on the EP's proposal for the IGC of Nice.[55] This report and the debate surrounding it is an important indicator of the attempts being made to institutionalize the Europarties from the top-down, and, indirectly, of their nature and function.

The report put together a host of ideas on how to foster the role of Europarties,[56] including the controversial proposal that by 2009 an additional quota of 10 per cent of the MEPs be elected in a single European Constituency by giving each voter two votes—one for the national list and one for the European list, the latter included at least one citizen from each member state. But a European party statute with the quality of law was the main objective for those seeking a constitutional solution to the European party formation. The statute was to define precisely what 'parties at the European level' are and stipulate under which conditions their organizations and activities could be entitled to *cooperate with* and *receive support from* EU institutions. The European party statute was in fact presented in February 2000 by almost all Europarties and it was a far-reaching code governing their recognition and funding. With regard to finance, the document stated that it was 'desirable and justified to establish provisions for a EU regulation for European Political Parties strengthening the democratic basis of the EU while assuring transparency'. The European political parties were defined as 'associations of national and/or regional parties in European countries'

---

[55] European Parliament, 'Committee on Constitutional Affairs, Final report (A5–0058/2000) on the preparation of the reform of the Treaties and the next Intergovernmental Conference', Reporters Giorgios Dimitrakopoulos and Jo Leinen, 27 March 2000.

[56] See Johansson, K. M. and P. Zervakis, 'Historical Institutional Framework', in K. M. Johansson and P. Zervakis (eds.), *European Political Parties Between Cooperation and Integration* (Baden-Baden: Nomos, 2002), 11–28. The authors reconstruct the process leading to Art. 138a of the Maastricht Treaty and the subsequent developments.

and the political groups in the European Parliament were regarded as possible constituents of European political parties next to national parties.[57]

In the statute, the activities and the role of the parties are institutionalized by stringent and constraining conditions. To be recognized and licensed as 'European', the party: (*a*) must have constituted or aimed at constituting or joining a political group in the EP; (*b*) must adopt a common programme and share the same objectives and aims for the election of the EP, and such programme must respect the fundamental constitutional principles enshrined in the TEU of democracy, respect of human rights and the rule of law; (*c*) must be represented at national and/or regional level in 'at least one third of the member states' by parties recognized as such in accordance with the relevant national party laws or similar provisions; and (*d*) must have spelled out organizational provisions, a written statute, be democratically legitimized and accountable, have periodic meetings, consultative and management organs, democratic and transparent procedures. The official recognition of a European Political Party shall be made by an 'independent committee' and appeals against a rejection decision should be registered with the ECJ. Finally, a most telling clause specifies the tasks that Europarties are meant to perform: establish a forum for expressing the political will of the citizens; facilitate coordination among and between national parties and EU institutions; inform the public about EU issues and prepare policy proposals; encourage the citizens to actively participate; draft programmes for shaping EU policies; contribute to candidate selection for EP elections; influence the Commission, Council and EP decisions.

The document states that European political parties are entitled 'to receive EU funding'. However, their own resources (memberships and donations) must 'constitute a significant part of their annual budget' (it is not specified how much is meant by 'significant'). The total amount of EU funding will be distributed among the constituent parties on the basis of the results obtained in the most recent EP elections. Accounts should be public, transparent, and checked by the Court of Auditors. Through the voice of Michel Barnier in the EP, the Commission committed itself to proposing a change of the party article to make it operational and did indeed respect this commitment.

This parliamentary document represented the view of the parliamentary groups. The Commission accepted the document with minor revisions for a proposal to the Council following the procedure of Art. 308 EC, requiring

---

[57] See 'European Party Statute', Working Document of European Political Parties, by the secretary-generals of the parties and parliamentary groups of the EPP, ED, PES, ELDRP, Group of Greens/Europe Free Alliance and the Federation of the Green Party, Democratic Party of the Peoples of Europe-European Free Alliance, 15 February 2000.

consultation of the EP and unanimity in the Council.[58] The final regulation was approved in November 2003[59] and it sets slightly less demanding conditions for the recognition of a European party than the original parliamentary proposal did. It immediately fostered the doubling of new European parties, from the four-five present in 2003 to the eight that have been actually financed in 2004 on the basis of the new rules.

The purpose of the institutional recognition of the European party federations is meant to solve the unsatisfactory situation in which they (their small staffs and campaign initiatives) existed in a rather *a-legal* situation and were financed by national parties and, above all, by the European parliamentary groups. Therefore, quite clearly, the more mundane reason for the recent attention paid to party federations, and, more generally, for the surprising institutionalization of party families, is that they represent the best way to obtain additional public finance essential to further strengthen the Europarties. In this sense Europarty federations are in the interest of both EP parliamentary groups and national parties. At the same time, other EU institutions have an interest in institutionalizing the role of extra-parliamentary parties as the debate about their functions is clearly evident. Parties seek recognition from EU institutions by offering their legitimating role with the citizens in exchange for economic support. Rather than claiming to 'represent' something or someone, European parties argue that they will use the money and statute to inform and solicit the participation and the support of the citizens. The clauses of institutionalization/constitutionalization, and the conditions of access and recognition are so stringent that parties tend to become institutions of support to the EU. The expression of dissenting or radical alternative views exposes them to the risk of not qualifying for the status of Europarties. In other words, the conditions for forming a party have high entry barriers that largely predefine the role of the parties themselves. As a result of the need to formalize the conditions of financing and of operational survival, the organization of political parties may experience a further institutionalization moving from the current network form to a more hierarchical and authoritative organization at the EU level. Europarties may become more organized because this is the only way to legally obtain the money they need to survive. Finally, it is important to note that in the debate

---

[58] See Commission Européenne, 'Proposition de règlement du Conseil sur le statut et le financement des partis politiques européens' (Bruxelles: 13 February 2001). For a discussion of the differences between the Parliament's and Commission's texts see Kulahci, E., 'Le status et le financement des fédérations européennes de partis: vers un renforcement du phénomène partisan européen?' (Brussels: Association Belge de science politique, 2002), Conference Paper, 14–15 March.

[59] 'Regulation (EC) No 2004/2003 on the EP and of the Council of 4 November 2003 on the regulation governing political parties at European level and the rules regarding their funding', *Official Journal of the European Union*, 15 November 2003, L 297/1.

that took place between the Maastricht and the Nice Treaties the Europarties did not request substantial changes in the constitutional balance of the EU. Europarties seek incorporation without constitutional power, and clearly declare their supportive role.

In conclusion, the European parliamentary groups and party federations evidence a tendency to become more inclusive and cohesive and structure along a left–right alignment. It is difficult, however, to find any clear explanation of this given the lack of interlinkage between European and national electoral markets. It is also surprising in view of the unfriendly institutional environment of the EP and European elections. It can be interpreted as a deliberate attempt by national and European political elite to develop mechanisms and institutions to legitimize their continued rule by institutionalizing from the top rather artificial forms of citizen participation, support and recognition. The Council-Commission offers financial support and recognition in exchange for indirect popular legitimacy, control and exclusion of critical subelite of anti-EU parties, and the necessary disciplining of behaviour in view of the organization of the work of the EP. An additional reason that transpires is the positive effect of strong Europarties on the parties of incoming member countries. There is recognition that European parties will never manage to fulfil these functions if left to themselves, without institutional support and friendly attitudes by the EU institutions. The attempts by the European and national parties to overcome the collective action problems by engaging in organizational innovation at the EU level through the top-down institutionalization of a European 'party system' may be successful in the longer run. Much depends on whether the Europarties are (or will be) in fact able to perform the function of 'informing and soliciting the participation, and the support of the citizens' as they claim. This last point also depends on how much these parties will shape and represent the attitudes of European citizens towards the EU.

Europarties and the Mass Public

Do the national and European parties represent the orientations of the European mass public towards the EU? For a long time analyses of levels of public support for the EU have concentrated on cross-countries variations, reflecting the basic understanding that the fundamental differences were among countries. The gap in national support was seen in terms of old members versus newcomers;[60] more or less favourable 'national traditions' (the 'geopolitical'

---

[60] The Germans were the most supportive in the 1950s; by the mid-1970s the Italians and French had become equally supportive; the British, on the contrary, showed a

interpretation; see supra); macrovariables such as inflation, GDP and un-employment; political mobilization factors like referenda; EC benefit evalu-ation in terms of budget ratio and intra-EC export rate.[61] Since then, new studies have mapped the attitudes of European citizens towards the EU by considering their individual support for unification or for membership, for specific EU institutions, and for specific policy areas.[62] Finally, since the 1990s, there has been growing attention to the 'structuring' of citizens' attitudes towards the EU, that is, to the underlying dimensions, if any, that unify and structure the varieties of single issues/institutions/field/policy preferences. The focus in this latter case is the relationship between ideational visions, political organizations, and citizens' attitudes to policies and politics of the EU.

Citizens' attitudes towards political objects are 'structured' when they are both salient and unified by some underlying dimensions that account for the covariation in the policy positions and preferences. The many possible posi-tions and preferences are reduced to a few dimensions. When this structuring process has occurred, we are in principle capable of inferring the position or preference of a citizen on one issue from his/her position on other issues. This definition, however, assumes that citizens have positions and preferences that are later subsumed, rationalized or unified by underlying dimensions. An alternative starting point is that citizens have no specific positions and pref-erences on many policies and issues. They only have general orientations to some predominant concern from which they derive positions and preferences on other policies and issues. In both cases, structuring implies a reduction of potentially scattered preferences, opinions and ideas about institutions and policies into a low number of definable dimensions. There is no agreement concerning the extent to which the individual bases of support and opposition to the European integration are 'structured' or remain 'indistinct'. According to some scholars, in the mass public there is no such thing as support or opposition, but rather an undifferentiated, uninformed, uninterested and incompetent orientation deprived of solid structure.[63] On the contrary,

declining support until their entry in 1973, after which it slowly grew. New members have generally been less supportive than the founding ones, although Spanish and Portuguese support has, since the beginning, been higher that that of the new members of the 1970s, Ireland, Britain and Denmark.

[61] For this type of study see Inglehart, R., Rabier, J.-R. and Reif, K., 'The Evolution of Public Attitudes towards European Integration, 1976–1986', *Revue d'Intégration europé-enne*, 10 (1987), 135–55; K. Reif and R. Inglehart (eds.), *Eurobarometer: The Dynamic of European Public Opinion* (London: Macmillan, 1993); Eichenberg, R. C. and Dalton, R. J., 'Europeans and the European Community: the dynamics of public support for European Integration', *International Organization*, 49 (1993), 507–34.

[62] A review of these studies can be found in the various articles in Marks and Steenbergen, *European Integration and Political Conflict*.

[63] The explanations of low turnout take this line of interpretation. See Blodel, J., Sinnott, R., and Svensson, P., *People and Parliament in the European Union: Participation, Dem-ocracy and Legitimacy* (Oxford: Oxford University Press, 1998).

other analyses point out that an attitudinal structure concerning the EU is emerging among the mass public along lines not too different from those prevailing at the national level.

The debate on the structuring of attitudes concerning the EU in parties and voters has therefore evolved around three closely connected issues: (*a*) whether those attitudes are sufficiently salient to become structured; (*b*) whether national and European parties and elite are in tune with their voters' attitudes on EU issues and institutions; and, in such a case, (*c*) what is (are) the dimension(s) along which such structuring is taking place. Concerning the *salience* of the European issues, observers disagree on their importance for political behaviours at the mass level; with regard to the *fit* between voters and their representatives, observers disagree about the extent to which representative elites adequately represent their voters' opinions; with regard to the *dimensionality* of attitudes to the EU, disagreements exist concerning whether a left–right dimension or a more complex dimensionality— including a pro-against integration or even other dimensions—prevail and on the extent to which these dimensions correlate with one another.

Salience

Are the European integration issues sufficiently important in the mind of the public? In a temporal perspective the answer is unquestionably yes. Through increasingly frequent ratification referenda, European direct elections, continuous debates about membership enlargement, wider publicity and media coverage of IGC, unexpected implications of EU legislation for everyday life and economic activities, and the physical tangibleness of the single currency, the public opinion is now more directly involved in the integration process than ever before. It is difficult to directly demonstrate this growing salience, but it is indirectly witnessed by the fact that national political elites have been dedicating more and more time to convince their domestic audience that the benefits of further integration outweigh the costs. The salience of European issues is often deduced from how much political parties—rather than voters—emphasize them in their programmes and activities. A study explicitly devoted to this problem reaches the conclusion that certain parties mute or downplay European integration either because they have an unpopular stance on these issues or because they are divided on them.[64] Conversely, other parties presumably try to keep this issue alive on the agenda because they are united, they believe they have a popular stance, or they perceive an

---

[64] Steenbergen, M. R. and Scott, D. J., 'Contesting Europe. The Salience of European Integration as a party issue', in Marks and Steenbergen, *European Integration and Political Conflict*, 165–93.

advantage deriving to them from the unpopular stance or the non-united position of their national competitors.

A direct challenge to the salience of integration issues is represented, however, by those studies that suggest that referendum outcomes and second-order European elections are contaminated by popular feelings about the incumbent government and parties (and the leader)[65] and by the institutional context of the choice.[66] According to this view, the level of information and competence about the EU and the treaties is insufficient to justify the claim of their direct significance. Voters react mostly on the basis of domestic issues and on the unity of their parties with regard to EU questions. However, the correlation between negative support for a government and an anti-EU vote (such as, for instance, a NO vote in a referendum) does not necessarily imply that such a vote is due purely to domestic reasons. This finding is also consistent with the interpretation suggesting that those who are worried by further steps in integration deem the incumbent government responsible for supporting them. Disapproval of a government and a vote against integration may well go hand in hand.

Fit

Political alignment problems emerge from the existence of a salient and prolonged misfit between the policy preferences of political parties and those of their electorates. If we assume that European issues are sufficiently salient, to what extent are the preferences of the voters on the European issues congruent with or do they diverge from those of their traditionally preferred party? Figure 6.1, taking the imaginary example of the issue of more national border control versus more EU openness, plots the attitude of the voters against the perceived attitudes of their party. It helps to define a number of polar situations with different implications for party alignments. Parties may all misrepresent voters' preferences in the same direction, for instance, as in Figure 6.1, being all more favourable to integration and less border control then their voters are. In this case one expects a low realignment potential, as all parties would coalesce to mould public opinion and voters' preferences. The constant Y line represents a situation in which voters have a fixed or very similar position while parties diverge. In this case, if the issues were to be salient, it would favour those parties nearer to the voters'

[65] Franklin, M. N., March, M., and McLaren, L., 'Uncorking the bottle: popular opposition to European Unification in the wake of Maastricht', *Journal of Common Market Studies*, 32 (1994), 455–72; Franklin, M. N., Van der Eijk, C., and Marsh, M., 'Referendum Outcomes and Trust in Government: Public Support for Europe in the Wake of Maastricht', *West European Politics*, 18 (1995), 101–17.

[66] Hug, *Voices of Europe*.

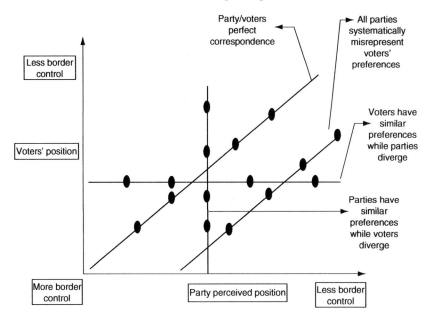

FIGURE 6.1. Party/voters fit in issue position (e.g. border control versus EU openness)

stable preference. The constant X line represents the case in which the voters' positions widely diverge while all the parties have a similar (e.g. pro-integration) stance. In this case, if the issue is salient, there will be room for the emergence of new parties, rather than realignment in favour of some of the existing parties.

The evidence of recent research can be organized in reference to these polar situations. In a study based on the 1989 parliamentary elections, Van der Eijk and Franklin[67] compare the attitude of voters towards the EC and the attitude of the main national parties as perceived by the voters themselves. Their general conclusion is that, on the whole, party-voters show quite a strong similarity of position. The general Rsq was 0.6213 for all parties and only in Britain, Italy, the Netherlands, and Ireland was the fit poor. The parties for which a general misfit was more evident (generally with voters more in favour than the party) were the Orthodox-Protestant combination in the Netherlands, the Workers Party in Ireland, the Italian MSI and the Greens in several countries (Germany, the Netherlands, Ireland, Luxembourg). The data, however, give the impression that all regression lines fall

[67] Van der Eijk, C. and Franklin, M., 'European Community Politics and Electoral Representation: evidence from the 1989 European Elections Study', *European Journal of Political Research*, 19 (1991), 105–27.

below the diagonal that represents a perfect party-voters fit,[68] and that most parties were perceived to be more in favour of EU integration than voters were. Basing his research on the 1994 Elections data, Schmitt[69] studied parties/voters congruence comparing voters' self-placement on a number of key issues with the placement of 'their party'. He came to the similar conclusion that, on the whole, the European party system reflects quite well the voters' preferences. Even in Schmitt's issue scattergrams party attitudes are systematically perceived as more pro-integration than voter attitudes.

Ten years later, Van der Eijk and Franklin[70] document that a considerable proportion of the European electorate have preferences on European main issues that are not represented by the positioning of their respective parties. They cannot, therefore, choose a party on the basis of its EU position while at the same time choosing on the basis of the party's left–right position. They argue that political entrepreneurs may soon seize the opportunity offered by this rather polarized distribution of EU opinions to create movements that differentiate themselves from the other parties on EU issues. Other studies by Schmitt and Thomassen have documented that mass–elite agreement on specific EU policies is poor.[71] Their data show that, while on a broad ideological characterization like left–right, the voters' and the representatives' positions are largely similar and are clearly constrained by the European party groups to which individual parties belong, when individual issues are considered (they analyse border control and common currency) the discrepancy between voters of the same party and party representatives are such that one wonders what the two have in common. Voters and their representatives are living in two different worlds, and the positions of those voters who are sceptical or opposed are totally or almost totally ignored in the representation channels.[72] These authors do not conclude, however, that voters are far less European-minded than their representatives. They suggest that voters might be merely insecure about the outcomes of particular EU policies and therefore tend to prefer what they perceive as the status quo to

[68] Admittedly it is difficult to trace this diagonal precisely because of difference of scale; the voters' position is measured on a five-point scale, while the party position on a four-point scale.

[69] Schmitt, H., 'National Party Systems and the Policies of the European Union. First Results from the 1994 European Election Study' (Berlin: 16th IPSA World Congress, 1994), 21–25August.

[70] Van der Eijk, C and Franklin, M. N., 'Potential for Contestation on European matters at national elections in Europe', in Marks and Steenbergen, *European Integration and Political Conflict*, 32–50.

[71] Thomassen, J. and Schmitt, H., 'Issue Representation', *European Journal of Political Research*, 32 (1997), 165–84; Schmitt, H. and Thomassen, J. (eds.), *Political Representation and Legitimacy in the European Union* (Oxford: Oxford University Press, 1999), Chapter 9.

[72] Thomassen, J. and Schmitt, H., 'Policy Representation', *European Journal of Political Research*, 32 (1997), 165–84, 181.

be. They argue that while policy preferences diverge, integrationist orientations of voters and party elite match approximately as closely as their left–right orientation, which is a very close match.[73] They conclude that political representation in the EU might be deficient as regards specific EU policies, but functions well as far as the main orientations of public opinion are concerned. This interpretation based on the distinction between concrete integration policies and integration in general is not, however, immediately evident. A different interpretation could be that voters have more precise opinions about specific policies (like the common currency), while they tend to give generic answers to general questions concerning integration. Moreover, figures 2 to 4 in their study on party-voter positions on integration and the left–right dimension do not clearly support the idea that the fit is as good on both dimensions. The Rsq is similar but as far as attitudes to integration are concerned most parties are more integrationists than their voters and outliers are crucial. Excluding five outlying cases out of forty-six it is difficult to see a linear association for the integration issue.

These studies conclude that there are variations across countries and parties, but, on the whole, the latter reflects quite well voters' preferences on very general attitudes towards integration, but very much less well when integration issues are made specific. It seems also that everywhere, and growing more so over time, the parties are seen as more supportive of integration than voters are. This is consistent with the qualitative information we have about the efforts several parties make to convince their rank and file of the necessity to support integration, and also with the evidence that in new member countries even those parties more clearly anti-EU before the entry, moderate their position after their membership is decided upon. This situation may slowly modify the position of the voters, but might also demonstrate a general problem of representation. If parties differentiate their positions sufficiently (even if these are always more integrationist than their voters) voters can move to the party that best satisfies their preference, if these are salient to them (with the exception of the more extreme positions that may require specific anti-integration new parties to be satisfied). However, the situation is quite different in the case parties have all developed the same profile on the integration issue. In this case, the politicization of integration issues cannot be reabsorbed by interparty realignment but may trigger more conspicuous changes.

[73] Schmitt, H. and Thomassen, J., 'Dynamic Representation: The Case of European Integration', *European Union Politics*, 1 (2000), 318–39, Table 1.

Dimensionality

Attitudes to institutions and policies get 'dimensional' to the extent that rather than remaining scattered and unrelated, they acquire transitivity along a given dimension. Dimensionality entails the capacity to incorporate new issues into pre-existing dimensions and opposition lines. Are the attitudes towards European integration related to some general dimension and how does this relate to pre-existing dimensions of alignment? The historical dimensionality of national party systems was assisted by powerful institutional factors pertaining to the dualistic nature of the government/opposition and majority/minority relationship, and by the territorial competition for votes. The lack of these features at the European level may make a dimensional structuring of the European party system very difficult.

As discussed earlier on in this chapter, it is difficult to relate parties' attitudes towards European integration to their national left–right placement or to any other national alignment. Several studies have concluded that for national parties, Europarties and voters the addition of a second dimension to the dominant left–right is necessary, which is generally labelled nationalist versus supranationalist, or integration versus independence.[74] Moreover, with the reconciliation of some left parties with and the growing opposition of some right-wing parties to the integration process, the two dimensions have become more independent from each other.[75] Within the EP, roll-call data and survey interviews have been used to show that a left–right alignment is the most important one, followed by the for–against integration.[76] Even if there are internal divisions concerning the EU, particularly in those groups (such as the EPP) that have expanded the most beyond their original scope, parliamentary groups are regarded as not ephemeral but characterized by a common ideology, leading to cohesive roll-call behaviour whenever they face those issues that reproduce the left–right dimensionality prevailing in national politics.

But as soon as these studies move from those issues I have defined 'isomorphic' to issues pertaining to the constitutive dimension of EU

---

[74] Marks and Wilson, 'The Past and the Present'; Marks, Wilson, and Ray, 'National Political Parties and European Integration'; Hix, S., 'Dimensions and Alignments in European Union Politics: Cognitive Constraints and Partisan Responses', *European Journal of Political Research* 35 (1999), 69–106; Hix, S., 'Legislative Behaviour and Party Competition in European Parliament: An Application of Nominate to the EU'.

[75] See Schmitt and Thomassen, 'Dynamic Representation'.

[76] Thomassen, J., Noury, A. G. and Voeten, E., 'Political Competition in the European Parliament. Evidence from Roll Call and Survey Analyses', in Marks and Steenbergen, *European Integration and Political Conflict*, 141–64.

politics—membership, competences, institutional design—the within parliamentary groups' cohesion and the between parliamentary groups' dimensionality collapse. On such issues national differences dramatically weaken the cohesiveness available on isomorphic issues.[77] The positions of the ESP, the EPP and the ELDR on EU constitutive issues are deeply divided internally and, therefore, externally undifferentiated. Any attempt by Europarties to take a clear stand on these problems would simply split and tear them apart. To put it crudely, the Europarties are quite meaningless on European constitutive issues, and there is no chance whatsoever that they may organize and compete by structuring opinions on the integration dimension. The conclusion to be drawn from these consistent data coming from different studies and techniques is that the European parties have a chance to structure their relationships and to influence and mould public opinion only if, and to the extent they organize the dimensionality of their relationships on issues isomorphic with the national ones, collude among themselves to keep the constitutive issue of European integration out of the EP political agenda, and prevent the European voters from expressing themselves on such issues.

For this reason, at the present and in the foreseeable future, attempts to organize the EU level party system along lines that allow voters in European elections to have a meaningful say about the membership, competences and institutional design of the EU project are impossible. The EP cannot articulate opinions and policies in these crucial domains. Cross-parliamentary groups alliances regrouping MEPs with similar opinions and concerns on EU constitutive issues—like the *Kangaroo Group*, dedicated to complete market liberalization, or the federalist *Crocodile Group*—are disturbing elements rather than precursors of an European party system *in nuce*. I share the conclusion that if European constitutive alignments became dominant in European politics, 'the remedy might be worse than the disease. Not only would such parties be internally divided on almost any other political issue [apart from their attitude to the EU] but given that policy view on this dimension are strongly related to national background, it would articulate national rather than cross-national political cleavages. Therefore, such a

---

[77] This is recognized even by those studies that conclude that a left-right dimension is the dominant structuring one. Simon Hix argues that 'voting in the EP is driven by national party preferences and membership' (694); and it 'is the principals that control candidate selection (the national parties) who ultimately determine how MEPs behave. When the national parties in the same parliamentary group decide to vote together, the EP parties look highly cohesive. But when these parties take opposing policy positions, the cohesion of the EP parties break down' (696); Hix, S., 'Parliamentary Behavior with Two Principals: Preferences, Parties, and Voting in the European Parliament', *American Journal of Political Science*, 46 (2002), 688–98.

party system would almost likely be a factor of disintegration rather than of integration of the Union'.[78] This consideration offers a key to understanding the paradox of European elections that still remain second-order elections[79] after a quarter of a century. The fact that European elections are fought on national, normal, and common policy issues rather than European issues is in this perspective a positive sign of development towards a supranational integrated or aggregated party system.[80] One can add that discussing EU constitutive issues will make the EP decisional rules, and the conditions in which the minority is expected to accept the majority decisions, very contentious.

In short, because national party systems are based on the differentiation of interests and ideological positions within established and bounded political communities, their isomorphic alignments are not suited to discuss the issues of the geographical and functional boundaries (membership, competence, institutional design) of a newly created political community. They fail to organize those alternatives that may be relevant to voters in the European context. So far, we know that there have been both cases of the left–right dimension splitting anti-European parties (the Danish anti-European movement) and cases of the independence/integration dimension splitting left or right parties (the French UDF and PS). We also know that the different orientations of traditional class groups, sector groups, and (subnational) territorial groups (see Chapter 5) make parties unable to frame the integration dimension without facing exorbitant internal costs. They respond by colluding and by de-emphasizing the competition on the integration dimension. In doing so they leave wide open an enormous political space for third parties, but have so far reduced the internal costs of the impact of European integration.

The attention and the support with which Europarties (parliamentary groups as well as federations) are viewed by the European and national elites is a sign of the latter's interest in engineering a policy-dimension based party system that can work as a source of demotic or popular legitimacy to compensate the divisions that prevail at the intergovernmental level in the relationship among member countries. The question is whether it will be possible to organize a Europarty system mainly based on the national

[78] Thomassen, Noury, and Voeten, 'Political Competition in the European Parliament. Evidence from Roll Call and Survey Analyses', 164.

[79] Reif, K-H. and Schmitt, H., 'Nine Second-Order National Elections: A Conceptual Framework for the Analysis of European Election Results', *European Journal of Political Research*, 8 (1980), 3–44.

[80] This is in fact the conclusion by Thomassen and Schmitt, 'Policy representation', 169: 'the more the Community develops, the more we would expect political debate to be dominated by "normal" policy issues, like the problems of unemployment, or of organized crime, rather than by more constitutional issues'.

isomorphic left–right alignment while the most crucial issues agitating the EU project concern problems of community definition, competence attribution, and decision rules. The constitutive issues concerning the boundary of the polity, which are not on the agenda of Europarties, are the crucial issues for EU institutions, states representatives, and also broad publics.

The strategy of integrating national left–right cleavage structures at the EU party system level while keeping the European constitutional issues at the top intergovernmental level may be successful, but this 'division of labour' is hard to maintain. The integration of national cleavage systems into the EP left–right dimension requires that domestic political organization: (*a*) let prevail those isomorphic issues and dimensions of conflict on which they can best integrate across Europe; (*b*) keep organizational unity and control over national voters while integrating their differentiated profiles into an overarching European profile; and (*c*) adapt the variety of national formations to a relatively few European political families. However, the politicizing of the EU constitutional issues, if it spills over from intergovernmental circles to parties and mass publics: (*a*) generates non-isomorphic issues and dimension of conflict that cannot be integrated in Europarty families; (*b*) reduce the potential control of national political organizations over their voters; and (*c*) challenges the cohesion of national political formation and makes it difficult to integrate them at the EP level. If, on the one hand, it seems unrealistic and unlikely that the left–right alignments of the current EP will represent the political alignment 'about Europe', on the other hand, one must acknowledge the powerful national and European forces that push towards this solution. So far, this has resulted in a somewhat unrealistic European left–right competition being reproduced at the EU level, whose chances of long-term survival are indeed difficult to evaluate.

The general problem of dimensionality can finally be looked at from the point of view of what we know about the individual determinants of support/opposition to the EU and the extent to which they relate to dimensions of national politics. Individual positive orientation towards the EU is generally related to the level of political awareness[81] and to political values that are less nationalistic and more committed to individual liberty and equality.[82] Other studies suggest that voters' attitudes generally reflect the evaluation of domestic issues and governments.[83] Utilitarian hypotheses suggest individuals

---

[81] The origins of this approach go back to Inglehart, R., 'Cognitive Mobilization and European Identity', *Comparative Politics*, 3 (1970), 45–70.

[82] See Inglehart, R. and Reif, K., 'Analysing Trends in Western European Opinion: The Role of the Eurobarometer Surveys', in Reif and Inglehart, *Eurobarometer*, 1–26.

[83] Franklin, March, and McLaren, 'Uncorking the bottle'; Van der Eijk and Franklin, 'European Community Politics and Electoral Representation'; Van der Eijk, C., Franklin, M., et al., *Choosing Europe? The European Electorate and National Politics in the Face of Union*

will favour the EU according to their social status and human capital position.[84] Early Eurobarometer studies[85] pointed out that significant class polarization was more evident in Denmark[86] and Britain than in the other countries, with manual workers and unemployed less favourable than higher income, higher status occupations, executives and professionals. However, across all classes and status groups those who perceive that they are doing well attribute it to the EU and those who are doing poorly do the same. On the cognitive mobilization dimension, those who are better educated, informed, active, and with a less parochial view feel more comfortable with remote large-scale institutions such as the EU. Those individuals with higher scores in scales concerning political discussion and partisanship are more in favour of the integration. Yet, again, this difference was marginal in the 1970s newcomers (Britain, Ireland, Denmark), indicating that national factors overcome the cognitive factor. Moreover, the same study points out that at the end of the 1980s the 'European movement no longer captured the imagination of the most educated and politically involved stratum to the extent that it once did'. The same holds true for young people.[87]

An analysis testing these various hypotheses on French anti-EU feeling concludes that lower level categories and farmers are always less supportive. Education is a stronger predictor of support than occupation. Political dissatisfaction and xenophobia become powerful determinants of anti-integration after social background and party identification have been controlled. Class and occupation affect attitudes only for exacerbated categories. The study documents that attitudes towards Europe now cut across other political attitudes, but concludes that a realignment over the EU-integration issue in the French electorate, and in particular between Communist Party and National Front voters, is unlikely.[88] In France several

(Ann Arbor, MI: University of Michigan Press, 1996); Van der Eijk, C., Franklin, M., and March, M., 'What Voters Teach Us About Europe-Wide Elections: What Europe-Wide Elections Teach Us about voters', *Electoral Studies*, 15 (1996), 149–56; Eichenberg and Dalton, 'Europeans and the European Community: the dynamics of public policy support for European Integration'.

[84] See Gabel, M. and Palmer, H., 'Understanding Variation in Public Support for European Integration', *European Journal of Political Research*, 27 (1995), 3–19; Gabel, M., 'Public Support for European Integration; an Empirical Test of Five Theories', *Journal of Politics*, 60 (1998), 333–54.

[85] Inglehart, R., Rabier, J.-R. and Reif, K., 'The Evolution of Public Attitudes towards European Integration, 1976–86', *Revue d'Intégration européenne*, 10 (1987), 135–55.

[86] Support for the EU is very weak among the working class and those in public employment. Siune, K., Svensson, P. and Tonsgaard, O., 'The European Union: The Danes Said "No" in 1992 but "Yes" in 1993: How and Why?', *Electoral Studies*, 13 (1994), 107–16, 111.

[87] Inglehart and Reif, 'Analysing Trends in Western European Opinion'.

[88] Evans, J., 'Contrasting attitudinal bases to Euroscepticism amongst the French Electorate', *Electoral Studies*, 19 (2000), 539–61.

divisions re-emerged or surfaced under the very close vote on the Maastricht Treaty in 1992.[89] There was a significant urban–rural divide, with rural regions voting 'no' and urban centres voting 'yes'; the 'yes' vote was predominant in the higher and better-educated socio-economic groups. A sort of progressive/repressive division line was also evident in the fact that the 'no' votes were associated with the death penalty, anti-immigration, and other populist issues. More important, in France, the 'no' to Maastricht progressively revealed a discourse in which Europe is associated with an open door to immigration; it is linked to and made responsible thereafter for high unemployment, insecurity, and cultural standardization and homogenization (if not globalization tout court).[90]

National surveys concerning nine EC referenda from 1972 to 1994[91] demonstrate that individuals located on the right scale vote more in favour than individuals located on the left (except in France and Switzerland); males vote on average more frequently in favour than women;[92] the level of the favourable vote increases with age and with education; voters without religious affiliation vote more in favour then voters with strong Catholic and Protestant affiliations; single persons vote more heavily in favour than married, divorced, and widowed persons; members of trade unions vote more against than unaffiliated workers; higher income categories vote more strongly for integration.

According to a study based on pooled cross-sectional data for the 1973–89 Eurobarometers, general support is related to proximity to borders, individual 'human capital', and income.[93] The EC policies affect individuals differently according to their ability to benefit from the liberalized labour and financial markets and support varies consistently with cross-sectional differences in an individual's potential benefit from the EC policies. Occupational skill and education level are positively related to the potential benefits from EC policies and thereby to support for the EU. Europeans with higher educational levels and more marketable occupational skills are better prepared to apply their talents in diverse international settings and to adapt to economic changes in their production sector and region. In contrast, less

[89] See Perrineau, P., 'L'enjeu européen, révélateur de la mutation des clivages politiques dans les années 1990', in F. Arcy and L. Rouban (eds.), *De la V République à l'Europe. Hommage à Jean-Louis Quermonne* (Paris: Presses de la Fondation Nationale des Sciences Politiques, 1996), 45–59.

[90] Mayer, N., 'L'offre identitaire du Front National', *Revue Internationale de Politique Comparé*, 5 (1998), 179–87.

[91] Hug, S. and Sciarini, P., 'Referendums on European Integration. Do Institutions Matter in the Voter's Decision?', *Comparative Political Studies*, 33 (2000), 3–36.

[92] Nelsen, B. F. and Guth, J. L., 'Exploring the Gender Gap. Women, Men and Public Attitudes towards European Integration', *European Union Politics* 1 (2000), 267–91.

[93] Gabel, M. and Palmer, H. D., 'Understanding Variations in Public Support for European Integration', *European Journal of Political Research*, 27 (1995), 3–19.

educated and poorly skilled Europeans have less valuable job experiences, possess less mutable skills and qualifications, are less likely to seek additional job training, and are more expendable in times of economic downturn. In terms of income, lower income citizens are more dependent on social welfare while higher income citizens prize more open financial markets, less public sector spending, and low inflation.

Analysis of the attitudes of party elites and interest groups towards entry in the four referenda held in Austria and Finland, Sweden and Norway underline that in all four cases the opposition and the campaign was between centre and periphery in cultural, economic, and political terms, between the 'resourceful establishment against the less-established groups', both trying to persuade a large proportion of undecided voters.[94]

In an extensive Italian 1998 survey[95] directly concerning the advantages and disadvantages of integration and single currency for social groups the data reveals an astonishing consistency: the groups that would profit more from further economic integration were identified with the large distribution storehouses, the banking system, the multinational firms, the big national firms, the shareholders, and the liberal professions. The disadvantaged groups were the small dealers, the saving families, the small firms, the house-owners and those with a fixed income (pensioners, employees). The single currency was seen as having negative consequences for family savings and for salaries. This distinction between the big and the small, the mobile capital and resources and the fixed incomes, property and skills, the resourceful and resourceless, the centrally located, and the peripheral in the socio-economic system emerged in all questions.

Pending judgement about the level of consolidation of citizens' attitudes to the EU, it is difficult to recognize in these orientations a resemblance with the historical combination of class and religious alignments typical of the left–right dimension. In my opinion, it is equally difficult to clearly relate these orientations to the new value dimensions identified by national electoral studies in the last twenty years and opposing duty, law and order, productive efficiency and achievement values versus individualistic orientations towards creativity, spontaneity, self-actualization and hedonism;[96] and dichotomies

---

[94] See the data and the discussion thereof in Detlef, J. and Storsved, A-S., 'Legitimacy through Referendum? The Nearly Successful Domino-Strategy of the EU Referendums in Austria, Finland, Sweden and Norway', *West European Politics*, 18 (1995), 18–37, 33.

[95] Barometro Sociale Abacus, *Italia al Microscopio*. Quaderno no. 5, 11–24 July 1998.

[96] Inglehart, R., 'The Silent Revolution in Europe: Intergenerational Change in Six Countries', *American Political Science Review*, 65 (1971), 991–1017; and Inglehart, R., 'The Changing Cleavage Structure of Political Cleavages in Western Society', in Dalton, Flanagan, and Beck, *Electoral Change in Industrial Democracies*, 25–69; Klages, H., 'Buildung und Wertewandelt', in L. Burkhart (ed.), *Soziologie und gesellschaftiche Entwicklung* (Frankfurt/New York: Campus, 1985), 224–41; Noelle-Neumann, E., 'Wir rüsten

like authoritarian versus libertarian, solidarity versus prosperity, security and prosperity versus ecology, and participation versus security.[97] With almost no exceptions the attitudes towards European integration tend to polarize along a dimension that stresses the opposition line between the perception of new opportunities and mobility options versus the perception of the costs of these. People characterized by objective new life chances and by elements of strong empathy (such as the capacity to see oneself projected in a different existential situation) tend to manifest higher support for integration. People who are less potentially mobile tend to oppose the integration process of their country. The distinction seems to cut across traditional social classes as well as productive sector divisions and also the above-mentioned cultural orientations. The enormous opening up of new opportunities of socio-economic interaction by the integration process seems to be interpreted by people in view of the concrete material opportunities and life chances that they see as implicit in it. The integration process may foster a stronger relationship between these life-chance perceptions and those value orientations more in line with 'option-centred' versus 'roots-centred' preferences.[98]

Conclusions: Electoral Representation Between National and European Arenas

This chapter investigates the electoral representation of the integration issues. It documents the extent to which European issues differentiate the attitudes of voters and parties alike. It argues that the attitudes of national and European parties, of political elites and public opinion towards the constitutive issues of the integration process are hard to interpret referring to historical cleavages or to a left–right dimension. These attitudes are not homogeneous to the traditional national socio-political alignments. If they become salient neither the national nor the European parties are unified and they do not represent their voters. Although we cannot predict the extent to

ab—im Arbeitsleben', *Frankfurter Allgemeine Zeitung*, 25 January1985, 10–11; Vester, M., Von Oertzen, P., Geiling, H., Hermann T., and Müller, D., *Soziale Milieus im gesellschaftlichen Strukturwandel. Zwischen Integration und Ausgrenzung* (Köhl: Bund-Verlag, 1993).

[97] Flanagan, S. C., 'Value Change in Industrial Societies', *American Political Science Review*, 81 (1987), 1303–19; Hertz, T., 'Werte, sozio-politische Konflikte und Generationen. Eine Überprüfung der Theorie des Postmaterialismus', *Zeitschrift für Soziologie*, 16 (1987), 56–69.

[98] It is therefore more in line with the opposition between orientations towards transnationalization and 'informationalisation' versus orientations towards territorial cultural and functional conflicts. See Luke, T. W., 'Class Contradictions and Social Cleavages in Informationalising Post-Industrial Societies: On the Rise of New Social Movements', *New Political Science*, 16/17 (1989), 125–53.

which these latent oppositions will be politicized and mobilized, we can, however, expect that the political preferences based on such oppositions will not be closely aligned with the political divisions on which domestic politics has traditionally been founded.

Constitutive issues such as adhesion, enlargement, democratization, competence definition and institutional powers, refer to the definition of the EU political community and constitutional order, and eventually to its legitimacy. Within the nation-state, these issues had to be solved before the democratic structuring of the polity could take place and political debates could concentrate on polity issues. When this did not happen, and a polity was democratized without legitimation by its community and constitutional order, democratization was likely to challenge the same territorial and constitutional bases of the polity. Within a consolidated political formation differences of opinion/interests on specific issues can be organized in a dimensional and transitive way, and majority decisions are more easily legitimated. On the contrary, differences of opinion/interests on constitutive issues of the political formation cannot be organized in a single dominant continuum without breaking the policy issues dimension, and the resort to majoritarian decision-making is likely to be regarded as illegitimate. One cannot have at the same time a system of representation that concerns the territorial and functional boundaries of a polity and its internal differentiation of opinions/interests. The two alignments delegitimize and destructure each other.

Notwithstanding this, national parties regroup into families at the European level in a European 'party system' made up by vertical and horizontal coordination between national arenas and the European arena. They seem to be able to do so thanks to the decisive support of the EU institutions, to the concentration on national isomorphic issues, and to the capacity to avoid taking stands on constitutive EU issues. Given the negative institutional incentives and the weak representational linkages with their electorates, the Europarties manifest an institutional development that is difficult to explain. This was interpreted as a top-down attempt by political elites to institutionalize an isomorphic party system at the EU level that tends to select those nation-like issues on which a structuring is likely. At the same time, both national and Europarties mute and collude as much as they can on those constitutive EU issues on which their divisions appear insurmountable and that would undermine their effective existence. The European political elites—who are in fact national party political elites—seem to believe that the more integration encompasses broader areas of delegation to the supranational centre, the more the traditional form of electoral legitimation is needed, and the more it becomes necessary to engineer a 'Europarty system'. However, this must stop short of further institutional 'democratization' of the EU. In the light of the above analysis, it is very doubtful that the European party system could perform a political structuring role even if the institutional frame of the EU were to allow and require this. Party families are so inconsistent and divided on EU constitutive issues and on issues of boundary control versus openness that they would find it very difficult to select or even simply sustain a EU executive forced to take clear stands on such issues.

If we cross-tabulate the nature of the issues concerning integration (isomorphic versus constitutive) and the arenas where they can be politicized (national and European), we can describe a set of potential developments (Table 6.2). If national type issues prevail in both arenas, we have the maximum likelihood of the structuring of a European party system that is isomorphic to the national ones (*isomorphic structuring*). If EU constitutive issues politicize in the national arenas while the European arena continues to be structured along national type issues, we will witness the development of a *split party system*, with the two levels dealing with different kinds of issues and characterized by different kinds of alignments of the same parties. In this case national alignments suffer the biggest strain. However, EU issues can be politicized in the national arenas with relatively limited consequences as the EU system allows for considerable flexibility with its intergovernmental component (postponing a treaty ratification or other legislative incorporations; not joining some functional regime of the EU, etc.). A split party system also results if national elections continue to be fought around national issues while in the European arena constitutive issues are politicized. However, as EU-constitutive issues tend to nationalize European party families, they cannot be discussed in the European parliamentary arena without disruptive consequences for its own autonomy and legitimation as a supranational body (different from the intergovernmental Council). The 'unified' EP does not allow the same flexibility as the multiple national

TABLE 6.2. *Predominant issues, arenas, and types of party system structuring*

	National Arena	Type of party system structuring	EU Arena
National issues	Domestic politicization of functional issues	Isomorphic structuring	EU politicization of functional issues
		Split party system	
EU constitutive issues	Domestic politicization of constitutive issues	European mass politics	EU politicization of constitutive issues

arenas, whose differences are mediated by the intergovernmental negotiations. Finally, if constitutive issues were politicized both at the national and European levels, we would observe the development of a *mass politics party system* with destructuring effect for the prevailing alignment at both levels: a party system in which left–right alignments are destructured by territorial and EU constitutive issues alignments, and EU constitutive issue alignments are destructured by left–right ideological families.

In the present situation, Europarties perform only one role among the many played in national politics: they organize the infrastructure of the working of the EP, structuring the election outcomes into a small set of options; organizing MPs in parliamentary groups and in legislative coalitions, disciplining their members' behaviour in the chamber, committees, and agenda-setting processes. Europarties do not bring up, solicit, channel, aggregate citizens' and groups' demands; they do not identify and voice a political demand that is wanting. If anything, they actively engage in diluting, hiding and muting every demand that could engender their cohesion. Europarties do not compete—that is, argue different thinks, try to embarrass each other, seek places and leadership positions, and select policy stands and political tactics—*in view of electoral rewards*. The mentioned incipient party competition refers to policy differentiation and voting behaviour differences, but none of what is done in the EP has a bearing on the electoral fortunes of national and Europarties. Europarties do not guarantee political *responsibility* by selecting the top political personnel and, therefore, ultimately conferring, either directly or indirectly, a decision-making power.

In this situation an empowerment of Europarties can only originate from the institutional empowerment of their arena: the EP. This can indeed result from (*a*) the unintended effects of the high interinstitutional competition at the EU level, or (*b*) the intended reactions resulting from a radical and common challenge. The two main EU hierarchical orders of the Council and the Commission are bound to live together, in cooperation and in conflict. As a third institutional order, the EP and the Europarties may draw advantages from their conflicts and deadlocks. Unintended empowerment via interinstitution competition closely resembles those national experiences where parties carved their way into the institutions taking advantage of conflicts between the Crown and its bureaucracy, the non-elective higher chambers and the elective lower ones. In their attempts to check the power of the dynastic circles, those of the bureaucracy and of hereditary first chambers, early liberal forces did not intend to establish extensive parliamentarization, disciplined parliamentary groups, and even less so party-government. These were largely unintended effects from their point of view. Similarly, it cannot be excluded that the increasing role of the EP and of the Europarties may result from second-best compromises in the institutional and competence conflicts among the top institutions of the EU. A commonly perceived radical challenge could derive instead from a loss of control of voters, groups, and personnel *at the national level*, where parties continue to draw their sources of power and existence. The losing control of the national policy agenda in a growing number of areas and the growing salience of European issues in national electorates may suggest that exclusive national strategies are insufficient, particularly in view of the fact that main parties see further integration as necessary and unavoidable. In the present configuration, national parties will care about the EU arenas and will try to control them more directly, if and when this lack of control jeopardizes the bases of their national existence. This latter point requires a little *coda* about the impact of integration on national electoral representation.

If the weakness of the European party system is not contingent and accidental, but structural, how big is the challenge for national parties embedded in the integration process? Table 6.3 summarizes the impact of integration on the national electoral representation distinguishing the level (the political system, the party system, the party and within-party) and a direct and indirect effect. If we extend the study beyond the more direct effects discussed in the chapter (new parties; new issue dimensions; electoral realignments; organizational problems of vertical and horizontal coordination; internal cohesion), a set of indirect domestic consequences emerge. They pertain mainly to (*a*) the changing balance between electoral and other channels of representation (corporate and territorial) as a result of the redistribution of national-resource control within the multilevel supranational system; (*b*) the consequences for partisan identities of the collusive pushes among national parties on EU related issues; and (*c*) the potential loosening of the internal hierarchical structure of the parties themselves as a result of new factional and new territorial conflicts. In fact, integration affects both the *effective* and *identifying* representation activities of national parties; [99] that is, those activities that aim at either improving or preserving the positions of the collective groups they want to represent, and those activities that aim at building, maintaining and strengthening collective partisan identities through symbolic initiatives.

At the national level, parties may find it difficult to continue to perform that role of national harmonizers of the inconsistencies and conflicts among the different principles, structures and agents of territorial, corporate and electoral representation referred to in the introduction of this chapter. There, it was argued that this harmonizing role resulted from a high capacity to

---

[99] See Pizzorno, A., 'Sulla razionalità della scelta democratica', *Stato e Mercato*, 7 (1983), 3–46, 33–4.

TABLE 6.3. *Impact of European integration on national electoral representation: synthetic summary*

Level	Problem	Direct impact	Indirect impact
Political system	Role of the parties	-	Further reduction of resource control at the national level Changes in the balance among different channels of representation
Party system	Format changes	New parties	Collusive pushes among established parties
	Electoral alignments	New issue dimensions	
	Pattern of competition	Latent or open realignments	
Party	Coordination with transnational federations	Problems of vertical coordination and supranational alliances Organizational changes	-
Within party	Factional and centre–periphery divisions	Party splits	Loosening of the internal hierarchical order

induce conformity of mass political behaviours combined with a high capacity to harmonize different inputs within the institutional configuration of the political system. This historical role is affected by the parties' loss of control over national resources (material, regulative, jurisdictional) and over 'unlocked' national actors that is implicit in the supranational integration. This loss of control is reflected in a changing balance with the corporate and the territorial channels of representation. So far the development of the EU has empowered far more interest groups and territorial subnational units than national or transnational political parties. The institutional assistance that is offered to Europarties can be seen as a way of re-balancing the legitimation system. But electoral representation rests on far more demanding preconditions than the loose system of interest and territorial entities consultation and incorporation. Therefore, integration tends to challenge the national harmonizing role of national parties opening a wider set of representational options and new spaces for the organization of representation through other channels. Parties may continue to structure the alternatives for national electorates, but they will tend to lose the capacity to control and to discipline actors and resources in the other two channels.

Citizens as voters are still locked in the national political representation system, which cannot be exited except by physically walking away. Therefore, parties will continue to depend on national elections and on national representation systems for their survival, and citizens will continue to be offered national partisan alternatives. On the contrary, citizens in their capacities other than that of voters—as savers, as consumers, as investors, as litigants, as welfare recipients, etc.—enjoy growing opportunities to exit the national political system, to find and access new avenues to express their interests and ideas, to pressurize for alternative centres of decision-making, to access material, regulative and jurisdictional resources different from those once monopolized by the nation-state and its party elites. The EU's institutions and negotiations shift the balance of domestic political power and redistribute control over policy initiative, open and close channels for domestic actors to influence the initiation of policy, and contribute towards a decline in policy competition among parties in the direction of what I elsewhere labelled 'collusive democracy'.[100] Parties have a weak capacity to react to these changes in the spheres of territorial, corporate group and individual redefinition of interests and identities and they make considerable efforts to manoeuvre and to collude in order to keep them under control. They largely define the EU issues as valence issues, but these collusive pushes provide quite large opportunities for anti-EU peripheral elites to exploit the tacit consensus against the established parties. This explains why most of the debates, conflicts and mobilization from below concerning EU affairs cannot be organized but 'against the EU' and must take an 'anti' and negative overtone.

Moreover, such collusive pushes contribute further to the general problems of parties in their 'identifying representation' role. Every process of formation, maintenance and consolidation of identity—political and partisan identities included—requires the normative construction of the responsibility and of a system of sanctions. For quite a long time parties have remained the central site for the formation of partisan identifications and of the norms of solidarity on which the former could be moulded and restated. Now, in the context of the EU system characterized by more *vertical levels* [101] and also by multiple *horizontal sites* of decision-making, the traditional image of those who hold hierarchically ordered competences and

---

[100] Bartolini, S., 'Collusion, Competition and Democracy', Part 1 and 2, *Journal of Theoretical Politics*, 11 (1999), 435–70; 12 (2000), 33–65.

[101] See Marks, G., Scharpf, F., Schmitter, P., and Streek, W., *Multi-level Governance in the Emerging Euro-Polity* (London: Sage, 1997).

responsibilities has crumbled. The pluralization of the regimes and the inter-twining of the decisional levels complicate the perception of the systemic dynamics; competences are vague and ambiguously defined, and this com-plexity allows the various subsystems—each with its own rationality of action: competence, resource control, legitimacy, etc.—to shift to the exterior the consequences of their actions. This makes it difficult to distinguish to whom to attribute responsibility and direct expectations, and confounds the definition and reinforcement of partisan identities.

Narrowing the adversarial political agenda may trivialize public life and make it useless. The integration process and institutions attribute the respon-sibility for actions to politically uncontrollable potencies, agencies, and networks of bargaining relationships. Problems are referred to international and intergovernmental institutions, courts, and technical regulatory bodies. Issues which are crucial for group identity and solidarity are depoliticized and transferred to higher or lower decisional loci because they are politically intractable, or because the political elite find it inconvenient to deal with them. But whatever is expelled from the adversarial political competition and from the attribution of direct political responsibility can no longer constitute the basis for significant partisan allegiances. The group attachments related to these *non*-issues will no longer provide a basis for politically salient group solidarity. Just as political competition may reinforce political identities, it can also undermine them. The attachments of these groups' will either give rise to social movements outside the party system, or they will tend to decline as a focus for group political identity.[102]

In this way, the competition avoidance and the issue displacement to other domains which is implicit in many aspects of the integration process contrib-utes to national political dealignment, depriving political contestation of those issues that constitute the stronger basis of politically salient group solidarity, and correspondingly weakening the 'identifying representation' aspect of partisan activities. The changing style of national party competition which is implied by the devolution of issues to the supranational level and to the corporate, territorial and intergovernmental channel of pressure and negotiation is a dynamics that reinforces the party system dealignment tendencies at the societal and institutional level in this historical period. National parties may soon discover the importance of the development of

---

[102] This, of course, applies also to national issues that have little or nothing to do with the EU. If religious feelings, preferences and customs are depoliticized and transferred into private preference matters by specific constitutional solutions, then religious attachment can no longer constitute the long-term basis for significant political allegiances. If issues of private versus public schools, pension pillars, and health care are removed from the political debate via legal or constitutional provisions which empower every individual citizen with the right of choice, then another issue is depoliticized, with consequences for those individuals for whom this was a politically salient and identity building issue.

the European issues and of the European arenas for the *national* control of their voters.

At the present time, not much can be done to strengthen electoral representation in the European party system, and not much can be done to insulate the national party system from the consequences of integration. The current situation witnesses an imbalance between the lack of party system structuring at the EU level and the growing potential for party system destructuring at the national level.

7

Restructuring Europe

In this final chapter I will review the main arguments of this work as they were presented. First, I interpret European integration in a long-term historical perspective and in relation to the preceding phases of the development of the European system of states, as sketched in Chapter 2. I then discuss analytically the macro and micro consequences of the boundary-redrawing activities for different types of actors, following the outline of Chapter 1. Finally, I relate the institutional and boundary configuration of the new EU centre (as discussed in Chapters 3 and 4) to the main structures of representation at the national and EU level (the subject of Chapters 5 and 6). This third part is more speculative in relation to possible developments.

European Integration in Historical Perspective:
The Sixth Developmental Process of the European Nation-State

At the beginning of the sixteenth century, early territorial states with weak markets predominated in the west maritime, and north and east continental peripheries of Europe. In the continental city and trade belt, extensive market networks prevailed over the weak universalistic hierarchies of the empire and the papacy, without states. The opposition between 'marketless peripheral states' and 'stateless central networks' captures the essential openness of the system at that stage. In the subsequent four centuries, states won over markets, with the trend moving towards the extension and imitation of the state model throughout the continent and towards the boundedness of the market forces within such state capsule. There were shorter-term fluctuations, the last of which was the 'great transformation'[1] from the attempt to set a global self-regulating market in the second half of the nineteenth century to the state interventionism of the corporatist, communist and social

[1] Polanyi, K., *The Great Transformation. The Political and Economic Origins of Our Times* (Boston, MA: Beacon Press, 1957 (1944)).

democratic models that materialized at the beginning of the twentieth century and culminated after the Second World War. In the last phase of the twentieth century we have witnessed a 'striking back' of the market at the expense of the state. It remains to be seen whether this is only one short-term fluctuation or the beginning of a more profound redefinition of the role of the state in European civilization.

In a broad historical perspective, European integration can be conceived as the sixth major developmental trend in the history of Europe since the sixteenth century. As discussed in Chapter 2, the first was *state building*, with its historical progressive coincidence of regulatory orders into administrative and military spheres under the supremacy of a single set of hierarchically organized territorial institutions. The second was the *development of capitalism*, which, notwithstanding its potential un-boundedness, was nourished within the capsule of the state with the formation of the national markets. The third was *nation formation*, with the strengthening of cultural boundaries and the creation of equality areas of cultural solidarity and common cultural standards. The fourth was the process of *democratization*, with the progressive articulation, recognition and legitimation of the institutional channels and political agencies for internal voice structuring. The fifth was the formation of *welfare systems*, with the development of the social sharing institutions for culturally homogeneous national communities.

State and nation building created the wrapping within which capitalism developed. These processes produced the accretion of national centre power and capacities and the building of a system of loyalties and identities within which the right of participation to collective decision-making and the policies of social sharing could develop. Party systems and welfare institutions constituted the crucial mechanisms of identification and legitimation that politically stabilized societies characterized by high rates of socio-economic changes and the coincidence of different boundaries that characterized the nation-state generated processes of political structuring on all fronts. As the state engaged in the nationalization of the masses and in cultural standardization, it engendered opposition and resistance from culturally distinctive groups. Economic oppositions in the market were politicized and brought to bear on the central decision-making arenas, particularly if and where the state appeared more openly as the defender of particular economic groups of the landed and/or bourgeois type. Politico-administrative resistance and opposition concerned the reach and scope of the state competencies and regulative/extractive capacities. Cultural, economic and politico-administrative lines of conflict and opposition thus overlapped and sometimes reinforced each other, contributing to the political 'vertebration' of civic society and to the accommodation of different interests within the state through representation and incorporation.

The hundred years running from the 1860s to the 1960s were crucial. Up to the First World War, trade and financial markets were not regulated either at the national or international level. Most states were not yet fully democratic and their political elites were only partially and incompletely submitted to political responsibility towards the enlarged citizenry. After the First World War, the gold standard and freedom of exchanges were re-established, but were accompanied by suffrage extension, the legalization and generalization of union activities, and the beginning of social insurance policies. When, in the 1920s, the international economic crisis generated mass unemployment, nation-states reacted differently but in general they developed new forms of control of economic activities within their borders, as well as reintroducing some of the old ones. Protectionist and autarchic strategies, tariffs, competitive devaluations, rigid control of capitals transfer, subvention to exports and quantitative restrictions to imports led the boundaries of the markets to coincide to a large extent with the politico-administrative boundaries of the state. In addition, all sorts of socio-economic practices were renationalized. Together with the mass nationalistic mobilization of the two world wars, franchise expansion, social right institutionalization, and the channelling of voice via mass parties and welfare bureaucracies strengthened the boundaries with the outside people, reinforcing the equality area within which the most striking health, wealth, and status inequalities were defined as unacceptable among fellow citizens. As a result, the cultural costs to exit increased together with the material ones.

After the Second World War, a balance was reached by which governments could exploit the capitalist capacity to generate profit and innovation by using the macro management of the economy without constraining excessively the choices of producers and consumers. An effective locking in of capital allowed the development of a wider set of public goods to be produced by the political system and forced capital and investors to accept negotiated orders yielding parts of their profits to domestic redistribution. The costs of these regulations were thus transferred to consumers, who had few exit opportunities given the controls and restrictions on exchanges. Political competition by vote and organization pressure with a view to influence the expanded public policy domain became more important. Mass political organizations increased their political legitimacy by offering political support to the essential rights and interests of capital and private property in exchange for the concessions of the key resource controllers.

In short, the considerable extension of the social practices following various forms of political, social and economic mobilization was made to strongly overlap with the rules for collective deliberation and with the socially important means for individual orientation. If people shared a sense of being part of one collectivity, and if most social practices were

bounded territorially, then the polity had legitimate rules for taking collectivized decisions, including those that implied redistribution choices. In the
twentieth century, through the agony of dramatic security and economic
crisis, the triangle of the nation-state was completed, linking cultural identities and solidarities closely to political participation institutions and to
social sharing institutions, each of them depending on and reinforced by
the others.

Integration, as a sixth powerful phase in the development of the European
system of states, economies, nations, democracies, and welfares, necessarily
relates to each of the five preceding phases. Figure 7.1 succinctly summarizes
the argument that follows via a set of arrows. The process of European
integration was triggered by two main problem-pressures. On the one
hand, it was driven by the unbearable costs of the rivalries of the state
systems in an era of war technologies whose destructive power had become
disproportionate to the stake of the rivalries themselves. On the other, it was
driven by the growing pressure deriving from the slow but significant economic peripheralization of Europe in the post-Second World War world
economy and the corresponding perception of the inadequacy of the European state as a unit of economic organization in world competition.
European integration can therefore be historically interpreted as a response
by national elites to the weakening of the European state system and to the
new pressure brought to bear by capitalist world development.

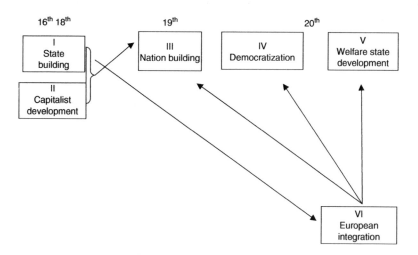

FIGURE 7.1. The six developmental trends in European
history since the sixteenth century

The history of the European integration cannot be adequately explained by reference to the intellectual and political debates preceding its birth and generated by the plans and proposals such as those of Aristide Briand and his associates in France, Brailsford and his associates in Britain, the movement around the Manifesto di Ventotene, or the many others initiatives following along these lines between the end of the First World War and 1951–57.[2] A careful analysis of the way in which interests were perceived nationally should not be considered as any less important. Nevertheless, a strong opposition between 'interests' and 'ideas' among the European political elites is equally unrealistic, if not naive. Without the post-war climate of the historical failure and inadequacy of the European state system—which the leaders, intellectuals and relatively marginal opinion movements mentioned were particularly sensitive about—no attempts would have been made to overcome the deep interest differentiations that existed. At the same time, negotiations for integration were able to concentrate on the areas of trade and policy coordination thanks to the overall situation as a result of which the monetary and military integration of the Western European states was guaranteed by their Atlantic integration. The 'rationality' of the states engaging in the cooperation cannot be understood without making recourse to this widespread perception of failure of the previous state system, on the one hand, and, on the other, the removal of monetary and military issues that was guaranteed by the Atlantic integration.[3] To posit that European integration was the result of a reaction by the European political elites against the inadequacy of the state as a capsule of economic and military competition is therefore non inconsistent with the idea that the *concrete outcomes* of the integration resulted from economic interest-based negotiations among asymmetric power actors.[4]

The integration process was conceived at the height of the phase of bounded national communities, but started to produce its more significant effects in conjunction with other international processes from the mid-1970s onwards.[5] Since then, its need to come to grips with the other features of the

---

[2] Documented in Lipgens, W., *A History of European Integration*, Vol. 1 (1945–1950) (Oxford: Clarendon Press, 1982).

[3] This idea is consistent with the difficult and unenthusiastic participation of France and Great Britain, as old nation-states, countries victorious in both World Wars, and persisting colonial powers. For the early French and British positions see Gilbert, M., 'Il processo storico dell'Europa Integrata', in S. Fabbrini (ed.), *L'Unione Europea. Le istituzioni e gli attori di un sistema sovranazionale* (Roma-Bari: Editori Laterza, 2002), 39–72, 43–56.

[4] Both Milward, A. S., *The European Rescue of the Nation State* (London: Routledge, 1992); and Moravcsik, A., *The Choice for Europe. Social Purpose and State Power from Messina to Maastricht* (Ithaca, NY: Cornell University Press, 1998) forcefully argue this thesis.

[5] In this work I have not used the much-abused term 'globalization'. The pages that follow discuss the relationship between European integration and what could be generally

state that were left outside the initial project has become more obvious: the national, democratic and welfare features. This relationship gives the impression of being problematic and contradictory. Nation building, democratization and welfare state development were closely linked to the state as a bounded territory and to its internal cultural homogeneity.[6] The founding and legitimation of the political obligations binding citizens make continuous reference to the cultural homogeneity and solidarity on which their state rests; at the same time, the democratic decision-making and the redistribution of material resources similarly rest on strong collective identities and solidarity ties—that is, on high cultural costs of exit—and on the difficulty of subtracting resources from the social obligations contracted on a territorial basis—that is, on high material costs of exit. The process of European economic integration is predicated upon the removal of boundaries among the pre-existing system of states with the aim of achieving a 'scale' sufficient to overcome their inadequacy. On the contrary, the national, democratic and welfare features of the states are predicated upon their continued control over redistributive capacities, cultural symbols and political authority. In this sense, European integration progressively represents a direct challenge to the latter.

European integration has opened up a new phase of wide-ranging expansion of social practices that breaks up the three-layered coherence between

called 'globalization' without resorting to this term. This, perhaps, requires a brief clarification of how 'globalization' fits into my argument. On the one hand, given the large literature and the many meanings associated with it, the definition and precise use of the term 'globalization' requires an extensive review and discussion which I have considered unnecessary in this context. On the other, its generic use does not really demand a special term. In my perspective, the generic term of 'globalization' point to the process of 'lowering' and growing 'permeability' of the boundaries of territorial systems, particularly accentuated in the economic and cultural spheres. In historical terms, 'globalization' enters my argument as the growing perception by the European political and economic elites of the inadequacy of the nation-state as efficient capsule of economic and military competition. Therefore, at the analytical level the meaning of 'globalization' and 'integration' can be both referred to boundary transcendence among the (global and European) system of states. The crucial difference clearly lies in the fact that boundary transcendence is governed through the process of new supranational centre formation at the European level, and it is, therefore, more intense and institutionally assisted within Europe than at the global level. Moreover, the presence of a centre in and of European integration obviously points to the possibility that the latter be directed towards the setting of new external boundaries, and to be, or become, a check or countervailing force to the global boundary transcendence (i.e. to what is usually labelled 'globalization'). In other words, European integration can be interpreted in terms of the relationship between boundary removing and boundary building, while 'globalization' is predominantly, if not exclusively seen as boundary transcendence (although there are some references in the literature to the trend towards the formation of new 'global' centres of governance).

[6] Miller emphasizes this link to the extent of making democracy and social sharing rest entirely on the nationality principle; Miller, D., *On Nationality* (Oxford: Oxford University Press, 1995).

identities, practices and institutions, or—following the terminology used in Chapter 1—dismantles the coincidence among the different types of state economic, cultural, politico-administrative and coercion boundaries. Within the EU, there is increasingly less overlap among the economic, political, and cultural boundaries and the dissonance between the spheres of social identities and the enlarged socio-economic practices is growing. The formation of social identities is also freer than in the past from the determination of cultural and social policies controlling cross-boundaries exchange of people, messages, and goods. This situation is embedded in the fundamental *openness* of the new system, and in its limited capacity to generate European-wide territorial consolidation while actively removing within-Europe boundaries.

To a certain extent, the limited capacity of EU system building reflects the limitations of the role of the state in highly decentralized contexts, which have a lower propensity to public spending and social protection[7] as well as a less penetrating nationwide political organization and thinner territorial identities. However, the weakness of the EU system building goes beyond this scale limitation and can be observed both in its market boundaries as well as in its legal and territorial ones.

The cornerstones of the integration process remain: (*a*) the formation of a transnational space for transactions within which the demands and supply of the European economic agents can operate without any interference of customs, fiscal, exchange, or other measures of discrimination (a common market); (*b*) the formation of a transnational space with uniform legal foundations for economic interactions through the convergence and centralized administration of the juridical foundations of economic activity; and (*c*) the monetary integration and centralized administration of the currency.

The 'common market' should be a 'protected' space for economic relations and its level of closure should be collectively regulated as a result of the general goals of the EU. However, this protection is limited. Since the 1980s,

---

[7] A large literature supports this thesis: Wilensky, A., *The welfare state and equality* (Berkeley, CA: University of California Press, 1975), 52; Cameron, D., 'The expansion of the public economy: A comparative analysis', *American Political Science Review*, 72 (1978), 1243–61; Castles, F. G. and McKinlay, R., 'Does politics matter? An analysis of the public welfare commitment in advanced democratic states', *European Journal of Political Research*, 7 (1979), 169–86; Huber, E., Ragin, C. and Stephens, J. D., 'Social democracy, Christian democracy, constitutional structure and the welfare state', *American Journal of Sociology*, 99 (1993), 711–49; Schmidt, M. G., 'When Parties Matter: A Review of the Possibilities and Limits of Partisan Influence on Public Policy', *European Journal of Political Research*, 30 (1996), 155–83; Castles, F. G., 'Decentralization and the Post-War Political Economy', *European Journal of Political Research*, 36 (1999), 27–53. For opposite opinions see Korpi, W., 'Power, Politics and the State Autonomy in the Development of Social Citizenship', *American Sociological Review*, 54 (1989), 309–29; and Pampel, F. C. and Williamson, J. B., *Age, Class, Politics and the Welfare State* (Cambridge: Cambridge University Press, 1989).

the internationalization of European economies has progressed hand in hand with European integration. In the 1950s and 1960s, the removal of economic boundaries was a political project that advanced economic integration beyond what the economic forces might have wanted. In the 1980s and 1990s, this boundary removal became a simple ratification of trends that were imposed on the Community by the internationalization not only of trade, but also of capital markets, technologies, etc. The integration process thus characterized over a long period by the careful control of the amount of goods and capitals entering and exiting the system. Within the context of the formation of a market big enough to take advantage of scale economies, the system was kept sufficiently closed to guarantee the attainment of the economic goals fixed politically. In the last twenty years, the process of internationalization has transformed from being an intrinsic tendency to be regulated to one that needs to be fostered. The liberalization of international exchanges has become an instrument by which to pursue the goal of economic growth and it has gained an ideological value in the public debate. The EU is loosing the instruments of control of the evolution of the economic system. Viewed in this perspective, the European 'common' market is losing most of its earlier meaning, which was related to a certain degree of external closure of the European economic system. A market exists through its relational boundaries; if there is no relation to some level of operational closure, a single market simply becomes a section of the global market.

The important correlate of this 'openness' is that the process of internationalization also erodes the idea of a European juridical space. The de-differentiation of the European juridical foundations of economic (and related) activities is one of the EU developments that has had the most wideranging effects.[8] This legal integration has possibly been facilitated by the longstanding pre-nation-state European legal tradition, in which law developed quite independently from state structures rather then being, as rationalized later, their quintessential element.[9] Until the sixteenth and seventeenth centuries European jurists used a common legal grammar and referred to a *jus commune* that had for a long time constituted a unified European legal culture based on the heritage of Roman (and canon) law. From the eleventh-century rediscovery of the Digest,[10] law and legal

---

[8] Weiler, J. H. H., 'The Transformation of Europe', *Yale Law Journal*, 50 (1991), 2403–83.

[9] On the medieval juridical order interpreted as 'law without state' see the fundamental work by Grossi, P., *L'ordine giuridico medievale* (Roma-Bari: Laterza, 1997).

[10] The origin of European legal theory and science is to be found in Justinian's '*corpus juris civilis*', as it was taught at the University of Bologna during the eleventh century, when a teacher of rhetoric (Irnerius) obtained a transcribed version of Justinian's Digest copied directly from the Digest of the sixth century. Since then, the Digest had disappeared from Italy and from Italian legal practice but maintained its place in Constantinople and the

reasoning were understood as an application of 'universal' legal principles, which were not based on context dependent customary law but on the formal rigour of methodical, disciplined, and scientific reasoning. Lawyers were trained in Roman and canon law regardless of where they came from, and the mobility of lawyers as academics and practitioners highlighted the 'universality' of law and legal training and its 'portability'.[11]

It the eighteenth century, this common heritage deprived of ethno-culturally or state specific bases, began to change through a process of legal territorial differentiation. The territorial state, first, and the nation-state, later, emerged as the imagined a priori element of law and the legal system, accompanied by the nationalization of legal training. Legal education thus acted as a fostering element of loyalty towards the nation-state. The latter regulated the opportunity to access knowledge, to be educated within its own framework of reference, to control credentials for practitioners, and to limit territorially the mobility of legally trained citizens. The trend for the modern state was in fact to legitimize its role, scope and reach of activities by 'nationalizing' the law and the legal system. This development also occurred because the absolute sovereignty of states militated against the idea of their being bounded any longer by universal legal principles.[12] In the end, the idea that law can exist independently of the framework of the nation-state lost grounds with respect to the idea that it can maintain itself and be realized only within the hierarchical structures of the state.[13]

On this view, the EU can be interpreted as supporting a new tendency moving towards the de-differentiation of law and legal traditions and giving rise to a new legal universalism, where law is no longer intrinsically linked to and only viable within the state.[14] In this perspective, the state becomes one jurisdiction among many, which needs to take into account the decisions taken by other legal instances when faced with similar matters. WTO law, for instance, is sometimes interpreted[15] as a sort of constitutional law which is

Byzantine Empire, where it remained a prevailing legal source until the fall of the empire in the fifteenth century.

[11] For these notes on law history see Mannori, L. and Sordi, B., *Storia del diritto amministrativo* (Roma: Editori Laterza, 2001 (1957)).

[12] Even if elements of legal universalism continued to be upheld by some theorists, as in Kant's '*Weltburger*' and legal order for all mankind.

[13] As, for instance, Kelsen, H., *The Pure Theory of Law* (Berkeley/Los Angeles: University of California Press, 1967).

[14] For a theory aiming at separating law from the state see MacCormick, N., *Questioning Sovereignty. Law, State and Nation in the European Commonwealth* (Oxford: Oxford University Press, 1999), Chapters 7 and 8.

[15] For instance Petersmann, E.-U., 'The WTO Constitution and Human Rights', *Journal of International Economic Law*, 3 (2000), 19–25; Petersmann, E.-U., 'The Transformation of the World Trading System through the 1994 Agreement Establishing the World Trade Organization', *European Journal of International Law*, 6 (1995), 161–89. The

even higher than the 'constitutional' treaties of the EU, in line and in agreement with the internal European economic constitution understood as a deregulatory constitution. This constitutional role is linked to the interpretation of substantive WTO law as functional to realizing the basic individual freedom of choice of entrepreneurs and consumers, giving rights to individuals against domestic legislation and other acts of public authorities under the supervising principle of 'economic rationality'.[16] In connection with economic activities, this new legal universalism assumes that the role of supranational orders is to limit regulatory and legislative intervention by the domestic political systems, and bring to an end the historical phase characterized by the close grip of politics on the economy through law.[17]

This openness of the national as well as the European legal systems can be seen as the 'crumbling' of the special status of the state as a positive law producer;[18] as the emergence of autonomous spheres of societal relations that are 'liberated' from all concrete spatial references and independent of the state intervention, as well as protected from it;[19] as a new form of 'hybrid governance' challenging constitutional law across national jurisdictions via the hybridization of public-private and national-foreign governing bodies;[20] as a 'privatization' and 'de-territorialization' of the production of rights and of a stabilized and generalized behavioural conformity associated with the truly transnational nature of the new 'Lex Mercatoria', and, more generally, with the development of supranational or transnational

question of the direct effect of WTO law is the object of a controversial debate in international trade law. On EU and WTO law see the collection by De Burca, G. and Scott, J. (eds.), *The EU and the WTO. Legal and Constitutional Issues* (Oxford: Hart Publishing, 2001).

[16] The protection of the operating of the economic process in its wealth-creating function against interfering political majorities using sub-optimal instruments is, of course, one of the longstanding demands of liberal economic theory. See Friedman, M., *Capitalism and Freedom* (Chicago: University of Chicago Press, 1962), 13–15.

[17] For a discussion of the normative implications of this thesis see Bogdandy, A. Von, 'Law and Politics in the WTO. Strategies to Cope with a Deficient Relationship', *Max Planck Yearbook of United Nation Law*, 5 (2001), 609–74. For general concerns about the relationship between lego-economic globalization and democracy see Dahrendorf, R., 'Anmerkungen zur Globalisierung', in U. Beck (ed.), *Perspektiven der Weltgesellschaft* (Frankfurt am Main: Suhrkamp Verlag, 1998), 41–54 ; Guéhenno, J.-M., 'From Territorial Communities to Communities of Choice: Implications for Democracy', in W. Streek (ed.), *Internationale Wirtschaft, nationale Demokratie* (Frankfurt: Campus Verlag, 1998), 137–40.

[18] Willke, H., 'The Tragedy of the State. Prolegomena to a Theory of the State in Polycentric Society', *Archiv für Rechts und Sozialphilosophie*, 72 (1987), 455–67, 465–7.

[19] Vesting, T., 'The Network economy as a Challenge to Create New Public Law (beyond the state)' (Florence: European University Institute, 2001), Workshop on Global Governance, 6–7 April.

[20] The term 'hybrid governance' is coined by Engel, C., 'Hybrid Governance Across National Jurisdictions as a Challenge to Constitutional Law', *European Business Organization Law Review*, 2 (2001), 569–83.

regimes.[21] Whatever the interpretation, de facto, the European legal de-differentiation does not translate into the building of an integrated European legal system of positive law.

Therefore, the internationalization of the economic process that moves a significant part of the value and profit formation outside the borders of Europe, in countries with profoundly different systems of economic and property rights, is accompanied by the openness of the EU common market and legal framework. Thus, the system of property rights within a given territorial space is losing its meaning if the well-being of European citizens ends up by depending on transactions with agents from other countries who operate on the basis of different legal foundations, which are often in contrast with those of Europe. Different systems of property represent different systems of incentives and of constraints and, in the end, of production conditions, and the market cannot therefore determine an 'equitable' exchange starting from legal foundations that are profoundly in contrast.

For this reason, the early idea of a common market was linked to the need to harmonize and homogenize the legal foundation of property rights and of economic interactions across Europe. In a situation of open boundaries between the European common market and broader markets without any common legal foundation, the European economic performance will eventually depend on factors on the suppression of which we have grounded the moral legitimacy of the European project (the elimination of the differential legal foundations).[22] The convergence of European legal foundations is a crucial integration development, but the model of market relations towards which to converge—which one could define as the 'political' or 'ethical' dimension of the project of convergence—tends to get lost in the process, or is simply reduced to a model of generalized openness that undermines the capacity for a political production of rights and titles by the new integrated system.

Paradoxically, two recent developments like the monetary unification and the continuous territorial enlargement contribute to this situation of weak political production. While monetary unification is the quintessential process

---

[21] As a private system of legal arbitration the new Lex Mercatora offers jurisdiction on the basis of norms that are defined autonomously and collectively. This law production is addressed to corporations and firms, bypassing national and international judicial and jurisdictional systems. It represents a new form of political production based on reputation sanctions that affect the possibility to reiterate the mutually advantageous relationship of market exchange. It is, therefore, unrelated to a specific territory and is not based on the threat of coercion or physical violence. See Stone, A., 'Islands of Transnational Governance', in C. Ansell and G. Di Palma (eds.), *Restructuring Territoriality: Europe and the United States Compared* (Cambridge: Cambridge University Press, 2004), 122–44.

[22] See on this point Calafati, A., 'L'Italia e la de-costruzione economica dell'Europa', *Foedus*, no. 6 (2003), 19–33.

of economic boundary building, continuous enlargement is a quintessential process of continuous political community redefinition. If the lack of a centralized coercion power makes the difference between a 'community' and a real 'federal' structure, in monetary policy the transfer of power to the federal level is full and the monetary subsystem is a federal subsystem in a non-federal system. The currency powers given to the ECB and the European System of Central Banks is directly operational, with no intermediation. The direct implication and effectiveness of the decisions achieve the perfect identity between the juridical and the economic orders, in which all powers are transferred in an exclusive way—and no subordinate state implementation is necessary—and where the direct relationship between citizens and the federal state is guaranteed by the function of the currency itself.

However, the setting up of this powerful subsystem, transforming national economic disequilibria into European economic disequilibria, has taken place without any new configuration of the mechanisms of regulation made necessary by the new common currency being set up. That is, none of the nationally abolished mechanisms of regulation (rates of exchange, rates of interest, currency supply) have been restored at the European level. Indeed, the pre- (and self-) defined goals of the ECB limit the possibility of using this new strong boundary for the achievement of any other specific goal beyond price stability. As a result, the EMU cannot in its present form be used as an instrument to govern the internationalization of the European economies; neither can it be used to set the limits of the scale economies sought or of the volume and directions of commercial transactions. In other words, the EMU cannot be used to reintroduce a level of closure for the European economies that is coherent and useful to the desired structure of the European system, and, in the end, functional to the EU interests and economic hegemony.

Similarly, the current ongoing and apparently unbound enlargement process (beyond the twenty-five, towards unknown east and south-east territories), continuously redefining the borders of the system, also continuously redefines the scale and complexity of its decision-making processes. Clearly, no system can have an institutional structure that is independent of the scale of its processes. The current and foreseen enlargements move the size of the European system to limits beyond which the current process of formation of the economic and territorial policies of the EU becomes impracticable, and beyond which it becomes almost impossible to plan a system of transnational regulation different from a mere custom union or free trade area. It is difficult to imagine the viability of a common monetary policy, a CAP, a coordinated budget policy (leaving aside the definition of common geopolitical interests), etc., extending its effects to an economic reality and a geographical space stretching from Finland to Cyprus (or Turkey) and from Portugal to

Rumania (or Ukraine).[23] There is, indeed, room for wide doubt as to whether the limited instruments so far developed for intervention in the economic sphere can be practicable or effective on this new territorial scale.

Historically, therefore, European integration is a new phase of nation-state boundary transcendence, resulting in the de-differentiation of European polities after five centuries of a progressive differentiation in their legal and administrative systems, social practices and cultural and linguistic codes, economic transactions and regulations of the market, and social and political institutions. The integration process disjoins the hitherto overlapping and coinciding economic, cultural and politico-administrative boundaries of the state, but seems unable to reproduce some new form of closure and overlapping boundaries at its own level. Boundaries are more easily transcended for economic activities and rights and for legal-administrative practices and regulations, while they still remain hard to trespass in the areas of cultural identifications and political and social rights, and, indeed, the limited integration that exists in these latter three areas is derivative, resulting from the functional needs of market integration. The economic and legal territorially expanded scope places the legitimation triangle of the nation-state (see Chapter 2) under severe pressure, based as it is on cultural homogeneity, political participation and social sharing institutions. The 'interests' and, more broadly, the 'social practices' to which politics refer are no longer easily confinable to any one space and therefore it becomes increasingly difficult to define membership groups for political deliberation. It is, equally, difficult to build a community of this size with a significant degree of shared values, and, therefore, a substantive base for common deliberation and the sharing of social risks becomes less likely too. This places European integration at the core of a potential contradiction between the process of overcoming the European state-system and of further capitalist development, on the one hand, and the process of 'national' legitimation on the other. The tension between the project of a stateless market building at the wider European level and the nationally bounded cultural, redistributive and political capacities is not a pure growth imbalance. This justifies viewing the integration as a further 'critical juncture' in European history and focusing attention on its impact on European political structures.[24]

---

[23] On the implications of enlargement in terms of EU functional versus territorial boundaries see Zielonka, J., 'How New Enlarged Borders will Reshape the European Union', *Journal of Common Market Studies*, 39 (2001), 507–36.

[24] Rokkan does not define this concept precisely. In his usage, 'critical junctures' are identified by their producing outcome differentiation. The critical juncture is a powerful source of the differentiation of territorial and membership groups in the historical process. For instance, the Protestant reform generated variation in the religious homogeneity of the territories (mixed versus homogeneous) and variation in the role of the church cultural agency (as state bureaucracy versus cross-national organization). Critical junctures are usually identified *ex post*.

European Integration in Analytical Perspective:
The Macro and Micro Consequences of Boundary Transcendence

The differential and unbalanced boundary transcendence that is embedded in the integration process has significant consequences for the domestic political structures and agencies, and, via these, for the level of politicization/depoliticization of key domestic problems. These consequences can be defined at the (macro) system level and at the (micro) actor level.

Macro Consequences

At the *macro system level*, integration redefines the configuration of actors/ resources that are 'locked in' a given territorial polity; that is, that are 'obliged' to consume territorial public goods. Five propositions make up this reconfiguration.

1. European integration considerably expands the capacity of intrastate institutional (e.g. local regional governments), collective (membership groups), and individual (firms, corporations, individuals) actors to access external, extra nation-state resources, and therefore to exit the consumption of a number of nationally produced private and public goods. *Regulation, jurisdictional*, and *material* external resources have become increasingly accessible without any need for physical mobility. Against the regulations of their state, actors can invoke regulations issued by the supranational hierarchy. Against the jurisdiction of their state, actors can invoke the arbitration of international courts and other judicial regimes. Against the potential limitation in access to state material resources, actors can autonomously access EU funds, international financial markets, rating agencies, etc.[25] This access to external resources transforms the production of generalized and guaranteed behavioural conformity that was once monopolized by the state. The EU is therefore no longer a 'natural' arena of interstate relations in which only the direct exercise of power and influence guarantees outcomes in the form of unstable and insecure short-term pacts. It has become a 'governmental' arena in which the distribution of rights and titles is generalized (valid for all other actors) and stabilized (over time) not only for states, but also for individuals, groups, firms, etc. Therefore, the right/titles conferred by the state may be challenged by the rights/titles conferred by the regulative and jurisdictional supranational authorities.

---

[25] Another of the fiscal nightmares that is likely to come into being for governments is represented by private internet currencies that are stored electronically on satellites, and which will drastically curtail their tax intake.

The EU functions as an additional competing provider of stabilized and generalized behavioural conformity towards every actor's endowment of right/titles. Therefore, the formation of the new centre is accompanied by uncertainties about the effective stability and generality of the existing national actors' rights-titles.

2. The capacity, scope and effectiveness of the political production of public goods are dependent on the control of the boundaries between different authority arenas. The higher the control of the transaction across them, the more extensive and effective is the capacity of autonomous production of public goods and the higher the capacity of the internal hierarchy to stabilize and legitimize its domination position. European integration considerably reduces the capacity of territorial hierarchies to autonomously set and modulate the level of boundary transcendence in the economy, cultural, administrative and even coercion domains. The growing accessibility of external regulatory, jurisdictional and material resources makes national policies to be more often based on the anticipated reactions of potentially mobile actors/resources, and the domestic political production is considerably constrained by these exit options. The level of boundary transcendence allowed in various domains is increasingly more rarely the result of domestic political decision relative to struggles of power and/or cooperative negotiations within the territorial polity.

3. European integration distributes in an uneven and differential way access to extraterritorial resources and partial exit options associated with the possibility of subtracting oneself from the consumption of territorial public goods. Actors are endowed with different 'structural capacity' and 'interest orientation' to transcend boundaries. Therefore, considerable redistribution of market, political, and institutional power is likely to result within the state. At the same time, partial exit options impinge on how far the state can extract resources for the building of territorial solidarity and how far the political system can spread such resources through (weak and peripheral) strata and sectors.

4. As a result of points 1, 2, and 3, European integration modifies the terms of the established domestic 'political exchanges'. Such political exchanges are less based on the 'locking in' of relevant actors/resources and are therefore less shaped by the effective production of behavioural conformity by the territorial hierarchy. The different types of domestic resources (votes, political participation, organizational strength, capital and investment control, institutional authority, policy implementation control, professional credentials) lose their centralized 'convertibility'. They are less likely to be exchanged at the centre of the system with a view to reaching territorial specific negotiated orders and compromises.

Some actors/resources can remove themselves from the costs involved in national political exchanges by exiting, transcending the boundaries, and leaving the domestic games, and, obviously, the actors/resources that are more territorially bounded find their negotiation strength devalued by the new boundary transcendence capacity of the former. The integration process shifts the configuration of resources from a primary use of internal to a primary use of external resources, and correspondingly devalues the internal convertibility of resources in domestic political exchanges. It also tends to produce interest polarization along the dimension of access to external resources.

Micro Consequences

This new macro configuration opens up new behavioural opportunities at the *micro individual level*. In highly bounded territorial systems, the behavioural alternatives of actors are indicated by the thinner arrows in Table 7.1. If actors do not perceive the quality of public goods, they will have no commitment, no involvement and no response in or to the political production of their system ('apolitical' actor). If the quality of public goods is perceived, political commitment and action are more likely, but they depend on the belief in the possibility to improve the public goods output and on the subjective perception of efficacy. The lack of belief in improvements and belief in improvement but lack of a sense of political efficacy both lead to 'apathetic' or 'loyal' actors, who may trust established political agencies. On the other hand, those who believe that improvements are possible and perceive themselves as holding effective means by which to achieve these are more likely to actively engage and participate in the production of public goods (the 'participant').

In loosely bounded polities, the possibility of consuming alternative regulative, jurisdictional and material public goods modifies this set of behavioural options by adding the 'partial exit' option to them. Partial exiters become potential instrumentally-oriented consumers of alternative public goods, who consider the opportunity costs of a participant strategy as opposed to the exit possibilities. This is likely to depress their interest and engagement in the improvement of territorial public goods. This option, or even its sheer likelihood, radically alters the perceptions and behavioural options not only of those who have the know-how and the structural conditions to consider exit, but also of those who do not. In principle, for each level of structural capacity and interest orientation to exiting, the most likely exiters are those who have no belief in the improvement of territorial public goods, and those who, while believing in a possible improvement, do not feel subjectively influential or effective enough to achieve it (the dotted lines in

TABLE 7.1. *Behavioural options in closed nation-states versus loosely bounded confederations*

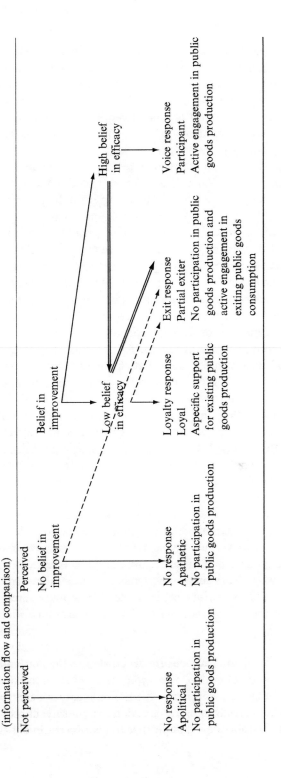

Quality differential in public goods (information flow and comparison)

Not perceived

No response
Apolitical
No participation in public goods production

Perceived

No belief in improvement

No response
Apathetic
No participation in public goods production

Belief in improvement

Low belief in efficacy

Loyalty response
Loyal
Aspecific support for existing public goods production

Exit response
Partial exiter
No participation in public goods production and active engagement in exiting public goods consumption

High belief in efficacy

Voice response
Participant
Active engagement in public goods production

Table 7.1). Those with a high sense of effectiveness, the participants, should, in principle, opt for a continued national strategy of influence.

However, in the long run, even the participants may have their perceptions modified by the new options available to the exiters, and, therefore, reconsider their behavioural options. Even if the exiters and the fields of exit are few, the political production is shaped by the political elites' concern with the implications of potential exiters' behaviour. Political elites may become so attentive and reactive to possible exit as to produce policies that try to preempt it by reducing its incentives. The absence of voice of the potential exiters may produce a bigger impact over public policy than the voice of the 'locked-in' participants. Non-participants, which were before confined to apolitical, apathetic or loyal responses, may become disproportionately influential. In this situation, the 'participants' are likely to be disappointed by the extent to which their voice options are circumscribed and made ineffective by the potential exit of the others. Their sense of efficacy may be reduced and they may, therefore, consider exit opportunities more effective and less costly than participation (the double lines in Table 7.1).

In analytical terms, growing partial exit possibilities from territorial public goods consumption (assuming, for instance, that you contribute to your national health care system, but that you consume medical care wherever you want over the EU territory) generate significant consequences on the political structuring of a polity. If exit options from public goods consumption are available, the individual transforms him/herself from a citizen-voter into a customer-taxpayer, whose preferences are best indicated by his/her consumption pattern rather than by any form of participation. To ascertain preferences through the political process becomes, therefore, less relevant. Governments need to be alerted less by the political voice of the citizens about the quality of their political production, as they are informed by their policy choices. In this world, there is less need for 'politicization' or political participation, except, maybe, by the permanent locked-in losers. The analytical model given here is extreme. However, it convincingly links the concrete development of European integration in the field of public goods production/consumption with the pushes away from active engagement in the production of territorial public policies. This powerful mechanism of radical political restructuring is embedded into the current mode of European integration.

The Political Destructuring of the Nation-State

Most studies of the impact of the EU on member states concern the domains of policy and institutional adaptation. Attention focalizes on the effect of EU policies on domestic policy latitude, on national administrative traditions, on practices and styles of regulation, and on policy fit–misfit and consequent adaptation needs.[26] In the institutional field, attention is given to changes in the relative power of executives and parliaments[27] and to the adaptation capacity of 'simple' as opposed to 'compounded' polities.[28] In this work, I have concentrated more on the less studied field of the changes in the political structures of representation that link citizens to the state and to its political elites. If we make reference to Figure 2.3 in Chapter 2, the argument is that via its effect on centre formation (policies, institutions, systemic boundaries), the macro and micro consequences of the project of differential boundary redrawing in the EU have significant repercussions also on the national 'system building' and 'political structuring'. It affects the national system building because the less bounded nature of the new polity unlocks resources and actors in an European (or world) wider area in which social solidarity, participation rights, and shared identities are missing or very weak. It affects political structuring, weakening the national political structures without producing alternative European political structures. To the extent that boundary transcendence and boundary redrawing among European territories and between them and the external world modify the opportunities for exit of individuals, groups and territories, they also affect the

[26] See in particular Knill, C., *The Europeanization of National Administrations. Patterns of Institutional Change and Persistence* (Cambridge: Cambridge University Press, 2001); and Schmidt V. A. and Scharpf, F., 'Europeanization and Domestic Structural Change: A Question of Fit' (Florence: European University Institute, 1998), Conference on 'Europeanization and domestic change'; Schmidt, V. A., 'Europeanization and the Dynamic and Mechanics of Economic Policy Adjustment' (Florence: European University Institute, 2001) Forum of the Robert Schuman Centre Seminar Paper, April.

[27] See Judge, D., 'The Failure of National Parliaments', *West European Politics*, 18 (1995), 79–100; Meunreither, K., 'The Democratic Deficit of the European Union: Towards Closer Cooperation between the European Parliament and National Parliaments', *Government and Opposition*, 29 (1994), 299–314; Shackleton, M., 'Democratic Accountability in the European Union', in F. Brouwer, V. Lintner, and M. Newman (eds.), *Economic Policy Making and the European Union* (London: Federal Trust, 1994), 91–101; Chiti, M. P., 'Il Trattato dell'Unione Europea e la sua influenza sulla costituzione italiana', *Rivista italiana di diritto pubblico comunitario*, 3 (1993), 343–66, coins the forceful term of 'communitarization of the executives'; Paladin, L., 'Forma italiana di governo e appartenenza dell'Italia all'Unione Europea', *Quaderni Costituzionali*, 14 (1994), 403–11; Moravcsik, A., 'Why the European Community Strengthen the State: Domestic Politics and International Cooperation' (Cambridge: Center for European Studies, 1994), European Studies Working Paper 52.

[28] See Schmidt, V. A., 'The Europeanization of Representation in "simple" and "compounded" systems: Changes in National Practices, challenges to national ideas and discourse' (Florence: University of Florence, 2002), Seminar Paper, June; Tuschhoff, C., 'The Compounding Effect. The Impact of Federalism on the Concept of Representation', *West European Politics*, 22 (1999), 16–33; Ladrech, R., 'Europeanization of domestic politics and institutions: The case of France', *Journal of Common Market Studies*, 32 (1994), 69–88; Hirsch, B. and Ernst, M. H., 'The European Constitution of the Netherlands. Reflections on Interdependent Statehood', *Acta Politica*, 33 (1998), 281–99.

conditions for and the modalities of their voice. In Chapters 5 and 6, I have discussed this aspect for each of the three main historical structures of political representation within the nation-state: the territorial, the corporate, and the electoral. Table 7.2 summarizes the main aspects of this process of restructuring as discussed in this work.

The impact on national political representation was analysed from three different perspectives. The first concerns the specific *balance* among the three main forms of territorial, corporate and electoral/plebiscitarian political representation. The second refers to the predominant pattern of *systemic interaction* within each channel. Finally, the third concerns the specific implications for the *individual actors* prevalent in each subsystem.

I have argued that the integration process switches the *balance* among representation channels to the advantage of those where territorial and corporate interests are expressed, and to the disadvantage of the politico-electoral channel. The theoretical underpinning for this generalization is that the shift to external resources implies a drastic decline in domestic resource convertibility. If the public goods production is constrained at the national level and alternative public goods are accessible beyond that level, general resources (votes, organizational strength, partisanship, representativeness, etc.) can be exchanged with greater difficulty at the same rate with specific corporate and territorial resource control.

The specific model of EU governance based on horizontal negotiations among actors/resources and bureaucracy devalues the resources controlled by domestic political-electoral agents such as parties, political movements, and legislative assemblies. EU governance is centred on organized actors and their institutional frameworks. The population groups, as sets of individuals who may react uniformly to the stimuli of a given public policy, are usually considered only as destination groups. In other words, the connection between the attempt at coordination of the organized actors and the collective behaviours of social groups is left out of the governance. In the institutional design and governance of the EU, the linkage that was historically established between market exchange processes, negotiations and deals among organized actors, authoritative interventions, and collective movements and behaviours is cut. In the new context, attention to collective movements and behaviours is very weak and the accent is put wholly on the interaction between authoritative decisions and market and coordination games. In this situation, the exchange and convertibility of resources become highly limited because traditional political resources (which remain bounded to the nation-state level) cannot be used in exchange in the new international or transnational settings. To the extent that areas of policies are demonopolized, decentralized, and supranationalized, resources for imposing domestic centralized political exchanges are thus 'externalized'. Those organizations that

TABLE 7.2. *The destructuring of the nation-state*

	System building			Outcomes		
	Identity solidarity	Social sharing	Political participation	Balance among channels	Systemic interactions within channels	Individual units
Centre-periphery structures	Reinforcement and rebirth of subnational identity/solidarity ties	Differentiation of interests among substate units concerning territorial social sharing institutions	Reinforcement of local coalitions weakening the cohesion of national political organizations	Empowered	More competitive structure	Territorial 'winners' and 'losers'
Interest intermediation structures	Declining cohesion of established national peak associations	Differentiation of interests concerning attachment to national social sharing versus supranational opening up and/or subnational narrowing down	Declining participation to national negotiated order production	Empowered	More fragmented and pluralistic structure	Interest organization cohesion and solidarity
Cleavage structures	Weakening and narrowing of areas of solidarity and of risk communities	Weakening relations between social sharing coalitions and cleavage alignments	Dealignment and depoliticization	Disempowered	More collusive structure	New parties, party splits, new electoral alignments

Political structuring

preside over such centralized political exchanges—politico-electoral organizations—are devalued together with the resources that they control.

Beyond the changes in the balance among channels, there are also pressures for changes in the *systemic interaction* among the stable set of key actors within each channel. It was argued that the predominant national patterns of interest intermediation, party competition and centre–periphery relations are affected by the development of new sets of such relationships at the European level and by the inconsistencies between European and national interaction patterns.

For the territorial channel, I have argued that the loosening grip of state boundaries is likely to lead to the re-emergence of territorial oppositions as a result of within-state progressive cultural, institutional, and economic differentiation. Within highly bounded political units territorial adjustments exist for disadvantaged regions, but most policies concern non-territorial sectors (industry, agriculture, education, welfare) and distributive and regulatory conflicts tend to be shaped primarily by functional alternatives. Integration challenges the unity of the territorial framework within which the functional policy choices are exercised and makes the relevance of the territorial dimension in the policy choice more salient. Not only does Europe have a territorial policy that adds to the national one, but also, in general, territorial alternatives become more important with respect to functional choices, or, to put it differently, functional choices can be neither framed nor legitimated without a strong territorial component. In addition, the multiplication of governmental levels increases the number of systemic interactions and modifies their hierarchical nature. In the nation-state, centre–periphery relations were bilateral and more hierarchical. Adding the European level increases the number of governmental centres with triangular and polygonal relationships. The European policy impact on subnational territories may foster a territorial redefinition of interests and even of cultural loyalties. Policies directed to territories within and across the boundaries of the nation-state may increase claims to politico-administrative decentralization and strengthen local forms of external representation. In this new constellation, possibilities for cross-boundary resource mobilization and alliance building are more accessible and it is less likely that these will be faced by coherent and cohesive repression or isolation response from established national elites. Therefore the lower boundedness of the new enlarged polity and the new forms of mobility tend to make territorial relationships more *competitive*.

In reference to the corporate channel, I have investigated the extent to which integration generates differentiation of interest among established interest organizations and, more importantly, within them. It was argued that internal boundary removing tends to destructure the ideological and organizational cohesiveness of long established national interest groups.

While corporate representation is enhanced in general, 'corporatist' types of interest intermediation are subject to stronger pressures for internal interest differentiation, but exercise more policy control at the national level and are characterized by stronger agencies and higher loyalty and identity resources. Pluralist types of interest intermediation structures are likely to experience lower pressure, but enjoy lower national policy control and have weaker loyalty/identity resources. Intermediate types of interest intermediation structures may face high interest differentiation with lower policy control and identity resources. Further, the multilevel and multisite institutional structure of the EU fosters the pluralism of interest groups' access points. This deprives those groups whose cohesion was based on the centralized exchange of their resources (mainly organizational and electoral), of a single centralized locus where to seek, negotiate, and achieve these exchanges. Finally, if subnational territorial differentiation generates local coalitions of interest groups and political elites engaged in strategies of 'external' representation of their 'common' territorial interests, this reverberates on the cohesiveness and centralization of national peak organizations. These effects combine, making the system of intermediation of corporate interests more *fragmented* and *pluralistic*.

In the electoral channel, the main implication concerns the declining capacity of political organizations to discipline corporate and territorial interests and actions. Historical alignments between social sharing coalitions and cleavage systems are weakened. Similarly, the tendency to narrow down the areas of solidarity and the risk communities territorially and by sector affects the capacity of national political organizations to reproduce political loyalties and identifications. Moreover, the changes affecting territorial and corporate channels weaken the historically interlocking relations between them and political-electoral organizations. Partisan alignments are weakened because they are no longer capable of integrating corporate and territorial interests' into solid political alliances coherently. At the same time, main national parties silence those EU constitutive issues of membership, competence and institutional design that are more likely to agitate national voters and anti-EU *lumpenelites*. The lack of any party thematization of EU issues leaves the mass public attitudes towards the EU largely unstructured, but it also leaves ample room for manoeuvring by anti-EU elites. The integration process then accrues to the already conspicuous tendency to more *collusive* relationships among the established actors within the channel of political-electoral representation.

The conclusion is that a similar mechanism seems to be at work in the three channels of representation. It is a mechanism of internal differentiation based on the perception of new opportunities or threats resulting from economic, administrative and cultural boundaries-transcendence and

cemented by pre-existing cultural orientations towards the opposition between 'roots' and 'options'. A link between material opportunities and
cultural orientations might well generate more stable conflicts and oppositions concerning the role of the EU.

Political Restructuring of the Union?

That supranational integration strains the national roots defined by the mix
of collective identities, social sharing and political rights, is in line with the
experience of state formation. Processes of new centre formation on an
enlarged territorial and membership scale tend to destructure the previous
locally rooted political structures and systems of representation to the advantage of the new mainly cross-local ones. In other words, territorial
expansion and consolidation has, first, a 'destructuring' effect on the lower
level system of representation, while it tends later to 'restructure' them at the
higher level. What are the prospects for a European-level system building and
political structuring? The conclusion of this work is that these prospects are
uncertain, if not gloomy. The environment of the EU does not welcome
internal political structuring without the development of fixed boundaries,
a system of territorial policies more complex, wide ranging and ambitious
than the current one, and a level of closure of the European economies.[29]

In every process of territorial integration-expansion, the first oppositions
necessarily concern the process of *'centre formation'*, implying the resistance
of peripheral territories against the accretion of resources, competencies, and
functions of the new centre. The second kind of oppositions is linked to the
processes of *'system building'*, with resistances against cultural standardization and centralization and the building of enlarged loyalties, identities, and
social solidarities. The third type of oppositions develops mainly along
functional lines based on the process of interest differentiation within the
newly consolidated polity, with conflicts and alignments concerning the
distribution mechanisms of the market and the redistribution mechanisms
of the state.

Some degree of consolidation and legitimation of the territorial and membership groups' boundaries are necessary for the development of oppositions
and alignments cutting across the territorial axis. Territorial cleavages concerning the centre formation and cultural cleavages concerning system building tend to militate against, to postpone and even to mute cleavages based

---

[29] Very interestingly, Habermas uses the expression of a 'renewed closure' of political
institutions to be achieved after the phase of opening up of the national political institutions. See Habermas, J., 'The Post-National Constellation and the Future of Democracy',
in J. Habermas, *The Post-National Constellation* (Oxford: Polity, 2001), 58–112, 83–4.

mainly on functional interest differentiation. The continued predominance of territorial and cultural oppositions can delay the process of system building, make it permanently precarious and actually lead to its breakdown in the phases of mass mobilization and democratization—as witnessed by the cases of the Ottoman, Habsburg, and Russian/Soviet large-scale empires.

If the formation of large-scale territorial political units proceeds from the coercion to the politico-administrative domain, the centralization of military and bureaucratic resources precedes the formation of the market as an inherent 'exit structure'. In these systems of military-administrative centralization, the possibility of physical exit is distributed according to the distance from the border and from the centre and according to the opportunity offered by neighbouring territorial units. The difficulty of exit associated with growing scale corresponds to the difficulty of voice at the same level. The structures of centralized politico-administrative guidance need to be liberalized and democratized to serve as channels for voice articulation. The process of voice structuring is naturally more complex, the wider the territory is. Thus voice is presumably more likely to be mobilized when the area to which it extends is not too large, from which comes the plea for democratic decentralization.[30] In this sense, in large-scale military and administrative centralized political units, the difficulties of exit and voice balance each other out.

If territorial integration starts from market formation and has only limited spill over in the politico-administrative (or coercion) domain, voice needs to be articulated at the larger-scale level while the mobility of economic factors and actors within the broadened territorial unit actually works against the political structuring. In fact, from the historical point of view we have no examples of inherent exit structures, like the market, fostering the formation of hierarchical political centres (and their democratization); while, on the contrary, we have examples of territorial hierarchical structures forming a market (and being later on democratized).

What type of political structures could develop out of the EU configuration of boundaries? In Table 7.3, the six phases of formation of the European system of states are synthetically reproduced, highlighting for each of them the main processes of boundary definition and the corresponding process of political structuring. At the EU level, the accomplishment of an internal market combined with the peculiarity of its institutional design makes it difficult to evaluate the extent to which the EU will be structured

[30] Young was the first to point out the paradox of exit and voice in large territories. Young, D. R., 'Consolidation or Diversity: Choices in the Structure of Urban Governance', *American Economic Review*, 66 (1976), 378–85. See also Hirschman, A. O., 'Exit and Voice: some further distinctions', in A. O. Hirschman, *Essays in Trespassing. Economics to Politics and Beyond* (Cambridge: Cambridge University Press, 1981), 236–45, 239–40.

TABLE 7.3. *Nation-state and EU political structuring*

	State Formation	Capitalist development	Nation formation	Democratization/ welfare state development	European integration
Boundaries' Definition	Territorial consolidation	National market formation	Cultural standardization	Citizenship, political participation and social-sharing institutions	Opening of economic and administrative nation-state boundaries
	Closure of military, administrative state boundaries	Opening of substate economic boundaries	Closure of cultural-state boundaries	Further closure of socio-political boundaries	Formation of new across-states boundaries
Main Processes of structuring	Territorial conflicts between local rulers and centre builders	Economic conflicts based on functional interests differentiation	Cultural conflicts between standardization and distinctiveness	Organizational mobilization of territorial, economic, and cultural conflicts	Domestic voice destructuring under growing exit options?
				Structuring of 'voice' under conditions of limited exit	Organizational restructuring of voice at the supranational level?

and the lines along which this can happen, as indicated by the question marks in the bottom-right box in the Table. We can only discuss various possible scenarios, organizing them along two dimensions. The first concerns the stratarchic alliances among actors; the second concerns the dichotomy between pure forms of territorial structuring versus pure forms of functional structuring.

The consolidation of the nation-state in modern Europe was dominated by a clear stratarchic structure with alignments based on the relationship between ordinary people, their local rulers, and the new centre (national) claimants to power.[31] Alliances between local rulers and ordinary people tended to produce highly decentralized local consolidation, as in city-states or confederated provinces. Alliances and integration between local rulers and national claimants tended to produce elite-based forms of large-scale territorial consolidation. Alliances between ordinary people and national claimants, cutting out local rulers, tended to produce more pronounced central consolidation. This historical and pre-modern stratarchic relationship of state building is reappearing in the process of territorial expansion associated with the development of the EU. Pure intergovernmentalism can be considered as a form of 'elite-consolidation' based on an accommodation between central claimants (the new Brussels centre) and local rulers (state executives and central institutions). Pure supranationalism, on the contrary, represents a form of 'central-consolidation' based on an alliance between ordinary people and central claimants at the expense of the local national rulers. A 'local-consolidation', based on an alliance of ordinary people and local national rulers, implies a redefinition of the current institutional design and dynamics towards a more decentralized and confederal structure.

On the second dimension, political structuring can be analysed along the territorial versus functional dimensions. In the first case, existing territorial entities are the natural focus for representation and their internal divisions tend to be either suppressed or politically diffused. In the second case, the internal social differentiation of the territorial units becomes the basis for cross-local organizational alliances. In Europe, the predominant political structure might remain dominated by purely territorial alternatives and alliances, for which territorial governments (national, but also subnational)

---

[31] For this stratarchic organization of relevant actors see Rokkan, S., 'Nation Building, Cleavage Formation and the Structuring of Mass Politics', in S. Rokkan (ed.), *Citizens, Elections, Parties. Approaches to Comparative Study of the Processes of Development* (Oslo: Universitetsforlaget, 1970), 72–144; for the distinction between these different forms of 'consolidation' see te Brake, W., *Making History: Ordinary People in European Politics, 1500–1700* (Berkeley, CA: University of California Press, 1997), whose terminology is adopted here. Sidney Tarrow has the merit to envisage the possibility to adapt te Brake concepts to the EU; see Tarrow, S., 'Center-Periphery Alignments and Political Contention in Late-Modern Europe', in Ansell and Di Palma, *Restructuring Territoriality*, 45–66.

would be almost the only agencies, and conflicts would mainly concern the asymmetric distribution of power and influence among them. Alternatively, the political structure could be characterized by the combination of a territorial principle of representation complemented with the growing importance of European cross-local alliances among corporate and political actors integrating their organizations along lines similar to those prevalent at the national level. Finally, we can imagine the third alternative that the emerging political structure will be dominated by a new functional cleavage specifically generated by integration, and which interacts with and reshapes those predominant at the national level. This would imply that the process of new cleavage formation would create new corporate and political agencies.

The territorial and functional dimensions of structuring interact. The prevailing stratarchic alliances offer different opportunities to transform territorial oppositions into functional ones. Local consolidations are strong obstacles to the spreading of functional oppositions, while central consolidations are more likely to generate them. On the other hand, the types of conflict that are politicized—functional or territorial—have an impact on the likely stratarchic alliances. For these reasons, the political structuring of the EU is an open process.

The Persistence of a Predominant Territorial Structuring

The persisting of an almost exclusively territorial structuring of the EU is the 'null hypothesis'. The early growth of the Eurobureaucracy produced essentially territorial oppositions, represented by the intergovernmental mutual veto and generalized mistrust of the new centre. However, territorial political structuring is unlikely to remain geared to the state units. As argued above, European integration makes substate territorial alternatives become more important and accrues territorial competition within the single market. At the same time, it challenges the national open and hidden mechanisms of territorial redistribution. In the European common market, discretionary territorial redistributions are often regarded as unfair state aids. Richer regions have less 'interest' to raise the purchasing power of their nation's poorer regions, as their goods and services can be sold under the same conditions in every other region of another nation-state without incurring the cost of territorial redistribution. In addition, the additional purchasing power due to national territorial redistribution is not necessarily directed towards the goods produced by richer territories of the same state. Finally, but no less important, the EU single market eradicates the economic costs of territorial forms of autonomy (or even of secession). It is likely, therefore, that the differentiation of territorial interests will foster forms of territorial representation involving substate territories and cross-state territories together with the state ones. Strong regions will be able to impose territorial choices and act as players in the new complex system of multilevel decision-making. Other regions will be too weak, and their territories will be unable to impose their own needs and will become increasingly dependant on the international market, the state and the EU itself.[32]

However, pure territorial forms of representation based on states or on a more complex set of territorial substate actors, present a problem. If the political structure of the EU remains dominated by territorial agents, the continuing enlarged scope of the EU competences and powers cannot be sustained, given that it generates growing tensions for which the territorial principle of representation has no clear and accepted means of conflict resolution. The early experience of the EU shows that the strengthening of the new centre can progress even in a system that is rigidly structured on territorial bases. The formal representation of member countries in the powerful Council was no guarantee of limited centre accretion. In fact, in the EU institutional design, nation-states are not constitutive units whose role, competencies, and attributions are constitutionally defended (i.e. defended even by those decisions that governments could take by unanimity or majority). Rather, *governments* are represented at the centre and endowed with (more or less) veto powers, but they can, if unanimous, encroach on the competencies of the nation-states fairly widely. In other words, the EU is a typical form of 'elite consolidation', which, in contrast to local consolidations, allows for a considerable expansion of the centre competencies.

Notwithstanding this, if territory remains the only principle of representation there is the risk that the social and economic implications of opening the domestic markets will be tainted with cultural conflicts. Distributive and redistributive issues may tend to become boundary and border issues, no longer interpreted as internal problems of culturally homogeneous areas and groups—for which established political mechanisms and decision-making rules exist—but as problems combining economic with identity and cultural dimensions. This may constitute the premise for a fundamentalist restructuring on the basis of primary interests legitimized in the name of roots-democracy. Within a complex system of economic interdependence based on territorial representation, cultural differences may become more important, and the regression of the levels of identification to the primary basic groups would be a plausible reaction.

---

[32] For a discussion of the differential territorial impact of the EMU on Italian regions suggesting that the EMU may generate territorial disadvantages in the south of Italy see Radaelli, C. M. and Bruni, M. G., 'Beyond Charlemagne's Europe: A Sub-National Examination of Italy within the EMU', *Regional and Federal Studies*, 18 (1998), 34–51.

In reference to the EU, 'identity' issues are dealt with almost exclusively in terms of new identity building: the need, possibility, desirability of creating a layer of European identification among the mass publics. This has gone to the detriment of a closer analysis of the potential for old identity re-politicization, including national and subnational identities. This imbalance is rooted in the devaluation of the positive contribution of the nation-state to the domestication of cultural conflict in the complex cultural infrastructure of Europe. Nation-states made cultural conflicts less important by 'internalizing' them and reducing ethno-linguistic, religious and identity conflicts to a lower ranking. Cultural conflicts in the large-scale European territorial system were 'solved' and transformed into relations among states, no longer directly dividing the 'European people'.[33] The formation of a system of nation-states created tensions in their relationships, but also solved tensions that would otherwise have been difficult to manage. This creation of territorially restricted but relatively homogeneous cultural environments made possible the development of functional cleavages that would otherwise have been obfuscated by cultural and identity oppositions. There is at least the possibility that an extended space organized on merely territorial principles will witness a decline in 'homogeneity-based' cleavages and the re-emergence of cultural differences and identities. The institutional design of the EU, characterized by the impact of the centralized regimes (competition, monetary, legal interpretation, etc.) over the decentralized ones (fiscal, representation, welfare, etc.), might lead to risks of nationalistic responses and reactions if these are organized on a mere territorial base.

The Isomorphic Functional Political Structuring

The EU could develop a political structure over time in which the territorial structuring is coupled with a cross-border coordination among national social, political, and corporate actors with similar interests/values. This is the core of the 'Europeanization' hypothesis, according to which the creation of vertical linkages—assisted institutionally by the Commission and other EU institutions—may eventually foster the development of horizontal cross-national contacts for sector or corporate groups, for political organizations, and even protest and social movements across Europe. Next to the above-mentioned alignments *among territories*, others are increasingly *across territories*, as the attempts at building Europarties, the growing network of

---

[33] Peter Flora underlines this crucial aspect of nation-state formation: Flora, P., 'Externe Grenzbildung und interne Strukturierung—Europa und seine Nationen, Eine Rokkanische Forschungsperspektive', *Berliner Journal für Soziologie*, 10 (2000), 157–66.

communication and exchange among sector interests groups, and even the development of contentious collective action and European social movements go to show.[34]

This possibility also presents several weak features. At present, notwithstanding the Commission's active role in fostering cross-state contacts and linkages, national groups find it hard to organize and act at the European level. The main problem is that, in enlarged membership and territorial groups, collective strategies of protection tend to become weaker. Cross-local functional alliances for interest protection are undermined by territorial competition and by the universalization of broader territory and membership group's rights. In the context of accrued economic competition, the political production of the new centre is bounded and limited. Therefore, European-level attempts by groups to seek protection and advantages for the appropriation of market opportunities via collective strategies are inevitably weakened.

In addition to this general problem, the European coordination of national political, social and corporate groups finds an obstacle in the number and fragmentation of the new sites of power and decision-making, which lowers their organizational cohesion. Just as there are differences in the capacity to access different layers and different sites of the EU, national and local decisional structures, there are within-organization divisions over the vertical decisional centre towards which to act. The organizational domain of the coordination efforts of all sorts of groups will necessarily cover narrower territorial capacities than the market.[35] Moreover, the specific organizations active in the corporate channel, party organizations mobilizing for electoral action, and specific protest and social movements have no effective organizational or ideological interlocking at the EU level. At best, these are erratic and unstable relationships.

Finally, in the mass publics, attitudes concerning the EU cut across the lines of EU-level coordination among interest groups and political organizations. Cues about integration are generated and transmitted mainly through non-partisan channels (EU legislation and its direct impact on citizens' economic and professional life, EU symbolic outputs, interests groups and

[34] Much attention has been focused on these, particularly by S. Tarrow and R. Balme See Imig, D. and Tarrow, S. (eds.), *Contentious Europeans: Protest and Politics in a Europeanizing Polity* (Lanham, MD: Rowman & Littlefield, 2001); R. Balme, D. Chabanet, and V. Wright (eds.), *L'action collective en Europe* (Paris: Presses de Sciences Po., 2002).

[35] See on this point Streek, W. and Schmitter, P., 'From National Corporatism to Transnational Pluralism: Organized Interests in the Single European Market', *Politics and Society*, 19 (1991), 133–64, 156.

professional associations information, the media)[36] and are poorly linked to partisan orientations. It was argued that the location of class and sector interests, parties, social movements and interest groups in the national cleavage system is not homogeneous with their location on the integration/ independence dimension. This makes it difficult for them to thematize this issue and to avoid internal divisions. These same aspects of integration, which bring about a growing differentiation of public opinion and of sector and social interests, also force a declining differentiation among the parties. In other words, the European coordination of groups along lines that are isomorphic to the national divisions rest on very thin mass support and necessarily silence the mass public differentiation of attitudes towards the EU.

In short, although the role of Europarties, interest Eurogroups, and social Euromovements is the object of considerable scholarly attention and institutional assistance, their becoming real structures of representation is uncertain and problematic. The issues generated by the integration process cannot be easily reconciled with nation-state based cleavage structures, as they considerably redefine the basic interests and identities on which those cleavages were built. These difficulties are due to the objective alien nature of those issues that pertain to territorial expansion and integration with respect to those which belong to the institutionalization of voice in economically and administratively closed and culturally homogeneous environments. For this reason, so far the European level fora, channels and organizations of corporate and political representation are more a system of legitimation for the techno-bureaucratic central hierarchy than effective mechanisms of representation and of (non-territorial) conflict resolution. In the current state of affairs, therefore, a stratarchic territorial representation, based mainly on the interaction between substate elites, national rulers, and centre-builders at the EU level seems to be more likely than the new formation of European-wide cross-territorial functional alliances.[37]

The Structuring of a New Cleavage Line

The third hypothesis to be investigated is whether the integration process could generate an additional cleavage line based on a social polarization

---

[36] What Wallace, W. calls 'informal integration' as that less visible and dispersed process by which sectoral and professional relations, networks of experts, informal practices within private associations slowly develop as a result of formal istitutional integration. Wallace, W., 'Introduction: the dynamics of European Integration', in W. Wallace (ed.), *The Dynamics of European Integration* (London: Pinter, 1990), 9.

[37] Bartolini, S., 'Old and New Peripheries in the Processes of European Territorial Integration', in Ansell and Di Palma, *Restructuring Territoriality*, 19–44.

linked directly to the integration process—as previous historical critical junctures have done. In Table 7.4, the comparison between the nation-state and the EU suggests that the predefined boundary-removing goals, the unclear legitimacy bases and division of powers, and the incorporation rather than representation features of the *internal hierarchical structure* provide for few mechanisms of social closure and for ineffective collective strategies of protection. At the same time, the weak *external territorial control* provides for a much weaker distinction in membership rights, privileges, and obligations between natives and foreigners than was the case in the nation-state.

Therefore, the main new source of *internal role differentiation* among the EU's natives concerns the differential distribution of total and partial exits associated with the lowering of the various boundaries. The new *social polarization* line concerning the integration process could therefore relate to the costs and advantages of exit versus those of renewed closure. This new cleavage could be rooted in the life chances and material opportunities perceived by different actors as a differentiation of their interests concerning the territorial integration process. It could also culturally cement values and beliefs about integration with wider normative visions of the self, the good life, and justice and equity. It could also relate to concrete issues concerning the conflicts generated by boundary transcendence versus boundary control options, like economic openness, immigration, multiculturalism, and national welfare autonomy. It could be politically organized by *new* agencies.

The discussion of the orientations to the integration process made in Chapters 5 and 6 offers some elements to support this scenario. To map such orientations at the level of party elites, groups, and individual citizens, I propose the scheme in Figure 7.2. The figure is based on four ideas. The first is that the left–right dimension of alignment and competition prevalent at the national level (and at the EP level) is not sufficient to reproduce the set of orientations and alignments that prevail when integration/independence issues are at stake. The second idea is that the meaning of the independence/integration dimension has been bifurcated by its widening, deepening, and accelerating. More integration may mean more market competition and openness, but it may also mean a greater European-level control of the market itself, of immigration fluxes, and of the exit options of globalized capital. More integration may mean breaking the unions' strength via economic liberalization, decentralizing bargaining and dismantling neo-corporatist structures, but it can also mean the exact opposite: regaining at the EU level that control over macroeconomic policies, negotiated orders and centralized bargaining which is being lost within the national context. More integration may be seen as a way to defend 'European' cultural traditions and diversity from globalizing multiculturalism, but more independence can similarly be argued as a way to defend national cultural

TABLE 7.4. *A comparison of the nation-state and the EU*

	Internal hierarchical structure Institutional form and legitimation principle of the ruled/rulers relationship	External territorial control Differences in membership rights, privileges, obligations **between** natives and foreigners	Internal role differentiation Differences in membership rights, privileges, obligations **among** natives	Social polarization Conflicts and oppositions
Nation-state	Predominant political legitimacy/responsibility Representation Legislative/executive relationships Politically defined goals and open competencies	Areas of equality among natives: Cultural: national identity Social: sharing institutions Political: participation right	Appropriation, acquisitive capacity, education, welfare and social rights, institutional endowments	Social polarization about internal distribution of resources, obligations, institutional rights
European Union	Mixed and unclear legitimacy sources Incorporation Unclear divisions of institutional powers Predefined goals and selected, expandable competencies	Weak area of equality among natives Weak distinction between 'we' and the 'others' No or weak cultural identity Inexistent social sharing institutions Limited and ineffective participation rights	As above, plus differential distribution of total and partial exit options	Cultural, territorial, and social polarization concerning the costs/advantages of exit versus losure

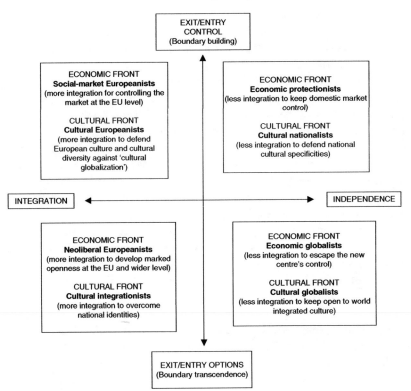

EXIT/ENTRY
CONTROL
(Boundary building)

ECONOMIC FRONT
Social-market Europeanists
(more integration for controlling the
market at the EU level)

CULTURAL FRONT
Cultural Europeanists
(more integration to defend
European culture and cultural
diversity against 'cultural
globalization')

ECONOMIC FRONT
Economic protectionists
(less integration to keep domestic market
control)

CULTURAL FRONT
Cultural nationalists
(less integration to defend national
cultural specificities)

INTEGRATION

INDEPENDENCE

ECONOMIC FRONT
Neoliberal Europeanists
(more integration to develop marked
openness at the EU and wider level)

CULTURAL FRONT
Cultural integrationists
(more integration to overcome
national identities)

ECONOMIC FRONT
Economic globalists
(less integration to escape the new
centre's control)

CULTURAL FRONT
Cultural globalists
(less integration to keep open to world
integrated culture)

EXIT/ENTRY OPTIONS
(Boundary transcendence)

FIGURE 7.2. European integration and partisan issue dimensions

distinctiveness. More independence may mean more protectionism and less international competition, but it can also mean escaping the growing bureaucratic control emanating from Brussels and its regulatory encroachment on globalized markets. More independence can also be advocated to defend the achievements of national welfare and democracy, but more integration can be advocated with similar goals, arguing that European national welfare states can only be defended at the level of the European market.

The third idea is that this bifurcation of attitudes towards integration can be captured by the new social polarization between the 'exit/entry controls' versus 'exit/entry options' discussed earlier. This second dimension in Figure 7.2 refers to the political goals of the project to be pursued through more or less integration, that is, it specifies for what integration is to be used. The exit/entry options versus exit/entry control dimension does not correlate any better with the left–right dimension than the integration/independence dimension does. The fourth idea is that on both dimensions of Figure 7.2 there is a low coincidence of the cultural and economic fronts. Those who support more independence, with a view of strengthening the national control of the boundaries (limiting thereafter entries and exits options: 'economic protectionists'), are not necessarily also 'cultural nationalists'. On the other hand, neither are those who support EU economic integration as a step towards global market openness by escaping the control of the new EU centre ('neoliberal Europeanists'), necessarily also 'cultural globalists'. Global markets can be supported together with national culture. Those supporting more integration in order to control the market exit options may be more positively oriented towards multiculturalism. The list of these inconsistencies could be extended, but the essential point is that market orientation and cultural orientation in the integration process may diverge sharply and that those who are bedfellows on the economic front are not necessarily bedfellows on the cultural front.

The dimensions charted in Figure 7.2 should be valid for *territories*, *groups*, and *individuals* and have both a 'material basis' as well as an 'ideological underpinning'. At the territorial level, attitudes to integration were related to the divide between early and newcomers. European integration initiated at the historical core of the continental territories of the Frankish kingdoms and the Holy Roman Empire, and did not originally include the Protestant north, east, south-east and south-west peripheries. The distinction between earlycomers and latecomers is, in fact, a distinction that runs along the north-south axis of distance from Catholic Rome and the unification attempts by the Holy Roman Empire and its successors, and a distinction along the east-west axis of distance from the core of continental capitalist development. Therefore, the early versus latecomers distinction does not in fact explain the amount of territorial resistance to integration, but, rather, the latter explains the former.

A 'Rokkanian' geopolitical map that combines these two historical dimensions with other macro historical variables such as the timing and contentiousness of national unification, the level of centralization of resources and decision-making, the inherited traditions of representative institutions and the territorial international status (all these suggesting more resistance to integration), offers a general guide to the macro variations in territorial support for integration. However, differences between states are now becoming less significant with respect to subnational differences. For substate territories, this latent opposition line can be conceptualized as a new centre–periphery dimension, pointing to territories whose distinctiveness is threatened by the integration drive pursued by the centre and which are the 'losers' in the new contest for the exploitations of the opportunities offered by the new loose boundaries. As loosely bounded territories are subject to the mobility options of crucial factors such as capital, taxpayers, patients, pensioners, consumers, skilled professions, winning/losing territories are defined by their capacity to access external resources made available by the new centre, to attract new mobile factors, resources and skills, and to remove themselves from the obligations and duties of the territorial state.

For social and sector interest groups, the material basis of the integration cleavage can be conceptualized as a functional/economic divide between groups whose economic interests and 'market' capacities are threatened or fostered by integration. Class coalitions may be weakened by sector differentiation. If the creation of the European market and administrative regimes tend to produce a within-group differentiation of interests based on a perception of the opportunities and the costs that these new exit/entry options may offer, even two key actors such as capital and labour may divide internally. Sectors oriented towards the world market versus those oriented towards the domestic market may divorce in the face of integration. Export-oriented sectors (including financial services and tourism) benefit from the removal of barriers; domestically-oriented sectors (including the public sector and agriculture) instead face increasing competition.[38]

For single individuals, the assets revalued by the new opportunities for exit/entry are linked to languages that give access to other cultures and to special skills and professional credentials that are marketable across national boundaries. Even if they are less dependent on passports, visas, and residential and labour permissions, most people remain 'nationalized'; they see their life chances as depending on the territorialized systems of social sharing, identity and political participation rights and on the monopolistic production of related public goods by national and local authorities. The less educated and unskilled, the poorly paid, and those in unstable positions may have more limited prospects for occupational mobility, are less well equipped to deal with the socio-cultural aspects of the opening of the boundaries, may be more affected by the retrenchment of the welfare state, more directly threatened by immigration and by new industrializing competitors in former Third World countries. They are more likely to oppose of exit/entry options and to be more in favour of their control.

However, even within the categories of those endowed with better economic, cultural and social resources, material and cultural opportunities may produce processes of interest differentiation. The findings concerning individuals' orientations towards integration mentioned in Chapter 6 are compatible with a general interpretation that emphasizes the opposition between the perception and positive evaluation of new material and cultural opportunities and mobility options versus the perception of their costs. People

---

[38] For an discussion of 'winning' and 'losing' groups in a context of globalization' rather than 'Europeanization' see Kriesi, H., 'The Transformation of the National Political Space in a Globalizing World', in P. Ibarra (ed.), *Social Movements and Democracy* (London: Palgrave Macmillan, 2003), 195–210.

characterized by stronger elements of empathy (such as the capacity to see themselves projected into a different existential situation) and by 'portable' cultural and material resources tend to show greater support to integration. There is some evidence to advance the hypothesis that the integration dimension correlates significantly with other traits of an *'option-centred'* versus *'roots-centred'* material interests and value orientation.

At the cultural level, the 'roots-centred' ideological base is identified by themes of ethnic purity and tradition; of the rediscovery of old cultural traditions; of local democracy and the themes of government closeness to citizens; of local fiscal transparency versus central fiscal opacity; of anti-central bureaucracy feelings. The individualist 'roots-centred' ideological base highlights ongoing lack of confidence and interest in the 'foreign' and 'foreigners'; a security ideology insisting on proximity and the local community; an attempt to reunite identity space and decision space; rejection of the standardizing effects of global communication and competition; support for the setting up of protective barriers to defend identity in cultural, economic and administrative matters; support for the reconstitution of 'meaningful' frontiers for the nation-state or for new forms of regionalism; a request for new boundaries against the 'nomadism' of culture, trade, and administrative practices.

In contrast, the 'option-centred' ideological syndrome is represented by a criticism and dislike of limits placed on communication, trade, cultural exchange, etc., embedded within state boundaries; an extensive reliance on networks of communication (electronic as well as hertzian, postal or traditional); an ideology of instantaneous information covering the world; a conviction that the global flow allows the rewards of the market to enrich all of us; identification with supranational institutions and a positive view of a transnational civic society of NGOs to ensure the international order. Within any authority arena, the most advanced, core and outwards-oriented individuals, groups and territories will be the ideological defenders of the openness of the organization, while the more immobile and peripheral may be at the centre of anti-openness ideology.

In conclusion, we can imagine the development of a dividing line that opposes material interests and cultural values of a *'nomadic'* versus *'standing'* nature.[39] These terms must be taken in a non-literal way, as for neither

[39] I owe these two terms to the creativity of Dupuy, H., 'Perspectives politiques et institutionnelles en Europe' (Florence: European University Institute, 1995), Seminar Paper, no. 8. There are resemblances between this dichotomy and that used by Bauman, between 'globalites' versus 'localites' (Bauman, Z., *Globalization* (London: Routledge, 1997)), and by Maier, between 'globalists' and 'territorialists' (Maier, C. S., 'Territorialisten und Globalistes. Die beiden 'Parteien' in den heitigen Demokratie', *Transit Helf* , 14 (1997), 5–14); and Maier, C. S., 'Does Europe need frontiers? From Territorial to

TABLE 7.5. *Conflict lines of the main phases of European historical development*

	Nation-state formation (exit versus voice alternatives)	Industrial revolution (voice versus loyalty alternatives)	Integration 'revolution' (again exit versus voice alternatives)
Territorial axis	Centre versus periphery		Loosing/winning territories in international/EU competition for attracting mobile factors
Functional axis	Church versus state	Primary versus secondary	'Nomadic'/ 'standing' individuals, groups, and corporate organizations
		Workers versus owners	

individuals nor groups or territories does this opposition impinge exclusively—as was the case in the past—on the physical capacity to move, migrate, delocate, and secede. One should speak, in fact, of the possibility of using competing functional and regulative boundaries to one's advantage.

The European national revolution was about the cultural limitations of exit options that were still available on the territorial (centre–periphery) and functional (church–state) axis. The rural/urban cleavage had strong territorial implications, but it was mainly expressed through functional conflicts between social groups in the production and distribution domains. The Industrial Revolution produced functional conflicts among groups linked to the division of labour within a consolidated territory. The *integration* revolution would instead oppose allegiance to a relatively closed territorial entity versus the internationalization of chances and opportunities (Table 7.5).

European territorial integration could well be the catalyst cementing these old and new value orientations and material interests, thanks to the highly institutionalized nature of conflicts over boundary building and boundary removing at the EU level. Like any previous cleavage, the integration

redistributive community', in J. Zielonka (ed.), *Europe Unbound: Enlarging and Reshaping the Boundaries of the European Union* (London: Routledge, 2002), 17–37. In my opinion, these dichotomies represent ideological characterizations that make few references to the material sources that sustain this cultural orientation they define.

cleavage can be viewed in various ways. It can take the form of a centre–
periphery opposition, pointing to groups and territories whose distinctiveness is threatened by the integration drive. It can be conceptualized as a
functional/economic divide between groups whose economic interests are
threatened or fostered by integration. It can also be conceptualized as a
cultural opposition to Brussels' bureaucracy and its standardizing practices,
administrative procedures and political culture. It is difficult, in fact, to
predict whether the scattered lines of opposition on the economic, cultural
and politico-administrative fronts have a potential for convergence and
ideological integration into an encompassing cleavage. The new social
polarization may prove very difficult to be politically structured in the wide
European space. However, even if social polarization stays latent, the
consequences of the European project of boundary redrawing will not
come to an end, and the material and cultural possibility of supranational
and subnational transcendence will probably restructure the nation-states to
such an extent as to lead to their declining integration.

This integration cleavage will have to combine with the already existing
European and domestic cleavage structures, and four scenarios can be envisaged.[40]

Containment: the internalization of the 'integration' cleavage. In this scenario, the generation of conflicts and oppositions concerning European integration would be contained within the national cleavage system and
therefore kept at the national level. National parties and national groups
would incorporate the issues of integration within their electoral packages
and main dimensions of competition. Their voters, members and leaders
would have different European preferences, which could be strong enough to
jeopardize the internal organizational unity of these organizations. Anti-EU
splinter parties or new small parties which campaign on divisive EU-policies/
issues could emerge. The organizational cohesion and unity of the main
interest groups could also be strained by strong intragroup differentiations.
Contacts and cooperation across the national communities among likeminded parties and interest groups could emerge, but these would be unable
to consolidate into true cross-national organizations, would be deeply
affected by internal coordination problems, and would be internally divided
along territorial lines on crucial European issues. The EU representation structures—the fora for elections-parties, interests groups and
substate territories—would retain their 'second-order' nature. In this
scenario, specific divisions concerning the integration process would be

---

[40] For two of these scenarios I am indebted to Peter Flora. See his intriguing paper,
'Externe Grenzbildung und interne Strukturierung'.

successfully 'contained' within the predominant national alignments by the adaptation of the socio-political elites.

Reproduction: the Europeanization of the nation-state cleavages. The second scenario suggests that the latent integration cleavage could be successfully managed by national agencies reproducing at the EU level a political alignment that would be isomorphic with the predominant national cleavage systems. To avoid the untenable fragmentation that would come about through simply 'translating' national organizations onto the EU level, national parties and interest organizations would regroup into European organizations. The growing powers of the EP, its stronger linkage with the Commission, and the logic of parliamentary groups attraction would progressively stabilize this isomorphic alignment, incorporating new member states' parties and interest groups into the existing ones after a period of 'socialization'. Territorial divisions would persist within European organizations, but would be slowly eroded by the fact that coordination would be strengthened, actively assisted by the material and ideological support of the EU central institutions and elites. If European organizations were successfully institutionalized along alignments that are isomorphic with national ones—and which, therefore, do not undermine the support and legitimacy of the national elites—they could slowly contribute to the constitution of some elements of system building at the EU level. The new European centre could thus rely on them to build elements of social and political citizenship, and even components of a European 'civic' identity. National political elites would not feel threatened by these developments to the extent that they would remain in firm control of the new representation agencies and channels. Anti-European groups and parties would continue to generate short-term signs of dissatisfaction, but would remain marginal, positioned at the periphery of the core representation groups and fora, negatively discriminated by the institutional setting.

Splitting: the Europeanization of the 'integration' cleavage. In a third scenario, the specific conflicts and oppositions concerning integration would appear only in the EU representation fora, implying that parties and groups would successfully shield national competition from integration issues. This would generate a 'split' or 'two-level' representation system with a relatively clear-cut division of labour and, therefore, with the possibility of different political alignments at each level. In European elections, specific Europarties (not campaigning at national elections) would represent this integration dimension. Voters and group members would thus perceive different but equally important concerns when participating in national and European elections and negotiations, and national parties would attract different votes in national and European elections (when the left–right divisions will combine with the pro–against Europe one). Similarly, in the interest intermediation system, national peak organizations would still be important at the national level, while at the EU level different sector, subsector, and even cross-firm alignments and alliances could prevail. However, since a 'split' representation system rests on a more clear-cut division of competencies between the levels and a stronger defence of the principle of 'subsidiary', this therefore would imply an important redefinition of the institutional design of the EU in a federal direction. Under the current institutional structure, a clear-cut splitting of the representation system is impossible. A two-level split party system would require to change the current situation in which the EP deals with detailed and specific legislation and has few competences in 'federal' matters, while the national parliaments have little opportunity to overview the detailed EU regulations to be implemented on their territories, while they retain formal competence on the important 'federal' choices of the EU.

Externalization: the mass politicization of the 'European integration' cleavage. In the fourth scenario, the new European integration cleavage would cut heavily across, reshuffle, and reshape the national party and interest groups and would also be externalized into the European representation arenas, with the building up of new trans-European alliances that do not fit with the traditional ones.[41] New political alignments about alternatives concerning European integration and related policies would be politicized. This new opposition line would interact with the (at this point) loose cleavage line represented by a mix of class and religion. The concomitant politicization of the integration process at both the national and European level would externalize national cleavages into the European arenas and internalize integration conflicts into the national one, contributing to a powerful politicization of territorial (interstate) oppositions. National party organizations and elites could find it difficult to maintain control over the political agenda, and could undergo splits within their national electorates and loss of control over the bulk of 'their' voters. The EU would thus truly enter the age of 'mass politics', although in a situation in which neither its territorial external borders nor the layered separation of its competencies or the identity and solidarity areas of its cultural boundaries would be clearly defined. This new mass politics would therefore politicize these poorly defined and unconsolidated boundaries. In the language of the political development literature of the 1960s, Europe would in this case cumulate the crises of legitimation, participation, and redistribution with the crises of system formation (territorial consolidation and identity formation). Under these conditions, the

---

[41] Andeweg, R., 'The Reshaping of National Party Systems', *West European Politics*, 18 (1995), 58–78 elaborates on this scenario.

consequences of politicization and 'democratization' could be fatal for any prospect of territorial integration.

Conclusion: Democratizing Without Political Structuring?

The tension between problem-solving and political legitimacy is crucial in every territorial system. Ruling elites need to deal with objective problems—such as economic conditions, international relations, etc.—as well as the problem of mobilizing political support in their favour. The connection between these two aspects was tenuous in pre-liberalized and pre-democratized European polities, but became much closer in the democratized nation-state. It has become loose and tenuous again in the EU integration process, in which any emphasis on solving objective coordination problems has been detached from support mobilization. This renewed independence between problem-solving and political support has come about as a result of the pooling of the problem-solving role at the EU level. Thanks to the separating of the criteria of economic rationality (reserved to the EU) from the other political, cultural, and social objectives (reserved to the nation-state), the EU has enjoyed a privileged position, being able to leave the latter problems outside its competence. As time has gone by, however, this possibility seems to have reduced. Euronational political elites now perceive a renewed tension between their problem-solving capacity—for which they pool efforts and sovereignty at the supranational level—and the nurturing of their sources of ruleship—for which they rest on national legitimation processes.

The national-European political elites are victims of the constraints that they have decided to impose on themselves, on their countries, and on their citizens. These constraints were progressively introduced to force exogenous discipline on the respective national communities in a phase in which democratic accountability and responsiveness make it difficult to endogenously produce such discipline. Even if it can be justified by the pressure to solve the objective problems of the European state system, the integration process can also be seen as a way for national political elites to bypass the constraints of national political production.

Therefore, the conflicts that oppose the member states' representatives in the Council to the more supranational orientation of the Commission (and the Parliament) should not be seen from the perspective of the 'realist' opposition between selfish state interests and idealistic supranational projects. They instead reflect the fundamental ambivalence of the Euronational political elites. The latter (institutionally identified with the Council) are sensitive to electoral pressures, which are, in turn, influenced by socio-political movements and diffuse interests. The EU institutions and bureaucracies are largely shielded from these influences and are generally more responsive towards the powerful but electorally weak groups of resource controllers. However, the elites that are electorally responsible are the same elites that actively engage in moving objective problem-solving into areas of techno-bureaucratic non-responsibility. The complementarity of the intergovernmentalist and supranationalist 'theories' is embedded in this contradictory position of Euronational political elites, engaged in a supranational attempt to improve the economic and security viability of their capsule of survival and, at the same time, remaining responsible to and drawing legitimacy from this capsule.

Nevertheless, the destructuring and restructuring capacity of the integration process is not limited to what is done in Brussels and how it is decided. Europe restructures domestic policy mainly via the indirect impact of its boundary-removing policies. The ECJ decisions concerning health care and pensions are supranational decisions; the Council decisions not to deal with pensions and health care are intergovernmental decisions. Their combination restructures national health and pension systems equally. The argument that only the Council has powers in key areas may satisfy the supporters of the intergovernmental thesis; the expansion of competencies and the role of the Commission/Parliament/Court of Justice may be used to support the supranational development thesis. However, whether the Euronational political elites decide to reserve decisions for their direct negotiation or to delegate supranational competencies, the core historical interpretation of European integration lies in the momentous consequences that come about for domestic political structuring as the result of both types of positive and negative decisions.

In one superbly clear and concise description the EU has been characterized as an 'enlightened administration on behalf of uninformed publics, in cooperation with affected interests and subject to the approval of national governments'.[42] This situation is unproblematic if one believes that the triangles of the nation-state (see Figure 2.3) are unaffected by this. According to this view, the nation-states, relinquishing sovereignty over the economic rights of their citizens and the Keynesian control of the national economy, successfully resist any attempt to intrude on their role as the upholders of effective political participation rights, social citizenship, and cultural identity. The ideas I have presented in this work have argued that this retrenchment of the nation-state into its cultural, social and political boundaries is incompatible with its relinquishing control over its economic and lego-administrative boundaries.

---

[42] Wallace, W. and Smith, J., 'Democracy or Technocracy? European Integration and the Problem of Popular Consent', *West European Politics*, 18 (1995), 138–57, 143.

In principle, one cannot exclude that political stability can be maintained even under conditions of very high international economic interdependence if citizens can be persuaded that the economic and social outcomes of this are de facto the result of forces outside the reach of the nation-state and of the political and social rights that they exercise within it. What cannot be maintained is the thesis of a 'division of labour' between the EU and the nation-state, according to which the EU should be exclusively responsible for the regulation/deregulation of the market (in a way that is as independent as possible from political pressures) while the state should retain responsibility for introducing the necessary compensatory measures both as intergovernmental decisions and as pure nation-state decisions.[43] This thesis conceals the fact that this compensatory function of the state cannot be easily performed given the regulatory nature of the EU. That is, the institutional mechanisms at the EU level and the constitutionalized core of its market defence make it difficult for a single state to enforce this compensatory action when similar actions is not taken by the other states as well. The EU has been able to impose the consequences of its policy of economic integration on the member states until these had sufficient national flexibility of legal and economic adaptation. Monetary integration and the centralized legal administration of the infringements of market freedoms and competition have largely reduced the adaptation elasticity offered to member states. One of the aims of this book has been to show that this very unbalanced 'division of labour' is likely to have serious consequences on the forms of national political representation and national identity definition, as well as on the national social sharing institutions.

This situation, in which national political destructuring occurs without European political structuring, also explains why Euronational political elites and the bureaucratic structures of the EU frantically try to foster the building up of some principle of EU legitimation and the institutionalization of fora of representation in the territorial, corporate and electoral channels from the top, while a considerable amount of scholarly energy goes into defending the need and desirability of 'democratization', or, alternatively, into inventing new 'discourses' on different standards of democracy and/or alternative principles of legitimation. If one does not take into account the above-mentioned problem in which the European political elites have entrapped themselves, this situation can even be seen as amusing: there are few historical examples of politicians, bureaucrats, and scholars searching so frenetically for 'democracy' and 'legitimacy' that no citizen has demanded.

---

[43] Among the many possible references see Streit, M. E., 'The Economic Constitution of the European Community: From "Rome" to "Maastricht" ', *European Law Journal*, 1 (1995), 5–30; Majone, G., 'The Regulatory State and its Legitimacy Problems', *West European Politics*, 22 (1999), 1–24.

The main thrust of my argument in this work is that the institutional design of the EU militates to date against any stable form of political structuring for its representative actors, while its growing political production tends to undermine national mechanisms of political representation and legitimation. Institutional democratization is, in principle, easy to achieve, but any institutional democratization without political structuring is potentially catastrophic, and political structures cannot be created without important advances in system buildings that, for now, are completely nonexistent. Undoubtedly, a top-down enforcement of majority principles in the decision-making process and the introduction of responsible government mechanisms in the EU would be one possiblity of strengthening intermediary political structures of representation. However, it is hard to identify these effects *ex ante*, and they could, in reality, be less benign than expected by the supporters of 'democratization'. This is so because political structures are vehicles for the representation of different ideas, interests and identities, and their specific content cannot be engineered before coming into being. In other words, historically, the elements of what we usually call 'democracy' were largely the unintended results of situations of equilibrium in resource control among different institutional, political and social forces. Today it is felt— although not yet demonstrated—that 'democracy' can be more easily than before exported or taught and that top-down democratization can lead later on to the political structuring of the polity. The extent to which this gives rise to only 'façade' democracies is still the object of heated debates, however. This is the main reason why I have paid little attention to the wide debate about the EU 'democratic deficit' and institutional engineering, and I have concentrated instead on political structures. There is, however, some room to come back to it in this conclusion.

My thesis is that the EU institutions cannot substitute the national political institutions not because they are not democratic enough, but because they are not operating within closed boundaries, and there is little point— and many risks—in 'democratizing' loosely bounded and non-legitimate territories. Only if the EU closes its economic and administrative boundaries more firmly will the possibility to shape European policies emerge. The more the possibilities of exit (flexibility, etc.) are open and available, the less the EU will be able to enforce 'positive' costly integration and the fewer will be the incentives to 'structure' voice at the European level. The possibility that a mutual strengthening of institutional democratization, contentious mass politics development, and legal founding of European citizenship and constitutional identity[44] will take place piecemeal cannot be dismissed. In my

[44] These are the three main lines of thinking in this area. The first argument suggests that the structuring of actors' political representation requires prior institutional democratization and that the latter will actually stimulate the former. A second argument

opinion, however, it is difficult for any new polity to define its political community and to infuse in it even a 'thin' sense of identity without its being able to institutionalize its internal distribution of territorial competencies and its external economic and politico-administrative (let alone cultural) boundaries. Institutional democratization and mass politics development under such conditions are likely to lead to the immediate politicization of those same issues which are defining the polity: Who are 'we' and who are the 'others'? What should the common goods to be collectively regulated be, and which decision rules should be followed to do so? Past experience suggests that this may prove an explosive mixture of problems in the process of democratization.

This scepticism has, therefore, nothing to do with the hypothesized need for a demos conceived in ethno-linguistic terms or for a level of trust and solidarity as preconditions for further integration.[45] The EU is obviously lacking in the primordial and ethno-cultural linkages to define itself. However, identities are not built exclusively on 'primordial' codes of closures. Civic codes, for instance, can also be the sources of system-building processes. Commitments to constitutional values and civic duties, a citizenship conception of the political community, and the development of a 'republican' patriotism could be enough to define a layer of political community built upon the ethno-cultural differentiation of the European peoples.

However, these 'constitutional' or 'civic' codes of closure and identity can only be created by the EU's eventual definition of these rights, duties, and obligations beyond the *economic rights* of the Europeans. That is, they require a considerable injection of specifically *political* and *social rights* to substantiate the European constitutional citizenship. This analysis suggests that the current institutional architecture of the EU is unlikely to achieve this level of political production given the un-boundedness of its territorial and membership spaces. The internal hierarchy of the EU does not seem to achieve a level of control over the boundaries with the broader environment that allows it to lock in those actors and resources whose cooperation or

contends that forms of contentious structuring of European public opinion, expressed through political agencies discussing European issues would create that European public sphere that will eventually lead to successful pressure for institutional democratization. Finally, a third strand of thinking suggests that the definition of the European political community through the establishment of civic, social and political rights enforceable by court action will achieve the result of increasing pressure for democratic development in other domains.

[45] For the first thesis see Grimm, D., 'Does Europe need a constitution?', *European Law Journal*, 1 (1995), 282–302; for the second see Offe, C., 'Demokratie und Wohlfahrtsstaat: Eine europäische Regimenform unter dem Strea der europäischen Integration', in W. Streek (ed.), *Internationale Wirtschaft, nationale Demokratie* (Frankfurt: Campus Verlag, 1998), 99–136.

compliance is essential to the production of those rights and titles necessary to substantiate the 'civic' system building. In the meantime, the 'constitutionalization' of European economic rights and of the market-making goals continues to produce boundary removing whose political consequences are then borne by national governments and representative institutions. The system-building weakness of the EU is thus rooted in the specific design of its centre formation, which is geared to its constitutionally prescribed project of differential boundary transcendence.

The European experience in the formation of nation-states has been interpreted in this work as a specific historical process in which the development of a wide-ranging (beyond local) identity (the national one, primarily) interacted with the creation of other political and social equality areas within which interest conflict was disciplined by the development of social-sharing principles and of collective(ized) decision-making capacities. Therefore, the historical *structural profile* of the nation-state is provided through the forming of a close relationship between identities, interests, and the institutions of social solidarity and political decision-making. With respect to this structural profile, the *dynamic processes* of integration challenge the historical boundaries of the state through their growing transcendence (total and partial); challenge the coincidence of such boundaries due to the uneven boundary transcendence in different domains; reduce the capacity to lock in relevant actors/resources endowed with new opportunities of exit; and challenge the domestic institutions of social sharing and those of representation and political decision-making.

Therefore, integration challenges the very essence of modernization theory: the idea that *some degree of coherence* between cultural identities, socioeconomic practices, and rules/institutions is necessary, or, to put the same idea differently, *some level of coincidence* and mutual reinforcement is necessary among the cultural, economic, coercion and politico-administrative boundaries of any modern political formation.[46] This coherence/coincidence has created the conditions for individuals to share a common understanding about what is important in their lives, to mostly interact with each other inside the collectivity, and to have accepted ways of deciding how to regulate their lives in common. However, the European integration project defines a sphere of enormous expansion of socio-economic practices that bear no or little relation to social identities and to decisional rules. The discussion in this book has focused on the consequences of this 'disjunction' and of the absence of some form of coherence between identities, social practices and rules/institutions.

---

[46] This issue of 'coherence' or 'coincidence' has an impressive genealogy in classical sociology and modernization theory. See Wagner, P., *Theorizing Modernity : Inescapability & Attainability in Social Theory* (London and New York : Sage, 2001).

Some observers view the European and global extension of socio-economic practices as unproblematic. If the individual and her/his economic rights is the sole methodological reference point and communities and collective entities are seen as based on highly contingent social and moral bases, then social identities and their transformations are unproblematic or irrelevant. Consequently, any boundary coincidence and any coherence between identities, social practices and rule setting is no longer possible, and no longer necessary. This split can also be welcomed and praised: the colossal expansion of socio-economic practices beyond localities and nations will have some sort of self-regulating capacity and the corresponding empowerment of individuals will make them freer. Viewed from this perspective, the European integration is mainly a solution to the growing problems of instrumental coordination of this enormous extension of socio-economic practices and the fragmentation of interests and identities. As political agency is unnecessary, the EU can be presented as a gigantic 'forum' for coordination games. Collective and collectivized decisions no longer need to rest on well-defined membership groups or on practices of participation and representation. A variety of different forms of access and an enriched set of actors (among whom experts, bureaucrats and lobbyists are especially important), can legitimize the fragmented decision-making process, and new legitimizing discourses concerning this disjointed order can be 'constructed'. In this perspective, a polity with a 'rational' and stable order can be constructed and legitimized even if identities, practices, and institutions do not tend towards some form of coherence, and even if the triangle of identity, social sharing, and legitimated decision-making, which is the historical achievement of the nation-state, has been definitely broken.

Clearly, the perspective underlining this work is different. It is based on the interaction between 'options' and 'roots', 'exits' and 'locking in', 'collective burdens' and 'individual free-riding', 'opportunities' and 'costs' involved in the process of functional and territorial boundary redefinition in Europe. In my opinion, paradoxically, it is in fact the complex European cultural infrastructure (language, religion, region, national identity, etc.) that has actually contained to date the levels of actors and resources' exit-entry envisaged by the current mode of integration, as well as the social disintegration problems they could generate. I have tried to interpret the integration process in the tradition of classical sociology that takes the existence of a certain overlap between social identities, political boundaries and social practices as a precondition for establishing political agency and a 'rational' political order. The scattered elements of identities, interests, and institutions need to be reconciled in some way into a new coherent order. If this reconstruction does not occur at some level other than that of the nation-state, then tensions, conflicts, and problems are likely to emerge that could jeopardize the features specific to European civilization. On this view, the EU is both a source of problems but also the only possible solution to them. It can be seen as a project for regaining some degree of coherence between extended social practices, social identities, solidarity ties and rules of deliberation at the European level. Most of the ideas expressed in this book show how problematic I believe this project to be.

Although the above-mentioned different interpretative schemes concerning the ultimate nature and meaning of integration bear some resemblance to different epistemological schools and cultural traditions, they also point to and imply different and concrete political projects, which can purposely be pursued by actors and agencies. In the end, as Stein Rokkan would have put it, the real issue is *which boundaries are built and removed, by whom, and for what purpose.*

INDEX